D0333502

ONE-YEAR READING PLAN WITH BIBLE TEXT

THE

BIG STORY

REVEALING
GOD'S COVENANT PLAN
FOR EVERYONE

PHILIP GREENSLADE
WITH DEVOTIONAL THOUGHTS BY SELWYN HUGHES

CWR

Copyright © CWR 2001.
First published without the Bible text by CWR 2001 as *Cover to Cover God's Story: Through the Bible Promise by Promise*. Reprinted 2004.

This revised edition published 2010 by CWR, Waverley Abbey House, Waverley Lane, Farnham, Surrey GU9 8EP England. CWR is a Registered Charity - Number 294387 and a Limited Company registered in England - Registration Number 1990308.

The right of Philip Greenslade to be identified as the author of this work has been asserted by him in accordance with the Copyright, Designs and Patents Act 1988, sections 77 and 78.

All rights reserved. No part of this publication may be reproduced, stored in a retrieval system, or transmitted, in any form or by any means, electronic, mechanical, photocopying, recording or otherwise, without the prior permission in writing of CWR. See back of book/visit website for list of National Distributors.
Unless otherwise indicated, all Scripture references are from the Holman Christian Standard Bible®, copyright 1999,2000,2002,2003 by Holman Bible Publishers. Used by permission. Holman Christian Standard Bible®, Holman CSB®, and HCSB® are federally registered trademarks of Holman Bible Publishers. Further information and an introduction to the Holman CSB translation can be found on CWR's website: www.cwr.org.uk/hcsbintro
Whereas HCSB mark OT quotes in the NT in bold, in this edition they are instead in quotation marks.

Other versions used are marked:
NIV: the Holy Bible: New International Version (NIV), copyright © 1973, 1978, 1984 by the International Bible Society.
NKJV:New King James Version, © 1982, Thomas Nelson Inc.
The Message: Scripture taken from *The Message*. Copyright © 1993, 1994,1995, 1996, 2000, 2001, 2002. Used by permission of NavPress Publishing Group.

Concept development, editing, design and production by CWR
Printed in India by Thomson Press Ltd
ISBN: 978-1-85345-562-9

CONTENTS

FOREWORD

Nothing in my opinion is more spiritually rewarding and exciting than tracing God's story as it is unfolded for us in the Scriptures. Nor have I ever come across one as competent at presenting this concept as Phil Greenslade. He not only has a unique ability to delineate this most tremendous truth but does it with a passion that shows through in almost every sentence he writes.

How I wish that more Christians would take the point that Eugene Peterson makes, namely that the Bible comes to us as a story. 'It does not come to us systematised into doctrine,' he says, 'or arranged as moral instruction. It is a story and the story form is as important as the truth it tells.'

One of the greatest things we can do as believers is to open our ears to Scripture and one of the best ways we can develop our spiritual lives is by allowing ourselves to be drawn into the action of God through history, a story that began in the eternity past and will end in the eternity to come.

I shall never forget the moment when the concept first hit me, that God is not only writing a story but that I am in it also. It did more than anything I know to develop a sense of journeying and discipleship.

I suspect that the time you will spend going through this Bible-reading programme will turn out to be one of the highlights of your Christian life so far.

Be blessed.
Selwyn Hughes, 2004
Rev Dr Selwyn Hughes (1928–2006) was the founder of CWR, an internationally acclaimed speaker and a widely published author.

NOTE TO READER

On days when the text focuses on only one Bible verse we have put the previous day's (or days') verses in grey, followed by the current day's reading to help you to see the context and to be reminded of the narrative or thought. It may be helpful to read it again or skim its content.

A DEVOTIONAL INTERLUDE
The purpose of the devotional interlude at the end of each day's commentary is to help you respond to the day's Scripture reading and teaching in a way that will apply the truth to both heart and mind. Sometimes it will be a prayer or a devotional thought arising out of the reading; at other times, a question, an affirmation, something to act upon or an issue for thanksgiving or praise. Note that the difference between a 'thought' and 'something to ponder' is this: the 'thought' is something to think about immediately following the day's reading. Something to 'ponder' might occupy your thoughts throughout the day and is deserving of deeper and further consideration.

INTRODUCTION

Welcome to this journey of discovery through the Bible. I trust you will be moved as I have been by following God's story from cover to cover, from first creation to final creation.

Throughout this year, you will see how the familiar Bible stories fit into the larger, coherent story of the Bible which climaxes in the story of Jesus.

I hope you will marvel, as I do, at the covenantal commitments God has made to bring salvation to us and to the whole created order.

Let me explain how *The Big Story* works.

The first two sections show that Jesus taught us to 'read' the Bible as God's story. This story centres on Jesus Himself, and encompasses the stories of the world, of Israel and of ourselves.

At the heart of this year-long programme are the major covenants by which God expresses His loving commitment to save the world He has made. The motif at the foot of each page represents the way these covenants sustain the progress of God's promise-plan through history.

In each of these central sections, *The Big Story* first looks at the key biblical passages where each covenant is described, and then shows how this works out from Genesis to Revelation.

Eventually, all the threads are pulled together in Jesus (as indicated in the diagram which prefaces each section) and are then elaborated through the voices of Paul and John who represent the New Testament witness.

As the year closes, we learn how we can respond to God's story and so find our personal narratives caught up in the large-scale adventure of what God is doing.

If you read in sequence, the effect is cumulative. So be patient and watch as each stage of the story gathers up clues from previous stages. Notice, especially, how particular themes reoccur with added significance. As you stay with the project, you will begin to make the connections which make the Bible so compelling.

The scope of the story is creation-wide. We start with Noah because covenant language is first explicitly used with him and because he marks the first major step on the recovery of Adam's position.

References supporting the biblical theology expressed here have not been included but may be found in my book *A Passion for God's Story* published by Paternoster Press.

So, we invite you to:

- experience the Bible as an enthralling narrative and learn of the five interlocking stories which help us interpret 'God's master story' that points the way to Jesus;
- discover with Noah that God loves His creation so much that He pledges to preserve the planet in order to redeem it;
- join the adventure of faith with father Abraham as God sets in motion through him the promise-plan to bless all nations;
- stand with Moses at Sinai as God chooses Israel as His covenant partner for the sake of the world.
- sit awestruck with David as God entrusts to his 'son-king' the 'charter by which the whole of humanity's future is directed';

- feel the acute anguish and fierce hope of the prophets of the Exile as they forge out of 'death' a new vision of God who so empowers His people as to make the covenant partnership with Him work;
- meet Jesus again, as if for the first time, as He re-enacts all that Israel and her kings were meant to be and so brings God's promise-plan to strange but successful fulfilment;
- stagger with Paul as he unveils the amazing mystery of God's secret strategy to bring everything together under the lordship of Jesus, and glimpse with John the stunning glory of God's new creation.

Above all we invite you to make a sincere response of wonder, worship and faith – perhaps for the first time – perhaps for a fresh time.

Paul told Timothy that in the last days people would love themselves, their money and their pleasure and would become 'allergic to God' (*The Message*).

The Big Story is our contribution to reversing that trend. It seeks to help you swim against the cultural tide by becoming a passionate lover of God.

So let's 'roll up the sleeves of our minds' and ask the Holy Spirit to be our Teacher as we travel together through God's story.

Wishing you all joy on the journey,

Philip Greenslade 2010

SECTION

SECTION 1 JESUS' BURNING-HEART
BIBLE SCHOOL

JESUS' BURNING-HEART BIBLE SCHOOL
(Luke 24:13-49)

Noah and his ark, Joseph and his 'technicolour dreamcoat', Moses 'Prince of Egypt', David and Goliath, Daniel in the lions' den – these are some of the Bible stories that people of my generation grew up to be familiar with. But being familiar with Bible stories is one thing; *knowing the Bible story* is another thing altogether!

This, I believe, is what Jesus wanted His followers to grasp after His resurrection, as He makes clear to the two disciples on the road to Emmaus and to the rest of the disciple band back in Jerusalem: 'Then beginning with Moses and all the Prophets, He interpreted for them the things concerning Himself in all the Scriptures. ... everything written about Me in the Law of Moses, the Prophets, and the Psalms must be fulfilled' (Luke 24:27,44).

It is unlikely that Jesus was merely listing certain proof-texts which in some way or other pointed to Him. More likely, He was seeking to show the disciples how the whole of the earlier part of the story of Israel told in the Old Testament had come to a climax in Him. 'So that the Scriptures might be fulfilled' cannot be reduced to those scattered predictions which land on target in Jesus. Jesus is, in effect, drawing the whole of the Old Testament story onto Himself. He is connecting up the well-loved Bible stories and showing how they add up to the one big story of what God is doing. This is the approach adopted in this study.

God's pledge to Noah to withhold further judgment on His first creation until His redemptive work is completed and He can bring in a new creation now converges with Christ's cross and resurrection. Here, in the cross, God absorbs and defeats the pain, sin and mortality of the old fallen creation. Here, in Christ's resurrection, the one Creator God both endorses the goodness of His first creation and relaunches it as a new creation.

God's promise to Abraham to bless all the nations through him sets in motion the long story of faith that comes to fulfilment in Jesus, Abraham's true 'seed', through whom the curse is turned to blessing for the world.

As Messiah and King, He assumes Israel's role as God's obedient Son, faithful covenant partner and servant who suffers for the sake of the world. What Israel's history was intended to achieve but left undone, He completes; what Israel was called to be but failed to do, He successfully re-enacts.

All God's dreams for kingship, first focused on David, by which Israel's King was destined to be Lord of the world – dreams turned to dust by five centuries of faithless monarchs – finally come good in Him!

What the prophets envisaged as salvation beyond the Exile when they saw God returning as King, and restoring His people on the other side of death and resurrection, is concentrated in Him. His blood is the blood of the new covenant shed for many, and His rising is the glory of His people Israel and the light of revelation to the Gentiles.

Every covenantal connection eventually leads to Him, every stream of truth flows into His river, every promise of God finds its 'Yes' and 'Amen' in Him, each aspect of God's overall strategy is filled-full in Him! This is what He wants them to grasp!

And the way He opens up the themes and traces the threads of God's purpose in Scriptures 'warms the heart'. Hearts which have iced up with despair or frozen over with false views of reality are thawed out with truth! And by opening up the Book in His own unique way He rekindles a lost passion. Later the apostle John would relive his first encounter when, with tears wiped from his eyes, he sees the slain Lamb standing, worthy to open the scroll of God's purposes for history.

For this *our eyes have to be opened, the Bible has to be opened, our minds need to be opened.*

It is quite possible, as some in Israel did, to follow Jesus on the road in admiration of His teaching right up to the cross. But if then we stop short of the cross we miss His whole reason for living since He enters into His real glory only through suffering.

It is perfectly possible to fall in with Jesus even after His resurrection but as though He were an unrecognised stranger who makes no difference to the direction our lives are taking.

It is even possible to have had a gloriously personal experience of Jesus as alive today and yet to remain in the dark about His central place in God's big story which alone explains Him.

Even then, though we have met the risen Christ and heard Him explain Himself from the big story, we will not know its truth until we join with other disciples in the community and learn to live out the story in our own lives in obedient joy.

So discover God's amazing story with us by enlisting in the Bible School of Jesus. And let's ask the Holy Spirit to be our teacher.

WHEN WE LOSE hope it is as if we are relinquishing our hold on life itself. We feel we are closing the door on the future and reaching a dead end.

It was in just such a mood that two disciples of Jesus went back to their home village of Emmaus in the bitter aftermath of His crucifixion. Their personal correspondence with Jesus was now closed; the great adventure was over.

Emmaus is where we all tend to go at such times. Frederick Buechner puts it well: 'Emmaus is whatever we do or wherever we go to make ourselves forget that the world holds nothing sacred; that even the wisest and bravest and loveliest decay and die; that even the noblest ideas that men have had – ideas about love and justice and freedom – have always in time been twisted out of shape by selfish men for selfish ends. Emmaus is where we go to forget.'

Emmaus is the 'comfort-zone' we retreat into as we attempt to piece together the shattered fragments of our own stories into something that makes sense.

DAY 01
LUKE 24:1-14

Luke 24:1-14

BIBLE READING

RESURRECTION MORNING

24 On the first day of the week, very early in the morning, they came to the tomb, bringing the spices they had prepared. ²They found the stone rolled away from the tomb. ³They went in but did not find the body of the Lord Jesus. ⁴While they were perplexed about this, suddenly two *— angels* men stood by them in dazzling clothes. ⁵So the women were terrified and bowed down to the ground.

"Why are you looking for the living among the dead?" asked the men. ⁶"He is not here, but He has been resurrected! Remember how He spoke to you when He was still in Galilee, ⁷saying, 'The Son of Man must be betrayed into the hands of sinful men, be crucified, and rise on the third day'?" ⁸And they remembered His words.

⁹Returning from the tomb, they reported all these things to

the Eleven and to all the rest. [10]Mary Magdalene, Joanna, Mary the mother of James, and the other women with them were telling the apostles these things. [11]But these words seemed like nonsense to them, and they did not believe the women. [12]Peter, however, got up and ran to the tomb. When he stooped to look in, he saw only the linen cloths. So he went home, amazed at what had happened.

THE EMMAUS DISCIPLES

[13]Now that same day two of them were on their way to a village called Emmaus, which was about seven miles from Jerusalem. [14]Together they were discussing everything that had taken place.

THOUGHT: Are you travelling along an Emmaus Road at this moment? Is your heart feeling dejected because God has not come through for you in the way you expected? Don't lose hope. Your own story (your plans and ambitions) may have to be shattered in order for God's big story to be acted out. Though it hurts to have one's own plans thwarted, always remember this: God's plans are not only the best for Him but also the best for us. *Amen.*

DAY
02

LUKE 24:15-16

DULLED BY DESPAIR and preoccupied with grief, the two disciples trudge home to Emmaus. Jesus had once assured them that there *was* a key even to death's door and they had believed that He held that key. But that glimmer of hope had been overtaken and buried by events.

They are so absorbed in their sad recriminations that they fail to recognise the Stranger who falls in alongside them on the road! They have lost the plot of whatever story it was that had held their lives together. Now they grope like bewildered characters in search of an author.

It is precisely in this context and mood that Easter is good news. There is a Stranger who falls in beside us on the uncertain road ahead to surprise us with hope.

There is something that makes all the difference in the world; there is Someone who makes all the difference to the world!

The good news we celebrate is the resurrection of Jesus Christ from the dead!

Luke 24:15-16

THE EMMAUS DISCIPLES

¹³Now that same day two of them were on their way to a village called Emmaus, which was about seven miles from Jerusalem. ¹⁴Together they were discussing everything that had taken place.

¹⁵And while they were discussing and arguing, Jesus Himself came near and began to walk along with them. ¹⁶But they were prevented from recognizing Him.

PRAYER: My Father and my God, forgive me that sometimes I allow myself to be so overcome by despair that my soul becomes oblivious of Your presence. Help me to understand that though I cannot feel Your presence, it is there nevertheless. One of the purposes of Your Son being raised from the dead was to be with me - always. I am so grateful that the message of the empty tomb is not just for Easter Day but for every day. Thank You, my Father. Amen.

UNABLE YET TO appreciate His aliveness, the two disciples explain to Jesus their sense of despair. 'But we were hoping that He was the One who was about to redeem Israel' (v.21). '... we *were hoping* ...' exactly sums up their disillusionment. Their dream was a proud one, kept alive in various forms within Israel for over five hundred years ever since the returning exiles had trudged back from Babylonian captivity.

These two, like so many before them, had hoped for someone to 'redeem Israel' from its deeper exile in

DAY
03
LUKE 24:17-21

alienation from God and under His judgment. They had pinned their hopes on Jesus of Nazareth. They had joined those who thought they could get Him elected Messiah. They had thought this was their moment of destiny, the moment to engage with the cogs of history's big wheel. They had felt sure that 'there is a life about to start when tomorrow comes'. Only tomorrow never came, except as Good Friday.

Now death has slammed shut the door of their lives.

BIBLE READING

Luke 24:17-21

THE EMMAUS DISCIPLES

[13]Now that same day two of them were on their way to a village called Emmaus, which was about seven miles from Jerusalem. [14]Together they were discussing everything that had taken place.

[15]And while they were discussing and arguing, Jesus Himself came near and began to walk along with them.

[16]But they were prevented from recognizing Him.

[17]Then He asked them, "What is this dispute that you're having with each other as you are walking?" And they stopped [walking and looked] discouraged.

[18]The one named Cleopas answered Him, "Are You the only visitor in Jerusalem who doesn't know the things that happened there in these days?"

[19]"What things?" He asked them.

So they said to Him, "The things concerning Jesus the Nazarene, who was a Prophet powerful in action and speech before God and all the people, [20]and how our chief priests and leaders handed Him over to be sentenced to death, and they crucified Him. [21]But we were hoping that He was the One who was about to redeem Israel. Besides all this, it's the third day since these things happened.

THOUGHT: Faith, said someone, is 'believing in the dark what you discovered in the light'. If the two Emmaus disciples had done this do you think they would have been in such a sad state spiritually? Had not Christ told His disciples over and over again that He would die but would be raised from the dead? When you next find yourself in spiritual darkness cast your mind back to the things you saw when your path was bathed in light.

at P's & G's — dynamic fellowship, lve of people in a busy, happy life.

IT IS IMPORTANT to realise that the resurrection is not some happy ending tacked on to the Jesus story. Without its final chapter, the gospel of Jesus Christ is no gospel at all. Now, as then, the resurrection of Jesus Christ opens the way into God's new creation and leaves a gaping hole in all failed, alternative versions of reality – be they scientific materialism, Marxism, or whatever.

DAY 04
LUKE 24:22-24

Of course, nothing affronts modern sensibilities more than talk of resurrection from the dead! But we need not be deterred by those who say you cannot fit incredible happenings such as resurrection into the modern way of looking at the world. As Lesslie Newbigin said so well: 'The resurrection cannot be accommodated in any way of understanding the world *except one of which it is the starting-point* ... the starting-point of a whole new way of understanding the cosmos and the human situation in the cosmos.'

The resurrection of Jesus has to be the ultimate postmodern event! It opens up a completely new way of viewing the world around us, as the two Emmaus-bound travellers were soon to discover. A *resurrection-view-of-reality* is now about to break in and open everything up for them!

Luke 24:22-24

[15]And while they were discussing and arguing, Jesus Himself came near and began to walk along with them. [16]But they were prevented from recognizing Him. [17]Then He asked them, "What is this dispute that you're having with each other as you are walking?" And they stopped [walking and looked] discouraged. [18]The one named Cleopas answered Him, "Are You the only visitor in Jerusalem who doesn't know the things that happened there in these days?" [19]"What things?" He asked them.

So they said to Him, "The things concerning Jesus the Nazarene, who was a Prophet powerful in action and speech before God and all the people, [20]and how our chief priests and leaders handed Him over to be sentenced to death, and they crucified Him. [21]But we were hoping that He was the One who was about to redeem Israel. Besides all this, it's the third day since these things happened.

[22]Moreover, some women from our group astounded us. They arrived early at the tomb, [23]and when they didn't find His body, they came and reported that they had seen a vision of angels who said He was alive. [24]Some of those who were with us went to the tomb and found it just as the women had said, but they didn't see Him."

PRAYER: Heavenly Father, help me to have a resurrection-view of reality and not allow myself to be brainwashed by an age which cannot conceive of Your miraculous interventions in the world. Help me understand that all alternative versions of reality are roads that lead nowhere. May the truth of Your resurrection fill and thrill my soul every moment of the day. In Jesus' name I pray. Amen.

IF WE PAUSE today to consider the situation in which Jesus speaks, we will marvel at His order of priorities. After all, what would any one of us have done immediately after being raised from the dead and vindicated as Messiah? What might He have been expected to do? Empty all the sick beds in Israel perhaps? Not so, it seems. Throw Himself off the pinnacle of the Temple to prove His divinity? No, He'd faced that one before! March to Rome to claim the world's throne? No, that was His for the asking!

His priority is different and very striking! He spends much of those precious forty days before His ascension in *Bible teaching*, explaining the Scriptures to His disciples as He does here to the two. Verses 25 to 27 give us a strong clue as to what He was up to: 'Then beginning with Moses and all the Prophets, *He interpreted for them the things concerning Himself in all the Scriptures'* (v.27).

This must mean that without the story of Jesus, the Old Testament makes no final sense. It also means that without the Old Testament we cannot understand Jesus, and that it takes the whole of the Old Testament story to explain who Jesus is.

To repeat what we have said before: this is not a matter of finding scattered proof-texts or predictions which somehow anticipate Jesus but of seeing how the whole Old Testament story reaches its climax in Him.

Luke 24:25-27

[18]The one named Cleopas answered Him, "Are You the only visitor in Jerusalem who doesn't know the things that happened there in these days?"
[19]"What things?" He asked them.
So they said to Him, "The things concerning Jesus the Nazarene, who was a Prophet powerful in action and speech before God and all the people, [20]and how our chief priests and leaders handed Him over to be sentenced to

death, and they crucified Him. ²¹But we were hoping that He was the One who was about to redeem Israel. Besides all this, it's the third day since these things happened. ²²Moreover, some women from our group astounded us. They arrived early at the tomb, ²³and when they didn't find His body, they came and reported that they had seen a vision of angels who said He was alive. ²⁴Some of those who were with us went to the tomb and found it just as the women had said, but they didn't see Him."

²⁵He said to them, "How unwise and slow you are to believe in your hearts all that the prophets have spoken! ²⁶Didn't the Messiah have to suffer these things and enter into His glory?" ²⁷Then beginning with Moses and all the Prophets, He interpreted for them the things concerning Himself in all the Scriptures.

THOUGHT: Imagine having an audio tape of that thrilling scriptural exposition given by Jesus during the walk to Emmaus. How greatly do you think you would value it? The Holy Spirit has not seen fit to give us a record of it but we do know its central theme: 'the things concerning Himself'. Never forget that the key to understanding both Old and New Testaments is *Jesus*. He is the hub of the Bible. Is He the hub of your heart and life?

DAY
06
LUKE 24:28-31

LUKE DESCRIBES THE impact of the resurrection by using three times in this chapter the verb 'to open' - open eyes, open Book (NIV), open minds (vv.31,32,45). The opened tomb of Jesus truly works wonders.

Notice first how their eyes are opened. As evening approaches, He seems intent on moving on, but they urge Him: "'Stay with us ...'" It was as He reclined at the table with them that He took the bread, blessed and broke it, and gave it to them. Then *their eyes were opened, and they recognized Him ...*' (vv.29-31). This wonderful recognition scene grips the imagination - as it has done for many great artists, including

Rembrandt! The fact of resurrection is brought home to them as they personally experience His risenness.

Such an experience will be different for each of us, of course, but every believer can testify to some moment of sudden or growing realisation that Jesus is truly alive and facing us, as it were, across the table! Those who have met Him in this way never forget the moment. And though called to walk by faith and not by sight, again and again – most likely in broken bread and poured-out wine – they meet Him afresh and know His presence as the living Christ.

Luke 24:28-31

BIBLE READING

¹⁵And while they were discussing and arguing, Jesus Himself came near and began to walk along with them. ¹⁶But they were prevented from recognizing Him.

¹⁷Then He asked them, "What is this dispute that you're having with each other as you are walking?" And they stopped [walking and looked] discouraged.

¹⁸The one named Cleopas answered Him, "Are You the only visitor in Jerusalem who doesn't know the things that happened there in these days?"

¹⁹"What things?" He asked them.

So they said to Him, "The things concerning Jesus the Nazarene, who was a Prophet powerful in action and speech before God and all the people, ²⁰and how our chief priests and leaders handed Him over to be sentenced to death, and they crucified Him. ²¹But we were hoping that He was the One who was about to redeem Israel. Besides all this, it's the third day since these things happened. ²²Moreover, some women from our group astounded us. They arrived early at the tomb, ²³and when they didn't find His body, they came and reported that they had seen a vision of angels who said He was alive. ²⁴Some of those who were with us went to the tomb and found it just as the women had said, but they didn't see Him."

²⁵He said to them, "How unwise and slow you are to believe in your hearts all that the prophets have

spoken! ²⁶Didn't the Messiah have to suffer these things and enter into His glory?" ²⁷Then beginning with Moses and all the Prophets, He interpreted for them the things concerning Himself in all the Scriptures.

²⁸They came near the village where they were going, and He gave the impression that He was going farther. ²⁹But they urged Him: "Stay with us, because it's almost evening, and now the day is almost over." So He went in to stay with them.

³⁰It was as He reclined at the table with them that He took the bread, blessed and broke it, and gave it to them. ³¹Then their eyes were opened, and they recognized Him, but He disappeared from their sight.

> QUESTION: When were you last vividly aware of the closeness of the risen Christ? If your encounters with the Saviour are few and far between then ask yourself 'Why?' Is it because your prayer times are rushed and you do not linger in His presence? Is there some unconfessed sin in your life? Throughout the centuries Christians have testified that prayer - unrushed prayer, that is - more than anything makes the risen Christ real.

DAY 07

LUKE 24:32-35

SUCH EYE-OPENING ENCOUNTERS with Jesus can hardly fail to be life-changing experiences. All the more remarkable, then, when the Emmaus Two reflect upon it, is what stood out for them in such an experience: 'Were not our hearts burning within us while he talked with us on the road and *opened the Scriptures to us*?' (v.32, NIV). This explains why, for me, Luke 24 is almost holy ground. I call this the 'Burning Heart Bible School', and it is surely the one we would all like to attend!

The sequence of events is striking and very revealing. First, Jesus *opens the Scriptures* to them (v.32c) and sets their hearts on fire with the breathtaking purposes of the big picture from Scripture! Then, while breaking bread over supper, their eyes are opened to recognise Him.

In our day it is cause for great rejoicing that more and more eyes are being opened by the Holy Spirit to the truth of the gospel and to the reality of the risen Jesus. The narrative strongly suggests that such a meeting with Jesus sets us on a lifetime of learning. It is precisely those *whose eyes are being opened* to His aliveness and personal presence who are the prime candidates for enrolment in His 'Burning Heart Bible School' and who, in turn, see Jesus in a fresh way.

Luke 24:32-35

BIBLE READING

²⁵He said to them, "How unwise and slow you are to believe in your hearts all that the prophets have spoken! ²⁶Didn't the Messiah have to suffer these things and enter into His glory?" ²⁷Then beginning with Moses and all the Prophets, He interpreted for them the things concerning Himself in all the Scriptures.

²⁸They came near the village where they were going, and He gave the impression that He was going farther. ²⁹But they urged Him: "Stay with us, because it's almost evening, and now the day is almost over." So He went in to stay with them.

³⁰It was as He reclined at the table with them that He took the bread, blessed and broke it, and gave it to them. ³¹Then their eyes were opened, and they recognized Him, but He disappeared from their sight.

³²So they said to each other, "Weren't our hearts ablaze within us while He was talking with us on the road and explaining the Scriptures to us?" ³³That very hour they got up and returned to Jerusalem. They found the Eleven and those with them gathered together, ³⁴who said, "The Lord has certainly been raised, and has appeared to Simon!" ³⁵Then they began to describe what had happened on the road and how He was made known to them in the breaking of the bread.

ACTION: Many have never had the opportunity to attend a Bible school. But everyone can be a student in the 'Burning Heart Bible School'. All you have to do each time you open your Bible is to make this your prayer: 'Open my eyes so that I may see wonderful things in Your law' (Psa. 119:18). Realise, as you read, that through the written Word you are meeting up with the living Word – the Word who is bigger than men's words.

DAY
08

LUKE 24:36-44

'EVERYTHING WRITTEN about Me in the Law of Moses, the Prophets, and the Psalms must be fulfilled' (v.44).

Once more, it is important to emphasise what Jesus is asserting here. Without Him the Old Testament revelation of God is incomplete. Conversely, we cannot understand who Jesus is and why He has come without understanding something of God's story in the first half of our Bible. Again, it is vital to realise that it is not a matter of finding isolated prophetic predictions that somehow land on target in Him. Something much grander is afoot! The very language used – 'must' and 'be fulfilled' – implies, as we shall find later, a coherent thread of divine purpose.

As I see it, what Jesus is doing is connecting up the familiar Bible stories and showing how they form the one big story told in the Bible of what God is doing. He is, in effect, gathering to Himself the whole of the story the Old Testament tells. He brings the long-range strategy of God to its successful conclusion. He is showing these disciples the larger story of God's strategic plan.

BIBLE READING

Luke 24:36-44

THE REALITY OF THE RISEN JESUS

³⁶And as they were saying these things, He Himself stood among them. He said to them, "Peace to you!" ³⁷But they were

startled and terrified and thought they were seeing a ghost. ³⁸"Why are you troubled?" He asked them. "And why do doubts arise in your hearts? ³⁹Look at My hands and My feet, that it is I Myself! Touch Me and see, because a ghost does not have flesh and bones as you can see I have." ⁴⁰Having said this, He showed them His hands and feet. ⁴¹But while they still could not believe because of [their] joy and were amazed, He asked them, "Do you have anything here to eat?" ⁴²So they gave Him a piece of a broiled fish, ⁴³and He took it and ate in their presence.

⁴⁴Then He told them, "These are My words that I spoke to you while I was still with you—that everything written about Me in the Law of Moses, the Prophets, and the Psalms must be fulfilled."

THOUGHT: So many believers in this busy modern age neglect or ignore the reading of the Old Testament. You can be sure of this: no true or complete picture of Jesus or of God's story can be built up if the Old Testament is disregarded. While enjoying the little stories of the Bible, be careful that you don't get so caught up in them that you miss the big story of what God is doing. That's like not seeing the wood for the trees.

WHAT HAPPENS NOW in Jerusalem is similar to what happened at Emmaus. After appearing before the disciples and convincing them of His aliveness, Luke tells us, 'He opened their minds to understand the Scriptures' (v.45).

DAY
09
LUKE 24:41-46

As was stressed in the introduction, it was – and is – vital that everyone, with heart on fire and eyes wide open to Christ's risenness, should have their *minds opened so they can understand the Scriptures.* Our modern minds are often shut by the limits set by materialism and unbelief. The resurrection breaks into the rationalist's closed system and opens it up to new possibilities.

But what were the disciples slow of heart to believe? Where are the obvious prophecies of suffering leading to glory? How is this connected to the story of Israel told in the law, the psalms and prophets?

Like the first disciples, we are slow of heart to believe the paradoxical message of the prophets that Israel's rejection and vindication is a pattern of suffering and glory which has settled on her anointed King and Messiah. Only slowly does it dawn on us that losing our life is the way to find it, that dying is the way to live again! Our minds certainly need to be opened to see all this, otherwise we will mistakenly believe the path of discipleship is too hard for us and step off the narrow way that leads to life.

| BIBLE READING | **Luke 24:41-46** |

[41]But while they still could not believe because of [their] joy and were amazed, He asked them, "Do you have anything here to eat?" [42]So they gave Him a piece of a broiled fish, [43]and He took it and ate in their presence. [44]Then He told them, "These are My words that I spoke to you while I was still with you—that everything written about Me in the Law of Moses, the Prophets, and the Psalms must be fulfilled."

[45]Then He opened their minds to understand the Scriptures. [46]He also said to them, "This is what is written: the Messiah would suffer and rise from the dead the third day ..."

PRAYER: Lord Jesus Christ, I acknowledge that while I enjoy the emotional side of Christian experience, that is never enough. I long to have a heart that feels like Yours but also a mind that thinks like Yours. Enable me, dear Lord, to think Christianly about all of life's issues. Help me to keep my mind open to the truth of God as it is found in the Scriptures, especially to the idea of God's big story. In Jesus' name. Amen.

NOT ONLY DO we need our minds opened to the wonder of God's big story in Christ, but we need to have our minds stretched if we are to take in the worldwide implications of what God has done in Jesus and commissions us to tell. We have been caught up in a story that reaches beyond private faith and personal experience into the realm of *public truth*. '... and repentance for forgiveness of sins [will] be proclaimed in His name to all the nations, beginning at Jerusalem' (v.47). The gospel is a call to the nations to forego their nationalist agendas, to rally to the flag of the Lord of the nations, and to lay their tribute at His feet. It challenges every one of us, whatever our race, skin colour or social status, to tear up the script of our own self-made stories and to enlist with a clean start in God's big drama of redemption.

This is a bold claim to make in a pluralistic world, one regarded as arrogant. But the uniqueness of Jesus is the only way to the whole world's salvation. Only by being exclusive to Him can the story be inclusive of all. His unprecedented suffering and unheard-of resurrection form the unique centre-piece of all the stories He redeems.

This is His story, this is our song. And it is the world's story. If we Christians could only stay together, we might even teach the world to sing this song in perfect harmony!

DAY 10
LUKE 24:47-48

Luke 24:47-48

BIBLE READING

⁴⁴Then He told them, "These are My words that I spoke to you while I was still with you—that everything written about Me in the Law of Moses, the Prophets, and the Psalms must be fulfilled." ⁴⁵Then He opened their minds to understand the Scriptures. ⁴⁶He also said to them, "This is what is written: the Messiah would suffer and rise from the dead the third day ...

⁴⁷and repentance for forgiveness of sins would be proclaimed

in His name to all the nations, beginning at Jerusalem. ⁴⁸You are witnesses of these things."

THOUGHT: One Christian leader has said that the biggest challenge facing the Church in the twenty-first century is remaining true to the uniqueness and exclusivity of Jesus. This means holding fast to Jesus' own claim that He is the only way to God. Christianity is not one religion among others but in a category all by itself. Are you strong on this issue? You may be tested on this matter sooner than you think.

DAY
11
LUKE 24:48-53

AS WITH THE Emmaus Two, our personal stories are redeemed from insignificance and futility by being reattached to God's big story of salvation for the world! Because 'the End of the story' has already lived among us, we can be sure we are included in a story which had a good beginning and will have a satisfactory conclusion.

Since this is wholly God's work, we must rely utterly on being empowered by His Holy Spirit (vv.48-49). God creates and redeems. God appoints and assigns and works out His long-term covenantal purposes through the painfully human story of Israel. Having brought that stage of the story to its intended destination in the cross of His Son Jesus, God raises Him from the dead, so vindicating Him as Messiah and Lord. As the head of a great family invested blessing in his sons, or as a priest pronounced a lasting benediction on the worshippers, so the risen Lord blesses His witnessing disciples with all the creative potential of resurrection-life. No wonder they are overwhelmed with joy and overflow with praise. Who could ask for a better story to be part of than this?

Luke 24:48-53

⁴⁴Then He told them, "These are My words that I spoke to you while I was still with you—that everything written about Me in the Law of Moses, the Prophets, and the Psalms must be fulfilled." ⁴⁵Then He opened their minds to understand the Scriptures. ⁴⁶He also said to them, "This is what is written: the Messiah would suffer and rise from the dead the third day,

⁴⁷and repentance for forgiveness of sins would be proclaimed in His name to all the nations, beginning at Jerusalem.

⁴⁸You are witnesses of these things. ⁴⁹And look, I am sending you what My Father promised. As for you, stay in the city until you are empowered from on high."

THE ASCENSION OF JESUS

⁵⁰Then He led them out as far as Bethany, and lifting up His hands He blessed them. ⁵¹And while He was blessing them, He left them and was carried up into heaven. ⁵²After worshiping Him, they returned to Jerusalem with great joy. ⁵³And they were continually in the temple complex blessing God.

PRAYER: O Father, what a thought this is to carry into my day. My little personal story, when caught up into Your big story, is invested with a dignity and a meaning that almost blows my mind. I am part of a story that has a good beginning and a perfect ending because I belong to You. There is no story in the world I would rather be a part of than this. Thank You my Father. Hallelujah! All honour and glory be to Your peerless name. Amen.

SECTION 2 THE BIBLE AS GOD'S STORY

| THE BIBLE AS GOD'S STORY

In approaching the Bible, we must keep in mind that it has been given to us largely in the form of a *narrative*, or *story*. This should drastically affect the way we handle it.

In fact, as Eugene Peterson has reminded us: 'The *way* the Bible is written is every bit as important as *what* is written in it: Narrative – this huge, capacious story that pulls us into its plot and shows us our place in its development from beginning to ending. It takes the whole Bible to read any part of the Bible.' Of course, not every part of the Bible is 'narrative' in a literary sense. It includes laws and songs and words of wisdom. 'Sometimes,' says Peterson again, 'we are told that the Bible is a library made up of many kinds of writing: poems and hymns, sermons and letters, visions and dreams, genealogical lists and historical chronicles, moral teaching and admonition and proverbs. And, of course, story. But that is not so. It is all story.'

In one sense, then, even the non-narrative parts of the Bible – the wisdom literature, for instance – take for granted the particular story-line we are following of the one Creator God and His people, Israel, among whom such literature was treasured and preserved.

The Bible exhibits the features common to all gripping narratives. There is a *vivid opening*, acting like the rousing overture to a stirring symphony, which determines the shape of the plot. Every great drama has its *catastrophe*, disaster or fall which, in turn, calls forth a *rescue mission*. It has depth of *character development* which usually determines the quality of the story and distinguishes a classic novel from a 'pot-boiler' paperback bought at an airport bookstall to help time fly! And the best stories don't leave the plot hanging in the air but have a *satisfactory ending*. They are – to use the theologian's jargon – 'eschatological'; that is, they end well.

GOD'S STORY

The starting-point, then, for this journey of discovery is the fresh realisation that *the Bible is essentially God's story*. As Stanley Hauerwas and William Willimon note: 'We are forever getting confused into thinking that Scripture is mainly about what we are supposed to do, rather than a picture of who God is.' God is the chief actor in the drama that unfolds through the Bible. God reveals Himself to us by participating with us in the story.

The word 'God' refers simply to a deity whose character is not known before we start the story. Only by reading His story will we discover who the real 'God' is and find out, through interaction with events and people, what He says and feels and plans and does.

In *The Sacred Romance* Brent Curtis and John Eldredge ask: 'What if? Just what if we saw God not as Author, the cosmic mastermind behind all human experience, but as the central character in the larger story? What could we learn about his heart?'

PLOT-LINE

But, if the Bible tells the story of God, our next move is to ask: Is there a plot? Is God, in fact, working to a purpose or is He simply seen as reacting to events in a random way? Does God merely have a 'devotional' relationship with believers or has He a plan for human history and for His creation?

The whole Bible presupposes that He has, and psalmists, prophets and apostles celebrate it (Psa. 33:10-11; Isa. 46:10-11; Eph. 1:9-10).

PROMISE-PLAN

We can gain more purchase on what this plan entails by adopting Old Testament scholar Walter Kaiser's designation of it as the *'promise-plan of God'* – referred to in over forty passages in the New Testament simply as the *'promise'* (eg, Acts 26:6).

KINGDOM AND COVENANT

We can bring the promise-plan of God into even sharper focus by employing two key categories: *the kingdom of God* and *the concept of covenant*.

The kingdom of God is the overarching theme, viewed as God's lordly rule over creation and demonstrated partially in Israel's calling and kingship. It can be seen as decisively established in Jesus, especially in His cross, resurrection and exaltation to be Lord and Christ. God's kingdom is anticipated in the Church by the ruling presence of the Holy Spirit, and looked for as the eventual outcome of Christ's second coming. In other words, we enjoy the presence of God's kingdom and yet still pray 'your kingdom come'.

THE CONCEPT OF COVENANT

Covenant spells relationship and mutual agreement. William Dyrness defines covenant as 'a solemn promise made binding by an oath', often accompanied by signs, whether verbal or symbolic. In O. Palmer Robertson's words, 'a covenant is a bond-in-blood sovereignly administered'.

Covenants were made in the ancient world between individuals – as in the biblical case of David and Saul's son Jonathan – but our aim will be to trace the covenantal arrangements God makes.

The biblical story, then, can be seen in the broadest way as the implementing of *God's kingdom rule* in history through a series of *covenantal arrangements*: God's covenants with Noah, Abraham, Israel, David, and the new covenant promised by the prophets – all in pursuit of that coherent goal.

The approach adopted here has been graphically illustrated to show the five major Old Testament covenants across which the promise-plan of God makes its way to Christ.

He takes the weight of all the previous covenant commitments of God, launching the worldwide promised blessings and inaugurating the still future kingdom. This feature appears intermittently as a helpful reminder:

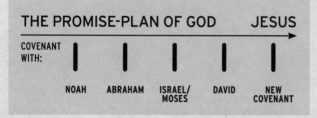

At the heart of God's promise-plan, as we shall see, is undoubtedly the promises and *covenant made with Abraham*. Genesis 12:1-3 is the launching pad for the redemptive story in Scripture.

Before we look at this, we first need to embrace the fact that *the Bible is our story too*.

To accept the gift of life is to acknowledge the call to participate in the flawed but glorious human story. To accept the call of grace is to accept the call to join the divine story, the redemptive, covenantal story of the kingdom of God, and to gain the recovery of our true humanness.

Abraham's faith was not that of a man seeking to fit God into his world, to make God useful to his success or family or even retirement. Abraham – whose faith-footsteps we all follow in – was enticed away from his culture by the glimpse of God's glory, lifted out of his world to be fitted amazingly and riskily into God's world and into God's adventure story.

THE DAILY READINGS which start today invite you to view human history as the unfolding of a great drama in which God is the chief actor.

DAY
12
ROMANS 15:7-9

I have found it helpful to view it as five overlapping, interlocking stories, which can be compared to the Olympic rings: the story of *God*; the story of God's *world*; the story of *Israel* in the Old Testament; the central story of *Jesus* as gathering in all the other stories; *our story* as the people of God, including your story and mine as we personally by faith participate in God's big story.

As an example of how these stories interact we can take Paul's brilliant summary statement in Romans 15:8-9, which encapsulates the whole biblical story. Here the *Jesus story* is viewed as the culmination of the *story of Israel*, among whom He comes as the Jewish Messiah (Christ) to bring to fruition God's promises to Abraham and the patriarchs. The result is that blessing reaches the whole *Gentile world* and, in this way, the *story is told of a God* who is both truthful and merciful.

At conversion, this story became the Roman Christian's story, and by grace it becomes *our* story too. Like Paul's original readers, we too are called to be characters in this story and invited to live it out by accepting one another in the Church and glorifying God together.

Romans 15:7-9

GLORIFYING GOD TOGETHER

⁷Therefore accept one another, just as the Messiah also accepted you, to the glory of God. ⁸Now I say that Christ has become a servant of the circumcised on behalf of the truth of God, to confirm the promises to the fathers, ⁹and so that Gentiles may glorify God for His mercy. As it is written:

> "Therefore I will praise You among the Gentiles,
> and I will sing psalms to Your name."

QUESTION: How secure are you in your relationship with the Lord? One of the characteristics of the human soul, say many psychologists, is the need to 'belong'. Those who do not feel they belong tend to be deeply insecure. This sense of belonging is extremely important in our relationship with the Lord. If it doesn't exist to a high degree then talk to your minister or a counsellor. And do so without delay.

DAY
13

2 CORINTHIANS 13:13
1 JOHN 3:19-21; 4:7-15

THE FORM TAKEN by the biblical narrative makes it clear that only by tracing the unfolding *story of God* in His interaction with history can we know who God really is.

'Story' – in the sense in which we are using the term – is therefore not inferior to 'doctrine', as if the matter could be better told in theological concepts. In fact, doctrines are essentially only shorthand ways of defining the terms in which we retell the story. The Christian doctrine of God as Trinity is a case in point, for it was an inevitable outcome of the story told in the New Testament. The apostles, who were heirs to the Jewish Old Testament relationship with the one Creator God, encountered Jesus, who reintroduced them to God as His Father and theirs. Through experiencing God's Spirit as the personal Spirit of

Jesus they were pressed, post-resurrection, to include Jesus in the same categories normally reserved for the one Creator God – and this without dissolving the unique 'oneness' of God! The story they lived was the raw material for the finished doctrine.

Through hearing God's story we encounter the real God, get to know His character, and find out what He's really like. In worship and through discipleship we relive God's story with Him, and in so doing find our true selves shaped by it.

2 Corinthians 13:13

BIBLE READING

[13]The grace of the Lord Jesus Christ, and the love of God, and the fellowship of the Holy Spirit be with all of you.*

1 John 3:19-21

BIBLE READING

[19]... that is how we will know we are of the truth, and will convince our hearts in His presence, [20]because if our hearts condemn us, God is greater than our hearts and knows all things.

[21]Dear friends, if our hearts do not condemn [us] we have confidence before God ...

1 John 4:7-15

BIBLE READING

KNOWING GOD THROUGH LOVE

[7]Dear friends, let us love one another, because love is from God, and everyone who loves has been born of God and knows God. [8]The one who does not love does not know God, because God is love. [9]God's love was revealed among us in this way: God sent His One and Only Son into the world so that we might live through Him. [10]Love consists in this: not that we loved God, but that He loved us and sent His Son to be the propitiation for our

*Some translations divide vv.12-13 into three verses so that v.13 becomes v.14.

sins. ¹¹Dear friends, if God loved us in this way, we also must love one another. ¹²No one has ever seen God. If we love one another, God remains in us and His love is perfected in us.

¹³This is how we know that we remain in Him and He in us: He has given to us from His Spirit. ¹⁴And we have seen and we testify that the Father has sent the Son as Savior of the world. ¹⁵Whoever confesses that Jesus is the Son of God—God remains in him and he in God.

THOUGHT: Do you realise that the story which the Trinity summarises is at its core a romantic one? The three Persons who form the Trinity enjoy a loving relationship in which there is perfect harmony. In this atmosphere a plan was devised to draw you into that inner circle. God thought it, Christ bought it, the Holy Spirit wrought it, and now, through grace, you've got it. No wonder it has been called 'The Greatest Story Ever Told'.

DAY
14
ROMANS 8:18-21

IN TELLING THE world's story, the Bible moves from first creation to new creation, addressing the concerns of the whole earth and all humankind. The story of Adam, of Israel – called to renew humanity – and Jesus – the Last Adam – are directly linked.

If we bear this in mind, we will not limit the Bible to private devotional exercises, but relish its power to speak truthfully across the whole range of human affairs. This will not provide us with all the answers to every question we decide to put on our agenda, but we will gain a wholly new and true vantage-point on reality. This creational approach will save us from devaluing the material and physical realm in favour of the 'spiritual' realm. Hopefully, it will incite our thinking to a world-view and our mission to world-vision.

In his stunning prophetic vision, Paul sees the destiny of believers and the future of creation mysteriously intertwined. As we know, our sin dragged creation down into fallenness and frustration. Now, strangely, our redemption offers hope to a groaning world. 'The creation is on tiptoe to see the wonderful sight of the sons of God coming into their own' (v.19, Phillips).

Romans 8:18-21

FROM GROANS TO GLORY

[18]For I consider that the sufferings of this present time are not worth comparing with the glory that is going to be revealed to us. [19]For the creation eagerly waits with anticipation for God's sons to be revealed. [20]For the creation was subjected to futility—not willingly, but because of Him who subjected it—in the hope [21]that the creation itself will also be set free from the bondage of corruption into the glorious freedom of God's children.

FOR PRAISE: Creation plays a great part in God's story. The old creation, because of sin, groans under the burden. Who can doubt it? Everything that lives is subject to disease. Life seems strangely poisoned at the fount. But hear with wonder the promise that the power released through the new creation will one day affect the old creation. The last word in the universe will not be a groan but Joy! Joy! Joy!

TO READ THE Bible well we must take history seriously and pay close attention to the *story of Israel* told in the Old Testament.

'... *salvation is from the Jews*' (v.22). This teaches us not only that the Messiah is a Jew but that the previous revelation, which God gave to Israel, is the birthplace of the world's salvation. In other words, Israel's story encapsulates the world's story. Israel was made the steward of our human vocation to reflect God's image by being 'holy as God is holy'. Israel was the nation entrusted with the revelation of the one Creator God which she was to pass on to the world so that none should live by bread alone. Israel was fated

DAY
15

JOHN 4:19-42

to bear the strange burden of the world's hopes.

The paradox of the Bible story is that only by being exclusively Jewish can it ever transcend all cultures. The specifically Jewish Messiah comes to slake the thirst of all so that we no longer need drink at Jacob's well or any other. This very Jewish Messiah leads all lost worshippers home to the Father to worship God neither at Samaritan shrines nor the Jerusalem Temple but 'in spirit and truth' (v.24) to which He alone gives access.

Salvation is truly 'from the Jews', for from them and their history comes the *Saviour of the world* (v.42).

BIBLE READING	**John 4:19-42**

[19]"Sir," the woman replied, "I see that You are a prophet. [20]Our fathers worshiped on this mountain, yet you [Jews] say that the place to worship is in Jerusalem."

[21]Jesus told her, "Believe Me, woman, an hour is coming when you will worship the Father neither on this mountain nor in Jerusalem. [22]You Samaritans worship what you do not know. We worship what we do know, because salvation is from the Jews. [23]But an hour is coming, and is now here, when the true worshipers will worship the Father in spirit and truth. Yes, the Father wants such people to worship Him. [24]God is spirit, and those who worship Him must worship in spirit and truth."

[25]The woman said to Him, "I know that Messiah is coming" (who is called Christ). "When He comes, He will explain everything to us."

[26]"I am [He]," Jesus told her, "the One speaking to you."

THE RIPENED HARVEST

[27]Just then His disciples arrived, and they were amazed that He was talking with a woman. Yet no one said, "What do You want?" or "Why are You talking with her?"

[28]Then the woman left her water jar, went into town, and told the men, [29]"Come, see a man who told me everything I ever did! Could this be the Messiah?" [30]They left the town and made their way to Him.

³¹In the meantime the disciples kept urging Him, "Rabbi, eat something."

³²But He said, "I have food to eat that you don't know about."

³³The disciples said to one another, "Could someone have brought Him something to eat?"

³⁴"My food is to do the will of Him who sent Me and to finish His work," Jesus told them. ³⁵"Don't you say, 'There are still four more months, then comes the harvest'? Listen [to what] I'm telling you: Open your eyes and look at the fields, for they are ready for harvest. ³⁶The reaper is already receiving pay and gathering fruit for eternal life, so the sower and reaper can rejoice together. ³⁷For in this case the saying is true: 'One sows and another reaps.' ³⁸I sent you to reap what you didn't labor for; others have labored, and you have benefited from their labor."

THE SAVIOR OF THE WORLD

³⁹Now many Samaritans from that town believed in Him because of what the woman said when she testified, "He told me everything I ever did." ⁴⁰Therefore, when the Samaritans came to Him, they asked Him to stay with them, and He stayed there two days. ⁴¹Many more believed because of what He said. ⁴²And they told the woman, "We no longer believe because of what you said, for we have heard for ourselves and know that this really is the Savior of the world."

FOR ACTION: The Samaritan woman represents all who are thirsty everywhere. Like her, many have tried every sensual experience and remained unsatisfied. True soul satisfaction is found only in God, who offers us living water in Jesus. But in order to receive it, all must bow the knee to Him. When we humble ourselves and drink from the source of a Jewish Messiah, we find Him to be the Saviour of the world. Nothing satisfies like Jesus.

AS WE HAVE seen in the first part of our introduction, the *story of Jesus* is the key that unlocks the whole Bible. To miss this is to miss everything. The Pharisees were diligent in their Bible study. But keen Bible students though they were, they refused to acknowledge Jesus and so deprived themselves of the life-changing impartation of the truth of God's Word. *The Big Story* takes an unashamedly Christ-centred approach to the Bible. Not that we read Jesus back into Old Testament in an artificial or contrived way. We do, however, see the Lord Jesus Christ as the central figure in God's plans. Into His safe keeping is entrusted the fulfilment of all previous Old Testament types and patterns. We repeat once more: we will not understand Jesus without understanding the Old Testament which leads up to Him; nor, on the other hand, will we understand the Old Testament without seeing it in the light of its completion in Him.

As the Samaritan woman said to Jesus: 'I do know that the Messiah is coming. When he arrives, we'll get the whole story' (4:25, *The Message*). In Him, the final Word made flesh, the *story of Israel* is successfully rewritten, the *story of God* is fully revealed, and the *story of the world* redeemingly redrawn.

BIBLE READING

John 5:31-40

FOUR WITNESSES TO JESUS

³¹"If I testify about Myself, My testimony is not valid. ³²There is Another who testifies about Me, and I know that the testimony He gives about Me is valid. ³³You have sent [messengers] to John, and he has testified to the truth. ³⁴I don't receive man's testimony, but I say these things so that you may be saved. ³⁵John was a burning and shining lamp, and for a time you were willing to enjoy his light.

³⁶"But I have a greater testimony than John's because of the works that the Father has given Me to accomplish. These very

works I am doing testify about Me that the Father has sent Me. ³⁷The Father who sent Me has Himself testified about Me. You have not heard His voice at any time, and you haven't seen His form. ³⁸You don't have His word living in you, because you don't believe the One He sent. ³⁹You pore over the Scriptures because you think you have eternal life in them, yet they testify about Me. ⁴⁰And you are not willing to come to Me that you may have life."

THOUGHT: Have you heard the expression 'All roads lead to Rome'? Something similar can be said about the Bible. Wherever you start in Scripture there is a road that leads to Jesus. Every time you open up your Bible remember this: it wasn't Jesus who came out of the Bible, it was the Bible that came out of Jesus. To understand it you have to know Him.

DAY
17
ROMANS 15:1-4

'EVEN IF IT was written in Scripture long ago, you can be sure it's written for *us*' (v.4, *The Message*, my italics). So the Bible is telling *our* story too.

We can take the Word 'personally' and 'corporately'.

When you and I believingly receive the biblical story we are drawn into the action and find ourselves caught up in the saving movement of God. As the late Lesslie Newbigin taught us well, we will learn to *indwell* the story so that we begin to look out *from within* the biblical world with new eyes onto the world in which we live.

Rather than striving to make the Bible relevant to our lives, it might be better to begin to allow our lives to be made relevant to the Bible! By faith, we can trade in the dog-eared, self-written script of our own self-directed lives in order to be written into the larger script of God's big story. When this happens, 'my' story becomes 'our' story as we are joined to a community of faith, the one covenant family of God. We gain, at once, a new history, and in the Church we become new chapters written by the Spirit into the script of the ongoing story.

Romans 15:1-4

PLEASING OTHERS, NOT OURSELVES

15 Now we who are strong have an obligation to bear the weaknesses of those without strength, and not to please ourselves. ²Each one of us must please his neighbor for his good, in order to build him up. ³For even the Messiah did not please Himself. On the contrary, as it is written, "The insults of those who insult You have fallen on Me." ⁴For whatever was written before was written for our instruction, so that through our endurance and through the encouragement of the Scriptures we may have hope.

PRAYER: My Father and my God, help me to grasp more clearly this concept of the bigger story - and to live in wonder of the fact that I am part of it. Help me also to understand that without demeaning my family attachments or depriving my loved ones of my affection, I can relate to my Christian brothers and sisters with a deeper sense of kinship than it is possible to experience with my blood family. Amen.

DAY
18

RUTH 4

A NOTABLE FEATURE of the biblical story is that seemingly minor stories gain their significance from the part they play in the overall narrative of God. This warns us against using Bible characters solely to draw moral or even spiritual lessons unless at the same time we take the trouble to place these characters in the story and to show how integral they are to it. In fact, many biblical characters make decidedly shaky moral examples! Far better to see them as stories about how unlikely people can, by grace, be grafted onto God's story.

Ruth is a shining example. This simple story of a young widow and the redemptive friendships which change her life gains its significance from the way the book is placed in the canon. There it is a beacon of light in the darkest days of the judges (1:1). Even more strikingly, it forges another link by joining the ancient patriarchs with the future King David (4:13-22). In short, Ruth serves both to offset the terrible 'Bethlehem' stories of Judges 18-21 and to carry forward the promise-plan of God to the model Davidic king and eventually to the Messianic Davidic King who shared the same birthplace.

Ruth says to each of us: 'You can make a difference. Your small-scale domestic story - if lived faithfully before God - can be of strategic importance to God!'

Ruth 4

BIBLE READING

RUTH AND BOAZ MARRY

4 Boaz went to the gate [of the town] and sat down there. Soon, the family redeemer Boaz had spoken about came by. Boaz called him by name and said, "Come over here and sit down." So he went over and sat down. ²Then Boaz took 10 men of the city's elders and said, "Sit here." And they sat down. ³He said to the redeemer, "Naomi, who has returned from the land of Moab, is selling a piece of land that belonged to our brother Elimelech. ⁴I thought I should inform you: Buy [it] back in the presence of those seated here and in the presence of the elders of my people. If you want to redeem [it], do so. But if you do not want to redeem [it], tell me, so that I will know, because there isn't anyone other than you to redeem [it], and I am next after you."

"I want to redeem [it]," he answered.

⁵Then Boaz said, "On the day you buy the land from Naomi, you will also acquire Ruth the Moabitess, the wife of the deceased man, to perpetuate the man's name on his property."

⁶The redeemer replied, "I can't redeem [it] myself, or I will ruin my [own] inheritance. Take my right of redemption, because I can't redeem it."

⁷At an earlier period in Israel, a man removed his sandal and gave [it] to the other party in order to make any matter [legally] binding concerning the right of redemption or the exchange of property. This was [the method of] legally binding a transaction in Israel.

⁸So the redeemer removed his sandal and said to Boaz, "Buy back [the property] yourself."

⁹Boaz said to the elders and all the people, "You are witnesses today that I am buying from Naomi everything that belonged to Elimelech, Chilion, and Mahlon. ¹⁰I will also acquire Ruth the Moabitess, Mahlon's widow, as my wife, to perpetuate the deceased man's name on his property, so that his name will not disappear among his relatives or from the gate of his home. You are witnesses today."

¹¹The elders and all the people who were at the gate said, "We are witnesses. May the LORD make the woman who is entering your house like Rachel and Leah, who together built the house of Israel. May you be powerful in Ephrathah and famous in Bethlehem. ¹²May your house become like the house of Perez, the son Tamar bore to Judah, because of the offspring the LORD will give you by this young woman."

¹³Boaz took Ruth and she became his wife. When he was intimate with her, the LORD enabled her to conceive, and she gave birth to a son. ¹⁴Then the women said to Naomi, "Praise the LORD, who has not left you without a family redeemer today. May his name be famous in Israel. ¹⁵He will renew your life and sustain you in your old age. Indeed, your daughter-in-law, who loves you and is better to you than seven sons, has given birth to him." ¹⁶Naomi took the child, placed him on her lap, and took care of him. ¹⁷The neighbor women said, "A son has been born to Naomi," and they named him Obed. He was the father of Jesse, the father of David.

DAVID'S GENEALOGY FROM JUDAH'S SON

¹⁸Now this is the genealogy of Perez:

Perez fathered Hezron.
¹⁹ Hezron fathered Ram,
who fathered Amminadab.
²⁰ Amminadab fathered Nahshon,
who fathered Salmon.
²¹ Salmon fathered Boaz,
who fathered Obed.
²² And Obed fathered Jesse,
who fathered David.

QUESTION: Does the phrase 'You can make a difference' fall flat on your ears? Maybe you feel your life is humdrum and you struggle to see how it can be of strategic importance to God. Though it may be hard for you to see the truth we are presenting here be assured of this: faithfulness in small things - a character quality - has a part in God's story that is equal to the exploits of the renowned and the great. It really does.

DAY
19

PSALM 33

EVEN IF WE accept that the Bible is God's story, we do need to ask: Is there a plot? Does God merely react randomly to events by stage-managing an occasional show of force to indicate His existence? Or does He, perhaps, have a personal relationship with believers and nothing more?

No, the Bible, including this psalm, assures us that God has *plans*. These plans are implemented by His *covenant word* which forges a reliable covenant partnership with His people (v.4), just as His *creative word* well ordered everything at the beginning (vv.6-9). So the *plans of the Lord* shape the way the world is going. Despite appearances to the contrary, it is not military hardware that determines the outcome of history (vv.16-17). And the *eyes of the Lord* oversee His purpose (vv.18-19). The righteous are not promised success and wealth but - even in famine and death - a covenant love that will not let them go (v.19).

The power which made the world, the plans that steer it to its intended goal, the providential care that watches over the process - all are symptoms of that unfailing love of God which we dare to hope will be the last word in the universe.

Psalm 33

PRAISE TO THE CREATOR

¹ Rejoice in the Lord, you righteous ones;
  praise from the upright is beautiful.
² Praise the Lord with the lyre;
  make music to Him with a ten-stringed harp.
³ Sing a new song to Him;
  play skillfully on the strings, with a joyful shout.

⁴ For the word of the Lord is right,
  and all His work is trustworthy.
⁵ He loves righteousness and justice;
  the earth is full of the Lord's unfailing love.

⁶ The heavens were made by the word of the Lord,
  and all the stars, by the breath of His mouth.
⁷ He gathers the waters of the sea into a heap;
  He puts the depths into storehouses.
⁸ Let the whole earth tremble before the Lord;
  let all the inhabitants of the world stand in awe of Him.
⁹ For He spoke, and it came into being;
  He commanded, and it came into existence.

¹⁰ The Lord frustrates the counsel of the nations;
   He thwarts the plans of the peoples.
¹¹ The counsel of the Lord stands forever,
   the plans of His heart from generation to generation.
¹² Happy is the nation whose God is the Lord—
   the people He has chosen to be His own possession!

¹³ The Lord looks down from heaven;
   He observes everyone.
¹⁴ He gazes on all the inhabitants of the earth
   from His dwelling place.
¹⁵ He alone crafts their hearts;
   He considers all their works.
¹⁶ A king is not saved by a large army;
   a warrior will not be delivered by great strength.

¹⁷ The horse is a false hope for safety;
   it provides no escape by its great power.

¹⁸ Now the eye of the LORD is on those who fear Him—
   those who depend on His faithful love
¹⁹ to deliver them from death
   and to keep them alive in famine.

²⁰ We wait for the LORD;
   He is our help and shield.
²¹ For our hearts rejoice in Him,
   because we trust in His holy name.
²² May Your faithful love rest on us, LORD,
   for we put our hope in You.

TO PONDER: It may be hard to believe as one looks at the world that a providential God is working out all things according to His purpose. But He is. Scripture may not tell us all we would like to know about why God allows bad things to happen to good people, but the psalmists shed some light on the darkened way by telling us, as in this psalm, that despite the God-denying look of things, He is in control. Ours is not to trace but to trust.

DAY
20
ISAIAH 46

AS WE PREPARE to trace the unfolding story of God in the Bible we note that Isaiah, too, is confident that God has a *plan and purpose* (vv.10-11). The prophet is seeking to raise the spirits and sights of the exiles in Babylon, swamped as they are with Babylonian propaganda and values. But God's plans are sovereign and *rooted in a long history* of sustaining His people from birth to old age and grey hair (v.4). Our memory of God's 'proven track record' plays no tricks, for God's actions are based not on whim but on the forethought of *long-term plans* (vv.9-10). Yet God 'moves in mysterious ways His wonders to perform', summoning 'a bird of prey' from the East – the Medo-Persian

Emperor, Cyrus - who will conquer Babylon and let God's people go (v.11). This is a strange way to effect a new exodus, but all God's plans are *saving plans* to those who believe (v.13). Not that knowing God's plans makes us party to privileged, 'insider' information which we can proudly use to control events or people. Rather, it evokes a deep, daring *trust*.

In the end, there is all the difference in the world between a god you carry and *a God who carries you* - between a god you include in your plans and a God who includes you in His!

Isaiah 46

BIBLE READING

THERE IS NO ONE LIKE GOD

46 Bel crouches; Nebo cowers.
Their idols are consigned to beasts and cattle.
The [images] you carry are loaded,
as a burden for the weary [animal].
² The gods cower; they crouch together;
they are not able to rescue the burden,
but they themselves go into captivity.

³ "Listen to Me, house of Jacob,
all the remnant of the house of Israel,
who have been sustained from the womb,
carried along since birth.
⁴ I will be the same until [your] old age,
and I will bear [you] up when you turn gray.
I have made [you], and I will carry [you];
I will bear and save [you].

⁵ "Who will you compare Me or make Me equal to?
Who will you measure Me with,
so that we should be like each other?
⁶ Those who pour out their bags of gold
and weigh out silver on scales—
they hire a goldsmith and he makes it into a god.
Then they kneel and bow down to it.

7 They lift it to their shoulder and bear it along;
   they set it in its place, and there it stands;
   it does not budge from its place.
   They cry out to it but it doesn't answer;
   it saves no one from his trouble.

8 "Remember this and be brave;
   take it to heart, you transgressors!
9 Remember what happened long ago,
   for I am God, and there is no other;
   [I am] God, and no one is like Me.
10 I declare the end from the beginning,
   and from long ago what is not yet done,
   saying: My plan will take place,
   and I will do all My will.
11 I call a bird of prey from the east,
   a man for My purpose from a far country.
   Yes, I have spoken; so I will also bring it about.
   I have planned it; I will also do it.
12 Listen to me, you hardhearted,
   far removed from justice:
13 I am bringing My justice near;
   it is not far away,
   and My salvation will not delay.
   I will put salvation in Zion,
   My splendor in Israel."

QUESTION: An elderly Christian talking to a group of young believers told them how his life had changed since he resigned as 'Director of the Universe'. One day he had awakened to the truth that he had been carrying God rather than letting God carry him. Here's the question: Are you trying to hold God up or is He holding you? Relax. Let God carry you. He has been holding up the world for aeons and is hardly likely to let you slip.

IN A MARVELLOUS movement of grace, the Father's eternal love reaches out to draw us back into His covenant family, sweeps into history in the incarnate love of His Son Jesus to forgive us our sins, and is vividly brought home to our experience through the impact of His Spirit by whom we are sealed as God's own possession.

DAY
21

EPHESIANS 1:1-14

Just as Israel was entrusted with the wisdom of God in the form of the law, so now, 'in Christ', and through the Spirit, Christian believers are privileged to share God's secret wisdom. We are initiated into 'the mystery of His will', the strategic plan of God to redeem His creation (vv.9-10).

The scope of this is breathtaking. God intends to reunite everything, to restore the original harmony to a fractured world, and to reconcile people to each other and to Himself. 'Everything will again be united in Him,' wrote Dr Martyn Lloyd-Jones. 'That is the message and that is God's plan. This is the mystery which has been revealed to us. Do you know that these things are so marvellous that you will never hear anything greater, either in this world or in the world to come?' And everything in the working out of this plan by the Father, Son and Holy Spirit tends to the praise of the glory of God's grace (vv.6,12,14).

Ephesians 1:1-14

BIBLE
READING

GREETING

1 Paul, an apostle of Christ Jesus by God's will:
To the saints and believers in Christ Jesus at Ephesus. ²Grace to you and peace from God our Father and the Lord Jesus Christ.

GOD'S RICH BLESSINGS

³Blessed be the God and Father of our Lord Jesus Christ, who has blessed us with every spiritual blessing in the heavens, in Christ; ⁴for He chose us in Him, before the foundation of

the world, to be holy and blameless in His sight. In love [5]He predestined us to be adopted through Jesus Christ for Himself, according to His favor and will, [6]to the praise of His glorious grace that He favored us with in the Beloved.

[7]In Him we have redemption through His blood, the forgiveness of our trespasses, according to the riches of His grace [8]that He lavished on us with all wisdom and understanding. [9]He made known to us the mystery of His will, according to His good pleasure that He planned in Him [10]for the administration of the days of fulfillment —to bring everything together in the Messiah, both things in heaven and things on earth in Him.

[11]In Him we were also made His inheritance, predestined according to the purpose of the One who works out everything in agreement with the decision of His will, [12]so that we who had already put our hope in the Messiah might bring praise to His glory.

[13]In Him you also, when you heard the word of truth, the gospel of your salvation—in Him when you believed—were sealed with the promised Holy Spirit. [14]He is the down payment of our inheritance, for the redemption of the possession, to the praise of His glory.

PRAYER: O Father, thank You that You have given me the gift of Your Holy Spirit, who seals me as Your possession and continues to reveal to me Your redemptive plans. I am so thankful, too, that in Jesus You bring together all the divided strands of history. Surely there can be nothing greater in earth or heaven than that Jesus my Saviour will bring all things to a glorious conclusion. Everlasting praise be to Your holy name. Amen.

DAY
22

ACTS 3:17-26

THIS STIRRING NARRATIVE reinforces what we have discovered so far. In the dramatic aftermath of the day of Pentecost, Peter preaches Jesus as the One who fulfils all Israel's long-held prophetic hopes (v.18).

In the mystery of His ways, God achieves this despite - even because of - the ignorant rejection of Jesus by the people He had prepared to receive

Him! And just as Jesus, by dying and rising, validates all God's dealings in the *past*, so His second coming is the guarantee of God's *future* plans for the restoration of all things (vv.20-21). Whether past, present or future, Jesus is clearly the crux of all God's purposes. All the prophets spoke of these days and they related them to Jesus (v.24).

The privileged natural heirs of a covenant which promises blessing for 'all peoples on earth' should have known this better than anyone. To them the Christ makes His first appeal. But for all of us, Jesus is the *one* prophet who embodies what all the prophets announced. We cannot pick and mix here; He is all or nothing! To listen to Him in obedient faith is to embrace God's vision of worldwide blessing. To refuse to hear Him is to miss the plot entirely.

Acts 3:17-26

BIBLE READING

[17]"And now, brothers, I know that you did it in ignorance, just as your leaders also did. [18]But what God predicted through the mouth of all the prophets—that His Messiah would suffer—He has fulfilled in this way. [19]Therefore repent and turn back, that your sins may be wiped out so that seasons of refreshing may come from the presence of the Lord, [20]and He may send Jesus, who has been appointed Messiah for you. [21]Heaven must welcome Him until the times of the restoration of all things, which God spoke about by the mouth of His holy prophets from the beginning. [22]Moses said:

'The Lord your God will raise up for you a Prophet like me from among your brothers. You must listen to Him in everything He will say to you. [23]And it will be that everyone who will not listen to that Prophet will be completely cut off from the people.'

[24]"In addition, all the prophets who have spoken, from Samuel and those after him, have also announced these days. [25]You are the sons of the prophets and of the covenant that

God made with your forefathers, saying to Abraham, 'And in your seed all the families of the earth will be blessed.' [26]God raised up His Servant and sent Him first to you to bless you by turning each of you from your evil ways."

THOUGHT: When Peter, James and John saw Jesus transfigured before them, we read that Moses and Elijah were present also (Matt. 17:1-13). Moses was the one who gave the law to the people of Israel; Elijah was the one who called them back to it. You can be sure of this: had Jesus not come and paid our debt to the law on Calvary, Moses and Elijah would never have been accorded a place in heaven. We are all what we are because Jesus is what He is.

DAY
23
ACTS 26:1-23

WE HAVE ALREADY noted that in the Bible there is *one* promise, God's single plan of salvation. Paul's defence before Agrippa illustrates the point: 'And now I am standing trial for the hope of *the promise* made by God to our fathers' (v.6, NASB). 'Paul's confidence then,' says Walter Kaiser, 'rested on a single promise, not a prediction, nor a number of scattered prognostications. It was a definite singular plan of God to benefit one man and through him to bless the whole world.'

Meeting the risen Jesus on the Damascus Road transformed Paul's view of the promise-plan of God. Nothing but the resurrection could have convinced the arch-Pharisee that the dead and discredited Messianic pretender, Jesus of Nazareth, was, in fact, the long-hoped-for Messiah and the key to our hopes and all God's dreams. Clearly, Paul did not convert to a new religion; all he now experiences 'in Christ' and understands of God's plan is the résumé of all the previous stages of the story. This remains the Jewish hope (v.7) until the light of Christ dawns (v.23).

Paul risks his life to tell this story because he knows it 'was not done in a corner' so as to become merely a matter of private religion but is 'public truth' to be proclaimed on the world stage to Jew and Gentile alike as the light of freedom and grace (vv.17-18, 23-26).

Acts 26:1-23

PAUL'S DEFENSE BEFORE AGRIPPA

26 Agrippa said to Paul, "It is permitted for you to speak for yourself."

Then Paul stretched out his hand and began his defense: [2]"I consider myself fortunate, King Agrippa, that today I am going to make a defense before you about everything I am accused of by the Jews, [3]especially since you are an expert in all the Jewish customs and controversies. Therefore I beg you to listen to me patiently.

[4]"All the Jews know my way of life from my youth, which was spent from the beginning among my own nation and in Jerusalem. [5]They had previously known me for quite some time, if they were willing to testify, that according to the strictest party of our religion I lived as a Pharisee. [6]And now I stand on trial for the hope of the promise made by God to our fathers, [7][the promise] our 12 tribes hope to attain as they earnestly serve Him night and day. Because of this hope I am being accused by the Jews, O king! [8]Why is it considered incredible by any of you that God raises the dead? [9]In fact, I myself supposed it was necessary to do many things in opposition to the name of Jesus the Nazarene. [10]This I actually did in Jerusalem, and I locked up many of the saints in prison, since I had received authority for that from the chief priests. When they were put to death, I cast my vote against them. [11]In all the synagogues I often tried to make them blaspheme by punishing them. Being greatly enraged at them, I even pursued them to foreign cities.

PAUL'S ACCOUNT OF HIS CONVERSION AND COMMISSION

[12]"Under these circumstances I was traveling to Damascus with authority and a commission from the chief priests. [13]At midday, while on the road, O king, I saw a light from heaven brighter than the sun, shining around me and those traveling with me. [14]When we had all fallen to the ground, I heard a voice

speaking to me in the Hebrew language, 'Saul, Saul, why are you persecuting Me? It is hard for you to kick against the goads.'

[15]"But I said, 'Who are You, Lord?'

"And the Lord replied: 'I am Jesus, whom you are persecuting. [16]But get up and stand on your feet. For I have appeared to you for this purpose, to appoint you as a servant and a witness of things you have seen, and of things in which I will appear to you. [17]I will rescue you from the people and from the Gentiles, to whom I now send you, [18]to open their eyes that they may turn from darkness to light and from the power of Satan to God, that they may receive forgiveness of sins and a share among those who are sanctified by faith in Me.'

[19]"Therefore, King Agrippa, I was not disobedient to the heavenly vision. [20]Instead, I preached to those in Damascus first, and to those in Jerusalem and in all the region of Judea, and to the Gentiles, that they should repent and turn to God, and do works worthy of repentance. [21]For this reason the Jews seized me in the temple complex and were trying to kill me. [22]Since I have obtained help that comes from God, to this day I stand and testify to both small and great, saying nothing else than what the prophets and Moses said would take place— [23]that the Messiah must suffer, and that as the first to rise from the dead, He would proclaim light to our people and to the Gentiles."

QUESTION: Has someone broken a promise to you lately? There is hardly a human being on earth who has not had this experience. The saying goes like this: 'Promises are made to be broken.' Not God's promises, however. It has been calculated that there are 365 promises in the Bible, one for every day of the year. And every promise of God can be banked on. Hold fast to this: others may break their promises but the Almighty - never.

LUKE'S FINAL VIEW of Paul shows him under some kind of house arrest, still taken up with 'the hope of Israel' for the coming of God's kingdom. Connected by the prophets to the arrival of the eagerly awaited Messiah, this stream of hope, Paul argues, had flowed into Jesus, and he worked tirelessly to convince others about this (v.23).

DAY
24
ACTS 28:17-31

Again we notice that the apostles viewed the gospel not as an innovation, a brand-new religion that had popped up without precedent, but as the fulfilment of texts and teaching, promises and prophecies deeply embedded in the Jewish Scriptures. But, in a tragic and ironic twist to the story, those whom God had prepared to receive their Messiah repeated their own history and closed their ears to His truth. In God's sovereignty, however, even this is turned to good. Since it was God's intention all along that Israel should bear His gospel to the world, He achieves this not through their co-operation but despite it – so sending the message to the Gentiles who, Paul asserts, 'will listen' (vv.26-28).

How persistent God is in His plans to bless the world! In the Greek text, Luke's very last words here are 'without hindrance' (v.31). How apt, for the story of God's kingdom and its King, the Lord Jesus Christ, is an ongoing story in which we are challenged to take part.

Acts 28:17-31

BIBLE
READING

PAUL'S FIRST INTERVIEW WITH ROMAN JEWS

¹⁷After three days he called together the leaders of the Jews. And when they had gathered he said to them: "Brothers, although I have done nothing against our people or the customs of our forefathers, I was delivered as a prisoner from Jerusalem into the hands of the Romans ¹⁸who, after examining me, wanted to release me, since I had not committed a capital offense. ¹⁹Because the Jews objected, I was compelled to appeal to Caesar; it was not as though I had any accusation against my nation. ²⁰So, for this reason I've

asked to see you and speak to you. In fact, it is for the hope of Israel that I'm wearing this chain."

²¹And they said to him, "We haven't received any letters about you from Judea; none of the brothers has come and reported or spoken anything evil about you. ²²But we consider it suitable to hear from you what you think. For concerning this sect, we are aware that it is spoken against everywhere."

THE RESPONSE TO PAUL'S MESSAGE

²³After arranging a day with him, many came to him at his lodging. From dawn to dusk he expounded and witnessed about the kingdom of God. He persuaded them concerning Jesus from both the Law of Moses and the Prophets. ²⁴Some were persuaded by what he said, but others did not believe.

²⁵Disagreeing among themselves, they began to leave after Paul made one statement: "The Holy Spirit correctly spoke through the prophet Isaiah to your forefathers ²⁶when He said,

'Go to this people and say:
"You will listen and listen, yet never understand;
and you will look and look, yet never perceive.
²⁷ For this people's heart has grown callous, their ears are
    hard of hearing,
and they have shut their eyes; otherwise
    they might see with their eyes
and hear with their ears, understand with their heart,
and be converted—and I would heal them."'

²⁸Therefore, let it be known to you that this saving work of God has been sent to the Gentiles; they will listen!" [²⁹After he said these things, the Jews departed, while engaging in a prolonged debate among themselves.]

PAUL'S MINISTRY UNHINDERED

³⁰Then he stayed two whole years in his own rented house. And he welcomed all who visited him, ³¹proclaiming the kingdom of God and teaching the things concerning the Lord Jesus Christ with full boldness and without hindrance.

THOUGHT: How persistent God is in His plans to bless the world. He will let nothing hinder or deter Him. Persistency has been defined as the ability to keep going no matter what obstacles are in the way. The good news is that God is able to help us develop that same characteristic in our own hearts but it won't happen automatically. It comes by spending time with Him. There is no other way.

IN DEFENDING HIMSELF against the charge of being inconsistent, Paul offers us this gem: 'For every one of God's promises is "Yes" in Him [Christ]' (v.20). That all the promises of God find their 'Yes' in Jesus does not mean He randomly rubber stamps these promises but rather that they *all converge on Him* as the focal point of a coherent plan that occasions them all.

DAY
25
2 CORINTHIANS 1:12-22

It is my conviction that nothing from the Old Testament bypasses Jesus. Every promise and prophecy goes through Him and in the process is fulfilled and transformed. Every covenantal connection connects with Him, every tributary of truth flows into His river, each aspect of God's strategy focuses and is filled-full in Him! All the prophetic affirmations God has ever given add up to one mighty 'Yes' which is Jesus! He is truly the final Word.

No wonder in Him we are established, empowered, owned as belonging to God, and guaranteed a future by the Spirit of God (vv.21-22). What would all our 'Amens' amount to if they were not responses to His resounding 'Yes'?

2 Corinthians 1:12-22

BIBLE
READING

A CLEAR CONSCIENCE

¹²For our boast is this: the testimony of our conscience that we have conducted ourselves in the world, and especially toward you, with God-given sincerity and purity, not by

fleshly wisdom but by God's grace. [13]Now we are writing you nothing other than what you can read and also understand. I hope you will understand completely— [14]as you have partially understood us—that we are your reason for pride, as you are ours, in the day of our Lord Jesus.

A VISIT POSTPONED

[15]In this confidence, I planned to come to you first, so you could have a double benefit, [16]and to go on to Macedonia with your help, then come to you again from Macedonia and be given a start by you on my journey to Judea. [17]So when I planned this, was I irresponsible? Or what I plan, do I plan in a purely human way so that I say "Yes, yes" and "No, no" [simultaneously]? [18]As God is faithful, our message to you is not "Yes and no." [19]For the Son of God, Jesus Christ, who was preached among you by us—by me and Silvanus and Timothy—did not become "Yes and no"; on the contrary, "Yes" has come about in Him. [20]For every one of God's promises is "Yes" in Him. Therefore the "Amen" is also through Him for God's glory through us. [21]Now the One who confirms us with you in Christ, and has anointed us, is God; [22]He has also sealed us and given us the Spirit as a down payment in our hearts.

TO PONDER: A great Bible translator of the early twentieth century was a man called James Moffatt. He translated 2 Corinthians 1:20 in this way: 'The divine "yes" has at last sounded in him [Jesus], for in him is the "yes" that affirms all the promises of God.' Many think Christianity is a 'No' religion – 'No' to this, 'No' to that. Instead it says 'Yes' to life – life more abundant. And Jesus is that life. Aren't you glad you have said 'Yes' to God's 'Yes'?

PAUL TALKS INTRIGUINGLY of the *'covenants of the promise'.* In other words, there are several covenants - in the plural - which all serve the one singular promise-plan of God.

The approach being followed in *The Big Story* looks at the five major Old Testament covenants across which the promise-plan of God makes its way to Christ (as illustrated in the diagram - see, for example, page 29).

Such a diagram, of course, conceals the uneven progress of God's plan. It masks the many occasions when God makes Himself strangely vulnerable to rebuff, or when He enters into risky intercessory negotiations with His praying people.

But what it does show is that all the covenantal commitments God makes are intended to further the progress of His promise-plan on its way through history to its crucial goal in Jesus and its ultimate goal in the renewal of His whole creation. What a plan! What a prospect!

At the heart of God's promise-plan, as we shall see, is undoubtedly the promise and the covenant made with Abraham in Genesis 12:1-3 where Abraham is promised *descendants*, a *land* and a *relationship with God characterised by blessing.* And the bottom line of His promise - later guaranteed by covenant - is God's intention to bring *blessing to all the nations of the world.* The exclusive relationship with Abraham and his descendants, in other words, tokens the commitment of the one Creator God to redeem the whole of His creation, which is why our story will begin with Noah.

Ephesians 2:11-22

BIBLE
READING

UNITY IN CHRIST

[11]So then, remember that at one time you were Gentiles in the flesh—called "the uncircumcised" by those called "the circumcised," done by hand in the flesh. [12]At that time you

were without the Messiah, excluded from the citizenship of Israel, and foreigners to the covenants of the promise, with no hope and without God in the world. [13]But now in Christ Jesus, you who were far away have been brought near by the blood of the Messiah. [14]For He is our peace, who made both groups one and tore down the dividing wall of hostility. In His flesh, [15]He did away with the law of the commandments in regulations, so that He might create in Himself one new man from the two, resulting in peace. [16][He did this so] that He might reconcile both to God in one body through the cross and put the hostility to death by it. [17]When [Christ] came, He proclaimed the good news of peace to you who were far away and peace to those who were near. [18]For through Him we both have access by one Spirit to the Father. [19]So then you are no longer foreigners and strangers, but fellow citizens with the saints, and members of God's household, [20]built on the foundation of the apostles and prophets, with Christ Jesus Himself as the cornerstone. [21]The whole building is being fitted together in Him and is growing into a holy sanctuary in the Lord, [22]in whom you also are being built together for God's dwelling in the Spirit.

PRAYER: My Father and my God, I pause before moving on into whatever lies before me to once again give You praise and thanks that I am on the pathway of faith because of Your commitment to redeem Your creation. Drive this truth deeper into my spirit, dear Lord, so that I shall see, and see even more clearly, that salvation is mine not because of my merit but because of Your mercy. All honour and glory be to Your name. Amen.

SECTION

NOAH
ALL CREATION

ABRAHAM
ALL NATIONS

ISRAEL
ONE NATION

DAVID
REPRESENTATIVE KING

NEW COVENANT
FAITHFUL COVENANT PARTNER

JESUS
FAITHFUL COVENANT PARTNER

JESUS
DAVIDIC KING MESSIAH

JESUS
THE NEW ISRAEL

JESUS
THE WORLD'S LORD

JESUS
THE TRULY HUMAN ONE
CROWNED WITH GLORY AND HONOUR

JESUS
COSMIC RULER IN GOD'S NEW CREATION
NEW HEAVENS AND NEW EARTH

SECTION 3   GOD'S COVENANT WITH NOAH

COMMITTED TO PRESERVING THE WORLD FOR FUTURE REDEMPTION – GOD'S COVENANT WITH NOAH

This dramatic story starts with the pain God feels at the tragedy that has overcome His world.

Noah's story puts us in touch with the turbulent emotions of a God who is grief-stricken over the way evil has spoilt His 'good' creation. But Noah finds grace in the eyes of the Lord and is burdened with the terrible secret of what God plans to do to judge the world and to save it.

God's judgment in unleashing the floodwaters represents an undoing of the act of creation. The waters out of which the world was formed – according to Genesis 1 – and which were set within bounds, now return unchecked to overwhelm Noah's world in judgment. It becomes clear, however, that judgment changes nothing. Despite the flood of God's judgment, our propensity to evil and wickedness remains the same.

Remarkably, it is God who freely chooses to change! He resolves 'never again' to destroy His creation in this way, by flood. Instead of cancelling His creation experiment, God renews His determination to uphold and eventually to redeem His world. He opts for patience and forbearance in His long-term dealings with His world.

To mark this, God makes a startling *covenant with Noah, with the animals, and even with the earth itself* (Gen. 9:12–13). To signify His enduring commitment, God hangs His war-bow in the sky as the rainbow-reminder of His pledge of grace.

Although we are far distant from Noah, we are, like him, 'saved through water' (1 Pet. 3:20). Drawn by faith-baptism 'into Christ' – and into His dying and rising – we pass through the waters of judgment,

leaving behind our old selves and world, to emerge as part of the 'new creation' (2 Cor. 5:17). As Noah did, we can stake everything on the covenant faithfulness of this tough and tender God.

Through faith, we too may prove to be the firstfruits of a new human race. Like Noah, we can be preachers of righteousness, not a self-righteousness that condemns, but a saving righteousness that through the cross offers hope of redemption. In this hope, we refuse to call down floods of wrath upon the heads of sinners and can instead bend to wash their dusty feet.

When Noah stepped into the ark he saved himself and his family; when he stepped out of the ark he saved the world! By God's grace we, too, can take those small steps of faith and obedience which may truly make a difference to our world beyond our wildest dreams as we wait for the world to come.

Let's look more closely at how one small step for Noah was one giant leap for mankind!

DAY 27

GENESIS 5:29
ROMANS 5:12-21

AS WE CONSIDER the heart of Noah's story, we soon begin to realise that what makes Noah significant is that he is the pioneer of God's intention to renew His creation and redeem His world. *Noah's role, in effect, is to be a new Adam,* as the many echoes of Genesis chapters 1 to 3 indicate.

The first point to notice is that Noah's role as a new Adam is anticipated in the name given to him by his father, Lamech: 'he named him Noah saying, "Out of the *ground* that the Lord has *cursed* this one shall bring us *comfort* from our painful toil"' (Gen. 5:29, NRSV, adapted). Noah's name is said to be derived not from the Hebrew word for 'rest' (*nwh*) but, by a bit of word-play, from the word (*nhm*) which means 'comfort'. Noah is a gift to the world from the 'God of all comfort'. Lamech prophetically announces an antidote to the judgment of Genesis 3:17 where the earth is 'cursed' and made the scene of Adam's 'painful labor'. And there is almost a hint of something incarnational in the statement that it will be out of the very ground cursed that the comforter will come!

BIBLE READING

Genesis 5:29

²⁹And he named him Noah, saying, "This one will bring us relief from the agonizing labor of our hands, caused by the ground the LORD has cursed."

BIBLE READING

Romans 5:12-21

DEATH THROUGH ADAM AND LIFE THROUGH CHRIST

¹²Therefore, just as sin entered the world through one man, and death through sin, in this way death spread to all men, because all sinned. ¹³In fact, sin was in the world before the law, but sin is not charged to one's account when there is no law. ¹⁴Nevertheless, death reigned from Adam to Moses, even over those who did not sin in the likeness of Adam's transgression.

He is a prototype of the Coming One.

¹⁵But the gift is not like the trespass. For if by the one man's trespass the many died, how much more have the grace of God and the gift overflowed to the many by the grace of the one man, Jesus Christ. ¹⁶And the gift is not like the one man's sin, because from one sin came the judgment, resulting in condemnation, but from many trespasses came the gift, resulting in justification. ¹⁷Since by the one man's trespass, death reigned through that one man, how much more will those who receive the overflow of grace and the gift of righteousness reign in life through the one man, Jesus Christ.

¹⁸So then, as through one trespass there is condemnation for everyone, so also through one righteous act there is life-giving justification for everyone. ¹⁹For just as through one man's disobedience the many were made sinners, so also through the one man's obedience the many will be made righteous. ²⁰The law came along to multiply the trespass. But where sin multiplied, grace multiplied even more, ²¹so that, just as sin reigned in death, so also grace will reign through righteousness, resulting in eternal life through Jesus Christ our Lord.

FOR ACTION: Noah was a gift to the world from the God of all comfort. His preaching and teaching was largely rejected, but despite that he remained faithful. In a sense everyone who is a Christian is a gift to the world from this same God of comfort. With appropriate humility keep this thought ever before you: I am God's gift to the world. He has blessed you so that you might bless others. Go out and in His name bless someone today.

WHAT WE NEED to notice here, particularly, is that Noah has been drawn so deeply into the drama only because of God's own deeper interest in the fate of His creation. The text highlights *what God saw, what God felt,* and *what God decided.* First, 'the LORD saw ...'. What the Lord sees is how evil and wicked the earth has become since the Fall. He sees how His untrusting human partners have succumbed to demonic

DAY
28
GENESIS 6:5
ROMANS 3:9-18

seduction. He sees them accusing and blaming one another in an early exercise in scapegoating. He has watched as their mounting anger eventually turns to blood feuds and murder, culminating in a strange and illicit involvement with angelic beings. And God looks not only on the outward appearances but deep into the human heart out of which, Jesus was to say, comes all manner of evils. Fantasies relished in the hotel bedroom conjure up the pornography and adultery that follow. Radical dreams of social engineering darkly imagined by Pol Pot and his fellow Paris-educated comrades spawn the 'killing fields' of Cambodia. Ideas always have consequences. And the Lord sees it all.

BIBLE READING

Genesis 6:5

JUDGMENT DECREED

[5]When the LORD saw that man's wickedness was widespread on the earth and that every scheme his mind thought of was nothing but evil all the time ...

BIBLE READING

Romans 3:9-18

THE WHOLE WORLD GUILTY BEFORE GOD

[9]What then? Are we any better? Not at all! For we have previously charged that both Jews and Gentiles are all under sin, [10]as it is written:

"There is no one righteous, not even one;
[11] there is no one who understands,
there is no one who seeks God.
[12] All have turned away,
together they have become useless;
there is no one who does good,
there is not even one.
[13] Their throat is an open grave;
they deceive with their tongues.
Vipers' venom is under their lips.
[14] Their mouth is full of cursing and bitterness.

¹⁵ Their feet are swift to shed blood;
¹⁶ ruin and wretchedness are in their paths,
¹⁷ and the path of peace they have not known.
¹⁸ There is no fear of God before their eyes."

PRAYER: Gracious and loving heavenly Father, help me see as You see, feel as You feel, and make only those decisions that fit in with Your plans. I am so prone to take my way in everything. Forgive me for my self-interest and self-centredness, and dwell so deeply in me that self will become marginal and You will become central. This I ask in Christ's precious name. Amen.

OUR ATTENTION IS now riveted on *what God felt!* The Lord sees the serious betrayal of His trust. And seeing this: *'The Lord was grieved ... and his heart was filled with pain'* (Gen. 6:6, NIV). These strong words show the emotions of someone who loves deeply and is deeply hurt. They invite us to feel the fierce pain in the heart of God.

DAY 29

GENESIS 6:6
HOSEA 11:8-9

The Bible tells us that God cannot change, in the sense that external pressures cannot control Him. He is always unthwarted in His sovereignty. But that understanding must not cancel out for us this equally biblical insight into a God who is not detached or unfeeling, but who is deeply moved by the world's tragedy. We are being given a glimpse into the deep pathos in God. God is emotionally affected by our human condition. The narrative does not focus on the Flood, as if to highlight only the severe judgment of God, but on the profound feelings of God, as if to emphasise His depth of mercy and grace.

Looking through this window into God's heart, we may perhaps begin to see that when He finally defeats the evil that plagues His fallen creation, it will involve Him in becoming vulnerable to its pain and wickedness, and in some strange way taking it upon Himself.

| BIBLE READING | ## Genesis 6:6 |

JUDGMENT DECREED

⁵When the LORD saw that man's wickedness was widespread on the earth and that every scheme his mind thought of was nothing but evil all the time,

⁶the LORD regretted that He had made man on the earth, and He was grieved in His heart.

| BIBLE READING | ## Hosea 11:8-9 |

⁸ How can I give you up, Ephraim?
How can I surrender you, Israel?
How can I make you like Admah?
How can I treat you like Zeboiim?
I have had a change of heart;
My compassion is stirred!
⁹ I will not vent the full fury of My anger;
I will not turn back to destroy Ephraim.
For I am God and not man,
the Holy One among you;
I will not come in rage.

TO PONDER: How glad we should be that God *feels*. Some theologians believe in the 'impassibility of God' - the idea that God does not feel. However, where there is love there must, inevitably, be vulnerability to the pain of rejection. How our rejection of the Almighty must have pained His heart. But now how much pleasure it must give Him to have us on His side. Let's live in such a way that our lives will bring Him pleasure, not pain.

HAVING GLIMPSED WHAT God saw and having been made aware of God's feelings, we now learn *what God has decided:* 'Then the LORD said, "I will wipe off the face of the earth: man, whom I created ..."'

God decides for justice. Whereas before He had looked on His creation and seen that it was 'good' (1:31), now He sees only corruption and violence. He resolves to judge the world by bringing everything to a watery end (6:13,17). The Flood, it is important to notice, will soon be portrayed as the unravelling of God's creative work. The fountains of the deep are about to burst forth and the windows of the heavens to open to drown the world in judgment (7:11) - language which harks back directly to Genesis 1 verses 2 and 7. In other words, the Flood will seem to be an undoing of God's original creation, as though He is going to press the rewind button and allow His created order to return to the watery chaos out of which it had been formed.

So God decides on the Flood. He calls 'time' on His grand creation experiment. The final curtain falls. Or does it?

Genesis 6:7

BIBLE READING

JUDGMENT DECREED

[5]When the LORD saw that man's wickedness was widespread on the earth and that every scheme his mind thought of was nothing but evil all the time, [6]the LORD regretted that He had made man on the earth, and He was grieved in His heart.

[7]Then the LORD said, "I will wipe off the face of the earth: man, whom I created, together with the animals, creatures that crawl, and birds of the sky—for I regret that I made them."

FOR PRAISE: Do you know this song: 'Ascribe greatness to our God, the Rock; His work is perfect and all His ways are just'?* If you do then sing it now. If you don't then make up your own song of praise in words that glorify God for His sense of justice. 'Justice,' commented C.S. Lewis, 'is an old name for what we now call fairness ... it includes honesty, give-and-take, truthfulness and keeping promises.' Praise God in your heart for that.

*by Mary K. Barthow and Mary Lou King

DAY 31

GENESIS 6:8

SUDDENLY THE TEXT strikes a new note: *'But Noah found grace in the eyes of the Lord'* (AV). Suddenly Noah emerges from the gloom as a significant figure. He finds favour from God, and when he does the whole human race finds itself a future.

But what strange grace it is! It is a strange grace that makes you the sole survivor of an environmental disaster of cosmic proportions! It is a tough grace that lifts Noah fearfully into the larger drama of God. When anyone receives such grace they cannot help but look at the world through God's eyes and see what He sees and inevitably – though the text does not explicitly say so of Noah – begin to feel what God feels.

And the grace which relieves our fears lets us in on God's awesome secrets and daring dreams. All who live under this grace submit their lives to the overruling providence of God's redemptive activity. This is what grace does to you! In this way, we gain a strange new vantage-point from which to see that *judgment is not God's final word*. We begin to discern that plans are afoot that provide hope.

BIBLE READING

Genesis 6:8

JUDGMENT DECREED

⁵When the LORD saw that man's wickedness was widespread on the earth and that every scheme his mind

thought of was nothing but evil all the time, ⁶the LORD regretted that He had made man on the earth, and He was grieved in His heart. ⁷Then the LORD said, "I will wipe off the face of the earth: man, whom I created, together with the animals, creatures that crawl, and birds of the sky—for I regret that I made them."

⁸Noah, however, found favor in the eyes of the LORD.

PRAYER: A Scottish preacher used to pray a prayer that stressed the pre-eminence of grace. Why not pray it today? 'Lord Jesus, from whom all grace is given and from whom all blessings flow, give me grace to feel my need of grace, and give me grace to ask for grace, then give me grace to receive grace. And when grace is given to me give me grace to use that grace and, above all, give me grace to be grateful for the grace I am given. Amen.'

DAY 32
GENESIS 6:11-22

AS WE BEGIN to trace the threads of God's redemptive purpose, it is helpful to distinguish two overall strands to this purpose which involve Noah.

First, what God is doing here is *saving one family for the sake of the whole world!* The narrative explaining this in several ways.

The first point to notice is that *God confides in Noah* (6:13,17) about the judgment about to be let loose. As with Abraham later in the story (18:16-33), God acts as if He would rather not bear the burden alone but seeks to take Noah into His confidence. When Noah is instructed to make the ark, everything depends, not for the last time, on one man's obedience. And not for the last time, when the storm winds of divine judgment beat upon the house and rain pours down, the man whose house survives is the one who hears the word of God and does it. It seems that Noah obeyed at every turn (6:22; 7:5).

We come now to another turning-point in the story. As part of His plan to save a family for the world's sake, *God promises to establish His covenant with Noah* (6:18). In contrast to the threat of verse 17 we read: 'But I will establish My covenant with you ...' God is now building a bridge across which all His plans will pass into fulfilment in the future. On this God stakes His redemptive dreams.

| BIBLE READING | **Genesis 6:11-22** |

[11]Now the earth was corrupt in God's sight, and the earth was filled with violence. [12]God saw how corrupt the earth was, for all flesh had corrupted its way on the earth. [13]Then God said to Noah, "I have decided to put an end to all flesh, for the earth is filled with violence because of them; therefore I am going to destroy them along with the earth.

[14]"Make yourself an ark of gofer wood. Make rooms in the ark, and cover it with pitch inside and outside. [15]This is how you are to make it: The ark will be 450 feet long, 75 feet wide, and 45 feet high. [16]You are to make a roof, finishing [the sides of the ark] to within 18 inches [of the roof.] You are to put a door in the side of the ark. Make it with lower, middle, and upper [decks].

[17]"Understand that I am bringing a deluge—floodwaters on the earth to destroy all flesh under heaven with the breath of life in it. Everything on earth will die. [18]But I will establish My covenant with you, and you will enter the ark with your sons, your wife, and your sons' wives. [19]You are also to bring into the ark two of every living thing of all flesh, male and female, to keep them alive with you. [20]Two of everything—from the birds according to their kinds, from the livestock according to their kinds, and from every animal that crawls on the ground according to its kind—will come to you so that you can keep them alive. [21]Take with you every kind of food that is eaten; gather it as food for you and for them." [22]And Noah did this. He did everything that God had commanded him.

FOR ACTION: To quote C.S. Lewis again, he once said: 'Obedience is the key to all doors in the Christian life; feelings come and go.' Do you know the hymn that begins: 'When we walk with the Lord, in the light of His Word'? The chorus goes like this: 'Trust and obey! For there's no other way, to be happy in Jesus, but to trust and obey.' Lift your heart in a hymn of prayer and praise right now and affirm your decision to obey Him in all things.

DAY
33
GENESIS 7:1-12

IN THE MEANTIME, judgment has to be done and be seen to be done. The Flood, as we have said, is pictured as the dismantling of God's creative work. The waters that burst forth from the depths and from the windows of the heavens (v.11) undo the process of creation as recorded in Genesis 1. *The Flood is an act of decreation!*

This is a key point to grasp. From here on, throughout the Bible, God's acts of judgment within history are often described, figuratively, in the *language of decreation* (eg, Isa. 9:1-10:34; Jer. 4:23-28). In this way, language which sounds as if it is describing the end of the world is used to give ultimate significance and theological weight to historical events which might otherwise be regarded as accidental. With this use of language, events within history become parables, and portents, of the final end of history.

Jesus spoke like this to show how important was the imminent destruction of Jerusalem and the Temple which would, paradoxically, vindicate Him in glory as the Son of Man (Matt. 24:29-31). Conversely, God's salvation is characteristically described as an act of *new creation* (eg, Isa. 41:17-20; 43:18-21; 65:17; 2 Cor. 5:17). There is life beyond judgment, it seems.

BIBLE READING

Genesis 7:1-12

ENTERING THE ARK

7 Then the LORD said to Noah, "Enter the ark, you and all your household, for I have seen that you [alone] are righteous before Me in this generation. ²You are to take with you seven pairs, a male and its female, of all the clean animals, and two of the animals that are not clean, a male and its female, ³and seven pairs, male and female, of the birds of the sky—in order to keep offspring alive on the face of the whole earth. ⁴Seven days from now I will make it rain on the earth 40 days and 40 nights, and I will wipe off the face of the earth every living thing I have made." ⁵And Noah did everything that the LORD commanded him.

⁶Noah was 600 years old when the deluge came [and] water covered the earth. ⁷So Noah, his sons, his wife, and his sons' wives entered the ark because of the waters of the deluge. ⁸From the clean animals, unclean animals, birds, and every creature that crawls on the ground, ⁹two of each, male and female, entered the ark with Noah, just as God had commanded him. ¹⁰Seven days later the waters of the deluge came on the earth.

THE DELUGE

¹¹In the six hundredth year of Noah's life, in the second month, on the seventeenth day of the month, on that day all the sources of the watery depths burst open, the floodgates of the sky were opened, ¹²and the rain fell on the earth 40 days and 40 nights.

PRAYER: O Father, how can I express the gratitude that begins to well up in my soul as I realise I am part of a new creation - a creation that is more marvellous and wondrous than anything that was part of Your first creation? The old will pass away, but the new - the salvation You have given through Jesus, Your Son - will last eternally. Life of my life, Being of my being, my heart belongs to You for ever. Amen.

SO NOAH FINDS himself shut inside this strange vessel by the Lord and therefore shut in to God's grace as his only hope (7:16). Noah and his entourage sit out the Flood as the sole survivors (7:23).

What were Noah's feelings as he entered the ark facing the prospect of sharing living space with a volatile assortment of animals! And who can possibly imagine how Mrs Noah coped with domestic management inside that gloomy and increasingly smelly ark? Above all, what did it feel like to be in a tiny boat – the only hope of life afloat on a sea of death and destruction? Presumably the Noah clan found grace for all this too! But the text offers us not one word from Noah through the entire episode!

What matters above everything else to the narrator is *what God is thinking and doing: 'God remembered Noah ...'* (8:1). Remembering Noah, God remembers mercy, and causes the Flood to recede and the earth to dry out.

Genesis 7:13-8:1

THE DELUGE

¹¹In the six hundredth year of Noah's life, in the second month, on the seventeenth day of the month, on that day all the sources of the watery depths burst open, the floodgates of the sky were opened, ¹²and the rain fell on the earth 40 days and 40 nights.

¹³On that same day Noah along with his sons Shem, Ham, and Japheth, Noah's wife, and his three sons' wives entered the ark with him. ¹⁴They [entered it] with all the wildlife according to their kinds, all livestock according to their kinds, every creature that crawls on the earth according to its kind, all birds, every fowl, and everything with wings according to their kinds. ¹⁵Two of all flesh that has the breath of life in it entered the ark with Noah. ¹⁶Those that entered, male and female of all flesh, entered just as God had commanded him. Then the LORD shut him in.

[17]The deluge continued 40 days on the earth; the waters increased and lifted up the ark so that it rose above the earth. [18]The waters surged and increased greatly on the earth, and the ark floated on the surface of the water. [19]Then the waters surged even higher on the earth, and all the high mountains under the whole sky were covered. [20]The mountains were covered as the waters surged [above them] more than 20 feet. [21]All flesh perished—creatures that crawl on the earth, birds, livestock, wildlife, and all creatures that swarm on the earth, as well as all mankind. [22]Everything with the breath of the spirit of life in its nostrils—everything on dry land died. [23]He wiped out every living thing that was on the surface of the ground, from mankind to livestock, to creatures that crawl, to the birds of the sky, and they were wiped off the earth. Only Noah was left, and those that were with him in the ark. [24]And the waters surged on the earth 150 days.

THE FLOOD RECEDES

8 God remembered Noah, as well as all the wildlife and all the livestock that were with him in the ark. God caused a wind to pass over the earth, and the water began to subside.

FOR THANKSGIVING: Consider where you would be today were it not for God's mercy. It will not be difficult for you, no doubt, to enter into these words of the psalmist with a true sense of understanding. Repeat them out loud and don't forget to say 'Amen' at the end. 'Oh, give thanks to the LORD, for He is good! For His mercy endures forever. Let the redeemed of the LORD say so, whom He has redeemed from the hand of the enemy' (Psa. 107:1-2, NKJV).

DAY 35

WHEN NOAH DISEMBARKS (v.15), he is recommissioned to the calling of Adam and Eve to be fruitful and multiply and, in worshipful response, builds an altar. But God's response is even more striking: '... *I will never again curse the ground because of man, even though man's inclination is evil from his youth*' (v.21). What is extraordinary here is that despite the judgment which has taken place, human wickedness continues. The floodwaters of judgment have abated but the tide of evil has not! Remarkably, it is God who freely chooses to change: 'I will never again ...'!

In the face of continuing human rebellion, God deepens His commitment to His creation. It seems that He intends, whatever it costs Him, to persist with His creation purposes until they come to fruition. In judging the world He reduced it to temporary disorder; now He pledges to maintain the regularity of the seasons, and to uphold the stability of the created order (v.22). Great is His faithfulness - it stabilises the natural world, and so makes life livable and makes it possible to do science.

At almost any time in the future God will have ample reason to destroy the earth and its inhabitants. But His 'never again' changes the picture to one where grace reigns.

BIBLE READING

Genesis 8:15-22

THE LORD'S PROMISE

¹⁵Then God spoke to Noah, ¹⁶"Come out of the ark, you, your wife, your sons, and your sons' wives with you. ¹⁷Bring out every living thing of all flesh that is with you—birds, livestock, creatures that crawl on the ground—and they will spread over the earth and be fruitful and multiply on the earth." ¹⁸So Noah, along with his sons, his wife, and his sons' wives, came out. ¹⁹All wildlife, all livestock, every bird, and every creature that crawls on the earth came out of the ark by their groups.

²⁰Then Noah built an altar to the LORD. He took some of every kind of clean animal and every kind of clean bird

and offered burnt offerings on the altar. ²¹When the LORD smelled the pleasing aroma, He said to Himself, "I will never again curse the ground because of man, even though man's inclination is evil from his youth. And I will never again strike down every living thing as I have done.

> ²² As long as the earth endures,
> seedtime and harvest, cold and heat,
> summer and winter, and day and night
> will not cease."

FOR ACTION: You will be familiar, no doubt, with the hymn 'Great is Thy faithfulness'. One line goes like this: 'Morning by morning new mercies I see!' Besides lifting up your heart in grateful adoration as you sing it yourself, once again make a list of all God's mercies you can recall over the past few days. Here is one to get you started: you awoke this morning to face a new day. That's the first; now add some more.

LONG BEFORE NEIL Armstrong stepped onto the moon, Noah had stepped onto the post-Flood world and taken a giant leap for mankind. As if he were a new Adam on a new earth, Noah is blessed as at the beginning (v.1).

DAY 36

GENESIS 9:1-6

Nothing, of course, can turn the clock back completely. The way back is already barred; there is only a way forward towards the cross and resurrection. God is not reinstating the old creation just as it was; He has His sights already on a new creation. We can never regain 'paradise', and our relationship with the animal world is now shadowed with fear. Our human calling to exercise dominion over nature becomes fraught with risk, and demands we do so with delicate skill if we are not to ruin our earthly environment.

After the Flood, God lays down three new ground rules – all of which aim to preserve and dignify human life. First, perhaps as a concession, the eating of meat is now allowed (v.3), though we might hear a warning against ranking animal rights higher than human life. Second, the command to reverence all 'lifeblood' encourages respect for all forms of life, but chiefly puts a premium on human life so that murder is construed as an attack on God in whose image humans are made (vv.4-6).

BIBLE READING

Genesis 9:1-6

GOD'S COVENANT WITH NOAH

9 God blessed Noah and his sons and said to them, "Be fruitful and multiply and fill the earth. ²The fear and terror of you will be in every living creature on the earth, every bird of the sky, every creature that crawls on the ground, and all the fish of the sea. They are placed under your authority. ³Every living creature will be food for you; as [I gave] the green plants, I have given you everything. ⁴However, you must not eat meat with its lifeblood in it. ⁵I will require the life of every animal and every man for your life and your blood. I will require the life of each man's brother for a man's life.

⁶ Whoever sheds man's blood,
his blood will be shed by man,
for God made man
in His image.

FOR PRAISE: Give praise to God as you repeat this prayer and reflect on the glory of God that fills both earth and heaven:

'Almighty God, whose glory the heavens are telling and whose skies proclaim the work of Your hands, we give You thanks that by Your Spirit You renew the face of the earth and give breath to every living creature. We will give You praise, Lord God, for as long as we live, as creatures who are made in Your image and who have been redeemed and restored by Jesus Christ, our Lord and Saviour. Amen.'

IN CONTINUING TO portray Noah as a new Adam, the narrative now tells us of the third directive which is to govern human life after the Fall and Flood. God reiterates His desire to see the world populated: 'Be fruitful and multiply ...' (9:7).

DAY
37
GENESIS 9:7

This is a striking statement in view of the fact that human sinfulness has outlived the Flood (8:21b). Here, the text is probably refuting those Mesopotamian flood stories in which the gods grow increasingly annoyed by the number of babies and the amount of noise humans make, and act to cull the human race by officially promoting infanticide and childlessness. By contrast, the one Creator God apparently loves making people too much to abort His creative experiment for ever!

Even modern research grudgingly admits that our world's greatest problem is not so much overpopulation as the unequal distribution of resources. Nor must we be resigned to exhausting our sources of supply in the light of God's commitment: 'I now give you everything' (9:3c, NIV). From now on, it will certainly be harder to be truly human, but Noah's God refuses to hand in His resignation and entrusts Noah with the future of His creation.

In picturing Noah as a representative head of a new human family, standing on new ground, we can see that God *has preserved a family for the sake of the world.*

Genesis 9:7

BIBLE
READING

GOD'S COVENANT WITH NOAH

9 God blessed Noah and his sons and said to them, "Be fruitful and multiply and fill the earth. ²The fear and terror of you will be in every living creature on the earth, every bird of the sky, every creature that crawls on the ground, and all the fish of the sea. They are placed under your authority. ³Every living creature will be food for you; as [I gave] the green plants, I have given you everything. ⁴However, you must not eat meat with its lifeblood in it.

⁵I will require the life of every animal and every man for your life and your blood. I will require the life of each man's brother for a man's life.

⁶Whoever sheds man's blood,
his blood will be shed by man,
for God made man
in His image.

⁷But you, be fruitful and multiply; spread out over the earth and multiply on it."

TO PONDER: Take a moment to respond to today's reading by turning to Psalm 65 and linking your heart with that of the psalmist. There is hardly a psalm or passage in the whole of Scripture that surpasses this in terms of giving thanks to God for the way He sustains the earth. We take the blessings of God for granted so often, but change all that today by deciding in future to take them with gratitude.

DAY 38

GENESIS 9:8-13

TODAY WE TEASE out the second major strand in God's strategic plan and say: *God preserves the world for the sake of His future - and that future is redemption.* In inviting us to see Noah as a new Adam, the text shows us the post-Flood world as a renewed creation. If, as we have noted before, the judgment of the Flood represented an act of *decreation,* then the receding of the Flood signals a new beginning.

Just as before, the creative Spirit-wind of God - His *ruach* - blows over the waters to dry out the earth (8:1). And just as His life-giving word once was 'Let there be ...' so now the earth resonates with God's gracious vow: 'I will never again ...' (8:21).

In this way, this stage of the story reaches its climax. '*I now establish my covenant with you and with your descendants ...*' (9:9, NIV), '*and with every living creature ...*' (9:10), and - this is remarkable - *even with the earth itself* (9:13). In this staggering covenantal promise, God commits Himself to keeping planet

Earth in existence, sustaining its fruitfulness and the regularity of the seasons. God pledges to maintain life on planet Earth by continuing to breathe into it His life-giving Spirit to replenish its resources.

Genesis 9:8-13

BIBLE READING

GOD'S COVENANT WITH NOAH

9 God blessed Noah and his sons and said to them, "Be fruitful and multiply and fill the earth. ²The fear and terror of you will be in every living creature on the earth, every bird of the sky, every creature that crawls on the ground, and all the fish of the sea. They are placed under your authority. ³Every living creature will be food for you; as [I gave] the green plants, I have given you everything. ⁴However, you must not eat meat with its lifeblood in it. ⁵I will require the life of every animal and every man for your life and your blood. I will require the life of each man's brother for a man's life.

⁶Whoever sheds man's blood,
his blood will be shed by man,
for God made man
in His image.

⁷But you, be fruitful and multiply; spread out over the earth and multiply on it."

⁸Then God said to Noah and his sons with him, ⁹"Understand that I am confirming My covenant with you and your descendants after you, ¹⁰and with every living creature that is with you—birds, livestock, and all wildlife of the earth that are with you—all the animals of the earth that came out of the ark. ¹¹I confirm My covenant with you that never again will all flesh be wiped out by the waters of a deluge; there will never again be a deluge to destroy the earth."

¹²And God said, "This is the sign of the covenant I am making between Me and you and every living creature with you, a covenant for all future generations: ¹³I have placed My bow in the clouds, and it will be a sign of the covenant between Me and the earth.

FOR THANKSGIVING: Do you ever pause to thank God for the fruitful earth? If so, good. But do so again now. God did not set us on the earth to have food merely by wishing for it. It is produced by toil and sweat and foresight. However, sweat and toil would be useless without the added blessing of God. Think of the fruitful earth, the predictability of the seasons, the framework of a universe shaped in love and given to men and women. Think and give thanks.

DAY
39

2 PETER 3:3-13

IF WE ASK *why* God pledges to the human and animal family that He will keep this old earth going, we have to turn to the New Testament and to the apostle Peter for the clue.

Writing to Christians who are being mocked by unbelievers for the seeming delay in the return of Jesus, Peter reminds them of the creation and the Flood (vv.4-6). When this present creation is brought to an end, it will not be by water, says Peter. God's 'never again' sees to that. Next time it will be fire that will reconstitute the elements of this old order (v.7). What will emerge are 'a new heaven and a new earth, the home of righteousness' (v.13, NIV). Until then, do we conclude that God is slow or forgetful? No; He is patient because He does *not want 'any to perish, but all to come to repentance'* (v.9). Here is the clue we are looking for as to why God chooses to sustain this old world still, even in its sin. It is because, under the terms of this Noahic covenant, God has pledged to preserve the earth until His redemptive purposes are completed. He is committed to the upkeep of this first, old creation until the fruition of His plans to bring in a new creation.

2 Peter 3:3-13

³First, be aware of this: scoffers will come in the last days to scoff, following their own lusts, ⁴saying, "Where is the promise of His coming? For ever since the fathers fell asleep, all things continue as they have been since the beginning of creation." ⁵They willfully ignore this: long ago the heavens and the earth existed out of water and through water by the word of God. ⁶Through these the world of that time perished when it was flooded by water. ⁷But by the same word the present heavens and earth are held in store for fire, being kept until the day of judgment and destruction of ungodly men.

⁸Dear friends, don't let this one thing escape you: with the Lord one day is like 1,000 years, and 1,000 years like one day. ⁹The Lord does not delay His promise, as some understand delay, but is patient with you, not wanting any to perish, but all to come to repentance.

¹⁰But the Day of the Lord will come like a thief; on that [day] the heavens will pass away with a loud noise, the elements will burn and be dissolved, and the earth and the works on it will be disclosed. ¹¹Since all these things are to be destroyed in this way, [it is clear] what sort of people you should be in holy conduct and godliness ¹²as you wait for and earnestly desire the coming of the day of God, because of which the heavens will be on fire and be dissolved, and the elements will melt with the heat. ¹³But based on His promise, we wait for new heavens and a new earth, where righteousness will dwell.

PRAYER: My Father and my God, I am in awe of the fact that in Your patient commitment to Your redemptive purposes You waited for me to come to repentance and become part of Your new creation. I ask myself: What if You had not been patient? And what if I had missed hearing of Your redemption? But all is well. I am Yours and You are mine. Our paths have crossed – and how! I am so grateful. Thank You, dear Father. Amen.

DAY 40

GENESIS 9:14-17

WE NOTED THAT God's covenant with Noah and the earth was not merely an ecological pronouncement, important as that is for us today, but a statement of redemptive intent.

The permanent sign God has given of His intention is the *the rainbow* (v.13). God's later covenant with Abraham will be marked with the sign of circumcision, and with Israel by the Sabbath, but now, with Noah, it is the rainbow in the clouds. The rainbow is God's 'preservation order' on this decaying but still beautiful old 'house' of creation. Having used His arrows of judgment, God can now hang His 'war-bow' in the sky as a sign of peace. Just as God's original Sabbath-rest showed that He has completed His *creation* work, so the war-bow at rest is the sign that He has ended His *decreation* work.

What is wonderful is that the bow is there not so much to remind *us* as to *remind God* (vv.15-16)! God continues to look down on human sin, but when He does, He sees too His rainbow-sign in the sky and remembers His covenant! For God to remember His covenant in this way spells salvation for us (Psa. 105:8-9), just as, in its own way, His forgetting does too (Jer. 31:34; Isa. 43:25)! This shows how determined God is to preserve this present world as the stage on which the future acts in His drama of redemption can be played out.

BIBLE READING

Genesis 9:14-17

[14]Whenever I form clouds over the earth and the bow appears in the clouds, [15]I will remember My covenant between Me and you and every living creature of all flesh: water will never again become a deluge to destroy all flesh. [16]The bow will be in the clouds, and I will look at it and remember the everlasting covenant between God and every living creature of all flesh on earth." [17]God said to Noah, "This is the sign of the covenant that I have confirmed between Me and all flesh on earth."

A LITANY: We praise You for the creation of the world and all living creatures in it. Thank You, Lord. We especially praise You that each time we see a rainbow, we can realise afresh Your commitment to Your covenant with the earth itself. Thank You, Lord. We praise You for the vision of a future kingdom in which all living creatures dwell in peace and security. Thank You, Lord. Hasten the coming of this glorious kingdom, we pray. Through Jesus Christ our Lord. Amen.

AS WE TRACE the implications of God's covenant with Noah and the earth, we first of all look back to the picture painted in the opening chapters of Genesis. From this dramatic opening to its end in the book of Revelation, the whole Bible story sweeps majestically *from creation to new creation.* But we soon realise that progress is going to be neither smooth nor inevitable. The story moves through Fall and Flood, Exodus and Exile, death and resurrection, to secure its outcome.

DAY
41

GENESIS 1:1-25

This section – Genesis chapters 1 to 9 – describes a dramatic sequence of events in which God, who creates in love, decreates in judgment, and recreates in grace.

This chapter affirms the uniqueness of the one Creator God over against all possible rivals. It celebrates the God-given beauty, light and order of creation. Like a peal of bells, it seven times affirms the essential goodness in God's eyes of all that He has made.

Our starting-point is God, not ourselves or our experience – a God who took the responsibility of creating because He knew He had the power to redeem.

Genesis 1:1-25

BIBLE
READING

THE CREATION

1 In the beginning God created the heavens and the earth.
²Now the earth was formless and empty, darkness covered the surface of the watery depths, and the Spirit of God was

hovering over the surface of the waters. ³Then God said, "Let there be light," and there was light. ⁴God saw that the light was good, and God separated the light from the darkness. ⁵God called the light "day," and He called the darkness "night." Evening came, and then morning: the first day.

⁶Then God said, "Let there be an expanse between the waters, separating water from water." ⁷So God made the expanse and separated the water under the expanse from the water above the expanse. And it was so. ⁸God called the expanse "sky." Evening came, and then morning: the second day.

⁹Then God said, "Let the water under the sky be gathered into one place, and let the dry land appear." And it was so. ¹⁰God called the dry land "earth," and He called the gathering of the water "seas." And God saw that it was good. ¹¹Then God said, "Let the earth produce vegetation: seed-bearing plants, and fruit trees on the earth bearing fruit with seed in it, according to their kinds." And it was so. ¹²The earth brought forth vegetation: seed-bearing plants according to their kinds and trees bearing fruit with seed in it, according to their kinds. And God saw that it was good. ¹³Evening came, and then morning: the third day.

¹⁴Then God said, "Let there be lights in the expanse of the sky to separate the day from the night. They will serve as signs for festivals and for days and years. ¹⁵They will be lights in the expanse of the sky to provide light on the earth." And it was so. ¹⁶God made the two great lights—the greater light to have dominion over the day and the lesser light to have dominion over the night—as well as the stars. ¹⁷God placed them in the expanse of the sky to provide light on the earth, ¹⁸to dominate the day and the night, and to separate light from darkness. And God saw that it was good. ¹⁹Evening came, and then morning: the fourth day.

²⁰Then God said, "Let the water swarm with living creatures, and let birds fly above the earth across the expanse of the sky." ²¹So God created the large sea-creatures and every living creature that moves and swarms in the water, according to their kinds. [He also created] every winged bird according to its kind. And God saw that it was good. ²²So God blessed them, "Be fruitful, multiply, and fill the waters of the seas, and let the birds multiply on the earth." ²³Evening came, and then morning: the fifth day.

²⁴Then God said, "Let the earth produce living creatures according to their kinds: livestock, creatures that crawl, and the wildlife of the earth according to their kinds." And it was so. ²⁵So God made the wildlife of the earth according to their kinds, the livestock according to their kinds, and creatures that crawl on the ground according to their kinds. And God saw that it was good.

AFFIRMATION: In the light of today's reading use these words of St Francis of Assisi to affirm the uniqueness of God: 'You are holy, Lord, You are the only God, and all Your works are wondrous. You are strong, You are great, You are the Most High, You are the Almighty King! You are the mystery of Three in One, the Lord above all gods. You are good, You are *all* good.'

IT AROUSES AN almost unbearable heartache and awakens a deep longing to be told that our human story was birthed in unconditional blessing (1:28). We have already seen that when God blessed Noah after the Flood, He was reaffirming His original blessing on Adam and Eve. 'Blessing' in the Bible is never an empty word or casual wish, but the imparting of life and prosperity. Blessing was an act of empowerment and destiny. We are truly human only when we live by the blessing of God.

DAY
42
GENESIS 1:26-2:16

Blessing, and its opposite, curse, become in time the semi-legal language of covenant arrangements. This led earlier Christians to posit an original covenant between God and Adam. Be that as it may, what we see here is a powerful combination of God's word (1:26) and God's Spirit (*ruach*, wind, breath, 2:7) which, in wonderful harmony, continue to be God's creative agents in shaping the unique dignity of men and women. Men and women are equal bearers of God's image, partners with God in ruling His world wisely. They are called to populate the planet to the glory of God (1:26-28). Our role as workers is a worthy one, which is dignified by the fact that God adopts a six-day working week! Yet we are more than workers; we are worshippers, invited to enjoy with God the Sabbath-rest of His creative accomplishment.

| BIBLE READING | **Genesis 1:26-2:16** |

²⁶Then God said, "Let Us make man in Our image, according to Our likeness. They will rule the fish of the sea, the birds of the sky, the livestock, all the earth, and the creatures that crawl on the earth."

²⁷ So God created man in His own image;
He created him in the image of God;
He created them male and female.

²⁸God blessed them, and God said to them, "Be fruitful, multiply, fill the earth, and subdue it. Rule the fish of the sea, the birds of the sky, and every creature that crawls on the earth." ²⁹God also said, "Look, I have given you every seed-bearing plant on the surface of the entire earth, and every tree whose fruit contains seed. This food will be for you, ³⁰for all the wildlife of the earth, for every bird of the sky, and for every creature that crawls on the earth—everything having the breath of life in it. [I have given] every green plant for food." And it was so. ³¹God saw all that He had made, and it was very good. Evening came, and then morning: the sixth day.

2 So the heavens and the earth and everything in them were completed. ²By the seventh day, God completed His work that He had done, and He rested on the seventh day from all His work that He had done. ³God blessed the seventh day and declared it holy, for on it He rested from His work of creation.

MAN AND WOMAN IN THE GARDEN

⁴These are the records of the heavens and the earth, concerning their creation at the time that the Lord God made the earth and the heavens. ⁵No shrub of the field had yet [grown] on the land, and no plant of the field had yet sprouted, for the Lord God had not made it rain on the land, and there

was no man to work the ground. ⁶But water would come out of the ground and water the entire surface of the land. ⁷Then the LORD God formed the man out of the dust from the ground and breathed the breath of life into his nostrils, and the man became a living being.

⁸The LORD God planted a garden in Eden, in the east, and there He placed the man He had formed. ⁹The LORD God caused to grow out of the ground every tree pleasing in appearance and good for food, including the tree of life in the midst of the garden, as well as the tree of the knowledge of good and evil.

¹⁰A river went out from Eden to water the garden. From there it divided and became the source of four rivers. ¹¹The name of the first is Pishon, which encircles the entire land of the Havilah, where there is gold. ¹²Gold from that land is pure; bdellium and onyx are also there. ¹³The name of the second river is Gihon, which encircles the entire land of Cush. ¹⁴The name of the third river is the Tigris, which flows to the east of Assyria. And the fourth river is the Euphrates.

¹⁵The LORD God took the man and placed him in the garden of Eden to work it and watch over it. ¹⁶And the LORD God commanded the man, "You are free to eat from any tree of the garden ..."

BLESSING: Think of someone you would like God to bless especially today. Picture that person in your mind's eye and pronounce this blessing on them: 'The LORD bless you and keep you; the LORD make His face shine upon you, and be gracious to you; the LORD lift up His countenance upon you, and give you peace' (Num. 6:24-26, NKJV). Now expect God to do what you have asked, and give Him thanks for the blessing that person will receive.

DAY 43

GENESIS 2:15-25

TODAY, WE FACE the *realism* of the creation narrative. Whilst a God-given environment, the Garden of Eden is not a paradise in some Utopian sense.

The human condition in Eden even before the Fall is marked by *challenge* (2:15), *limitation* (2:16-17), *loneliness* (2:18) and *temptation* (3:1ff.).

For a start, there is challenging work to be done! Called to subdue the earth, men and women must exercise skill, energy and sensitivity in managing the natural world, without exploiting or despoiling it. As we care for and nurture God's creation, we find ample scope for every legitimate human art, from ground-level cultivation to high culture.

And God sets boundaries not to cramp our style but to keep us humble and to stimulate our respect for others. Our essential aloneness stirs us to reach out for loving relationship. The possibility of temptation creates space for obedient choices that make a difference.

Adam's privilege of naming other creatures, shows how, uniquely, human beings share God's authority to define the world (2:19; cf.1:5, etc). As for sexuality, and in light of the fact that humans are made in God's image as male–female counterparts, it is questionable whether same-gender sex can be truly complementary or be construed as anything other than a form of self-love. On the other hand, Adam's outburst of joy (2:23), the first song in the Bible, celebrates intimacy with one who is part of oneself yet truly other.

BIBLE READING

Genesis 2:15-25

¹⁵The Lord God took the man and placed him in the garden of Eden to work it and watch over it. ¹⁶And the Lord God commanded the man, "You are free to eat from any tree of the garden, ¹⁷but you must not eat from the tree of the knowledge of good and evil, for on the day you eat from it, you will certainly die." ¹⁸Then the Lord God said, "It is not good for

the man to be alone. I will make a helper who is like him." [19]So the Lord God formed out of the ground each wild animal and each bird of the sky, and brought each to the man to see what he would call it. And whatever the man called a living creature, that was its name. [20]The man gave names to all the livestock, to the birds of the sky, and to every wild animal; but for the man no helper was found who was like him. [21]So the Lord God caused a deep sleep to come over the man, and he slept. God took one of his ribs and closed the flesh at that place. [22]Then the Lord God made the rib He had taken from the man into a woman and brought her to the man. [23]And the man said:

> This one, at last, is bone of my bone,
> and flesh of my flesh;
> this one will be called woman,
> for she was taken from man.

[24]This is why a man leaves his father and mother and bonds with his wife, and they become one flesh. [25]Both the man and his wife were naked, yet felt no shame.

FOR ACTION: God has given us a great deal of freedom in life, but with that freedom comes responsibility. Adam and Eve in the Garden of Eden chose wrong rather than right and thus used their freedom in a way that violated the divine commands. Ask God today, in your own words, to enable you to choose good and not evil, life and not death, truth and not lies. Your choices make a difference, either for right or wrong. Let it always be for right.

DAY 44

GENESIS 3:1-7

NOW THE SHADOWS lengthen over the lovely land of God's creation as the darkening reality of our human sinfulness unfolds. Later, but not here, the serpent is associated with the devil. Here, the text will not allow us to off-load any responsibility for our mistrust and rebellion. The insidious voice comes from *within* creation, not from outside.

What the serpent says constitutes a *threefold attack*: on God's word (v.1), on God's authority (v.4), and on God's goodness (v.5). The last thrust is to insinuate to the couple that God is not really out for their best interests but is keeping something from them that would advantage them! What the woman perceives has a *threefold attraction*: it is good for food, delights the eyes and is desirable for gaining wisdom (v.6). This triple attraction, characterised later by the apostle John as 'the lust of the flesh, the lust of the eyes, and the pride in one's lifestyle' (1 John 2:16) is crucially mirrored and mastered in the victory of Jesus in the Judean desert (Matt. 4:1-11; Luke 4:1-13).

BIBLE READING

Genesis 3:1-7

THE TEMPTATION AND THE FALL

3 Now the serpent was the most cunning of all the wild animals that the LORD God had made. He said to the woman, "Did God really say, 'You can't eat from any tree in the garden'?"

²The woman said to the serpent, "We may eat the fruit from the trees in the garden. ³But about the fruit of the tree in the middle of the garden, God said, 'You must not eat it or touch it, or you will die.'"

⁴"No! You will not die," the serpent said to the woman. ⁵"In fact, God knows that when you eat it your eyes will be opened and you will be like God, knowing good and evil." ⁶Then the woman saw that the tree was good for food and delightful to look at, and that it was desirable for obtaining wisdom. So she took some of its fruit and ate [it]; she also gave [some] to

her husband, [who was] with her, and he ate [it]. ⁷Then the eyes of both of them were opened, and they knew they were naked; so they sewed fig leaves together and made loincloths for themselves.

TO PONDER: Spend a few moments meditating on Jesus' victory during His temptation in the wilderness (Luke 4:1-13). What was the secret of His triumph over Satan? His trust in God and His knowledge of the Word. His rebuttal of Satan was based on texts all drawn from the book of Deuteronomy. If you were faced with a powerful attack of Satan would you know what scripture to use against him? Worth thinking about isn't it?

DAY 45
GENESIS 3:8-4:16

HERE OUR HUMAN story starts on its terrible slide into that degeneration which will culminate with the Flood. The Fall leads to embarrassment and shame (cf.2:25; 3:7); to escape from God in fear (3:8); and to evasion of responsibility - either by confessing symptoms rather than sin (3:10) or by shifting the blame to someone else (3:12).

God's initial response to His sinful creatures is to ask a series of penetrating questions (3:9,11,13; 4:6,9)! And each question is intended to rouse them to *take responsibility* again for their lives.

The divine judgmental curse signifies that the spiritual battle has been joined (3:14-15), but carries with it a hint of promised salvation and victory on the human battlefield. The battle of the sexes also follows (3:16), as does our estrangement from the natural world (3:17-19).

Eden is barred for ever (3:24); there is no going back to lost innocence. The only way is forward to atonement and reconciliation. Behind us is the first Adam who sinned, but ahead of us is the Last Adam whose 'agony in the garden [of Gethsemane] heals all the agony of the race' (P.T. Forsyth). As we have seen, God's dealings with Noah constituted the first major step on that journey.

BIBLE READING

Genesis 3:8-4:16

SIN'S CONSEQUENCES

⁸Then the man and his wife heard the sound of the LORD God walking in the garden at the time of the evening breeze, and they hid themselves from the LORD God among the trees of the garden. ⁹So the LORD God called out to the man and said to him, "Where are you?"

¹⁰And he said, "I heard You in the garden, and I was afraid because I was naked, so I hid."

¹¹Then He asked, "Who told you that you were naked? Did you eat from the tree that I had commanded you not to eat from?"

¹²Then the man replied, "The woman You gave to be with me—she gave me [some fruit] from the tree, and I ate."

¹³So the LORD God asked the woman, "What is this you have done?"

And the woman said, "It was the serpent. He deceived me, and I ate."

¹⁴Then the LORD God said to the serpent:

> Because you have done this,
> you are cursed more than any livestock
> and more than any wild animal.
> You will move on your belly
> and eat dust all the days of your life.
> ¹⁵ I will put hostility between you and the woman,
> and between your seed and her seed.
> He will strike your head,
> and you will strike his heel.

¹⁶He said to the woman:

> I will intensify your labor pains;
> you will bear children in anguish.
> Your desire will be for your husband,
> yet he will dominate you.

¹⁷And He said to Adam, "Because you listened to your wife's voice and ate from the tree about which I commanded you,

'Do not eat from it':

> The ground is cursed because of you.
> You will eat from it by means of painful labor
> all the days of your life.
> ¹⁸ It will produce thorns and thistles for you,
> and you will eat the plants of the field.
> ¹⁹ You will eat bread by the sweat of your brow
> until you return to the ground,
> since you were taken from it.
> For you are dust,
> and you will return to dust."

²⁰Adam named his wife Eve because she was the mother of all the living. ²¹The LORD God made clothing out of skins for Adam and his wife, and He clothed them.

²²The LORD God said, "Since man has become like one of Us, knowing good and evil, he must not reach out, and also take from the tree of life, and eat, and live forever." ²³So the LORD God sent him away from the garden of Eden to work the ground from which he was taken. ²⁴He drove man out, and east of the garden of Eden He stationed cherubim with a flaming, whirling sword to guard the way to the tree of life.

CAIN MURDERS ABEL

4 Adam knew his wife Eve intimately, and she conceived and gave birth to Cain. She said, "I have had a male child with the LORD's help." ²Then she also gave birth to his brother Abel. Now Abel became a shepherd of a flock, but Cain cultivated the land. ³In the course of time Cain presented some of the land's produce as an offering to the LORD. ⁴And Abel also presented [an offering]—some of the firstborn of his flock and their fat portions. The LORD had regard for Abel and his offering, ⁵but He did not have regard for Cain and his offering. Cain was furious, and he was downcast.

⁶Then the LORD said to Cain, "Why are you furious? And why are you downcast? ⁷If you do right, won't you be accepted? But if you do not do right, sin is crouching at the door. Its desire is for you, but you must master it."

⁸Cain said to his brother Abel, "Let's go out to the field."

And while they were in the field, Cain attacked his brother Abel and killed him.

⁹Then the Lᴏʀᴅ said to Cain, "Where is your brother Abel?"

"I don't know," he replied. "Am I my brother's guardian?"

¹⁰Then He said, "What have you done? Your brother's blood cries out to Me from the ground! ¹¹So now you are cursed [with alienation] from the ground that opened its mouth to receive your brother's blood you have shed. ¹²If you work the land, it will never again give you its yield. You will be a restless wanderer on the earth."

¹³But Cain answered the Lᴏʀᴅ, "My punishment is too great to bear! ¹⁴Since You are banishing me today from the soil, and I must hide myself from Your presence and become a restless wanderer on the earth, whoever finds me will kill me."

¹⁵Then the Lᴏʀᴅ replied to him, "In that case, whoever kills Cain will suffer vengeance seven times over." And He placed a mark on Cain so that whoever found him would not kill him. ¹⁶Then Cain went out from the Lᴏʀᴅ's presence and lived in the land of Nod, east of Eden.

PRAYER: Gracious and loving heavenly Father, how grateful I am for the fact that although the first Adam failed in a garden of beauty, You triumphed in the midst of the most humiliating conditions. As I think of Your agony in the Garden of Gethsemane and Your sufferings on the cross my heart cries out: Thank You, dear Lord. Your agony has healed my agony. Amen.

DAY
46

EXODUS 25:1-9; 31:1-17

IN CONTINUING TO explore the creational dimension to the redemptive story, we move beyond Noah and the patriarchs to the nation of Israel. God selected Israel to be His covenant partner in bringing blessing to the whole world. To that end, God redeemed His people from slavery in Egypt so that they might embody what a truly human race might look like which lived by God's grace and for God's glory. The book of Exodus is shaped throughout by a theology of creation, not least in the parallels between Exodus and Genesis. The plagues on Egypt, like the Flood, are ecological judgments; deliverance is through water (15:1ff.); and chapters 25 to 40, like Genesis 1 to 9, may be seen as a sequence of creation-decreation-recreation.

In particular, the building of the tabernacle in chapters 35 to 40 can be seen in terms of recreation. The parallels are intriguing. The creative Spirit is again at work (31:1-11; cf. Gen. 1:2); seven speeches in chapters 25 to 31 mirror the seven days of creation, climaxing, like them, in the Sabbath (31:16-17) which, as the sign of God's special covenant with Israel, reminds His people also of its role in His wider purposes for His creation. In this portable worship-centre then, and with His pilgrim people, the mobile God is on His way to the new creation!

Exodus 25:1-9

OFFERINGS TO BUILD THE TABERNACLE

25 The Lord spoke to Moses: [2]"Tell the Israelites to take an offering for Me. You are to take My offering from everyone whose heart stirs him [to give]. [3]This is the offering you are to receive from them: gold, silver, and bronze; [4]blue, purple, and scarlet yarn; fine linen and goat hair; [5]ram skins dyed red and manatee skins; acacia wood; [6]oil for the light; spices for the anointing oil and for the fragrant incense; [7]and onyx along with [other] gemstones for mounting on the ephod and breastpiece.

[8]"They are to make a sanctuary for Me so that I may dwell among them. [9]You must make [it] according to all that I show you—the design of the tabernacle as well as the design of all its furnishings."

BIBLE READING

Exodus 31:1-17

GOD'S PROVISION OF THE SKILLED WORKERS

31 The LORD also spoke to Moses: ²"Look, I have appointed by name Bezalel son of Uri, son of Hur, of the tribe of Judah. ³I have filled him with God's Spirit, with wisdom, understanding, and ability in every craft ⁴to design artistic works in gold, silver, and bronze, ⁵to cut gemstones for mounting, and to carve wood for work in every craft. ⁶I have also selected Oholiab son of Ahisamach, of the tribe of Dan, to be with him. I have placed wisdom within every skilled craftsman in order to make all that I have commanded you: ⁷the tent of meeting, the ark of the testimony, the mercy seat that is on top of it, and all the [other] furnishings of the tent— ⁸the table with its utensils, the pure [gold] lampstand with all its utensils, the altar of incense, ⁹the altar of burnt offering with all its utensils, the basin with its stand— ¹⁰the specially woven garments, both the holy garments for Aaron the priest and the garments for his sons to serve as priests, ¹¹the anointing oil, and the fragrant incense for the sanctuary. They must make [them] according to all that I have commanded you."

OBSERVING THE SABBATH

¹²The LORD said to Moses: ¹³"Tell the Israelites: You must observe My Sabbaths, for it is a sign between Me and you throughout your generations, so that you will know that I am the LORD who sets you apart. ¹⁴Observe the Sabbath, for it is holy to you. Whoever profanes it must be put to death. If anyone does work on it, that person must be cut off from his people. ¹⁵For six days work may be done, but on the seventh day there must be a Sabbath of complete rest, dedicated to the LORD. Anyone who does work on the Sabbath day must be put to death. ¹⁶The Israelites must observe the Sabbath, celebrating it throughout their generations as a perpetual covenant. ¹⁷It is a sign forever between Me and the Israelites, for in six days the LORD made the heavens and the earth, but on the seventh day He rested and was refreshed."

TO PONDER: A key passage to focus on is Deuteronomy 26:16-19. Note particularly verse 17: 'Today you have affirmed that the Lord is your God and that you will walk in His ways, keep His statutes, commands, and ordinances, and obey Him.' God selected the Israelites to be His covenant partner. How sad that so often they failed. We too are God's covenant partners – let's draw daily on God's grace to ensure we do not fail.

DAY
47

EXODUS 39:43-40:38

STILL PURSUING OUR creation theme we note that, in building the tabernacle, Moses draws together materials and skills which God has invested in His creation. It is as if the whole material world and all human craftsmanship is being redirected to its original goal of glorifying God. The sanctuary itself exhibits beauty, order, design and colour – just those features most evident in God's original 'good' world.

As in Genesis 1, so here the work is finished, evaluated as satisfactory, and blessed (39:43). The tabernacle is dedicated on the first day of the first month, corresponding liturgically to the first day of creation (40:2,17). In other words, the tabernacle symbolically celebrates, within a disordered world, the beauty and order of God's creation.

This makes worship hugely significant. Worship becomes, for us, the one spot in the midst of a fractured world where we declare God's redemptive reordering of the world. In worship we exult in God's promise of a new creation. We take the holy time and make holy space which God can fill with His glorious presence (40:34).

Exodus 39:43-40:38

BIBLE
READING

⁴³Moses inspected all the work they had accomplished. They had done just as the LORD commanded. Then Moses blessed them.

SETTING UP THE TABERNACLE

40 The Lord spoke to Moses: [2]"You are to set up the tabernacle, the tent of meeting, on the first day of the first month. [3]Put the ark of the testimony there, and screen off the ark with the veil. [4]Then bring in the table and lay out its arrangement; also bring in the lampstand and set up its lamps. [5]Place the gold altar for incense in front of the ark of the testimony. Put up the screen for the entrance to the tabernacle. [6]Position the altar of burnt offering in front of the entrance to the tabernacle, the tent of meeting. [7]Place the basin between the tent of meeting and the altar, and put water in it. [8]Assemble the surrounding courtyard and hang the screen for the gate of the courtyard.

[9]"Take the anointing oil, and anoint the tabernacle and everything in it; consecrate it along with all its furnishings so that it will be holy. [10]Anoint the altar of burnt offering and all its utensils; consecrate the altar so that it will be especially holy. [11]Anoint the basin and its stand, and consecrate it.

[12]"Then bring Aaron and his sons to the entrance to the tent of meeting and wash them with water. [13]Clothe Aaron with the holy garments, anoint him, and consecrate him, so that he can serve Me as a priest. [14]Have his sons come forward and clothe them in tunics. [15]Anoint them just as you anointed their father, so that they may also serve Me as priests. Their anointing will serve to inaugurate a permanent priesthood for them throughout their generations."

[16]Moses did everything just as the Lord had commanded him. [17]The tabernacle was set up in the first month of the second year, on the first [day] of the month. [18]Moses set up the tabernacle: he laid its bases, positioned its planks, inserted its crossbars, and set up its posts. [19]Then he spread the tent over the tabernacle and put the covering of the tent on top of it, just as the Lord had commanded Moses.

[20]Moses took the testimony and placed [it] in the ark, and attached the poles to the ark. He set the mercy seat on top of the ark. [21]He brought the ark into the tabernacle, put up the veil for the screen, and screened off the ark of the testimony, just as the Lord had commanded him.

[22]Moses placed the table in the tent of meeting on the north side of the tabernacle, outside the veil. [23]He arranged the bread on it before the Lord, just as the Lord had commanded him.

[24]He also put the lampstand in the tent of meeting opposite the table on the south side of the tabernacle [25]and set up the lamps before the LORD, just as the LORD had commanded him.

[26]Moses also installed the gold altar in the tent of meeting, in front of the veil, [27]and burned fragrant incense on it, just as the LORD had commanded him. [28]He put up the screen at the entrance to the tabernacle. [29]Then he placed the altar of burnt offering at the entrance to the tabernacle, the tent of meeting, and offered the burnt offering and the grain offering on it, just as the LORD had commanded him.

[30]He set the basin between the tent of meeting and the altar and put water in it for washing. [31]Moses, Aaron, and his sons washed their hands and feet from it. [32]They washed whenever they came to the tent of meeting and approached the altar, just as the LORD had commanded Moses.

[33]Next Moses set up the surrounding courtyard for the tabernacle and the altar and hung a screen for the gate of the courtyard. So Moses finished the work.

THE LORD'S GLORY

[34]The cloud covered the tent of meeting, and the glory of the LORD filled the tabernacle. [35]Moses was unable to enter the tent of meeting because the cloud rested on it, and the glory of the LORD filled the tabernacle.

[36]The Israelites set out whenever the cloud was taken up from the tabernacle throughout all the stages of their journey. [37]If the cloud was not taken up, they did not set out until the day it was taken up. [38]For the cloud of the LORD was over the tabernacle by day, and there was a fire inside the cloud by night, visible to the entire house of Israel throughout all the stages of their journey.

> THOUGHT: Worship, it has been said, is 'inner health made audible'. What is meant by this? We are made for worship, and when we engage in true worship our souls are drawn to health. Those who do not worship may have physical health but not spiritual health. The worship of God is the way to achieve spiritual health. But remember, there can be no true worship where there is no trust. You cannot worship someone you do not trust.

DAY
48

JOB 38:1-7; 40; 42:1-7

OUR STORY NOW takes us to a mini-drama all its own; a series of tense dialogues between a suffering man and his so-called friends and spurious theological experts, and, lastly, his encounter with the Creator God in person! Job's 'advisers' finally grind to a halt. Having stubbornly refused to deny his own integrity, Job, too, falls silent. When at last God speaks, He overwhelms Job with a dazzling recital of His power as Creator. Is God browbeating Job into submission? Or is He, perhaps, taking drastic measures to break through Job's defences? In his pain, Job has often complained that he hates being human (7:17-21; cf. Psa. 8). But we do not glorify God by loathing ourselves.

God's rebuke is not meant to cut Job down to size, but to rouse him to measure up as a worthy conversation partner and co-worker. On one possible reading of the text of 42:6, Job repents *of*, not *in*, 'dust and ashes'. That is, he repudiates his low sense of self-worth, turning from his own self-hatred to re-engage with the One in whose image he is made. God summons Job to stand on his feet 'like a man', to look Him in the eye (38:3; 40:6-7).

One glimpse of this majestic God cleanses and clarifies as no judgmental friends or self-condemnation can ever do (42:5). This is the wisdom Job finds in the end, albeit through suffering.

BIBLE READING

Job 38:1-7

THE LORD SPEAKS

38 Then the LORD answered Job from the whirlwind. He said:

2 Who is this who obscures [My] counsel
   with ignorant words?
3 Get ready to answer Me like a man;
   when I question you, you will inform Me.
4 Where were you when I established the earth?

Tell [Me], if you have understanding.
5 Who fixed its dimensions? Certainly you know!
Who stretched a measuring line across it?
6 What supports its foundations?
Or who laid its cornerstone
7 while the morning stars sang together
and all the sons of God shouted for joy?

Job 40

BIBLE
READING

40 The LORD answered Job:

2 Will the one who contends with the Almighty
correct [Him]?
Let him who argues with God give an answer.

3 Then Job answered the LORD:

4 I am so insignificant. How can I answer You?
I place my hand over my mouth.
5 I have spoken once, and I will not reply;
twice, but [now] I can add nothing.

6Then the LORD answered Job from the whirlwind:

7 Get ready to answer Me like a man;
When I question you, you will inform Me.
8 Would you really challenge My justice?
Would you declare Me guilty to justify yourself?
9 Do you have an arm like God's?
Can you thunder with a voice like His?

10 Adorn yourself with majesty and splendor,
and clothe yourself with honor and glory.
11 Unleash your raging anger;
look on every proud person and humiliate him.
12 Look on every proud person and humble him;
trample the wicked where they stand.
13 Hide them together in the dust;

imprison them in the grave.

¹⁴ Then I will confess to you
that your own right hand can deliver you.

¹⁵ Look at Behemoth,
which I made along with you.
He eats grass like an ox.

¹⁶ Look at the strength of his loins
and the power in the muscles of his belly.

¹⁷ He stiffens his tail like a cedar tree;
the tendons of his thighs are woven firmly together.

¹⁸ His bones are bronze tubes;
his limbs are like iron rods.

¹⁹ He is the foremost of God's works;
[only] his Maker can draw the sword against him.

²⁰ The hills yield food for him,
while all [sorts of] wild animals play there.

²¹ He lies under the lotus plants,
hiding in the protection of marshy reeds.

²² Lotus plants cover him with their shade;
the willows by the brook surround him.

²³ Though the river rages, Behemoth is unafraid;
he remains confident, even if the Jordan surges up to his
mouth.

²⁴ Can anyone capture him while he looks on,
or pierce his nose with snares?

BIBLE READING

Job 42:1-7

JOB REPLIES TO THE LORD

42 Then Job replied to the LORD:

² I know that You can do anything
and no plan of Yours can be thwarted.

³ [You asked,] "Who is this who conceals [My] counsel
with ignorance?"
Surely I spoke about things I did not understand,
things too wonderful for me to know.

⁴ [You said,] "Listen now, and I will speak.

When I question you, you will inform Me."
⁵ I had heard rumors about You,
 but now my eyes have seen You.
⁶ Therefore I take back [my words]
 and repent in dust and ashes.

⁷After the LORD had finished speaking to Job, He said to Eliphaz the Temanite: "I am angry with you and your two friends, for you have not spoken the truth about Me, as My servant Job has."

PRAYER: Gracious and loving Father, forgive me if I tell You what I think *You* should do rather than listening to You to learn what *I* should do. How I pray that the drastic steps You took to silence Job may not be necessary with me. If I have been focusing more on speaking than listening, then help me through this problem. In Jesus' name. Amen.

DAY 49
PSALM 8

IN THE MOONLIGHT, under a star-studded sky, how big and majestic God seems; how tiny and insignificant I feel! When I glimpse the big picture, it seems to dwarf my little domestic story.

Undeterred, the singer celebrates by setting Genesis 1:26-28 to music. '... made him little less than God ...' (v.5) helps us find our bearings. We neither *deify* human beings as gods nor *denigrate them* as junk! In the vastness of the universe we may seem fragile and insignificant. But God *considers us*, and what we are in His eyes is what counts! Not, as the famous philosopher said: 'I think, therefore I am.' But rather: 'God thinks of me, therefore I am'! Neither the planets nor the apes determine who we are! *It is our relationship with God that defines us most accurately.*

Crowned with glory and honour ... and 'made lord' over the works of His hands (vv.5-6), we have a calling that ennobles us. Although sin and suffering can make it seem an oppressive burden (Job 7:17-21), being human is a royal vocation.

Our text awaits the victory of the truly human One who, conquering evil and death, emerges with everything – even death – successfully 'under His feet' (1 Cor. 15:20-28; Eph. 1:16-23; Heb. 2:5-8). 'The head that once was crowned with thorns is crowned with glory now.'

| BIBLE READING | **Psalm 8** |

GOD'S GLORY, MAN'S DIGNITY

For the choir director: on the *Gittith*. A Davidic psalm.

1 LORD, our Lord,
how magnificent is Your name throughout the earth!

You have covered the heavens with Your majesty.
2 Because of Your adversaries,
You have established a stronghold
from the mouths of children and nursing infants,
to silence the enemy and the avenger.

3 When I observe Your heavens,
the work of Your fingers,
the moon and the stars,
which You set in place,
4 what is man that You remember him,
the son of man that You look after him?
5 You made him little less than God
and crowned him with glory and honor.
6 You made him lord over the works of Your hands;
You put everything under his feet:
7 all the sheep and oxen,
as well as animals in the wild,
8 birds of the sky,
and fish of the sea
passing through the currents of the seas.

9 LORD, our Lord,
how magnificent is Your name throughout the earth!

TO PONDER: Someone has commented: 'I am not what I think I am. I am not what you think I am. I am what I think you think I am.' In other words, the way we think about ourselves is not the way others think of us but the way we think they think of us. How do you think God thinks about you? He thinks you are special, someone in whom He delights. Now think that way about yourself. Remember: 'It is our relationship with God that defines us most accurately.'

DAY 50

PSALM 19

GOD SPEAKS IN both the *sky* (vv.1-6) and the *Scriptures* (vv.7-14). In the *sky* the 'voice' of His creation declares His glory and proclaims His handiwork in morning lectures and evening classes. As joyfully as a bridegroom is meant for his bride, and an athlete is meant for the finishing tape, so the sun, by rising and setting, adds its witness to the glorious purpose of things.

In the *Scriptures* (vv.7-14) God speaks firsthand in the words of the law. The psalmist exults in what the law *is* – God's testimony and precepts – and also in what the law is *like* – perfect, sure, radiant, pure, sweet. Above all he relishes what the law *does*: it revives the soul, makes wise the simple, gives joy to the heart and light to the eyes! The fear of God this evokes does not deter but attracts (v.10), enabling us to breathe moral fresh air (vv.11-13). In the end we fear to mar such beauty, deny such truth, grieve such love.

This remarkable song joins what God reveals in creation (general revelation) with what He reveals through the story told in Israel's Scriptures (special revelation). Both invite *saving* revelation. God is the Rock which His creation reveals Him to be and becomes the Redeemer His law needs Him to be. But to tell *that* story and declare *that* glory we must follow another star.

BIBLE READING

Psalm 19

THE WITNESS OF CREATION AND SCRIPTURE

For the choir director. A Davidic psalm.

1 The heavens declare the glory of God,
and the sky proclaims the work of His hands.
2 Day after day they pour out speech;
night after night they communicate knowledge.
3 There is no speech; there are no words;
their voice is not heard.
4 Their message has gone out to all the earth,
and their words to the ends of the inhabited world.

In the heavens He has pitched a tent for the sun.
5 It is like a groom coming from the bridal chamber;
it rejoices like an athlete running a course.
6 It rises from one end of the heavens
and circles to their other end;
nothing is hidden from its heat.

7 The instruction of the LORD is perfect,
reviving the soul;
the testimony of the LORD is trustworthy,
making the inexperienced wise.
8 The precepts of the LORD are right,
making the heart glad;
the commandment of the LORD is radiant,
making the eyes light up.
9 The fear of the LORD is pure,
enduring forever;
the ordinances of the LORD are reliable
and altogether righteous.
10 They are more desirable than gold—
than an abundance of pure gold;
and sweeter than honey—
than honey dripping from the comb.
11 In addition, Your servant is warned by them;
there is great reward in keeping them.

¹² Who perceives his unintentional sins?
Cleanse me from my hidden faults.
¹³ Moreover, keep Your servant from willful sins;
do not let them rule over me.
Then I will be innocent,
and cleansed from blatant rebellion.
¹⁴ May the words of my mouth
and the meditation of my heart
be acceptable to You,
LORD, my rock and my Redeemer.

FOR THANKSGIVING: Two thrilling verses that join creation and redemption are found in the book of Revelation: 'Our Lord and God, You are worthy to receive glory and honor and power, because You have created all things ...' (Rev. 4:11). 'You made them a kingdom and priests to our God, and they will reign on the earth' (Rev. 5:10). How wonderful God is in creation, but how much more wonderful is He in redemption.

WE PAUSE TO reflect further on how the prophetic singers of Israel praised the one Creator God and celebrated His works of creation.

Dramatically, in the first stanza, the psalmist pictures God clothed majestically in a robe of light, striding through His world, painting the world in glorious colours, sparking into life everything He touches. Here is no distant God, locked outside His world. This is the biblical God, pouring out His creative energies and love all the time from *inside* His world.

Echoing what we have seen of God's commitment to Noah and the earth, the song relishes the way God's faithfulness guarantees the world's *stability* (vv.5-9), His creativity funds its *fruitfulness* (vv.10-18), His design shapes its *orderliness* (vv.19-23), and His multifaceted wisdom is prodigal in its *variety* (vv.24-26). Unless we act irresponsibly and ransack the earth, we can be sure its resources will never run out! God's

DAY
51
PSALM 104

Spirit renews the face of the earth (v.30).
Feasting, working, researching, praising – it's a
wonderful world!

| BIBLE READING | **Psalm 104** |

GOD THE CREATOR

¹ My soul, praise the LORD!
  LORD my God, You are very great;
  You are clothed with majesty and splendor.
² He wraps Himself in light as if it were a robe,
  spreading out the sky like a canopy,
³ laying the beams of His palace
  on the waters [above],
  making the clouds His chariot,
  walking on the wings of the wind,
⁴ and making the winds His messengers,
  flames of fire His servants.

⁵ He established the earth on its foundations;
  it will never be shaken.
⁶ You covered it with the deep
  as if it were a garment;
  the waters stood above the mountains.
⁷ At Your rebuke the waters fled;
  at the sound of Your thunder they hurried away—
⁸ mountains rose and valleys sank—
  to the place You established for them.
⁹ You set a boundary they cannot cross;
  they will never cover the earth again.

¹⁰ He causes the springs to gush into the valleys;
  they flow between the mountains.
¹¹ They supply water for every wild beast;
  the wild donkeys quench their thirst.
¹² The birds of the sky live beside [the springs];
  they sing among the foliage.
¹³ He waters the mountains from His palace;

the earth is satisfied by the fruit of Your labor.

¹⁴ He causes grass to grow for the livestock
and [provides] crops for man to cultivate,
producing food from the earth,
¹⁵ wine that makes man's heart glad—
making his face shine with oil—
and bread that sustains man's heart.
¹⁶ The trees of the LORD flourish,
the cedars of Lebanon that He planted.
¹⁷ There the birds make their nests;
the stork makes its home in the pine trees.
¹⁸ The high mountains are for the wild goats;
the cliffs are a refuge for hyraxes.

¹⁹ He made the moon to mark the seasons;
the sun knows when to set.
²⁰ You bring darkness, and it becomes night,
when all the forest animals stir.
²¹ The young lions roar for their prey
and seek their food from God.
²² The sun rises; they go back
and lie down in their dens.
²³ Man goes out to his work
and to his labor until evening.

²⁴ How countless are Your works, LORD!
In wisdom You have made them all;
the earth is full of Your creatures.
²⁵ Here is the sea, vast and wide,
teeming with creatures beyond number—
living things both large and small.
²⁶ There the ships move about,
and Leviathan, which You formed to play there.

²⁷ All of them wait for You
to give them their food at the right time.
²⁸ When You give it to them,
they gather it;
when You open Your hand,

they are satisfied with good things.
²⁹ When You hide Your face,
they are terrified;
when You take away their breath,
they die and return to the dust.
³⁰ When You send Your breath,
they are created,
and You renew the face of the earth.

³¹ May the glory of the LORD endure forever;
may the LORD rejoice in His works.
³² He looks at the earth, and it trembles;
He touches the mountains,
and they pour out smoke.
³³ I will sing to the LORD all my life;
I will sing praise to my God while I live.
³⁴ May my meditation be pleasing to Him;
I will rejoice in the LORD.

³⁵ May sinners vanish from the earth
and the wicked be no more.
My soul, praise the LORD!
Hallelujah!

FOR PRAISE: 'Jesus is Lord, creation's voice proclaims it.' Think about the fact that throughout the whole of creation there are evidences of Christ's creative hand. It is the same in the Christian life. His resources - grace, love, joy, peace, and so on - will never be exhausted. For that also give Him praise.

DAY
52

PROVERBS 8

THIS REMARKABLE FLIGHT of prophetic imagination pictures the wisdom of God as God's creative partner in making the world, dancing beside Him in the sheer joy of creativity (vv.30-31).

Scholars argue over whether or not this is strictly a personification of wisdom. Be that as it may, we can find the wisdom of God at street level (v.2). Following the Maker's instructions, we learn the life-skills to raise a family, run a business, rule our tongues or rule a nation! When moral choices must be made we can find God's wisdom along the paths of righteousness (v.20). And this wisdom, we discover, is nothing less than the very wisdom with which God made the world (vv.22-31)!

From Proverbs 8 the trajectory of wisdom travelled through the Jewish writings *The Wisdom of Solomon* and *Ecclesiasticus* until it lodged in the mind-set of the apostles. There it provided the key categories which enabled them to speak of the divinity of Jesus without compromising the oneness of God (see Col. 1:15ff.; cf. 1 Cor. 1:18-2:4; 8:4-6). For the apostles and for us, the wisdom of God finally came down to earth *in Person* in the words and work of Jesus of Nazareth.

BIBLE READING

Proverbs 8

WISDOM'S APPEAL

8 Doesn't Wisdom call out?
Doesn't Understanding make her voice heard?
² At the heights overlooking the road,
at the crossroads, she takes her stand.
³ Beside the gates at the entry to the city,
at the main entrance, she cries out:
⁴ "People, I call out to you;
my cry is to mankind.
⁵ Learn to be shrewd, you who are inexperienced;
develop common sense, you who are foolish.
⁶ Listen, for I speak of noble things,

and what my lips say is right.
7 For my mouth tells the truth,
and wickedness is detestable to my lips.
8 All the words of my mouth are righteous;
none of them are deceptive or perverse.
9 All of them are clear to the perceptive,
and right to those who discover knowledge.
10 Accept my instruction instead of silver,
and knowledge rather than pure gold.
11 For wisdom is better than precious stones,
and nothing desirable can compare with it.
12 I, Wisdom, share a home with shrewdness
and have knowledge and discretion.
13 To fear the LORD is to hate evil.
I hate arrogant pride, evil conduct,
and perverse speech.
14 I possess good advice and competence;
I have understanding and strength.
15 It is by me that kings reign
and rulers enact just law;
16 by me, princes lead,
as do nobles [and] all righteous judges.
17 I love those who love me,
and those who search for me find me.
18 With me are riches and honor,
lasting wealth and righteousness.
19 My fruit is better than solid gold,
and my harvest than pure silver.
20 I walk in the way of righteousness,
along the paths of justice,
21 giving wealth as an inheritance to those who love me,
and filling their treasuries.

22 The LORD made me
at the beginning of His creation,
before His works of long ago.
23 I was formed before ancient times,
from the beginning, before the earth began.
24 I was brought forth
when there were no watery depths

and no springs filled with water.

25 I was brought forth
before the mountains and hills were established,
26 before He made the land, the fields,
or the first soil on earth.
27 I was there when He established the heavens,
when He laid out the horizon on the surface
of the ocean,
28 when He placed the skies above,
when the fountains of the ocean gushed forth,
29 when He set a limit for the sea
so that the waters would not violate His command,
when He laid out the foundations of the earth.
30 I was a skilled craftsman beside Him.
I was His delight every day,
always rejoicing before Him.
31 I was rejoicing in His inhabited world,
delighting in the human race.

32 And now, [my] sons, listen to me;
those who keep my ways are happy.
33 Listen to instruction and be wise;
don't ignore it.
34 Anyone who listens to me is happy,
watching at my doors every day,
waiting by the posts of my doorway.
35 For the one who finds me finds life
and obtains favor from the LORD,
36 but the one who sins against me harms himself;
all who hate me love death."

TO PONDER: The difference between knowledge and wisdom, it has been said, is this: knowledge is what one knows, wisdom is knowing how best to use that knowledge. Jesus is described as 'God's power and God's wisdom' (1 Cor. 1:24). What an apt description. Not only does He have all the information He needs to run the universe but He also knows the best way to use it. And that wisdom is available to you and me - any time (see James 1:5).

THE EXPERIENCE OF the Babylonian Exile was so traumatic that the prophets who lived through it harked back to the old Flood story to define it! It was Jeremiah who pictured the impending Babylonian invasion of Judah as a catastrophe on a scale which could only be described as an act of decreation (Jer. 4:19-28). The great 'Israel adventure' seemed to have come to an end with the people of God engulfed in a 'flood' of judgment. So severe is the crisis that not even Noah, Ezekiel said, could have made a difference (Ezek. 14:12-20)!

But it was just at this point that talk of Noah gives hope. For Isaiah, God's commitment to Noah in covenant not only guarantees creation but becomes a pattern and a promise of God's renewing work after the Exile (Isa. 54:5-10). We recall that after the deluge of water and destruction, God swore that the Flood of His judgment would never happen again. Now, says Isaiah, the God of all the earth swears never again to desert His people or loosen the grip of His covenant love upon them. This pledge of reconciliation Isaiah calls a 'covenant of peace' (54:10). The Creator resolves to be Redeemer, ultimately on an unprecedented scale (Isa. 65:17-25).

DAY
53
ISAIAH 54

Isaiah 54

BIBLE READING

FUTURE GLORY FOR ISRAEL

54 "Rejoice, barren one, who did not give birth;
burst into song and shout,
you who have not been in labor!
For the children of the forsaken one will be more
than the children of the married woman,"
says the LORD.
² "Enlarge the site of your tent,
and let your tent curtains be stretched out;
do not hold back;
lengthen your ropes,

and drive your pegs deep.
³ For you will spread out to the right and to the left,
and your descendants will dispossess nations
and inhabit the desolate cities.

⁴ "Do not be afraid, for you will not be put to shame;
don't be humiliated, for you will not be disgraced.
For you will forget the shame of your youth,
and you will no longer remember
the disgrace of your widowhood.
⁵ For your husband is your Maker—
His name is Yahweh of Hosts—
and the Holy One of Israel is your Redeemer;
He is called the God of all the earth.
⁶ For the LORD has called you,
like a wife deserted and wounded in spirit,
a wife of one's youth when she is rejected,"
says your God.
⁷ "I deserted you for a brief moment,
but I will take you back with great compassion.
⁸ In a surge of anger
I hid My face from you for a moment,
but I will have compassion on you
with everlasting love,"
says the LORD your Redeemer.
⁹ "For this is like the days of Noah to Me:
when I swore that the waters of Noah
would never flood the earth again,
so I have sworn that I will not be angry with you
or rebuke you.
¹⁰ Though the mountains move and the hills shake,
My love will not be removed from you
and My covenant of peace will not be shaken,"
says your compassionate LORD.

¹¹ "Poor [Jerusalem], storm-tossed, and not comforted,
I will set your stones in black mortar,
and lay your foundations in sapphires.
¹² I will make your battlements of rubies,
your gates of sparkling stones,

and all your walls of precious stones.

13 Then all your children will be taught by the LORD,
their prosperity will be great,

14 and you will be established
on [a foundation of] righteousness.
You will be far from oppression,
you will certainly not be afraid;
you will be far from terror,
it will certainly not come near you.

15 If anyone attacks you, it is not from Me;
whoever attacks you will fall before you.

16 Look, I have created the craftsman
who blows on the charcoal fire
and produces a weapon suitable for its task;
and I have created the destroyer to work havoc.

17 No weapon formed against you will succeed,
and you will refute any accusation
raised against you in court.
This is the heritage of the LORD's servants,
and their righteousness is from Me."

[This is] the LORD's declaration.

PRAYER: My Father and my God, how my heart rejoices at this truth that You have sworn never to desert Your people or loosen the grip of Your covenant love upon them. How secure it makes me feel that as one of Your covenant people my name is written on Your hands. This means I cannot be forgotten. My name is before You for eternity. How can I ever sufficiently thank You for that tremendous fact? My heart is Yours for ever. Amen.

DAY
54

JOHN 1

JOHN HERE RECALLS Genesis 1, introducing Jesus as both one with the eternal Creator God and as head of a new creation. John calls Him 'the Word' (*logos*), a term known in Greek thought, but, more importantly, with Old Testament roots. There, God's word is world-making, powerful and effective (eg, Gen. 1:2ff.; Psa. 33:6ff.; Isa. 55:10-11). This 'word' is now concentrated in a Person, Jesus Christ.

John draws on two other sources. First, is the Old Testament and Jewish concept of 'personified' wisdom as God's agent in creation (Prov. 8:22ff.). Secondly, John is, no doubt, echoing the early Christians' experience of the gospel as the powerful 'Word' that saves (eg, Rom. 1:16; 10:17; Col. 1:5). John celebrates this Word as eternal, as personal, as light and life, and, above all, as truly human (v.14). God's openly spoken word and God's deep, underlying wisdom come into sharp focus in the face of Jesus. God's grace and truth have taken on flesh-and-blood reality (cf. 1 John 1:1ff.). His glory fulfils and eclipses all that's come before, even through Moses. The incarnate Word is the 'exegesis' or 'narration' of God (v.18). *The story of Jesus is the story of God.*

Reading His script and singing His song, we, too, behold God's glory in Jesus Christ.

BIBLE READING

John 1

1 In the beginning was the Word,
and the Word was with God,
    and the Word was God.
² He was with God in the beginning.
³ All things were created through Him,
    and apart from Him not one thing was created
    that has been created.
⁴ Life was in Him,
    and that life was the light of men.
⁵ That light shines in the darkness,
    yet the darkness did not overcome it.

[6] There was a man named John
who was sent from God.
[7] He came as a witness
to testify about the light,
so that all might believe through him.
[8] He was not the light,
but he came to testify about the light.
[9] The true light, who gives light to everyone,
was coming into the world.

[10] He was in the world,
and the world was created through Him,
yet the world did not recognize Him.
[11] He came to His own,
and His own people did not receive Him.
[12] But to all who did receive Him,
He gave them the right to be children of God,
to those who believe in His name,
[13] who were born,
not of blood,
or of the will of the flesh,
or of the will of man,
but of God.

[14] The Word became flesh
and took up residence among us.
We observed His glory,
the glory as the One and Only Son from the Father,
full of grace and truth.
[15] (John testified concerning Him and exclaimed,
"This was the One of whom I said,
'The One coming after me has surpassed me,
because He existed before me.'")
[16] Indeed, we have all received grace after grace
from His fullness,
[17] for although the law was given through Moses,
grace and truth came through Jesus Christ.
[18] No one has ever seen God.
The One and Only Son—
the One who is at the Father's side—

He has revealed Him.

JOHN THE BAPTIST'S TESTIMONY

[19]This is John's testimony when the Jews from Jerusalem sent priests and Levites to ask him, "Who are you?"

[20]He did not refuse to answer, but he declared: "I am not the Messiah."

[21]"What then?" they asked him. "Are you Elijah?"

"I am not," he said.

"Are you the Prophet?"

"No," he answered.

[22]"Who are you, then?" they asked. "We need to give an answer to those who sent us. What can you tell us about yourself?"

[23]He said, "I am 'a voice of one crying out in the wilderness: Make straight the way of the Lord'—just as Isaiah the prophet said."

[24]Now they had been sent from the Pharisees. [25]So they asked him, "Why then do you baptize if you aren't the Messiah, or Elijah, or the Prophet?"

[26]"I baptize with water," John answered them. "Someone stands among you, but you don't know [Him]. [27]He is the One coming after me, whose sandal strap I'm not worthy to untie."

[28]All this happened in Bethany across the Jordan, where John was baptizing.

THE LAMB OF GOD

[29]The next day John saw Jesus coming toward him and said, "Here is the Lamb of God, who takes away the sin of the world! [30]This is the One I told you about: 'After me comes a man who has surpassed me, because He existed before me.' [31]I didn't know Him, but I came baptizing with water so He might be revealed to Israel."

[32]And John testified, "I watched the Spirit descending from heaven like a dove, and He rested on Him. [33]I didn't know Him, but He who sent me to baptize with water told me, 'The One you see the Spirit descending and resting on—He is the One who baptizes with the Holy Spirit.' [34]I have seen and testified that He is the Son of God!"

[35]Again the next day, John was standing with two of his disciples. [36]When he saw Jesus passing by, he said, "Look! The

Lamb of God!"

[37]The two disciples heard him say this and followed Jesus. [38]When Jesus turned and noticed them following Him, He asked them, "What are you looking for?"

They said to Him, "Rabbi" (which means "Teacher"), "where are You staying?"

[39]"Come and you'll see," He replied. So they went and saw where He was staying, and they stayed with Him that day. It was about 10 in the morning.

[40]Andrew, Simon Peter's brother, was one of the two who heard John and followed Him. [41]He first found his own brother Simon and told him, "We have found the Messiah!" (which means "Anointed One"), [42]and he brought [Simon] to Jesus.

When Jesus saw him, He said, "You are Simon, son of John. You will be called Cephas" (which means "Rock").

PHILIP AND NATHANAEL

[43]The next day He decided to leave for Galilee. Jesus found Philip and told him, "Follow Me!"

[44]Now Philip was from Bethsaida, the hometown of Andrew and Peter. [45]Philip found Nathanael and told him, "We have found the One Moses wrote about in the Law (and so did the prophets): Jesus the son of Joseph, from Nazareth!"

[46]"Can anything good come out of Nazareth?" Nathanael asked him.

"Come and see," Philip answered.

[47]Then Jesus saw Nathanael coming toward Him and said about him, "Here is a true Israelite; no deceit is in him."

[48]"How do you know me?" Nathanael asked.

"Before Philip called you, when you were under the fig tree, I saw you," Jesus answered.

[49]"Rabbi," Nathanael replied, "You are the Son of God! You are the King of Israel!"

[50]Jesus responded to him, "Do you believe [only] because I told you I saw you under the fig tree? You will see greater things than this." [51]Then He said, "I assure you: You will see heaven opened and the angels of God ascending and descending on the Son of Man."

FOR THANKSGIVING: Dr E. Stanley Jones told of a little boy who stood in front of a picture of his absent father and then said wistfully to his mother: 'How I wish Father would step out of the picture.' Throughout the Old Testament we can almost hear the same cry: 'If only the Father would step out of the picture.' Well, He has. He did so at Bethlehem. It shouldn't be only at Christmas time that we thank Him for stepping out of the picture. Do so now.

DAY 55

ROMANS 1:16-32

IN THIS DEVASTATING analysis of sin, Paul argues that creation displays unmistakable evidence of God's power and personality; enough, at least, to damn us if not enough to save us (v.20)! Failure in *worship* is the root sin (1:21). Our inbuilt drive to worship is then diverted into idolatry. Rejecting the Creator, we make a threefold 'exchange': God for idols, the truth for a lie, the natural for the unnatural (1:23,25,26).

Of persistent rebels, God is said, in judicial language, to 'deliver them over' or 'give them up' (NIV) to experience the inevitable consequences of rebellion (1:24,26,28). Sexual perversions are seen here not so much as acts which incur God's wrath but as *signs of a society already under God's wrath*. Homosexuality is highlighted, of course, not because it is more heinous a sin than gossip or envy (1:29ff.), rather, it graphically illustrates how sin destroys God's creation order, and how society has lost its way. The practice of homosexuality is vivid idolatry, perhaps the ultimate form of self-love. But this passage is a devastating indictment of *all* human sin and leaves no one in a position to judge others (2:1).

Thankfully, the gospel is more than adequate to redeem the human condition even in cities such as Rome (1:15-17).

Romans 1:16-32

THE RIGHTEOUS WILL LIVE BY FAITH

[16]For I am not ashamed of the gospel, because it is God's power for salvation to everyone who believes, first to the Jew, and also to the Greek. [17]For in it God's righteousness is revealed from faith to faith, just as it is written: "The righteous will live by faith."

THE GUILT OF THE GENTILE WORLD

[18]For God's wrath is revealed from heaven against all godlessness and unrighteousness of people who by their unrighteousness suppress the truth, [19]since what can be known about God is evident among them, because God has shown it to them. [20]From the creation of the world His invisible attributes, that is, His eternal power and divine nature, have been clearly seen, being understood through what He has made. As a result, people are without excuse. [21]For though they knew God, they did not glorify Him as God or show gratitude. Instead, their thinking became nonsense, and their senseless minds were darkened. [22]Claiming to be wise, they became fools [23]and exchanged the glory of the immortal God for images resembling mortal man, birds, four-footed animals, and reptiles.

[24]Therefore God delivered them over in the cravings of their hearts to sexual impurity, so that their bodies were degraded among themselves. [25]They exchanged the truth of God for a lie, and worshiped and served something created instead of the Creator, who is blessed forever. Amen.

FROM IDOLATRY TO DEPRAVITY

[26]This is why God delivered them over to degrading passions. For even their females exchanged natural sexual intercourse for what is unnatural. [27]The males in the same way also left natural sexual intercourse with females and were inflamed in their lust for one another. Males committed shameless acts with males and received in their own persons the appropriate penalty for their perversion.

[28]And because they did not think it worthwhile to have God in their knowledge, God delivered them over to a worthless

mind to do what is morally wrong. ²⁹They are filled with all unrighteousness, evil, greed, and wickedness. They are full of envy, murder, disputes, deceit, and malice. They are gossips, ³⁰slanderers, God-haters, arrogant, proud, boastful, inventors of evil, disobedient to parents, ³¹undiscerning, untrustworthy, unloving, and unmerciful. ³²Although they know full well God's just sentence—that those who practice such things deserve to die—they not only do them, but even applaud others who practice them.

RESPONSE: What better response could we give to today's reading than to reflect on the words of the well-known hymn by Isaac Watts. Say it or sing it now: 'When I survey the wondrous cross, on which the Prince of glory died, my richest gain I count but loss, and pour contempt on all my pride.'

DAY 56

COLOSSIANS 1:1-2:7

IT IS EXCITING to make the biblical connections and to see how the whole story hangs together. So it is with this stunning 'hymn' (1:15-20) which celebrates the supremacy of Jesus and is the hub around which the whole letter to the Colossians revolves.

This breathtaking vision is couched in language employed in the Old Testament and in Jewish writings to describe the creative wisdom of God. *In relation to God*, Jesus is the image (*icon*). *In relation to the cosmos*, He is the 'firstborn' of all creation (1:18), which does not imply that He ranks merely as a created being (the next verse precludes this). The likely background here is the inheritance rights of the eldest son in Old Testament families. Paul is stressing that *Jesus has priority, precedence, and stands to inherit the whole world*.

This is in line with the King's destiny as Son of God (Psa. 2). Amazingly, He is also the 'glue' that holds all things together (1:17). *In relation to the Church*, He is its Head (1:18). Applied to someone who had been crucified as a false prophet only some thirty years earlier, Paul's description is truly staggering! This is Jesus who, by virtue of His death and resurrection, is the climax of the old creation and the starting-point of the new creation where all things are reconciled to God's loving will.

Colossians 1:1-2:7

BIBLE READING

GREETING

1 Paul, an apostle of Christ Jesus by God's will, and Timothy our brother:
²To the saints and faithful brothers in Christ in Colossae. Grace to you and peace from God our Father.

THANKSGIVING

³We always thank God, the Father of our Lord Jesus Christ, when we pray for you, ⁴for we have heard of your faith in Christ Jesus and of the love you have for all the saints ⁵because of the hope reserved for you in heaven. You have already heard about [this hope] in the message of truth, the gospel ⁶that has come to you. It is bearing fruit and growing all over the world, just as it has among you since the day you heard it and recognized God's grace in the truth. ⁷You learned this from Epaphras, our much loved fellow slave. He is a faithful minister of the Messiah on your behalf, ⁸and he has told us about your love in the Spirit.

PRAYER FOR SPIRITUAL GROWTH

⁹For this reason also, since the day we heard this, we haven't stopped praying for you. We are asking that you may be filled with the knowledge of His will in all wisdom and spiritual understanding, ¹⁰so that you may walk worthy of the Lord, fully pleasing [to Him], bearing fruit in every good work and growing in the knowledge of God. ¹¹May you be strengthened with all power, according to His glorious might, for all endurance and patience, with joy ¹²giving thanks to the Father, who has enabled you to share in the saints' inheritance in the light. ¹³He has rescued us from the domain of darkness and transferred us into the kingdom of the Son He loves, ¹⁴in whom we have redemption, the forgiveness of sins.

THE CENTRALITY OF CHRIST

15 He is the image of the invisible God,
the firstborn over all creation;

16 because by Him everything was created,
in heaven and on earth, the visible and the invisible,
whether thrones or dominions or rulers or authorities—
all things have been created through Him and for Him.

17 He is before all things, and by Him all things
hold together.

18 He is also the head of the body, the church;
He is the beginning, the firstborn from the dead,
so that He might come to have first place in everything.

19 For God was pleased [to have] all His fullness dwell
in Him,

20 and through Him to reconcile everything to Himself
by making peace through the blood of His cross—
whether things on earth or things in heaven.

21And you were once alienated and hostile in mind because of your evil actions. 22But now He has reconciled you by His physical body through His death, to present you holy, faultless, and blameless before Him— 23if indeed you remain grounded and steadfast in the faith, and are not shifted away from the hope of the gospel that you heard. [This gospel] has been proclaimed in all creation under heaven, and I, Paul, have become a minister of it.

PAUL'S MINISTRY

24Now I rejoice in my sufferings for you, and I am completing in my flesh what is lacking in Christ's afflictions for His body, that is, the church. 25I have become its minister, according to God's administration that was given to me for you, to make God's message fully known, 26the mystery hidden for ages and generations but now revealed to His saints. 27God wanted to make known to those among the Gentiles the glorious wealth of this mystery, which is Christ in you, the hope of glory. 28We proclaim Him, warning and teaching everyone with all wisdom, so that we may present everyone mature in Christ. 29I labor for this, striving with His strength that works powerfully in me.

2 For I want you to know how great a struggle I have for you, for those in Laodicea, and for all who have not seen me in person. ²[I want] their hearts to be encouraged and joined together in love, so that they may have all the riches of assured understanding, and have the knowledge of God's mystery—Christ. ³In Him all the treasures of wisdom and knowledge are hidden.

CHRIST VERSUS THE COLOSSIAN HERESY

⁴I am saying this so that no one will deceive you with persuasive arguments. ⁵For I may be absent in body, but I am with you in spirit, rejoicing to see your good order and the strength of your faith in Christ.

⁶Therefore as you have received Christ Jesus the Lord, walk in Him, ⁷rooted and built up in Him and established in the faith, just as you were taught, and overflowing with thankfulness.

FOR ACTION: Though many 'hymns to Christ' have been developed over the centuries, nothing comes near to the inspired words of the apostle Paul in the passage we have read today. Consider composing your own 'hymn to Christ'. List all the things He has done for you - saving you, delivering you, and so on. Remember that the law of expression deepens impression. The more you express something the deeper it penetrates. You'll see.

IT SEEMS a long journey from Noah, but the trajectories being traced are now converging again and again on Jesus. Here, the majestic opening statement (1:1-4), and the seven Old Testament references that support it (1:5-14), magnificently declare once more that Jesus is God's 'last word' to His old creation and the 'first word' on the new creation. From this we learn that Jesus can be explained only as One who comes out of God, from outside creation.

Chapter 2 then claims that He comes, at the same

DAY
57

HEBREWS 1:1-2:18

time, from our human side of things, from within the created order! The writer builds his case on Psalm 8 (Day 49, Psa. 8) to show that the transcendent Son of God made the human condition fully His own. In His real humanity He became like us, liable to temptation, suffering, and even death, in order to restore us to the glory of our God-given human destiny (2:9). As the truly human One Jesus has lived our life, died our death, and now wears our crown. This is the guarantee that, in Him, we shall make it back to the glory from which we so tragically fell (2:10).

We see now only glimpses of this future but we do see *Jesus crowned* ... and holding to His cross, we trust in His achievement.

| BIBLE READING | **Hebrews 1:1-2:18** |

THE NATURE OF THE SON

1 Long ago God spoke to the fathers by the prophets at different times and in different ways. [2]In these last days, He has spoken to us by [His] Son, whom He has appointed heir of all things and through whom He made the universe. [3]He is the radiance of His glory, the exact expression of His nature, and He sustains all things by His powerful word. After making purification for sins, He sat down at the right hand of the Majesty on high. [4]So He became higher in rank than the angels, just as the name He inherited is superior to theirs.

THE SON SUPERIOR TO ANGELS

[5]For to which of the angels did He ever say, "You are My Son; today I have become Your Father," or again, "I will be His Father, and He will be My Son"? [6]When He again brings His firstborn into the world, He says, "And all God's angels must worship Him." [7]And about the angels He says:

"He makes His angels winds,
and His servants a fiery flame;"

[8]but about the Son:

"Your throne, O God, is forever and ever,
and the scepter of Your kingdom is a scepter of justice.
⁹ You have loved righteousness and hated lawlessness;
this is why God, Your God, has anointed You,
rather than Your companions, with the oil of joy."

¹⁰And:

"In the beginning, Lord, You established the earth,
and the heavens are the works of Your hands;
¹¹ they will perish, but You remain.
They will all wear out like clothing;
¹² You will roll them up like a cloak,
and they will be changed like a robe.
But You are the same,
and Your years will never end."

¹³Now to which of the angels has He ever said:

"Sit at My right hand
until I make Your enemies Your footstool"?

¹⁴Are they not all ministering spirits sent out to serve those who are going to inherit salvation?

WARNING AGAINST NEGLECT

2 We must therefore pay even more attention to what we have heard, so that we will not drift away. ²For if the message spoken through angels was legally binding, and every transgression and disobedience received a just punishment, ³how will we escape if we neglect such a great salvation? It was first spoken by the Lord and was confirmed to us by those who heard Him. ⁴At the same time, God also testified by signs and wonders, various miracles, and distributions [of gifts] from the Holy Spirit according to His will.

JESUS AND HUMANITY

⁵For He has not subjected to angels the world to come that we are talking about. ⁶But one has somewhere testified:

"What is man, that You remember him,
or the son of man, that You care for him?
7 You made him lower than the angels for a short time;
You crowned him with glory and honor
8 and subjected everything under his feet."

For in "subjecting everything" to him, He left nothing not subject to him. As it is, we do not yet see "everything subjected" to him. 9But we do see Jesus— "made lower than the angels for a short time" so that by God's grace He might taste death for everyone—crowned with glory and honor because of the suffering of death.

10For it was fitting, in bringing many sons to glory, that He, for whom and through whom all things exist, should make the source of their salvation perfect through sufferings. 11For the One who sanctifies and those who are sanctified all have one Father. That is why He is not ashamed to call them brothers, 12saying:

"I will proclaim Your name to My brothers;
I will sing hymns to You in the congregation."

13Again, "I will trust in Him." And again, "Here I am with the children God gave Me."

14Now since the children have flesh and blood in common, He also shared in these, so that through His death He might destroy the one holding the power of death—that is, the Devil— 15and free those who were held in slavery all their lives by the fear of death. 16For it is clear that He does not reach out to help angels, but to help Abraham's offspring. 17Therefore He had to be like His brothers in every way, so that He could become a merciful and faithful high priest in service to God, to make propitiation for the sins of the people. 18For since He Himself was tested and has suffered, He is able to help those who are tested.

FOR PRAISE: There is but one response we can make to today's reading; it is to say or sing these words:

> Crown Him with many crowns,
> The Lamb upon His throne;
> Hark! how the heavenly anthem drowns
> All music but its own.
> Awake, my soul, and sing
> Of Him who died for thee,
> And hail Him as thy matchless King through all eternity.

DAY 58

ROMANS 8

AS WE ROUND off the implications of God's covenant with Noah, we reach this exalted vantage-point from which we see laid out before us the breathtaking panorama of God's saving plans. Fresh from the Exodus, Israel was claimed as 'God's son' and pointed towards the promised land (Exod. 4:22-23).

But it was Jesus alone, centuries later, who succeeded, through suffering as the obedient 'Son of God', in the role created for Israel and her anointed king (2 Sam. 7:12-14). For us who are now 'in Christ' to fulfil our destiny as God's sons is both an incomparable privilege and a bracing challenge (vv.15-18).

Since our sinful failure mysteriously dragged creation down with us into frustration, so, by a miracle of grace, our faithfulness raises hopes of creation's renewal (v.19). We too wait in hope for the redemption of our bodies. Meanwhile, with those who love God, the Spirit works all things together for God's good purpose in our lives. This Spirit takes the dumb sighs of nature for release, the uttered cries of human beings for liberty, joins them to the groaning prayers of believers, and makes mysterious intercession that this decaying world may one day find its redemption and come to share in the glorious freedom of the sons of God. To this end Love has spared no expense (v.32) and suffers no separation (vv.38-39).

BIBLE READING

Romans 8

THE LIFE-GIVING SPIRIT

8 Therefore, no condemnation now exists for those in Christ Jesus, [2]because the Spirit's law of life in Christ Jesus has set you free from the law of sin and of death. [3]What the law could not do since it was limited by the flesh, God did. He condemned sin in the flesh by sending His own Son in flesh like ours under sin's domain, and as a sin offering, [4]in order that the law's requirement would be accomplished in us who do not walk according to the flesh but according to the Spirit. [5]For those whose lives are according to the flesh think about the things of the flesh, but those whose lives are according to the Spirit, about the things of the Spirit. [6]For the mind-set of the flesh is death, but the mind-set of the Spirit is life and peace. [7]For the mind-set of the flesh is hostile to God because it does not submit itself to God's law, for it is unable to do so. [8]Those whose lives are in the flesh are unable to please God. [9]You, however, are not in the flesh, but in the Spirit, since the Spirit of God lives in you. But if anyone does not have the Spirit of Christ, he does not belong to Him. [10]Now if Christ is in you, the body is dead because of sin, but the Spirit is life because of righteousness. [11]And if the Spirit of Him who raised Jesus from the dead lives in you, then He who raised Christ from the dead will also bring your mortal bodies to life through His Spirit who lives in you.

THE HOLY SPIRIT'S MINISTRIES

[12]So then, brothers, we are not obligated to the flesh to live according to the flesh, [13]for if you live according to the flesh, you are going to die. But if by the Spirit you put to death the deeds of the body, you will live. [14]All those led by God's Spirit are God's sons. [15]For you did not receive a spirit of slavery to fall back into fear, but you received the Spirit of adoption, by whom we cry out, "*Abba*, Father!" [16]The Spirit Himself testifies together with our spirit that we are God's children, [17]and if children, also heirs—heirs of God and co-heirs with Christ—seeing that we suffer with Him so that we may also be glorified with Him.

FROM GROANS TO GLORY

[18]For I consider that the sufferings of this present time are not worth comparing with the glory that is going to be revealed to us. [19]For the creation eagerly waits with anticipation for God's sons to be revealed. [20]For the creation was subjected to futility—not willingly, but because of Him who subjected it—in the hope [21]that the creation itself will also be set free from the bondage of corruption into the glorious freedom of God's children. [22]For we know that the whole creation has been groaning together with labor pains until now. [23]And not only that, but we ourselves who have the Spirit as the firstfruits—we also groan within ourselves, eagerly waiting for adoption, the redemption of our bodies. [24]Now in this hope we were saved, yet hope that is seen is not hope, because who hopes for what he sees? [25]But if we hope for what we do not see, we eagerly wait for it with patience.

[26]In the same way the Spirit also joins to help in our weakness, because we do not know what to pray for as we should, but the Spirit Himself intercedes for us with unspoken groanings. [27]And He who searches the hearts knows the Spirit's mind-set, because He intercedes for the saints according to the will of God.

[28]We know that all things work together for the good of those who love God: those who are called according to His purpose. [29]For those He foreknew He also predestined to be conformed to the image of His Son, so that He would be the firstborn among many brothers. [30]And those He predestined, He also called; and those He called, He also justified; and those He justified, He also glorified.

THE BELIEVER'S TRIUMPH

[31]What then are we to say about these things?

If God is for us, who is against us?
[32] He did not even spare His own Son,
but offered Him up for us all;
how will He not also with Him grant us everything?
[33] Who can bring an accusation against God's elect?
God is the One who justifies.
[34] Who is the one who condemns?
Christ Jesus is the One who died, but even more,
has been raised;

He also is at the right hand of God and intercedes for us.

35 Who can separate us from the love of Christ?
Can affliction or anguish or persecution
or famine or nakedness or danger or sword?

36 As it is written:
"Because of You we are being put to death all day long;
we are counted as sheep to be slaughtered."

37 No, in all these things we are more than victorious
through Him who loved us.

38 For I am persuaded that neither death nor life,
nor angels nor rulers,
nor things present, nor things to come, nor powers,

39 nor height, nor depth, nor any other created thing
will have the power to separate us
from the love of God that is in Christ Jesus our Lord!

QUESTION: How astonishing - a groan in the heart of God. The *Spirit* groans. And what for? That sin and its effects will at the right time be removed from the universe for ever. One preacher has said: 'All progress in this world is by the echo of the groan of God in the heart of man.' Here's a question to consider today: Can I hear the echo of God's groan over creation in my own heart? Little progress will be made in prayer unless you do.

DAY
59

MATTHEW 24:36-44

JESUS MENTIONED NOAH'S name only once but, when He did, He issued two urgent warnings: *'stay awake'* and *'don't speculate'*! 'Spiritual sleeping sickness' can afflict any of us. As in the days of Noah, we can become so preoccupied with everyday affairs that we forget the larger drama we are meant to take part in. Unlike Rip Van Winkle we Christians cannot sleep through the revolution but must *stay awake*.

An opposite danger is the fevered *speculation* of armchair experts on the end times. One brand of pop-prophecy harks back to verse 31 to support its theories about the 'rapture'. It assumes that those 'taken' (in verses 40 to 41) are believers, and those 'left behind' are unbelievers. In fact, in context, the exact opposite is likely to be the case. Those 'taken' are those who, as in the Flood (v.39), are taken away by judgment, while those left behind are God's vindicated people!

Jesus says plainly about the present: don't fix dates. The timing and exact sequence of future events can safely be left in the Father's hands. Staying awake (being spiritually aware) is evidently not something to lose sleep over (make a worrying obsession)!

In passionate trust, faith walks with God into an unknown but not uncertain future, looking for the light of His Son's coming. And that leads us to reflect on Abraham's part in the story!

Matthew 24:36-44

BIBLE READING

NO ONE KNOWS THE DAY OR HOUR

[36]"Now concerning that day and hour no one knows—neither the angels in heaven, nor the Son—except the Father only. [37]As the days of Noah were, so the coming of the Son of Man will be. [38]For in those days before the flood they were eating and drinking, marrying and giving in marriage, until the day Noah boarded the ark. [39]They didn't know until the flood came and swept them all away. So this is the way the coming of the Son of Man will be: [40]Then two men will be in the field: one will be taken and one left. [41]Two women will be grinding at the mill: one will be taken and one left. [42]Therefore be alert, since you don't know what day your Lord is coming. [43]But know this: If the homeowner had known what time the thief was coming, he would have stayed alert and not let his house be broken into. [44]This is why you also must be ready, because the Son of Man is coming at an hour you do not expect.

PRAYER: Gracious and loving Father, help me not to become preoccupied with dates and seasons but to remain spiritually awake, knowing that the future is in Your safe hands. Watch over my spirit and keep me free of all speculation, content in the knowledge that in the end everything is going to work out as You have planned it. Drive that conviction deeper and deeper into my spirit. In Jesus' name I pray. Amen.

NOAH
ALL CREATION

ABRAHAM
ALL NATIONS

ISRAEL
ONE NATION

DAVID
REPRESENTATIVE KING

NEW COVENANT
FAITHFUL COVENANT PARTNER

JESUS
FAITHFUL COVENANT PARTNER

JESUS
DAVIDIC KING MESSIAH

JESUS
THE NEW ISRAEL

JESUS
THE WORLD'S LORD

JESUS
.THE TRULY HUMAN ONE
CROWNED WITH GLORY AND HONOUR

JESUS
COSMIC RULER IN GOD'S NEW CREATION
NEW HEAVENS AND NEW EARTH

SECTION 4 ABRAHAM'S
ADVENTURE

GOD IS COMMITTED TO BLESSING ALL NATIONS ON EARTH – GOD'S COVENANT WITH ABRAHAM

Abraham surprised himself, late in life, by becoming an adventurer. When the great Polar explorer, Sir Ernest Shackleton, planned his ambitious and ultimately unsuccessful trans-Antarctic expedition of 1914, which turned into an epic survival story, he reputedly advertised for recruits with this notice: 'Men wanted for hazardous journey. Small wages, bitter cold, long months of complete darkness, constant danger, safe return doubtful. Honour and recognition in case of success.' Five thousand men are said to have answered the call.

When Abraham responded to God's call, the hazards ahead were different, but, in its own way, the challenge he faced was every bit as daunting.

Abram – as he was known then – is called to exchange a settled and reasonably comfortable lifestyle in what, by ancient standards, was a sophisticated society, for a nomadic existence trekking to and through foreign, and for him, unexplored territory. Abram chooses to break the close ties of clan and kinship, to leave the 'comfort-zone' of social standing and acceptance, to forsake the traditional gods of his fathers, for the sake of this risky journey into the unknown.

Glimpsing God's glory is evidently enough to disenchant Abram of anything Babylon had to offer. God's lordly command clearly overrides all Babylonian claims upon him (Acts 7:2-3; Gen. 12:1). Childless and dispossessed, Abram is promised multiplied descendants, and a land for them to inherit (Gen. 12:7) – a famous name and great nation and, eventually, an extended family beyond his wildest dreams, too numerous to count. This new God promises to bless him

THE PROMISE-PLAN OF GOD

JESUS

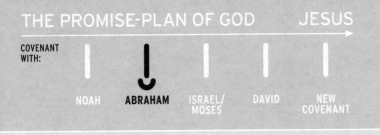

COVENANT
WITH:

NOAH   **ABRAHAM**   ISRAEL/   DAVID   NEW
MOSES   COVENANT

and his descendants, and make him the pivotal figure through whom He can bring blessing to all the nations on the earth (Gen. 12:2-3).

Abram's role is global. He has been lifted out of his domestic story and made part of God's big story. Abram obeyed and left.

As the years drag by, however, without children, and Abram begins to question God's promise, God steps in again with the staggering new promise that Abram's descendants will be as numerous as the stars in the night sky. Abram responds by trusting God utterly and 'He credited it to him as righteousness' (Gen. 15:6), so establishing the abiding scriptural principle that faith alone brings us into a righteous relationship with God. To reinforce His commitment, God then makes a covenant in a ritual which sounds bizarre to us but which, in the ancient world, meant that the parties to the agreement swore to their own death should either break it (Gen. 15).

Even when Abram's patience runs so thin that he takes matters into his own hand, and he has a son, Ishmael, by Hagar, Sarah's maidservant (Gen. 16), God does not write him off.

Just as the covenant of chapter 15 reassured Abram about the descendants and the land, so now God makes a covenant again to reassure Abraham about the third strand to the promise – 'blessing for all nations on the earth' – this time in a challenging mutual exchange of vows (Gen. 17). His name is now changed to 'Abraham', meaning 'father of many nations' (Gen. 17:5). The patriarch is later tested by God, who asked for the sacrifice of his beloved son, Isaac (Gen. 22:1-18). Though Isaac is spared, the oath this elicits from God commits God, in effect, to matching Abraham's offering of his son in order to maintain the integrity of His long-term plans for redemption.

With the promises made to Abraham, sealed in covenant, God has laid down His permanent intentions to redeem His world. Nothing less than the establishment of His kingdom on a global scale, and the blessing of all nations with salvation, is the goal of the Abrahamic covenant.

THE BIBLE CAN be viewed as the 'tale of two cities': Babylon and Jerusalem. City-building reveals our best and worst. On the one hand, God-given creativity worked out in community; on the other, the arrogant pursuit of the glory of man.

The tower of Babel, perhaps an ancient ziggurat reaching to the heavens, seems construed by the text as an attempt to displace God or the gods. The resolve not to 'be scattered over the face of the whole earth' (11:4) directly contradicts the Creator's original command to fill the earth (1:26). In short, we have a vivid cameo of a God-defying civilisation. With delicious irony, the text tells us that the Lord had to 'come down' to inspect the tower, so infinitesimal was it! The repeated 'come, *let us* ...' parodies the original divine *'Let Us make'* (1:26), only to be matched by a further divine *'let Us'* (11:7). God scrambles human languages to a 'babble' – 'Babel' – the root of 'Babylon'!

We glimpse two cities, then, which will reappear in the Bible's final vision: one that man is building for his own short-lived fame, the other which God is building for His eternal glory. Abraham left the one for the other in the service of God's promise-plan of salvation. For the same reason, you and I rise each morning to trust and travel with God in pursuit of His dreams.

Genesis 11:1-10,24-12:1

THE TOWER OF BABYLON

11 At one time the whole earth had the same language and vocabulary. ²As people migrated from the east, they found a valley in the land of Shinar and settled there. ³They said to each other, "Come, let us make oven-fired bricks." They had brick for stone and asphalt for mortar. ⁴And they said, "Come, let us build ourselves a city and a tower with its top in the sky. Let us make a name for ourselves; otherwise, we will be scattered over the face of the whole earth."

⁵Then the LORD came down to look over the city and the tower that the men were building. ⁶The LORD said, "If, as one people all having the same language, they have begun to do this, then nothing they plan to do will be impossible for them. ⁷Come, let Us go down there and confuse their language so that they will not understand one another's speech." ⁸So the LORD scattered them from there over the face of the whole earth, and they stopped building the city. ⁹Therefore its name is called Babylon, for there the LORD confused the language of the whole earth, and from there the LORD scattered them over the face of the whole earth.

FROM SHEM TO ABRAM

¹⁰These are the family records of Shem. Shem lived 100 years and fathered Arpachshad two years after the deluge.

· · · · · · · · · ·

²⁴Nahor lived 29 years and fathered Terah. ²⁵After he fathered Terah, Nahor lived 119 years and fathered [other] sons and daughters. ²⁶Terah lived 70 years and fathered Abram, Nahor, and Haran.

²⁷These are the family records of Terah. Terah fathered Abram, Nahor, and Haran, and Haran fathered Lot. ²⁸Haran died in his native land, in Ur of the Chaldeans, during his father Terah's lifetime. ²⁹Abram and Nahor took wives: Abram's wife was named Sarai, and Nahor's wife was named Milcah. She was the daughter of Haran, the father of both Milcah and Iscah. ³⁰Sarai was barren; she had no child.

³¹Terah took his son Abram, his grandson Lot (Haran's son), and his daughter-in-law Sarai, his son Abram's wife, and they set out together from Ur of the Chaldeans to go to the land of Canaan. But when they came to Haran, they settled there. ³²Terah lived 205 years and died in Haran.

THE CALL OF ABRAM

12 The LORD said to Abram:

> Go out from your land,
> your relatives,
> and your father's house
> to the land that I will show you.

TO PONDER: When you awoke this morning did you consider yourself as a modern-day Abraham led by God to pursue His dreams? Probably not. But consider now: whose dreams are you pursuing? Yours or His? Are your working for the 'city' or are your eyes focused on the one to come? We must not ignore our responsibilities on earth, but they must always be balanced by the recognition that this world is not our home – we are just passing through.

ABRAHAM – WE SHALL CALL him by the longer form of his name throughout these notes – left Ur. But why? What made him do it?

DAY 61

ACTS 7:1-8,17-36,44-60

When the first Christian martyr, Stephen, reviewed Israel's history, he said that 'The God of glory appeared to our father Abraham when he was in Mesopotamia ...' (v.2). Was this the vision that impelled Abraham to uproot from his own country and journey to the land of promise? Did the glimpse of God's glory outshine the splendour of Babylonia?

Stephen's speech goes on to suggest that Abraham's decision to leave embraced his father, Terah, too – no small thing in such a patriarchal society. Stephen's whole prophetic review of the Old Testament story strongly implies that God's people have been most in touch with Him when they lived outside the land rather than in it. If so, then again it was Abraham who pioneered a relationship with God which did not depend on territory or Temple but followed in faith a God on the move who was going places.

Merely to glimpse His dazzling glory is to be spoiled for the attractions of Babylon. It makes living as a nomad in a foreign land bearable and even – as Stephen immediately discovered – dying as a martyr meaningful (v.55)!

| BIBLE READING | **Acts 7:1-8,17-36,44-60** |

STEPHEN'S ADDRESS

7 "Is this true?" the high priest asked.

²"Brothers and fathers," he said, "listen: The God of glory appeared to our father Abraham when he was in Mesopotamia, before he settled in Haran, ³and said to him:

"Get out of your country and away from your relatives,
and come to the land that I will show you."

⁴"Then he came out of the land of the Chaldeans and settled in Haran. And from there, after his father died, God had him move to this land in which you now live. ⁵He didn't give him an inheritance in it, not even a foot of ground, but He promised to give it to him as a possession, and to his descendants after him, even though he was childless. ⁶God spoke in this way:

"His descendants would be strangers
in a foreign country,
and they would enslave and oppress them
for 400 years.
⁷ I will judge the nation that they will serve as slaves,"
God said.
"After this, they will come out and worship Me
in this place."

⁸Then He gave him the covenant of circumcision. This being so, he fathered Isaac and circumcised him on the eighth day; Isaac did the same with Jacob, and Jacob with the 12 patriarchs.

· · · · · · · · · ·

MOSES, A REJECTED SAVIOR

¹⁷"As the time was drawing near to fulfill the promise that God had made to Abraham, the people flourished and multiplied in Egypt ¹⁸until a different king ruled over Egypt who did not know Joseph. ¹⁹He dealt deceitfully with our race and oppressed our forefathers by making them leave their

infants outside so they wouldn't survive. [20]At this time Moses was born, and he was beautiful before God. He was nursed in his father's home three months, [21]and when he was left outside, Pharaoh's daughter adopted and raised him as her own son. [22]So Moses was educated in all the wisdom of the Egyptians, and was powerful in his speech and actions.

[23]"As he was approaching the age of 40, he decided to visit his brothers, the sons of Israel. [24]When he saw one of them being mistreated, he came to his rescue and avenged the oppressed man by striking down the Egyptian. [25]He assumed his brothers would understand that God would give them deliverance through him, but they did not understand. [26]The next day he showed up while they were fighting and tried to reconcile them peacefully, saying, 'Men, you are brothers. Why are you mistreating each other?'

[27]"But the one who was mistreating his neighbor pushed him away, saying:

"Who appointed you a ruler and a judge over us? [28]Do you want to kill me, the same way you killed the Egyptian yesterday?"

[29]"At this disclosure, Moses fled and became an exile in the land of Midian, where he fathered two sons. [30]After 40 years had passed, an angel appeared to him in the desert of Mount Sinai, in the flame of a burning bush. [31]When Moses saw it, he was amazed at the sight. As he was approaching to look at it, the voice of the Lord came: [32]I am the God of your forefathers—the God of Abraham, of Isaac, and of Jacob. So Moses began to tremble and did not dare to look.

[33]"Then the Lord said to him:

"Take the sandals off your feet, because the place where you are standing is holy ground. [34]I have certainly seen the oppression of My people in Egypt; I have heard their groaning and have come down to rescue them. And now, come, I will send you to Egypt."

[35]"This Moses, whom they rejected when they said, "Who appointed you a ruler and a judge?"—this one God sent as

a ruler and a redeemer by means of the angel who appeared to him in the bush. [36]This man led them out and performed wonders and signs in the land of Egypt, at the Red Sea, and in the desert for 40 years.

● ● ● ● ● ● ● ● ●

GOD'S REAL TABERNACLE

[44]"Our forefathers had the tabernacle of the testimony in the desert, just as He who spoke to Moses commanded him to make it according to the pattern he had seen. [45]Our forefathers in turn received it and with Joshua brought it in when they dispossessed the nations that God drove out before our fathers, until the days of David. [46]He found favor in God's sight and asked that he might provide a dwelling place for the God of Jacob. [47]But it was Solomon who built Him a house. [48]However, the Most High does not dwell in sanctuaries made with hands, as the prophet says:

[49] "Heaven is My throne,
and earth My footstool.
What sort of house will you build for Me? says the Lord,
or what is My resting place?
[50] Did not My hand make all these things?"

RESISTING THE HOLY SPIRIT

[51]"You stiff-necked people with uncircumcised hearts and ears! You are always resisting the Holy Spirit; as your forefathers did, so do you. [52]Which of the prophets did your fathers not persecute? They even killed those who announced beforehand the coming of the Righteous One, whose betrayers and murderers you have now become. [53]You received the law under the direction of angels and yet have not kept it."

THE FIRST CHRISTIAN MARTYR

[54]When they heard these things, they were enraged in their hearts and gnashed their teeth at him. [55]But Stephen, filled by the Holy Spirit, gazed into heaven. He saw God's glory, with Jesus standing at the right hand of God, and he said, [56]"Look! I see the heavens opened and the Son of Man standing at the right hand of God!"

⁵⁷Then they screamed at the top of their voices, stopped their ears, and rushed together against him. ⁵⁸They threw him out of the city and began to stone him. And the witnesses laid their robes at the feet of a young man named Saul. ⁵⁹They were stoning Stephen as he called out: "Lord Jesus, receive my spirit!" ⁶⁰Then he knelt down and cried out with a loud voice, "Lord, do not charge them with this sin!" And saying this, he fell asleep.

THOUGHT: Paul reminds us in 2 Corinthians 5:20 that we are ambassadors for Christ. An ambassador, as you know, represents his country in a foreign land. Think of it: you are a personal representative of a heavenly King! What is more, an ambassador has direct access to the ruler of his native country. And so do you! Make sure you maintain daily communication with your heavenly King. A vision of His glory makes every other vision dim.

DAY 62

GENESIS 12:1
ISAIAH 52:10-12

IF SEEING GOD'S glory unsettles Abraham, causing his disenchantment with Babylonian culture, then it is hearing God's word which cuts him loose from it, launching him on the flowing tide of faith in search of an alternative.

That God has spoken His word to us is the foundation of all biblical faith. Abraham, however, has long been exposed exclusively to Babylonian versions of truth. All Abraham has heard are Babylonian promises and propaganda, information and misinformation. But when God speaks, Abraham hears a voice he's never heard before. God speaks a piercing word which cuts through all settled convictions, all unexamined dogmas and ideological slogans, all undisturbed assumptions about the way things are and must be. God speaks like a crystal clear stream in a desert, like blissfully cool water to a parched throat, like a clear trumpet call above the confused cacophony of human opinions.

So Abraham obeys and goes. And so must we, not

in the old pietistic and passive sense of 'Let go and let God' but in the more bracing and adventurous Abrahamic sense of 'Let God and let's go'!

| BIBLE READING | **Genesis 12:1** | |

THE CALL OF ABRAM

12 The Lord said to Abram:

Go out from your land,
your relatives,
and your father's house
to the land that I will show you.

| BIBLE READING | **Isaiah 52:10-12** |

¹⁰ The Lord has displayed His holy arm
in the sight of all the nations;
all the ends of the earth will see
the salvation of our God.

¹¹ Leave, leave, go out from there!
Do not touch anything unclean;
go out from her, purify yourselves,
you who carry the vessels of the Lord.
¹² For you will not leave in a hurry,
and you will not have to take flight;
because the Lord is going before you,
and the God of Israel is your rear guard.

QUESTION: When in prayer, do you take time to listen for God's voice? The art of listening is the product of long practice. Those who would cultivate the ability must set time aside specifically for the purpose, and set it aside every day. Be quiet before God. At first you will not be able to disentangle His voice from your thoughts. But be patient. Eventually you will hear His voice, and when you do it will be well worth the wait.

GOD'S PROMISE TO Abraham has three vital elements. First, God promises Abraham *land* (12:1,7) or, at least, a sight of the land of Canaan which his descendants will possess as the land of promise, *the promised land*. But to receive it Abraham must leave and let go of his old securities.

The tension between promise and fulfilment which is a recurring pattern in the story, is heightened as we see Abraham, a stranger wandering through the land but not settling in it! Even when he returns from Egypt where famine has driven him (12:10), Abraham is a 'resident alien', pacing out the length and breadth of the land as if to lay claim to it, but oddly never taking root in it (13:17). And by his death, he owns nothing of the land except the burial place he has paid good money for in which to bury his beloved Sarah (23:4-20)!

In this way Abraham pioneers what it means to live by God's grace: to have nothing yet possess all things, to be gifted a homeland but to sit light to it and to continue to live a semi-nomadic existence. There was a clear lesson here for Abraham's descendants when they eventually possessed the land if only they could have heard it: never take the land for granted, it is pure gift; respect the gift and the Giver or it will be lost; and never stake everything on occupying the land at all costs.

DAY 63

GENESIS 12:1-10; 13:17

Genesis 12:1-10

BIBLE READING

THE CALL OF ABRAM

12 The LORD said to Abram:

Go out from your land,
your relatives,
and your father's house
to the land that I will show you.
² I will make you into a great nation,

> I will bless you,
> I will make your name great,
> and you will be a blessing.
> ³ I will bless those who bless you,
> I will curse those who treat you with contempt,
> and all the peoples on earth
> will be blessed through you.

⁴So Abram went, as the LORD had told him, and Lot went with him. Abram was 75 years old when he left Haran. ⁵He took his wife Sarai, his nephew Lot, all the possessions they had accumulated, and the people he had acquired in Haran, and they set out for the land of Canaan. When they came to the land of Canaan, ⁶Abram passed through the land to the site of Shechem, at the oak of Moreh. At that time the Canaanites were in the land. ⁷But the LORD appeared to Abram and said, "I will give this land to your offspring." So he built an altar there to the LORD who had appeared to him. ⁸From there he moved on to the hill country east of Bethel and pitched his tent, with Bethel on the west and Ai on the east. There he built an altar to the LORD and worshiped Him. ⁹Then Abram journeyed by stages to the Negev.

ABRAM IN EGYPT

¹⁰There was a famine in the land, so Abram went down to Egypt to live there for a while because the famine in the land was severe.

BIBLE READING

Genesis 13:17

¹⁷"Get up and walk from one end of the land to the other, for I will give it to you."

PRAYER: O Father, help me, I pray, to understand that I am not a proprietor but a steward. You are the true Owner of everything. May I therefore hang on to things lightly, knowing that one day I shall leave them all behind to be with You. Give me the wisdom to use the resources that are in my hands wisely so that when I face You I will hear the words: 'Well done, good and faithful servant ... enter into the joy of your Lord.' Amen.

SECOND, GOD PROMISES Abraham's *descendants* (12:2).

DAY 64

GENESIS 12:2
REVELATION 7:9-12

'I will make you into a great nation' is bold talk to a childless man whose wife is barren (11:30) and beyond the age of child-bearing.

Once more dramatic tension is built into the narrative. The tension mounts as God speaks of offspring like the dust of the ground and the stars in the sky (13:16; 15:5) while the reality of Abraham and Sarah's condition becomes laughable (17:17). For over twenty-five years the question hangs in the air: Will there be any son at all? Even when the miracle child arrives, the suspense is maintained as the reader wonders whether or not he will survive the sacrificial knife. Will the sons survive each other's jealousy? The later chapters also seem to show the promise under threat since not only Sarah but then both Rebekah (25:21) and Rachel (29:31) are said to be barren.

These stories will in time remind the 'great nation', Israel, that she does not exist on her own merit but solely from God's grace. Israel is an impossibility which exists only because God wills and works miracles of grace.

BIBLE READING

Genesis 12:2

THE CALL OF ABRAM

12 The LORD said to Abram:

Go out from your land,
your relatives,
and your father's house
to the land that I will show you.
² I will make you into a great nation,
I will bless you,
I will make your name great,
and you will be a blessing.

BIBLE READING

Revelation 7:9-12

A MULTITUDE FROM THE GREAT TRIBULATION

⁹After this I looked, and there was a vast multitude from every nation, tribe, people, and language, which no one could number, standing before the throne and before the Lamb. They were robed in white with palm branches in their hands. ¹⁰And they cried out in a loud voice:

Salvation belongs to our God,
who is seated on the throne,
and to the Lamb!

¹¹All the angels stood around the throne, the elders, and the four living creatures, and they fell on their faces before the throne and worshiped God, ¹²saying:

Amen! Blessing and glory and wisdom
and thanksgiving and honor
and power and strength,
be to our God forever and ever. Amen.

QUESTION: Do you long for a miracle at this present time? Then reflect on these words: 'Is anything impossible for the Lᴏʀᴅ? At the appointed time I will come back to you, and in about a year she will have a son' (Gen. 18:14). God's Word is written for our admonition and encouragement. Let this verse encourage you today to ask God for the miracle you desire. However, first make sure that the miracle is what you *need*, not merely something you want.

DAY
65
GENESIS 12:2; 24:1,34-35

GOD PROMISES ABRAHAM, thirdly, a relationship with Him which is characterised by *blessing* (12:2-3). In the Old Testament, to bless someone is not to make a merely formal gesture of goodwill but to speak a life-changing word. This word not only transmits happiness and material success – which Abraham certainly enjoyed in abundance (eg, 24:1,35) – but, at an even deeper level, connects the recipient with God's original empowerment of humankind.

God's 'I will bless you' is therefore doubly significant, not only aligning Abraham with future prosperity but connecting him back through Noah to Adam and God's original creation-blessing and mandate (Gen. 9:1; 1:26).

So Abraham is presented to us, like Noah before him, as a 'new Adam', the forerunner of a new humanity, though with an added vital dimension. Where God's covenant with Noah was largely preservative, maintaining the earth as a settled environment for human beings in general, His promise to Abraham launches His specific redemptive programme for blessing the human race.

Significantly, the fivefold mention of blessing here seems to mirror the fivefold curse of Genesis chapters 1 to 11 (3:14,17; 4:11; 5:29; 9:25). Evidently, Abraham's call is crucial if worldwide curse is to be turned into a worldwide blessing.

BIBLE READING

Genesis 12:2

THE CALL OF ABRAM

12 The LORD said to Abram:

Go out from your land,
your relatives,
and your father's house
to the land that I will show you.

² I will make you into a great nation,
I will bless you,
I will make your name great,
and you will be a blessing.

BIBLE READING

Genesis 24:1,34-35

A WIFE FOR ISAAC

24 Abraham was now old, getting on in years, and the LORD had blessed him in everything.

• • • • • • • • •

³⁴"I am Abraham's servant," he said. ³⁵"The LORD has greatly blessed my master, and he has become rich. He has given him sheep and cattle, silver and gold, male and female slaves, and camels and donkeys.

FOR ACTION: One of the greatest joys in life is to have God's blessing. But there are conditions to receiving God's blessing. Read again the first verses of Matthew chapter 5 to see those conditions. You will see that the scope of God's blessings is endless but the conditions have to be obeyed. Do you want to be blessed? Then take the eight Beatitudes and work out how many apply in your life and how many are missing.

EVERY PHRASE IN these texts is important for understanding God's plan of salvation, so we must linger another day on this verse.

God's promise, 'I will make your name great', almost certainly implies royal status, as is soon confirmed by the explicit anticipation that 'kings will come from you' (17:6,16). This connects Abraham to Israel's future kings, especially David, of whose line the same promise is made (2 Sam. 7:9). Abraham's God-shaped royal future also sets him in sharp contrast to the inhabitants of Babel whose stated objective was to make a name for themselves (Gen. 11:4). Abraham will owe his fame and place in history to God alone! Furthermore, he will make his reputation by being made the means of blessing to others. And there is an astonishing scope to this.

God decides that Abraham and his seed, insignificant players though they seem to be on the world-stage, will become the touchstone by which all nations are measured (12:3). The destiny of all nations is mysteriously and critically bound up with the future of Abraham's descendants!

As we shall see all along our route, what makes people great – or sometimes famous – is the extent to which their faith is not self-serving but makes them willing participants in God's plan to bless the whole world.

DAY 66

GENESIS 12:2
ROMANS 11:28-32

Genesis 12:2

BIBLE READING

THE CALL OF ABRAM

12 The LORD said to Abram:

> Go out from your land,
> your relatives,
> and your father's house
> to the land that I will show you.

² I will make you into a great nation,
I will bless you,

I will make your name great,
and you will be a blessing.

| BIBLE READING | **Romans 11:28-32** |

[28]Regarding the gospel, they are enemies for your advantage, but regarding election, they are loved because of their forefathers, [29]since God's gracious gifts and calling are irrevocable. [30]As you once disobeyed God, but now have received mercy through their disobedience, [31]so they too have now disobeyed, [resulting] in mercy to you, so that they also now may receive mercy. [32]For God has imprisoned all in disobedience, so that He may have mercy on all.

TO PONDER: 'Life,' said Dr Martyn Lloyd-Jones, 'is all about service.' That being so, we have to decide: Do we serve ourselves or others? Our Lord put the needs of others before His own, eventually giving up His life on a cross. Has this mark of the Saviour been written into your life? To live effectively you must serve somebody. Ask yourself now: How well do I serve others? 'Whatever He says to you, do it' (John 2:5, NKJV).

DAY 67

GENESIS 12:3
GALATIANS 3:26-29

GOD'S ULTIMATE INTENTION, the bottom line of His promise-plan, is that 'all the peoples on earth will be blessed through you' (v.3b). By staying close to these Abraham stories, Israel could embrace the challenge to remain sharply different from other nations yet without becoming exclusive or self-serving.

But throughout the story, Abraham's 'great nation', Israel, betrays its calling by allowing its special nation status to degenerate into an inward-looking nationalism. Just such a situation confronted Jesus and faced the Jewish-Christian apostles as they battled to get the gospel to the Gentile world in the teeth of often fierce Jewish opposition.

Tragically, Israel, entrusted with blessing for the world,

would be unready to receive the blessing for herself when offered it *first* through her own Messiah and then through His apostles, as Peter did in the immediate aftermath of Pentecost when he pleaded with the people of God not to disown their ancient destiny (Acts 3:25).

Paul, for his part, strove to convince his fellow-countrymen, both inside and outside the Church, that Gentile acceptance of God's blessing of salvation in Christ was exactly what God always intended in the promise-plan announced to Abraham as the 'gospel in advance' (Gal. 3:8, NIV).

BIBLE READING

Genesis 12:3

THE CALL OF ABRAM

12 The LORD said to Abram:

Go out from your land,
your relatives,
and your father's house
to the land that I will show you.
² I will make you into a great nation,
I will bless you,
I will make your name great,
and you will be a blessing.
³I will bless those who bless you,
I will curse those who treat you with contempt,
and all the peoples on earth
will be blessed through you.

BIBLE READING

Galatians 3:26-29

²⁶for you are all sons of God through faith in Christ Jesus.

SONS AND HEIRS

²⁷For as many of you as have been baptized into Christ have put on Christ. ²⁸There is no Jew or Greek, slave or free, male or female; for you are all one in Christ Jesus.

²⁹And if you are Christ's, then you are Abraham's seed, heirs according to the promise.

FOR THANKSGIVING: How grateful we should be that the gospel is being spread throughout the whole earth. Have you ever thought how many people have been involved over the centuries in making known the gospel? Preachers, missionaries, evangelists, open-air speakers, tract distributors, and many others. Some have given their lives to spread the gospel. Give God thanks today for this great army of men and women.

DAY 68

GENESIS 14:17-20; 15:1

WE COME NOW to the next major move God makes and Abraham's reaction to it. First, we find Abraham evidently afraid, and after the crises reported in chapter 14, he might well have felt physically and emotionally exhausted and so fallen prey to anxiety. A 150-mile route march and a night battle against superior forces are taxing enough for an old man. But, in addition, Abraham has had a close encounter of a strange kind with a mysterious, almost supernatural, royal figure called Melchizedek, and has turned down the King of Sodom's offer to make him a rich man!

In the anticlimax, following momentous events, the human spirit is often vulnerable to fear and self-doubt. 'Will my enemies return to seek revenge? What was a shrewd business operator like me doing rejecting such a generous financial package? Can God be trusted in the end?'

Sensing Abraham's mood, God reassures him through a prophetic vision. Abraham sees what looks like a covenant ceremony in which the king rewards the conquering hero with his royal weaponry and pledge of royal protection. It is as if God were saying to him: 'Everything I have is at your disposal. I am committed to being at your side to protect you. Your battles are My battles, My victories are your victories.' Already, it seems, there's a covenantal gleam in God's eye.

BIBLE READING

Genesis 14:17-20

MELCHIZEDEK'S BLESSING

[17]After Abram returned from defeating Chedorlaomer and the kings who were with him, the king of Sodom went out to meet him in the Valley of Shaveh (that is, the King's Valley). [18]Then Melchizedek, king of Salem, brought out bread and wine; he was a priest to God Most High. [19]He blessed him and said:

> Abram is blessed by God Most High,
> Creator of heaven and earth,
> [20] and give praise to God Most High
> who has handed over your enemies to you.

And Abram gave him a tenth of everything.

BIBLE READING

Genesis 15:1

THE ABRAHAMIC COVENANT

15 After these events, the word of the LORD came to Abram in a vision:

> Do not be afraid, Abram.
> I am your shield;
> your reward will be very great.

PRAYER: O Father, how reassuring it is when I am troubled by doubts and fears to know that You are present at my side. When next I am called to deal with something that causes me concern, or I face an overwhelming test, then may I realise that Your promise holds firm - You will never leave me nor forsake me. But let this be more than mere theory, dear Lord. Help me to really *feel* Your presence - to *sense* that You are near. Amen.

THE REASSURANCE GOD gives now encourages Abraham to question Him about the promised descendants (15:2-3) and the promised land (15:7-8).

First, Abraham takes God up on the promise of children. This is Abraham 'in God's face': 'You can be my benefactor, Lord, but of all that You can give me, what I want above everything else is the promised child!' Abraham even offers to help God out of a fix by adopting Eliezer, his servant, as his legal heir, but God emphatically rules this out: 'one who comes from your own body will be your heir' (15:4).

Given Abraham and Sarah's condition, nothing short of a miracle will do, and God seems committed to acting supernaturally to make good His promise. Under the night sky, God reaffirms His pledge to give descendants as numerous as the 'dust of the earth' (13:16) who will be as countless as the stars in the sky (15:5)! Abraham is being forced to turn away from looking down or at himself for any half-baked alternative solution. He is being encouraged to look up to the God who made the stars, a promise-keeping, miracle-working God.

Abraham's response is striking and crucial to the unfolding story in the rest of the Bible: *'Abram believed the LORD, and He credited it to him as righteousness'* (15:6). Abraham takes God at His word in a moment of faith.

DAY
69

GENESIS 15:2-6

Genesis 15:2-6

BIBLE
READING

THE ABRAHAMIC COVENANT

15 After these events, the word of the LORD came to Abram in a vision:
Do not be afraid, Abram.
I am your shield;
your reward will be very great.

²But Abram said, "Lord GOD, what can You give me, since I am childless and the heir of my house is Eliezer of Damascus?" ³Abram continued, "Look, You have given me no offspring, so a slave born in my house will be my heir."

⁴Now the word of the LORD came to him: "This one will not be your heir; instead, one who comes from your own body will be your heir." ⁵He took him outside and said, "Look at the sky and count the stars, if you are able to count them." Then He said to him, "Your offspring will be that [numerous]."

⁶Abram believed the LORD, and He credited it to him as righteousness.

QUESTION: Many years ago a little boy in Sunday School, when asked to define 'faith', took the letters FAITH and gave this as his reply: 'Forsaking All I Trust Him'. Here's a question to consider as you make your way into the day: How strong is your faith in God? Can you trust Him when all ahead is dark and confusing? It's so easy to trust when the road ahead is clear, but what about when a fog descends? You will never know how strong your trust is until you are called upon to exercise it.

DAY 70

GENESIS 15:6

ABRAHAM'S DECLARATION OF faith and God's endorsement of it are among the most important elements in the whole scriptural story. On the basis of his faith, God credits Abraham with righteousness.

'Righteousness' in the Old Testament is primarily a relational term, so that what Abraham is granted is a 'right relationship with God' – one shortly to be sealed by the covenant. This is not reckoned to Abraham because he keeps religious observances or matches up to ethical demands, and Abraham does not immediately become noticeably more ethical as a result of this. The key point is that righteousness is counted to him on the basis of his *faith alone*! This is a revolutionary move. Just as blessing is more original than sin, so, long before the law was given, even before circumcision was enjoined, Abraham is credited with a covenant relationship.

No statement proves more foundational to the apostolic understanding of God's grace in the gospel (see Rom. 4:3; Gal. 3:6). 'Justification' or 'righteousness' (synonymous translations of the same word in Greek) is by faith alone! Paul can argue that this has been the case right from the beginning so that it is not the 'works' of the Law but the 'faith story' of Abraham told in the Law that provides the key to a true relationship with God.

Genesis 15:6

BIBLE READING

THE ABRAHAMIC COVENANT

15 After these events, the word of the LORD came to Abram in a vision:

Do not be afraid, Abram.

I am your shield;

your reward will be very great.

²But Abram said, "Lord GOD, what can You give me, since I am childless and the heir of my house is Eliezer of Damascus?" ³Abram continued, "Look, You have given me no offspring, so a slave born in my house will be my heir."

⁴Now the word of the LORD came to him: "This one will not be your heir; instead, one who comes from your own body will be your heir." ⁵He took him outside and said, "Look at the sky and count the stars, if you are able to count them." Then He said to him, "Your offspring will be that [numerous]."

⁶Abram believed the LORD, and He credited it to him as righteousness.

FOR PRAISE: In response to today's reading make this a special day of praise, and reflect on the fact that through the grace of God you are saved, made righteous and put into a covenant relationship with the God of Abraham. Ask God also to deepen your understanding of this fact. To grasp it, and grasp it clearly, will cause a spirit of praise to burst inside you like an artesian well. So once again - think and praise.

DAY 71

GENESIS 15:7-21

HAVING BEEN REMINDED of God's promise, Abraham asks about the land (v.8). How God responds is crucial for Abraham and for the outworking of His redemptive purposes for the rest of history!

At God's command, Abraham kills three animals, and arranges the split carcasses in two parallel lines, with a bird at the end of each line. After a day in the sun, Abraham falls into a deep and dreadful stupor, during which he is shown his people's future slavery and release.

In ancient covenant ritual, as far as we can tell, each party walked between the pieces in a figure-of-eight manner to settle their agreement. The shedding of the substitute blood probably invoked a 'maledictory oath', so that each party swore death to itself if it defaulted on the arrangement. Significantly, in this ceremony only God, in the form of fire, passes between the pieces to 'make a covenant with Abram' (v.18). Here is no negotiated settlement but an amazingly one-sided commitment on God's part, which puts the sleeping Abraham on the receiving end of the sovereign grace of a God who is acting unilaterally.

God pledges unconditionally to bless Abraham and the nation that comes from him as the means of blessing all the nations of the world! No wonder this covenant with Abraham has been called the 'very backbone of the Bible'.

Genesis 15:7-21

THE ABRAHAMIC COVENANT

15 After these events, the word of the LORD came to Abram in a vision:

Do not be afraid, Abram.

I am your shield;

your reward will be very great.

²But Abram said, "Lord GOD, what can You give me, since I am childless and the heir of my house is Eliezer of Damascus?" ³Abram continued, "Look, You have given me no offspring, so a slave born in my house will be my heir."

⁴Now the word of the LORD came to him: "This one will not be your heir; instead, one who comes from your own body will be your heir." ⁵He took him outside and said, "Look at the sky and count the stars, if you are able to count them." Then He said to him, "Your offspring will be that [numerous]."

⁶Abram believed the LORD, and He credited it to him as righteousness.

⁷He also said to him, "I am the LORD who brought you from Ur of the Chaldeans to give you this land to possess."

⁸But he said, "Lord GOD, how can I know that I will possess it?"

⁹He said to him, "Bring Me a three-year-old cow, a three-year-old female goat, a three-year-old ram, a turtledove, and a young pigeon."

¹⁰So he brought all these to Him, split them down the middle, and laid the pieces opposite each other, but he did not cut up the birds. ¹¹Birds of prey came down on the carcasses, but Abram drove them away. ¹²As the sun was setting, a deep sleep fell on Abram, and suddenly a terror and great darkness descended on him.

¹³Then the LORD said to Abram, "Know this for certain: Your offspring will be strangers in a land that does not belong to them; they will be enslaved and oppressed 400 years. ¹⁴However, I will judge the nation they serve, and afterwards they will go out with many possessions. ¹⁵But you will go to

your fathers in peace and be buried at a ripe old age. [16]In the fourth generation they will return here, for the iniquity of the Amorites has not yet reached its full measure."

[17]When the sun had set and it was dark, a smoking fire pot and a flaming torch appeared and passed between the divided [animals]. [18]On that day the LORD made a covenant with Abram, saying, "I give this land to your offspring, from the brook of Egypt to the Euphrates River: [19][the land of] the Kenites, Kenizzites, Kadmonites, [20]Hittites, Perizzites, Rephaim, [21]Amorites, Canaanites, Girgashites, and Jebusites."

PRAYER: Father, the ancient ceremonies sound strange to me but I thank You that they are recorded to show Your unconditional love and Your commitment to us. Every one of Your covenant moves and gracious initiatives is so wonderful that they stretch the natural mind. But I thank You that You have given the Holy Spirit to be my teacher. Continue to enlighten me by Your Spirit as I read on. In Jesus' name. Amen.

DAY 72

GENESIS 16:15-17:1

TODAY'S TEXT CONFIRMS that God's promise-plan sealed in covenant with Abraham determines the future of God's dealings with His world. Whereas chapter 15 revolved around the issues of descendants and land – affecting domestic family and future nationhood – here the focus is on the *third*, international, strand of God's promise in Genesis 12:1-3: blessing for all nations. Once more Abraham needs God's reassurance.

Years before, Abraham had finally lost patience with this dilatory God who keeps making 'promises, promises', and slept with Sarah's maid, Hagar, and fathered Ishmael, now thirteen years old! Of course, Ishmael's presence is a standing indictment of every attempt to force God's hand, to speed up His workings by taking things into our own hands! Abraham had made a terrible mistake and stepped outside God's will for his life. But had he blown his chances for good?

Again God's reassurance is covenantal – announced with a *new name for God*: 'I am El Shaddai, God Almighty.' Is this comfort or rebuke? Perhaps both. 'I am the Almighty. I am full of resources, I can cope with impossible situations, and I can do this on My own, thank you very much; I don't need your misguided efforts to help Me out; I can make this promise-plan and covenant work!'

Genesis 16:15-17:1

¹⁵So Hagar gave birth to Abram's son, and Abram gave the name Ishmael to the son Hagar had. ¹⁶Abram was 86 years old when Hagar bore Ishmael to him.

COVENANT CIRCUMCISION

17 When Abram was 99 years old, the LORD appeared to him, saying, "I am God Almighty. Live in My presence and be devout.

THOUGHT: One translation of the great Hebrew name for God, El Shaddai, is *God the Enough.* Have you grasped the implication of this? There is only one way the human heart can have enough, or, to be more exact, only one Being who can satisfy it, and that is God. Only He is sufficient for us. Only He can really satisfy our souls. You may think you do not have enough of many things, but when you have God, He is *Enough.* Worth thinking about?

DAY 73

GENESIS 17:2-5

GOD ISSUES ABRAHAM with the new challenge of walking blamelessly before Him. This obligation, however, also sounds like an invitation to experience God's ongoing presence!

Then God gives him new hope of the promised increase in numbers (v.2). Embarrassed by grace, Abraham prostrates himself before the Lord.

God reassures Abraham, but this time spells out the mutual obligations of the covenant. In doing so, God deepens relationship into partnership by an exchange of vows: 'As for Me' (v.4) ... 'As for you' (v.9; cf.vv.15,20). For His part, God re-emphasises the strategic role Abraham plays on the world scene by giving him a *new name*, endorsing him as the father of many nations (v.4) - a significant upgrading of the original promise that Abraham would produce a great nation.

Unlike the men of Babel, Abraham had foregone the right to make a name for himself, trusting God to do it for him, and God rewards that faith by changing his name from Abram (which means 'exalted father') to Abraham, 'father of many' (v.5).

BIBLE READING

Genesis 17:2-5

COVENANT CIRCUMCISION

17 When Abram was 99 years old, the LORD appeared to him, saying, "I am God Almighty. Live in My presence and be devout.

[2] I will establish My covenant between Me and you, and I will multiply you greatly."

[3] Then Abram fell to the ground, and God spoke with him: [4] "As for Me, My covenant is with you, and you will become the father of many nations. [5] Your name will no longer be Abram, but your name will be Abraham, for I will make you the father of many nations.

PRAYER: O Father, from the bottom of my heart I want to tell You that my greatest longing is to walk blamelessly before You. Yet I fail so often. Forgive me, dear Father. The fault is never Yours, but mine. You have promised me grace, yet frequently I spurn it and rely on my own resources. Help me from now on to turn to You in utter dependence and rely on Your strength, not my own. All this I ask in the precious name of Jesus. Amen.

BY MENTIONING ABRAHAM'S promised fruitfulness, the text connects Abraham *back* to the earlier story of Noah and Adam, and *forward* to Abraham's descendants in Egypt (Exod. 1:6), and – with the promise of kingship – even further forward to the Davidic kingship (2 Sam. 7) in which Sarah is included (vv.15-16). For his part, Abraham must walk blamelessly before the Lord and must commit himself to circumcision (vv.9-14); and he does. A year later, with the birth of Isaac, God has the last laugh on Abraham and Sarah!

DAY 74

GENESIS 17:6-22

Ishmael, too, is to be blessed but, crucially, is not in the line of covenant purpose. In the redemptive future neither circumcision nor uncircumcision will count for anything, neither ethnic roots nor genealogical status will matter, but only grace and promise and faith (Rom. 4).

All this the God who is 'El Shaddai' will do for Abraham and for you, making His resources available, time and time again. Our God is Abraham's God and He is not a puny, under-achieving God. Right from the start of the story we are invited to be joined to a God who, as Creator of the universe, is well able to redeem it. This is God's story. God is the prime mover at every stage of it. We will always fall back on this grace; He is 'the author and finisher of our faith' (Heb. 12:2, NKJV).

| BIBLE
READING | **Genesis 17:6-22** |

COVENANT CIRCUMCISION

17 When Abram was 99 years old, the LORD appeared to him, saying, "I am God Almighty. Live in My presence and be devout.

²I will establish My covenant between Me and you, and I will multiply you greatly."

³Then Abram fell to the ground, and God spoke with him: ⁴"As for Me, My covenant is with you, and you will become the father of many nations. ⁵Your name will no longer be Abram, but your name will be Abraham, for I will make you the father of many nations.

⁶I will make you extremely fruitful and will make nations and kings come from you. ⁷I will keep My covenant between Me and you, and your offspring after you throughout their generations, as an everlasting covenant to be your God and the [God] of your offspring after you. ⁸And to you and your offspring after you I will give the land where you are residing—all the land of Canaan—as an eternal possession, and I will be their God."

⁹God also said to Abraham, "As for you, you and your offspring after you throughout their generations are to keep My covenant. ¹⁰This is My covenant, which you are to keep, between Me and you and your offspring after you: Every one of your males must be circumcised. ¹¹You must circumcise the flesh of your foreskin to serve as a sign of the covenant between Me and you. ¹²Throughout your generations, every male among you at eight days old is to be circumcised. This includes a slave born in your house and one purchased with money from any foreigner. The one who is not your offspring, ¹³a slave born in your house, as well as one purchased with money, must be circumcised. My covenant will be in your flesh as an everlasting covenant. ¹⁴If any male is not circumcised in the flesh of his foreskin, that man will be cut off from his people; he has broken My covenant."

¹⁵God said to Abraham, "As for your wife Sarai, do not call her Sarai, for Sarah will be her name. ¹⁶I will bless her; indeed, I will give you a son by her. I will bless her, and she will produce nations; kings of peoples will come from her."

¹⁷Abraham fell to the ground, laughed, and thought in his heart, "Can a child be born to a hundred-year-old man? Can Sarah, a ninety-year-old woman, give birth?" ¹⁸So Abraham said to God, "If only Ishmael could live in Your presence!"

¹⁹But God said, "No. Your wife Sarah will bear you a son, and you will name him Isaac. I will confirm My covenant with him as an everlasting covenant for his offspring after him. ²⁰As for Ishmael, I have heard you. I will certainly bless him; I will make him fruitful and will multiply him greatly. He will father 12 tribal leaders, and I will make him into a great nation. ²¹But I will confirm My covenant with Isaac, whom Sarah will bear to you at this time next year." ²²When He finished talking with him, God withdrew from Abraham.

QUESTION: At this stage in the journey how clear is the concept of God's story to you? Can you see how God has been pursuing a theme from all eternity which has taken in priests, prophets, the whole nation of Israel, and that you have a part in it too? Consider the words: 'He is "the author and finisher of our faith"'. He started it and He will finish it. Be assured of this: the more the thought of story grips you, the more exciting the Christian faith becomes.

WE PAUSE IN this chapter to comment on Abraham's commitment to circumcision. Circumcision, which was widely practised in the ancient world, was set to become the key identity marker for Israel. By commanding it God was saying three things:

DAY
75
GENESIS 17:23-27

'I want your whole body, Abraham. Marked "in your flesh" (v.13) you henceforth belong to Me.'

'I want your whole family, Abraham. By the mark in your reproductive organ I lay claim to your seed, your descendants, your children.'

'I want your whole heart, Abraham.'

Circumcision, of course, is intended to be the sign not of outward conformity but of inner covenant loyalty. So, in Deuteronomy and the prophets, circumcision becomes a metaphor for that inner 'cutting' of the heart that marks the repentant, humbled member of God's covenant people. Paul picks this up when he writes to the Romans that 'it's not the cut of the knife that makes a Jew' but the 'mark of God on your heart' (Rom. 2:29, *The Message*).

BIBLE READING

Genesis 17:23-27

[9]God also said to Abraham, "As for you, you and your offspring after you throughout their generations are to keep My covenant. [10]This is My covenant, which you are to keep, between Me and you and your offspring after you: Every one of your males must be circumcised. [11]You must circumcise the flesh of your foreskin to serve as a sign of the covenant between Me and you. [12]Throughout your generations, every male among you at eight days old is to be circumcised. This includes a slave born in your house and one purchased with money from any foreigner. The one who is not your offspring, [13]a slave born in your house, as well as one purchased with money, must be circumcised. My covenant will be in your flesh as an everlasting covenant. [14]If any male is not circumcised in the flesh of his foreskin, that man will be cut off from his people; he has broken My covenant."

[15]God said to Abraham, "As for your wife Sarai, do not call her Sarai, for Sarah will be her name. [16]I will bless her; indeed, I will give you a son by her. I will bless her, and she will produce nations; kings of peoples will come from her."

[17]Abraham fell to the ground, laughed, and thought in his heart, "Can a child be born to a hundred-year-old man? Can Sarah, a ninety-year-old woman, give birth?" [18]So Abraham said to God, "If only Ishmael could live in Your presence!"

[19]But God said, "No. Your wife Sarah will bear you a son, and you will name him Isaac. I will confirm My covenant with him as an everlasting covenant for his offspring after him. [20]As for Ishmael, I have heard you.

I will certainly bless him; I will make him fruitful and will multiply him greatly. He will father 12 tribal leaders, and I will make him into a great nation. ²¹But I will confirm My covenant with Isaac, whom Sarah will bear to you at this time next year." ²²When He finished talking with him, God withdrew from Abraham.

²³Then Abraham took his son Ishmael and all the slaves born in his house or purchased with his money—every male among the members of Abraham's household—and he circumcised the flesh of their foreskin on that very day, just as God had said to him. ²⁴Abraham was 99 years old when the flesh of his foreskin was circumcised, ²⁵and his son Ishmael was 13 years old when the flesh of his foreskin was circumcised. ²⁶On that same day Abraham and his son Ishmael were circumcised. ²⁷And all the men of his household—both slaves born in his house and those purchased with money from a foreigner— were circumcised with him.

TO PONDER: Reflect on these great verses from Paul's letter to the Thessalonians: 'May God himself, the God of peace, sanctify you through and through. May your whole spirit, soul and body be kept blameless at the coming of our Lord Jesus Christ' (1 Thess. 5:23-24, NIV). Do these verses come alive to you now in the light of today's reading? Whatever else they mean they mean at least this: God wants the whole of us, not just a part.

THIS STRANGE SCENE in which the Lord appears in the form of the three mysterious visitors has long inspired reflection, notably expressed in Andrei Rublev's famous and much imitated icon of *The Trinity*. It first shows us God talking to Himself, reminding Himself of Abraham's strategic importance, and so resolving to take Abraham into His confidence (vv.17-19). The cry that arises from Sodom is voiced presumably by those being sexually violated and economically oppressed (cf.Ezek. 16:49-50). God is

DAY
76
GENESIS 18

moved (cf.Exod. 2:23-25) to go down and inspect the city (cf.Gen. 11:7). But if God has already decided what to do, why tell Abraham?

Abraham discovers that to know God's secrets is a mixed blessing! To share the long-term redemptive plan of God is also to be burdened with the short-term pain of God.

What follows is Abraham's extraordinary intercessory negotiation as the 'friend of God' (cf.2 Chron. 20:7). It is almost as if Abraham's 'You could not possibly do that!' (v.25) is helping a sovereign God decide what kind of God to be! This is a remarkable tribute to the potential of covenant partnership. Out of it comes a new revelation of God, and even Sodom is blessed!

| BIBLE READING | **Genesis 18** |

ABRAHAM'S THREE VISITORS

18 Then the LORD appeared to Abraham at the oaks of Mamre while he was sitting in the entrance of his tent during the heat of the day. ²He looked up, and he saw three men standing near him. When he saw them, he ran from the entrance of the tent to meet them and bowed to the ground. ³Then he said, "My lord, if I have found favor in your sight, please do not go on past your servant. ⁴Let a little water be brought, that you may wash your feet and rest yourselves under the tree. ⁵I will bring a bit of bread so that you may strengthen yourselves. This is why you have passed your servant's [way]. Later, you can continue on."

"Yes," they replied, "do as you have said."

⁶So Abraham hurried into the tent and said to Sarah, "Quick! Knead three measures of fine flour and make bread." ⁷Meanwhile, Abraham ran to the herd and got a tender, choice calf. He gave it to a young man, who hurried to prepare it. ⁸Then Abraham took curds and milk, and the calf that he had prepared, and set [them] before the men. He served them as they ate under the tree.

SARAH LAUGHS

[9]"Where is your wife Sarah?" they asked him.

"There, in the tent," he answered.

[10]The LORD said, "I will certainly come back to you in about a year's time, and your wife Sarah will have a son!" Now Sarah was listening at the entrance of the tent behind him.

[11]Abraham and Sarah were old and getting on in years. Sarah had passed the age of childbearing. [12]So she laughed to herself: "After I have become shriveled up and my lord is old, will I have delight?"

[13]But the LORD asked Abraham, "Why did Sarah laugh, saying, 'Can I really have a baby when I'm old?' [14]Is anything impossible for the LORD? At the appointed time I will come back to you, and in about a year she will have a son."

[15]Sarah denied it. "I did not laugh," she said, because she was afraid.

But He replied, "No, you did laugh."

ABRAHAM'S PLEA FOR SODOM

[16]The men got up from there and looked out over Sodom, and Abraham was walking with them to see them off. [17]Then the LORD said, "Should I hide from Abraham what I am about to do? [18]Abraham is to become a great and powerful nation, and all the nations of the earth will be blessed through him. [19]For I have chosen him so that he will command his children and his house after him to keep the way of the LORD by doing what is right and just. This is how the LORD will fulfill to Abraham what He promised him." [20]Then the LORD said, "The outcry against Sodom and Gomorrah is immense, and their sin is extremely serious. [21]I will go down to see if what they have done justifies the cry that has come up to Me. If not, I will find out."

[22]The men turned from there and went toward Sodom while Abraham remained standing before the LORD. [23]Abraham stepped forward and said, "Will You really sweep away the righteous with the wicked? [24]What if there are 50 righteous people in the city? Will You really sweep it away instead of sparing the place for the sake of the 50 righteous people who are in it? [25]You could not possibly do such a thing: to kill the righteous with the wicked, treating the righteous and the

wicked alike. You could not possibly do that! Won't the Judge of all the earth do what is just?"

²⁶The LORD said, "If at Sodom I find 50 righteous people in the city, I will spare the whole place for their sake."

²⁷Then Abraham answered, "Since I have ventured to speak to the Lord—even though I am dust and ashes— ²⁸suppose the 50 righteous lack five. Will you destroy the whole city for lack of five?"

He replied, "I will not destroy [it] if I find 45 there."

²⁹Then he spoke to Him again, "Suppose 40 are found there?"

He answered, "I will not do [it] on account of 40."

³⁰Then he said, "Let the Lord not be angry, and I will speak further. Suppose 30 are found there?"

He answered, "I will not do [it] if I find 30 there."

³¹Then he said, "Since I have ventured to speak to the Lord, suppose 20 are found there?"

He replied, "I will not destroy [it] on account of 20."

³²Then he said, "Let the Lord not be angry, and I will speak one more time. Suppose 10 are found there?"

He answered, "I will not destroy [it] on account of 10." ³³When the LORD had finished speaking with Abraham, He departed, and Abraham returned to his place.

FOR ACTION: A ministry of intercession is probably the crowning ministry of the Christian life. Today why not ask God to give you the name of someone or something to intercede for. Then plead for them. Hold them there in your heart before God for as long as you feel it is right. Pray passionately for their needs. There is no ministry greater than the ministry of intercession. With that statement the whole Church must surely agree.

OUR FINAL MOVE in this stage of the story is to watch as God tests His covenant partner, Abraham, in a way that sounds incomprehensible to modern ears. Challenged perhaps to match the devotion of the pagan child-sacrificers to their gods, Abraham is asked to offer up the miracle child on whom the promise-plan hangs!

DAY
77
GENESIS 22:1-14

The text is sparse and poignant in its details. 'Take your son [does God really mean the miracle child of promise?], your only son Isaac ['only', but what about Ishmael?], whom you love [what an understatement since in the East to sacrifice oneself was less than to sacrifice one's son and therefore one's lineage and future] ...'

To his credit, Abraham doesn't dismiss this as a bad dream but seems able to discern the voice of God. Rising early, in prompt obedience, Abraham makes three great faith statements on the way: *we will worship* (v.5), for Yahweh is worthy to receive back His best gifts; *we will return* (v.5), which the writer to the Hebrews interprets as faith in resurrection (see Heb. 11:17-19); *God will provide* (v.8). So it proves. God does provide and Isaac is spared.

Of course, Abraham is a test case; we are not asked to sacrifice our children in just this way. But his kind of faith has passed its fiercest test; and to those with Abraham-like faith, the promise is certain (see Rom. 4:16).

Genesis 22:1-14

BIBLE READING

THE SACRIFICE OF ISAAC

22 After these things God tested Abraham and said to him, "Abraham!"

"Here I am," he answered.

²"Take your son," He said, "your only [son] Isaac, whom you love, go to the land of Moriah, and offer him there as a burnt offering on one of the mountains I will tell you about."

³So early in the morning Abraham got up, saddled his donkey, and took with him two of his young men and his son Isaac. He split wood for a burnt offering and set out to go to the place God had told him about. ⁴On the third day Abraham looked up and saw the place in the distance. ⁵Then Abraham said to his young men, "Stay here with the donkey. The boy and I will go over there to worship; then we'll come back to you." ⁶Abraham took the wood for the burnt offering and laid it on his son Isaac. In his hand he took the fire and the sacrificial knife, and the two of them walked on together.

⁷Then Isaac spoke to his father Abraham and said, "My father."

And he replied, "Here I am, my son."

Isaac said, "The fire and the wood are here, but where is the lamb for the burnt offering?"

⁸Abraham answered, "God Himself will provide the lamb for the burnt offering, my son." Then the two of them walked on together.

⁹When they arrived at the place that God had told him about, Abraham built the altar there and arranged the wood. He bound his son Isaac and placed him on the altar, on top of the wood. ¹⁰Then Abraham reached out and took the knife to slaughter his son.

¹¹But the Angel of the LORD called to him from heaven and said, "Abraham, Abraham!"

He replied, "Here I am."

¹²Then He said, "Do not lay a hand on the boy or do anything to him. For now I know that you fear God, since you have not withheld your only son from Me." ¹³Abraham looked up and saw a ram caught by its horns in the thicket. So Abraham went and took the ram and offered it as a burnt offering in place of his son. ¹⁴And Abraham named that place The LORD Will Provide, so today it is said: "It will be provided on the LORD's mountain."

FOR PRAISE: As you consider Abraham's great faith, give praise to his God and yours – the God who delights in responding to a believing heart.

> The God of Abraham praise, who reigns enthroned above,
> Ancient of everlasting days, and God of love.
> Jehovah! Great I AM! By earth and heaven confessed;
> We bow and bless the sacred Name, for ever blessed.
> (Thomas Olivers, c. 1770)

DAY
78
GENESIS 22:15-18

IN A REMARKABLE response to Abraham's act of obedient faith, God swears an oath which confirms the international aspects of the original promise-plan (vv.17-18). Abraham will have a multitude of descendants that no one can number; they will be triumphant over their enemies; through them the nations of the world will know God's blessing. God makes this commitment on oath because Abraham has not withheld his only son.

Is God here demonstrating His willingness to match Abraham in offering up His only beloved Son? This is the theological time bomb buried in the Abraham narrative. At the point where God seems to demand most He gives most. He will not be outdone in sacrifice by any of His creatures. Here is a hint of the gospel 'in advance', telling us that God is not a God who demands sacrifice but a God who makes sacrifice. Our salvation lies not in the sacrifices we make but in the sacrifice we trust. 'Bring me a 33-year-old man; cut Him to the heart; let His blood be shed.'

In the deep darkness, the all-consuming fire of God's holy love 'passes between the pieces'. And the covenant is sealed by blood. Whenever we break bread and drink blood-red wine we remind ourselves that God will provide; that where Isaac was spared, Jesus was not (Rom. 8:32).

| BIBLE READING | **Genesis 22:15-18** |

THE SACRIFICE OF ISAAC

22 After these things God tested Abraham and said to him, "Abraham!"

"Here I am," he answered.

²"Take your son," He said, "your only [son] Isaac, whom you love, go to the land of Moriah, and offer him there as a burnt offering on one of the mountains I will tell you about."

³So early in the morning Abraham got up, saddled his donkey, and took with him two of his young men and his son Isaac. He split wood for a burnt offering and set out to go to the place God had told him about. ⁴On the third day Abraham looked up and saw the place in the distance. ⁵Then Abraham said to his young men, "Stay here with the donkey. The boy and I will go over there to worship; then we'll come back to you." ⁶Abraham took the wood for the burnt offering and laid it on his son Isaac. In his hand he took the fire and the sacrificial knife, and the two of them walked on together.

⁷Then Isaac spoke to his father Abraham and said, "My father."

And he replied, "Here I am, my son."

Isaac said, "The fire and the wood are here, but where is the lamb for the burnt offering?"

⁸Abraham answered, "God Himself will provide the lamb for the burnt offering, my son." Then the two of them walked on together.

⁹When they arrived at the place that God had told him about, Abraham built the altar there and arranged the wood. He bound his son Isaac and placed him on the altar, on top of the wood. ¹⁰Then Abraham reached out and took the knife to slaughter his son.

¹¹But the Angel of the LORD called to him from heaven and said, "Abraham, Abraham!"

He replied, "Here I am."

¹²Then He said, "Do not lay a hand on the boy or do anything to him. For now I know that you fear God,

since you have not withheld your only son from Me." [13]Abraham looked up and saw a ram caught by its horns in the thicket. So Abraham went and took the ram and offered it as a burnt offering in place of his son. [14]And Abraham named that place The LORD Will Provide, so today it is said: "It will be provided on the LORD's mountain."

[15]Then the Angel of the LORD called to Abraham a second time from heaven [16]and said, "By Myself I have sworn, says the LORD: Because you have done this thing and have not withheld your only son, [17]I will indeed bless you and make your offspring as numerous as the stars in the sky and the sand on the seashore. Your offspring will possess the gates of their enemies. [18]And all the nations of the earth will be blessed by your offspring because you have obeyed My command."

THOUGHT: 'The God who demands most gives most.' God has a perfect right to ask sacrifice of us because He has given His own Son as a sacrifice for our sin on the cross. He does not ask of us what He is not prepared to do Himself. A poet has put this same thought in these words: 'By all that God requires of me, I know that He Himself must be.' 'He will not be outdone in sacrifice by any of His creatures.'

DAY 79

GENESIS 28

TODAY WE SEE how God's promise-plan is carried a stage further by being reiterated to Jacob, as it had been to Isaac (26:3-5). Like his father and grandfather before him, Jacob is made party to the covenant purposes of God for the world, becoming for a symbolic moment the meeting-point between heaven and earth (28:2,17).

Surely the Lord is in the most surprising places and with the most surprising people! The text is frank about Jacob's character, showing that God enlists the most unlikely people in His story. That God should be the *God of Jacob* the con man, from whom you wouldn't buy a used camel, is the scandal of grace.

Jacob, intent on survival, is promised salvation. Alone and in exile, Jacob feels heaven to be remote, but heaven comes down to earth with one man at one particular spot on the earth. The seeds of incarnation are sown that will one day see some surprising people surprised by grace by a man from an unlikely place (John 1:51)! Only through brokenness will this happen, as Genesis 32 affirms.

Crippled in a strange wrestling match with God, Jacob limps off into the sunrise of a new day to give his new name to the nation that would treasure both his story and God's story.

| BIBLE READING | **Genesis 28** |

JACOB'S DEPARTURE

28 Isaac summoned Jacob, blessed him, and commanded him: "Don't take a wife from the Canaanite women. ²Go at once to Paddan-aram, to the house of Bethuel, your mother's father. Marry one of the daughters of Laban, your mother's brother. ³May God Almighty bless you and make you fruitful and multiply you so that you become an assembly of peoples. ⁴May God give you and your offspring the blessing of Abraham so that you may possess the land where you live as an alien, the land God gave to Abraham." ⁵So Isaac sent Jacob to Paddan-aram, to Laban son of Bethuel the Aramean, the brother of Rebekah, the mother of Jacob and Esau.

⁶Esau noticed that Isaac blessed Jacob and sent him to Paddan-aram to get a wife there. When he blessed him, Isaac commanded Jacob not to marry a Canaanite woman. ⁷And Jacob listened to his father and mother and went to Paddan-aram. ⁸Esau realized that his father Isaac disapproved of the Canaanite women, ⁹so Esau went to Ishmael and married, in addition to his other wives, Mahalath daughter of Ishmael, Abraham's son. She was the sister of Nebaioth.

JACOB AT BETHEL

¹⁰Jacob left Beer-sheba and went toward Haran. ¹¹He reached a certain place and spent the night there because the sun had set. He took one of the stones from the place, put it there at

his head, and lay down in that place. ¹²And he dreamed: A stairway was set on the ground with its top reaching heaven, and God's angels were going up and down on it. ¹³The LORD was standing there beside him, saying, "I am the LORD, the God of your father Abraham and the God of Isaac. I will give you and your offspring the land that you are now sleeping on. ¹⁴Your offspring will be like the dust of the earth, and you will spread out toward the west, the east, the north, and the south. All the peoples on earth will be blessed through you and your offspring. ¹⁵Look, I am with you and will watch over you wherever you go. I will bring you back to this land, for I will not leave you until I have done what I have promised you."

¹⁶When Jacob awoke from his sleep, he said, "Surely the LORD is in this place, and I did not know it." ¹⁷He was afraid and said, "What an awesome place this is! This is none other than the house of God. This is the gate of heaven."

¹⁸Early in the morning Jacob took the stone that was near his head and set it up as a marker. He poured oil on top of it ¹⁹and named the place Bethel, though previously the city was named Luz. ²⁰Then Jacob made a vow: "If God will be with me and watch over me on this journey, if He provides me with food to eat and clothing to wear, ²¹and if I return safely to my father's house, then the LORD will be my God. ²²This stone that I have set up as a marker will be God's house, and I will give to You a tenth of all that You give me."

TO PONDER: Have you ever wrestled with God over some issue you were reluctant to surrender? At such a time, as with Jacob, He will ask your name. What is it? Pride, ego, self-sufficiency? Confess it and God will change your name and your nature too, just as He did with Jacob. Instead of 'Inferiority' it will be 'Confidence', instead of 'Self-pity' it will be 'Faith', and so on. But remember: no new name until you confess the old one.

DAY
80

PSALM 105

IN WORSHIP, ISRAEL regularly celebrated her history as a record of the mighty acts of God. No reference is made here to the Sinai covenant as the basis of Israel's identity, suggesting that this song came out of the experience of the Babylonian Exile. In exile, without land or Temple or kingship, only God's *word* remains to define who Israel is (vv.5,19). Specifically, Israel praises God for His *covenant word* to Abraham (vv.8-11,42).

The psalm celebrates the power of the promise to generate energy and faithfulness across the generations and to shape the course of history. Israel's whole history – from the patriarchal wanderings (vv.12-15) and Joseph's sojourn in Egypt (vv.16-25) to the exodus under Moses (vv.26-43) and the conquest (vv.44) – is brought under the one original covenant promise (vv.8,42).

The good news is always that *God remembers His covenant with Abraham,* and this turns out to be not a mere episode but the start of an epic story running through all of time and in which every believer in every generation is caught up. This is our story, this is our song!

BIBLE READING

Psalm 105

GOD'S FAITHFULNESS TO HIS PEOPLE

¹ Give thanks to the LORD, call on His name;
  proclaim His deeds among the peoples.
² Sing to Him, sing praise to Him;
  tell about all His wonderful works!
³ Honor His holy name;
  let the hearts of those who seek the LORD rejoice.
⁴ Search for the LORD and for His strength;
  seek His face always.
⁵ Remember the wonderful works He has done,
  His wonders, and the judgments
    He has pronounced,

⁶ you offspring of Abraham His servant,
 Jacob's descendants—
   His chosen ones.

⁷ He is the LORD our God;
 His judgments [govern] the whole earth.
⁸ He forever remembers His covenant,
 the promise He ordained
 for a thousand generations—
⁹ [the covenant] He made with Abraham,
 swore to Isaac,
¹⁰ and confirmed to Jacob as a decree
 and to Israel as an everlasting covenant:
¹¹ "I will give the land of Canaan to you
 as your inherited portion."

¹² When they were few in number,
 very few indeed,
 and temporary residents in Canaan,
¹³ wandering from nation to nation
 and from one kingdom to another,
¹⁴ He allowed no one to oppress them;
 He rebuked kings on their behalf:
¹⁵ "Do not touch My anointed ones,
 or harm My prophets."

¹⁶ He called down famine against the land
 and destroyed the entire food supply.
¹⁷ He had sent a man ahead of them—
 Joseph, who was sold as a slave.
¹⁸ They hurt his feet with shackles;
 his neck was put in an iron collar.
¹⁹ Until the time his prediction came true,
 the word of the LORD tested him.
²⁰ The king sent [for him] and released him;
 the ruler of peoples set him free.
²¹ He made him master of his household,
 ruler over all his possessions—
²² binding his officials at will
 and instructing his elders.

²³ Then Israel went to Egypt;
   Jacob lived as a foreigner in the land of Ham.
²⁴ The LORD made His people very fruitful;
   He made them more numerous than their foes,
²⁵ whose hearts He turned to hate His people
   and to deal deceptively with His servants.
²⁶ He sent Moses His servant,
   and Aaron, whom He had chosen.
²⁷ They performed His miraculous signs among them,
   and wonders in the land of Ham.
²⁸ He sent darkness, and it became dark—
   for did they not defy His commands?
²⁹ He turned their waters into blood
   and caused their fish to die.
³⁰ Their land was overrun with frogs,
   even in their kings' chambers.
³¹ He spoke, and insects came—
   gnats throughout their country.
³² He gave them hail for rain,
   and lightning throughout their land.
³³ He struck their vines and fig trees
   and shattered the trees of their territory.
³⁴ He spoke and locusts came—
   young locusts without number.
³⁵ They devoured all the vegetation in their land
   and consumed the produce of their soil.
³⁶ He struck all the firstborn in their land,
   all their first progeny.

³⁷ Then He brought Israel out with silver and gold,
   and no one among His tribes stumbled.
³⁸ Egypt was glad when they left,
   for dread of Israel had fallen on them.
³⁹ He spread a cloud as a covering
   and [gave] a fire to light up the night.
⁴⁰ They asked, and He brought quail
   and satisfied them with bread from heaven.
⁴¹ He opened a rock, and water gushed out;
   it flowed like a stream in the desert.
⁴² For He remembered His holy promise

to Abraham His servant.
⁴³ He brought His people out with rejoicing,
His chosen ones with shouts of joy.
⁴⁴ He gave them the lands of the nations,
and they inherited
what other peoples had worked for.

⁴⁵ [All this happened]
so that they might keep His statutes
and obey His laws.
Hallelujah!

FOR ACTION: Just as in Old Testament times worship involved thinking about and focusing on the record of God's mighty acts so we too should look back over our own lives and recollect what God has done for us in times past. Make a list of all the great things you can recollect that God has done for you. Do you know the advantage of this? John Newton put it in these words: 'His love in time past forbids me to think He'll leave me at last in trouble to sink.'

WHEN WORLD EVENTS are in turmoil, as they are here, we grope for a reason. The idol factories go into over-production to secure the tottering faith of their adherents (v.7). But to the prophet, God's ways are traceable even in the most turbulent times. Behind the tumult of nations, the movements of armies, the rise and fall of empires – such as that of the Medo-Persian ruler, Cyrus, here – the prophet detects the sovereign authority and even initiative of the one Creator God.

Israel can be confident, as God's servant nation, of being at the disposal of these larger plans and purposes, though only, like Abraham, through being God's 'friend' (v.8).

We sometimes loosely say that God 'uses' people. He certainly overrules His enemies and commandeers

DAY
81
ISAIAH 41:1-20

godless warlords such as Cyrus for His purpose. But He does not 'use' His own people. Such a term is too mechanical, too utilitarian to describe the relationship God desires with them. God works in, through and with His own people; but He never 'uses' them. Rather, they are called in love to intimate friendship. Burdened with God's dreams, entrusted with His painful secrets - as Abraham was over Sodom's fate - they hold their heads high with the privilege of being friends of this humbly sovereign God!

BIBLE READING

Isaiah 41:1-20

THE LORD VERSUS THE NATIONS' GODS

41 "Be silent before Me, islands!
And let peoples renew their strength.
Let them approach, then let them testify;
let us come together for the trial.
2 Who has stirred him up from the east?
He calls righteousness to his feet.
The LORD hands nations over to him,
and he subdues kings.
He makes [them] like dust [with] his sword,
like wind-driven stubble [with] his bow.
3 He pursues them, going on safely,
hardly touching the path with his feet.
4 Who has performed and done [this],
calling the generations from the beginning?
I, the LORD, am the first,
and with the last—I am He."

5 The islands see and are afraid,
the ends of the earth tremble.
They approach and arrive.
6 Each one helps the other,
and says to another, "Take courage!"
7 The craftsman encourages the metalworker;
the one who flattens with the hammer
[supports] the one who strikes the anvil,

saying of the soldering, "It is good."
He fastens it with nails so that it will not fall over.

⁸ But you, Israel, My servant,
Jacob, whom I have chosen,
descendant of Abraham, My friend—
⁹ I brought you from the ends of the earth
and called you from its farthest corners.
I said to you: You are My servant;
I have chosen you and not rejected you.
¹⁰ Do not fear, for I am with you;
do not be afraid, for I am your God.
I will strengthen you; I will help you;
I will hold on to you with My righteous right hand.

¹¹ Be sure that all who are enraged against you
will be ashamed and disgraced;
those who contend with you
will become as nothing and will perish.
¹² You will look for those who contend with you,
but you will not find them.
Those who war against you
will become absolutely nothing.
¹³ For I, the LORD your God,
hold your right hand
and say to you: Do not fear,
I will help you.
¹⁴ Do not fear, you worm Jacob,
you men of Israel:
I will help you—the LORD's declaration.
Your Redeemer is the Holy One of Israel.
¹⁵ See, I will make you into a sharp threshing board,
new, with many teeth.
You will thresh mountains and pulverize [them],
and make hills like chaff.
¹⁶ You will winnow them
and a wind will carry them away,
and a gale will scatter them.
But you will rejoice in the LORD;
you will boast in the Holy One of Israel.

[17] The poor and the needy seek water, but there is none;
 their tongues are parched with thirst.
 I, the Lord, will answer them;
 I, the God of Israel, do not forsake them.
[18] I will open rivers on the barren heights,
 and springs in the middle of the plains.
 I will turn the desert into a pool of water
 and dry land into springs of water.
[19] I will plant cedars in the desert,
 acacias, myrtles, and olive trees.
 I will put cypress trees in the desert,
 elms and box trees together,
[20] so that all may see and know,
 consider and understand,
 that the hand of the Lord has done this,
 the Holy One of Israel has created it.

QUESTION: Do you doubt that God can work in and through you? Are you held back by feelings of inadequacy? Then focus on your Abrahamic roots. God is the God of the impossible. The One who worked a miracle for Abraham and Sarah is just the same today. God's covenant with Abraham stretches through time to encircle you too. Rise up and face whatever is your need at this hour. Exercise faith and see that the God of Abraham is your God also.

THE PROPHET URGES those exiles whose hearts are set on covenant integrity ('righteousness', cf.v.7), to look to the Lord and to be inspired by the early chapters of their story. The Lord is the rock from which His people have been hewn (cf.Deut. 32:18) - in particular His miraculous and covenantal beginnings with Abraham and Sarah. To live out of these Abrahamic roots is to live by faith in the impossibilities of divine grace and power.

Abraham felt hopeless and helpless - one man among many - when God called and blessed him; the exiles, feeling a beleaguered minority, should take heart from this. Abraham was as good as dead, and Sarah was dead in her womb, when God acted; so, out of the womb of the 'death' of exile, God will bring His people into fruitful new life (cf.Isa. 54:1ff.).

The memory of the Creator God's conquest of chaotic forces at the exodus (vv.9-10) inspires hope that God will comfort and save His people once more.

For, if God can carve a people out of the rock of barrenness or exile, making somebodies out of nobodies, then His people should avoid presumption or complacency and 'awake' to seize the opportunities for faith presented by the hour (vv.17ff.). Then they will see God's covenant faithfulness acting in salvation (vv.5-6,8).

DAY 82
ISAIAH 51

Isaiah 51

BIBLE READING

SALVATION FOR ZION

51 Listen to Me, you who pursue righteousness,
you who seek the LORD:
Look to the rock from which you were cut,
and to the quarry from which you were dug.
2 Look to Abraham your father,
and to Sarah who gave birth to you in pain.
When I called him, he was only one;
I blessed him and made him many.
3 For the LORD will comfort Zion;

He will comfort all her waste places,
and He will make her wilderness like Eden,
and her desert like the garden of the Lord.
Joy and gladness will be found in her,
thanksgiving and melodious song.

4 Pay attention to Me, My people,
and listen to Me, My nation;
for instruction will come from Me,
and My justice for a light to the nations.
I will bring it about quickly.
5 My righteousness is near,
My salvation appears,
and My arms will bring justice to the nations.
The coastlands will put their hope in Me,
and they will look to My strength.
6 Look up to the heavens,
and look at the earth beneath;
for the heavens will vanish like smoke,
the earth will wear out like a garment,
and its inhabitants will die in like manner.
But My salvation will last forever,
and My righteousness will never be shattered.

7 Listen to Me, you who know righteousness,
the people in whose heart is My instruction:
do not fear disgrace by men,
and do not be shattered by their taunts.
8 For the moth will devour them like a garment,
and the worm will eat them like wool.
But My righteousness will last forever,
and My salvation for all generations.

9 Wake up, wake up!
Put on the strength of the Lord's power.
Wake up as in days past,
as in generations of long ago.
Wasn't it You who hacked Rahab to pieces,
who pierced the sea monster?
10 Wasn't it You who dried up the sea,

the waters of the great deep,
who made the sea-bed into a road
for the redeemed to pass over?
¹¹ And the ransomed of the LORD will return
and come to Zion with singing,
crowned with unending joy.
Joy and gladness will overtake [them],
and sorrow and sighing will flee.

¹² I—I am the One who comforts you.
Who are you that you should fear man who dies,
or a son of man who is given up like grass?
¹³ But you have forgotten the LORD, your Maker,
who stretched out the heavens
and laid the foundations of the earth.
You are in constant dread all day long
because of the fury of the oppressor,
who has set himself to destroy.
But where is the fury
of the oppressor?
¹⁴ The prisoner is soon to be set free;
he will not die [and go] to the Pit,
and his food will not be lacking.
¹⁵ For I am the LORD your God
who stirs up the sea so that its waves roar—
His name is Yahweh of Hosts.
¹⁶ I have put My words in your mouth,
and covered you in the shadow of My hand,
in order to plant the heavens,
to found the earth,
and to say to Zion, "You are My people."

¹⁷ Wake yourself, wake yourself up!
Stand up, Jerusalem,
you who have drunk the cup of His fury
from the hand of the LORD;
you who have drunk the goblet to the dregs—
the cup that [causes people] to stagger.
¹⁸ There is no one to guide her
among all the children she has raised;

there is no one to take hold of her hand
among all the offspring she has brought up.
¹⁹ These two things have happened to you:
devastation and destruction,
famine and sword.
Who will grieve for you?
How can I comfort you?
²⁰ Your children have fainted;
they lie at the head of every street
like an antelope in a net.
They are full of the LORD's fury,
the rebuke of your God.

²¹ So listen to this, afflicted
and drunken one—but not with wine.
²² This is what your Lord says—
Yahweh, even your God,
who defends His people—
"Look, I have removed
the cup of staggering from your hand;
that goblet, the cup of My fury.
You will never drink it again.
²³ I will put it into the hands of your tormenters,
who said to you:
Lie down, so we can walk over you.
You made your back like the ground,
and like a street for those who walk on it.

FOR ACTION: Read through Isaiah 51 once more. Consider what God says and give your response. For example, God says, 'Listen to me ...' Respond by saying, 'Yes, Lord, I will listen. Again He says, 'Look.' Respond by saying, 'Yes, Lord, I will look.' Go through the whole chapter, making your response to each of God's challenges. God challenges us in order to change us. But there can be no change without a positive response.

LUKE HERE DESCRIBES just the kind of faithful, covenant-keeping remnant envisaged by Isaiah, now forming the 'welcoming committee' for Jesus. Christmas, for all its wonderful freshness, does not come out of the blue but is the decisive turning-point in the age-old story which began with Abraham. This remnant has kept alive the dream of what God promised Abraham, interpreting what happens now, as Mary does, as God remembering His covenant to Abraham (vv.54-55).

Zechariah, filled with the Spirit, is singing from the same hymn-book, interpreting events within his own family as the stirrings of a great move of God prompted by His remembrance of the oath and covenant He long ago swore to Abraham (vv.72-73).

In this way Luke highlights the historic significance of the babies born to Elizabeth and Mary. Already we begin to see that Jesus is the fulfilment, the climactic chapter of the much older story of Israel and her patriarchs. Sarah's barrenness, Abraham's childlessness, and the details of their story, are mirrored in the miracles of grace of Elizabeth and Zechariah and Mary. Zechariah hails the dawning of the age of forgiveness and mercy. Mary, stirred by the recreative energies of God within her, celebrates a new exodus when tyranny is overthrown and the oppressed are given freedom.

DAY 83

LUKE 1:39-80

Luke 1:39-80

BIBLE READING

MARY'S VISIT TO ELIZABETH

³⁹In those days Mary set out and hurried to a town in the hill country of Judah ⁴⁰where she entered Zechariah's house and greeted Elizabeth. ⁴¹When Elizabeth heard Mary's greeting, the baby leaped inside her, and Elizabeth was filled with the Holy Spirit. ⁴²Then she exclaimed with a loud cry:

"You are the most blessed of women,
and your child will be blessed!

⁴³How could this happen to me, that the mother of my Lord should come to me? ⁴⁴For you see, when the sound of your greeting reached my ears, the baby leaped for joy inside me! ⁴⁵She who has believed is blessed because what was spoken to her by the Lord will be fulfilled!"

MARY'S PRAISE

⁴⁶And Mary said:

My soul proclaims the greatness of the Lord,
⁴⁷ and my spirit has rejoiced in God my Savior,
⁴⁸ because He has looked with favor
   on the humble condition of His slave.
   Surely, from now on all generations
   will call me blessed,
⁴⁹ because the Mighty One
   has done great things for me,
   and His name is holy.
⁵⁰ His mercy is from generation to generation
   on those who fear Him.
⁵¹ He has done a mighty deed with His arm;
   He has scattered the proud
   because of the thoughts of their hearts;
⁵² He has toppled the mighty from their thrones
   and exalted the lowly.
⁵³ He has satisfied the hungry with good things
   and sent the rich away empty.
⁵⁴ He has helped His servant Israel,
   mindful of His mercy,
⁵⁵ just as He spoke to our ancestors,
   to Abraham and his descendants forever.

⁵⁶And Mary stayed with her about three months; then she returned to her home.

THE BIRTH AND NAMING OF JOHN

⁵⁷Now the time had come for Elizabeth to give birth, and she had a son. ⁵⁸Then her neighbors and relatives heard that the Lord had shown her His great mercy, and they rejoiced with her.

⁵⁹When they came to circumcise the child on the eighth day,

they were going to name him Zechariah, after his father. ⁶⁰But his mother responded, "No! He will be called John."

⁶¹Then they said to her, "None of your relatives has that name." ⁶²So they motioned to his father to find out what he wanted him to be called. ⁶³He asked for a writing tablet and wrote:

HIS NAME IS JOHN

And they were all amazed. ⁶⁴Immediately his mouth was opened and his tongue [set free], and he began to speak, praising God. ⁶⁵Fear came on all those who lived around them, and all these things were being talked about throughout the hill country of Judea. ⁶⁶All who heard about [him] took [it] to heart, saying, "What then will this child become?" For, indeed, the Lord's hand was with him.

ZECHARIAH'S PROPHECY

⁶⁷Then his father Zechariah was filled with the Holy Spirit and prophesied:

⁶⁸ Praise the Lord, the God of Israel,
because He has visited
and provided redemption for His people.
⁶⁹ He has raised up a horn of salvation for us
in the house of His servant David,
⁷⁰ just as He spoke by the mouth
of His holy prophets in ancient times;
⁷¹ salvation from our enemies
and from the clutches of those who hate us.
⁷² He has dealt mercifully with our fathers
and remembered His holy covenant—
⁷³ the oath that He swore to our father Abraham.
He has given us the privilege,
⁷⁴ since we have been rescued
from our enemies' clutches,
to serve Him without fear
⁷⁵ in holiness and righteousness
in His presence all our days.
⁷⁶ And child, you will be called
a prophet of the Most High,

for you will go before the Lord
to prepare His ways,
[77] to give His people knowledge of salvation
through the forgiveness of their sins.
[78] Because of our God's merciful compassion,
the Dawn from on high will visit us
[79] to shine on those who live in darkness
and the shadow of death,
to guide our feet into the way of peace.

[80]The child grew up and became spiritually strong, and he was in the wilderness until the day of his public appearance to Israel.

PRAYER: My Father and my God, I see more clearly day by day the wonder of Your covenant-keeping abilities. Help me, I pray, to increase my understanding of this concept of covenant. I sense that the more I can comprehend it, the more secure I will be and feel as a Christian. You are a God who keeps His covenant and allows into my life only that which will work for my highest good. Blessed be Your wonderful name for ever. Amen.

DAY
84

ACTS 3:11-26

BY STAYING CLOSE to the old Abraham stories, the Israel that first cherished them might have remained sharply different from other nations without becoming exclusive or nationalistically self-seeking. Israel's failure in this mission and her attendant suffering were - as her prophets anticipated - brought mysteriously to concentrated fulfilment in her suffering Messiah, the Servant-Son of God, the final Moses-like prophet who must be listened to (vv.18, 22-23; cf.Deut. 18:15). In Him and through Him the ancient patriarchal promise of blessing for the world, paradoxically entrusted to one nation, was now seen to be redeemable. So the apostle Peter pleads with the heirs of the prophets and the descendants of Abraham not to renege on their God-given destiny and so miss

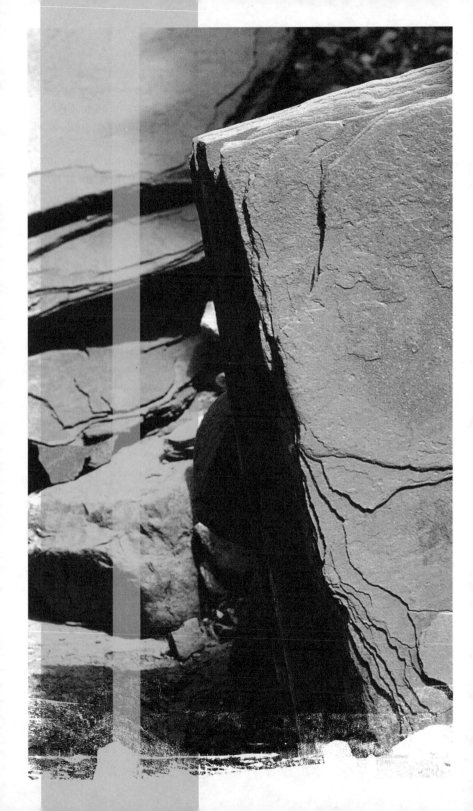

their hour of decision (vv.18ff.; cf.Joel 2:1-3:21).

The dramatic healing of one lame man symbolised the healing of a broken nation, guaranteed further times of refreshing and heralded the restoration of all things. Meanwhile, Abraham's promised inheritance of blessing for all the nations was gloriously available through the gospel. This was something - and still is - to make a song and dance about!

BIBLE READING

Acts 3:11-26

PREACHING IN SOLOMON'S COLONNADE

[11]While he was holding on to Peter and John, all the people, greatly amazed, ran toward them in what is called Solomon's Colonnade. [12]When Peter saw this, he addressed the people: "Men of Israel, why are you amazed at this? Or why do you stare at us, as though by our own power or godliness we had made him walk? [13]The God of Abraham, Isaac, and Jacob, the God of our fathers, has glorified His Servant Jesus, whom you handed over and denied in the presence of Pilate, when he had decided to release Him. [14]But you denied the Holy and Righteous One, and asked to have a murderer given to you. [15]And you killed the source of life, whom God raised from the dead; we are witnesses of this. [16]By faith in His name, His name has made this man strong, whom you see and know. So the faith that comes through Him has given him this perfect health in front of all of you.

[17]"And now, brothers, I know that you did it in ignorance, just as your leaders also did. [18]But what God predicted through the mouth of all the prophets—that His Messiah would suffer—He has fulfilled in this way. [19]Therefore repent and turn back, that your sins may be wiped out so that seasons of refreshing may come from the presence of the Lord, [20]and He may send Jesus, who has been appointed Messiah for you. [21]Heaven must welcome Him until the times of the restoration of all things, which God spoke about by the mouth of His holy prophets from the beginning. [22]Moses said:

"The Lord your God will raise up for you a Prophet like me from among your brothers. You must listen to

Him in everything He will say to you. [23]And it will be that everyone who will not listen to that Prophet will be completely cut off from the people."

[24]"In addition, all the prophets who have spoken, from Samuel and those after him, have also announced these days. [25]You are the sons of the prophets and of the covenant that God made with your forefathers, saying to Abraham, 'And in your seed all the families of the earth will be blessed.' [26]God raised up His Servant and sent Him first to you to bless you by turning each of you from your evil ways."

TO PONDER: Christians are called to weep with those who weep and rejoice with those who rejoice. And frequently the two emotions are expressed within a short space of time; for instance, when we rejoice for those who see the Abrahamic covenant in Jesus, and then weep for those who have not yet entered into it. Today, while rejoicing for those of your loved ones who know Christ, spend a little time praying for those who do not yet know Him.

RICHARD HAYS PARAPHRASES Paul's

question: 'Have we found Abraham to be our forefather according to the flesh?' (4:1). In expecting the answer 'No' Paul is able to advance the argument of 3:27-31. Jews have never relied for their status only on physical descent from Abraham. The gospel of grace, therefore, does not contradict the Law but upholds it (3:31) – that is, if we view the Torah rightly as embracing the narratives of Abraham in Genesis. God has always intended a worldwide family of faith. So Abraham is set to inherit not merely the land of Canaan but the entire world (4:13). And what kind of faith is Abraham-faith? It is faith which, as with Isaac, believes in a God who can raise the dead, for even a 'dead' Israel is 'resurrectable' (cf.Ezek. 37). It is a faith which believes in a God who, as at creation, can call into existence the things that

DAY
85
ROMANS 4

do not exist so that even Gentiles who, in terms of the covenant, are non-existent 'no-people' (cf.Rom. 9:25-26) are included through Christ in the people of God.

Covenant status (what Paul calls 'righteousness' or 'justification') comes by grace to those who believe in Him who raised His own 'Isaac', Jesus, from the dead (4:25). No wonder Abraham's faith was so pivotal or that Paul describes him as the father of all who believe (4:16).

BIBLE READING

Romans 4

ABRAHAM JUSTIFIED BY FAITH

4 What then can we say that Abraham, our forefather according to the flesh, has found? ²If Abraham was justified by works, then he has something to brag about—but not before God. ³For what does the Scripture say?

> "Abraham believed God,
> and it was credited to him for righteousness."

⁴Now to the one who works, pay is not considered as a gift, but as something owed. ⁵But to the one who does not work, but believes on Him who declares righteous the ungodly, his faith is credited for righteousness.

DAVID CELEBRATING THE SAME TRUTH

⁶Likewise, David also speaks of the blessing of the man to whom God credits righteousness apart from works:

> ⁷ "How happy those whose lawless acts are forgiven
> and whose sins are covered!
> ⁸ How happy the man whom
> the Lord will never charge with sin!"

ABRAHAM JUSTIFIED BEFORE CIRCUMCISION

⁹Is this blessing only for the circumcised, then? Or is it also for the uncircumcised? For we say, "Faith was credited to Abraham for righteousness." ¹⁰How then was it credited—while he was circumcised, or uncircumcised? Not while he was

circumcised, but uncircumcised. [11]And he received the sign of circumcision as a seal of the righteousness that he had by faith while still uncircumcised. This was to make him the father of all who believe but are not circumcised, so that righteousness may be credited to them also. [12]And he became the father of the circumcised, not only to those who are circumcised, but also to those who follow in the footsteps of the faith our father Abraham had while still uncircumcised.

THE PROMISE GRANTED THROUGH FAITH

[13]For the promise to Abraham or to his descendants that he would inherit the world was not through the law, but through the righteousness that comes by faith. [14]If those who are of the law are heirs, faith is made empty and the promise is canceled. [15]For the law produces wrath; but where there is no law, there is no transgression.

[16]This is why the promise is by faith, so that it may be according to grace, to guarantee it to all the descendants—not only to those who are of the law, but also to those who are of Abraham's faith. He is the father of us all [17]in God's sight. As it is written: "I have made you the father of many nations." He believed in God, who gives life to the dead and calls things into existence that do not exist. [18]Against hope, with hope he believed, so that he became "the father of many nations," according to what had been spoken: "So will your descendants be." [19]He considered his own body to be already dead (since he was about a hundred years old), and the deadness of Sarah's womb, without weakening in the faith. [20]He did not waver in unbelief at God's promise, but was strengthened in his faith and gave glory to God, [21]because he was fully convinced that what He had promised He was also able to perform. [22]Therefore, "it was credited to him for righteousness." [23]Now "it was credited to him" was not written for Abraham alone, [24]but also for us. It will be credited to us who believe in Him who raised Jesus our Lord from the dead. [25]He was delivered up for our trespasses and raised for our justification.

> **FOR PRAISE**: The movement of God that has taken those of us who were outside the covenants of promise and put us on the inside deserves endless praise. To be 'in Christ' is, in a sense, to be 'in Abraham' by believing in the resurrection. Lift your heart now in praise that we who were 'excluded from citizenship of Israel, and foreigners to the covenants of the promise ... have been brought near by the blood of the Messiah' (Eph. 2:12-13).

DAY 86

GALATIANS 3:1-9

THE QUESTION PAUL pursues here is: Who are the true sons of Abraham? He concludes that all who believe in Christ - whether Jew or Gentile - are sons of God and offspring of Abraham (vv.26-29). This global faith community was in view in God's original promise to Abraham that 'All the nations will be blessed in you' (v.8), the gospel in advance. Just as 'Abraham believed God, and it was credited to him for righteousness', so, Paul argues, with us all.

As we have seen from Genesis 15, Abraham's relationship was soon defined in covenantal terms so that thereafter in the Old Testament to be righteous was not so much an indication of moral character as of covenant status and identity. Similarly, to refer to the 'righteousness of God' - as the Psalms and Isaiah do particularly - will be to speak primarily of God's own *covenant faithfulness* which prompts Him to *saving action*.

Paul seizes on Genesis 15:6 not as a quick proof-text but because he is tracing the trajectory of faith right back to its Abrahamic launching pad. He is not merely illustrating faith but is convinced that Christian believers stand in unbroken continuity with God's covenant people stretching back to the patriarch Abraham, the father of all who believe. To be 'in Christ' is to be 'in Abraham'.

Galatians 3:1-9

JUSTIFICATION THROUGH FAITH

3 You foolish Galatians! Who has hypnotized you, before whose eyes Jesus Christ was vividly portrayed as crucified? ²I only want to learn this from you: Did you receive the Spirit by the works of the law or by hearing with faith? ³Are you so foolish? After beginning with the Spirit, are you now going to be made complete by the flesh? ⁴Did you suffer so much for nothing—if in fact it was for nothing? ⁵So then, does God supply you with the Spirit and work miracles among you by the works of the law or by hearing with faith?

⁶Just as Abraham "believed God, and it was credited to him for righteousness," ⁷so understand that those who have faith are Abraham's sons. ⁸Now the Scripture foresaw that God would justify the Gentiles by faith and foretold the good news to Abraham, saying, "All the nations will be blessed in you." ⁹So those who have faith are blessed with Abraham, who had faith.

THOUGHT: Think about this truth a little more: to be in Christ is to be in Abraham. We come to Christ by faith, we live by faith (as did Abraham) and we will receive the promised reward by faith. Abraham's life was characterised by faith. His name is recorded in the 'Heroes of Faith' chapter - Hebrews 11. No higher commendation will be given to any Christian in heaven than the commendation given for having lived by faith.

DAY 87

COLOSSIANS 2

COVENANTAL LANGUAGE, THOUGH not prominent in Colossians, is never far from the surface of Paul's mind.

'The circumcision of the Messiah' (v.11) could, grammatically, be taken as referring to what Christ does *to us* in order to bring about that 'circumcision of the heart' which marks the new covenant transformation of believers. More likely it refers to something done *to Jesus* – most probably in His death on the cross, so that 'circumcision' is a gruesome metaphor for crucifixion. Not the neat and swift surgical removal of the foreskin by a skilled rabbi, but the tearing apart of Jesus' body by ruthless executioners – *this* is what brings us into covenant membership. As we put our faith in this circumcised-by-crucifixion and raised-from-the-dead Jesus, expressed in the 'baptismal burial' of our old life, we are joined to God's covenant community.

So Jesus proves entirely sufficient for our salvation and covenant membership; we need no extra qualifications provided by the 'dos' and 'don'ts' of legalism, the fantasies of mysticism, or the lashings of asceticism – whether of a Greek or Jewish or hybrid variety! His cross is our new identity-marker as God's people in Christ – not worn as an outward badge or decoration but written on our hearts and worked out in our lives in self-giving.

BIBLE READING

Colossians 2

2 For I want you to know how great a struggle I have for you, for those in Laodicea, and for all who have not seen me in person. ²[I want] their hearts to be encouraged and joined together in love, so that they may have all the riches of assured understanding, and have the knowledge of God's mystery—Christ. ³In Him all the treasures of wisdom and knowledge are hidden.

CHRIST VERSUS THE COLOSSIAN HERESY

⁴I am saying this so that no one will deceive you with persuasive arguments. ⁵For I may be absent in body, but I am with you in spirit, rejoicing to see your good order and the strength of your faith in Christ.

⁶Therefore as you have received Christ Jesus the Lord, walk in Him, ⁷rooted and built up in Him and established in the faith, just as you were taught, and overflowing with thankfulness.

⁸Be careful that no one takes you captive through philosophy and empty deceit based on human tradition, based on the elemental forces of the world, and not based on Christ. ⁹For in Him the entire fullness of God's nature dwells bodily, ¹⁰and you have been filled by Him, who is the head over every ruler and authority. ¹¹In Him you were also circumcised with a circumcision not done with hands, by putting off the body of flesh, in the circumcision of the Messiah. ¹²Having been buried with Him in baptism, you were also raised with Him through faith in the working of God, who raised Him from the dead. ¹³And when you were dead in trespasses and in the uncircumcision of your flesh, He made you alive with Him and forgave us all our trespasses. ¹⁴He erased the certificate of debt, with its obligations, that was against us and opposed to us, and has taken it out of the way by nailing it to the cross. ¹⁵He disarmed the rulers and authorities and disgraced them publicly; He triumphed over them by Him.

¹⁶Therefore don't let anyone judge you in regard to food and drink or in the matter of a festival or a new moon or a sabbath day. ¹⁷These are a shadow of what was to come; the substance is the Messiah. ¹⁸Let no one disqualify you, insisting on ascetic practices and the worship of angels, claiming access to a visionary realm and inflated without cause by his fleshly mind. ¹⁹He doesn't hold on to the head, from whom the whole body, nourished and held together by its ligaments and tendons, develops with growth from God.

²⁰If you died with Christ to the elemental forces of this world, why do you live as if you still belonged to the world? Why do you submit to regulations: ²¹"Don't handle, don't taste, don't touch"? ²²All these [regulations] refer to what is destroyed by being used up; they are human commands and doctrines. ²³Although these have a reputation of wisdom by promoting

ascetic practices, humility, and severe treatment of the body, they are not of any value against fleshly indulgence.

TO PONDER: One of the biggest threats to Christianity, said C.S. Lewis, is 'Christianity and'. The truth is that Jesus is entirely sufficient for our salvation and no add-ons are needed. Some think that living out the Beatitudes is what saves us. However, Jesus is not saying, 'Live like this and you will be saved', but, 'Be saved and you will live like this'. Good works cannot save us. Salvation is through Christ - and Christ alone.

DAY
88

HEBREWS 6:13-20

CONVENTIONAL CHRISTIANITY HAS

been described as 'an initial spasm followed by chronic inertia'! Unconventional Christianity imitates the patriarchs in overcoming sluggishness (v.12) and pressing on to inherit the promises.

God is so committed to His redemptive plan that He guarantees His promise to Abraham by swearing an oath - swearing 'by Himself' (v.13) - putting His own reputation as a God who does what He says, on the line. These two unalterable things - God's promise and His sworn oath - encourage us, on our leg of the journey, to travel with endurance and hope. Christian hope is no wishful thinking or mere optimism, but is pinned on Jesus who has pioneered the way into God's vivid presence and eternal future. This anchors hope in the permanent realities of the kingdom of God. A hymn I learned as a child poses the question: 'Will your anchor hold in the storms of life?' Hebrews answers 'Yes'.

Whether in the flux of a first-century or a post-modern world, this is the fixed point faith can rely on. We are not anchored 'downward to the sea-bed' so that we stay immovable, victims of chronic inertia, but 'upward to the Trailblazer on the summit' so that we keep climbing. This anchor takes the strain even when the ledges are narrow, the grip is weak and our hold on the rock face is precarious.

Hebrews 6:13-20

INHERITING THE PROMISE

¹³For when God made a promise to Abraham, since He had no one greater to swear by, He swore by Himself:

¹⁴ "I will most certainly bless you,
    and I will greatly multiply you."

¹⁵And so, after waiting patiently, Abraham obtained the promise. ¹⁶For men swear by something greater than themselves, and for them a confirming oath ends every dispute. ¹⁷Because God wanted to show His unchangeable purpose even more clearly to the heirs of the promise, He guaranteed it with an oath, ¹⁸so that through two unchangeable things, in which it is impossible for God to lie, we who have fled for refuge might have strong encouragement to seize the hope set before us. ¹⁹We have this [hope]—like a sure and firm anchor of the soul—that enters the inner sanctuary behind the curtain. ²⁰Jesus has entered there on our behalf as a forerunner, because He has become a "high priest forever in the order of Melchizedek."

QUESTION: Could your Christianity be described as 'an initial spasm followed by chronic inertia'? The Christian life is kept alive by many things, not the least *hope*. The common assessment of hope is that it is a poor, vain, deceptive thing. Cowley said: 'Hope is the most hopeless thing of all.' In worldly terms that may be so, but not in biblical terms. Christian hope has a specific object - Jesus. Joined to Him, despair is impossible.

DAY
89
HEBREWS 7:1-28

TRACING THE PATH of God's covenant with Abraham has brought us to the priesthood of Jesus! As the high priest in Israel entered the Holiest Place, symbolically bearing the people into the presence of the Most Holy God, so, even more and in reality, Jesus has secured permanent access to God for us by His atoning death and continuing life of intercession.

His priesthood, however, is not based on that of Aaron but on that of Melchizedek, the strangely superior priest-king to whom Abraham paid tithes. Since the seeds of the later Levitical priests were in his body when he did this, Abraham, symbolically, ranked the Levitical priesthood beneath that of Melchizedek! Melchizedek appears in Genesis out of the blue, with no mention of ancestors or successors. Hebrews exploits this literary gap to present Melchizedek as prefiguring Jesus, who has eternal roots and who continues His priestly activity, uninterrupted by death, in the power of an endless resurrection life (v.16)! Psalm 110 confirms this, linking the Abrahamic experience to a prophetic oracle made to the Davidic king which was also backed by an oath (7:17-21).

Who would have guessed that following in the footsteps of our faith-father Abraham would have taken us this far - to the very High King and High Priest of heaven Himself!

BIBLE READING

Hebrews 7:1-28

THE GREATNESS OF MELCHIZEDEK

7 For this Melchizedek—

> King of Salem, priest of the Most High God,
> who met Abraham and blessed him as he returned
>   from defeating the kings,
> ² and Abraham gave him a tenth of everything;
> first, his name means "king of righteousness,"
> then also, "king of Salem," meaning "king of peace";

³ without father, mother, or genealogy,
having neither beginning of days nor end of life,
but resembling the Son of God—

remains a priest forever. ⁴Now consider how great this man was, to whom even Abraham the patriarch gave a tenth of the plunder! ⁵The sons of Levi who receive the priestly office have a commandment according to the law to collect a tenth from the people—that is, from their brothers—though they have [also] descended from Abraham. ⁶But one without this lineage collected tithes from Abraham and blessed the one who had the promises. ⁷Without a doubt, the inferior is blessed by the superior. ⁸In the one case, men who will die receive tithes; but in the other case, [Scripture] testifies that he lives. ⁹And in a sense Levi himself, who receives tithes, has paid tithes through Abraham, ¹⁰for he was still within his forefather when Melchizedek met him.

A SUPERIOR PRIESTHOOD

¹¹If, then, perfection came through the Levitical priesthood (for under it the people received the law), what further need was there for another priest to arise in the order of Melchizedek, and not to be described as being in the order of Aaron? ¹²For when there is a change of the priesthood, there must be a change of law as well. ¹³For the One about whom these things are said belonged to a different tribe, from which no one has served at the altar. ¹⁴Now it is evident that our Lord came from Judah, and about that tribe Moses said nothing concerning priests.

¹⁵And this becomes clearer if an other priest like Melchizedek arises, ¹⁶who doesn't become a [priest] based on a legal command concerning physical descent but based on the power of an indestructible life. ¹⁷For it has been testified:

"You are a priest forever in the order of Melchizedek."

¹⁸So the previous commandment is annulled because it was weak and unprofitable ¹⁹(for the law perfected nothing), but a better hope is introduced, through which we draw near to God.

[20]None of this [happened] without an oath. For others became priests without an oath, [21]but He with an oath made by the One who said to Him:

> "The Lord has sworn, and He will not change
>   His mind,
> You are a priest forever."

[22]So Jesus has also become the guarantee of a better covenant.

[23]Now many have become [Levitical] priests, since they are prevented by death from remaining in office. [24]But because He remains forever, He holds His priesthood permanently. [25]Therefore He is always able to save those who come to God through Him, since He always lives to intercede for them.

[26]For this is the kind of high priest we need: holy, innocent, undefiled, separated from sinners, and exalted above the heavens. [27]He doesn't need to offer sacrifices every day, as high priests do—first for their own sins, then for those of the people. He did this once for all when He offered Himself. [28]For the law appoints as high priests men who are weak, but the promise of the oath, which came after the law, [appoints] a Son, who has been perfected forever.

FOR PRAISE: You will undoubtedly know this hymn. Sing it to yourself as you reflect on the reading today:

Be Thou my vision, O Lord of my heart,
Naught be all else to me, save that Thou art,
Be Thou my best thought in the day and the night,
Both waking and sleeping, Thy presence my light.

THE WRITER'S PASTORAL urgency is obvious as he warns and encourages his Christian friends not to shrink back from full-blooded commitment to Jesus Christ in face of the type of harassment that is the prelude to full-scale persecution (10:32-39). He has already made unfavourable reference to Israel's unbelief (4:2) but that isn't the whole story; there are also outstanding stories of faith to be told. But these are not simply held up before us as examples of how to believe from *another* story but presented to us as *earlier* chapters in the *same* story. What we have here is not simply a borrowed vocabulary but a common vocation. 'They' remain incomplete without 'us', and we without them (11:40)! Their story is our story, the story of decision-making faith.

For the builders of the Tower of Babel, 'Come, let us build ourselves a city ...' (Gen. 11:4), set the limit of their horizon. Abraham makes a radical counter-cultural statement by turning his back on the city that man is building – visible and tangible to all – for the sake of the city that God is building, which is still invisible except to faith. He refuses to sink his roots into that man-made city because, in the words of Hebrews again, 'he was looking forward to the city that has foundations, whose architect and builder is God' (Heb. 11:10).

Hebrews 11:1-12

HEROES OF FAITH

11 Now faith is the reality of what is hoped for, the proof of what is not seen. ²For by it our ancestors were approved.

³By faith we understand that the universe was created by the word of God, so that what is seen has been made from things that are not visible.

⁴By faith Abel offered to God a better sacrifice than Cain [did]. By this he was approved as a righteous man, because God approved his gifts, and even though he is dead, he still speaks through this.

[5]By faith, Enoch was taken away so that he did not experience death, and "he was not to be found because God took him away." For prior to his transformation he was approved, having pleased God. [6]Now without faith it is impossible to please God, for the one who draws near to Him must believe that He exists and rewards those who seek Him.

[7]By faith Noah, after being warned about what was not yet seen, in reverence built an ark to deliver his family. By this he condemned the world and became an heir of the righteousness that comes by faith.

[8]By faith Abraham, when he was called, obeyed and went out to a place he was going to receive as an inheritance; he went out, not knowing where he was going. [9]By faith he stayed as a foreigner in the land of promise, living in tents with Isaac and Jacob, co-heirs of the same promise. [10]For he was looking forward to the city that has foundations, whose architect and builder is God.

[11]By faith even Sarah herself, when she was barren, received power to conceive offspring, even though she was past the age, since she considered that the One who had promised was faithful. [12]And therefore from one man—in fact, from one as good as dead—came offspring as numerous as the stars of heaven and as innumerable as the grains of sand by the seashore.

TO PONDER: Some consider that keeping the vision of heaven in view hinders us from fulfilling our responsibilities here on earth. Such is not the case, however. Throughout time great Christians (such as General Booth of the Salvation Army) have claimed that the prospect of heaven nerved them on to do remarkable work here on earth. Thinking about heaven can give us the incentive to leave earth a better place than we found it.

THESE HEROES SHOW us just how radically counter-cultural faith is! In an age obsessed with self-fulfilment, we recall that Abraham was not moved to sacrifice Isaac in order to satisfy personal needs. In fact, as Heschel again reminds us, 'To believe in God is to fight for him, to fight whatever is against him within ourselves, including our interests when they collide with his will.'

What gives significance to the life of faith lies beyond visible satisfaction.

The negatives say it all: not seen, not visible, not knowing where he was going. This last is hardest for modern people who value self-determination above all. But beyond the ability to manage our own lives, faith marches to a louder drumbeat! A glory beckons.

This is a high-risk strategy, that stakes all on a 'better land' (v.16), an enduring city (13:14)! 'Otherworldly' is too tepid a word for such earthy faith.

The supreme example and the climax of the covenantal story of faith is Jesus Himself (12:2f). The story goes on but His is the crucial chapter. In His name our resolve is stiffened; we go on, we risk and obey, we endure and overcome, we forego pleasure and face pain, we fight to the finish and run the race. Our prize is to share in that same joy that was set before Him.

DAY
91

HEBREWS 11:13-19, 32-12:3

Hebrews 11:13-19,32-12:3

BIBLE READING

HEROES OF FAITH

11 Now faith is the reality of what is hoped for, the proof of what is not seen. ²For by it our ancestors were approved.

• • • • • • • • •

⁷By faith Noah, after being warned about what was not yet seen, in reverence built an ark to deliver his family. By this he condemned the world and became an heir of the righteousness that comes by faith.

[8]By faith Abraham, when he was called, obeyed and went out to a place he was going to receive as an inheritance; he went out, not knowing where he was going. [9]By faith he stayed as a foreigner in the land of promise, living in tents with Isaac and Jacob, co-heirs of the same promise. [10]For he was looking forward to the city that has foundations, whose architect and builder is God.

[11]By faith even Sarah herself, when she was barren, received power to conceive offspring, even though she was past the age, since she considered that the One who had promised was faithful. [12]And therefore from one man—in fact, from one as good as dead—came offspring as numerous as the stars of heaven and as innumerable as the grains of sand by the seashore.

[13]These all died in faith without having received the promises, but they saw them from a distance, greeted them, and confessed that they were foreigners and temporary residents on the earth. [14]Now those who say such things make it clear that they are seeking a homeland. [15]If they had been remembering that land they came from, they would have had opportunity to return. [16]But they now aspire to a better land—a heavenly one. Therefore God is not ashamed to be called their God, for He has prepared a city for them.

[17]By faith Abraham, when he was tested, offered up Isaac; he who had received the promises was offering up his unique son, [18]about whom it had been said, "In Isaac your seed will be called." [19]He considered God to be able even to raise someone from the dead, from which he also got him back as an illustration.

• • • • • • • • •

[32]And what more can I say? Time is too short for me to tell about Gideon, Barak, Samson, Jephthah, of David and Samuel and the prophets, [33]who by faith conquered kingdoms, administered justice, obtained promises, shut the mouths of lions, [34]quenched the raging of fire, escaped the edge of the sword, gained strength after being weak, became mighty in battle, and put foreign armies to flight. [35]Women received their dead raised to life again. Some men were tortured, not accepting release, so that they might gain a better resurrection,

[36]and others experienced mockings and scourgings, as well as bonds and imprisonment. [37]They were stoned, they were sawed in two, they died by the sword, they wandered about in sheepskins, in goatskins, destitute, afflicted, and mistreated. [38]The world was not worthy of them. They wandered in deserts, mountains, caves, and holes in the ground.

[39]All these were approved through their faith, but they did not receive what was promised, [40]since God had provided something better for us, so that they would not be made perfect without us.

THE CALL TO ENDURANCE

12 Therefore since we also have such a large cloud of witnesses surrounding us, let us lay aside every weight and the sin that so easily ensnares us, and run with endurance the race that lies before us, [2]keeping our eyes on Jesus, the source and perfecter of our faith, who for the joy that lay before Him endured a cross and despised the shame, and has sat down at the right hand of God's throne.

FATHERLY DISCIPLINE

[3]For consider Him who endured such hostility from sinners against Himself, so that you won't grow weary and lose heart.

FOR ACTION: The apostle Paul resolved to run the race set before him with an enthusiasm and determination that echoes the commitment of Jesus Himself. Read Philippians 3:12-14 and ask yourself: Am I willing to risk and obey, endure and overcome, forego everything necessary, face any pain, to win the prize - the joy that C.S. Lewis says 'is the business of heaven'? Now prayerfully renew your commitment to the Lord.

DAY
92

JAMES 2:14-26

WE HAVE SURELY seen enough of Abraham's story and the reverberations of it down the centuries to know one thing: faith is action and adventure. Faith has too often in modern Christianity become reduced either to an intellectual assent to certain dogmas or to a vague God-dependency characterised by a particularly religious state of mind.

Real faith of Abraham dimensions, takes risks, feeds the hungry, takes in the orphans. Faith like this goes beyond words into heroic deeds that authenticate the commitment.

The apostle James – like Paul – hears the contemporary power of the ancient text (Gen. 15:6) in which Abraham is declared righteous on the basis of his faith (v.23). Faith without its 'Isaac' is dead: faith which offers up its 'Isaac' is alive with resurrection life. Faith-doers are God's friends. This is the challenge of Abraham to us: to participate in God's story.

'I happen to believe,' said A.W. Tozer, 'that Abraham's encounters with the living God nearly 4,000 years ago leave modern men and women without excuse.'

Abraham, you've a lot to answer for!

This is the faith adventure: to have something to die for is to have something to live for.

BIBLE READING

James 2:14-26

FAITH AND WORKS

[14]What good is it, my brothers, if someone says he has faith, but does not have works? Can his faith save him?

[15]If a brother or sister is without clothes and lacks daily food, [16]and one of you says to them, "Go in peace, keep warm, and eat well," but you don't give them what the body needs, what good is it? [17]In the same way faith, if it doesn't have works, is dead by itself.

[18]But someone will say, "You have faith, and I have works."

Show me your faith without works, and I will show you faith from my works. [19]You believe that God is one; you do well. The demons also believe—and they shudder.

[20]Foolish man! Are you willing to learn that faith without works is useless? [21]Wasn't Abraham our father justified by works when he offered Isaac his son on the altar? [22]You see that faith was active together with his works, and by works, faith was perfected. [23]So the Scripture was fulfilled that says, "Abraham believed God, and it was credited to him for righteousness," and he was called God's friend. [24]You see that a man is justified by works and not by faith alone. [25]And in the same way, wasn't Rahab the prostitute also justified by works when she received the messengers and sent them out by a different route? [26]For just as the body without the spirit is dead, so also faith without works is dead.

PRAYER: My Father and my God, if I have been blocking Your power in my life by my lack of faith let this day be a day of release and deliverance. Help me take the steps that will lead me on a new adventure - one that goes beyond mere words and issues forth in actions. Show me what I can do to authenticate my commitment - some new task or project, a loving deed for someone. Help me my Saviour. No more words. It's time for action. Amen.

SECTIONS

NOAH
ALL CREATION

ABRAHAM
ALL NATIONS

ISRAEL
ONE NATION

DAVID
REPRESENTATIVE KING

NEW COVENANT
FAITHFUL COVENANT PARTNER

JESUS
FAITHFUL COVENANT PARTNER

JESUS
DAVIDIC KING MESSIAH

JESUS
THE NEW ISRAEL

JESUS
THE WORLD'S LORD

JESUS
THE TRULY HUMAN ONE
CROWNED WITH GLORY AND HONOUR

JESUS
COSMIC RULER IN GOD'S NEW CREATION
NEW HEAVENS AND NEW EARTH

SECTION 5   ISRAEL'S CALLING

GOD IS COMMITTED TO CALLING A PEOPLE FOR HIS OWN GLORY - ISRAEL'S VOCATION

Les Miserables, the world-famous musical, based on Victor Hugo's novel, celebrates the optimism of the students manning the barricades in revolutionary Paris and laments the dashing of their dreams. The origins of Israel's national story finds the people of Israel also among 'les miserables', oppressed as slaves in Egypt and clamouring for freedom. But, unlike Hugo's tragic heroes, their longing for liberation was realised, and realised, not by a man-made revolution, but by a God-wrought redemption.

Why God chose Israel is explained by the text as the mystery of love (Deut. 7:7-9). God set His love not on the more numerous or more powerful nations in existence at the time but on the enslaved sons of Jacob. God's love is a caring love which responds to the immediate painful plight of the people - 'God heard their groaning' - and a covenant-love which remembers His previous commitments to Abraham (Exod. 2:23-25). God hears and feels, sees and knows, remembers and acts to save His people. Choosing one man, Moses, whom He preserves and disciplines and prepares for His service, God makes Himself known to him as the God of the patriarchs in an eerie encounter at the burning bush. Pressing God for His real name, Moses soon learns that God is not only the God of the known past who made promises to Abraham but He is the God of the unknown future. To know God's future, Israel must trust and travel with Him, experiencing along the way that God will be what He will be as and when they need Him (Exod. 3:1-22)!

Suitably emboldened, Moses is told to demand that Pharaoh let God's 'firstborn son' go. God protects the Israelites - as the judgment of death 'passes over' the

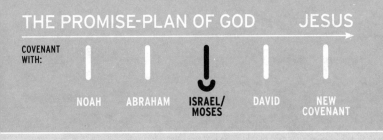
blood-marked homes of the Israelites – and then, even more dramatically, rescues them from Pharaoh's army by opening the Red Sea. This saving 'Exodus' is forever commemorated in the Passover Feast and the Song of Moses (Exod. 14-15).

Brought to Mount Sinai, Israel is made party to the covenant God had already made with Abraham to bring blessing to the world. There Israel is honoured as God's own treasured possession, called to be a holy nation, a kingdom of priests to represent God before the watching nations (Exod. 19:1-6). The Torah is given to show Israel how to live as covenant people. Israel is intended to be a showcase nation, her mandate to 'be holy as God is holy' aimed at taking up the discarded human mantle of being image-bearers of God in the world.

But before the 'ink is dry', as it were, Israel falls from grace in the golden calf incident, so proving to be as much part of the problem as the answer. But it remains Israel's privilege both to keep the Sabbath which sanctifies time so that God and His people can renew relationship, and to erect the tabernacle which sanctifies space where God can dwell in concentrated holiness with His people.

On the verge of entry to the promised land, Moses warns that covenant unfaithfulness will eventually incur the ultimate curse of judgment – exile from the land, so repeating the Adam and Eve pattern.

What a turbulent story it was – and remains. Israel, said Abraham Heschel is 'God's stake in history', a people burdened with 'dreaming the dreams of God'. In her proneness to suffer, Israel is, said Arthur Koestler, 'the exposed nerve of the human race'. This history is unusual in being history from the 'underside'. History is usually told by the 'winners' as the top-down record of conquest and domination, enshrined in the annals of the superpowers from Egypt to Rome. But Israel's is the story of ex-slaves and former exiles who are God's gift to the world and through whom God will give Himself to and for the world.

The whole Old Testament story of Israel revolves around the twin poles of Exodus and Exile, ironically from slavery to slavery again! Hopes beyond Exile look to a New Israel, a true son and covenant partner, who will bring salvation by faithfully acting out the story of Israel and her God by re-enacting the one and embodying the other.

ISRAEL'S KEY ROLE in the great story starts with a Great Escape. Abraham's descendants, Jacob's sons, have been enslaved in Egypt under a Pharaoh no longer favourable to them as his predecessor had been to Joseph and his kinsmen. But their cries for help and groaning under repression and injustice do not go unheard by God. In noting this, our text highlights the twin aspects of God's love that make Him concerned for the plight of the Israelites. First, God cares and is moved to respond to the immediate cries of His people. God is also stirred to remember His long-term commitment to the patriarchs, Abraham, Isaac and Jacob, in the earlier stages of the story. Already we see the kind of God disclosed by the story. This is a God who is passionately aroused by injustice, and plunges into emotional involvement with His people. Yet, at the same time, His love is not a fleeting pang of sympathy but a tough, enduring, steadfast love, grounded in covenant making and keeping.

As with Noah, and as in significant future situations, salvation will depend on God remembering His covenant promises as much as it does on God forgiving and forgetting sins! God 'remembers' not as if He suffers from occasional amnesia, but in the sense of acting to implement his previous commitments.

DAY
93
EXODUS 2:23-25

Exodus 2:23-25

BIBLE READING

²³After a long time, the king of Egypt died. The Israelites groaned because of their difficult labor, and they cried out; and their cry for help ascended to God because of the difficult labor. ²⁴So God heard their groaning, and He remembered His covenant with Abraham, Isaac, and Jacob. ²⁵God saw the Israelites, and He took notice.

TO PONDER: The point 'God "remembers" not as if He suffers from occasional amnesia' ought to be a tremendous personal encouragement to us. In other words God simply cannot forget us, and all our interests, even the tiniest detail, are ever before Him. Meditate on this text as you go through the day: 'The LORD remembers us and will bless us. He will bless the house of Israel; He will bless the house of Aaron ...' (Psa. 115:12).

DAY 94

EXODUS 3:1-10

TYPICALLY, IN REACHING out to rescue His people, God starts with one man, selecting Moses to be the agent of deliverance. Already God has sovereignly preserved Moses' life through the shrewd enterprise of his mother and sister, aided and abetted by Pharaoh's own daughter (2:1-10). Ironically, Moses is educated, all expenses paid, by the very regime he is called to undermine! God sets Himself against arrogant and God-defying powers. But Moses' first attempt to assert God's justice by taking matters into his own hands fails miserably and he has to flee the country (2:11-22). God will deal with the Egyptians in His time and in His way. Now, shepherding in the desert, Moses' attention is riveted by a burning bush which does not burn up and from which a voice speaks. Moses concedes to being on holy ground by taking off his sandals. This occurs in the shadow of Horeb, the mountain of God. Not that Horeb is special – it becomes special only because God appears there. Any old bush will do for God to incite your curiosity and so draw you deeper into His self-revelation. But when you do glimpse Him or hear Him, it will not be to enrich your stockpile of spiritual sensations but to implicate you further in the ongoing story of God's plans to bless and save the world.

Exodus 3:1-10

MOSES AND THE BURNING BUSH

3 Meanwhile Moses was shepherding the flock of his father-in-law Jethro, the priest of Midian. He led the flock to the far side of the wilderness and came to Horeb, the mountain of God. ²Then the Angel of the LORD appeared to him in a flame of fire within a bush. As Moses looked, he saw that the bush was on fire but was not consumed. ³So Moses thought: I must go over and look at this remarkable sight. Why isn't the bush burning up?

⁴When the LORD saw that he had gone over to look, God called out to him from the bush, "Moses, Moses!"

"Here I am," he answered.

⁵"Do not come closer," He said. "Take your sandals off your feet, for the place where you are standing is holy ground." ⁶Then He continued, "I am the God of your father, the God of Abraham, the God of Isaac, and the God of Jacob." Moses hid his face because he was afraid to look at God.

⁷Then the LORD said, "I have observed the misery of My people in Egypt, and have heard them crying out because of their oppressors, and I know about their sufferings. ⁸I have come down to rescue them from the power of the Egyptians and to bring them from that land to a good and spacious land, a land flowing with milk and honey—the territory of the Canaanites, Hittites, Amorites, Perizzites, Hivites, and Jebusites. ⁹The Israelites' cry for help has come to Me, and I have also seen the way the Egyptians are oppressing them. ¹⁰Therefore, go. I am sending you to Pharaoh so that you may lead My people, the Israelites, out of Egypt."

QUESTION: God called Moses and Moses answered, 'Here I am'. God called Samuel and Samuel answered, 'Here I am'. God called Isaiah and he answered, 'Here I am'. What a blessing they were there! Dr Alexander Whyte of Scotland once said in a sermon that God often calls but His children are not always listening. If God were to call you to do something for Him today are you there - listening, eager, willing and ready to do His bidding?

DAY
95

EXODUS 3:7-22

HAVING FIRST REASSURED the awestruck Moses that He is none other than the God of Abraham, God shares with Moses His determination to immerse Himself in His people's troubles and to act to redeem them.

So far so good. All this is music to Moses' ears until the words 'Therefore, go. I am sending you ...'. Moses then demonstrates how to have cold feet while hopping barefoot around a blazing fire! What God has in mind sounds to Moses like 'mission impossible'. With his 'Who am I?' Moses heads a long line of reluctant biblical heroes. We can understand his reaction; after all in view of what God has promised to do, why should He need Moses' help? God promises to be with him but offers no guarantees about the future. Moses' initial 'Who am I?' dissolves into a bigger question: 'Who are You? ... What is Your name? Who is authorising me to act in this way?' God's reply - a virtually untranslatable version of the verb 'to be' - has provoked philosophical speculation. But in context the accent is less on God's self-sufficiency, true as that is, than on His passion to be intimately involved with His people: 'I will be what I will be' to you and for you whenever and wherever you need Me.

BIBLE READING

Exodus 3:7-22

MOSES AND THE BURNING BUSH

3 Meanwhile Moses was shepherding the flock of his father-in-law Jethro, the priest of Midian. He led the flock to the far side of the wilderness and came to Horeb, the mountain of God. [2]Then the Angel of the LORD appeared to him in a flame of fire within a bush. As Moses looked, he saw that the bush was on fire but was not consumed. [3]So Moses thought: I must go over and look at this remarkable sight. Why isn't the bush burning up?

[4]When the LORD saw that he had gone over to look, God

called out to him from the bush, "Moses, Moses!"

"Here I am," he answered.

⁵"Do not come closer," He said. "Take your sandals off your feet, for the place where you are standing is holy ground." ⁶Then He continued, "I am the God of your father, the God of Abraham, the God of Isaac, and the God of Jacob." Moses hid his face because he was afraid to look at God.

⁷Then the LORD said, "I have observed the misery of My people in Egypt, and have heard them crying out because of their oppressors, and I know about their sufferings. ⁸I have come down to rescue them from the power of the Egyptians and to bring them from that land to a good and spacious land, a land flowing with milk and honey—the territory of the Canaanites, Hittites, Amorites, Perizzites, Hivites, and Jebusites. ⁹The Israelites' cry for help has come to Me, and I have also seen the way the Egyptians are oppressing them. ¹⁰Therefore, go. I am sending you to Pharaoh so that you may lead My people, the Israelites, out of Egypt."

¹¹But Moses asked God, "Who am I that I should go to Pharaoh and that I should bring the Israelites out of Egypt?"

¹²He answered, "I will certainly be with you, and this will be the sign to you that I have sent you: when you bring the people out of Egypt, you will all worship God at this mountain."

¹³Then Moses asked God, "If I go to the Israelites and say to them: The God of your fathers has sent me to you, and they ask me, 'What is His name?' what should I tell them?"

¹⁴God replied to Moses, "I AM WHO I AM. This is what you are to say to the Israelites: I AM has sent me to you." ¹⁵God also said to Moses, "Say this to the Israelites: Yahweh, the God of your fathers, the God of Abraham, the God of Isaac, and the God of Jacob, has sent me to you. This is My name forever; this is how I am to be remembered in every generation.

¹⁶"Go and assemble the elders of Israel and say to them: Yahweh, the God of your fathers, the God of Abraham, Isaac, and Jacob, has appeared to me and said: I have paid close attention to you and to what has been done to you in Egypt. ¹⁷And I have promised you that I will bring you up from the misery of Egypt to the land of the Canaanites, Hittites, Amorites, Perizzites, Hivites, and Jebusites—a land flowing

with milk and honey. ¹⁸They will listen to what you say. Then you, along with the elders of Israel, must go to the king of Egypt and say to him: The LORD, the God of the Hebrews, has met with us. Now please let us go on a three-day trip into the wilderness so that we may sacrifice to the LORD our God.

¹⁹"However, I know that the king of Egypt will not allow you to go, unless [he is forced] by a strong hand. ²⁰I will stretch out My hand and strike Egypt with all My miracles that I will perform in it. After that, he will let you go. ²¹And I will give this people such favor in the sight of the Egyptians that when you go, you will not go empty-handed. ²²Each woman will ask her neighbor and any woman staying in her house for silver and gold jewelry, and clothing, and you will put them on your sons and daughters. So you will plunder the Egyptians."

PRAYER: Father, strengthen me I pray for those times when You call me to do something for which I feel utterly inadequate. Help me know that when Your finger points the way, Your hand provides the resources I need. Drive this truth deeply into my spirit that the task ahead, whatever it may be, is never as great as the power that lies behind me. Teach me how to rely less on my sufficiency and more on Yours. In Jesus' name. Amen.

DAY 96

EXODUS 4:18-23

MOSES IS TOLD to call on Pharaoh to release Israel – God's 'firstborn son'. This crucial statement connects with the death of the firstborn in Egypt (v.23) and the later consecration of the Israelite firstborn to the Lord. Beyond this it shapes the role of the king in Israel who is called God's 'son' because he represents both God and the nation. It takes final form in the Sonship of Jesus who perfectly embodies Israel's destiny and fully incarnates her God. Suffice it to say here that God's fatherly image is not in conflict with the tough sovereign decisions He takes against the Egyptian regime. The Exodus story all along shows the absolute power of God over the opposition of despotic earthly rulers like Pharaoh. God's harsh threat to him is in the cause of justice and aims at unseating a cruel tyrant. God is clearly not a tame God as is shown by the way He threatens to kill Moses, who is saved, not for the first time, by a woman's wit. The incident serves to highlight the significance of the key covenant sign of circumcision which Moses has evidently neglected. Certainly when the people learn that God is concerned about their plight, they bow to worship this fatherly God whom they may not fully know but are beginning to trust.

Exodus 4:18-23

BIBLE READING

MOSES' RETURN TO EGYPT

[18]Then Moses went back to his father-in-law Jethro and said to him, "Please let me return to my relatives in Egypt and see if they are still living."

Jethro said to Moses, "Go in peace."

[19]Now in Midian the LORD told Moses, "Return to Egypt, for all the men who wanted to kill you are dead." [20]So Moses took his wife and sons, put them on a donkey, and set out for the land of Egypt. And Moses took God's staff in his hand.

[21]The LORD instructed Moses, "When you go back to Egypt, make sure you do in front of Pharaoh all the wonders I have put within your power. But I will harden his heart so that he won't let the people go. [22]Then you will say to Pharaoh: This is what the LORD says: Israel is My firstborn son. [23]I told you: Let My son go so that he may worship Me, but you refused to let him go. Now I will kill your firstborn son!"

FOR PRAISE: How diverse and wondrous are the ways of God. The more we read Scripture the more of the facets of His character we see. Lift your heart in praise as you sing or read Isaac Watts' song:

Give to our God immortal praise,
Mercy and truth are all His ways
Wonders of grace to Him belong,
Repeat His mercies in your song.

DAY 97

EXODUS 12:1-42

PHARAOH'S RELUCTANCE TO let the Israelites go elicits a series of plague-judgments, culminating in the death of all the firstborn. But God aims to preserve the Israelites, instructing them to daub their doorposts with lamb's blood so that judgment will 'pass over' their homes. Notice that God's controversy is not with things Egyptian, nor even with Pharaoh himself as an individual, but with the gods of Egypt (12:12). Since the cross, we now know that we do not fight flesh-and-blood people. But from the outset, the conflict has always been a spiritual battle between the true God and all false rivals to His unique glory. Pharaoh is a front for false gods but he tragically represents his people who suffer with him.

By the feast of Passover, which commemorates Israel's deliverance, Israel renewed its identity as God's redeemed people. Later sharers in the feast, through remembering, 'relived' the Exodus experience. So Israel escapes, clutching the unleavened bread as God has commanded and now weighed down with the treasures the panic-stricken Egyptians have pressed upon them. Pharaoh has been paid in full for his genocidal policy and cruel repression. Israel leaves, as it were, by the front door, heads held high and dressed no longer as slaves.

BIBLE READING

Exodus 12:1-42

INSTRUCTIONS FOR THE PASSOVER

12 The LORD said to Moses and Aaron in the land of Egypt: ²"This month is to be the beginning of months for you; it is the first month of your year. ³Tell the whole community of Israel that on the tenth day of this month they must each select an animal of the flock according to [their] fathers' households, one animal per household. ⁴If the household is too small for a [whole] animal, that person and the neighbor nearest his house are to select one based on the combined number of people; you should apportion the animal according to what each person

will eat. [5]You must have an unblemished animal, a year-old male; you may take it from either the sheep or the goats. [6]You are to keep it until the fourteenth day of this month; then the whole assembly of the community of Israel will slaughter the animals at twilight. [7]They must take some of the blood and put it on the two doorposts and the lintel of the houses in which they eat them. [8]They are to eat the meat that night; they should eat it, roasted over the fire along with unleavened bread and bitter herbs. [9]Do not eat any of it raw or cooked in boiling water, but only roasted over fire—its head as well as its legs and inner organs. [10]Do not let any of it remain until morning; you must burn up any part of it that does remain until morning. [11]Here is how you must eat it: dressed for travel, your sandals on your feet, and your staff in your hand. You are to eat it in a hurry; it is the LORD's Passover.

[12]"I will pass through the land of Egypt on that night and strike every firstborn [male] in the land of Egypt, both man and beast. I am the LORD; I will execute judgments against all the gods of Egypt. [13]The blood on the houses where you are staying will be a distinguishing mark for you; when I see the blood, I will pass over you. No plague will be among you to destroy [you] when I strike the land of Egypt.

[14]"This day is to be a memorial for you, and you must celebrate it as a festival to the LORD. You are to celebrate it throughout your generations as a permanent statute. [15]You must eat unleavened bread for seven days. On the first day you must remove yeast from your houses. Whoever eats what is leavened from the first day through the seventh day must be cut off from Israel. [16]You are to hold a sacred assembly on the first day and another sacred assembly on the seventh day. No work may be done on those [days] except for preparing what people need to eat—you may do only that.

[17]"You are to observe the [Festival of] Unleavened Bread because on this very day I brought your ranks out of the land of Egypt. You must observe this day throughout your generations as a permanent statute. [18]You are to eat unleavened bread in the first [month], from the evening of the fourteenth day of the month until the evening of the twenty-first day. [19]Yeast must not be found in your houses for seven days. If anyone eats something leavened, that person, whether a foreign resident

or native of the land, must be cut off from the community of Israel. [20]Do not eat anything leavened; eat unleavened bread in all your homes."

[21]Then Moses summoned all the elders of Israel and said to them, "Go, select an animal from the flock according to your families, and slaughter the Passover lamb. [22]Take a cluster of hyssop, dip it in the blood that is in the basin, and brush the lintel and the two doorposts with some of the blood in the basin. None of you may go out the door of his house until morning. [23]When the LORD passes through to strike Egypt and sees the blood on the lintel and the two doorposts, He will pass over the door and not let the destroyer enter your houses to strike [you].

[24]"Keep this command permanently as a statute for you and your descendants. [25]When you enter the land that the LORD will give you as He promised, you are to observe this ritual. [26]When your children ask you, 'What does this ritual mean to you?' [27]you are to reply, 'It is the Passover sacrifice to the LORD, for He passed over the houses of the Israelites in Egypt when He struck the Egyptians and spared our homes.'" So the people bowed down and worshiped. [28]Then the Israelites went and did [this]; they did just as the LORD had commanded Moses and Aaron.

THE EXODUS

[29]Now at midnight the LORD struck every firstborn [male] in the land of Egypt, from the firstborn of Pharaoh who sat on his throne to the firstborn of the prisoner who was in the dungeon, and every firstborn of the livestock. [30]During the night Pharaoh got up, he along with all his officials and all the Egyptians, and there was a loud wailing throughout Egypt because there wasn't a house without someone dead. [31]He summoned Moses and Aaron during the night and said, "Get up, leave my people, both you and the Israelites, and go, worship the LORD as you have asked. [32]Take even your flocks and your herds as you asked, and leave, and this will also be a blessing to me."

[33]Now the Egyptians pressured the people in order to send them quickly out of the country, for they said, "We're all going to die!" [34]So the people took their dough before it was leavened, with their kneading bowls wrapped up in their clothes on their shoulders.

[35]The Israelites acted on Moses' word and asked the Egyptians for silver and gold jewelry and for clothing. [36]And the LORD gave the people such favor in the Egyptians' sight that they gave them what they requested. In this way they plundered the Egyptians.

[37]The Israelites traveled from Rameses to Succoth, about 600,000 soldiers on foot, besides their families. [38]An ethnically diverse crowd also went up with them, along with a huge number of livestock, both flocks and herds. [39]The people baked the dough they had brought out of Egypt into unleavened loaves, since it had no yeast; for when they had been driven out of Egypt they could not delay and had not prepared any provisions for themselves.

[40]The time that the Israelites lived in Egypt was 430 years. [41]At the end of 430 years, on that same day, all the divisions of the LORD went out from the land of Egypt. [42]It was a night of vigil in honor of the LORD, because He would bring them out of the land of Egypt. This same night is in honor of the LORD, a night vigil for all the Israelites throughout their generations.

FOR ACTION: Paul, in Ephesians 6:12, says: 'For we do not wrestle against flesh and blood, but against principalities, against powers, against the rulers of the darkness of this age' (NJKV). A preacher suggested that many Christian lives could be summed up in the first five words of that text. Are you a wrestling or a resting Christian? Begin to use the power that you have been given against the forces of darkness. Don't just nestle, wrestle.

DAY
98
EXODUS 15

PURSUED TO THE sea, hemmed in by Pharaoh's army, Israel has been miraculously delivered by the parting of the waters. Redemption – release from the slave-market which was Egypt – is something now to be celebrated in song. To be saved and delivered is to be reinstated in the chorus of praise of a redeeming God. So, awestruck and relieved, the people stand on the banks of the Red Sea. And relief soon bursts into song as Moses and then Miriam lead them in celebrating their mighty warrior-God who has fought His people's battles and won a stunning victory over their enemies. Here is a pointer to true biblical praise. There is a better reason for praise than our fluctuating feelings. True praise is a thankful, joyful recital of God's character and saving deeds. And nobody sings about this God more than freed slaves. 'Les miserables' learn to sing 'the music of a people who will not be slaves again'. All the more sad then to see Israel, almost immediately in the following chapters of the story, descend into grumbling and complaining! Undeterred, God works wonders of bread and water to sustain His people in their risky new freedom. The 'eagles' wings' of a merciful God who is determined not to let His people go, picks them up and carries them forward to the next stage of the story.

BIBLE READING

Exodus 15

ISRAEL'S SONG

15 Then Moses and the Israelites sang this song to the LORD. They said:

> I will sing to the LORD,
> for He is highly exalted;
> He has thrown the horse
> and its rider into the sea.
> ² The LORD is my strength and my song;
> He has become my salvation.
> This is my God, and I will praise Him,

my father's God, and I will exalt Him.

³ The LORD is a warrior;
Yahweh is His name.

⁴ He threw Pharaoh's chariots
and his army into the sea;
the elite of his officers
were drowned in the Red Sea.
⁵ The floods covered them;
they sank to the depths like a stone.
⁶ LORD, Your right hand is glorious in power.
LORD, Your right hand shattered the enemy.
⁷ You overthrew Your adversaries
by Your great majesty.
You unleashed Your burning wrath;
it consumed them like stubble.
⁸ The waters heaped up at the blast of Your nostrils;
the currents stood firm like a dam.
The watery depths congealed in the heart of the sea.
⁹ The enemy said:
"I will pursue, I will overtake,
I will divide the spoil.
My desire will be gratified at their expense.
I will draw my sword;
my hand will destroy them."
¹⁰ But You blew with Your breath,
and the sea covered them.
They sank like lead
in the mighty waters.

¹¹ LORD, who is like You among the gods?
Who is like You, glorious in holiness,
revered with praises, performing wonders?
¹² You stretched out Your right hand,
and the earth swallowed them.
¹³ You will lead the people
You have redeemed
with Your faithful love;
You will guide [them] to Your holy dwelling
with Your strength.

¹⁴ When the peoples hear, they will shudder;
   anguish will seize the inhabitants of Philistia.
¹⁵ Then the chiefs of Edom will be terrified;
   trembling will seize the leaders of Moab;
   the inhabitants of Canaan will panic;
¹⁶ and terror and dread will fall on them.
   They will be as still as a stone
   because of Your powerful arm
   until Your people pass by, Lord,
   until the people whom You purchased pass by.

¹⁷ You will bring them in and plant them
   on the mountain of Your possession;
   Lord, You have prepared the place
   for Your dwelling;
   Lord, Your hands have established the sanctuary.
¹⁸ The Lord will reign forever and ever!

¹⁹When Pharaoh's horses with his chariots and horsemen went into the sea, the Lord brought the waters of the sea back over them. But the Israelites walked through the sea on dry ground. ²⁰Then Miriam the prophetess, Aaron's sister, took a tambourine in her hand, and all the women followed her with tambourines and dancing. ²¹Miriam sang to them:

Sing to the Lord,
   for He is highly exalted;
He has thrown the horse
   and its rider into the sea.

WATER PROVIDED

²²Then Moses led Israel on from the Red Sea, and they went out to the Wilderness of Shur. They journeyed for three days in the wilderness without finding water. ²³They came to Marah, but they could not drink the water at Marah because it was bitter—that is why it was named Marah. ²⁴The people grumbled to Moses, "What are we going to drink?" ²⁵So he cried out to the Lord, and the Lord showed him a tree. When he threw it into the water, the water became drinkable.

He made a statute and ordinance for them at Marah and

He tested them there. [26]He said, "If you will carefully obey the LORD your God, do what is right in His eyes, pay attention to His commands, and keep all His statutes, I will not inflict any illness on you I inflicted on the Egyptians. For I am the LORD who heals you."

[27]Then they came to Elim, where there were 12 springs of water and 70 date palms, and they camped there by the waters.

TO PONDER: Today consider the number of deliverances God has wrought in your life. Use biblical language to express your gratitude to God. For example: I will praise You O Lord for You have triumphed gloriously in my life, saving me from destruction, keeping me from sin. I will bless You O Lord for You have become my salvation . . . and so on. Using Bible language to express your thanks to God does something to your soul. Try it and see!

DAY 99

EXODUS 19:1-4

TODAY WE ARRIVE at Mount Sinai and the momentous events that made Israel into a nation. Here a bunch of ex-slaves were forged into God's covenant partner and entrusted with His redemptive plans for the world. Israel has truly been carried here 'on eagles' wings'. God has heard their cry for help, raised up Moses to lead them to freedom, performed signs to break Pharaoh's resistance, protected them from judgment, brought them through the Red Sea, provided food and water for them in the desert and brought them to His holy mountain. This is a record of grace!

Sometimes we make the serious mistake of offsetting the Old Testament God of law against the New Testament God of grace. But Israel was never intended to 'work her passage' into God's favour and covenant by doing good works. Rather, as we shall see, the Law was given to a people already delivered and assured of a relationship with God. "Tis grace has brought them safe thus far' and it will be 'grace that leads them home' to the promised land. Now grace is set to turn relationship into covenant partnership and give them the Law.

| BIBLE READING | **Exodus 19:1-4** |

ISRAEL AT SINAI

19 In the third month, on the same day [of the month] that the Israelites had left the land of Egypt, they entered the Wilderness of Sinai. ²After they departed from Rephidim, they entered the Wilderness of Sinai and camped in the wilderness, and Israel camped there in front of the mountain.

³Moses went up [the mountain] to God, and the LORD called to him from the mountain: "This is what you must say to the house of Jacob, and explain to the Israelites: ⁴You have seen what I did to the Egyptians and how I carried you on eagles' wings and brought you to Me."

FOR PRAISE: The more we ponder Israel's deliverance the more it seems right to focus on the theme of gratitude, thanks and praise. And how better than to sing the following song. Thousands will be singing it with you today.

Amazing grace, how sweet the sound,
That saved a wretch like me
I once was lost, but now I'm found,
Was blind but now I see.

(John Newton, 1725-1807)

AS WE SAW yesterday, it makes a great difference if the God who commands us is the same God who carries us. But that He does command us is a fact we must face squarely.

Obedience, of course, is almost a dirty word in our modern world, for we have been taught to believe that the self is autonomous, that is, answerable to no one and nothing outside itself.

But in the story we are following, willing obedience is the true pathway to fulfilment and human wholeness. Whereas, 'I feel therefore I am' is the order of our day, the true essence of being a human being, said the great Jewish scholar, Abraham Heschel, can be summed up as: 'I am commanded, therefore I am.'

The Israelites who had gone into Egypt to find bread ended up making bricks under very harsh commands! God's promised freedom was not meant to be a self-serving independence but a new kind of servitude under God's 'tender' commandments. A God who has extricated His people from a tyrannical, authoritarian regime in Egypt, is hardly likely to want to initiate them into an even more repressive rule. In fact, God loves freedom more than we do! To obey the One Creator God who makes covenant is to pave the way for a just and free society where neighbours and aliens work and worship Him together.

DAY
100

EXODUS 19:5

Exodus 19:5

BIBLE
READING

ISRAEL AT SINAI

19 In the third month, on the same day [of the month] that the Israelites had left the land of Egypt, they entered the Wilderness of Sinai. ²After they departed from Rephidim, they entered the Wilderness of Sinai and camped in the wilderness, and Israel camped there in front of the mountain.

³Moses went up [the mountain] to God, and the LORD

called to him from the mountain: "This is what you must say to the house of Jacob, and explain to the Israelites: ⁴You have seen what I did to the Egyptians and how I carried you on eagles' wings and brought you to Me.

⁵Now if you will listen to Me and carefully keep My covenant, you will be My own possession out of all the peoples, although all the earth is Mine ..."

BIBLE READING

John 8:31-32

³¹So Jesus said to the Jews who had believed Him, "If you continue in My word, you really are My disciples. ³²You will know the truth, and the truth will set you free."

A COLLECT:

Almighty and everlasting God,
increase in us Your gift of faith;
that, forsaking what lies behind
and reaching out to that which is before,
we may run the way of Your commandments
and win the crown of everlasting joy through
Jesus Christ our Lord.

DAY 101

EXODUS 19:5-6
MALACHI 3:17-18

GOD NOW GRACIOUSLY states His intention to make this bunch of ex-slaves partners in what He calls 'My covenant'. By calling it 'My covenant', God is emphasising that He is entering into a covenant relationship with Israel in order to take a stage further His original covenant promise to bless Abraham and through him bless all the nations of the earth. To this end, Israel will be His treasured possession – His personal property, which is what the Hebrew word 'segullah' basically means. The idea of value may be present too. Many of you reading this may have a jewellery box or precious-stone collection. As God's

treasured possession, God's people are infinitely precious to him (cf.Mal. 3:17).

But in case Israel should ever misconstrue this special place in God's heart as an exclusive, self-centred or nationalistic relationship, the text adds the telling comment: 'all the earth is Mine.' God has still got His sights firmly fixed on all the nations, even at the precise moment when He chooses one nation to serve Him in the world! What could be clearer? Israel is, undoubtedly, the jewel in God's crown, but the crown God wears is not that of a tribal or even a national god, but the One Creator God of all the world.

BIBLE READING

Exodus 19:5-6

[5]Now if you will listen to Me and carefully keep My covenant, you will be My own possession out of all the peoples, although all the earth is Mine, [6]and you will be My kingdom of priests and My holy nation. These are the words that you are to say to the Israelites."

BIBLE READING

Malachi 3:17-18

[17]"They will be Mine," says the LORD of Hosts, "a special possession on the day I am preparing. I will have compassion on them as a man has compassion on his son who serves him. [18]So you will again see the difference between the righteous and the wicked, between one who serves God and one who does not serve Him.

PRAYER: Gracious and loving God, I thank You from the depths of my heart that though Israel were Your chosen people, they were not Your exclusive people. Your love spilled over to the other nations of the world, and through the sufferings of Your Son on the cross I am now in the fold. There is no way I could be closer to You. I am Yours and You are mine. And we are going to spend eternity together. I am so deeply thankful. Amen.

PONDERING THESE WORDS, we note that Israel is called 'a kingdom of priests' who will enjoy living under God's direct kingly rule. But they do so as priestly mediators between God and His world! As a priestly kingdom, Israel is entrusted with God's Word so that others might come to know Him. The temptation for God's people – as it was for Israel – is to forget this challenging vocation and turn God into our exclusive possession or make religion into a private, self-serving experience. But we are chosen for mission. And the priestly calling inevitably works the other way too – not only from God to the world but from the world to God. Here we are on the edge of a mystery: that Israel is called in some strange way to intercede for the world, to echo its groaning for redemption and, in an even stranger way, to embody the world's sin and suffering on God's behalf. In the end, of course, only one true Israelite, the final priestly King, was up to doing this job.

And Israel is called to be God's holy nation, devoted to God, a showcase nation, showing God to the world. 'Be holy as I am holy' becomes Israel's national charter as a prototype new humanity, reflecting God's image to the world as Adam and Eve had been intended to do. Again, only in Jesus has God begun to achieve this, but this has always been His aim.

Exodus 19:5-6

BIBLE
READING

ISRAEL AT SINAI

19 In the third month, on the same day [of the month] that the Israelites had left the land of Egypt, they entered the Wilderness of Sinai. ²After they departed from Rephidim, they entered the Wilderness of Sinai and camped in the wilderness, and Israel camped there in front of the mountain.

³Moses went up [the mountain] to God, and the LORD called to him from the mountain: "This is what you must say to the house of Jacob, and explain to the Israelites:

⁴You have seen what I did to the Egyptians and how I carried you on eagles' wings and brought you to Me. ⁵Now if you will listen to Me and carefully keep My covenant, you will be My own possession out of all the peoples, although all the earth is Mine, ⁶and you will be My kingdom of priests and My holy nation. These are the words that you are to say to the Israelites."

BIBLE READING

Leviticus 11:45

⁴⁵For I am the LORD, who brought you up from the land of Egypt to be your God, so you must be holy because I am holy.

THOUGHT: Years ago a saying that was very popular in evangelistic churches was this: 'We are saved to serve.' New converts were told, now you are a Christian your job is to win others to Christ. This emphasis is missing in many of today's churches. How deep is the passion to tell others about Jesus in your heart? In 1 Corinthians 9 Paul appears to be saying that he would do anything short of sinning to bring people to Christ. Would you?

DAY 103

EXODUS 19:16-20:2

SPECTACULAR AS THE natural phenomena at Sinai were, what was crucial was what Israel heard God say, directly in the 'ten words', and indirectly through Moses in the rest of the laws.

To maintain Israel as God's holy nation, for the world's sake, God gives the law. The 'law', we recall, does not precede God's grace, but is given to a people already redeemed.

So, as Ron Mehl calls them, these are truly 'ten(der) commandments', that reflect God's loving desire that Israel should stay free. They are given to ensure Israel's freedom in a just and equal society - the very opposite of the oppressive, slave-driven regime in Egypt.

Our modern world mistakenly believes that we become

free by rebelling against God. Ours, it is rightly said, is not so much a permissive society as a transgressive one!

Not that the 'ten words' are meant merely to produce good citizens in a conventional society. Rather, they are the means by which the Creator God's ordering of chaos at creation is re-established at the social level so that heaven's will is done on earth. Rather than being relics of an outmoded social system, therefore, the 'ten words' are signposts to the renewal of human community in Christ. They come from the One Creator God as the 'Maker's instructions' for a better world, as an act of re-creation.

Exodus 19:16—20:2

BIBLE READING

[16]On the third day, when morning came, there was thunder and lightning, a thick cloud on the mountain, and a loud trumpet sound, so that all the people in the camp shuddered. [17]Then Moses brought the people out of the camp to meet God, and they stood at the foot of the mountain. [18]Mount Sinai was completely enveloped in smoke because the LORD came down on it in fire. Its smoke went up like the smoke of a furnace, and the whole mountain shook violently. [19]As the sound of the trumpet grew louder and louder, Moses spoke and God answered him in the thunder.

[20]The LORD came down on Mount Sinai, at the top of the mountain. Then the LORD summoned Moses to the top of the mountain, and he went up. [21]The LORD directed Moses, "Go down and warn the people not to break through to see the LORD; otherwise many of them will die. [22]Even the priests who come near the LORD must purify themselves or the LORD will break out [in anger] against them."

[23]But Moses responded to the LORD, "The people cannot come up Mount Sinai, since You warned us: Put a boundary around the mountain and consider it holy." [24]And the LORD replied to him, "Go down and come back with Aaron. But the priests and the people must not break through to come up to the LORD, or He will break out [in anger] against them." [25]So Moses went down to the people and told them.

THE TEN COMMANDMENTS

20 Then God spoke all these words:

² I am the LORD your God, who brought you out of the land of Egypt, out of the place of slavery.

FOR ACTION: Spend a few moments now reading through the Ten Commandments and after each one use this responsive prayer which is based on the *Baptist Hymn Book* (UK Edition): 'Lord have mercy on me and incline my heart to keep this law.' In reading these commandments you may think God lifts the standards to almost unbelievable heights, but never forget that He also provides the power by which we reach up to them.

DAY
104
EXODUS 20:3-21

IT IS BECAUSE God is Israel's Saviour that Israel is to have no rivals to Him.

Strictly speaking, what is commanded here is not monotheism – 'you must worship only one God' – but that among rivals, 'there is only One God who has lifted you on eagles' wings, who is worthy of your love, just Me and no one else!'

Likewise, the ban on idols is meant to safeguard not so much God's transcendence as His ability to relate to us. Idols are pilloried by Isarel's prophets for being inanimate objects, unable to communicate with their devotees. But Yahweh is the Living God who speaks.

His 'jealousy' – a term taken from close relationships like marriage – does not mean that God is spiteful or capricious but that He cares passionately about His involvement with His people so that He alone deserves their undivided loyalty.

From the first four commands which guard Israel's bond with God, flow the last six – governing Israel's relationships within the covenant community, and beyond. That free, just and loving society God wants His people to enjoy, depends entirely on their maintaining a right relationship with Him. The 'ten words' thus show us not only 'what we must do' but what God is like.

Israel is entrusted with the sacred task of embodying that God-likeness for the rest of the world.

Exodus 20:3-21

THE TEN COMMANDMENTS

20 Then God spoke all these words:

² I am the LORD your God, who brought you out of the land of Egypt, out of the place of slavery.

³ Do not have other gods besides Me.

⁴ Do not make an idol for yourself, whether in the shape of anything in the heavens above or on the earth below or in the waters under the earth. ⁵You must not bow down to them or worship them; for I, the LORD your God, am a jealous God, punishing the children for the fathers' sin, to the third and fourth [generations] of those who hate Me, ⁶but showing faithful love to a thousand [generations] of those who love Me and keep My commands.

⁷ Do not misuse the name of the LORD your God, because the LORD will punish anyone who misuses His name.

⁸ Remember to dedicate the Sabbath day: ⁹You are to labor six days and do all your work, ¹⁰but the seventh day is a Sabbath to the LORD your God. You must not do any work—you, your son or daughter, your male or female slave, your livestock, or the foreigner who is within your gates. ¹¹For the LORD made the heavens and the earth, the sea, and everything in them in six days; then He rested on the seventh day. Therefore the LORD blessed the Sabbath day and declared it holy.

¹² Honor your father and your mother so that you may have a long life in the land that the LORD your God is giving you.

¹³ Do not murder.

[14] Do not commit adultery.

[15] Do not steal.

[16] Do not give false testimony against your neighbor.

[17] Do not covet your neighbor's house. Do not covet your neighbor's wife, his male or female slave, his ox or donkey, or anything that belongs to your neighbor.

THE PEOPLE'S REACTION

[18] All the people witnessed the thunder and lightning, the sound of the trumpet, and the mountain [surrounded by] smoke. When the people saw [it] they trembled and stood at a distance. [19]"You speak to us, and we will listen," they said to Moses, "but don't let God speak to us, or we will die."

[20] Moses responded to the people, "Don't be afraid, for God has come to test you, so that you will fear Him and will not sin." [21]And the people remained standing at a distance as Moses approached the thick darkness where God was.

FOR PRAISE: In response to what has been said today, praise God that He is the only one who can fill your deepest longing, give you new life and answer your heart's cry. Then say or sing the following:

The dearest idol I have known
Whate'er that idol be
Help me tear it from Thy throne
And worship only Thee.

(William Cowper, 1731-1800)

AS GOD'S COVENANT with Israel is ratified, two features in the ritual involved merit our attention: the book and the blood.

Moses reads from the Book of the Covenant and gains the people's assent to what is said in God's Word. He sprinkles the blood over the people and on the altar, thus confirming the bond-in-blood between God and His people. The mention of burnt offerings and fellowship offerings reminds us that the sacrificial principle was at the heart of Israel's worship. This doubtless echoed the earlier substitutionary blood-shedding of the Passover Lamb and became institutionalised in Leviticus as the regular means of grace by which a sinful people could repair and sustain the covenant relationship.

What follows in our text is that Moses and the group with him 'see' God – or rather they see only what looked like a sapphire pavement beneath His feet. Their gaze is down and what they see is beyond words to describe. But 'seeing' what cannot be seen or uttered, they eat and drink before God's face. As we gaze on 'things unseen' and words fail us for joy, we too can re-affirm the bond-in-blood between us and the Lord. As we eat bread and drink wine in our never-to-be-forgotten covenant meal, we renew our participation in God's story.

Exodus 24:1-18

BIBLE
READING

THE COVENANT CEREMONY

24 Then He said to Moses, "Go up to the LORD, you and Aaron, Nadab, and Abihu, and 70 of Israel's elders, and bow in worship at a distance. ²Moses alone is to approach the LORD, but the others are not to approach, and the people are not to go up with him."

³Moses came and told the people all the commands of the LORD and all the ordinances. Then all the people responded with a single voice, "We will do everything that the LORD has

commanded." [4]And Moses wrote down all the words of the LORD. He rose early the next morning and set up an altar and 12 pillars for the 12 tribes of Israel at the base of the mountain. [5]Then he sent out young Israelite men, and they offered burnt offerings and sacrificed bulls as fellowship offerings to the LORD. [6]Moses took half the blood and set it in basins; the [other] half of the blood he sprinkled on the altar. [7]He then took the covenant scroll and read [it] aloud to the people. They responded, "We will do and obey everything that the LORD has commanded."

[8]Moses took the blood, sprinkled it on the people, and said, "This is the blood of the covenant that the LORD has made with you concerning all these words."

[9]Then Moses went up with Aaron, Nadab, and Abihu, and 70 of Israel's elders, [10]and they saw the God of Israel. Beneath His feet was something like a pavement made of sapphire stone, as clear as the sky itself. [11]God did not harm the Israelite nobles; they saw Him, and they ate and drank.

[12]The LORD said to Moses, "Come up to Me on the mountain and stay there so that I may give you the stone tablets with the law and commands I have written for their instruction."

[13]So Moses arose with his assistant Joshua, and went up the mountain of God. [14]He told the elders, "Wait here for us until we return to you. Aaron and Hur are here with you. Whoever has a dispute should go to them." [15]When Moses went up the mountain, the cloud covered it. [16]The glory of the LORD settled on Mount Sinai, and the cloud covered it for six days. On the seventh day He called to Moses from the cloud. [17]The appearance of the LORD's glory to the Israelites was like a consuming fire on the mountaintop. [18]Moses entered the cloud as he went up the mountain, and he remained on the mountain 40 days and 40 nights.

TO PONDER: Whenever you attend the Table of Communion (the Lord's Supper, Eucharist, etc) what are the thoughts that go through your mind? There are many no doubt. The main thought in our minds, however, ought to be this – Lord Jesus You have given Yourself for me, in a fresh act of commitment I now give myself to You.

Take my heart, Lord. Take my life – I offer myself to You completely. I am Yours. Amen.

DAY 106
EXODUS 25:1-22; 26:30

NO PART OF Scripture has suffered more from over-eager students in the search for spiritual analogies to the Christian life than this description of the tabernacle. But if the writer to the Hebrews is our guide, we must not overpress the details of our interpretation but rather ask: What does this tell us about God and His intentions towards His people?

Firstly, in line with his stated aim (Exod. 15:17), the tabernacle is a portable sanctuary for God so that He can dwell among His people (25:8) during their wilderness wanderings. From walking in the Garden of Eden conversing with Adam and Eve in the cool of the day, to the pillar of cloud and fire, God has already shown His intense desire to be present with His human partners.

Secondly, Moses was to build the tabernacle 'according to the plan for it that you have been shown on the mountain' (26:30). This implies that the earthly structure is a symbol of a heavenly reality. Because God is King over Israel, the tabernacle, and later the Temple, are not only His earthly address but His royal palace. The ark of the covenant – the chief article of furniture in the sanctuary – is later described as the footstool of His throne; that is, the earthly footstool of God's heavenly throne. When God's people worship, they know the King is among them.

BIBLE READING

Exodus 25:1-22

OFFERINGS TO BUILD THE TABERNACLE

25 The LORD spoke to Moses: [2]"Tell the Israelites to take an offering for Me. You are to take My offering from everyone whose heart stirs him [to give]. [3]This is the offering you are to receive from them: gold, silver, and bronze; [4]blue, purple, and scarlet yarn; fine linen and goat hair; [5]ram skins dyed red and manatee skins; acacia wood; [6]oil for the light; spices for the anointing oil and for the fragrant incense; [7]and onyx along with [other] gemstones for mounting on the ephod and breastpiece.

[8]"They are to make a sanctuary for Me so that I may dwell among them. [9]You must make [it] according to all that I show you—the design of the tabernacle as well as the design of all its furnishings."

THE ARK

[10]"They are to make an ark of acacia wood, 45 inches long, 27 inches wide, and 27 inches high. [11]Overlay it with pure gold; overlay it both inside and out. Also make a gold molding all around it. [12]Cast four gold rings for it and place [them] on its four feet, two rings on one side and two rings on the other side. [13]Make poles of acacia wood and overlay them with gold. [14]Insert the poles into the rings on the sides of the ark in order to carry the ark with them. [15]The poles are to remain in the rings of the ark; they must not be removed from it. [16]Put the [tablets of the] testimony that I will give you into the ark. [17]Make a mercy seat of pure gold, 45 inches long and 27 inches wide. [18]Make two cherubim of gold; make them of hammered work at the two ends of the mercy seat. [19]Make one cherub at one end and one cherub at the other end. Make the cherubim of one piece with the mercy seat at its two ends. [20]The cherubim are to have wings spread out above, covering the mercy seat with their wings, and are to face one another. The faces of the cherubim should be toward the mercy seat. [21]Set the mercy seat on top of the ark and put the testimony that I will give you into the ark. [22]I will meet with you there above the mercy seat, between the two cherubim that are over the ark of the testimony; I will speak with you from there about all that I command you regarding the Israelites.

Exodus 26:30

³⁰You are to set up the tabernacle according to the plan for it that you have been shown on the mountain.

PRAYER: My Father and my God I am so grateful that You are not only transcendent, far above all, but also imminent, close at hand. I do not have to go up to You; You are here in my heart. What love you must have, to come to earth in the Person of Your Son to live amongst us and die for our sins. You are so big that You fill the heavens yet so small that You can fill my heart. How can this be? Yet I know it to be so. Thank You, dear Father. Amen.

DAY 107

EXODUS 31:12-18

IF IT IS clear from Genesis that human beings are the crown of God's creation, then it is equally clear that the Sabbath is the goal of creation.

God's human creatures are indeed the peak of His work, with exalted responsibility over everything else He has made. But Sabbath represents what all creation – including humans – are moving towards. For Israel, God's immediate Sabbath rest was the promised land, but this in turn becomes a symbol of the ultimate rest of God's salvation in the coming kingdom when God 'rests' from His new creation labours. Israel was to keep this memory and hope alive in the world by keeping Sabbath. Israel kept Sabbath as a badge of its covenant identity as the steward of the world's future. The practical benefits of Sabbath were obvious, too, with animals and fields given regular respite from being worked. For ex-slaves above all, Sabbath was a treasured gift, reminding them of the grace that had rescued them from the round-the-clock production lines of Egypt's slave economy. Sabbath was not meant to rob life of fun or encourage the work-shy but to enable God's people to know God better (v.13). Just as God's six-day working week dignifies the work we do, so God's Sabbath-rest reminds us weekly that we are called to be worshippers not workaholics.

BIBLE READING

Exodus 31:12-18

OBSERVING THE SABBATH

[12]The LORD said to Moses: [13]"Tell the Israelites: You must observe My Sabbaths, for it is a sign between Me and you throughout your generations, so that you will know that I am the LORD who sets you apart. [14]Observe the Sabbath, for it is holy to you. Whoever profanes it must be put to death. If anyone does work on it, that person must be cut off from his people. [15]For six days work may be done, but on the seventh day there must be a Sabbath of complete rest, dedicated to the LORD. Anyone who does work on the Sabbath day must be put to death. [16]The Israelites must observe the Sabbath, celebrating it throughout their generations as a perpetual covenant. [17]It is a sign forever between Me and the Israelites, for in six days the LORD made the heavens and the earth, but on the seventh day He rested and was refreshed."

THE TWO STONE TABLETS

[18]When He finished speaking with Moses on Mount Sinai, He gave him the two tablets of the testimony, stone tablets inscribed by the finger of God.

THOUGHT: David Adam once wrote a prayer on the theme of 'Work'. Today you may like to pray the following words based on that prayer:

In the quiet of the morning, In the new day that is dawning
Thy Kingdom come
In my tasks and my employment, In my leisure and enjoyment
Thy Kingdom come
All day, until its very ending, Praise to You I shall be sending
Thy Kingdom come.

TODAY'S READING COMES as a shock after what we have been reading of Israel's redemption and covenant with God and God's desire to dwell among His people. It puts the whole Exodus experiment at risk. Barely is the ink dry on the precious bond between them than Israel falls from grace and lapses into idolatry. It is not so much that the people want another god, as that – unsettled perhaps by Moses' absence – they hanker after a visible symbol of God's presence. Whatever the reason, they now seek to honour God in an illegitimate way. Coming down the mountain, Joshua hears what he takes to be the noise of war in the camp. But Moses hears otherwise, hearing not the sound of heroes exulting, nor the sound of the vanquished lamenting but merely the sound of random singing! Such idolatrous worship is a sad parody of the praise of Exodus 15. Celebration without victory, rejoicing without reality, neither high praise nor deep lament, just a meaningless round of songs to make people feel good about themselves.

Aaron's excuse is that he was going with the flow of popular demand and giving the people what they want! That's where idolatry starts and immorality isn't far behind.

DAY
108
EXODUS 32:1-6,15-29

Exodus 32:1-6,15-29

BIBLE READING

THE GOLDEN CALF

32 When the people saw that Moses delayed in coming down from the mountain, they gathered around Aaron and said to him, "Come, make us a god who will go before us because this Moses, the man who brought us up from the land of Egypt—we don't know what has happened to him!"

²Then Aaron replied to them, "Take off the gold rings that are on the ears of your wives, your sons, and your daughters and bring [them] to me." ³So all the people took off the gold rings that were on their ears and brought [them] to Aaron.

⁴He took [the gold] from their hands, fashioned it with an engraving tool, and made it into an image of a calf.

Then they said, "Israel, this is your God, who brought you up from the land of Egypt!"

⁵When Aaron saw [this], he built an altar before it; then he made an announcement: "There will be a festival to the LORD tomorrow." ⁶Early the next morning they arose, offered burnt offerings, and presented fellowship offerings. The people sat down to eat and drink, then got up to revel.

· · · · · · · · · ·

¹⁵Then Moses turned and went down the mountain with the two tablets of the testimony in his hands. They were inscribed on both sides—inscribed front and back. ¹⁶The tablets were the work of God, and the writing was God's writing, engraved on the tablets.

¹⁷When Joshua heard the sound of the people as they shouted, he said to Moses, "There is a sound of war in the camp."

¹⁸But Moses replied:

> It's not the sound of a victory cry
> and not the sound of a cry of defeat;
> I hear the sound of singing!

¹⁹As he approached the camp and saw the calf and the dancing, Moses became enraged and threw the tablets out of his hands, smashing them at the base of the mountain. ²⁰Then he took the calf they had made, burned [it] up, and ground [it] to powder. He scattered [the powder] over the surface of the water and forced the Israelites to drink [the water].

²¹Then Moses asked Aaron, "What did this people do to you that you have led them into [such] a grave sin?"

²²"Don't be enraged, my lord," Aaron replied. "You yourself know that the people are [intent] on evil. ²³They said to me, 'Make us a god who will go before us because this Moses, the man who brought us up from the land of Egypt—we don't know what has happened to him!' ²⁴So I said to them, 'Whoever has gold, take it off,' and they gave [it] to me. When I threw it into the fire, out came this calf!"

²⁵Moses saw that the people were out of control, for

Aaron had let them get out of control, so that they would be vulnerable to their enemies. [26]And Moses stood at the camp's entrance and said, "Whoever is for the LORD, [come] to me." And all the Levites gathered around him. [27]He told them, "This is what the LORD, the God of Israel, says, 'Every man fasten his sword to his side; go back and forth through the camp from entrance to entrance, and each of you kill his brother, his friend, and his neighbor.'" [28]The Levites did as Moses commanded, and about 3,000 men fell dead that day among the people. [29]Afterwards Moses said, "Today you have been dedicated to the LORD, since each man went against his son and his brother. Therefore you have brought a blessing on yourselves today."

> TO PONDER: Is it possible that we can engage in singing 'the songs of Zion' in an effort to feel good about ourselves rather than focusing on how our singing can bring honour and glory to the Lord? How careful we should be that we enter into worship not for our own sake or to give ourselves a spiritual lift but to glorify the Lord. In the glorifying of God the lift comes, but we ought not to do it for our own sake but for His.

THIS TRAGIC INCIDENT with the golden calf, as we have seen, threatens to bring the Exodus story to an abrupt end and to unravel all God's future plans. God's reaction shows Him in a mood to disown Israel, because, as He insists to Moses, '... your people you brought up from the land of Egypt have acted corruptly' (v.7). As if to forestall any possible intervention from Moses, God then tells him, 'Now leave Me alone, so that My anger can burn against them ...' (v.10), even offering to start all over again with Moses as His new Abraham by making him into a 'great nation'!

DAY
109
EXODUS 32:7-14,30-35

Moses' intercession saves the day. He pleads God's previous saving power, argues that God's reputation is at stake - what will the neighbour-nations think? -

and then reminds God of His long-standing covenant promises made to the patriarchs. As a result the Lord relents. What a prayer. Boldly Moses holds God to His own integrity of word and action and offers his own life in Israel's stead. Prayer urges God to be God and to act in Godlike ways, true to His own nature. What an amazing God, too, who is willing to be entreated in ways that change the course of history. Even more amazingly, one day, this same God would offer His own life to make atonement for our sins.

BIBLE READING

Exodus 32:7-14,30-35

7The LORD spoke to Moses: "Go down at once! For your people you brought up from the land of Egypt have acted corruptly. 8They have quickly turned from the way I commanded them; they have made for themselves an image of a calf. They have bowed down to it, sacrificed to it, and said, 'Israel, this is your God, who brought you up from the land of Egypt.'" 9The LORD also said to Moses: "I have seen this people, and they are indeed a stiff-necked people. 10Now leave Me alone, so that My anger can burn against them and I can destroy them. Then I will make you into a great nation."

11But Moses interceded with the LORD his God: "LORD, why does Your anger burn against Your people You brought out of the land of Egypt with great power and a strong hand? 12Why should the Egyptians say, 'He brought them out with an evil intent to kill them in the mountains and wipe them off the face of the earth'? Turn from Your great anger and change Your mind about this disaster [planned] for Your people. 13Remember that You swore to Your servants Abraham, Isaac, and Israel by Yourself and declared to them, 'I will make your offspring as numerous as the stars of the sky and will give your offspring all this land that I have promised, and they will inherit [it] forever.'" 14So the LORD changed His mind about the disaster He said He would bring on His people.

• • • • • • • • •

[30]The following day Moses said to the people, "You have committed a great sin. Now I will go up to the LORD; perhaps I will be able to pay for your sin."

[31]So Moses returned to the LORD and said, "Oh, this people has committed a great sin; they have made for themselves a god of gold. [32]Now if You would only forgive their sin. But if not, please erase me from the book You have written."

[33]The LORD replied to Moses: "Whoever has sinned against Me I will erase from My book. [34]Now go, lead the people to the place I told you about; see, My angel will go before you. But on the day I settle accounts, I will hold them accountable for their sin." [35]And the LORD inflicted a plague on the people for what they did with the calf Aaron had made.

FOR PRAISE: Do you know the first verse of the hymn that follows? Sing it to the Lord. Let it be your response to the reading today.

Great God of wonders, all Thy ways
Display Thine attributes divine
But countless acts of pardoning grace
Beyond Thine other words shine
Who is a pardoning God like Thee?
Or who has grace so rich and free?

THAT ISRAEL'S 'FALL' has not aborted the story of redemption is due to Moses' timely intervention. But the situation is still serious as God refuses to travel any further with His stubborn people in case He destroys them en route. Has Moses' intercession changed nothing? If so then to build the tabernacle is pointless since God will not come and occupy it, and the first 31 chapters of Exodus are undone. Everything hangs in the balance. Moses again steps into the gap and presses his case like a faithful friend, in a 'face to face' meeting with God: 'You want me to lead, Lord, but who will follow me? I may have found favour with You

DAY
110
EXODUS 33:1-23

but what about the people, do they have a future?' 'My presence will go with you Moses.'

But Moses persists. Without Your ongoing presence we have an unenviable future (v.15), uncertain of Your favour (v.16). Without Your presence we will lose our distinctive identity in the world and who else will be Your witnesses? This is powerful persuasion encouraged by God's grace and matched by God's response. Emboldened further, Moses asks to see God's glory but is allowed a glimpse of God's back, not His face. This was the closest Moses got to the glory until, on another day and mountain, he found himself talking with Jesus who was transfigured before his very eyes.

BIBLE READING

Exodus 33:1-23

THE TENT OUTSIDE THE CAMP

33 The LORD spoke to Moses: "Go, leave here, you and the people you brought up from the land of Egypt, to the land I promised to Abraham, Isaac, and Jacob, saying: I will give it to your offspring. [2] I will send an angel ahead of you and will drive out the Canaanites, Amorites, Hittites, Perizzites, Hivites, and Jebusites. [3] [Go up] to a land flowing with milk and honey. But I will not go with you because you are a stiff-necked people; otherwise, I might destroy you on the way." [4] When the people heard this bad news, they mourned and didn't put on their jewelry.

[5] For the LORD said to Moses: "Tell the Israelites: You are a stiff-necked people. If I went with you for a single moment, I would destroy you. Now take off your jewelry, and I will decide what to do with you." [6] So the Israelites [remained] stripped of their jewelry from Mount Horeb [onward].

[7] Now Moses took a tent and set it up outside the camp, far away from the camp; he called it the tent of meeting. Anyone who wanted to consult the LORD would go to the tent of meeting that was outside the camp. [8] Whenever Moses went out to the tent, all the people would stand up, each one at the door of his tent, and they would watch Moses until he entered

the tent. [9]When Moses entered the tent, the pillar of cloud would come down and remain at the entrance to the tent, and [the LORD] would speak with Moses. [10]As all the people saw the pillar of cloud remaining at the entrance to the tent, they would stand up, then bow in worship, each one at the door of his tent. [11]The LORD spoke with Moses face to face, just as a man speaks with his friend. Then Moses would return to the camp, but his assistant, the young man Joshua son of Nun, would not leave the inside of the tent.

THE LORD'S GLORY

[12]Moses said to the LORD, "Look, You have told me, 'Lead this people up,' but You have not let me know whom You will send with me. You said, 'I know you by name, and you have also found favor in My sight.' [13]Now if I have indeed found favor in Your sight, please teach me Your ways, and I will know You and find favor in Your sight. Now consider that this nation is Your people."

[14]Then He replied, "My presence will go [with you], and I will give you rest."

[15]"If Your presence does not go," Moses responded to Him, "don't make us go up from here. [16]How will it be known that I and Your people have found favor in Your sight unless You go with us? I and Your people will be distinguished [by this] from all the other people on the face of the earth."

[17]The LORD answered Moses, "I will do this very thing you have asked, for you have found favor in My sight, and I know you by name."

[18]Then Moses said, "Please, let me see Your glory."

[19]He said, "I will cause all My goodness to pass in front of you, and I will proclaim the name Yahweh before you. I will be gracious to whom I will be gracious, and I will have compassion on whom I will have compassion." [20]But He answered, "You cannot see My face, for no one can see Me and live." [21]The LORD said, "Here is a place near Me. You are to stand on the rock, [22]and when My glory passes by, I will put you in the crevice of the rock and cover you with My hand until I have passed by. [23]Then I will take My hand away, and you will see My back, but My face will not be seen."

PRAYER: O Lord that is my prayer also. If Your Presence does not go with me into the day and every day that is ahead then I just don't want to go. The thought of You not being at my side is something I do not want to contemplate. You designed me to function best when I am dependent on You. You are my hope, my strength, my light, my way. I do not want to take one step into the future without You. Stay with me, dear Father. Always. In Jesus' name. Amen.

DAY 111

EXODUS 34:1-35

THESE VERSES REPRESENT the closest Israel came to God's autobiography.

The Lord is 'compassionate and gracious', tender towards sufferers and full of unmerited favour. When a partner has a short fuse, life is tense, but thankfully, God is 'slow to anger, and rich in faithful love' (v.6). God is full of '*hesed*' – that tough, covenant-love which matches His tenderness and guarantees the continuance of the covenant bond. The outflow of this is God's faithfulness – a consistency of purpose and commitment that reflects His own integrity. And this faithful loving 'abounds' (NIV) so that God is not grudging or frugal but is as quick to love as He is slow to anger. His reservoir of patience is no more depleted than is His readiness to be forgiving.

But the text reminds us sharply that God is not complacent about sin, that sin incurs judgment, and that seeds sown in one generation are often tragically reaped in another.

Moses, seeking reassurance about Israel's future, confesses the people's stubborn sinfulness, and is granted a renewal of the covenant (vv.10-28). Moses is personally reaffirmed in his mediatorial role by the radiance that streams from his face when he has spoken with the Lord. So awesome is this speech and sight that Moses has to veil his face whenever he speaks to the people on God's behalf (vv.33-35).

Exodus 34:1-35

NEW STONE TABLETS

34 The LORD said to Moses, "Cut two stone tablets like the first ones, and I will write on them the words that were on the first tablets, which you broke. ²Be prepared by morning. Come up Mount Sinai in the morning and stand before Me on the mountaintop. ³No one may go up with you; in fact, no one must be seen anywhere on the mountain. Even the flocks and herds are not to graze in front of that mountain."

⁴Moses cut two stone tablets like the first ones. He got up early in the morning, and taking the two stone tablets in his hand, he climbed Mount Sinai, just as the LORD had commanded him.

⁵The LORD came down in a cloud, stood with him there, and proclaimed [His] name Yahweh. ⁶Then the LORD passed in front of him and proclaimed:

Yahweh—Yahweh is a compassionate and gracious God, slow to anger and rich in faithful love and truth, ⁷maintaining faithful love to a thousand [generations], forgiving wrongdoing, rebellion, and sin. But He will not leave [the guilty] unpunished, bringing the consequences of the fathers' wrongdoing on the children and grandchildren to the third and fourth generation.

⁸Moses immediately bowed down to the ground and worshiped. ⁹Then he said, "My Lord, if I have indeed found favor in Your sight, my Lord, please go with us. Even though this is a stiff-necked people, forgive our wrongdoing and sin, and accept us as Your own possession."

COVENANT OBLIGATIONS

¹⁰And the LORD responded: "Look, I am making a covenant. I will perform wonders in the presence of all your people that have never been done in all the earth or in any nation. All the people you live among will see the LORD's work, for what I am doing with you is awe-inspiring. ¹¹Observe what I command you today. I am going to drive out before you the Amorites,

Canaanites, Hittites, Perizzites, Hivites, and Jebusites. [12]Be careful not to make a treaty with the inhabitants of the land that you are going to enter; otherwise, they will become a snare among you. [13]Instead, you must tear down their altars, smash their sacred pillars, and chop down their Asherah poles. [14]You are to never bow down to another god because the LORD, being jealous by nature, is a jealous God.

[15]"Do not make a treaty with the inhabitants of the land, or else when they prostitute themselves with their gods and sacrifice to their gods, they will invite you, and you will eat of their sacrifice. [16]Then you will take some of their daughters [as brides] for your sons. Their daughters will prostitute themselves with their gods and cause your sons to prostitute themselves with their gods.

[17]"Do not make cast images of gods for yourselves.

[18]"Observe the Festival of Unleavened Bread. You are to eat unleavened bread for seven days at the appointed time in the month of Abib as I commanded you. For you came out of Egypt in the month of Abib.

[19]"The firstborn male from every womb belongs to Me, including all your male livestock, the firstborn of cattle or sheep. [20]You must redeem the firstborn of a donkey with a sheep, but if you do not redeem [it], break its neck. You must redeem all the firstborn of your sons. No one is to appear before Me empty-handed.

[21]"You are to labor six days but you must rest on the seventh day; you must even rest during plowing and harvesting times.

[22]"Observe the Festival of Weeks with the firstfruits of the wheat harvest, and the Festival of Ingathering at the turn of the [agricultural] year. [23]Three times a year all your males are to appear before the Lord GOD, the God of Israel. [24]For I will drive out nations before you and enlarge your territory. No one will covet your land when you go up three times a year to appear before the LORD your God.

[25]"Do not present the blood for My sacrifice with anything leavened. The sacrifice of the Passover Festival must not remain until morning.

[26]"Bring the best firstfruits of your land to the house of the LORD your God.

"You must not boil a young goat in its mother's milk."

²⁷The Lord also said to Moses, "Write down these words, for I have made a covenant with you and with Israel based on these words."

²⁸Moses was there with the Lord 40 days and 40 nights; he did not eat bread or drink water. He wrote down on the tablets the words of the covenant—the Ten Commandments.

MOSES' RADIANT FACE

²⁹As Moses descended from Mount Sinai—with the two tablets of the testimony in his hands as he descended the mountain—he did not realize that the skin of his face shone as a result of his speaking with the Lord. ³⁰When Aaron and all the Israelites saw Moses, the skin of his face shone! They were afraid to come near him. ³¹But Moses called out to them, so Aaron and all the leaders of the community returned to him, and Moses spoke to them. ³²Afterwards all the Israelites came near, and he commanded them everything the Lord had told him on Mount Sinai. ³³When Moses had finished speaking with them, he put a veil over his face. ³⁴But whenever Moses went before the Lord to speak with Him, he would remove the veil until he came out. After he came out, he would tell the Israelites what he had been commanded, ³⁵and the Israelites would see that Moses' face was radiant. Then Moses would put the veil over his face again until he went to speak with the Lord.

THOUGHT: How balanced are the qualities of compassion and judgment in the heart of our heavenly Father. Verses 6 and 7 are 'the closest Israel came to God's autobiography'. Think about your own life for a moment: are you slow to anger, abounding in love and faithfulness, but not complacent about sin? These are qualities that all of us ought to possess – and they ought to be reflected in our autobiography too.

DAY
112

**EXODUS 35:4-11a,
29-36:1; 39:32,42-43;
40:16-38**

IF, AS WE noted a day or two ago, we stand back from over-elaborate attempts to interpret the details of the tabernacle, we see a big picture. In fact, the tabernacle is less a coded model of salvation and more a wonderful microcosm of creation. It represents a creation-in-miniature, marked by all the features found in the first chapter of Genesis. Notice the following: the seven times the Lord spoke to Moses, ending with the Sabbath; the bringing of all the rich resources of God's world into order and beauty; the action of the creative Spirit of God; the way the work is said to be completed; the way Moses inspects the work, pronounces himself satisfied and blesses it; the commencement date on the first day of the first month ... all of these features echo the Genesis 1 account.

In other words just as the Sabbath sanctifies time, so the tabernacle sanctifies space. In the midst of a fallen, disordered, rebellious world, there is one place where the original beauty and design and purpose of creation as a vehicle for God's glorious presence can be seen! Where God dwells with Israel, on this small scale it is 'just as it was at the beginning'.

The tabernacle also points forwards, a prophetic parable of 'what will be at the end' in the final splendour of God's new creation where He will dwell with His people for ever.

BIBLE
READING

Exodus 35:4-11a,29-36:1

BUILDING THE TABERNACLE

⁴Then Moses said to the entire Israelite community, "This is what the LORD has commanded: ⁵Take up an offering for the LORD among you. Let everyone whose heart is willing bring this as the LORD's offering: gold, silver, and bronze; ⁶blue, purple, and scarlet yarn; fine linen and goat hair; ⁷ram skins dyed red and manatee skins; acacia wood; ⁸oil for the light; spices for the anointing oil and for the fragrant incense; ⁹and onyx with gemstones to mount on the ephod and breastpiece.

[10]"Let all the skilled craftsmen among you come and make everything that the LORD has commanded: [11]the tabernacle—

. . . .

[29]So the Israelites brought a freewill offering to the LORD, all the men and women whose hearts prompted them to bring [something] for all the work that the LORD, through Moses, had commanded to be done.

BEZALEL AND OHOLIAB

[30]Moses then said to the Israelites: "Look, the LORD has appointed by name Bezalel son of Uri, son of Hur, of the tribe of Judah. [31]He has filled him with God's Spirit, with wisdom, understanding, and ability in every kind of craft [32]to design artistic works in gold, silver, and bronze, [33]to cut gemstones for mounting, and to carve wood for work in every kind of artistic craft. [34]He has also given both him and Oholiab son of Ahisamach, of the tribe of Dan, [the ability] to teach [others]. [35]He has filled them with skill to do all the work of a gem cutter; a designer; an embroiderer in blue, purple, and scarlet yarn and fine linen; and a weaver. They can do every kind of craft and design

36 artistic designs. [1]Bezalel, Oholiab, and all the skilled people are to work based on everything the LORD has commanded. The LORD has given them wisdom and understanding to know how to do all the work of constructing the sanctuary."

Exodus 39:32,42-43

MOSES' INSPECTION OF THE TABERNACLE

[32]So all the work for the tabernacle, the tent of meeting, was finished. The Israelites did everything just as the LORD had commanded Moses.

. . . .

[42]The Israelites had done all the work according to everything the LORD had commanded Moses. [43]Moses inspected all the work they had accomplished. They had done just as the LORD commanded. Then Moses blessed them.

BIBLE READING

Exodus 40:16-38

¹⁶Moses did everything just as the LORD had commanded him. ¹⁷The tabernacle was set up in the first month of the second year, on the first [day] of the month. ¹⁸Moses set up the tabernacle: he laid its bases, positioned its planks, inserted its crossbars, and set up its posts. ¹⁹Then he spread the tent over the tabernacle and put the covering of the tent on top of it, just as the LORD had commanded Moses.

²⁰Moses took the testimony and placed [it] in the ark, and attached the poles to the ark. He set the mercy seat on top of the ark. ²¹He brought the ark into the tabernacle, put up the veil for the screen, and screened off the ark of the testimony, just as the LORD had commanded him.

²²Moses placed the table in the tent of meeting on the north side of the tabernacle, outside the veil. ²³He arranged the bread on it before the LORD, just as the LORD had commanded him. ²⁴He also put the lampstand in the tent of meeting opposite the table on the south side of the tabernacle ²⁵and set up the lamps before the LORD, just as the LORD had commanded him.

²⁶Moses also installed the gold altar in the tent of meeting, in front of the veil, ²⁷and burned fragrant incense on it, just as the LORD had commanded him. ²⁸He put up the screen at the entrance to the tabernacle. ²⁹Then he placed the altar of burnt offering at the entrance to the tabernacle, the tent of meeting, and offered the burnt offering and the grain offering on it, just as the LORD had commanded him.

³⁰He set the basin between the tent of meeting and the altar and put water in it for washing. ³¹Moses, Aaron, and his sons washed their hands and feet from it. ³²They washed whenever they came to the tent of meeting and approached the altar, just as the LORD had commanded Moses.

³³Next Moses set up the surrounding courtyard for the tabernacle and the altar and hung a screen for the gate of the courtyard. So Moses finished the work.

THE LORD'S GLORY

³⁴The cloud covered the tent of meeting, and the glory of the LORD filled the tabernacle. ³⁵Moses was unable to enter

the tent of meeting because the cloud rested on it, and the glory of the LORD filled the tabernacle.

³⁶The Israelites set out whenever the cloud was taken up from the tabernacle throughout all the stages of their journey. ³⁷If the cloud was not taken up, they did not set out until the day it was taken up. ³⁸For the cloud of the LORD was over the tabernacle by day, and there was a fire inside the cloud by night, visible to the entire house of Israel throughout all the stages of their journey.

TO PONDER: How grateful we should be that God's presence is everywhere. Let these words rest on your heart: 'How lovely is Your dwelling place, LORD of Hosts. I long and yearn for the courts of the LORD; my heart and flesh cry out for the living God. Even a sparrow finds a home, and a swallow, a nest for herself ... near Your altars, LORD of Hosts, my King and my God' (Psa. 84:1-4).

FORTY YEARS OF disobedient wandering have elapsed since the Exodus and Sinai, and now, on the verge of the promised land, Moses gives a second reading of the law ('*deutero-nomos*') climaxed by a renewal and expansion of the original covenant.

DAY 113

DEUTERONOMY 4:1-40

Today's text urges Israel to live up to her unique story by remembering the Exodus (vv.15-20) and Sinai (vv.10-14) as they cross over into the land (vv.21-24), warning that failure will bring exile (vv.25-30).

Israel must not forget the covenant because God never will (vv.23,31).

Israel is distinctive because her God is unique.

No other nation has ever heard the Creator God speak out of the fire or been singled out for redemptive help, only Israel (vv.32-34). The world that watches and waits for Israel's story to unfold for its salvation depends upon a faithful Israel (v.6)! That God chooses to save the world through one particular nation has to many always been a scandal.

Old Testament scholar, Chris Wright, brilliantly draws out the implications of this when he says: 'The uniqueness of Jesus as the Messiah of Israel and thereby as Saviour of the world, is grounded in the uniqueness of Israel itself and of Yahweh as God, for according to the New Testament Jesus embodied the one and incarnated the other.'

BIBLE READING

Deuteronomy 4:1-40

CALL TO OBEDIENCE

4 "Now, Israel, listen to the statutes and ordinances I am teaching you to follow, so that you may live, enter, and take possession of the land the LORD, the God of your fathers, is giving you. ²You must not add anything to what I command you or take anything away from it, so that you may keep the commands of the LORD your God I am giving you. ³Your eyes have seen what the LORD did at Baal-peor, for the LORD your God destroyed every one of you who followed Baal of Peor. ⁴But you who have remained faithful to the LORD your God are all alive today. ⁵Look, I have taught you statutes and ordinances as the LORD my God has commanded me, so that you may follow them in the land you are entering to possess. ⁶Carefully follow [them], for this will [show] your wisdom and understanding in the eyes of the peoples. When they hear about all these statutes, they will say, 'This great nation is indeed a wise and understanding people.' ⁷For what great nation is there that has a god near to it as the LORD our God is [to us] whenever we call to Him? ⁸And what great nation has righteous statutes and ordinances like this entire law I set before you today?

⁹"Only be on your guard and diligently watch yourselves, so that you don't forget the things your eyes have seen and so that they don't slip from your mind as long as you live. Teach them to your children and your grandchildren. ¹⁰The day you stood before the LORD your God at Horeb, the LORD said to me, 'Assemble the people before Me, and I will let them hear My words, so that they may learn to fear Me all the days they live on the earth and may instruct their children.' ¹¹You came near

and stood at the base of the mountain, a mountain blazing with fire into the heavens and enveloped in a dense, black cloud. ¹²Then the LORD spoke to you from the fire. You kept hearing the sound of the words, but didn't see a form; there was only a voice. ¹³He declared His covenant to you. He commanded you to follow the Ten Commandments, which He wrote on two stone tablets. ¹⁴At that time the LORD commanded me to teach you statutes and ordinances for you to follow in the land you are about to cross into and possess.

WORSHIPING THE TRUE GOD

¹⁵"Be extremely careful for your own good—because you did not see any form on the day the LORD spoke to you at Horeb out of the fire— ¹⁶not to act corruptly and make an idol for yourselves in the shape of any figure: a male or female form, ¹⁷or the form of any beast on the earth, any winged creature that flies in the sky, ¹⁸any creature that crawls on the ground, or any fish in the waters under the earth. ¹⁹When you look to the heavens and see the sun, moon, and stars—all the array of heaven—do not be led astray to bow down and worship them. The LORD your God has provided them for all people everywhere under heaven. ²⁰But the LORD selected you and brought you out of Egypt's iron furnace to be a people for His inheritance, as you are today.

²¹"The LORD was angry with me on your account. He swore that I would not cross the Jordan and enter the good land the LORD your God is giving you as an inheritance. ²²I won't be crossing the Jordan because I am going to die in this land. But you are about to cross over and take possession of this good land. ²³Be careful not to forget the covenant of the LORD your God that He made with you, and make an idol for yourselves in the shape of anything He has forbidden you. ²⁴For the LORD your God is a consuming fire, a jealous God.

²⁵"When you have children and grandchildren and have been in the land a long time, and if you act corruptly, make an idol in the form of anything, and do what is evil in the sight of the LORD your God, provoking Him to anger, ²⁶I call heaven and earth as witnesses against you today that you will quickly perish from the land you are about to cross the Jordan to possess. You will not live long there, but you will certainly

be destroyed. [27]The LORD will scatter you among the peoples, and you will be reduced to a few survivors among the nations where the LORD your God will drive you. [28]There you will worship man-made gods of wood and stone, which cannot see, hear, eat, or smell. [29]But from there, you will search for the LORD your God, and you will find [Him] when you seek Him with all your heart and all your soul. [30]When you are in distress and all these things have happened to you, you will return to the LORD your God in later days and obey Him. [31]He will not leave you, destroy you, or forget the covenant with your fathers that He swore to them by oath, because the LORD your God is a compassionate God.

[32]"Indeed, ask about the earlier days that preceded you, from the day God created man on the earth and from one end of the heavens to the other: Has anything like this great event [ever] happened, or has anything like it been heard of? [33]Has a people ever heard God's voice speaking from the fire as you have, and lived? [34]Or has a god [ever] attempted to go and take a nation as his own out of [another] nation, by trials, signs, wonders, and war, by a strong hand and an outstretched arm, by great terrors, as the LORD your God did for you in Egypt before your eyes? [35]You were shown [these things] so that you would know that the LORD is God; there is no other besides Him. [36]He let you hear His voice from heaven to instruct you. He showed you His great fire on earth, and you heard His words from the fire. [37]Because He loved your fathers, He chose their descendants after them and brought you out of Egypt by His presence and great power, [38]to drive out before you nations greater and stronger than you and to bring you in and give you their land as an inheritance, as is now taking place. [39]Today, recognize and keep in mind that the LORD is God in heaven above and on earth below; there is no other. [40]Keep His statutes and commands, which I am giving you today, so that you and your children after you may prosper and so that you may live long in the land the LORD your God is giving you for all time."

FOR PRAISE: Turn right now to Psalm 147, and join your heart with the psalmist who furnishes us with one of the most delightful frameworks for praise found in the Bible. Note especially verse 20 where he says: 'He has not done this for any nation; they do not know His judgments [laws, NIV]. Hallelujah!' How grateful we should be that we have come to know His laws. And not only know them, but live by them. Blessed be His name for ever.

ISRAEL IS HERE reminded of her special vocation as God's holy people and is dared to be different (7:1-6).

DAY
114

DEUTERONOMY 7:1-18;
8:11-9:6,22-29

Israel exists only as a miracle of grace and choice of love (7:7-8) by a Lord who is faithful and keeps covenant (7:9).

God's people had been urged to love Him with all their heart in the Shema (6:4-5) but other voices would seek to seduce Israel from the path of whole-hearted trust. The thrice-repeated phrase: 'If you should say in your heart' (NKJV), highlights the three key temptations Israel will face in the land. Intimidated by larger nations, Israel will be tempted by militarism to put her faith in military power rather than trust in Yahweh (7:17). Forgetful of where the good things of the land come from, Israel will be tempted to listen to the voice of materialism and bow down to the god of self-sufficiency (8:17). When the voice of moralism is heeded Israel will forget the grace which saved her and exalt the god of national self-righteousness and communal pride (9:4).

The wilderness years were meant as discipline to show that a true son does not live by bread alone but by the ever-spoken word of a fatherly God. From here we might readily trace a trajectory to the One true Son in the wilderness who absorbed His people's failure in His own faithful compliance with this Deuteronomic covenant charter.

| BIBLE | **Deuteronomy 7:1-18** |
| READING | |

ISRAEL TO DESTROY IDOLATROUS NATIONS

7 "When the LORD your God brings you into the land you are entering to possess, and He drives out many nations before you—the Hittites, Girgashites, Amorites, Canaanites, Perizzites, Hivites and Jebusites, seven nations more numerous and powerful than you— ²and when the LORD your God delivers them over to you and you defeat them, you must completely destroy them. Make no treaty with them and show them no mercy. ³Do not intermarry with them. Do not give your daughters to their sons or take their daughters for your sons, ⁴because they will turn your sons away from Me to worship other gods. Then the LORD's anger will burn against you, and He will swiftly destroy you. ⁵Instead, this is what you are to do to them: tear down their altars, smash their standing pillars, cut down their Asherah poles, and burn up their carved images. ⁶For you are a holy people belonging to the LORD your God. The LORD your God has chosen you to be His own possession out of all the peoples on the face of the earth.

⁷"The LORD was devoted to you and chose you, not because you were more numerous than all peoples, for you were the fewest of all peoples. ⁸But because the LORD loved you and kept the oath He swore to your fathers, He brought you out with a strong hand and redeemed you from the place of slavery, from the power of Pharaoh king of Egypt. ⁹Know that Yahweh your God is God, the faithful God who keeps His gracious covenant loyalty for a thousand generations with those who love Him and keep His commands. ¹⁰But He directly pays back and destroys those who hate Him. He will not hesitate to directly pay back the one who hates Him. ¹¹So keep the command—the statutes and ordinances—that I am giving you to follow today.

¹²"If you listen to and are careful to keep these ordinances, the LORD your God will keep His covenant loyalty with you, as He swore to your fathers. ¹³He will love you, bless you, and multiply you. He will bless your descendants, and the produce of your soil—your grain, new wine, and oil—the young of your herds, and the newborn of your flocks, in the land He

swore to your fathers that He would give you. ¹⁴You will be blessed above all peoples; there will be no infertile male or female among you or your livestock. ¹⁵The LORD will remove all sickness from you; He will not put on you all the terrible diseases of Egypt that you know about, but He will inflict them on all who hate you. ¹⁶You must destroy all the peoples the LORD your God is delivering over to you and not look on them with pity. Do not worship their gods, for that will be a snare to you.

¹⁷"If you say to yourself, 'These nations are greater than I; how can I drive them out?' ¹⁸do not be afraid of them. Be sure to remember what the LORD your God did to Pharaoh and all Egypt:

Deuteronomy 8:11-9:6,22-29

BIBLE READING

¹¹"Be careful that you don't forget the LORD your God by failing to keep His command—the ordinances and statutes—I am giving you today. ¹²When you eat and are full, and build beautiful houses to live in, ¹³and your herds and flocks grow large, and your silver and gold multiply, and everything else you have increases, ¹⁴[be careful] that your heart doesn't become proud and you forget the LORD your God who brought you out of the land of Egypt, out of the place of slavery. ¹⁵He led you through the great and terrible wilderness with its poisonous snakes and scorpions, a thirsty land where there was no water. He brought water out of the flintlike rock for you. ¹⁶He fed you in the wilderness with manna that your fathers had not known, in order to humble and test you, so that in the end He might cause you to prosper. ¹⁷You may say to yourself, 'My power and my own ability have gained this wealth for me,' ¹⁸but remember that the LORD your God gives you the power to gain wealth, in order to confirm His covenant He swore to your fathers, as it is today. ¹⁹If you ever forget the LORD your God and go after other gods to worship and bow down to them, I testify against you today that you will perish. ²⁰Like the nations the LORD is about to destroy before you, you will perish if you do not obey the LORD your God.

WARNING AGAINST SELF-RIGHTEOUSNESS

9 "Listen, Israel: Today you are about to cross the Jordan to go and drive out nations greater and stronger than you [with] large cities fortified to the heavens. ²The people are strong and tall, the descendants of the Anakim. You know about them and you have heard it said about them, 'Who can stand up to the sons of Anak?' ³But understand that today the LORD your God will cross over ahead of you as a consuming fire; He will devastate and subdue them before you. You will drive them out and destroy them swiftly, as the LORD has told you. ⁴When the LORD your God drives them out before you, do not say to yourself, 'The LORD brought me in to take possession of this land because of my righteousness.' Instead, the LORD will drive out these nations before you because of their wickedness. ⁵You are not going to take possession of their land because of your righteousness or your integrity. Instead, the LORD your God will drive out these nations before you because of their wickedness, in order to keep the promise He swore to your fathers, Abraham, Isaac, and Jacob. ⁶Understand that the LORD your God is not giving you this good land to possess because of your righteousness, for you are a stiff-necked people.

* * * * * * * * * *

²²"You continued to provoke the LORD at Taberah, Massah, and Kibroth-hattaavah. ²³When the LORD sent you from Kadesh-barnea, He said, 'Go up and possess the land I have given you'; you rebelled against the command of the LORD your God. You did not believe or obey Him. ²⁴You have been rebelling against the LORD ever since I have known you.

²⁵"I fell down in the presence of the LORD 40 days and 40 nights because the LORD had threatened to destroy you. ²⁶I prayed to the LORD:

Lord GOD, do not annihilate Your people, Your inheritance, whom You redeemed through Your greatness and brought out of Egypt with a strong hand. ²⁷Remember Your servants Abraham, Isaac, and Jacob. Disregard this people's stubbornness, and their wickedness and sin. ²⁸Otherwise, those in the land you brought us from will say, 'Because the LORD wasn't able to bring them into the land He had promised them, and because He hated them, He brought them out to kill them in the wilderness.' ²⁹But they are Your people, Your inheritance, whom You brought out by Your great power and outstretched arm.

> **THOUGHT:** If the Israelites were tempted to think that they were favoured by God because of some special characteristics they possessed, then here they learned differently. They were loved not because of what was in them but what was in God - eternal boundless Love. It is the same with us. We are what we are because God is who He is. As the hymn writer put it:
>
> He has loved, He has loved us
> We cannot tell why.

DAY 115

DEUTERONOMY 27:9-10; 28:1-6,15-19; 29:1-15, 22-30:20

MOSES HERE LISTS the blessings of covenantal obedience and the judgmental curses that fall on disobedience. Moses anticipates that Israel's future covenantal unfaithfulness will incur God's ultimate judgmental curse of ejection from the promised land (28:63). Sadly, Israel's story replicates the human story. Israel's exile from Canaan - a place often portrayed in Scripture in Edenic language - mirrors the expulsion of Adam and Eve from the Garden of Eden. And Moses issues this warning before Israel has even entered the land!

Tragically, what Moses anticipated became grim reality 800 years later in the Babylonian Exile so that when the Torah takes final shape as Scripture, his warning is already in the past tense (29:28 'as it is now', NIV). Even more remarkably, Moses points to a hope beyond exile that is not based on the sacrificial system, Israel's conventional means of grace. Rather, pre-empting Jeremiah and Ezekiel, Moses looks to when God will create radically new covenant hearts in God's people. We can glimpse this hope by comparing Deuteronomy 10:16 – where God commands, '... circumcise your hearts ...' – with 30:6 where God does it. When commanded human action turns into promised divine action, the new covenant is on the horizon. The law is grace in the end.

BIBLE READING

Deuteronomy 27:9-10

THE COVENANT CURSES

⁹Moses and the Levitical priests spoke to all Israel, "Be silent, Israel, and listen! This day you have become the people of the LORD your God. ¹⁰Obey the LORD your God and follow His commands and statutes I am giving you today."

BIBLE READING

Deuteronomy 28:1-6,15-19

BLESSINGS FOR OBEDIENCE

28 "Now if you faithfully obey the LORD your God and are careful to follow all His commands I am giving you today, the LORD your God will put you far above all the nations of the earth. ²All these blessings will come and overtake you, because you obey the LORD your God:

³ You will be blessed in the city
  and blessed in the country.
⁴ Your descendants will be blessed,
  and your soil's produce,
  and the offspring of your livestock,
  including the young of your herds
  and the newborn of your flocks.
⁵ Your basket and kneading bowl will be blessed.
⁶ You will be blessed when you come in
  and blessed when you go out.

• • • • • • • • •

CURSES FOR DISOBEDIENCE

¹⁵"But if you do not obey the LORD your God by carefully following all His commands and statutes I am giving you today, all these curses will come and overtake you:

¹⁶ You will be cursed in the city
and cursed in the country.
¹⁷ Your basket and kneading bowl will be cursed.
¹⁸ Your descendants will be cursed,
and your soil's produce,
the young of your herds,
and the newborn of your flocks.
¹⁹ You will be cursed when you come in
and cursed when you go out.

Deuteronomy 29:1-15, 22-30:20

BIBLE READING

RENEWING THE COVENANT

29 These are the words of the covenant the LORD commanded Moses to make with the Israelites in the land of Moab, in addition to the covenant He had made with them at Horeb. ²Moses summoned all Israel and said to them, "You have seen with your own eyes everything the LORD did in Egypt to Pharaoh, to all his officials, and to his entire land. ³You saw with your own eyes the great trials and those great signs and wonders. ⁴Yet to this day the LORD has not given you a mind to understand, eyes to see, or ears to hear. ⁵I led you 40 years in the wilderness; your clothes and the sandals on your feet did not wear out; ⁶you did not eat bread or drink wine or beer—so that you might know that I am the LORD your God. ⁷When you reached this place, Sihon king of Heshbon and Og king of Bashan came out against us in battle, but we defeated them. ⁸We took their land and gave it as an inheritance to the Reubenites, the Gadites, and half the tribe of Manasseh. ⁹Therefore, observe the words of this covenant and follow them, so that you will succeed in everything you do.

¹⁰"All of you are standing today before the LORD your God—your leaders, tribes, elders, officials, all the men of Israel, ¹¹your children, your wives, and the foreigners in your camps who

cut your wood and draw your water— [12]so that you may enter into the covenant of the LORD your God, which He is making with you today, so that you may enter into His oath [13]and so that He may establish you today as His people and He may be your God as He promised you and as He swore to your fathers Abraham, Isaac, and Jacob. [14]I am making this covenant and this oath not only with you, [15]but also with those who are standing here with us today in the presence of the LORD our God and with those who are not here today.

• • • • • • • • •

[22]"Future generations of your children who follow you and the foreigner who comes from a distant country will see the plagues of the land and the sicknesses the LORD has inflicted on it. [23]All its soil will be a burning waste of sulfur and salt, unsown, producing nothing, with no plant growing on it, just like the fall of Sodom and Gomorrah, Admah and Zeboiim, which the LORD demolished in His fierce anger. [24]All the nations will ask, 'Why has the LORD done this to this land? Why this great outburst of anger?' [25]Then people will answer, 'It is because they abandoned the covenant of the LORD, the God of their fathers, which He had made with them when He brought them out of the land of Egypt. [26]They began to worship other gods, bowing down to gods they had not known—gods that the LORD had not permitted them [to worship]. [27]Therefore the LORD's anger burned against this land, and He brought every curse written in this book on it. [28]The LORD uprooted them from their land in [His] anger, fury, and great wrath, and threw them into another land where they are today.' [29]The hidden things belong to the LORD our God, but the revealed things belong to us and our children forever, so that we may follow all the words of this law.

RETURNING TO THE LORD

30 "When all these things happen to you—the blessings and curses I have set before you—and you come to your senses [while you are] in all the nations where the LORD your God has driven you, [2]and you and your children return to the LORD your God and obey Him with all your heart and all your soul by doing everything I am giving you today, [3]then

He will restore your fortunes, have compassion on you, and gather you again from all the peoples where the LORD your God has scattered you. ⁴Even if your exiles are at the ends of the earth, He will gather you and bring you back from there. ⁵The LORD your God will bring you into the land your fathers possessed, and you will take possession of it. He will cause you to prosper and multiply you more than [He did] your fathers. ⁶The LORD your God will circumcise your heart and the hearts of your descendants, and you will love Him with all your heart and all your soul, so that you will live. ⁷The LORD your God will put all these curses on your enemies who hate and persecute you. ⁸Then you will again obey Him and follow all His commands I am giving you today. ⁹The LORD your God will make you prosper abundantly in all the work of your hands with children, the offspring of your livestock, and your soil's produce. Indeed, the LORD will again delight in your prosperity, as He delighted in that of your fathers, ¹⁰when you obey the LORD your God by keeping His commands and statutes that are written in this book of the law and return to Him with all your heart and all your soul.

CHOOSE LIFE

¹¹"This command that I give you today is certainly not too difficult or beyond your reach. ¹²It is not in heaven, so that you have to ask, 'Who will go up to heaven, get it for us, and proclaim it to us so that we may follow it?' ¹³And it is not across the sea, so that you have to ask, 'Who will cross the sea, get it for us, and proclaim it to us so that we may follow it?' ¹⁴But the message is very near you, in your mouth and in your heart, so that you may follow it. ¹⁵See, today I have set before you life and prosperity, death and adversity. ¹⁶For I am commanding you today to love the LORD your God, to walk in His ways, and to keep His commands, statutes, and ordinances, so that you may live and multiply, and the LORD your God may bless you in the land you are entering to possess. ¹⁷But if your heart turns away and you do not listen and you are led astray to bow down to other gods and worship them, ¹⁸I tell you today that you will certainly perish and will not live long in the land you are entering to possess across the Jordan. ¹⁹I call heaven and earth as witnesses against you today that I have set before you

life and death, blessing and curse. Choose life so that you and your descendants may live, [20]love the LORD your God, obey Him, and remain faithful to Him. For He is your life, and He will prolong your life in the land the LORD swore to give to your fathers Abraham, Isaac, and Jacob."

PRAYER: My Father and my God, once again I lift my heart to You in deepest gratitude that Your law drove me to the place where my heart opened to grace. I shall never cease to praise You that You not only commanded righteousness but provided it through the innocent sufferings of Your Son on Calvary. The more I learn of Your Story, the more amazed I am that I am part of it - and grateful to the depths of my heart. Thank You, Father. Amen.

DAY 116

AMOS 3

TODAY WE DIP briefly into Israel's long-running love-hate relationship with the prophets whom God sent as prosecutors to hold Israel and her kings accountable to the covenant bond.

The prophetic oracles brought by prophets like Amos constitute 'covenant lawsuits' in which God indicts His people for turning away from Him and for failing to live covenantally. The outcome of God's plans told by the prophets is inescapable (vv.3-7).

Amos's own lion-like roar especially exposes the injustice at the heart of the nation's life - the poor exploited by corrupt economic practices, and all masked by hypocritical religion. Israel's unique privilege - 'You only have I chosen of all the families of the earth' (NIV) - automatically entails ('therefore') solemn responsibility and, in the case of failure, judgment - 'therefore, I will punish you for all your iniquities' (v.2). Even hardened international observers, well-versed in the black arts of oppression and injustice, will look askance at Israel (vv.9-12). If God's people are to be saved it will only be as a remnant, unflatteringly described here as the tattered leftovers of a lion's dinner! (v.12). Not much left for God to work with! But, as so often with God, these pitiful scraps are just enough for Him to begin to write a new chapter in the story.

Amos 3

GOD'S REASONS FOR PUNISHING ISRAEL

3 Listen to this message that the LORD has spoken against you, Israelites, against the entire clan that I brought from the land of Egypt:

² I have known only you
   out of all the clans of the earth;
   therefore, I will punish you for all your iniquities.
³ Can two walk together
   without agreeing to meet?
⁴ Does a lion roar in the forest
   when it has no prey?
   Does a young lion growl from its lair
   unless it has captured [something]?
⁵ Does a bird land in a trap on the ground
   if there is no bait for it?
   Does a trap spring from the ground
   when it has caught nothing?
⁶ If a ram's horn is blown in a city,
   aren't people afraid?
   If a disaster occurs in a city,
   hasn't the LORD done it?
⁷ Indeed, the Lord GOD does nothing
   without revealing His counsel
   to His servants the prophets.
⁸ A lion has roared;
   who will not fear?
   The Lord GOD has spoken;
   who will not prophesy?

⁹ Proclaim on the citadels in Ashdod
   and on the citadels in the land of Egypt:
   Assemble on the mountains of Samaria

and see the great turmoil in the city
and the acts of oppression within it.

10 The people are incapable of doing right—

the LORD's declaration—

those who store up violence and destruction
in their citadels.

11Therefore, the Lord GOD says:

An enemy will surround the land;
he will destroy your strongholds
and plunder your citadels.

12The LORD says:

As the shepherd snatches two legs
or a piece of an ear
from the lion's mouth,
so the Israelites who live in Samaria
will be rescued
with [only] the corner of a bed
or the cushion of a couch.

13 Listen and testify against the house of Jacob—

[this is] the declaration
of the Lord GOD,
the God of Hosts.

14 I will punish the altars of Bethel
on the day I punish Israel for its crimes;
the horns of the altar will be cut off
and fall to the ground.

15 I will demolish the winter house
and the summer house;
the houses [inlaid with] ivory will be destroyed,
and the great houses will come to an end—

the LORD's declaration.

FOR ACTION: How grateful we ought to be for those who in Old Testament times spoke the Word of the Lord to the people – and for those now who faithfully preach His Word. Willard F. Jabusch has taken an Israeli folk melody and put these words to it. Give God thanks for the fact that He spoke through His Word and that He speaks through it still.

God has spoken to His people; Hallelujah!
And His words are words of wisdom; Hallelujah!

DAY
117

HOSEA 11

THIS IS RIGHTLY regarded as one of the most moving chapters in the Bible. God's relationship to Israel is likened to that between parent and child and it yields an astonishing view of God's tenderness. '... out of Egypt I called My son' (v.1) echoes the claim made by Moses to Pharaoh at the Exodus (Exod. 4:22). Israel is pictured as a toddler nation unaware of being taught to walk by a patient and gentle God (v.3). For a moment the image fades into that of a good farmer sensitive to how young animals need to be nurtured and not over-driven (v.4). But again Israel fails to respond and turns away from God (v.7).

Should God repudiate His people? As we overhear His own self-questioning, we gain a remarkable insight into the agony of indecision in the heart of God. God is emotionally involved with Israel. He feels with and for His people.

But these human-like emotions paradoxically show God to be God not man (v.9)! Human patience would have been exhausted long ago but divine love will not let His people go. The God of our story is not woodenly acting out a pre-determined script, He is living out a passion for His people and for the world's redemption that will one day cost Him if He's not more careful! His prodigal sons will return home when the prodigal Father opens wide His arms of love.

BIBLE READING	Hosea 11

THE LORD'S LOVE FOR ISRAEL

11 When Israel was a child, I loved him,
and out of Egypt I called My son.

2 [The more] they called them,
[the more] they departed from Me.
They kept sacrificing to the Baals
and burning offerings to idols.

3 It was I who taught Ephraim to walk,
taking them in My arms,
but they never knew that I healed them.

4 I led them with human cords,
with ropes of kindness.
To them I was like one
who eases the yoke from their jaws;
I bent down to give them food.

5 Israel will not return to the land of Egypt
and Assyria will be his king,
because they refused to repent.

6 A sword will whirl through his cities;
it will destroy and devour the bars of his gates,
because of their schemes.

7 My people are bent on turning from Me.
Though they call to Him on high,
He will not exalt them at all.

8 How can I give you up, Ephraim?
How can I surrender you, Israel?
How can I make you like Admah?
How can I treat you like Zeboiim?
I have had a change of heart;
My compassion is stirred!

9 I will not vent the full fury of My anger;
I will not turn back to destroy Ephraim.
For I am God and not man,
the Holy One among you;
I will not come in rage.

10 They will follow the LORD;

He will roar like a lion.
When He roars,
His children will come trembling from the west.

¹¹ They will be roused like birds from Egypt
and like doves from the land of Assyria.
Then I will settle them in their homes.

[This is] the LORD's declaration.

¹² Ephraim surrounds me with lies,
the house of Israel, with deceit.
Judah still wanders with El
and is faithful to holy ones.

THOUGHT: One of the greatest aspects of the love of God is not just that He loves, but that it is a love that will never let us go. Let your response to today's reading be expressed in the words of one of the verses of the well-known hymn:

O Love, that wilt not let me go,
I rest my weary soul in Thee;
I give Thee back the life I owe,
That in Thine ocean depths its flow
May richer, fuller be.
(George Matheson, 1882)

WE TRACE THE fate of the divided kingdom down to the demise of the northern kingdom of Israel whose capital, Samaria, fell to the invading Assyrians in 720 BC, and to the exile of Judah to Babylonia, climaxing with the fall of Jersualem in 586 BC.

DAY
118
2 KINGS 17:7-23
2 CHRONICLES 36:11-23

In both cases, tragic judgment finally overtook God's people due to their covenant unfaithfulness and treatment of the prophets. In Israel's case, records the historian, they failed to trust God but '... worshiped other gods ... and rejected ... His covenant ... and the warnings He had given them' through the prophets' (2 Kings 17:7,15). Reneging on their unique calling to be a holy nation, believing and behaving no differently from the surrounding cultures, they '... imitated the nations around them ...' (2 Kings 17:15, NIV).

As for the people of Judah, surviving for another 120 years or so, they eventually succumbed to the Babylonians and were taken into exile because '... they kept ridiculing God's messengers ... until the LORD's wrath was so stirred up against His people that there was no remedy' (2 Chron. 36:16)! Or was there? In the marvellous paradox of grace, the prophetic word which, when rejected, sealed Judah's fate, also offered a glimmer of hope for future restoration. If the old covenant people could not be patched up, perhaps a new covenant people might be created, raised to life out of the 'death' of exile!

BIBLE READING

2 Kings 17:7-23

WHY ISRAEL FELL

[7][This disaster] happened because the people of Israel had sinned against the LORD their God who had brought them out of the land of Egypt from the power of Pharaoh king of Egypt and because they had worshiped other gods. [8]They had lived according to the customs of the nations that the LORD had dispossessed before the Israelites and the customs the kings of Israel had introduced. [9]The Israelites secretly did what was not right against the LORD their God. They built high places in all their towns from watchtower to fortified city. [10]They set up for themselves sacred pillars and Asherah poles on every high hill and under every green tree. [11]They burned incense on all the high places just like those nations that the LORD had driven out before them. They did evil things, provoking the LORD. [12]They served idols, although the LORD had told them, "You must not do this." [13]Still, the LORD warned Israel and Judah through every prophet and every seer, saying, "Turn from your evil ways and keep My commandments and statutes according to all the law I commanded your ancestors and sent to you through My servants the prophets."

[14]But they would not listen. Instead, they became obstinate like their ancestors who did not believe the LORD their God. [15]They rejected His statutes and His covenant He had

made with their ancestors and the warnings He had given them. They pursued worthless idols and became worthless themselves, following the surrounding nations the LORD had commanded them not to imitate.

¹⁶They abandoned all the commandments of the LORD their God. They made for themselves molded images—even two calves—and an Asherah pole. They worshiped the whole heavenly host and served Baal. ¹⁷They made their sons and daughters pass through the fire and practiced divination and interpreted omens. They devoted themselves to do what was evil in the LORD's sight and provoked Him.

¹⁸Therefore, the LORD was very angry with Israel, and He removed them from His presence. Only the tribe of Judah remained. ¹⁹Even Judah did not keep the commandments of the LORD their God but lived according to the customs Israel had introduced. ²⁰So the LORD rejected all the descendants of Israel, afflicted them, and handed them over to plunderers until He had banished them from His presence.

SUMMARY OF ISRAEL'S HISTORY

²¹When the LORD tore Israel from the house of David, Israel made Jeroboam son of Nebat king. Then Jeroboam led Israel away from following the LORD and caused them to commit great sin. ²²The Israelites persisted in all the sins that Jeroboam committed and did not turn away from them. ²³Finally, the LORD removed Israel from His presence just as He had declared through all His servants the prophets. So Israel has been exiled to Assyria from their homeland until today.

2 Chronicles 36:11-23

BIBLE READING

JUDAH'S KING ZEDEKIAH

¹¹Zedekiah was 21 years old when he became king; he reigned 11 years in Jerusalem. ¹²He did what was evil in the sight of the LORD his God and did not humble himself before Jeremiah the prophet at the LORD's command. ¹³He also rebelled against King Nebuchadnezzar who had made him swear allegiance by God. He became obstinate and hardened his heart against returning to the LORD God of Israel. ¹⁴All the leaders of the priests and

the people multiplied their unfaithful deeds, imitating all the detestable practices of the nations, and they defiled the LORD's temple that He had consecrated in Jerusalem.

THE DESTRUCTION OF JERUSALEM

[15]But the LORD God of their ancestors sent word against them by the hand of His messengers, sending them time and time again, for He had compassion on His people and on His dwelling place. [16]But they kept ridiculing God's messengers, despising His words, and scoffing at His prophets, until the LORD's wrath was so stirred up against His people that there was no remedy. [17]So He brought up against them the king of the Chaldeans, who killed their choice young men with the sword in the house of their sanctuary. He had no pity on young man and virgin or elderly and aged; He handed them all over to him. [18]He took everything to Babylon—all the articles of God's temple, large and small, the treasures of the LORD's temple, and the treasures of the king and his officials. [19]Then the Chaldeans burned God's temple. They tore down Jerusalem's wall, burned down all its palaces, and destroyed all its valuable utensils.

[20]Those who escaped from the sword he deported to Babylon, and they became servants to him and his sons until the rise of the Persian kingdom. [21]This fulfilled the word of the LORD through Jeremiah and the land enjoyed its Sabbath rest all the days of the desolation until 70 years were fulfilled.

THE DECREE OF CYRUS

[22]In the first year of Cyrus king of Persia, the word of the LORD spoken through Jeremiah was fulfilled. The LORD put it into the mind of King Cyrus of Persia to issue a proclamation throughout his entire kingdom and also [to put it] in writing:

> [23]This is what King Cyrus of Persia says: The LORD, the God of heaven, has given me all the kingdoms of the earth and has appointed me to build Him a temple at Jerusalem in Judah. Whoever among you of His people may go up, and may the LORD his God be with him.

TO PONDER: The thing that has puzzled the people of God through the ages is why some who have been delivered from so many things by the good hand of God can then turn against Him. Our natural minds might reason thus: if God foresees that some people He delivers will not stay faithful to Him then why deliver them in the first place? The answer must surely be this: God blesses us not for what we will be tomorrow but for who we are today.

WITH BREAKING HEART, Paul faces the mystery of Israel's unbelief. He sadly recalls the unique privileges Israel enjoyed, above all being the race that produced the Messiah (vv.1-5). So why has Israel rejected Him? Paul's answer starts from one rock-bottom conviction: that whoever or whatever has failed, it is not God or God's covenant faithfulness (v.6).

DAY
119
ROMANS 9:1-5

Paul reviews Israel's entire history from Abraham to the Exile (vv.6-29) and discerns that from the start there has been a selectivity of God at work. Always, Paul sees, there has been an Israel within Israel, for covenant relationship has rested on faith and obedience not on mere biological descent from Abraham. Grace not race explains God's workings.

And if a remnant exists - Jews who like Paul believe in Jesus as Messiah - then just as Isaiah saw, there is hope for the future (vv.27-29). Wonderfully, Paul expands Hosea's promised restoration of disowned Israelites, to explain the adoption of Gentiles into God's enlarged family (vv.25-26).

And if it had long been true that Israel could not be affirmed as she stood but needed to undergo renewal through judgment and mercy, exile and restoration, then was Israel's failure perhaps mysteriously built into the plan from the start? The mystery of Israel continues as the scandal of grace.

BIBLE READING

Romans 9:1-5

ISRAEL'S REJECTION OF CHRIST

9 I speak the truth in Christ—I am not lying; my conscience is testifying to me with the Holy Spirit — ²that I have intense sorrow and continual anguish in my heart. ³For I could wish that I myself were cursed and cut off from the Messiah for the benefit of my brothers, my countrymen by physical descent. ⁴They are Israelites, and to them belong the adoption, the glory, the covenants, the giving of the law, the temple service, and the promises. ⁵The forefathers are theirs, and from them, by physical descent, came the Messiah, who is God over all, blessed forever. Amen.

THOUGHT: Consider this - no one can ever bring a justifiable complaint against God. Whatever the Almighty does is always good. At times it may not seem so to us, but in the bigger scheme of things His goodness is at the heart of everything. When you find yourself doubting God's goodness, remind yourself of this - a God who gave His Son to die for us on a cross has got to be good. You will find this helps put things in proper perspective.

DAY 120

1 PETER 2:1-12

SO CRUCIAL IS Jesus to us that Peter, using Isaiah's words, sees Him as either the stepping-stone to salvation or the stumbling-block of judgment (vv.6-8). To highlight this, Peter applies to the Church, the classic descriptions of Israel's status, titles and role, culled from Exodus 19 and Isaiah 43 (v.7).

Like Paul, Peter extends Hosea's promised reinstatement of Israel to include Gentile believers in Christ (v.10). In Christ, 'nobodies' become 'somebodies', even alienated 'non-people' are now by grace in God's covenant family!

The Church then is not meant to be a Gentile innovation which replaces Israel in a simplistic way. Rather, it exists as a remade and enlarged Israel

on a world scale. Isn't this just what God promised Abraham? All believers in Jesus Christ inherit those promises. But with the privileges come the obligations. God's aim has never been to save random individuals for a privatised heaven but to create a people out of all nations for his own glory. Jesus is the one foundation that can bear the weight of such a vast and living Temple from which, whether in evangelism, worship or God-glorifying living, flows a stream of endless praise. The story we have been tracking from Noah to Abraham to Israel now narrows down to one individual – the king. To this we now turn.

| BIBLE READING | **1 Peter 2:1-12** | |

THE LIVING STONE AND A HOLY PEOPLE

2 So rid yourselves of all wickedness, all deceit, hypocrisy, envy, and all slander. [2]Like newborn infants, desire the unadulterated spiritual milk, so that you may grow by it in [your] salvation, [3]since "you have tasted that the Lord is good." [4]Coming to Him, a living stone— rejected by men but chosen and valuable to God— [5]you yourselves, as living stones, are being built into a spiritual house for a holy priesthood to offer spiritual sacrifices acceptable to God through Jesus Christ. [6]For it stands in Scripture:

> "Look! I lay a stone in Zion,
> a chosen and valuable cornerstone,
> and the one who believes in Him
> will never be put to shame!"

[7]So the honor is for you who believe; but for the unbelieving,

> "The stone that the builders rejected—
> this One has become the cornerstone,"

and

8 "A stone that causes men to stumble,
  and a rock that trips them up."

They stumble by disobeying the message; they were destined for this.

9 But you are "a chosen race, a royal priesthood,
  a holy nation, a people for His possession,
  so that you may proclaim
      the praises"
  of the One who called you out of darkness
  into His marvelous light.
10 Once you were not a people,
   but now you are God's people;
   you had not received mercy,
   but now you have received mercy.

A CALL TO GOOD WORKS

11Dear friends, I urge you as aliens and temporary residents to abstain from fleshly desires that war against you. 12Conduct yourselves honorably among the Gentiles, so that in a case where they speak against you as those who do evil, they may, by observing your good works, glorify God in a day of visitation.

PRAYER: My Father and my God how grateful I am for the fact that the foundation which has been laid in the Church is Jesus. Because He is the Eternal Rock, I am standing safe and secure on something that can never be moved. There are times when I may tremble on the Rock, but I am more grateful than words can convey for the fact that the Rock never trembles under me. All honour and glory be unto Your peerless and precious name for ever. Amen.

SECTION

NOAH
ALL CREATION

ABRAHAM
ALL NATIONS

ISRAEL
ONE NATION

DAVID
REPRESENTATIVE KING

NEW COVENANT
FAITHFUL COVENANT PARTNER

JESUS
FAITHFUL COVENANT PARTNER

JESUS
DAVIDIC KING MESSIAH

JESUS
THE NEW ISRAEL

JESUS
THE WORLD'S LORD

JESUS
THE TRULY HUMAN ONE
CROWNED WITH GLORY AND HONOUR

JESUS
COSMIC RULER IN GOD'S NEW CREATION
NEW HEAVENS AND NEW EARTH

SECTION 6   DAVID'S DESTINY

GOD IS COMMITTED TO CROWNING HIS SON KING - DAVID'S DESTINY

The second book of Samuel chapter 7 has been called a 'mountain peak in redemptive history'. It dramatises the frustration of David's plans to build a house or temple for God and the announcement by God through the prophet Nathan of God's intention to build a house for David! Even without this chapter, it would be hard to overestimate the importance of kingship to Israel. We recall that the promise of kings was part of the original covenantal promise to Abraham (Gen. 17:6) and prescriptions for kingship were written into the law (Deut. 17:14-20). Following the false start with Saul, David is seen to be the '... man after his own heart ...' (1 Sam. 13:14, NIV), who will shepherd God's people. But the commitment God makes to David and his kingly line goes beyond national interests. David is promised a dynasty, a throne, a kingdom that will last for ever, and a special father-son relationship with God.

This astonishing commitment which leaves David dumbfounded and humbled is celebrated as the Davidic 'covenant' in Psalm 89. One implication was that, in line with the ancient concept of 'sacral kingship', each subsequent king in Israel was regarded as God's representative on earth to whom was applied the privileged affirmation 'You are My Son; today I have become Your Father'. Psalm 2 from which these words come was probably a song sung at the king's coronation in which the prophetic singer declares that Israel's king in Zion is destined to become Lord of the whole world!

Not only does the king represent God but he represents the people. His subjects are so bound up with his interests and fate that what happens to him

happens to them. This is one reason why, with the rise of kingship – the Old Testament narrative about the children of Israel becomes the 'chronicles' of the kings of Israel.

So, as the ancient historian saw, God's covenant commitment to David remained as a lamp that would never go out even in the darkest days of the most evil kings (2 Kings 8:19).

In the unfolding of revelation, it was, no doubt, the failure of the kings to live up to the ideals of kingship that, in part, prompted hopes for the coming of an ideal ruler who would restore God's people and implement God's kingly rule. This vision, first glimpsed by Isaiah and Micah in the middle of the eighth century BC, comes into more urgent and clearer focus in the Exilic prophets, Jeremiah and Ezekiel. It is left to Isaiah to put a wholly new spin on the notion of kingship by unveiling the mysterious figure of God's anointed servant who will suffer as God's agent of salvation. Isaiah, at the same time, envisages the coming of God Himself as King to establish His kingdom of justice and peace. Only the New Testament will resolve these paradoxes. Suffice it to say that all this background of kingship – especially Psalm 2 – informs the language of the Evangelists when they describe Jesus at His baptism being anointed by the Spirit and singled out by the divine voice as God's royal 'Son'. This Sonship which begins as a national epithet and a royal vocation – reaffirmed at Jesus' transfiguration – blossoms into full-scale divine Sonship in the wake of the resurrection which acclaims Him as God's Messiah and therefore Lord of the world (Acts 2:36).

So with the Davidic covenant, God narrows down His

redemptive purpose, not in the sense of restricting its scope, but in the sense of concentrating on one representative figure. Where the covenant with Noah concerns the whole creation; the covenant with Abraham potentially affects all nations; and the covenant with Israel channels that purpose into the stewardship of just one nation – so now the plan of God is focused on a representative individual. To the king and his dynasty who represent God and the people is entrusted the plan of God. On the future ideal King rests the hopes of the people for national renewal and new covenant blessings, and in turn the hopes of the nations of being blessed through Abraham's seed. Kingship was always the truly human vocation. By recovering Adam's lost dominion, retrieving Israel's kingdom calling, and redeeming the office of kingship, Jesus, the Truly Human One, now wears the crown of honour and glory which alone guarantees us glory and offers creation hope of renewal.

THE EVENT DESCRIBED here is one of the supreme moments in Scripture.

Safely settled in his own palace in Jerusalem, David's thoughts turn to more grandiose schemes. Like a typical ancient king, David's ambition is to erect a palace for the god who sponsors his regime. He shares with his key advisors this desire to build a house for God.

No doubt anxious to please, his court-prophet, Nathan, readily rubber-stamps the proposal. But prophets are expected to be 'open all hours' and during the night Nathan is woken by God and told that God forbids the king to build Him a house. Instead, God will build a house for David and with it, a throne and a kingdom that will last for ever. Above all, the king is promised a special father–son relationship with God! With what trepidation, I wonder, did Nathan enter David's quarters the next morning with his bitter-sweet news? 'No, you are not to build a house for God ... but God will build a house for you!' The death of David's dream makes way for the bigger dreams of God who always does far more than we can ask or imagine.

Though the word does not appear in this text, God's commitment here to David is rightly recalled by later writers as God's 'covenant' with David. As such it is unconditional. Even though individual kings will fail, God's covenant love for the Davidic line will remain. On this hangs the success of God's plan.

DAY
121

2 SAMUEL 7:1-17

2 Samuel 7:1-17

BIBLE
READING

THE LORD'S COVENANT WITH DAVID

7 When the king had settled into his palace and the LORD had given him rest on every side from all his enemies, ²the king said to Nathan the prophet, "Look, I am living in a cedar house while the ark of God sits inside tent curtains."

³So Nathan told the king, "Go and do all that is on your heart, for the LORD is with you."

⁴But that night the word of the LORD came to Nathan: ⁵"Go to My servant David and say, 'This is what the LORD says: Are you to build a house for Me to live in? ⁶From the time I brought the Israelites out of Egypt until today I have not lived in a house; instead, I have been moving around with the tabernacle tent. ⁷In all My journeys with all the Israelites, have I ever asked anyone among the tribes of Israel, whom I commanded to shepherd My people Israel: Why haven't you built Me a house of cedar?'

⁸"Now this is what you are to say to My servant David: 'This is what the LORD of Hosts says: I took you from the pasture and from following the sheep to be ruler over My people Israel. ⁹I have been with you wherever you have gone, and I have destroyed all your enemies before you. I will make a name for you like that of the greatest in the land. ¹⁰I will establish a place for My people Israel and plant them, so that they may live there and not be disturbed again. Evildoers will not afflict them as they have done ¹¹ever since the day I ordered judges to be over My people Israel. I will give you rest from all your enemies.

"'The LORD declares to you: The LORD Himself will make a house for you. ¹²When your time comes and you rest with your fathers, I will raise up after you your descendant, who will come from your body, and I will establish his kingdom. ¹³He will build a house for My name, and I will establish the throne of his kingdom forever. ¹⁴I will be a father to him, and he will be a son to Me. When he does wrong, I will discipline him with a human rod and with blows from others. ¹⁵But My faithful love will never leave him as I removed it from Saul; I removed him from your way. ¹⁶Your house and kingdom will endure before Me forever, and your throne will be established forever.'"

¹⁷Nathan spoke all these words and this entire vision to David.

QUOTE: Following today's reading, consider this powerful quotation from Dr Larry Crabb: 'Shattered dreams are never random. They are always a piece in a larger puzzle, a chapter in a larger story. The Holy Spirit uses the pain of shattered dreams to help us discover our desire for God, to help us begin dreaming the highest dream. They are ordained opportunities for the Spirit first to awaken, then to satisfy our highest dream.'

DEEPLY DISAPPOINTED YET dumbstruck with wonder, the king tries to come to terms with the night's events. David has tried to fit God into his programme, but God refuses to be accommodated in this way and instead makes a place for David in the divine scheme of things. David is suitably humbled and awed – and asks, literally, 'Is this the law of man ...?' This is variously translated, with the NIV taking the minimal reading: 'Is this your usual way of dealing with man?'(v.19). But other Old Testament scholars see weightier issues here, noting that in some ancient languages the phrase 'the law of man' concerns human fate and destiny. So one scholar translates it, 'Is this the charter for humanity?' This is surely to be preferred. In the prophetic oracle Nathan has delivered to him, David rightly sees beyond the domestic or royal honour done to him and senses that the future of the whole human race is involved.

We know only too well that life does not conform to our expectations or desires and that control evades us. Only with time do we come to appreciate the strange grace that denies us our requests in the interests of God's bigger visions.

If God sometimes thwarts even our godliest plans it is only so as to include us in His larger, long-term plans.

In this case, David's disappointment is the world's destiny.

2 Samuel 7:18-29

BIBLE
READING

DAVID'S PRAYER OF THANKSGIVING

[18]Then King David went in, sat in the LORD's presence, and said, "Who am I, Lord GOD, and what is my house that You have brought me this far? [19]What You have done so far was a little thing to You, Lord GOD, for You have also spoken about Your servant's house in the distant future. And this is a revelation for mankind, Lord GOD. [20]What more can David say to You? You know Your servant, Lord GOD. [21]Because of

Your word and according to Your will, You have revealed all these great things to Your servant.

²²"This is why You are great, Lord GOD. There is no one like You, and there is no God besides You, as all we have heard confirms. ²³And who is like Your people Israel? God came to one nation on earth in order to redeem a people for Himself, to make a name for Himself, and to perform for them great and awesome acts, driving out nations and their gods before Your people You redeemed for Yourself from Egypt. ²⁴You established Your people Israel Your own people forever, and You, LORD, have become their God.

²⁵"Now, LORD God, fulfill the promise forever that You have made to Your servant and his house. Do as You have promised, ²⁶so that Your name will be exalted forever, when it is said, 'The LORD of Hosts is God over Israel.' The house of Your servant David will be established before You ²⁷since You, LORD of Hosts, God of Israel, have revealed this to Your servant when You said, 'I will build a house for you.' Therefore, Your servant has found the courage to pray this prayer to You. ²⁸Lord GOD, You are God; Your words are true, and You have promised this grace to Your servant. ²⁹Now, please bless Your servant's house so that it will continue before You forever. For You, Lord GOD, have spoken, and with Your blessing Your servant's house will be blessed forever."

TO PONDER: Have your plans been thwarted in some way? Then hold on to this – the Almighty dismantles our plans in order to build bigger and better ones – plans that fit into the story He is telling. It is disappointing when the things we want to do or accomplish do not have the divine approval, but learn to change the first letter of the word disappointment from 'd' to 'h'. Then rejoice in the change of perspective.

THE PSALMIST HERE reflects ruefully on the humiliating and shameful demise of kingship at the time of the Babylonian exile. The unthinkable appears to have happened; God seems to have repudiated His covenant promises to the Davidic monarchy (vv.38-45).

Yet still the psalmist's faith reaches out to grasp the faithfulness of God guaranteed by His covenant with David. 'Lord, where are the former acts of Your faithful love that You swore to David in Your faithfulness?' (v.49). Israel's hope for the future lies in recalling God's commitment to David which He said was inviolable (vv.19-37).

For the king to call God his 'Father' and to be called 'God's son' is an intensified form of the relationship Israel enjoyed with God (Exod. 4:22-23). This reaffirms the view that the king - in effect - assumes the role and responsibilities of the whole people. As a representative figure, when he fails, they are deemed to have failed. So the people's future is still bound up with that of God's promises to the king.

The world role of Israel's king is remembered, too (v.27). He is destined to be ruler of the world, lord of lords and king of kings. Now what will happen?

The answer told in Psalms 90 onwards is that God will re-assert His saving kingship in the world in His own way and person. What a prospect!

DAY **123**
PSALM 89

Psalm 89

BIBLE READING

PERPLEXITY ABOUT GOD'S PROMISES

A *Maskil* of Ethan the Ezrahite.

¹ I will sing about the LORD's faithful love forever;
with my mouth
I will proclaim Your faithfulness to all generations.
² For I will declare,
"Faithful love is built up forever;
You establish Your faithfulness in the heavens."

³ [The LORD said,]
"I have made a covenant with My chosen one;
I have sworn an oath to David My servant:
⁴ 'I will establish your offspring forever
and build up your throne for all generations.'"

Selah

⁵ LORD, the heavens praise Your wonders—
Your faithfulness also—
in the assembly of the holy ones.
⁶ For who in the skies can compare with the LORD?
Who among the heavenly beings is like the LORD?
⁷ God is greatly feared in the council of the holy ones,
more awe-inspiring than all who surround Him.
⁸ LORD God of Hosts,
who is strong like You, LORD?
Your faithfulness surrounds You.
⁹ You rule the raging sea;
when its waves surge, You still them.
¹⁰ You crushed Rahab like one who is slain;
You scattered Your enemies with Your powerful arm.
¹¹ The heavens are Yours; the earth also is Yours.
The world and everything in it—You founded them.
¹² North and south—You created them.
Tabor and Hermon shout for joy at Your name.
¹³ You have a mighty arm;
Your hand is powerful;
Your right hand is lifted high.
¹⁴ Righteousness and justice are the foundation
of Your throne;
faithful love and truth go before You.
¹⁵ Happy are the people who know the joyful shout;
LORD, they walk in the light of Your presence.
¹⁶ They rejoice in Your name all day long,
and they are exalted by Your righteousness.
¹⁷ For You are their magnificent strength;
by Your favor our horn is exalted.
¹⁸ Surely our shield belongs to the LORD,
our king to the Holy One of Israel.

¹⁹ You once spoke in a vision to Your loyal ones
and said: "I have granted help to a warrior;
I have exalted one chosen from the people.

²⁰ I have found David My servant;
I have anointed him with My sacred oil.

²¹ My hand will always be with him,
and My arm will strengthen him.

²² The enemy will not afflict him;
no wicked man will oppress him.

²³ I will crush his foes before him
and strike those who hate him.

²⁴ My faithfulness and love will be with him,
and through My name
his horn will be exalted.

²⁵ I will extend his power to the sea
and his right hand to the rivers.

²⁶ He will call to Me, 'You are my Father,
my God, the rock of my salvation.'

²⁷ I will also make him My firstborn,
greatest of the kings of the earth.

²⁸ I will always preserve My faithful love for him,
and My covenant with him will endure.

²⁹ I will establish his line forever,
his throne as long as heaven lasts.

³⁰ If his sons forsake My instruction
and do not live by My ordinances,

³¹ if they dishonor My statutes
and do not keep My commandments,

³² then I will call their rebellion
to account with the rod,
their sin with blows.

³³ But I will not withdraw
My faithful love from him
or betray My faithfulness.

³⁴ I will not violate My covenant
or change what My lips have said.

³⁵ Once and for all
I have sworn an oath by My holiness;
I will not lie to David.

³⁶ His offspring will continue forever,

his throne like the sun before Me,
³⁷ like the moon, established forever,
a faithful witness in the sky." *Selah*

³⁸ But You have spurned and rejected him;
You have become enraged with Your anointed.
³⁹ You have repudiated the covenant with Your servant;
You have completely dishonored his crown.
⁴⁰ You have broken down all his walls;
You have reduced his fortified cities to ruins.
⁴¹ All who pass by plunder him;
he has become a joke to his neighbors.
⁴² You have lifted high the right hand of his foes;
You have made all his enemies rejoice.
⁴³ You have also turned back his sharp sword
and have not let him stand in battle.
⁴⁴ You have made his splendor cease
and have overturned his throne.
⁴⁵ You have shortened the days of his youth;
You have covered him with shame. *Selah*

⁴⁶ How long, LORD? Will You hide Yourself forever?
Will Your anger keep burning like fire?
⁴⁷ Remember how short my life is.
Have You created everyone for nothing?
⁴⁸ What man can live and never see death?
Who can save himself from the power of Sheol? *Selah*
⁴⁹ Lord, where are the former acts of Your faithful love
that You swore to David in Your faithfulness?
⁵⁰ Remember, Lord, the ridicule against Your servants—
in my heart I carry [abuse] from all the peoples—
⁵¹ how Your enemies have ridiculed, LORD,
how they have ridiculed every step of Your anointed.

⁵² May the LORD be praised forever.
Amen and amen.

THOUGHT: How our hearts rejoice that one day the Saviour who first came to this world as a baby is going to return as King. But we must not forget that He is King now (Heb. 2:9). Join with thousands today in expressing praise and renewed dedication through the following verse:

Rise up O men of God
Have done with lesser things,
Give heart and soul and mind and strength
To serve the King of kings!   (William P. Merrill)

THIS PSALM WAS probably first sung at a king's coronation in Israel.

DAY
124

PSALM 2

The prophetic singer sings a vision of the nations in uproar, their leaders in fierce debate as if at a world-summit conference. For all their differences, they are perceived by the psalmist as conspiring together 'against the Lord and His Anointed One ...' (v.2). Beneath their well-spun political manifestos, the men of power intend to run God's world without Him.

But what our visionary singer sees and hears is very different: he sees God's throne and hears God laugh! It's not a cruel laughter but a divine derision which pricks the bubble of human arrogance. Now one voice rises authoritatively above the rest to declare that the decision about who rules the world is not open for discussion but has already been taken! 'I have installed my King on Zion, my holy hill' (v.6, NIV).

How incongruous it sounds to the world's empire-builders, to be supplanted by this King in Zion, a puny hill in the capital of an obscure, uninfluential, out-of-the-way nation.

But let the King speak: 'He said to Me, "You are My Son; today I have become Your Father. Ask of Me, and I will make the nations Your inheritance and the ends of the earth Your possession"' (vv.7–8).

Next time we hear this we will be with two men,

standing dripping wet on a river bank on the verge of
the kingdom of God.

BIBLE READING

Psalm 2

CORONATION OF THE SON

¹ Why do the nations rebel
and the peoples plot in vain?
² The kings of the earth take their stand
and the rulers conspire together
against the LORD and His Anointed One:
³ "Let us tear off their chains
and free ourselves from their restraints."

⁴ The One enthroned in heaven laughs;
the Lord ridicules them.
⁵ Then He speaks to them in His anger
and terrifies them in His wrath:
⁶ "I have consecrated My King
on Zion, My holy mountain."

⁷ I will declare the LORD's decree:
He said to Me, "You are My Son;
today I have become Your Father.
⁸ Ask of Me,
and I will make the nations Your inheritance
and the ends of the earth Your possession.
⁹ You will break them with a rod of iron;
You will shatter them like pottery."

¹⁰ So now, kings, be wise;
receive instruction, you judges of the earth.
¹¹ Serve the LORD with reverential awe,
and rejoice with trembling.
¹² Pay homage to the Son, or He will be angry,
and you will perish in your rebellion,
for His anger may ignite at any moment.
All those who take refuge in Him are happy.

FOR PRAISE: Have you ever considered how many times the Old Testament prophets were sustained by a vision of the throne - a place of power and authority? When things looked bad on earth they lifted their eyes to heaven and drew inspiration from the fact that ultimately God was in control. Earthly thrones may be toppled, but as the writer to the Hebrews says, 'Your throne O God is forever and ever'. Give God praise for that glorious fact.

WE PAUSE FOR a moment to acknowledge that God's commitment to the royal office is remarkable in the light of its inauspicious beginnings in Israel. Today's passage makes for sorry reading!

DAY
125

JUDGES 21

In pre-monarchical days, in the period of the Judges, Israel was meant to model social salvation by experiencing the blessings of living under a theocracy - that is, under the direct rule and government of God. Tragically, by the end of the Judges period, the divine experiment of Israel as a 'holy nation' in the promised land had degenerated into moral and social anarchy. The ancient historian sounds a society's epitaph like the dull tolling of a funeral bell: '... there was no king in Israel; everyone did what was right in his own eyes' (Judg. 21:25 NKJV). This repeated 'there was no king in Israel' is intended to alert the reader of the text to the deadly spiritual vacuum that preceded the rise of kingship in Israel. In Germany in the 1930s, social, moral and national disarray prompted a groundswell for a strong and authoritarian leader who would 'make the trains run on time'. The German people, resentful of their treatment by the Allies after World War I, and facing economic and social meltdown, got the Nazis and Adolf Hitler! Israel got Saul!

| BIBLE READING | **Judges 21** |

BRIDES FOR BENJAMIN

21 The men of Israel had sworn an oath at Mizpah: "None of us will give his daughter to a Benjaminite in marriage." ²So the people went to Bethel and sat there before God until evening. They wept loudly and bitterly, ³and cried out, "Why, LORD God of Israel, has it occurred that one tribe is [missing] in Israel today?" ⁴The next day the people got up early, built an altar there, and offered burnt offerings and fellowship offerings. ⁵The Israelites asked, "Who of all the tribes of Israel didn't come to the LORD with the assembly?" For a great oath had been taken that anyone who had not come to the LORD at Mizpah would certainly be put to death.

⁶But the Israelites had compassion on their brothers, the Benjaminites, and said, "Today a tribe has been cut off from Israel. ⁷What should we do about wives for the survivors? We've sworn to the LORD not to give them any of our daughters as wives." ⁸They asked, "Which city among the tribes of Israel didn't come to the LORD at Mizpah?" It turned out that no one from Jabesh-gilead had come to the camp and the assembly. ⁹For when the people were counted, no one was there from the inhabitants of Jabesh-gilead.

¹⁰The congregation sent 12,000 brave warriors there and commanded them: "Go and kill the inhabitants of Jabesh-gilead with the sword, including women and children. ¹¹This is what you should do: Completely destroy every male, as well as every female who has slept with a man." ¹²They found among the inhabitants of Jabesh-gilead 400 young virgins, who had not had sexual relations with a man, and they brought them to the camp at Shiloh in the land of Canaan.

¹³The whole congregation sent a message of peace to the Benjaminites who were at the rock of Rimmon. ¹⁴Benjamin returned at that time, and Israel gave them the women they had kept alive from Jabesh-gilead. But there were not enough for them.

¹⁵The people had compassion on Benjamin, because the LORD had made this gap in the tribes of Israel. ¹⁶The elders of the congregation said, "What should we do about wives

for those who are left, since the women of Benjamin have been destroyed?" ¹⁷They said, "There must be heirs for the survivors of Benjamin, so that a tribe of Israel will not be wiped out. ¹⁸But we can't give them our daughters as wives." For the Israelites had sworn: "Anyone who gives a wife to a Benjaminite is cursed." ¹⁹They also said, "Look, there's an annual festival to the Lᴏʀᴅ in Shiloh, which is north of Bethel, east of the highway that goes up from Bethel to Shechem, and south of Lebonah."

²⁰Then they commanded the Benjaminites: "Go and hide in the vineyards. ²¹Watch, and when you see the young women of Shiloh come out to perform the dances, each of you leave the vineyards and catch a wife for yourself from the young women of Shiloh, and go to the land of Benjamin. ²²When their fathers or brothers come to us and protest, we will tell them, 'Show favor to them, since we did not get enough wives for each of them in the battle. You didn't actually give [the women] to them, so you are not guilty [of breaking your oath].'"

²³The Benjaminites did this and took the number of women they needed from the dancers they caught. They went back to their own inheritance, rebuilt their cities, and lived in them. ²⁴At that time, each of the Israelites returned from there to his own tribe and family. Each returned from there to his own inheritance.

²⁵In those days there was no king in Israel; everyone did whatever he wanted.

PRAYER: O Father I am aware that deep down in my heart I have longed all my life for someone to rule and reign over the forces and energies within me that are too strong for my feeble will to control. Now I have made You the King of my life – things are so different. You have filled this 'deadly spiritual vacuum' that was in my heart. And how! Help me to give You sway over every part of my being. In Jesus' name I pray. Amen.

THE MORAL AND spiritual vacuum left by the period of the Judges stirs up popular clamour for a king and a deputation comes to Samuel to demand one. Sadly, the people ask for a king for the wrong reason and end up with the wrong man!

They ask for the wrong reason, demanding a king so as to be like every other nation – thus, directly repudiating Israel's destiny which was to be *unlike* any other nation.

Coming from a people meant to live theocratically – that is, directly under God's rule – it is tantamount to rejecting God Himself as King.

Furthermore, the 'wrong man', Saul, is installed, whose obvious 'head and shoulders' suitability, will soon compare poorly with David, the man 'after God's own heart', and His choice.

God through Samuel concedes to their demand, perhaps because, since Abraham and Sarah's time, kingship has always been within His plan for Israel. But Samuel warns the people of the dire consequences of humanly contrived monarchy, foreseeing just how oppressive and self-serving the kings would become.

But if bad and power-hungry kings – and with few exceptions they were bad – misused kingship for their own ends, God remained capable of using the royal category for His own purpose and glory. In God's hands, the office of kingship was redeemable and might become redemptive.

BIBLE READING

1 Samuel 8

ISRAEL'S DEMAND FOR A KING

8 When Samuel grew old, he appointed his sons as judges over Israel. ²His firstborn son's name was Joel and his second was Abijah. They were judges in Beer-sheba. ³However, his sons did not walk in his ways—they turned toward dishonest gain, took bribes, and perverted justice.

⁴So all the elders of Israel gathered together and went to Samuel at Ramah. ⁵They said to him, "Look, you are old, and your sons do not follow your example. Therefore, appoint a king to judge us the same as all the other nations have."

⁶When they said, "Give us a king to judge us," Samuel considered their demand sinful, so he prayed to the LORD. ⁷But the LORD told him, "Listen to the people and everything they say to you. They have not rejected you; they have rejected Me as their king. ⁸They are doing the same thing to you that they have done to Me, since the day I brought them out of Egypt until this day, abandoning Me and worshiping other gods. ⁹Listen to them, but you must solemnly warn them and tell them about the rights of the king who will rule over them."

¹⁰Samuel told all the LORD's words to the people who were asking him for a king. ¹¹He said, "These are the rights of the king who will rule over you: He can take your sons and put them to his use in his chariots, on his horses, or running in front of his chariots. ¹²He can appoint them for his use as commanders of thousands or commanders of fifties, to plow his ground or reap his harvest, or to make his weapons of war or the equipment for his chariots. ¹³He can take your daughters to become perfumers, cooks, and bakers. ¹⁴He can take your best fields, vineyards, and olive orchards and give them to his servants. ¹⁵He can take a tenth of your grain and your vineyards and give them to his officials and servants. ¹⁶He can take your male servants, your female servants, your best young men, and your donkeys and use them for his work. ¹⁷He can take a tenth of your flocks, and you yourselves can become his servants. ¹⁸When that day comes, you will cry out because of the king you've chosen for yourselves, but the LORD won't answer you on that day."

¹⁹The people refused to listen to Samuel. "No!" they said. "We must have a king over us. ²⁰Then we'll be like all the other nations: our king will judge us, go out before us, and fight our battles."

²¹Samuel listened to all the people's words and then repeated them to the LORD. ²²"Listen to them," the LORD told Samuel. "Appoint a king for them."

Then Samuel told the men of Israel, "Each of you, go back to your city."

TO PONDER: You take a certain risk when you ask God for something that you think is right for you, but does not conform to His will. He may give it to you, and you may not like it. Israel demanded a king but the one they got ended up ruining much of Israel and his life ended in tragedy. Be careful when you pray for something, to always add the phrase 'but only if it be Your will'. Remember, God always gives the best to those who leave the choice to Him.

DAY 127

2 SAMUEL 19:39–20:2

IN THE DISRUPTION that follows Absalom's rebellion, David flees for his life across the Jordan. After Absalom's death which grieves David deeply, a coalition of troops from David's own tribe of Judah and from Israel escort him back across the river. When the men of Israel complain at being upstaged by the men of Judah, they are told that such a course of action was obvious since David was a close kinsman of theirs. But, the men of Israel retort: 'We have 10 shares in the king ...' When this appeal cuts no ice, the Israelites are induced by a troublemaker to renounce their claim on the king and desert him by saying: 'We have no share in David ...' (NIV). And it's this language of having 'shares in David' which is intriguing. It suggests that the king is an incorporative person, one who embodies his people, so that allegiance to him gives them an interest in him and makes the follower a part of his people. It's not too fanciful to see here the germ of an idea which will blossom again with telling effect in gospel times when those who follow Jesus Christ, the true Messianic King, are said to be 'in Christ'. Once more we see how crucial the right king is to the ongoing plan of God.

2 Samuel 19:39-20:2

³⁹So all the people crossed the Jordan, and then the king crossed. The king kissed Barzillai and blessed him, and Barzillai returned to his home.

⁴⁰The king went on to Gilgal, and Chimham went with him. All the troops of Judah and half of Israel's escorted the king. ⁴¹Suddenly, all the men of Israel came to the king. They asked him, "Why did our brothers, the men of Judah, take you away secretly and transport the king and his household across the Jordan, along with all of David's men?"

⁴²All the men of Judah responded to the men of Israel, "Because the king is our relative. Why does this make you angry? Have we ever eaten anything of the king's or been honored at all?"

⁴³The men of Israel answered the men of Judah: "We have 10 shares in the king, so we have a greater [claim] to David than you. Why then do you despise us? Weren't we the first to speak of restoring our king?" But the words of the men of Judah were harsher than those of the men of Israel.

SHEBA'S REVOLT

20 Now a wicked man, a Benjaminite named Sheba son of Bichri, happened to be there. He blew the ram's horn and shouted:

> We have no portion in David,
> no inheritance in Jesse's son.
> Each man to his tent, Israel!

²So all the men of Israel deserted David and followed Sheba son of Bichri, but the men of Judah from the Jordan all the way to Jerusalem remained loyal to their king.

THOUGHT: Dr Deismann, the German scholar, said that the phrase 'in Christ' and its equivalent occurs no less than 164 times in Paul's writings. How much that concept must have meant to the apostle. How it sustained him in the work that he did for the Master. Let that same thought lie on your heart today. Meditate on it. Say to yourself 'I am in Christ ... and Christ is in me. I am safe from all that Satan would do to destroy me.'

DAY 128

PSALM 72

TRUE KINGSHIP IS here celebrated for its justice, righteousness and concern for the poor, the afflicted and the weak. The lovely image of rain falling on mown grass (v.6) - briefly scented in David's rule (2 Sam. 23:4), suggests how deeply satisfying such a kingdom might be. To such a kingdom, all kings are summoned to come, drawn as to a magnet (v.11, compare Rev.21:24). Through it will flow blessing for all nations as promised to Abraham (v.17).

This vision has inspired some of the greatest Christian hymns. In 'Jesus shall reign where'er the sun' Isaac Watts shrewdly notes that this ideal King will not merely return things to their original state but will bring to fruition all the unfulfilled potential in God's creation:

Where He displays His healing power
Death and the curse are known no more
In Him the tribes of Adam boast
More blessings than their father lost.

The 'more blessings' reminds us that redemption is an advance on creation, a decisive change for the better. And in 'Hail to the Lord's Anointed', James Montgomery glories in the one constant factor:

The tide of time shall never
His covenant remove;
His name shall stand for ever,
His changeless name of love.

On this empire of God's true King, the sun will never set, and for us and our needy world, it can't come quickly enough!

Psalm 72

A PRAYER FOR THE KING

Solomonic.

¹ God, give Your justice to the king
and Your righteousness to the king's son.
² He will judge Your people with righteousness
and Your afflicted ones with justice.
³ May the mountains bring prosperity to the people,
and the hills, righteousness.
⁴ May he vindicate the afflicted among the people,
help the poor,
and crush the oppressor.

⁵ May he continue while the sun endures,
and as long as the moon, throughout all generations.
⁶ May he be like rain that falls on the cut grass,
like spring showers that water the earth.
⁷ May the righteous flourish in his days,
and prosperity abound
until the moon is no more.

⁸ And may he rule from sea to sea
and from the Euphrates
to the ends of the earth.
⁹ May desert tribes kneel before him
and his enemies lick the dust.
¹⁰ May the kings of Tarshish
and the coasts and islands bring tribute,
the kings of Sheba and Seba offer gifts.
¹¹ And let all kings bow down to him,
all nations serve him.

¹² For he will rescue the poor who cry out
and the afflicted who have no helper.
¹³ He will have pity on the poor and helpless
and save the lives of the poor.
¹⁴ He will redeem them from oppression and violence,

for their lives are precious in his sight.

15 May he live long!
May gold from Sheba be given to him.
May prayer be offered for him continually,
and may he be blessed all day long.
16 May there be plenty of grain in the land;
may it wave on the tops of the mountains.
May its crops be like Lebanon.
May people flourish in the cities
like the grass of the field.
17 May his name endure forever;
as long as the sun shines,
may his fame increase.
May all nations be blessed by him
and call him blessed.

18 May the LORD God, the God of Israel, be praised,
who alone does wonders.
19 May His glorious name be praised forever;
the whole earth is filled with His glory.
Amen and amen.
20 The prayers of David son of Jesse are concluded.

PRAYER: Father, my heart awaits the dawning of that great day when Jesus the King will return to establish His rule of righteousness in the earth. And I see that Your coming will not only return things to their original condition but will bring out the potential that because of sin was never fully realised. How wonderful. For me and for my brothers and sisters in Christ, it can't come quickly enough. Even so come Lord Jesus!

THIS ROYAL SONG became the most quoted psalm in the New Testament applied to the Messiah.

First, the Lord - that is Yahweh - is heard by a subject of the king addressing his royal 'Lord'. The king is promised an elevated place alongside God as His co-regent who will share in God's victory over His enemies. His troops will not be conscripts but willing volunteers in the fight. Verse 3b may be read literally as, 'on the holy mountains, from the womb of the dawn, I have begotten you', so harking back to Psalm 2:7's picture of the king's coronation day. The dew at dawn imagery symbolises the life-giving hope offered by the king in a land noted for its parched summers.

The prophetic singer's second oracle singles out a priestly figure - modelled uniquely on the strange priest-king of Salem who met Abraham - who will triumph militarily, in the cause of God's just judgment. Verse 7 may echo Solomon's anointing as king at the Gihon Spring outside Jerusalem (1 Kings 1:38-39). It suggests the king being 'sacramentally resourced' (John Goldingay) for his vocation, and going on to victory with head held high. If this second declaration, like the first, was addressed to the Davidic king, then it is an unprecedented joining of the roles of priest and king - previously kept rigidly separate - in one person. The writer to the Hebrews, as we shall see, was not slow to exploit this prophetic song to glorify Jesus as the Son-Priest-King of God!

Psalm 110

DAY
129

PSALM 110

BIBLE
READING

THE PRIESTLY KING

A Davidic psalm.

¹ The LORD declared to my Lord:
    "Sit at My right hand
    until I make Your enemies Your footstool."
² The LORD will extend Your mighty scepter from Zion.

Rule over Your surrounding enemies.
³ Your people will volunteer
on Your day of battle.
In holy splendor, from the womb of the dawn,
the dew of Your youth belongs to You.
⁴ The LORD has sworn an oath and will not take it back:
"Forever, You are a priest
like Melchizedek."

⁵ The Lord is at Your right hand;
He will crush kings on the day of His anger.
⁶ He will judge the nations, heaping up corpses;
He will crush leaders over the entire world.
⁷ He will drink from the brook by the road;
therefore, He will lift up His head.

FOR PRAISE: Give thanks to God today for the ministry of our Lord, which encompasses the role of Priest and King. Realise and rejoice in all that this means. As our great High Priest He represents us before God, prays for us and pleads for our deliverance from Satan's bondage. As King He rules and reigns over sin, self and the world. Now in your own words give God thanks for all the implications of this great truth in your life.

DAY
130

PSALM 132

THE 'ARK OF the covenant' was that wooden chest surmounted by cherubim which was the key piece of sacred furniture in the Temple. It acted as the earthly footstool of God's heavenly throne where God's holy presence was concentrated.

The entrance of the ark into the tabernacle in Jerusalem had sparked wild rejoicing (2 Sam. 6:1-15) and continued to inspire sublime songs like today's well-crafted psalm.

This old 'ark song', once sung at the dedication of the Temple, would have stirred the faith of later pilgrims to the feasts (Psa. 132:8).

In it, four prayers of David (vv.1-10) are then perfectly

matched by God's fourfold prophetic answer (vv.11–18).

When David asks that his oath of allegiance to the Lord be remembered, the Lord reminds him of the divine oath that guarantees the Davidic covenant promises!

When David leads the pleas that God would arise and come to His resting place, the Lord reassures king and people that Zion is indeed His chosen resting place.

The prayer for the priest to be clothed with righteousness is answered by the Lord's promise.

Finally, when David asks not to be rejected, he is overwhelmed by lavish pledges of future glory.

Marvellously, the fears, doubts, questions and prayers, even of the anointed king, are met and matched by God's unswerving covenant commitment!

Psalm 132

BIBLE READING

DAVID AND ZION CHOSEN

A song of ascents.

¹ LORD, remember David
and all the hardships he endured,
² and how he swore an oath to the LORD,
making a vow to the Mighty One of Jacob:
³ "I will not enter my house
or get into my bed,
⁴ I will not allow my eyes to sleep
or my eyelids to slumber
⁵ until I find a place for the LORD,
a dwelling for the Mighty One of Jacob."

⁶ We heard of [the ark] in Ephrathah;
we found it in the fields of Jaar.
⁷ Let us go to His dwelling place;
let us worship at His footstool.
⁸ Arise, LORD, come to Your resting place,
You and the ark [that shows] Your strength.
⁹ May Your priests be clothed with righteousness,
and may Your godly people shout for joy.

¹⁰ Because of Your servant David,
do not reject Your anointed one.

¹¹ The LORD swore an oath to David,
a promise He will not abandon:
"I will set one of your descendants
on your throne.
¹² If your sons keep My covenant
and My decrees that I will teach them,
their sons will also sit on your throne, forever."

¹³ For the LORD has chosen Zion;
He has desired it for His home:
¹⁴ "This is My resting place forever;
I will make My home here
because I have desired it.
¹⁵ I will abundantly bless its food;
I will satisfy its needy with bread.
¹⁶ I will clothe its priests with salvation,
and its godly people will shout for joy.
¹⁷ There I will make a horn grow for David;
I have prepared a lamp for My anointed one.
¹⁸ I will clothe his enemies with shame,
but the crown he wears will be glorious."

FOR ACTION: We see in today's reading that the entrance of the ark into the tabernacle sparked off wild rejoicing and inspired songs of praise and gratitude to God. Think of this: our Lord Jesus Christ died on a cross, was buried in a tomb, rose from the dead and has returned to His rightful place in heaven. Is that not a cause for 'wild rejoicing'? Compose your own psalm of praise. Try it and see what it will do for your soul.

THE HISTORY OF kingship after Solomon in the divided kingdom of Israel and Judah is the sad but not unfamiliar story of how power corrupts and absolute power corrupts absolutely. The prophets voiced God's passionate protest at this trend as they sought to recall both kings and people to covenantal standards. Where false prophets defended the status quo with a false sense of security, the true prophets, like Micah, shattered such complacency for the sake of a deeper peace (3:5-12).

God can start again if necessary with the most unlikely material - such as the bruised and homeless - in order to build a new people for Himself. He will make the 'lame the nucleus of a nation ...' (4:6, Moffatt). They will be 'a showcase exhibit of God's rule in action' (*The Message*) to which the nations will stream (4:2-5), no longer tearing each other apart but secure and at rest in the king's greatness (5:4-5). 'He will stand and shepherd them [his flock, NIV] in the strength of Yahweh, in the majestic name of Yahweh His God' (5:4). This ideal king holds the key to Israel's hope and the whole world's peace (5:3,5). God's plans are safe in His hands. And where else could this ideal king originate but in David's birthplace? (5:2). As Micah says, when it comes to the future, it's back to Bethlehem!

DAY 131
MICAH 3:5-4:8; 5:1-4

Micah 3:5-4:8

BIBLE READING

FALSE PROPHETS JUDGED

⁵ This is what the LORD says
concerning the prophets
who lead my people astray,
who proclaim peace
when they have [food] to sink their teeth into
but declare war against the one
who puts nothing in their mouths.
⁶ Therefore, it will be night for you—

without visions;
it will grow dark for you—
without divination.
The sun will set on these prophets,
and the daylight will turn black over them.

⁷ Then the seers will be ashamed
and the diviners disappointed.
They will all cover their mouths
because there will be no answer from God.

⁸ But as for me, I am filled with power
by the Spirit of the Lord,
with justice and courage,
to proclaim to Jacob his rebellion
and to Israel his sin.

ZION'S DESTRUCTION

⁹ Listen to this, leaders of the house of Jacob,
you rulers of the house of Israel,
who abhor justice
and pervert everything that is right,

¹⁰ who build Zion with bloodshed
and Jerusalem with injustice.

¹¹ Her leaders issue rulings for a bribe,
her priests teach for payment,
and her prophets practice divination for money.
Yet they lean on the Lord, saying,
"Isn't the Lord among us?
No calamity will overtake us."

¹² Therefore, because of you,
Zion will be plowed like a field,
Jerusalem will become ruins,
and the hill of the temple mount
will be a thicket.

THE LORD'S RULE FROM RESTORED ZION

4 In the last days
the mountain of the Lord's house
will be established
at the top of the mountains

and will be raised above the hills.
Peoples will stream to it,

2 and many nations will come and say,
"Come, let us go up to the mountain of the LORD,
to the house of the God of Jacob.
He will teach us about His ways
so we may walk in His paths."
For instruction will go out of Zion
and the word of the LORD from Jerusalem.

3 He will settle disputes among many peoples
and provide arbitration for strong nations
that are far away.
They will beat their swords into plows,
and their spears into pruning knives.
Nation will not take up the sword against nation,
and they will never again train for war.

4 But each man will sit under his grapevine
and under his fig tree
with no one to frighten [him].
For the mouth of the LORD of Hosts
has promised [this].

5 Though all the peoples each walk
in the name of their gods,
we will walk in the name of Yahweh our God
forever and ever.

6 On that day—
[this is] the LORD's declaration—
I will assemble the lame
and gather the scattered,
those I have injured.

7 I will make the lame into a remnant,
those far removed into a strong nation.
Then the LORD will rule over them in Mount Zion
from this time on and forever.

8 And you, watchtower for the flock,
fortified hill of Daughter Zion,
the former rule will come to you,
sovereignty will come to Daughter Jerusalem.

BIBLE READING

Micah 5:1-4

FROM DEFEATED RULER TO CONQUERING KING

5 Now daughter [who is] under attack,
you slash yourself [in grief];
a siege is set against us!
They are striking the judge of Israel
on the cheek with a rod.
2 Bethlehem Ephrathah,
you are small among the clans of Judah;
One will come from you
to be ruler over Israel for Me.
His origin is from antiquity,
from eternity.
3 Therefore, He will abandon them until the time
when she who is in labor has given birth;
then the rest of His brothers will return
to the people of Israel.
4 He will stand and shepherd [them]
in the strength of Yahweh,
in the majestic name of Yahweh His God.
They will live securely,
for then His greatness will extend
to the ends of the earth.

PRAYER: O Father, I am so grateful that the plans You devise are guaranteed not to fail. They are in safe hands. I rejoice even more that my life is in Your hands. Scripture tells me that my life is hid with Christ in God. You have been holding up the universe for aeons and it is still intact, still runs with amazing mathematical precision. In Your hands I am safe and secure. Deepen that assurance within me. In Jesus' name. Amen.

AS WE SAID yesterday, the prophets clashed with the kings, holding them accountable to the covenant. This was particularly true of Isaiah, fighting for faith with a mistrustful king, Ahaz.

DAY
132
ISAIAH 8:16-9:7

In response to total lack of faith, God is hiding His face from the king (8:17). As dawn light fails, unbelief turns from the light of the Torah and gropes for occult meaning in the darkness that descends (8:19-20)! Over all, death casts its long shadow (9:2).

But those who rally to the prophet's word of truth and become his disciples are shown the shining vision of another kingdom, the birth of another king (9:1-7). This Prince with the four names - will take the government back from fallible rulers onto His own broad shoulders.

Humiliation gives way to honour, darkness to light, despair to joy.

And the joy is even sweeter than over a bumper harvest, a victory in battle or freedom from oppression! There is no decline and fall of His empire, only continuous increase! The Davidic covenant comes good in and through this Prince of Peace (9:7). And if our zeal for God's work ever cools, we can be sure that God's never does (9:7). God remains infinitely more enthusiastic for His work and plans than we ever do. His passionate commitments will see this through!

Isaiah 8:16-9:7

BIBLE READING

¹⁶ Bind up the testimony.
Seal up the instruction among my disciples.
¹⁷ I will wait for the LORD,
who is hiding His face from the house of Jacob.
I will wait for Him.

¹⁸Here I am with the children the LORD has given me to be signs and wonders in Israel from the LORD of Hosts who dwells on Mount Zion. ¹⁹When they say to you, "Consult the spirits of the dead and the spiritists who chirp and mutter," shouldn't a people

consult their God? [Should they consult] the dead on behalf of the living? ²⁰To the law and to the testimony! If they do not speak according to this word, there will be no dawn for them.

²¹They will wander through the land, dejected and hungry. When they are famished, they will become enraged, and, looking upward, will curse their king and their God. ²²They will look toward the earth and see only distress, darkness, and the gloom of affliction, and they will be driven into thick darkness.

BIRTH OF THE PRINCE OF PEACE

9 Nevertheless, the gloom of the distressed land will not be like that of the former times when He humbled the land of Zebulun and the land of Naphtali. But in the future He will bring honor to the Way of the Sea, to the land east of the Jordan, and to Galilee of the nations.

² The people walking in darkness
   have seen a great light;
   on those living in the land of darkness,
   a light has dawned.
³ You have enlarged the nation
   and increased its joy.
   [The people] have rejoiced before You
   as they rejoice at harvest time
   and as they rejoice when dividing spoils.
⁴ For You have shattered their burdensome yoke
   and the rod on their shoulders,
   the staff of their oppressor,
   just as [You did] on the day of Midian.
⁵ For the trampling boot of battle
   and the bloodied garments of war
   will be burned as fuel for the fire.
⁶ For a child will be born for us,
   a son will be given to us,
   and the government will be on His shoulders.
   He will be named
   Wonderful Counselor, Mighty God,
   Eternal Father, Prince of Peace.
⁷ The dominion will be vast,
   and its prosperity will never end.

He will reign on the throne of David
and over his kingdom,
to establish and sustain it
with justice and righteousness from now on
   and forever.
The zeal of the LORD of Hosts will accomplish this.

THOUGHT: How comforting to know that though
sometimes our enthusiasm wanes and our love cools God's
does not. Do you know someone whose love is consistent and
whose enthusiasm for life (and perhaps for you) never
changes? Multiply those qualities a billion times and you come
near to understanding something of the passion for the Big
Story to which God is committed. He is going to see this thing
through – right to the end.

LET'S RELISH AGAIN this stunning prophetic vision of the Prince with the fourfold name.

DAY 133

ISAIAH 9:2–7

Here is the Wonderful Counsellor in a darkened world where so many have lost the light of God's truth and grope for answers in the twilight realm of their own opinions or the murky underworld of occultism and pseudo-science.

His wisdom is wonderful. He is the bearer of supernatural counsel.

Entrusted with the grand strategy of God, He can surely be trusted for the details of your life and mine.

Mighty God or – better – Mighty Warrior, this almighty little One, is a child born to us, who tips the balance of power in God's favour and therefore in ours, our champion in the battle for faith.

And the Son is also the Everlasting Father! Given to us is a royal child who becomes the source of eternal life to those who embrace His rule and find Him to be the Prince of Peace. And this is not peace at any price, but peace as the costly foundation of His kingdom.

If your faith seems a flickering candle in the wind,

rekindle it at the great flame of this vision – a vision
which was one day enacted in a life on fire for
God, a bush that burned but was not consumed by
crucifixion, that burst forth from the shadow of death
in a blaze of resurrection light which will one day flood
the earth in glory.

| BIBLE
| READING

Isaiah 9:2-7

² The people walking in darkness
   have seen a great light;
   on those living in the land of darkness,
   a light has dawned.
³ You have enlarged the nation
   and increased its joy.
   [The people] have rejoiced before You
   as they rejoice at harvest time
   and as they rejoice when dividing spoils.
⁴ For You have shattered their burdensome yoke
   and the rod on their shoulders,
   the staff of their oppressor,
   just as [You did] on the day of Midian.
⁵ For the trampling boot of battle
   and the bloodied garments of war
   will be burned as fuel for the fire.
⁶ For a child will be born for us,
   a son will be given to us,
   and the government will be on His shoulders.
   He will be named
   Wonderful Counselor, Mighty God,
   Eternal Father, Prince of Peace.
⁷ The dominion will be vast,
   and its prosperity will never end.
   He will reign on the throne of David
   and over his kingdom,
   to establish and sustain it
   with justice and righteousness from now on
     and forever.
   The zeal of the LORD of Hosts will accomplish this.

TO PONDER: One Bible teacher claims that 'Wonderful Counsellor' can be translated: 'As a counsellor he is a wonder.' Jesus Christ is the only counsellor who doesn't need counselling Himself. The two main resources of a counsellor are knowledge (how problems arise) and wisdom (how to rightly apply that knowledge). Jesus is the fount of all knowledge and wisdom. And it's all available - free of charge - for you and me.

ISAIAH NOW SPEAKS of impossibilities happening, a new shoot from the root of Jesse, David's father.

DAY
134

ISAIAH 11

All along, Isaiah has been convinced that God cuts down only to start again, that from the decimated stump of judgment, grace can flow into new life (6:13). The Assyrian oppressors of God's people will themselves be cut down never to rise again (10:34) but from the stump and root of David's line, amazingly new life will sprout and grow into a Branch (11:1) to be the leader, judge and standard-bearer of the nations.

His humble beginnings (v.1) only highlight the fact that He qualifies to rule (vv.1-3) only by His endowment with God's Spirit. This reminds us of the wild 'wind of God' ('*ruach*') which had invaded David, marking him as God's appointee. The Spirit heightens our awareness of the solemn joys of living with the awesome majesty of God. He will draw breath in the fear of the Lord as if the very atmosphere is charged with grandeur. To fear God in this way is to know that rush of spiritual adrenaline in the presence of holiness.

With such a ruler comes a vision of a transformed earth (vv.6-9). Creation's unrest is pacified by an Adamic dominion cleansed of unrighteousness. Noah take note! The earth will be brimful of knowing God! The nations - Abraham are you watching? - will rally to His banner!

| BIBLE READING | **Isaiah 11** |

REIGN OF THE DAVIDIC KING

11 Then a shoot will grow from the stump of Jesse,
and a branch from his roots will bear fruit.
2 The Spirit of the LORD will rest on Him—
a Spirit of wisdom and understanding,
a Spirit of counsel and strength,
a Spirit of knowledge and of the fear of the LORD.
3 His delight will be in the fear of the LORD.
He will not judge
by what He sees with His eyes,
He will not execute justice
by what He hears with His ears,
4 but He will judge the poor righteously
and execute justice for the oppressed of the land.
He will strike the land
with discipline from His mouth,
and He will kill the wicked
with a command from His lips.
5 Righteousness and faithfulness
will be a belt around His waist.
6 The wolf will live with the lamb,
and the leopard will lie down with the goat.
The calf, the young lion, and the fatling
will be together,
and a child will lead them.
7 The cow and the bear will graze,
their young ones will lie down together,
and the lion will eat straw like an ox.
8 An infant will play beside the cobra's pit,
and a toddler will put his hand into a snake's den.
9 No one will harm or destroy
on My entire holy mountain,
for the land will be as full
of the knowledge of the LORD
as the sea is filled with water.

ISRAEL REGATHERED

¹⁰ On that day the root of Jesse
will stand as a banner for the peoples.
The nations will seek Him,
and His resting place will be glorious.

¹¹On that day the Lord will [extend] His hand a second time to recover—from Assyria, Egypt, Pathros, Cush, Elam, Shinar, Hamath, and the coasts and islands of the west—the remnant of His people who survive.

¹² He will lift up a banner for the nations
and gather the dispersed of Israel;
He will collect the scattered of Judah
from the four corners of the earth.
¹³ Ephraim's envy will cease;
Judah's harassment will end.
Ephraim will no longer be envious of Judah,
and Judah will not harass Ephraim.
¹⁴ But they will swoop down
on the Philistine flank to the west.
Together they will plunder the people of the east.
They will extend their power over Edom and Moab,
and the Ammonites will be their subjects.
¹⁵ The LORD will divide the Gulf of Suez.
He will wave His hand over the Euphrates
with His mighty wind
and will split it into seven streams,
letting people walk through on foot.
¹⁶ There will be a highway for the remnant of His people
who will survive from Assyria,
as there was for Israel
when they came up from the land of Egypt.

THOUGHT: Humble beginnings can be of great significance when God is in them. An unknown poet wrote this:

> I said, Master, where shall I work today?
> And my love flowed warm and free
> And he pointed to a little plot and said,
> There, tend that for me.
> But Lord, I said, not that, not that little place for me.
> And his voice when it spoke was soft and warm,
> Bethlehem was just a little place - and so was Galilee.

DAY
135
JEREMIAH 22:1-5,11-17; 23:1-8

BEING A KING during Jeremiah's time was often a very uncomfortable experience. The prophet gives the kings a hard time.

Chapter 22 is a savage indictment of the kings in Judah for their injustice, ostentation and self-seeking - a sadly familiar litany of abuses of power. In contrast to his father, Josiah, Shallum is upbraided for failing to defend the poor (22:11-17). Knowing the Lord is not a matter of having exalted religious experiences of God but of practising social justice. If you don't do justly, you don't 'know' God.

From this sorry scene, Jeremiah turns in a burst of prophetic hope to depict the grace that will emerge triumphant out of judgment. Uncaring, false shepherds who have misled and scattered God's sheep will be supplanted by God Himself who will regather and grow the flock (23:1-4). God will raise up a righteous Branch in David's line (v.5). This King will reign wisely and be known as 'The Lord Is Our Righteousness' (v.6). This is an ironic twist in the story. The name of Judah's last, disgraced king, Zedekiah, means 'Yahweh is righteous'. But where he failed to live up to his name, the future King will embody God's righteousness.

Through this King God will not only bring social stability and well-being (vv.4-6) but will bring His people home in a radical new exodus which will eclipse the memory of the first (vv.7-8)!

BIBLE READING

Jeremiah 22:1-5,11-17

JUDGMENT AGAINST SINFUL KINGS

22 This is what the LORD says: "Go down to the palace of the king of Judah and announce this word there. ²You are to say: Hear the word of the LORD, king of Judah, you who sit on the throne of David—you, your officers, and your people who enter these gates. ³This is what the LORD says: Administer justice and righteousness. Rescue the victim of robbery from the hand of his oppressor. Don't exploit or brutalize the alien, the fatherless, or the widow. Don't shed innocent blood in this place. ⁴For if you conscientiously carry out this word, then kings sitting on David's throne will enter through the gates of this palace riding on chariots and horses—they, their officers, and their people. ⁵But if you do not obey these words, then I swear by Myself"—[this is] the LORD's declaration—"that this house will become a ruin."

• • • • • • • • •

¹¹For this is what the LORD says concerning Shallum son of Josiah, king of Judah, who succeeded Josiah his father as king: "He has left this place—he will never return here again, ¹²but he will die in the place where they deported him, never seeing this land again."

A MESSAGE CONCERNING JEHOIAKIM

¹³ Woe for the one who builds his palace
   through unrighteousness,
   his upper rooms through injustice,
   who makes his fellow man serve without pay
   and will not give him his wages,
¹⁴ who says: I will build myself a massive palace,
   with spacious upper rooms.
   He will cut windows in it,
   and it will be paneled with cedar
   and painted with vermilion.
¹⁵ Are you a king because you excel in cedar?
   Your own father, did he not eat and drink?
   He administered justice and righteousness,

then it went well with him.
¹⁶ He took up the case of the poor and needy,
then it went well.
Is this not what it means to know Me?
[This is] the LORD's declaration.
¹⁷ But you have eyes and heart for nothing
except your own unjust gain,
shedding innocent blood
and committing extortion and oppression.

Jeremiah 23:1-8

THE LORD AND HIS SHEEP

23 "Woe to the shepherds who destroy and scatter the sheep of My pasture!" [This is] the LORD's declaration. ²"Therefore, this is what the LORD, the God of Israel, says about the shepherds who shepherd My people: You have scattered My flock, banished them, and have not attended to them. I will attend to you because of your evil acts"—the LORD's declaration. ³"I will gather the remnant of My flock from all the lands where I have banished them, and I will return them to their grazing land. They will become fruitful and numerous. ⁴I will raise up shepherds over them who will shepherd them. They will no longer be afraid or dismayed, nor will any be missing." [This is] the LORD's declaration.

THE RIGHTEOUS BRANCH OF DAVID

⁵"The days are coming"—[this is] the LORD's declaration—"when I will raise up a righteous Branch of David. He will reign wisely as king and administer justice and righteousness in the land. ⁶In His days Judah will be saved, and Israel will dwell securely. This is what He will be named: The LORD Is Our Righteousness. ⁷The days are coming"—the LORD's declaration—"when it will no longer be said: As the LORD lives who brought the Israelites from the land of Egypt, ⁸but: As the LORD lives, who brought and led the descendants of the house of Israel from the land of the north and from all the other countries where I had banished them. They will dwell once more in their own land."

HYMN: What better response can we give to today's reading than to sing with all the enthusiasm possible:

Rejoice, the Lord is King!
Your Lord and King adore;
Mortals, give thanks, and sing,
And triumph evermore:
Lift up your heart, lift up your voice;
Rejoice! Again I say: rejoice!

(Charles Wesley)

DAY 136

EZEKIEL 34

IN TRYING TO stay on the track of the promise given to David, we have already seen how the kings who followed him both in Israel and Judah proved, almost without exception, to be both unworthy recipients of the magnificent promises God had made to him, and unfaithful stewards of God's long-term plan to bless the world through them.

Nowhere are these royal failings more ruthlessly exposed than in this prophecy of Ezekiel.

Because the king carries within himself the whole nation's destiny, his disloyalty brings ruin to the people. So God holds the royal shepherds accountable and acts to remove them from office. But as is typical of the prophets, judgment is not God's final word. The demise of kingship in Judah at the Babylonian Exile, clears the way for a renewed appreciation of God as the only true King and Shepherd of His people.

And Ezekiel speaks a strangely ambiguous hope of the coming of a true Shepherd who, at one and the same time, is God Himself – come to do the shepherding job that has been so badly neglected – and a Prince of the house of David sent to restore His people. A good shepherd who is both God and the Davidic king? We haven't heard the last of this, that's for sure. And what is unambiguous is that He will usher in the long-awaited day of covenant fulfilment and salvation!

Ezekiel 34

THE SHEPHERDS AND GOD'S FLOCK

34 The word of the LORD came to me: [2]"Son of man, prophesy against the shepherds of Israel. Prophesy, and say to them: This is what the Lord GOD says to the shepherds: Woe to the shepherds of Israel, who have been feeding themselves! Shouldn't the shepherds feed their flock? [3]You eat the fat, wear the wool, and butcher the fatlings, but you do not tend the flock. [4]You have not strengthened the weak, healed the sick, bandaged the injured, brought back the strays, or sought the lost. Instead, you have ruled them with violence and cruelty. [5]They were scattered for lack of a shepherd; they became food for all the wild animals when they were scattered. [6]My flock went astray on all the mountains and every high hill. They were scattered over the whole face of the earth, and there was no one searching or seeking [for them].

[7]"Therefore, you shepherds, hear the word of the LORD. [8]As I live"—the declaration of the Lord GOD—"because My flock has become [prey and] food for every wild animal since [they] lack a shepherd, for My shepherds do not search for My flock, and [because] the shepherds feed themselves rather than My flock, [9]therefore, you shepherds, hear the word of the LORD!

[10]"This is what the Lord GOD says: Look, I am against the shepherds. I will demand My flock from them and prevent them from shepherding the flock. The shepherds will no longer feed themselves, for I will rescue My flock from their mouths so that they will not be food for them.

[11]"For this is what the Lord GOD says: See, I Myself will search for My flock and look for them. [12]As a shepherd looks for his sheep on the day he is among his scattered flock, so I will look for My flock. I will rescue them from all the places where they have been scattered on a cloudy and dark day. [13]I will bring them out from the peoples, gather them from the countries, and bring them into their own land. I will shepherd them on the mountains of Israel, in the ravines, and in all the inhabited places of the land. [14]I will tend them with good pasture, and their grazing place will be on Israel's lofty mountains. There they will lie down in a good grazing place; they will feed in

rich pasture on the mountains of Israel. [15]I will tend My flock and let them lie down." [This is] the declaration of the Lord GOD. [16]"I will seek the lost, bring back the strays, bandage the injured, and strengthen the weak, but I will destroy the fat and the strong. I will shepherd them with justice.

[17]"The Lord GOD says to you, My flock: I am going to judge between one sheep and another, between the rams and male goats. [18]Isn't it enough for you to feed on the good pasture? Must you also trample the rest of the pasture with your feet? Or [isn't it enough] that you drink the clear water? Must you also muddy the rest with your feet? [19]Yet My flock has to feed on what your feet have trampled, and drink what your feet have muddied.

[20]"Therefore, this is what the Lord GOD says to them: See, I Myself will judge between the fat sheep and the lean sheep. [21]Since you have pushed with flank and shoulder and butted all the weak ones with your horns until you scattered them all over, [22]I will save My flock, and they will no longer be prey for you. I will judge between one sheep and another. [23]I will appoint over them a single shepherd, My servant David, and he will shepherd them. He will tend them himself and will be their shepherd. [24]I, the LORD, will be their God, and My servant David will be a prince among them. I, the LORD, have spoken.

[25]"I will make a covenant of peace with them and eliminate dangerous animals in the land, so that they may live securely in the wilderness and sleep in the forest. [26]I will make them and the area around My hill a blessing: I will send down showers in their season—showers of blessing. [27]The trees of the field will give their fruit, and the land will yield its produce; My flock will be secure in their land. They will know that I am the LORD when I break the bars of their yoke and rescue them from the hands of those who enslave them. [28]They will no longer be prey for the nations, and the wild animals of the land will not consume them. They will live securely, and no one will frighten [them]. [29]I will establish for them a place renowned for [its] agriculture, and they will no longer be victims of famine in the land. They will no longer endure the insults of the nations. [30]Then they will know that I, the LORD their God, am with them, and that they, the house of Israel, are My people." [This is] the declaration of the Lord GOD. [31]"You are My flock, the human flock of My pasture, and I am your God." [This is] the declaration of the Lord GOD.

PRAYER: O Father, I pray today for those who are shepherding Your flock – Your precious under-shepherds – that You will keep them and protect them from evil. They are the special targets of the devil's strategies and they can easily get discouraged, become dysfunctional. Bind Satan's power in their lives and anoint them afresh to preach and teach Your Word. I ask this in and through the precious name of Jesus. Amen.

DAY
137
ISAIAH 55

IN A BUSTLING market-place, street-traders shout out their special offers to grab the attention of passers-by. In the Exile, as now, cultural airwaves are jammed with conflicting ideas and opinions.

Into this babble of competing truth-claims, God speaks the word which is above all words, an invitation of pure grace.

We are rightly suspicious of free offers but this one, while free, will cost us 'nothing less than everything' (vv.6-7)! But it invites us to satisfy our hunger and quench our thirst at the only source of true satisfaction for our souls.

Above all, God offers us a part in an alternative story to the one peddled by the Babylonian media, the true story of God's redemptive plans. Everyone is promised a role in making history with God. God's covenant with David – that 'charter for all humanity' through the Davidic king – is here democratised and opened up to all who repent and believe (vv.3-7)! David's 'sure mercies' are here extended to all who rally to the true King.

Like the earlier covenants, this 'everlasting covenant' (v.3) will have a sign attached to it – unlike before, an everlasting sign which is nothing less than a resplendently transformed creation (v.13).

God's final covenant will not cancel out all the previous ones – reviewed in chapter 54 – but will fulfil and perfect them. What a God!

BIBLE READING

Isaiah 55

COME TO THE LORD

55 "Come, everyone who is thirsty,
come to the waters;
and you without money,
come, buy, and eat!
Come, buy wine and milk
without money and without cost!
² Why do you spend money on what is not food,
and your wages on what does not satisfy?
Listen carefully to Me, and eat what is good,
and you will enjoy the choicest of foods.
³ Pay attention and come to Me;
listen, so that you will live.
I will make an everlasting covenant with you,
the promises assured to David.
⁴ Since I have made him a witness to the peoples,
a leader and commander for the peoples,
⁵ so you will summon a nation you do not know,
and nations who do not know you will run to you.
For the LORD your God,
even the Holy One of Israel,
has glorified you."

⁶ Seek the LORD while He may be found;
call to Him while He is near.
⁷ Let the wicked one abandon his way,
and the sinful one his thoughts;
let him return to the LORD,
so He may have compassion on him,
and to our God, for He will freely forgive.

⁸ "For My thoughts are not your thoughts,
and your ways are not My ways."
[This is] the LORD's declaration.
⁹ "For as heaven is higher than earth,
so My ways are higher than your ways,
and My thoughts than your thoughts.

¹⁰ For just as rain and snow fall from heaven,
    and do not return there
    without saturating the earth,
    and making it germinate and sprout,
    and providing seed to sow
    and food to eat,
¹¹ so My word that comes from My mouth
    will not return to Me empty,
    but it will accomplish what I please,
    and will prosper in what I send it [to do]."

¹² You will indeed go out with joy
    and be peacefully guided;
    the mountains and the hills will break into singing
      before you,
    and all the trees of the field will clap [their] hands.
¹³ Instead of the thornbush, a cypress will come up,
    and instead of the brier, a myrtle will come up;
    it will make a name for the LORD
    as an everlasting sign that will not be destroyed.

TO PONDER: What a God indeed! Have you ever considered that the way our personality works is like this: what we think about affects the way we feel and how we feel affects the way we act. Throughout the day ponder this truth: 'Everyone is promised a role in making history with God.' The more you think on that, the more it should affect your emotions and move you to deeper dedication. The best way to prove that theory is to put it to the test.

DAY
138

LUKE 1:26-56

WE HAVE TRACED the trajectory of the covenant made with David through the rise and fall of kingship in Israel and now to its fulfilment, a thousand years later, in a baby born to a young up-country girl in Nazareth. Betrothed but not yet married to Joseph, Mary knew that any son born to her would be a dim-distant descendant of David. But what kind of son and descendant was pure revelation to her.

Gabriel tells Mary that her child is set to inherit the enduring throne and never-ending kingdom promised to David.

As for the special father–son relationship with God, this would be assured from conception by God's creative Spirit who will 'overshadow' her as God's glory cloud 'overshadowed' the tabernacle. This royal Son's birth truly marks the dawn of a new creation, and a new start for God's people.

Through Mary's son, the Davidic covenant will find its climax and be fulfilled (v.32), Israel will be remembered by the Lord and mercifully restored (v.54), and the Abrahamic promises will be honoured (v.55)! Favoured by God, she joyfully responds with obedient co-operation – the very model of what it meant to be a true Israelite.

But what she had learned about her son remained a treasured secret for over thirty years until the joy she felt at His being part of her body was eclipsed by *her* being part of *His* body!

BIBLE READING

Luke 1:26-56

GABRIEL PREDICTS JESUS' BIRTH

²⁶In the sixth month, the angel Gabriel was sent by God to a town in Galilee called Nazareth, ²⁷to a virgin engaged to a man named Joseph, of the house of David. The virgin's name was Mary. ²⁸And [the angel] came to her and said, "Rejoice, favored woman! The Lord is with you." ²⁹But she was deeply troubled by this statement, wondering what kind of greeting this could be. ³⁰Then the angel told her:

Do not be afraid, Mary,
for you have found favor with God.
31 Now listen:
You will conceive and give birth to a son,
and you will call His name JESUS.
32 He will be great
and will be called the Son of the Most High,
and the Lord God will give Him
the throne of His father David.
33 He will reign over the house of Jacob forever,
and His kingdom will have no end.

34Mary asked the angel, "How can this be, since I have not been intimate with a man?"

35The angel replied to her:

"The Holy Spirit will come upon you,
and the power of the Most High will overshadow you.
Therefore the holy One to be born
will be called the Son of God.

36And consider your relative Elizabeth—even she has conceived a son in her old age, and this is the sixth month for her who was called barren. 37For nothing will be impossible with God."

38"I am the Lord's slave," said Mary. "May it be done to me according to your word." Then the angel left her.

MARY'S VISIT TO ELIZABETH

39In those days Mary set out and hurried to a town in the hill country of Judah 40where she entered Zechariah's house and greeted Elizabeth. 41When Elizabeth heard Mary's greeting, the baby leaped inside her, and Elizabeth was filled with the Holy Spirit. 42Then she exclaimed with a loud cry:

"You are the most blessed of women,
and your child will be blessed!

43How could this happen to me, that the mother of my Lord should come to me? 44For you see, when the sound of your greeting reached my ears, the baby leaped for joy inside me! [45]She who has believed is blessed because what was spoken to her by the Lord will be fulfilled!"

MARY'S PRAISE

[46]And Mary said:

My soul proclaims the greatness of the Lord,
[47] and my spirit has rejoiced in God my Savior,
[48] because He has looked with favor
on the humble condition of His slave.
Surely, from now on all generations
will call me blessed,
[49] because the Mighty One
has done great things for me,
and His name is holy.
[50] His mercy is from generation to generation
on those who fear Him.
[51] He has done a mighty deed with His arm;
He has scattered the proud
because of the thoughts of their hearts;
[52] He has toppled the mighty from their thrones
and exalted the lowly.
[53] He has satisfied the hungry with good things
and sent the rich away empty.
[54] He has helped His servant Israel,
mindful of His mercy,
[55] just as He spoke to our ancestors,
to Abraham and his descendants forever.

[56]And Mary stayed with her about three months; then she returned to her home.

QUESTION: In some sections of the Church Mary's role is overplayed while in others it is underplayed. What a choice young woman she must have been to be selected as the mother of Jesus. Consider the way in which she responded to the announcement that she had been impregnated by the Holy Spirit: 'May it be to me as you have said.' When God asks you to do something for Him is your response as quick and decisive?

IN HIS OPENING chapters, Luke is painting with broad brush strokes, writing what amounts to a remake of the story of kingship in Israel, especially its beginnings. So in Luke's parallelism, John the Baptist is acting as Samuel to Jesus' David. And this is set on the even larger canvas of the Roman Empire and its Caesars to make an immediate point. Jesus is Israel's true King, come at last to take His place on the throne of Israel and the world. Just as Samuel spelt judgment for the house of Saul and the priesthood of Eli, so the birth of John and the advent of Jesus spell judgment on King Herod and the current house of Israel. And the map of international power must be redrawn.

DAY 139

LUKE 2:1-15

Where Rome issued a 'euangellion' or 'gospel' to announce the emperor's birthday or success in battle, the angel declares the real good news in this baby's birth (2:10-11). The child born in Bethlehem is Israel's long-awaited Messiah who will reclaim from Caesar the self-appointed title of 'Saviour of the world'. And this Christ, as Psalm 2 had announced so long before, was destined to usurp the Caesars – and any other claimants – as the rightful Lord of God's world! His peace, unlike Rome's peace (the 'pax Romana') would be founded not on the crosses of its victims but on the cross on which He would suffer.

BIBLE READING

Luke 2:1-15

THE BIRTH OF JESUS

2 In those days a decree went out from Caesar Augustus that the whole empire should be registered. [2]This first registration took place while Quirinius was governing Syria. [3]So everyone went to be registered, each to his own town.

[4]And Joseph also went up from the town of Nazareth in Galilee, to Judea, to the city of David, which is called Bethlehem, because he was of the house and family line of David, [5]to be registered along with Mary, who was engaged to him and was pregnant. [6]While they were there, the time came for her to give birth. [7]Then she gave birth to her firstborn Son, and she wrapped Him snugly in cloth and laid Him in a feeding trough—because there was no room for them at the inn.

THE SHEPHERDS AND THE ANGELS

[8]In the same region, shepherds were staying out in the fields and keeping watch at night over their flock. [9]Then an angel of the Lord stood before them, and the glory of the Lord shone around them, and they were terrified. [10]But the angel said to them, "Don't be afraid, for look, I proclaim to you good news of great joy that will be for all the people: [11]today a Savior, who is Messiah the Lord, was born for you in the city of David. [12]This will be the sign for you: you will find a baby wrapped snugly in cloth and lying in a feeding trough."

[13]Suddenly there was a multitude of the heavenly host with the angel, praising God and saying:

[14] Glory to God in the highest heaven,
and peace on earth to people He favors!

[15]When the angels had left them and returned to heaven, the shepherds said to one another, "Let's go straight to Bethlehem and see what has happened, which the Lord has made known to us."

PRAYER: Lord Jesus Christ, I have thanked You time and time again for dying for me on the cross but I realise that I can never thank You enough! I am touched to the depth of my soul that You would give Your life for me, a sordid sinner, but even more for the fact that, in reclaiming this world for Yourself, you have included me in Your Story. It's almost too good to be true. But too good not to be true. Amen.

AS JESUS WAS baptised, the voice from heaven said: 'You are My Son.'

DAY 140

LUKE 3:21-23,30b-4:13

We last heard these words in Psalm 2 and 2 Samuel 7. There God promised the Davidic dynasty a unique father-son relationship with Him in which the king could call God his Father and God would look on the king as His son. So, as we fast forward to two men, standing, soaked through, on the bank of the River Jordan, we see the Holy Spirit single out one of them, and alight upon Him. At which the heavens open and God points out Jesus as His Son.

So, whatever else we come to know about Jesus of Nazareth, at least we know for sure that He is Israel's anointed King who inherits the Davidic mantle and promises. Luke underlines this by giving Jesus' family tree and tracing His ancestry back to David. Not only back to David, however, but through David right back to Adam, 'son of God'. Jesus, the Messiah, takes up the human mantle and inherits the vocation to have dominion.

It is precisely in His royal human vocation as Son of God that Jesus is then tested. But, like David before Him striding out to meet and defeat Goliath, Jesus meets and routs out the age-old enemy of humanity.

Where the first Adam failed, the second Adam succeeds and comes to our fight and rescue.

BIBLE READING

Luke 3:21-23,30b-4:13

THE BAPTISM OF JESUS

²¹When all the people were baptized, Jesus also was baptized. As He was praying, heaven opened, ²²and the Holy Spirit descended on Him in a physical appearance like a dove. And a voice came from heaven:

> You are My beloved Son.
> I take delight in You!

THE GENEALOGY OF JESUS CHRIST

²³As He began [His ministry], Jesus was about 30 years old and was thought to be the

> son of Joseph, [son] of Heli,
> ²⁴ [son] of Matthat, [son] of Levi,

. . . .

> [son] of Nathan, [son] of David,
> ³² [son] of Jesse, [son] of Obed,
> [son] of Boaz, [son] of Salmon,
> [son] of Nahshon, ³³[son] of Amminadab,
> [son] of Ram, [son] of Hezron,
> [son] of Perez, [son] of Judah,
> ³⁴ [son] of Jacob, [son] of Isaac,
> [son] of Abraham, [son] of Terah,
> [son] of Nahor, ³⁵[son] of Serug,
> [son] of Reu, [son] of Peleg,
> [son] of Eber, [son] of Shelah,
> ³⁶ [son] of Cainan, [son] of Arphaxad,
> [son] of Shem, [son] of Noah,
> [son] of Lamech, ³⁷[son] of Methuselah,
> [son] of Enoch, [son] of Jared,
> [son] of Mahalaleel, [son] of Cainan,
> ³⁸ [son] of Enos, [son] of Seth,
> [son] of Adam, [son] of God.

THE TEMPTATION OF JESUS

4 Then Jesus returned from the Jordan, full of the Holy Spirit, and was led by the Spirit in the wilderness ²for 40 days to be tempted by the Devil. He ate nothing during those days, and when they were over, He was hungry. ³The Devil said to Him, "If You are the Son of God, tell this stone to become bread."

⁴But Jesus answered him, "It is written: Man must not live on bread alone."

⁵So he took Him up and showed Him all the kingdoms of the world in a moment of time. ⁶The Devil said to Him, "I will give You their splendor and all this authority, because it has been given over to me, and I can give it to anyone I want. ⁷If You, then, will worship me, all will be Yours."

⁸And Jesus answered him, "It is written:

'Worship the Lord your God,
and serve Him only.'"

⁹So he took Him to Jerusalem, had Him stand on the pinnacle of the temple, and said to Him, "If You are the Son of God, throw Yourself down from here. ¹⁰For it is written:

'He will give His angels orders concerning you,
to protect you, ¹¹and
they will support you with their hands,
so that you will not strike
your foot against a stone.'"

¹²And Jesus answered him, "It is said: 'Do not test the Lord your God.'"

¹³After the Devil had finished every temptation, he departed from Him for a time.

THOUGHT: The story is told of Greig the composer who, sitting in a hotel in Oslo, heard one of his songs being sung by a woman in the next room. Unable to contain himself, he went to her door and said to her, 'That is how my songs should be sung!' God does something like this at our Lord's baptism. He breaks in, so to speak, on the life of Jesus and shouts: 'That is how My life should be lived.' What a life! What a death! What a Saviour.

DAY 141

MARK 1:1-18

AFTER HIS INVESTITURE at the Jordan River, Jesus proclaims the good news of God. The word 'gospel' needs serious attention. It is not a blank cheque to be filled in at our discretion. As Jesus uses it, it has two reference points: one that establishes its content; one that points up a contrast.

Its content stems from its Old Testament usage, particularly in Isaiah (Isa. 40:9; 52:7) who identifies the 'good news' as the announcement of God's return as King. The contrast is with the use of the concept by the Roman emperor who applied the term 'good news' to a public proclamation of his birthday or military victory.

The time for God's kingdom to come is here, says Jesus. The time for the Caesars to be upstaged and threatened by the world's real Lord is now! God's kingdom is not so much a realm or territory as His saving reign, His active rule in the affairs of this world. Because of its upside-down nature, God's kingdom is brought home to us in parable and metaphor. But its effects are felt in the miracles and healing and exorcisms Jesus performs. When Jesus forgives sins and welcomes sinners to eat with Him, then the kingdom has come.

It is to serve the cause of God's kingdom that Jesus commands recruits to His disciple band (vv.16-17). It's high time to repent, believe, come and follow!

Mark 1:1-18

THE MESSIAH'S HERALD

1 The beginning of the gospel of Jesus Christ, the Son of God. ²As it is written in Isaiah the prophet:

"Look, I am sending My messenger ahead of You,
who will prepare Your way.
³ A voice of one crying out in the wilderness:
'Prepare the way for the Lord;
make His paths straight!'"

⁴John came baptizing in the wilderness and preaching a baptism of repentance for the forgiveness of sins. ⁵The whole Judean countryside and all the people of Jerusalem were flocking to him, and they were baptized by him in the Jordan River as they confessed their sins. ⁶John wore a camel-hair garment with a leather belt around his waist and ate locusts and wild honey. ⁷He was preaching: "Someone more powerful than I will come after me. I am not worthy to stoop down and untie the strap of His sandals. ⁸I have baptized you with water, but He will baptize you with the Holy Spirit."

THE BAPTISM OF JESUS

⁹In those days Jesus came from Nazareth in Galilee and was baptized in the Jordan by John. ¹⁰As soon as He came up out of the water, He saw the heavens being torn open and the Spirit descending to Him like a dove. ¹¹And a voice came from heaven:

You are My beloved Son;
I take delight in You!

THE TEMPTATION OF JESUS

¹²Immediately the Spirit drove Him into the wilderness. ¹³He was in the wilderness 40 days, being tempted by Satan. He was with the wild animals, and the angels began to serve Him.

MINISTRY IN GALILEE

¹⁴After John was arrested, Jesus went to Galilee, preaching

the good news of God: [15]"The time is fulfilled, and the kingdom of God has come near. Repent and believe in the good news!"

THE FIRST DISCIPLES

[16]As He was passing along by the Sea of Galilee, He saw Simon and Andrew, Simon's brother. They were casting a net into the sea, since they were fishermen.

[17]"Follow Me," Jesus told them, "and I will make you fish for people!" [18]Immediately they left their nets and followed Him.

TO PONDER: The biblical equivalent of 'ponder' is meditate. And meditation has been described as 'holding a thought like a sweet on the tip of your tongue and sucking every precious drop from it'. Take the thought suggested that God's kingdom is upside down and suck every precious drop from it. Here are a few starters: We lose to gain, we die in order to live, we become slaves in order to be free. Now over to you.

DAY 142

MATTHEW 21:1-11

WHEN JESUS EVENTUALLY enters Jerusalem after three years of ministry, He causes great excitement.

He comes there for a final showdown. And there is a certain inevitability about His arrival.

After all, where else would a king in Israel come to be crowned?

The crowds certainly greet Him as a Messianic claimant, with their cries of 'Hosanna to the Son of David!'

But His manner of entering the city is strange and disturbing, reminiscent of David's own disconcerting entry a thousand years before (2 Sam. 6).

Clearly the procession Jesus is leading is purely a symbolic one. No heavily armed troops accompany Him. He is not making a serious attempt at a coup d'état or palace revolution. In the crowded city, Jesus causes a stir by enacting a piece of political street-theatre to symbolise what kind of kingdom He is bringing. He rides in on a donkey, the least militaristic animal available, in conscious echo of Zechariah's poignant prophecy. By this odd, almost eccentric action, He subverts current expectations of how kings act and, in particular, how Israel's king might act at a time when armed revolution against the occupying Romans was in the air. At the same time it is a winsome appeal to Israel to change before disaster strikes.

Matthew 21:1-11

THE TRIUMPHAL ENTRY

21 When they approached Jerusalem and came to Bethphage at the Mount of Olives, Jesus then sent two disciples, ²telling them, "Go into the village ahead of you. At once you will find a donkey tied there, and a colt with her. Untie them and bring them to Me. ³If anyone says anything to you, you should say that the Lord needs them, and immediately he will send them."

⁴This took place so that what was spoken through the prophet might be fulfilled:

⁵ "Tell Daughter Zion,
  'See, your King is coming to you,
  gentle, and mounted on a donkey,
  even on a colt,
  the foal of a beast of burden.'"

⁶The disciples went and did just as Jesus directed them. ⁷They brought the donkey and the colt; then they laid their robes on them, and He sat on them. ⁸A very large crowd spread their robes on the road; others were cutting branches from the trees and spreading them on the road. ⁹Then the crowds who went ahead of Him and those who followed kept shouting:

  "*Hosanna*" to the Son of David!
  "Blessed is He who comes
  in the name of the Lord!
  Hosanna" in the highest heaven!

¹⁰When He entered Jerusalem, the whole city was shaken, saying, "Who is this?" ¹¹And the crowds kept saying, "This is the prophet Jesus from Nazareth in Galilee!"

> THOUGHT: There is nothing dignified about a donkey - from any angle it lacks what we call 'presence'. Whoever heard of a conqueror riding on an ass? Yet we read that the Lord needed him. There is a parable in this. No matter how ordinary, ill educated, disabled, ill born, talented or obscure a man or woman may be Christ has use for them. The world may not know your name, but rejoice that it is written in the Lamb's book of life.

DAY 143
MATTHEW 21:12-17

THE TEMPLE HAD been David's original idea, his son Solomon built it, and two of Israel's better kings, Hezekiah and Josiah, had cleansed and restored it. It was the king's role to be the Temple builder.

But, like His entry on a donkey, Jesus' so-called cleansing of the Temple is, in effect, an acted parable of judgment

It is not simply a critique of economic corruption, since, in any case, it is doubtful if there was anything intrinsically wrong with changing common currency into Temple coinage in order to buy the requisite sacrifices. But the Temple was meant to be a 'house of prayer for all nations' (Isa. 56:7), and its current role as a focus of nationalism threatens to deny the Gentiles their intended blessings. And as if to dramatise how drastically different God's kingdom is, Jesus opens the Temple courts to the sick and ritually excluded. When David originally attacked Jerusalem, its Jebusite defenders mocked him, saying, 'Even the blind and lame can repel you ...' (2 Sam. 5:6). Afterwards, David turned the taunt back on the lame and blind who are David's enemies (2 Sam. 5:8). This, says the ancient historian, explains the proverb: 'The blind and lame shall not enter the palace!' But no proverbial saying is going to stop King Jesus opening His doors to the lame and blind and healing them!

Matthew 21:12-17

CLEANSING THE TEMPLE COMPLEX

¹²Jesus went into the temple complex and drove out all those buying and selling in the temple. He overturned the money changers' tables and the chairs of those selling doves. ¹³And He said to them, "It is written, 'My house will be called a house of prayer.' But you are making it 'a den of thieves'!"

CHILDREN CHEER JESUS

¹⁴The blind and the lame came to Him in the temple complex, and He healed them. ¹⁵When the chief priests and the scribes saw the wonders that He did and the children in the temple complex cheering, "*Hosanna* to the Son of David!" they were indignant ¹⁶and said to Him, "Do You hear what these [children] are saying?"

"Yes," Jesus told them. "Have you never read:

'You have prepared praise
from the mouths of children and nursing infants'"?

¹⁷Then He left them, went out of the city to Bethany, and spent the night there.

FOR PRAISE: What other response can we give to today's reading than to sing out in praise to God a verse taken from the hymn 'O for a thousand tongues to sing':

Hear Him, ye deaf; His praise, ye dumb,
Your loosened tongues employ;
Ye blind, behold your Saviour come,
And leap, ye lame, for joy.

(Charles Wesley)

DAY
144

ACTS 2:22-36

IF THIS SCRIPTURE teaches us anything it is that there is nothing superficial about events or people but that a deeper design is discernible beneath the surface. To all appearances, Jesus of Nazareth was a discredited Messianic pretender. But in reality He is the centrepiece of God's age-old plan to bring salvation to the world. The cross which looks like a defeat turns out to be the victorious crux of all God's aims. The worst that men can do turns out to be the best that God can do! Such deep paradox at the heart of God's workings requires the resurrection to overturn the verdict of God's enemies and stand scepticism on its head.

Similarly, when Peter quotes David's life and words, he is not simply finding useful analogies to Jesus but bringing to the surface the deep underlying connections in Scripture. So David is a prophetic person whose part in the plan of God carries the seeds of its greater fulfilment in Jesus. David both spoke and lived 'more than he knew' when he anticipated a triumph over death only realisable by the Messiah's resurrection from the dead (Psa. 16) and subsequent enthronement (Psa. 110).

God's tough and persistent determination – shown in Psalm 2 – to make His Anointed King in Israel, Lord of the world, comes good in Jesus, whom Peter proclaims as Lord and Christ.

BIBLE READING

Acts 2:22-36

²²"Men of Israel, listen to these words: This Jesus the Nazarene was a man pointed out to you by God with miracles, wonders, and signs that God did among you through Him, just as you yourselves know. ²³Though He was delivered up according to God's determined plan and foreknowledge, you used lawless people to nail Him to a cross and kill Him. ²⁴God raised Him up, ending the pains of death, because it was not possible for Him to be held by it. ²⁵For David says of Him:

"I saw the Lord ever before me;
because He is at my right hand,
I will not be shaken.
26 Therefore my heart was glad,
and my tongue rejoiced.
Moreover my flesh will rest in hope,
27 because You will not leave my soul in Hades,
or allow Your Holy One to see decay.
28 You have revealed the paths of life to me;
You will fill me with gladness in Your presence."

29"Brothers, I can confidently speak to you about the patriarch David: he is both dead and buried, and his tomb is with us to this day. 30Since he was a prophet, he knew that God had sworn an oath to him to seat one of his descendants on his throne. 31Seeing this in advance, he spoke concerning the resurrection of the Messiah:

"He was not left in Hades,
and" His flesh "did not experience decay."

32"God has resurrected this Jesus. We are all witnesses of this. 33Therefore, since He has been exalted to the right hand of God and has received from the Father the promised Holy Spirit, He has poured out what you both see and hear. 34For it was not David who ascended into the heavens, but he himself says:

"The Lord said to my Lord,
'Sit at My right hand
35 until I make Your enemies Your footstool.'"

36"Therefore let all the house of Israel know with certainty that God has made this Jesus, whom you crucified, both Lord and Messiah!"

PRAYER: O Father how grateful I am that I am in the hands of a God who can take the worst that men can do and turn it into the best You can do. The things I call stumbling-blocks are really stepping-stones, the setbacks are really springboards. All things serve me when I serve You. Whatever happens turns out through You to my advantage. I am so thankful. Amen.

DAY
145

ACTS 4

PSALM 2 AGAIN comes into its own to help explain the deeper issue at stake in the seemingly random crucifixion of a Galilean preacher.

Just as God's salvation comes to its climax in the events of Easter, so does the long battle with evil. By referring to Psalm 2, the apostles are not merely comforting themselves with an apt scripture, but rising to the conviction that they are part of God's bigger and better story.

Herod and Pilate are unlikely bedfellows, showing that sin dupes us all into being unwitting conspirators against God and His Anointed King. But Herod and Pilate, of course, are really mere stooges, the front men for darker forces.

Pit your puny pragmatism against God's mighty eternal plans and you find yourself outwitted and outdone at every turn.

Congratulating themselves on a job well done, His enemies might roll down their sleeves, having washed their hands of this troublesome young prophet. But He just won't go away. Their lasting frustration will be to discover just how much they have contributed to their own defeat and His own triumph!

If this is the case then the persecuted disciples of such a sovereign Lord and servant-King rebound from setbacks as irrepressible people, praying irresistible prayers, and proclaiming an unstoppable gospel.

Acts 4

PETER AND JOHN ARRESTED

4 Now as they were speaking to the people, the priests, the commander of the temple guard, and the Sadducees confronted them, ²because they were provoked that they were teaching the people and proclaiming in the person of Jesus the resurrection from the dead. ³So they seized them and put them in custody until the next day, since it was already evening. ⁴But many of those who heard the message believed, and the number of the men came to about 5,000.

PETER AND JOHN FACE THE JEWISH LEADERSHIP

⁵The next day, their rulers, elders, and scribes assembled in Jerusalem ⁶with Annas the high priest, Caiaphas, John and Alexander, and all the members of the high-priestly family. ⁷After they had Peter and John stand before them, they asked the question: "By what power or in what name have you done this?"

⁸Then Peter was filled with the Holy Spirit and said to them, "Rulers of the people and elders: ⁹If we are being examined today about a good deed done to a disabled man—by what means he was healed— ¹⁰let it be known to all of you and to all the people of Israel, that by the name of Jesus Christ the Nazarene—whom you crucified and whom God raised from the dead—by Him this man is standing here before you healthy. ¹¹This [Jesus] is

"The stone despised by you builders,
who has become the cornerstone."

¹²There is salvation in no one else, for there is no other name under heaven given to people by which we must be saved."

THE NAME FORBIDDEN

¹³When they observed the boldness of Peter and John and realized that they were uneducated and untrained men, they were amazed and knew that they had been with Jesus. ¹⁴And

since they saw the man who had been healed standing with them, they had nothing to say in response. [15]After they had ordered them to leave the Sanhedrin, they conferred among themselves, [16]saying, "What should we do with these men? For an obvious sign, evident to all who live in Jerusalem, has been done through them, and we cannot deny it! [17]But so this does not spread any further among the people, let's threaten them against speaking to anyone in this name again." [18]So they called for them and ordered them not to preach or teach at all in the name of Jesus.

[19]But Peter and John answered them, "Whether it's right in the sight of God [for us] to listen to you rather than to God, you decide; [20]for we are unable to stop speaking about what we have seen and heard."

[21]After threatening them further, they released them. They found no way to punish them, because the people were all giving glory to God over what had been done; [22]for the man was over 40 years old on whom this sign of healing had been performed.

PRAYER FOR BOLDNESS

[23]After they were released, they went to their own fellowship and reported all that the chief priests and the elders had said to them. [24]When they heard this, they raised their voices to God unanimously and said, "Master, You are the One who made the heaven, the earth, and the sea, and everything in them. [25]You said through the Holy Spirit, by the mouth of our father David Your servant:

> 'Why did the Gentiles rage,
> and the peoples plot futile things?
> [26] The kings of the earth took their stand,
> and the rulers assembled together
> against the Lord and against His Messiah.'

[27]"For, in fact, in this city both Herod and Pontius Pilate, with the Gentiles and the peoples of Israel, assembled together against Your holy Servant Jesus, whom You anointed, [28]to do whatever Your hand and Your plan had predestined to take place. [29]And now, Lord, consider their threats, and grant that

Your slaves may speak Your message with complete boldness, [30]while You stretch out Your hand for healing, signs, and wonders to be performed through the name of Your holy Servant Jesus." [31]When they had prayed, the place where they were assembled was shaken, and they were all filled with the Holy Spirit and began to speak God's message with boldness.

BELIEVERS SHARING

[32]Now the multitude of those who believed were of one heart and soul, and no one said that any of his possessions was his own, but instead they held everything in common. [33]And with great power the apostles were giving testimony to the resurrection of the Lord Jesus, and great grace was on all of them. [34]For there was not a needy person among them, because all those who owned lands or houses sold them, brought the proceeds of the things that were sold, [35]and laid them at the apostles' feet. This was then distributed to each person as anyone had a need.

[36]Joseph, a Levite and a Cypriot by birth, whom the apostles named Barnabas, which is translated Son of Encouragement, [37]sold a field he owned, brought the money, and laid it at the apostles' feet.

FOR PRAISE: Thank God that through His Word you have learned one of life's deepest secrets - namely that in Him nothing can work successfully against you. The wind can blow from any direction but it will only drive you towards the goal of making you more like Jesus Christ. Everything can be used by those who are in Christ. You may be knocked down but you cannot be kept down and when you come up you will come up smiling. All because of Him.

DAY 146

ACTS 13:13-52

THIS POWERFUL SERMON preached by Paul to the synagogue in Antioch is rich in Davidic allusions and echoes. Sweeping from Abraham through Moses and Israel's election down to the days of Samuel and Saul, Paul's survey of the earlier stages of God's story focuses on the link between Jesus and David. Scriptures that we have already recognised as significant – Psalm 2, Isaiah 55, Psalm 16 – feature in Paul's gripping account of how God's dealings with the patriarchs and chosen people have channelled down through David to Jesus. The framework which enables Paul to discern the coherence of God's plan in the Scriptures is that of 'promise and fulfilment'.

For Paul, God's over-arching promise-plan has reached its intended goal in Jesus (v.32). To preach the gospel is precisely to declare the good news that everything God promised to the fathers has now come to fruition in Jesus Christ. The raising of Jesus from the dead is His coronation as Son-King, in line with Psalm 2, the 'sure mercies' promised to David's people in Isaiah, and the protection from decay for which the royal psalmist hopefully sang.

The enormous emphasis on the resurrection in the proclamation of the good news may come as a surprise to us modern Christians. But to the apostles it was the beating heart of their message of hope.

BIBLE READING

Acts 13:13-52

PAUL'S SERMON IN ANTIOCH OF PISIDIA

¹³Paul and his companions set sail from Paphos and came to Perga in Pamphylia. John, however, left them and went back to Jerusalem. ¹⁴They continued their journey from Perga and reached Antioch in Pisidia. On the Sabbath day they went into the synagogue and sat down. ¹⁵After the reading of the Law and the Prophets, the leaders of the synagogue sent [word] to them, saying, "Brothers, if you have any message of encouragement for the people, you can speak."

[16]Then standing up, Paul motioned with his hand and spoke: "Men of Israel, and you who fear God, listen! [17]The God of this people Israel chose our forefathers, exalted the people during their stay in the land of Egypt, and led them out of it with a mighty arm. [18]And for about 40 years He put up with them in the desert; [19]then after destroying seven nations in the land of Canaan, He gave their land to them as an inheritance. [20]This all took about 450 years. After this, He gave them judges until Samuel the prophet. [21]Then they asked for a king, so God gave them Saul the son of Kish, a man of the tribe of Benjamin, for 40 years. [22]After removing him, He raised up David as their king, of whom He testified: "'I have found David" the son of Jesse, "a man after My heart," who will carry out all My will.'

[23]"From this man's descendants, according to the promise, God brought the Savior, Jesus, to Israel. [24]Before He came to public attention, John had previously proclaimed a baptism of repentance to all the people of Israel. [25]Then as John was completing his life work, he said, 'Who do you think I am? I am not the One. But look! Someone is coming after me, and I am not worthy to untie the sandals on His feet.'

[26]"Brothers, sons of Abraham's race, and those among you who fear God, the message of this salvation has been sent to us. [27]For the residents of Jerusalem and their rulers, since they did not recognize Him or the voices of the prophets that are read every Sabbath, have fulfilled their words by condemning Him. [28]Though they found no grounds for the death penalty, they asked Pilate to have Him killed. [29]When they had fulfilled all that had been written about Him, they took Him down from the tree and put Him in a tomb. [30]But God raised Him from the dead, [31]and He appeared for many days to those who came up with Him from Galilee to Jerusalem, who are now His witnesses to the people. [32]And we ourselves proclaim to you the good news of the promise that was made to our forefathers. [33]God has fulfilled this to us their children by raising up Jesus, as it is written in the second Psalm:

'You are My Son;
today I have become Your Father.'

[34]Since He raised Him from the dead, never to return to

decay, He has spoken in this way, 'I will grant you the faithful covenant blessings made to David.' [35]Therefore He also says in another passage, 'You will not allow Your Holy One to see decay.' [36]For David, after serving his own generation in God's plan, fell asleep, was buried with his fathers, and decayed. [37]But the One whom God raised up did not decay. [38]Therefore, let it be known to you, brothers, that through this man forgiveness of sins is being proclaimed to you, [39]and everyone who believes in Him is justified from everything, which you could not be justified from through the law of Moses. [40]So beware that what is said in the prophets does not happen to you:

[41]   'Look, you scoffers,
        marvel and vanish away,
        because I am doing a work in your days,
        a work that you will never believe,
        even if someone were to explain it to you.'"

PAUL AND BARNABAS IN ANTIOCH

[42]As they were leaving, they begged that these matters be presented to them the following Sabbath. [43]After the synagogue had been dismissed, many of the Jews and devout proselytes followed Paul and Barnabas, who were speaking with them and persuading them to continue in the grace of God.

[44]The following Sabbath almost the whole town assembled to hear the message of the Lord. [45]But when the Jews saw the crowds, they were filled with jealousy and began to oppose what Paul was saying by insulting him.

[46]Then Paul and Barnabas boldly said: "It was necessary that God's message be spoken to you first. But since you reject it, and consider yourselves unworthy of eternal life, we now turn to the Gentiles! [47]For this is what the Lord has commanded us:

        'I have appointed you as a light for the Gentiles,
        to bring salvation to the ends of the earth.'"

[48]When the Gentiles heard this, they rejoiced and glorified the message of the Lord, and all who had been appointed to eternal life believed. [49]So the message of the Lord spread

through the whole region. [50]But the Jews incited the religious women of high standing and the leading men of the city. They stirred up persecution against Paul and Barnabas and expelled them from their district. [51]But shaking the dust off their feet against them, they proceeded to Iconium. [52]And the disciples were filled with joy and the Holy Spirit.

THOUGHT: When did you last hear a sermon on Christ's resurrection? Today's Church tends to emphasise it only at Easter. The early disciples made much of the cross but seemed to make more of the resurrection. Consider this: had there been no resurrection there would be no salvation. The cross was a wonderful event, but had He not risen from the dead we would not be saved. Think about that today.

THE SYNOD IN Jerusalem, attended by apostles and elders, marks a crucial turning point in the early history of the Church.

DAY
147
ACTS 15:1-35

Under James's wise, Spirit-directed leadership, it resolved any doubts about the terms on which Gentiles could be included in God's covenant family. The prophets had said that God would first restore His people Israel and then the Gentiles would come in. Only this sequence, perhaps, explains why the apostles had strangely held back from obeying the great commission in order to concentrate on the Jewish mission. Events, however, had taken a seemingly different tack. How could they square a largely hostile Jewish reaction to Jesus with the eager response shown by the Gentiles now flocking into the kingdom? There could be only one answer: in some mysterious way, Israel must have already been restored in and through Jesus! For scriptural support for the conclusion of the council, James fastens on the prophet Amos's vision of a restored Davidic house. In David's unique tabernacle in Jerusalem, the psalms were sung that summoned the nations to praise the one true God (1 Chron. 16). It was a foretaste of worship in the Spirit in God's kingdom. Now, both Jew and Gentile in Christ call gladly and joyfully on the name of the Lord.

BIBLE READING

Acts 15:1-35

DISPUTE IN ANTIOCH

15 Some men came down from Judea and began to teach the brothers: "Unless you are circumcised according to the custom prescribed by Moses, you cannot be saved!" [2]But after Paul and Barnabas had engaged them in serious argument and debate, they arranged for Paul and Barnabas and some others of them to go up to the apostles and elders in Jerusalem concerning this controversy. [3]When they had been sent on their way by the church, they passed through both Phoenicia and Samaria, explaining in detail the conversion of the Gentiles, and they created great joy among all the brothers.

[4]When they arrived at Jerusalem, they were welcomed by the church, the apostles, and the elders, and they reported all that God had done with them. [5]But some of the believers from the party of the Pharisees stood up and said, "It is necessary to circumcise them and to command them to keep the law of Moses!"

THE JERUSALEM COUNCIL

[6]Then the apostles and the elders assembled to consider this matter. [7]After there had been much debate, Peter stood up and said to them: "Brothers, you are aware that in the early days God made a choice among you, that by my mouth the Gentiles would hear the gospel message and believe. [8]And God, who knows the heart, testified to them by giving the Holy Spirit, just as He also did to us. [9]He made no distinction between us and them, cleansing their hearts by faith. [10]Why, then, are you now testing God by putting on the disciples' necks a yoke that neither our forefathers nor we have been able to bear? [11]On the contrary, we believe we are saved through the grace of the Lord Jesus, in the same way they are."

[12]Then the whole assembly fell silent and listened to Barnabas and Paul describing all the signs and wonders God had done through them among the Gentiles. [13]After they

stopped speaking, James responded: "Brothers, listen to me! [14]Simeon has reported how God first intervened to take from the Gentiles a people for His name. [15]And the words of the prophets agree with this, as it is written:

[16] 'After these things I will return
and will rebuild David's tent, which has fallen down.
I will rebuild its ruins and will set it up again,
[17] so that those who are left of mankind
may seek the Lord—
even all the Gentiles who are called by My name,
says the Lord who does these things,
[18] which have been known from long ago.'

[19]Therefore, in my judgment, we should not cause difficulties for those who turn to God from among the Gentiles, [20]but instead we should write to them to abstain from things polluted by idols, from sexual immorality, from eating anything that has been strangled, and from blood. [21]For since ancient times, Moses has had in every city those who proclaim him, and he is read aloud in the synagogues every Sabbath day."

THE LETTER TO THE GENTILE BELIEVERS

[22]Then the apostles and the elders, with the whole church, decided to select men from among them and to send them to Antioch with Paul and Barnabas: Judas, called Barsabbas, and Silas, both leading men among the brothers. [23]They wrote this letter to be delivered by them:

From the apostles and the elders, your brothers,
To the brothers from among the Gentiles in Antioch,
Syria, and Cilicia:
Greetings.
[24]Because we have heard that some to whom we gave
no authorization went out from us and troubled you
with their words and unsettled your hearts, [25]we have
unanimously decided to select men and send them
to you along with our beloved Barnabas and Paul,
[26]who have risked their lives for the name of our Lord
Jesus Christ. [27]Therefore we have sent Judas and Silas,

who will personally report the same things by word of mouth. [28]For it was the Holy Spirit's decision—and ours—to put no greater burden on you than these necessary things: [29]that you abstain from food offered to idols, from blood, from eating anything that has been strangled, and from sexual immorality. If you keep yourselves from these things, you will do well.

Farewell.

THE OUTCOME OF THE JERUSALEM LETTER

[30]Then, being sent off, they went down to Antioch, and after gathering the assembly, they delivered the letter. [31]When they read it, they rejoiced because of its encouragement. [32]Both Judas and Silas, who were also prophets themselves, encouraged the brothers and strengthened them with a long message. [33]After spending some time there, they were sent back in peace by the brothers to those who had sent them. * [35]But Paul and Barnabas, along with many others, remained in Antioch teaching and proclaiming the message of the Lord.

[*Other mss add v.34: *But Silas decided to stay there.*]

PRAISE: Do you know this well-known hymn? If so lift your heart in praise and give thanks to God for the promise of His glorious return:

Sing we the King who is coming to reign,
Glory to Jesus, the Lamb that was slain;
Life and salvation His empire shall bring,
Joy to the nations when Jesus is King.

(Charles S. Horne)

THE GOSPEL RECALLS God's promises, and evokes God's initiatives.

God's promises, which stretch back to Abraham, explode with colour in the visions of Israel's great prophets. They see a kingdom coming, a new era of forgiveness and justice, of exile ended and homecoming to God's gracious rule. The gospel is the public declaration that God has kept His word!

Central to it is God's Son, Jesus. At one level, His Sonship is a royal and Jewish sonship as befits a descendant of King David. This Sonship was lived out on the level of our normal fleshly human existence, marked by weakness and limitation. But this same Jesus has been declared to be the 'Son-of-God-with-power' Son of God! Raised from the dead, He eclipses everything David was and fulfils everything David stood for. His resurrection has launched Him into a new sphere of human existence characterised by the unlimited power and possibilities of God's creative Spirit. The resurrection happened in history but came from beyond history as the mighty inrush of God's coming kingdom. This Jesus is truly Israel's Messiah and the world's true Lord, claiming the allegiance of everyone, everywhere, and commissioning heralds, like Paul, to go through the Roman Empire and beyond to announce His accession to the world's throne!

Romans 1:1-7

BIBLE
READING

GOD'S GOOD NEWS FOR ROME

1 Paul, a slave of Christ Jesus, called as an apostle and singled out for God's good news— ²which He promised long ago through His prophets in the Holy Scriptures— ³concerning His Son, Jesus Christ our Lord, who was a descendant of David according to the flesh ⁴and was established as the powerful Son of God by the resurrection from the dead according to the Spirit of holiness. ⁵We have received grace and apostleship through Him to bring about the obedi-

ence of faith among all the nations, on behalf of His name, ⁶including yourselves who are also Jesus Christ's by calling:

⁷To all who are in Rome, loved by God, called as saints.

Grace to you and peace from God our Father and the Lord Jesus Christ.

TO PONDER: Let this powerful and weighty text lie upon your mind throughout the day and draw from it the inspiration you need to face whatever difficulties are confronting you at this moment:

And if the Spirit of Him who raised Jesus from the dead lives in you, then He who raised Christ from the dead will also bring your mortal bodies to life through His Spirit who lives in you. (Rom. 8:11)

DAY 149

HEBREWS 1

GOD'S PREVIOUS REVELATION, varied and fragmented as it was, is now gathered up in completed form and offered to us in Jesus.

When I was young, a board stood outside our local newsagent on which was scrawled the breaking news only briefly covered in the midday editions of the newspapers but with the added promise of the 'full story in the final edition'.

This is exactly what Jesus is to the Old Testament stage of God's plan. What was only partially said before is now fully said in Jesus. What was provisional is now final in Him. Whereas, before, God spoke through God's servants, now He has spoken through His Son. Jesus, God's Son, is the full and final edition of all God wants to say to us.

God's story has already entered its 'last days' - not as the end of the space-time world as we know it - but as the culmination of the long progress of God's promise-plan.

Not surprisingly, the flood of Old Testament truth comes in like a tidal wave.

Seven quotations from the Old Testament in verses 5-14 rush to the spot like iron filings drawn to a magnet to confirm the vision of Jesus given in verses 1-3, of Jesus as royal heir apparent, as mediator of creation, as enjoying eternal glory, and as exalted to God's right hand.

It's all come together in God's time and God's Son! Who can say more or afford to neglect this (2:1-4)?

Hebrews 1

THE NATURE OF THE SON

1 Long ago God spoke to the fathers by the prophets at different times and in different ways. ²In these last days, He has spoken to us by [His] Son, whom He has appointed heir of all things and through whom He made the universe. ³He is the radiance of His glory, the exact expression of His nature, and He sustains all things by His powerful word. After making purification for sins, He sat down at the right hand of the Majesty on high. ⁴So He became higher in rank than the angels, just as the name He inherited is superior to theirs.

THE SON SUPERIOR TO ANGELS

⁵For to which of the angels did He ever say, "You are My Son; today I have become Your Father," or again, "I will be His Father, and He will be My Son"? ⁶When He again brings His firstborn into the world, He says, "And all God's angels must worship Him." ⁷And about the angels He says:

"He makes His angels winds,
and His servants a fiery flame;"

⁸but about the Son:

"Your throne, O God, is forever and ever,
and the scepter of Your kingdom is a scepter of justice.
⁹ You have loved righteousness and hated lawlessness;
this is why God, Your God, has anointed You,
rather than Your companions, with the oil of joy."

¹⁰And:

> "In the beginning, Lord, You established the earth,
> and the heavens are the works of Your hands;
> ¹¹ they will perish, but You remain.
> They will all wear out like clothing;
> ¹² You will roll them up like a cloak,
> and they will be changed like a robe.
> But You are the same,
> and Your years will never end."

¹³Now to which of the angels has He ever said:

> "Sit at My right hand
> until I make Your enemies Your footstool"?

¹⁴Are they not all ministering spirits sent out to serve those who are going to inherit salvation?

THOUGHT: People unread in comparative religions say one religion is as good as another, which is actually a judgment of ignorance. Certainly there are fine things in other faiths. But Christianity is not one religion amongst others, it is in a category all by itself. Christ is the Light of the world. We are not unmindful of other lamps but He is the only One who illuminates the world with the truth about God. For He is God.

DAY
150
REVELATION 1:4-7

WHEN JOHN WANTS to comfort and encourage the churches he pastors, his top priority is a fresh vision of Jesus. In his pastoral letter, top billing is given to Jesus, the faithful witness, answering any doubt about His reliability. In Him is true and trustworthy testimony to the reality of who God is. Intriguingly, the book of Revelation, while never explicitly quoting the Old Testament, is soaked through with allusions to it. Jesus is the climax to the Scriptures, the conclusive witness to all that God has said. That He is the firstborn from the dead answers any worries about His being still alive. Jesus inherits the ascription to which the Messianic King was entitled (Psa. 89:26f), giving Him priority in His Father's affairs. Because He has won this right through dying and rising, He is the pioneer of many who will follow Him in resurrection glory. He is the ruler of the kings of the earth, assuming the messianic mantle (Psa. 2:7; Psa. 89:27), so answering any fears as to who is ultimately in charge of our world. All this John's readers needed to know, oppressed as they were by a pervasive Roman Imperial power. And they need be in no doubt that this faithful firstborn, ever-living Jesus – whose death frees them from their sins – loves them still. He couldn't love us less; He can't love us more!

Revelation 1:4-7

⁴John:

To the seven churches in the province of Asia.

Grace and peace to you from the One who is, who was, and who is coming; from the seven spirits before His throne; ⁵and from Jesus Christ, the faithful witness, the firstborn from the dead and the ruler of the kings of the earth.

To Him who loves us and has set us free from our sins by His blood, ⁶and made us a kingdom, priests to His God and Father—to Him be the glory and dominion forever and ever. Amen.

⁷ "Look! He is coming with the clouds,
　and every eye will see Him,
　including those who pierced Him.
　And all the families of the earth
　will mourn over Him."
This is certain. Amen.

TO PONDER: How different is the love of God from human love! Our love changes with circumstances. Consider as you go through the day that 'Jesus could not love us less nor love us more'. Nothing in us gave rise to it, and nothing in us can extinguish it. 'There is no greater security in life,' said someone, 'than knowing that we are loved with a love that will never be taken away.' That's the kind of love that fills our hearts.

DAY
151
REVELATION 5

WE HAVE COME a long way from the image of David with his dreams dashed. But the outcome of God's promise-plan is still sufficiently uncertain as to reduce John to tears, that no one seems qualified to effect God's final will for the world's redemption. Then, in the Spirit, he sees the Lion-King silhouetted on the skyline of history. Here is David's descendant, custodian of the scroll of God's covenant purposes for all mankind, the only one worthy to implement God's plans. He has reclaimed, for His Father on the throne, the praise of every creature in heaven and on earth (v.13) of which Noah was a lonely pioneer. He is the Lord of the world and the King of kings, head over an international multitude no more capable of being counted than Abraham could count the stars in the night sky. And it all began with David's disappointment at the dashing of his dreams! But God can do 'far more than you could ever imagine or guess or request in your wildest dreams' (Eph. 3:20, *The Message*).

The evidence is Jesus, the High King of heaven, and heaven's bright sun; the keeper of the keys of David (Rev. 3:7) that open the door to God's eternal kingdom. Beyond this door, there are no tears or broken dreams, no disappointment or regret. Beyond this door, there is no night: it's always bright and sun-drenched morning.

Revelation 5

THE LAMB TAKES THE SCROLL

5 Then I saw in the right hand of the One seated on the throne a scroll with writing on the inside and on the back, sealed with seven seals. ²I also saw a mighty angel proclaiming in a loud voice, "Who is worthy to open the scroll and break its seals?" ³But no one in heaven or on earth or under the earth was able to open the scroll or even to look in it. ⁴And I cried and cried because no one was found worthy to open the scroll or even to look in it.

⁵Then one of the elders said to me, "Stop crying. Look! The Lion from the tribe of Judah, the Root of David, has been victorious so that He may open the scroll and its seven seals." ⁶Then I saw one like a slaughtered lamb standing between the throne and the four living creatures and among the elders. He had seven horns and seven eyes, which are the seven spirits of God sent into all the earth. ⁷He came and took [the scroll] out of the right hand of the One seated on the throne.

THE LAMB IS WORTHY

⁸When He took the scroll, the four living creatures and the 24 elders fell down before the Lamb. Each one had a harp and gold bowls filled with incense, which are the prayers of the saints. ⁹And they sang a new song:

> You are worthy to take the scroll
> and to open its seals;
> because You were slaughtered,
> and You redeemed [people] for God by Your blood
> from every tribe and language and people and nation.
> ¹⁰ You made them a kingdom and priests to our God,
> and they will reign on the earth.

¹¹Then I looked, and heard the voice of many angels around the throne, and also of the living creatures, and of the elders. Their number was countless thousands, plus thousands of thousands. ¹²They said with a loud voice:

The Lamb who was slaughtered is worthy
to receive power and riches
and wisdom and strength
and honor and glory and blessing!

¹³I heard every creature in heaven, on earth, under the earth, on the sea, and everything in them say:

Blessing and honor and glory and dominion
to the One seated on the throne,
and to the Lamb, forever and ever!

¹⁴The four living creatures said, "Amen," and the elders fell down and worshiped.

QUOTATION: 'Shattered dreams are never random,' Dr Larry Crabb says. 'They are always a piece in a larger puzzle, a chapter in a larger story. The Holy Spirit uses the pain of shattered dreams to help us discover our desire for God, to help us begin dreaming the highest dream which when realised will release a new song, sing with tears until God wipes them away and we sing with nothing but joy in our hearts.'

SECTION

NOAH
ALL CREATION

ABRAHAM
ALL NATIONS

ISRAEL
ONE NATION

DAVID
REPRESENTATIVE KING

NEW COVENANT
FAITHFUL COVENANT
PARTNER

JESUS
FAITHFUL COVENANT PARTNER

JESUS
DAVIDIC KING MESSIAH

JESUS
THE NEW ISRAEL

JESUS
THE WORLD'S LORD

JESUS
THE TRULY HUMAN ONE
CROWNED WITH GLORY AND HONOUR

JESUS
COSMIC RULER IN GOD'S NEW CREATION
NEW HEAVENS AND NEW EARTH

SECTION 7   THE PROPHETIC VISION

GOD IS COMMITTED TO CHANGING HIS PEOPLE FROM THE INSIDE OUT – THE PROPHETIC VISION

When the Babylonians over-ran Judah and started deportations to Babylonia around 606 BC, there began the most traumatic period in Israel's history since the Exodus.

Three pictures from Scripture vividly highlight for us both the reasons for the Exile and the reactions to it.

Firstly, in memorable imagery, Jeremiah lamented the persistent disobedience of kings and people and their deep-seated inability to alter their uncovenantal patterns of behaviour: 'Can the Ethiopian change his skin or the leopard its spots? Neither can you do good who are accustomed to doing evil' (Jer. 13:23, NIV).

This is the reason why God has judged His people and sent them into exile (cf.2 Chron. 15–21).

Secondly, the reaction to Exile when it happened is poignantly expressed in Psalm 137 with its vivid echoes of the 'day the music died' by the rivers of Babylon when harps were hung, discarded, on the willow trees and the plaintive question hung in the air: 'How can we sing the Lord's song on foreign soil?' (v.4).

The book of Lamentations is a great outpouring of grief which graphically captures the sense of national bereavement. Loss of kingship, Temple and land must have seemed terminal, ending Israel's unique identity and destiny – even perhaps spelling the death of God Himself.

So, in a third vivid metaphor, the prophet Ezekiel, himself one of the first to be taken to Babylon, pictured the state of Israel as a valley full of bleached and dry bones – one vast graveyard – and he too left a question hanging in the air: 'can these bones live?' (37:3).

But buried deep in the pain was a glimmer of hope: 'Because of the Lord's faithful love we do not perish,

for His mercies never end. They are new every
morning; great is Your faithfulness' (Lam. 3:22–23).

There is hope because God is faithful to His covenant.

Jeremiah's response is twofold.

With life in Babylonia an accomplished fact,
Jeremiah urges the exiles to accept their situation
in Exile with realism not wishful thinking (Jer. 23).
But he also urges them by a flight of imagination to
envisage salvation beyond Exile in the promise of a
new covenant (Jer. 31:31–34).

God will make the covenant effective with His people
by working on both sides of the covenant relationship.
He will give His people a new disposition to obey
Him, a fresh reassurance of belonging to Him, an
unprecedented knowledge of God that works social
justice, and a deep and lasting forgiveness of sins!

Ezekiel added to this hope with his vision of a
transformed people, washed and cleansed, with an
entirely new heart empowered by the very Spirit of
God to live in covenant loyalty with God! (Ezek. 36).

The question too, 'Can the dead bones live?' God
answers with a vision of 'resurrection from the dead'
(Ezek. 37).

But, of course, not only the people but the kings have
consistently failed and so the prophets of Exile, as we
have seen, begin to project hopes of a new kingship.

God would raise up a new David (Jer. 23:5),
accompanied by or identical with the coming of God
Himself to be the Shepherd-Ruler of His people
(Ezek. 34).

Isaiah proclaims the 'good news' of God's kingdom
as God Himself leads the Exiles home across the
desert, returning as King in Zion, at the centre of His

people's life again to establish justice and peace and salvation (Isa. 40:9-10; 52:7f).

But Isaiah's unique contribution is to show that none of this will take effect except through the shameful suffering and ignominious death of a mysterious servant of God.

We have noted the tragic irony before, that Exodus and Exile are the two poles around which the Old Testament story of Israel revolves. From slavery in Egypt - so the story runs - to slavery in Babylonia - where Abraham had come from to begin the faith journey over 1,000 years earlier! But the hopes of the Exilic prophets are even more remarkable.

Exodus gave birth to a nation for God out of slavery through deliverance and redemption. Exile yields promise of a new people of God redeemed this time out of the deeper slavery of sin through 'death and resurrection'.

Here then is the prophetic vision: the new covenant community - a community newly motivated to obey God, deeply secure in belonging to God and being His people, with an all-pervading God-consciousness - a grateful community of forgiven-forgivers; a community empowered by the creative Spirit of God, under the Lordship of God through His appointed Messiah, the foretaste of a brand new creation!

This depiction of new covenant realities begins to sound very much like a description of vibrant Christian experience - like that described in Acts 2! And, praise God, that's exactly what it is!

PSALM 137 POIGNANTLY captures emotions felt by the Exiles beside the 'rivers of Babylon' in shoulder-shrugging mood.

'There we hung up our lyres on the poplar trees' sums up the futility induced by despair. Pain has paralysed praise. Mockery mercilessly picks at their emotional wound (v.3). How can we sing the Lord's song in a strange land? Unwilling to forget Jerusalem, the exiles struggle with the bitter-sweet burden of memory. In the end, the dark violence of the victimised spirit erupts in a raging resentment from which we recoil (vv.8-9). But better that such anger is heaped on God in prayer than hurled at people in vengeance!

This emotional intensity caused by Exile is matched only in the book of Lamentations – the most 'tear-stained book in the Old Testament' – a grief-stricken litany of national bereavement.

From the first deportation in 606 BC down to the demise of Jerusalem in around 586, the protracted Babylonian conquest of Judah brought the long slow death of a nation.

But, although God's heart 'breaks' over His people's failure and disgrace, His heart does not 'fail' (3:19-25). His covenant faithfulness proves greater than our failure. A new day of His mercy dawns on the long night of our shame. Fresh hopes are pinned on this God who 'turns all our sunsets into sunrise'.

DAY
152

PSALM 137
LAMENTATIONS
3:1-3,16-27

Psalm 137

BIBLE
READING

LAMENT OF THE EXILES

¹ By the rivers of Babylon—
   there we sat down and wept
   when we remembered Zion.
² There we hung up our lyres
   on the poplar trees,
³ for our captors there asked us for songs,

and our tormentors, for rejoicing:
"Sing us one of the songs of Zion."

⁴ How can we sing the LORD's song
on foreign soil?
⁵ If I forget you, Jerusalem,
may my right hand forget [its skill].
⁶ May my tongue stick to the roof of my mouth
if I do not remember you,
if I do not exalt Jerusalem as my greatest joy!

⁷ Remember, LORD, [what] the Edomites said
that day at Jerusalem:
"Destroy it! Destroy it
down to its foundations!"
⁸ Daughter Babylon, doomed to destruction,
happy is the one who pays you back
what you have done to us.
⁹ Happy is he who takes your little ones
and dashes them against the rocks.

| BIBLE READING | **Lamentations 3: 1-3,16-27** |

HOPE THROUGH GOD'S MERCY

א *Alef*

3 I am the man who has seen affliction
under the rod of God's wrath.
² He has driven me away and forced [me] to walk
in darkness instead of light.
³ Yes, He repeatedly turns His hand
against me all day long.

· · · · · · · · · ·

ו *Vav*

¹⁶ He ground my teeth on gravel
and made me cower in the dust.
¹⁷ My soul has been deprived of peace;

I have forgotten what happiness is.
¹⁸ Then I thought: My future is lost,
   as well as my hope from the LORD.

ז Zayin

¹⁹ Remember my affliction and my homelessness,
   the wormwood and the poison.
²⁰ I continually remember [them]
   and have become depressed.
²¹ Yet I call this to mind,
   and therefore I have hope:

ח Khet

²² [Because of] the LORD's faithful love
   we do not perish,
      for His mercies never end.
²³ They are new every morning;
   great is Your faithfulness!
²⁴ I say: The LORD is my portion,
   therefore I will put my hope in Him.

ט Tet

²⁵ The LORD is good to those who wait for Him,
   to the person who seeks Him.
²⁶ It is good to wait quietly
   for deliverance from the LORD.
²⁷ It is good for a man to bear the yoke
   while he is [still] young.

PRAYER: My Father and my God, whenever I feel in exile help me let You be my home as well as bringing me home. Help me not only understand that You are my Hiding Place, my Shelter in the time of storm, my Rock and my Fortress, but show me how to lean on You, to trust You and give myself to You in such a way that the theory becomes fact. I want this to be my experience - always. Grant it Father in Jesus' name. Amen.

DAY 153

EZEKIEL 37

TO MANY OF the exiles taken to Babylonia, the loss of kingship, Temple and land must have seemed the virtual end of everything, the end of Israel's unique identity and destiny – even perhaps the death of God Himself.

The prophet, Ezekiel, himself one of the first deportees, saw the state of Israel, in prophetic vision, as a valley full of bleached and dry bones – one vast cemetery with the dead humiliatingly left unburied, for the vultures to strip the carcasses, and the elements to dismember the skeletons! But there is hope.

Challenged as to how these bones can live again, the prophet – shrewdly enough – puts the onus back on the Lord: 'Lord God, only You know.'

Commanded to prophesy to the bones, he does so and the bones come together again and flesh re-forms. Told to prophesy to the 'ruach' or 'breath' or 'wind', the prophet obeys and the very breath or Spirit of God enters into the bodies and they stand on their feet – a living army of God – raised, as it were, from the dead!

This establishes a crucial pattern or model for God's work.

Salvation and restoration, it appears, lie on the other side of Exile, that is, on the other side of 'death and resurrection' and by the Spirit's empowerment.

BIBLE READING

Ezekiel 37

THE VALLEY OF DRY BONES

37 The hand of the LORD was on me, and He brought me out by His Spirit and set me down in the middle of the valley; it was full of bones. ²He led me all around them. There were a great many of them on the surface of the valley, and they were very dry. ³Then He said to me, "Son of man, can these bones live?"

I replied, "Lord GOD, [only] You know."

⁴He said to me, "Prophesy concerning these bones and say to them: Dry bones, hear the word of the LORD! ⁵This is what the

Lord GOD says to these bones: I will cause breath to enter you, and you will live. ⁶I will put tendons on you, make flesh grow on you, and cover you with skin. I will put breath in you so that you come to life. Then you will know that I am the LORD."

⁷So I prophesied as I had been commanded. While I was prophesying, there was a noise, a rattling sound, and the bones came together, bone to bone. ⁸As I looked, tendons appeared on them, flesh grew, and skin covered them, but there was no breath in them. ⁹He said to me, "Prophesy to the breath, prophesy, son of man. Say to it: This is what the Lord GOD says: Breath, come from the four winds and breathe into these slain so that they may live!" ¹⁰So I prophesied as He commanded me; the breath entered them, and they came to life and stood on their feet, a vast army.

¹¹Then He said to me, "Son of man, these bones are the whole house of Israel. Look how they say: Our bones are dried up, and our hope has perished; we are cut off. ¹²Therefore, prophesy and say to them: This is what the Lord GOD says: I am going to open your graves and bring you up from them, My people, and lead you into the land of Israel. ¹³You will know that I am the LORD, My people, when I open your graves and bring you up from them. ¹⁴I will put My Spirit in you, and you will live, and I will settle you in your own land. Then you will know that I am the LORD. I have spoken, and I will do [it]." [This is] the declaration of the LORD.

THE REUNIFICATION OF ISRAEL

¹⁵The word of the LORD came to me: ¹⁶"Son of man, take a single stick and write on it: Belonging to Judah and the Israelites associated with him. Then take another stick and write on it: Belonging to Joseph—the stick of Ephraim—and all the house of Israel associated with him. ¹⁷Then join them together into a single stick so that they become one in your hand. ¹⁸When your people ask you: Won't you explain to us what you mean by these things?— ¹⁹tell them: This is what the Lord GOD says: I am going to take the stick of Joseph—which is in the hand of Ephraim—and the tribes of Israel associated with him, and put them together with the stick of Judah. I will make them into a single stick so that they become one in My hand.

20"When the sticks you have written on are in your hand and in full view of the people, 21tell them: This is what the Lord God says: I am going to take the Israelites out of the nations where they have gone. I will gather them from all around and bring them into their own land. 22I will make them one nation in the land, on the mountains of Israel, and one king will rule over all of them. They will no longer be two nations and will no longer be divided into two kingdoms. 23They will not defile themselves any more with their idols, their detestable things, and all their transgressions. I will save them from all their apostasies by which they sinned, and I will cleanse them. Then they will be My people, and I will be their God. 24My servant David will be king over them, and there will be one shepherd for all of them. They will follow My ordinances, and keep My statutes and obey them.

25"They will live in the land that I gave to My servant Jacob, where your fathers lived. They will live in it forever with their children and grandchildren, and My servant David will be their prince forever. 26I will make a covenant of peace with them; it will be an everlasting covenant with them. I will establish and multiply them, and will set My sanctuary among them forever. 27My dwelling place will be with them; I will be their God, and they will be My people. 28When My sanctuary is among them forever, the nations will know that I, the Lord, sanctify Israel."

THOUGHT: Before you go out into the day dwell for a few moments on the glorious fact that you have been re-born through the power of the Holy Spirit and have become part of a people empowered by the Holy Spirit. Think of it – the same Holy Spirit who rested on Jesus and filled His life with power and joy is resting on you and is in you. Could there be anything more wonderful in earth or in heaven? If so then we have still to hear of it.

AS WE LOOK back on the extraordinary start which Israel had as a nation, it would seem hard to improve on its dramatic evidence of God's power at work to save. From the plagues which tested Pharaoh's resolve, through the miraculous protection from death on Passover night, to the parting of the Red Sea, the Exodus seems unsurpassable as an intervention of God. But the first Exodus from enslavement in Egypt is destined to be eclipsed in a new and greater Exodus – this time from slavery in Babylon (vv.16-21)!

In fact so remarkably will God act to bring His people back from captivity that He urges them to forget the former things and not to dwell on the past (v.18)! Whereas once He made a dry way through the sea, now He proposes to make streams flow in the desert (vv.16,20). Either way, nothing is impossible to God when He acts to bring salvation to His people. The first Exodus is but a parable of a future, final Exodus. Israel's God is the One Creator God. He is not bound by His past, nor exhausted by His past achievements. Only our persistent sin and lack of trust in Him weary Him (v.24). But even our past cannot cripple God (v.25). He has a reputation to maintain for making new starts and so He forgives! And the forgiven – and only the forgiven – have a future.

DAY
154
ISAIAH 43

Isaiah 43

BIBLE
READING

43 Now this is what the LORD says—
the One who created you, Jacob,
and the One who formed you, Israel—
"Do not fear, for I have redeemed you;
I have called you by your name; you are Mine.
² I will be with you
when you pass through the waters,
and [when you pass] through the rivers,
they will not overwhelm you.
You will not be scorched

when you walk through the fire,
and the flame will not burn you.
3 For I the LORD your God,
the Holy One of Israel, and your Savior,
give Egypt as a ransom for you,
Cush and Seba in your place.
4 Because you are precious in My sight
and honored, and I love you,
I will give human beings in your place,
and peoples in place of your life.
5 Do not fear, for I am with you;
I will bring your descendants from the east,
and gather you from the west.
6 I will say to the north: Give [them] up!
and to the south: Do not hold [them] back!
Bring My sons from far away,
and My daughters from the ends of the earth—
7 everyone called by My name
and created for My glory.
I have formed him; indeed, I have made him."

8 Bring out a people who are blind, yet have eyes,
and are deaf, yet have ears.
9 All the nations are gathered together,
and the peoples are assembled.
Who among them can declare this,
and tell us the former things?
Let them present their witnesses
to vindicate [themselves],
so that people may hear and say, "It is true."
10 "You are My witnesses"—

the LORD's declaration—

"and My servant whom I have chosen,
so that you may know and believe Me
and understand that I am He.
No god was formed before Me,
and there will be none after Me.
11 I, I am the LORD,
and there is no other Savior but Me.
12 I alone declared, saved, and proclaimed—

and not some foreign god among you.
So you are My witnesses"—

the LORD's declaration—

"and I am God.
¹³ Also, from today on I am He [alone],
and no one can take [anything] from My hand.
I act, and who can reverse it?"

GOD'S DELIVERANCE OF REBELLIOUS ISRAEL

¹⁴This is what the LORD, your Redeemer, the Holy One of
Israel says:

Because of you, I will send to Babylon
and bring all of them as fugitives,
even the Chaldeans in the ships in which they rejoice.
¹⁵ I am the LORD, your Holy One,
the Creator of Israel, your King.

¹⁶ This is what the LORD says—
who makes a way in the sea,
and a path through surging waters,
¹⁷ who brings out the chariot and horse,
the army and the mighty one together
(they lie down, they do not rise again;
they are extinguished, quenched like a wick)—
¹⁸ "Do not remember the past events,
pay no attention to things of old.
¹⁹ Look, I am about to do something new;
even now it is coming. Do you not see it?
Indeed, I will make a way in the wilderness,
rivers in the desert.
²⁰ The animals of the field will honor Me,
jackals and ostriches,
because I provide water in the wilderness,
and rivers in the desert,
to give drink to My chosen people.
²¹ The people I formed for Myself
will declare My praise.

²² "But Jacob, you have not called on Me,

because, Israel, you have become weary of Me.

²³ You have not brought Me your sheep for burnt offerings
or honored Me with your sacrifices.
I have not burdened you with offerings
or wearied you with incense.

²⁴ You have not bought Me aromatic cane with silver,
or satisfied Me with the fat of your sacrifices.
But you have burdened Me with your sins;
you have wearied Me with your iniquities.

²⁵ "It is I who sweep away your transgressions
for My own sake
and remember your sins no more.

²⁶ Take Me to court; let us argue our case together.
State your [case], so that you may be vindicated.

²⁷ Your first father sinned,
and your mediators have rebelled against Me.

²⁸ So I defiled the officers of the sanctuary,
and gave Jacob over to total destruction
and Israel to abuse.

FOR ACTION: If it is true (and it is) that only the forgiven have a great and glorious future, then it follows that the unforgiven face an eternity where all is gloom and sadness. Ought not this stir our hearts to pray more passionately and persistently for those in our circle of loved ones and friends who do not yet know Christ? Put a fence around fifteen minutes of your day and intercede for them.

DAY
155
JEREMIAH 31:31-34

AS A KEY feature of the new and greater Exodus coming to His people, God will create a new and better covenant arrangement with them. The covenant promised now will not be like the covenant which bound Israel to God at Sinai but which has broken down (v.32). Not that there was anything wrong with that 'old' covenant.

The prophet makes clear that the fault lay not on

the 'divine side' of the covenant relationship but on the human side, with Israel's persistent inability and unwillingness to keep covenant: 'a covenant they broke' (32b).

Four elements of this wonderful new covenant promise are spelt out: first of all, God promises to give to His people what we might call 'a new disposition to obey Him' – He promises to 'place My law within them and write it on their hearts' (v.33).

This is not so much a change of law as a change in the way the covenant is administered. The law – previously external to the people, written on tablets of stone – is now to be internalised and imprinted on the hearts of God's covenant partners.

God's people will receive a new, inner motivation, empowering them to do God's will from the 'inside out'!

This in turn, can be expected to produce what Jeremiah later calls a 'singleness of heart and action' (32:39, NIV). God seems determined to have a people who will share His story with Him and live out that story to His glory.

Jeremiah 31:31-34

BIBLE READING

THE NEW COVENANT

³¹"Look, the days are coming"—[this is] the LORD's declaration—"when I will make a new covenant with the house of Israel and with the house of Judah. ³²[This one will] not be like the covenant I made with their ancestors when I took them by the hand to bring them out of the land of Egypt—a covenant they broke even though I had married them"—the LORD's declaration. ³³"Instead, this is the covenant I will make with the house of Israel after those days"—the LORD's declaration. "I will place My law within them and write it on their hearts. I will be their God, and they will be My people. ³⁴No longer will one teach his neighbor or his brother, saying: Know the LORD, for they will all know Me, from the least to the greatest of them"—the LORD's declaration. "For I will forgive their wrongdoing and never again remember their sin."

PRAYER: O Father, the more I read of Your determination and resolve to have a people with whom You will share Your story the more amazed I am that I am part of this great epic. How I praise You too for the fact that Your law is not outside me but inside me. I have a new disposition to obey and share Your glory through the power of Your Holy Spirit. Thank You my Father. Thank You. In Jesus' name. Amen.

DAY 156

DEUTERONOMY 30

WE PAUSE TO note that the first of the new covenant's blessings, as outlined by Jeremiah, recall words spoken long before and which we have previously touched on. Jeremiah's prophecy echoes a speech given by Moses at the end of the forty-year wilderness wanderings to the new generation poised to enter the promised land.

Even before Israel has entered to possess the land, Moses anticipates a tragic end of the story when by her persistent disobedience Israel will incur the ultimate covenantal judgment of forfeiting the land!

But in an extraordinary move, Moses offers the people hope.

Intriguingly – and prophetically – Moses does not refer for hope to the system of animal sacrifices, the appointed way of dealing with sin. No mention is made of this as part of the long-term solution. It is as if, in the end, sin will prove so deep-seated and stubborn a problem as to require an act of God beyond what the Torah provides. What Moses does say is that God will bring His people back from Exile to the land. God pledges then to turn His demand: 'circumcise your hearts' (Deut. 10:16) into a promise: 'The LORD your God will circumcise your heart ... and you will love Him with all your heart and all your soul, so that you will live' (30:6). God, it seems, is intent on having a covenant partnership that works, come what may!

Deuteronomy 30

RETURNING TO THE LORD

30 "When all these things happen to you—the blessings and curses I have set before you—and you come to your senses [while you are] in all the nations where the LORD your God has driven you, ²and you and your children return to the LORD your God and obey Him with all your heart and all your soul by doing everything I am giving you today, ³then He will restore your fortunes, have compassion on you, and gather you again from all the peoples where the LORD your God has scattered you. ⁴Even if your exiles are at the ends of the earth, He will gather you and bring you back from there. ⁵The LORD your God will bring you into the land your fathers possessed, and you will take possession of it. He will cause you to prosper and multiply you more than [He did] your fathers. ⁶The LORD your God will circumcise your heart and the hearts of your descendants, and you will love Him with all your heart and all your soul, so that you will live. ⁷The LORD your God will put all these curses on your enemies who hate and persecute you. ⁸Then you will again obey Him and follow all His commands I am giving you today. ⁹The LORD your God will make you prosper abundantly in all the work of your hands with children, the offspring of your livestock, and your soil's produce. Indeed, the LORD will again delight in your prosperity, as He delighted in that of your fathers, ¹⁰when you obey the LORD your God by keeping His commands and statutes that are written in this book of the law and return to Him with all your heart and all your soul.

CHOOSE LIFE

¹¹"This command that I give you today is certainly not too difficult or beyond your reach. ¹²It is not in heaven, so that you have to ask, 'Who will go up to heaven, get it for us, and proclaim it to us so that we may follow it?' ¹³And it is not across the sea, so that you have to ask, 'Who will cross the sea, get it for us, and proclaim it to us so that we may follow it?' ¹⁴But the message is very near you, in your mouth and in your heart, so that you may follow it. ¹⁵See, today I have set before you life

and prosperity, death and adversity. ¹⁶For I am commanding you today to love the LORD your God, to walk in His ways, and to keep His commands, statutes, and ordinances, so that you may live and multiply, and the LORD your God may bless you in the land you are entering to possess. ¹⁷But if your heart turns away and you do not listen and you are led astray to bow down to other gods and worship them, ¹⁸I tell you today that you will certainly perish and will not live long in the land you are entering to possess across the Jordan. ¹⁹I call heaven and earth as witnesses against you today that I have set before you life and death, blessing and curse. Choose life so that you and your descendants may live, ²⁰love the LORD your God, obey Him, and remain faithful to Him. For He is your life, and He will prolong your life in the land the LORD swore to give to your fathers Abraham, Isaac, and Jacob."

> **THOUGHT:** Sin (both Adam's sin and our own) has produced a stain on the soul that nothing could erase – except the blood of Christ. The old covenant, based on law, worked from the outside in but the new covenant based on grace reaches deep into our lives and changes us from the inside out. The law said: do this and you will live. Grace says: I will do it for you. Pause to give God praise for this great and glorious fact before moving out into the day.

DAY
157

JEREMIAH 31:31-34
HOSEA 2:21-23

THE SECOND PROMISE of the new covenant is the promise of a fresh sense of security in belonging to God.

God re-affirms the heart of the covenant: 'I will be their God, and they will be My people' (Jer. 31:33). These words crystallise as a formula, the bond of mutual commitment that was meant to characterise God's special relationship with Israel.

Despite failure and defeat the bond is now to be intensified and renewed. God's people are to be re-established as His own possession.

The repercussions of this promise would prove to be

truly amazing. Hosea - some two centuries earlier - had already held out the hope that God would one day say 'to Not My People: You are My people, and he will say: You are My God' (Hosea 2:23). But even such far-seeing prophets as Hosea and Jeremiah could scarcely have envisaged the day when those alien to God's original vow - the Gentiles scattered across the wider world - would lay hold of this promise for their own salvation and inclusion in God's covenant family (Rom. 9:25; 10:19; 2 Cor. 6:16)! The apostle Peter would, one day, be in a position to encourage the new covenant communities, in time-honoured terms, by reminding them - especially, no doubt, the Gentile believers among them - 'Once you were not a people, but now you are God's people' (1 Pet. 2:10).

Jeremiah 31:31-34

THE NEW COVENANT

[31]"Look, the days are coming"—[this is] the LORD's declaration—"when I will make a new covenant with the house of Israel and with the house of Judah. [32][This one will] not be like the covenant I made with their ancestors when I took them by the hand to bring them out of the land of Egypt—a covenant they broke even though I had married them"—the LORD's declaration. [33]"Instead, this is the covenant I will make with the house of Israel after those days"—the LORD's declaration. "I will place My law within them and write it on their hearts. I will be their God, and they will be My people. [34]No longer will one teach his neighbor or his brother, saying: Know the LORD, for they will all know Me, from the least to the greatest of them"—the LORD's declaration. "For I will forgive their wrongdoing and never again remember their sin."

BIBLE READING

Hosea 2:21-23

²¹ On that day I will respond—

the LORD's declaration.

I will respond to the sky,
and it will respond to the earth.
²² The earth will respond to the grain,
the new wine, and the oil,
and they will respond to Jezreel.
²³ I will sow her in the land for Myself,
and I will have compassion
on No Compassion;
I will say to Not My People:
You are My people,
and he will say: [You are] My God.

TO PONDER: How secure do you feel in your relationship with Jesus Christ? Psychologists tell us that there is no greater security than realising one belongs. Children who never feel they belong show evidences of deep insecurity. A sense of belonging it seems is essential to a secure personality. You belong to Jesus Christ; you are an heir of God and a joint heir with Jesus Christ. Dwell on that fact, but more - rejoice in it.

DAY
158

JEREMIAH 9:23-24;
31:31-34

TODAY, WE RELISH the next great promise of the new covenant: an unprecedented assurance of knowing God personally. No longer will 'knowing God' be second-hand, inherited or merely mediated, but first-hand and immediate. The emphasis on the word 'all' (31:34) implies what has been termed the 'democratisation of the knowledge of God'. No longer confined to priests or prophets, knowledge of God is accessible to everyone.

But knowing God is not a matter of having some

mystical or private religious experience. In fact the words 'from the least to the greatest of them' (v.34) alert us to the profound social implications of the new covenant. 'Knowing God' - especially in Jeremiah - always involves knowing what kind of God God is, namely that He is a God of justice (see 9:23-24).

As Jeremiah challenged King Jehoahaz, son of the godly Josiah: ' "Your own father, did he not eat and drink? He administered justice and righteousness, then it went well with him. He took up the case of the poor and needy, then it went well. Is this not what it means to know Me?" This is the LORD's declaration' (22:15-16).

Knowing God means loving your neighbour through loving God and loving God through loving your neighbour. Not to 'know' your neighbour in this way is not to know God - something on which the apostle John would later have much to say (cf.1 John 2:4ff.)!

Jeremiah 9:23-24

BIBLE READING

BOAST IN THE LORD

²³This is what the LORD says:

> The wise must not boast in his wisdom;
> the mighty must not boast in his might;
> the rich must not boast in his riches.
> ²⁴ But the one who boasts should boast in this,
> that he understands and knows Me—
> that I am the LORD, showing faithful love,
> justice, and righteousness on the earth,
> for I delight in these things.
>   [This is] the LORD's declaration.

BIBLE READING

Jeremiah 31:31-34

THE NEW COVENANT

³¹"Look, the days are coming"—[this is] the Lord's declaration—"when I will make a new covenant with the house of Israel and with the house of Judah. ³²[This one will] not be like the covenant I made with their ancestors when I took them by the hand to bring them out of the land of Egypt—a covenant they broke even though I had married them"—the Lord's declaration. ³³"Instead, this is the covenant I will make with the house of Israel after those days"—the Lord's declaration. "I will place My law within them and write it on their hearts. I will be their God, and they will be My people. ³⁴No longer will one teach his neighbor or his brother, saying: Know the Lord, for they will all know Me, from the least to the greatest of them"—the Lord's declaration. "For I will forgive their wrongdoing and never again remember their sin."

QUESTION: Ask yourself this important personal question: How well do I know God? Knowing *about* Him is one thing but knowing Him intimately as a friend and confidant is another. The way to get to know someone is to spend time with them. How much time do you spend with the Lord in personal prayer? Psalm 46:10 says: 'Be still, and know that I am God' (NIV). If you are too busy to develop intimacy with God then you are busier than God intends you to be.

DAY
159

JEREMIAH 31:34
MICAH 7:18-20

UNDERGIRDING ALL THE other promises of the new covenant is that of a radical forgiveness of sins.

God pledges a permanent solution to the deep-seated problem of human sin and covenant unfaithfulness: 'For I will forgive their wrongdoing and never again remember their sin.'

In one sense, this is nothing new. Forgiveness was always available under the old covenant arrangement, through repentant use of the sacrificial system.

Clearly, Old Testament sacrifices were effective, but only temporarily and needed to be constantly repeated – a point, which as we shall see, the writer to the Hebrews exploits in expounding the blessings of being in the new covenant (Heb. 8-10). As we have noted, neither here nor in Deuteronomy 30 which anticipates restoration beyond Exile, is the sacrificial system deemed adequate to deal with the deep-rooted sinfulness that has led to the judgment and 'death' of Exile!

God will need to do a 'new thing' to atone for such sin that will bring lasting forgiveness and a permanent state of non-condemnation where sins are remembered no more. But how He will do this Jeremiah is not told. At this stage in the story God is simply pledging to exercise His amazing grace, working on both sides of the relationship to make covenant work! Watch this space and watch this God!

Jeremiah 31:34

BIBLE READING

THE NEW COVENANT

³¹"Look, the days are coming"—[this is] the LORD's declaration—"when I will make a new covenant with the house of Israel and with the house of Judah. ³²[This one will] not be like the covenant I made with their ancestors when I took them by the hand to bring them out of the land of Egypt—a covenant they broke even though I had married them"—the LORD's declaration. ³³"Instead, this is the covenant I will make with the house of Israel after those days"—the LORD's declaration. "I will place My law within them and write it on their hearts. I will be their God, and they will be My people.

³⁴No longer will one teach his neighbor or his brother, saying: Know the LORD, for they will all know Me, from the least to the greatest of them"—the LORD's declaration. "For I will forgive their wrongdoing and never again remember their sin."

BIBLE READING

Micah 7:18-20

¹⁸ Who is a God like You,
  removing iniquity and passing over rebellion
  for the remnant of His inheritance?
  He does not hold on to His anger forever,
  because He delights in faithful love.
¹⁹ He will again have compassion on us;
  He will vanquish our iniquities.
  You will cast all our sins
  into the depths of the sea.
²⁰ You will show loyalty to Jacob
  and faithful love to Abraham,
  as You swore to our fathers
  from days long ago.

PRAYER: O Father what a joy it is to live in a permanent state of non-condemnation. The thought has never gripped me in this way before. I can sing with Wesley: 'No condemnation now I dread, Jesus and all in Him is mine.' What a blessed sense of freedom this gives me. Help me never to forget that to bring me into this place it cost Your Son His precious blood. My heart is grateful more than words can ever convey. Thank You, Father. Amen.

DAY
160
EZEKIEL 36:16-38

AS BEFITS A man who was trained as a priest, Ezekiel uses cultic or sacrificial language. He talks of the 'washing and cleansing' by which God will effect a complete change of heart in His covenant people. God will give a new heart – one which is soft and responsive to God – to replace an obdurate and unresponsive one.

Furthermore, God's very life-breath will pour into us to invigorate our covenant instincts, an action which matches the original in-breathing of Adam to make him a living being (Gen. 2:7).

As in Jeremiah's version, so in Ezekiel's: God's own

creative Spirit will empower God's covenant people to faithful covenant behaviour and practice.

This, says Ezekiel, will happen in the midst of Israel in the very land where unfaithfulness had led to Exile. So God's name will be hallowed which is His first concern and, according to Jesus, our first priority in prayer. By new covenant people, filled with His Spirit, God aims to redeem His reputation and to have the covenant people He has always set His heart on. As we have seen, this will amount to a 'resurrection' of God's people from the dead, achieved by the prophetic word and powerful Spirit of God (Ezek. 37). The Spirit of life animates the new covenant community.

Ezekiel 36:16-38

BIBLE READING

RESTORATION OF ISRAEL'S PEOPLE

[16]The word of the LORD came to me: [17]"Son of man, while the house of Israel lived in their land, they defiled it with their conduct and actions. Their behavior before Me was like menstrual impurity. [18]So I poured out My wrath on them because of the blood they had shed on the land, and because they had defiled it with their idols. [19]I dispersed them among the nations, and they were scattered among the countries. I judged them according to their conduct and actions. [20]When they came to the nations where they went, they profaned My holy name, because it was said about them: These are the people of the LORD, yet they had to leave His land [in exile]. [21]Then I had concern for My holy name, which the house of Israel profaned among the nations where they went.

[22]"Therefore, say to the house of Israel: This is what the Lord GOD says: It is not for your sake that I will act, house of Israel, but for My holy name, which you profaned among the nations where you went. [23]I will honor the holiness of My great name, which has been profaned among the nations—the name you have profaned among them. The nations will know that I am Yahweh"—the declaration of the Lord GOD—"when I demonstrate My holiness through you in their sight.

[24]"For I will take you from the nations and gather you from

all the countries, and will bring you into your own land. ²⁵I will also sprinkle clean water on you, and you will be clean. I will cleanse you from all your impurities and all your idols. ²⁶I will give you a new heart and put a new spirit within you; I will remove your heart of stone and give you a heart of flesh. ²⁷I will place My Spirit within you and cause you to follow My statutes and carefully observe My ordinances. ²⁸Then you will live in the land that I gave your fathers; you will be My people, and I will be your God. ²⁹I will save you from all your uncleanness. I will summon the grain and make it plentiful, and will not bring famine on you. ³⁰I will also make the fruit of the trees and the produce of the field plentiful, so that you will no longer experience reproach among the nations on account of famine.

³¹"Then you will remember your evil ways and your deeds that were not good, and you will loathe yourselves for your iniquities and abominations. ³²It is not for your sake that I will act"—the declaration of the Lord GOD—"let this be known to you. Be ashamed and humiliated because of your ways, house of Israel!

³³"This is what the Lord GOD says: On the day I cleanse you from all your iniquities, I will cause the cities to be inhabited, and the ruins will be rebuilt. ³⁴The desolate land will be cultivated instead of lying desolate in the sight of everyone who passes by. ³⁵Then they will say: This land that was desolate has become like the garden of Eden. The cities that were once ruined, desolate, and destroyed are [now] fortified and inhabited. ³⁶Then the nations that remain around you will know that I, the LORD, have rebuilt what was destroyed and have replanted what was desolate. I, the LORD, have spoken and I will do [it].

³⁷"This is what the Lord GOD says: I will respond to the house of Israel and do this for them: I will multiply them in number like a flock. ³⁸So the ruined cities will be filled with a flock of people, just as the flock of sheep for sacrifice is filled in Jerusalem during its appointed festivals. Then they will know that I am the LORD."

THOUGHT: To be part of the new covenant community means we are told that God 'aims to redeem his reputation'. The people of the old covenant acted shamefully at times and brought the name of God into disrepute. It is our task now, aided by the Holy Spirit, to show the world that it is possible to live the life He wants us to live and to keep His commandments. The challenge is tremendous but then so is the power available to us.

DAY
161
JOEL 2:1-3,10-32

THIS IS PERHAPS an appropriate point to consider the undated prophecy of Joel with its vision of a Spirit-drenched future.

But the prophet warns the people against complacently assuming that this future 'Day of the Lord' will be like a good-natured school prizegiving! When the day comes it will bring judgment as well as grace and will be as terrible as it is wonderful (v.11).

Joel warns God's people not to presume on God's grace but to be morally and spiritually ready for God's day. His message is a trumpet-call to Israel to reckon with the sobering reality of the coming Day and to return repentantly to the Lord.

Joel echoes the new covenant language of Jeremiah when he urges his hearers to 'Tear your hearts, not just your clothes' – in short, to change their habits not just their habit (v.13)! In a moving call, young and old, newly-weds and priests at worship, are urged to drop everything else in order to implore God with tears to remove His people's reproach and to silence the pagans' sneering, 'Where is their God?'

Some of the greatest prophetic promises are at stake here: 'I will make up for the years the locusts have eaten' (v.25, *The Message*). 'I will pour out My Spirit on all humanity ... everyone who calls on the name of Yahweh will be saved ...' (vv.28,32).

BIBLE READING

Joel 2:1-3,10-32

2 Blow the horn in Zion;
sound the alarm on My holy mountain!
Let all the residents of the land tremble,
for the Day of the LORD is coming;
in fact, it is near—
² a day of darkness and gloom,
a day of clouds and dense overcast,
like the dawn spreading over the mountains;
a great and strong people [appears],
such as never existed in ages past
and never will again
in all the generations to come.

³ A fire destroys in front of them,
and behind them a flame devours.
The land in front of them
is like the Garden of Eden,
but behind them,
it is like a desert wasteland;
there is no escape from them.

• • • • • • • • •

¹⁰ The earth quakes before them;
the sky shakes.
The sun and moon grow dark,
and the stars cease their shining.
¹¹ The LORD raises His voice
in the presence of His army.
His camp is very large;
Those who carry out His command are powerful.
Indeed, the Day of the LORD is terrible and dreadful—
who can endure it?

GOD'S CALL FOR REPENTANCE

¹² Even now—

[this is] the LORD's declaration—
turn to Me with all your heart,

with fasting, weeping, and mourning.
¹³ Tear your hearts,
not just your clothes,
and return to the LORD your God.
For He is gracious and compassionate,
slow to anger, rich in faithful love,
and He relents from sending disaster.
¹⁴ Who knows? He may turn and relent
and leave a blessing behind Him,
[so you can] offer grain and wine
to the LORD your God.

¹⁵ Blow the horn in Zion!
Announce a sacred fast;
proclaim an assembly.
¹⁶ Gather the people;
sanctify the congregation;
assemble the aged;
gather the children,
even those nursing at the breast.
Let the bridegroom leave his bedroom,
and the bride her honeymoon chamber.
¹⁷ Let the priests, the LORD's ministers,
weep between the portico and the altar.
Let them say:
"Have pity on Your people, LORD,
and do not make Your inheritance a disgrace,
an object of scorn among the nations.
Why should it be said among the peoples,
'Where is their God?'"

GOD'S RESPONSE TO HIS PEOPLE

¹⁸Then the LORD became jealous for His land and spared His
people. ¹⁹The LORD answered His people:

Look, I am about to send you
grain, new wine, and olive oil.
You will be satiated with them,
and I will no longer make you
a disgrace among the nations.

²⁰ I will drive the northerner far from you
   and banish him to a dry and desolate land,
   his front ranks into the Dead Sea,
   and his rear guard into the Mediterranean Sea.
   His stench will rise;
   yes, his rotten smell will rise,
   for he has done catastrophic things.

²¹ Don't be afraid, land;
   rejoice and be glad,
   for the LORD has done great things.
²² Don't be afraid, wild animals,
   for the wilderness pastures have turned green,
   the trees bear their fruit,
   and the fig tree and grapevine yield their riches.
²³ Children of Zion, rejoice and be glad
   in the LORD your God,
   because He gives you the autumn rain
   for your vindication.
   He sends showers for you,
   both autumn and spring rain as before.
²⁴ The threshing floors will be full of grain,
   and the vats will overflow
   with new wine and olive oil.

²⁵ I will repay you for the years
   that the swarming locust ate,
   the young locust, the destroying locust,
   and the devouring locust—
   My great army that I sent against you.
²⁶ You will have plenty to eat and be satisfied.
   You will praise the name of Yahweh your God,
   who has dealt wondrously with you.
   My people will never again be put to shame.
²⁷ You will know that I am present in Israel
   and that I am the LORD your God,
   and there is no other.
   My people will never again be put to shame.

GOD'S PROMISE OF HIS SPIRIT

²⁸ After this

I will pour out My Spirit on all humanity;

then your sons and your daughters will prophesy,

your old men will have dreams,

and your young men will see visions.

²⁹ I will even pour out My Spirit

on the male and female slaves in those days.

³⁰ I will display wonders

in the heavens and on the earth:

blood, fire, and columns of smoke.

³¹ The sun will be turned to darkness

and the moon to blood

before the great and awe-inspiring Day

of the LORD comes.

³² Then everyone who calls

on the name of Yahweh will be saved,

for there will be an escape

for those on Mount Zion and in Jerusalem,

as the LORD promised,

among the survivors the LORD calls.

TO PONDER: How wonderful to be alive in a day that is 'Spirit-drenched'. In Old Testament times the Holy Spirit seemed to come upon people for temporary purposes. His visitations were special and occasional. Since Pentecost, however, His presence is continuous and perpetual, bringing us to repentant praise and restoring to us the years which the locusts have eaten. Let the wonder of that fill your mind this day.

IN TRACING THE trajectory of the Davidic covenant, we noted that it was not only the people but the kings who failed and needed renewal. From the emergence of kingship in Israel (1 Sam. 9:9), it seems that one of the most important roles a prophet had to play was to act as a standing reminder to the kings that they held their kingship

DAY
162
JEREMIAH 33

in trust as stewards of God's sovereign rule.

Wherever kings abused their power, the prophets boldly threatened their continued claim to the privileges of the Davidic covenant. But when the dismal failure of the kings became evident, the prophets of Exile - as we have seen - began to project hopes of a new kingship.

God would raise up a new David, 'a Branch of righteousness ... [a king who] will administer justice and righteousness in the land' (vv.15-16).

Jeremiah envisages what seems a twofold office, blending the roles of Davidic king and Levitical priest, backed by God's covenant commitment (vv.19-21). Significantly, he links the emergence of this fascinating priest-king with God's foundational promise to Abraham of descendants as 'countless as the stars of the sky and as measureless as the sand on the seashore' (v.22, NIV, cf.Gen. 15). In the thread of God's great strategic plan of redemption, the stories of Jacob and David are joined to the future hope of one faithful Israelite (v.26)!

BIBLE READING

Jeremiah 33

ISRAEL'S RESTORATION

33 While he was still confined in the guard's courtyard, the word of the LORD came to Jeremiah a second time: [2]"The LORD who made the earth, the LORD who forms it to establish it, the LORD is His name, says this: [3]Call to Me and I will answer you and tell you great and wondrous things you do not know. [4]For this is what the LORD, the God of Israel, says concerning the houses of this city and the palaces of Judah's kings, the ones torn down [for defense] against the siege ramps and the sword: [5]The people coming to fight the Chaldeans will fill the houses with the corpses of [their own] men I strike down in My wrath and rage. I have hidden My face from this city because of all their evil. [6]Yet I will certainly bring health and healing to it and will indeed heal them. I will let them experience the abundance of peace and truth. [7]I will restore the fortunes of Judah and of Israel and will rebuild them as in former times. [8]I will purify them from all the wrongs they have committed against Me, and I will forgive all the wrongs they have committed against Me, rebelling against Me. [9]This city will bear on My behalf a name of joy, praise, and glory before all the nations of the earth, who will hear of all the good I will do for them. They will tremble with awe because of all the good and all the peace I will bring about for them.

[10]"This is what the LORD says: In this place which you say is a ruin, without man or beast—that is, in Judah's cities and Jerusalem's streets that are a desolation without man, without inhabitant, and without beast—there will be heard again [11]a sound of joy and gladness, the voice of the bridegroom and the bride, and the voice of those saying,

> Praise the LORD of Hosts,
> for the LORD is good;
> His faithful love endures forever

as they bring thank offerings to the temple of the LORD. For I will restore the fortunes of the land as in former times, says the LORD.

[12]"This is what the LORD of Hosts says: In this desolate place—without man or beast—and in all its cities there will once more be a grazing land where shepherds may rest flocks. [13]The flocks will again pass under the hands of the one who counts them in the cities of the hill country, the cities of the Judean foothills, the cities of the Negev, the land of Benjamin—the cities surrounding Jerusalem and Judah's cities, says the LORD.

GOD'S COVENANT WITH DAVID

[14]"Look, the days are coming"—[this is] the LORD's declaration—"when I will fulfill the good promises that I have spoken concerning the house of Israel and the house of Judah. [15]In those days and at that time I will cause a Branch of righteousness to sprout up for David, and He will administer justice and righteousness in the land. [16]In those days Judah will be saved, and Jerusalem will dwell securely, and this is what she will be named: The LORD Is Our Righteousness. [17]For this is what the LORD says: David will never fail to have a

man sitting on the throne of the house of Israel. [18]The Levitical priests will never fail to have a man always before Me to offer burnt offerings, to burn grain offerings, and to make sacrifices."

[19]The word of the LORD came to Jeremiah: [20]"This is what the LORD says: If you can break My covenant with the day and My covenant with the night so that day and night cease to come at their regular time, [21]then also My covenant with My servant David may be broken so that he will not have a son reigning on his throne, and the Levitical priests will not be My ministers. [22]The hosts of heaven cannot be counted; the sand of the sea cannot be measured. So, too, I will make the descendants of My servant David and the Levites who minister to Me innumerable."

[23]The word of the LORD came to Jeremiah: [24]"Have you not noticed what these people have said? They say: The LORD has rejected the two families He had chosen. My people are treated with contempt and no longer regarded as a nation among them. [25]This is what the LORD says: If I do not [keep] My covenant with the day and with the night and fail to establish the fixed order of heaven and earth, [26]then I might also reject the seed of Jacob and of My servant David—not taking from his descendants rulers over the descendants of Abraham, Isaac, and Jacob. Instead, I will restore their fortunes and have compassion on them."

FOR PRAISE: God's plan to have a worldwide family of faith has threaded its way through history until this very moment - and that great plan includes you. It is as if a great river runs down to water one little daisy. Let your heart overflow in praise right now as once again you dwell on the fact that God's story includes you. 'Praise,' said C.S. Lewis, 'is always the right response to the discovery of God's mercies.'

ISAIAH CHAPTERS 40-55 constitute the high point of Old Testament revelation. By portraying, in vivid imagery, the future stages of God's story, these chapters are the seedbed from which springs the Evangelists' understanding of Jesus and the apostolic understanding of the gospel. It is to Isaiah that we owe the very meaning of the concept of 'gospel'.

For Isaiah, the gospel which the herald announces is, 'Here is your God!' (v.9). God Himself, in grace and for glory, will return as King to Zion - leading the homecoming exiles on the road across the desert. This God who comes as strong soldier and sensitive shepherd (vv.10-11), is no less a deliverer than the One Creator God, the mastermind behind the whole teeming, multi-coloured creation project (vv.12-14). This God both grasps the big picture and notices the detail of a falling star. This is the independent, all-sufficient, incomparable Holy One of Israel, who never suffers compassion-fatigue or brain-drain (v.28)! The Creator is the Redeemer who aims at nothing less than a renewal of His whole creation.

Today we can replenish our supply from His strength and resume our homeward journey with the buoyancy of soaring eagles, the energy of relentless runners and the dogged persistence of tireless walkers.

DAY
163
ISAIAH 40

Isaiah 40

BIBLE
READING

GOD'S PEOPLE COMFORTED

40 "Comfort, comfort My people,"
says your God.

² Speak tenderly to Jerusalem,
and announce to her
that her time of servitude is over,
her iniquity has been pardoned,
and she has received from the LORD's hand
double for all her sins.

³ A voice of one crying out:

> Prepare the way of the L<small>ORD</small> in the wilderness;
> make a straight highway for our God in the desert.

⁴ Every valley will be lifted up,
and every mountain and hill will be leveled;
the uneven ground will become smooth,
and the rough places a plain.

⁵ And the glory of the L<small>ORD</small> will appear,
and all humanity will see [it] together,
for the mouth of the L<small>ORD</small> has spoken.

⁶ A voice was saying, "Cry out!"
Another said, "What should I cry out?"
"All humanity is grass,
and all its goodness is like the flower of the field.

⁷ The grass withers, the flowers fade
when the breath of the L<small>ORD</small> blows on them;
indeed, the people are grass.

⁸ The grass withers, the flowers fade,
but the word of our God remains forever."

⁹ Zion, herald of good news,
go up on a high mountain.
Jerusalem, herald of good news,
raise your voice loudly.
Raise it, do not be afraid!
Say to the cities of Judah,
"Here is your God!"

¹⁰ See, the Lord G<small>OD</small> comes with strength,
and His power establishes His rule.
His reward is with Him,
and His gifts accompany Him.

¹¹ He protects His flock like a shepherd;
He gathers the lambs in His arms
and carries [them] in the fold of His [garment].
He gently leads those that are nursing.

¹² Who has measured the waters in the hollow
of his hand

or marked off the heavens with the span [of his hand]?
Who has gathered the dust of the earth in a measure
or weighed the mountains in a balance
and the hills in scales?

¹³ Who has directed the Spirit of the Lord,
or who gave Him His counsel?

¹⁴ Who did He consult with?
Who gave Him understanding
and taught Him the paths of justice?
Who taught Him knowledge
and showed Him the way of understanding?

¹⁵ Look, the nations are like a drop in a bucket;
they are considered as a speck of dust on the scales;
He lifts up the islands like fine dust.

¹⁶ Lebanon is not enough for fuel,
or its animals enough for a burnt offering.

¹⁷ All the nations are as nothing before Him;
they are considered by Him
as nothingness and emptiness.

¹⁸ Who will you compare God with?
What likeness will you compare Him to?

¹⁹ To an idol?—[something that] a smelter casts,
and a metalworker plates with gold
and makes silver welds [for it]?

²⁰ To one who shapes a pedestal,
choosing wood that does not rot?
He looks for a skilled craftsman
to set up an idol that will not fall over.

²¹ Do you not know?
Have you not heard?
Has it not been declared to you
from the beginning?
Have you not considered
the foundations of the earth?

²² God is enthroned above the circle of the earth;
its inhabitants are like grasshoppers.
He stretches out the heavens like thin cloth
and spreads them out like a tent to live in.

23 He reduces princes to nothing
and makes the judges of the earth to be irrational.
24 They are barely planted, barely sown,
their stem hardly takes root in the ground
when He blows on them and they wither,
and a whirlwind carries them away like stubble.

25 "Who will you compare Me to,
or who is My equal?" asks the Holy One.
26 Look up and see:
who created these?
He brings out the starry host by number;
He calls all of them by name.
Because of His great power and strength,
not one of them is missing.

27 Jacob, why do you say,
and Israel, why do you assert:
"My way is hidden from the LORD,
and my claim is ignored by my God"?
28 Do you not know?
Have you not heard?
Yahweh is the everlasting God,
the Creator of the whole earth.
He never grows faint or weary;
there is no limit to His understanding.
29 He gives strength to the weary
and strengthens the powerless.
30 Youths may faint and grow weary,
and young men stumble and fall,
31 but those who trust in the LORD
will renew their strength;
they will soar on wings like eagles;
they will run and not grow weary;
they will walk and not faint.

QUESTION: Are you feeling tired and weary? Do you feel you are running out of spiritual or physical resources? Then hold on to the thought, 'we can replenish our supply from His strength'. Let your weakness lie limp on God's shoulder. Draw from His endless resources which so immeasurably exceed our demands. Lift your heart in believing prayer at this moment and take God at His word. He will not fail you.

SO FAR WE have traced God's promise-plan as it makes its way through history, implemented by God's covenant commitments: with Noah and the earth, with Abraham for the nations, through Moses for Israel, and with David for the sake of the future. Now has come Exile, and the judgment and grace God speaks through His prophets of the time.

DAY 164

2 CHRONICLES
36:15-23
ISAIAH 41:2-4;
44:24-45:7

From a wider perspective we can see that Exodus and Exile are the two poles around which the Old Testament story of Israel revolves. Ironically, Israel's story which began in slavery in Egypt, effectively ends in captivity in Babylonia from where Abraham had come over a millennium earlier!

But the hopes of the Exilic prophets are remarkable.

If, in the first Exodus, Egypt gave birth to a nation for God, out of slavery through deliverance, so, now, Exile yields promise of a new people of God, redeemed this time in a greater exodus, out of the deeper slavery of sin through 'death and resurrection'.

So two problems need to be addressed.

To get God's people physically back to the land, God raises up Cyrus, who does not know Yahweh.

But to restore God's people to Himself, cleansed, forgiven and reconstituted, is an issue way beyond the scope of political warlords like Cyrus. For that God will need another, altogether different kind of 'servant'!

BIBLE READING

2 Chronicles 36:15-23

THE DESTRUCTION OF JERUSALEM

[15]But the LORD God of their ancestors sent word against them by the hand of His messengers, sending them time and time again, for He had compassion on His people and on His dwelling place. [16]But they kept ridiculing God's messengers, despising His words, and scoffing at His prophets, until the LORD's wrath was so stirred up against His people that there was no remedy. [17]So He brought up against them the king of the Chaldeans, who killed their choice young men with the sword in the house of their sanctuary. He had no pity on young man and virgin or elderly and aged; He handed them all over to him. [18]He took everything to Babylon—all the articles of God's temple, large and small, the treasures of the LORD's temple, and the treasures of the king and his officials. [19]Then the Chaldeans burned God's temple. They tore down Jerusalem's wall, burned down all its palaces, and destroyed all its valuable utensils.

[20]Those who escaped from the sword he deported to Babylon, and they became servants to him and his sons until the rise of the Persian kingdom. [21]This fulfilled the word of the LORD through Jeremiah and the land enjoyed its Sabbath rest all the days of the desolation until 70 years were fulfilled.

THE DECREE OF CYRUS

[22]In the first year of Cyrus king of Persia, the word of the LORD spoken through Jeremiah was fulfilled. The LORD put it into the mind of King Cyrus of Persia to issue a proclamation throughout his entire kingdom and also [to put it] in writing:

[23]This is what King Cyrus of Persia says: The LORD, the God of heaven, has given me all the kingdoms of the earth and has appointed me to build Him a temple at Jerusalem in Judah. Whoever among you of His people may go up, and may the LORD his God be with him.

Isaiah 41:2-4

² Who has stirred him up from the east?
He calls righteousness to his feet.
The LORD hands nations over to him,
and he subdues kings.
He makes [them] like dust [with] his sword,
like wind-driven stubble [with] his bow.
³ He pursues them, going on safely,
hardly touching the path with his feet.
⁴ Who has performed and done [this],
calling the generations from the beginning?
I, the LORD, am the first,
and with the last—I am He."

Isaiah 44:24-45:7

RESTORATION OF ISRAEL THROUGH CYRUS

²⁴This is what the LORD, your Redeemer who formed you
from the womb, says:

I am the LORD, who made everything;
who stretched out the heavens by Myself;
who alone spread out the earth;
²⁵ who destroys the omens of the false prophets
and makes fools of diviners;
who confounds the wise
and makes their knowledge foolishness;
²⁶ who confirms the message of His servant
and fulfills the counsel of His messengers;
who says to Jerusalem: She will be inhabited,
and to the cities of Judah: They will be rebuilt,
and I will restore her ruins;
²⁷ who says to the depths of the sea: Be dry,
and I will dry up your rivers;
²⁸ who says to Cyrus: My shepherd,
he will fulfill all My pleasure
and say to Jerusalem: She will be rebuilt,

and of the temple: Its foundation will be laid.

45 The LORD says this to Cyrus, His anointed,
whose right hand I have grasped
to subdue nations before him,
to unloose the loins of kings,
to open the doors before him
and the gates will not be shut:
2 "I will go before you
and level the uneven places;
I will shatter the bronze doors
and cut the iron bars in two.
3 I will give you the treasures of darkness
and riches from secret places,
so that you may know that I, the LORD,
the God of Israel call you by your name.
4 I call you by your name,
because of Jacob My servant
and Israel My chosen one.
I give a name to you,
though you do not know Me.
5 I am the LORD, and there is no other;
there is no God but Me.
I will strengthen you,
though you do not know Me,
6 so that all may know from the rising of the sun
to its setting
that there is no one but Me.
I am the LORD, and there is no other.
7 I form light and create darkness,
I make success and create disaster;
I, the LORD, do all these things.

THOUGHT: We have seen that it was one thing for God to bring His people back to the land He had given them, but it was quite another thing to bring them back to Himself. The men God used in Old Testament times to achieve this were flawed, but now God's servant, because He is both human and divine, joins us to the Father and journeys with us, helping us day by day to develop a deeper intimacy with God. To Him be eternal praise.

IT IS GIVEN to the prophet Isaiah movingly to unveil the figure of this mysterious servant who alone will achieve God's greatest work. He does so particularly in what have been called the 'servant songs'.

DAY
165

ISAIAH 42

In the first of these songs, we learn that God will select and endorse this servant. The servant will know God's approval and anointing and will nourish His true self-identity in God's delight in Him. His manner of ministry will run counter to worldly methods by showing self-restraint, neither raucously promoting Himself nor blusteringly protecting Himself. He will win people's allegiance but not by trampling over them. When He meets the weak He does not overpower or crush them. His own strength of purpose will remain uncrushed and undimmed. And His mission will be the establishment of God's justice in the earth (vv.1,3-4). As Creator, God guarantees the success of the servant's cause.

As covenant-maker, God will cause the servant to embody the covenant, so that He becomes the means by which people enter into a covenant relationship with God (v.6). His light shines not only in Israel but to the world of nations, working wonders of healing and freedom that demonstrate the unrivalled glory and unprecedented newness of God, and spark riots of rejoicing and praise (vv.6-13).

BIBLE READING

Isaiah 42

THE SERVANT'S MISSION

42 "This is My Servant;
I strengthen Him,
[this is] My Chosen One; I delight in Him.
I have put My Spirit on Him;
He will bring justice to the nations.

2 He will not cry out or shout
or make His voice heard in the streets.

3 He will not break a bruised reed,
and He will not put out a smoldering wick;
He will faithfully bring justice.

4 He will not grow weak or be discouraged
until He has established justice on earth.
The islands will wait for His instruction."

5 This is what God the LORD says—
who created the heavens and stretched them out,
who spread out the earth and what comes from it,
who gives breath to the people on it
and life to those who walk on it—

6 "I, the LORD, have called you
for a righteous [purpose],
and I will hold you by your hand.
I will keep you, and I make you
a covenant for the people
[and] a light to the nations,

7 in order to open blind eyes,
to bring out prisoners from the dungeon,
[and] those sitting in darkness from the prison house.

8 I am Yahweh, that is My name;
I will not give My glory to another,
or My praise to idols.

9 The past events have indeed happened.
Now I declare new events;
I announce them to you before they occur."

A SONG OF PRAISE

¹⁰ Sing a new song to the LORD;
[sing] His praise from the ends of the earth,
you who go down to the sea with all that fills it,
you islands with your inhabitants.

¹¹ Let the desert and its cities shout,
the settlements where Kedar dwells [cry aloud].
Let the inhabitants of Sela sing for joy;
let them cry out from the mountaintops.

¹² Let them give glory to the LORD,
and declare His praise in the islands.

¹³ The LORD advances like a warrior;
He stirs up His zeal like a soldier.
He shouts, He roars aloud,
He prevails over His enemies.

¹⁴ "I have kept silent from ages past;
I have been quiet and restrained Myself.
[But now,] I will groan like a woman in labor,
gasping breathlessly.

¹⁵ I will lay waste mountains and hills,
and dry up all their vegetation.
I will turn rivers into islands,
and dry up marshes.

¹⁶ I will lead the blind by a way they did not know;
I will guide them on paths they have not known.
I will turn darkness to light in front of them,
and rough places into level ground.
This is what I will do for them,
and I will not forsake them.

¹⁷ They will be turned back [and] utterly ashamed—
those who trust in idols
and say to metal-plated images:
You are our gods!

ISRAEL'S BLINDNESS AND DEAFNESS

¹⁸ "Listen, you deaf!
Look, you blind, so that you may see.

¹⁹ Who is blind but My servant,
or deaf like My messenger I am sending?

Who is blind like [My] dedicated one,
or blind like the servant of the Lord?
20 Though seeing many things, you do not obey.
Though [his] ears are open, he does not listen."

21 The Lord was pleased, because of His righteousness,
to magnify [His] instruction and make it glorious.
22 But this is a people plundered and looted,
all of them trapped in holes
or imprisoned in dungeons.
They have become plunder,
with no one to rescue them,
and loot, with no one saying "Give [it] back!"
23 Who among you will pay attention to this?
Let him listen and obey in the future.
24 Who gave Jacob to the robber,
and Israel to the plunderers?
Was it not the Lord?
Have we not sinned against Him?
They were not willing to walk in His ways,
and they would not listen to His instruction.
25 So He poured out on Jacob His furious anger
and the power of war.
It surrounded him with fire, but he did not know [it];
it burned him, but he paid no attention.

FOR PRAISE: Embarking upon the theme of the 'servant songs' brings to mind the chorus from Graham Kendrick's wonderful hymn: 'The Servant King'. Sing it with praise and gratitude in your heart for the One who stooped to serve.

This is our God, the Servant King
He calls us now to follow Him
To bring our lives as a daily offering
Of worship to the Servant King.

Copyright © 1983 Thankyou Music. Used by permission.

DAY
166

ISAIAH 49

IN THIS 'SERVANT song', the mystery deepens as to who or what this strange agent of God can be. There is a puzzling ambiguity about the prophet's description of Him. It seems that, on the one hand, the servant is to be identified with Israel (v.3) but that, on the other, He will have a ministry to Israel and will thus fulfil Israel's vocation of being a saving light to the Gentiles. How can this be? We are reminded, perhaps, of the way in which the king, as a representative figure, carries the nation in himself. Perhaps this is our clue here. It helps to remember that 'Israel' was a name first given to an individual, the father of the nation, Jacob. This servant then, by living out Israel's covenant faithfulness, will, as it were, 'father' a new people of God.

He will be both the glory of His people Israel and the light for the Gentile nations. Again, God's own faithfulness guarantees the servant's mission, once more by making Him an embodiment of the covenant (vv.7-8). It is as if all the covenant promises and dreams will converge on Him so that everyone must come to Him to receive the blessings of salvation.

When that day comes it will be a day of favour and opportunity none can afford to miss (v.8) and none would want to. From dark dungeons captives will step out in the fresh air and daylight of God's freedom.

BIBLE READING

Isaiah 49

THE SERVANT BRINGS SALVATION

49 Coastlands, listen to me;
distant peoples, pay attention.
The LORD called me before I was born.
He named me while I was in my mother's womb.
² He made my words like a sharp sword;
He hid me in the shadow of His hand.
He made me like a sharpened arrow;
He hid me in His quiver.

3 He said to me, "You are My servant, Israel;
  I will be glorified in him."
4 But I myself said: I have labored in vain,
  I have spent my strength for nothing and futility;
  yet my vindication is with the LORD,
  and my reward is with my God.
5 And now, says the LORD,
  who formed me from the womb to be His servant,
  to bring Jacob back to Him
  so that Israel might be gathered to Him;
  for I am honored in the sight of the LORD,
  and my God is my strength—
6 He says,
  "It is not enough for you to be My servant
  raising up the tribes of Jacob
  and restoring the protected ones of Israel.
  I will also make you a light for the nations,
  to be My salvation to the ends of the earth."
7 This is what the LORD,
  the Redeemer of Israel, his Holy One says
  to one who is despised,
  to one abhorred by people,
  to a servant of rulers:
  "Kings will see and stand up,
  and princes will bow down,
  because of the LORD, who is faithful,
  the Holy One of Israel—and He has chosen you."

8 This is what the LORD says:

  I will answer you in a time of favor,
  and I will help you in the day of salvation.
  I will keep you, and I will appoint you
  to be a covenant for the people,
  to restore the land,
  to make them possess the desolate inheritances,
9 saying to the prisoners: Come out,
  and to those who are in darkness: Show yourselves.
  They will feed along the pathways,
  and their pastures will be on all the barren heights.

¹⁰ They will not hunger or thirst,
  the scorching heat or sun will not strike them;
  for their compassionate One will guide them,
  and lead them to springs of water.
¹¹ I will make all My mountains into a road,
  and My highways will be raised up.
¹² See, these will come from far away,
  from the north and from the west,
  and from the land of Sinim.

¹³ Shout for joy, you heavens!
  Earth, rejoice!
  Mountains break into joyful shouts!
  For the LORD has comforted His people,
  and will have compassion on His afflicted ones.

ZION REMEMBERED

¹⁴ Zion says, "The LORD has abandoned me;
  The Lord has forgotten me!"
¹⁵ "Can a woman forget her nursing child,
  or lack compassion for the child of her womb?
  Even if these forget,
  yet I will not forget you.
¹⁶ Look, I have inscribed you on the palms of My hands;
  your walls are continually before Me.
¹⁷ Your builders hurry;
  those who destroy and devastate you will leave you.
¹⁸ Look up, and look around.
  They all gather together; they come to you.
  As I live"—

                              the LORD's declaration—
  "you will wear all your children as jewelry,
  and put them on as a bride does.
¹⁹ For your waste and desolate places
  and your land marked by ruins—
  will now be indeed too small for the inhabitants,
  and those who swallowed you up will be far away.
²⁰ The children that you have been deprived of
  will yet say in your hearing:
  This place is too small for me;

make room for me so that I may settle.
21 Then you will say within yourself:
Who fathered these for me?
I was deprived of my children and barren,
exiled and wandering—
but who brought them up?
See, I was left by myself—
but these, where did they come from?"

²²This is what the Lord GOD says:

Look, I will lift up My hand to the nations,
and raise My banner to the peoples.
They will bring your sons in their arms,
and your daughters will be carried on their shoulders.
23 Kings will be your foster fathers,
and their queens your nursing mothers.
They will bow down to you
with their faces to the ground,
and lick the dust at your feet.
Then you will know that I am the LORD;
those who put their hope in Me
will not be put to shame.

24 Can the prey be taken from the mighty,
or the captives of the righteous be delivered?
25 For this is what the LORD says:
"Even the captives of a mighty man will be taken,
and the prey of a tyrant will be delivered;
I will contend with the one who contends with you,
and I will save your children.
26 I will make your oppressors eat their own flesh,
and they will be drunk with their own blood
as with sweet wine.
Then all flesh will know
that I, the LORD, am your Savior,
and your Redeemer, the Mighty One of Jacob."

PRAYER: O Father how can I ever thank You enough for reaching down into the dungeon of my life, shattering the chains of sin that bound me, and delivering me from the bondage I was in. In Wesley's words: 'My chains fell off, my heart was free, I rose went forth and followed Thee.' Now I want to be Your willing slave for ever. All honour and glory be to Your peerless and precious name. Amen.

DAY 167

ISAIAH 50

THROUGH THE PROPHET, God once more gently chides His people that He has not divorced them nor has He settled a debt by selling them off. God's people have been 'sent away' into Exile not because God has failed but because they refused to recognise His presence and power. One exception stands out - a servant of God who speaks for Himself in this third 'servant song' (vv.4-9). When God came and called no one responded except God's servant who is 'all ears', listening for the voice of the Lord as a true disciple of the Lord. He hears 'morning by morning' (NIV), giving priority to God's Word, as prophets did (cf.Jer. 7:25).

Daily He will speak words that sustain the weary, offering an easy yoke to replace a burdensome law - only to be beaten and spat upon for His pains. The servant's vigilance makes Him vulnerable to humiliation ('tore out My beard ... scorn and spitting') and violence ('beat Me'). Undaunted, He endures with flint-like determination, trusting to God to vindicate Him (vv.6-9). As a result, He forces everyone else to make a life-or-death decision whether to walk by faith though in the dark or to walk by the light of their own self-lit fires. God's long redemptive story seems to come down in the end to the trust of this one faithful Israelite. Who on earth is He? And when on earth will He appear?

Isaiah 50

50 This is what the LORD says:

Where is your mother's divorce certificate
that I used to send her away?
Or who were My creditors that I sold you to?
Look, you were sold for your iniquities,
and your mother was put away
because of your transgressions.

² Why was no one there when I came?
Why was there no one to answer when I called?
Is My hand too short to redeem?
Or do I have no power to deliver?
Look, I dry up the sea by My rebuke;
I turn the rivers into a wilderness;
their fish rot because of lack of water
and die of thirst.

³ I dress the heavens in black
and make sackcloth their clothing.

THE OBEDIENT SERVANT

⁴ The Lord GOD has given Me
the tongue of those who are instructed
to know how to sustain the weary with a word.
He awakens [Me] each morning;
He awakens My ear to listen like those being instructed.

⁵ The Lord GOD has opened My ear,
and I was not rebellious;
I did not turn back.

⁶ I gave My back to those who beat Me,
and My cheeks to those who tore out My beard.
I did not hide My face from scorn and spitting.

⁷ The Lord GOD will help Me;
therefore I have not been humiliated;
therefore I have set My face like flint,
and I know I will not be put to shame.

⁸ The One who justifies Me is near;
who will contend with Me?

Let us confront each other.
Who has a case against Me?
Let him come near Me!

⁹ In truth, the Lord GOD will help Me;
who is he who will condemn Me?
Indeed, all of them will wear out like a garment;
a moth will devour them.

¹⁰ Who among you fears the LORD,
listening to the voice of His servant?
Who [among you] walks in darkness,
and has no light?
Let him trust in the name of the LORD;
let him lean on his God.

¹¹ Look, all you who kindle a fire,
who encircle yourselves with firebrands;
walk in the light of your fire
and in the firebrands you have lit!
This is what you'll get from My hand:
you will lie down in a place of torment.

QUESTION: When God calls you to walk in the darkness of confusion and wait for His answers, what do you do? Cling to Him in deep trust or seek to illuminate your surroundings by lighting your own fire? (See again vv.10-11.) There is nothing like confusion to erode our sense of competence, but it is in such situations that the muscles of faith and trust are exercised. How good are you at trusting God when you cannot see the way ahead?

DAY
168

ISAIAH 52

AS WE HAVE said, no other prophet so vividly anticipates the gospel as Isaiah does. He heralds the return of God as King to be at the centre of His people's life again (40:3-10); declares the joyous prospect of forgiveness for the nation's sin (43:25ff.; 44:22ff.) and envisages the establishment of this kingdom of grace paradoxically through the suffering of God's servant. Here in 52:7-12, particularly, we find promises which become 'thematic for the whole work of Jesus' (Tom Wright).

Isaiah presents powerful images and hopes about how life might look on the other side of Exile.

Watchmen on the ruined ramparts of Jerusalem will shout for joy as they glimpse a distant runner with 'beautiful feet' that convey good news of God's kingdom. God is always King over creation and history but, as we have learned, His redemptive plan is to implement His rule in a dynamic, active sense that changes conditions on earth and ultimately renews His created world. The herald's gospel proclamation announces 'peace' and 'salvation', where and when 'Your God reigns!'

From the outset, as we have seen, Abraham's inheritance and Israel's hope were always meant to spell hope for the whole world, so that, when salvation finally comes to God's people, the ends of the earth hear of it (v.10).

Isaiah 52

BIBLE READING

52 "Wake up, wake up;
  put on your strength, Zion!
  Put on your beautiful garments,
  Jerusalem, the Holy City!
  For the uncircumcised and the unclean
  will no longer enter you.
² Stand up, shake the dust off yourself!
  Take your seat, Jerusalem.
  Remove the bonds from your neck,
  captive Daughter Zion."
³ For this is what the LORD says:
  "You were sold for nothing,
  and you will be redeemed without silver."
⁴ For this is what the Lord GOD says:
  "At first My people went down to Egypt to live there,
  then Assyria oppressed them without cause.

⁵ So now what have I here"—

> the LORD's declaration—

"that My people are taken away for nothing?
Its rulers wail"—

> the LORD's declaration—

"and My name is continually blasphemed all day long.
⁶ Therefore My people will know My name;
therefore [they will know] on that day
that I am He who says:
Here I am."

⁷ How beautiful on the mountains
are the feet of the herald,
who proclaims peace,
who brings news of good things,
who proclaims salvation,
who says to Zion, "Your God reigns!"
⁸ The voices of your watchmen—
they lift up their voices,
shouting for joy together;
for every eye will see
when the LORD returns to Zion.
⁹ Be joyful, rejoice together,
you ruins of Jerusalem!
For the LORD has comforted His people;
He has redeemed Jerusalem.
¹⁰ The LORD has displayed His holy arm
in the sight of all the nations;
all the ends of the earth will see
the salvation of our God.

¹¹ Leave, leave, go out from there!
Do not touch anything unclean;
go out from her, purify yourselves,
you who carry the vessels of the LORD.
¹² For you will not leave in a hurry,
and you will not have to take flight;
because the LORD is going before you,
and the God of Israel is your rear guard.

THE SERVANT'S SUFFERING AND EXALTATION

¹³ See, My servant will act wisely;
He will be raised and lifted up and greatly exalted.

¹⁴ Just as many were appalled at You—
His appearance was so disfigured
that He did not look like a man,
and His form did not resemble a human being—

¹⁵ so He will sprinkle many nations.
Kings will shut their mouths because of Him,
For they will see what had not been told them,
and they will understand what they had not heard.

FOR PRAISE: It seems appropriate to respond once again in a song of praise. Join in with the thousands who sing these lines by Leonard E. Smith:

You watchmen lift your voices joyfully as one ...
Your God reigns, your God reigns.

He does. He is our King, He is our Lord.
Blessed be His name for ever!

GOD'S SERVANT SUFFERS as a free and willing partner who submits to the consequence of doing the Lord's will.

DAY 169
ISAIAH 53

He at last will be despised, rejected and crushed - cut off from the land of the living - cast forth into the land of Exile and forsakenness. He achieves the salvation which could not be achieved by either animal sacrifices offered in the appointed way at the Temple or repeated prophetic calls to repentance. Only beyond Exile, as Israel attaches itself to this strange figure and goes down into death with Him, is there hope for the future.

Mysteriously God's suffering servant will atone for the sins of the people. His solo work will achieve the vindication of the justified many and, as a result,

He will be raised and lifted up and highly exalted
(52:13-53:12)

This exaltation unveils the strangest form of kingship
ever seen. Stooping to conquer, suffering in order
to save, He is the wise fool, the wounded Healer, the
Servant King!

Who is this servant? Did Isaiah know?

Probably not, is the answer to the second question.

As G.B. Caird said of the prophet, 'It was as though
he was publishing an advertisement: "Wanted: Servant
of the Lord: all applications welcome' accompanied by
a job description.'

As we now know there was only one applicant for
the job who fitted the description!

BIBLE READING	Isaiah 53

53 Who has believed what we have heard?
And who has the arm
of the LORD been revealed to?

2 He grew up before Him like a young plant
and like a root out of dry ground.
He had no form or splendor that we should look at Him,
no appearance that we should desire Him.

3 He was despised and rejected by men,
a man of suffering who knew what sickness was.
He was like one people turned away from;
He was despised, and we didn't value Him.

4 Yet He Himself bore our sicknesses,
and He carried our pains;
but we in turn regarded Him stricken,
struck down by God, and afflicted.

5 But He was pierced because of our transgressions,
crushed because of our iniquities;
punishment for our peace was on Him,
and we are healed by His wounds.

6 We all went astray like sheep;
we all have turned to our own way;

and the LORD has punished Him
for the iniquity of us all.

⁷ He was oppressed and afflicted,
yet He did not open His mouth.
Like a lamb led to the slaughter
and like a sheep silent before her shearers,
He did not open His mouth.
⁸ He was taken away because of oppression and judgment;
and who considered His fate?
For He was cut off from the land of the living;
He was struck because of My people's rebellion.
⁹ They made His grave with the wicked,
and with a rich man at His death,
although He had done no violence
and had not spoken deceitfully.

¹⁰ Yet the LORD was pleased to crush Him,
and He made Him sick.
When You make Him a restitution offering,
He will see [His] seed, He will prolong His days,
and the will of the LORD will succeed by His hand.
¹¹ He will see [it] out of His anguish,
and He will be satisfied with His knowledge.
My righteous servant will justify many,
and He will carry their iniquities.
¹² Therefore I will give Him the many as a portion,
and He will receive the mighty as spoil,
because He submitted Himself to death,
and was counted among the rebels;
yet He bore the sin of many
and interceded for the rebels.

THOUGHT: How privileged we are to look back to the cross and see the suffering servant, the one whom Old Testament saints saw as just a vague figure in the future. Now we know this suffering servant is none other than the second Person of the Trinity - our Lord Jesus Christ Himself;

With what rapture, with what rapture
Gaze we on those glorious scars!

DAY
170

**ISAIAH 35;
65:17-19; 66:1**

FROM THE COVENANT with Noah, God has made clear His intention to reclaim His once-good creation.

Isaiah picks up this divine ambition and sees further into its future than any prophet before him. He sees that the triumphant outcome of all the servant's labours will be not only the restoration of God's people to include the Gentiles, but the eventual renewal of all God's works - the re-creation of new heavens and a new earth (65:17; 66:22)!

Isaiah's visions of hope had, from the beginning, been cast in extravagant creational language.

'The wilderness and the dry land will be glad; the desert will rejoice and blossom like a rose. It will blossom abundantly' (35:1). God will provide water in the wilderness, streams in the desert (35:6); 'the mountains and the hills will break into singing ... and all the trees of the field will clap their hands' (55:12). In contrast to the fallen, sin-cursed old world, the new world will be a thornless world.

Isaiah consistently links creation and redemption. Just as God pledges to redeem what He has created, so the power by which He creates guarantees His ability to redeem. Isaiah, for one, is convinced that the God who created is the same God who redeems. 'No half God could redeem a world it took a whole God to create' (P.T. Forsyth).

Final salvation will be a new act of creation, as the

apostles Paul and John will one day celebrate even more confidently in the light of Christ.

Isaiah 35

THE RANSOMED RETURN TO ZION

35 The wilderness and the dry land will be glad;
the desert will rejoice and blossom like a rose.
² It will blossom abundantly
and will also rejoice with joy and singing.
The glory of Lebanon will be given to it,
the splendor of Carmel and Sharon.
They will see the glory of the LORD,
the splendor of our God.
³ Strengthen the weak hands,
steady the shaking knees!
⁴ Say to the faint-hearted:
"Be strong; do not fear!
Here is your God; vengeance is coming.
God's retribution is coming; He will save you."
⁵ Then the eyes of the blind will be opened,
and the ears of the deaf unstopped.
⁶ Then the lame will leap like a deer,
and the tongue of the mute will sing for joy,
for water will gush in the wilderness,
and streams in the desert;
⁷ the parched ground will become a pool of water,
and the thirsty land springs of water.
In the haunt of jackals, in their lairs,
there will be grass, reeds, and papyrus.
⁸ A road will be there and a way;
it will be called the Holy Way.
The unclean will not travel on it,
but it will be for him who walks the path.
Even the fool will not go astray.
⁹ There will be no lion there,
and no vicious beast will go up on it;
they will not be found there.
But the redeemed will walk [on it],

¹⁰ and the ransomed of the LORD will return
and come to Zion with singing,
crowned with unending joy.

**BIBLE
READING**

Isaiah 65:17-19

A NEW CREATION

¹⁷ "For I will create a new heaven and a new earth;
the past events will not be remembered or come
to mind.
¹⁸ Then be glad and rejoice forever
in what I am creating;
for I will create Jerusalem to be a joy,
and its people to be a delight.
¹⁹ I will rejoice in Jerusalem
and be glad in My people.
The sound of weeping and crying
will no longer be heard in her.

**BIBLE
READING**

Isaiah 66:1

FINAL JUDGMENT AND JOYOUS RESTORATION

66 This is what the LORD says:

Heaven is My throne,
and earth is My footstool.
What house could you possibly build for Me?
And what place could be My home?

FOR PRAISE: Such a revelation of creative power deserves to be responded to by an abundant outpouring of praise. Praise God in your own way and in your own words as you consider once more the fact that the same God who created the world is the One who redeemed it. Let the thought from P.T. Forsyth, 'No half God could redeem a world it took a whole God to create', stir you to express your deepest gratitude to God for dying for you on Calvary.

EXILE AS A physical separation from the land lasted barely seventy years as Jeremiah had promised. But 'Exile' as a state or condition of being under judgment and awaiting the fulfilment of promises of restoration and new covenant - that was an entirely different matter.

Both Daniel and Ezra in words written after the physical return to the land, pray as if Israel were still slaves in Exile (Dan. 9:3-19; Ezra 9:8-9; Neh. 9:36).

For the next four centuries, while Israel - except for a brief period with the Maccabees - remained under foreign domination, there were perceptive Jewish writers who considered Israel to be still under God's judgment 'in Exile'.

Right up to the time of Jesus, no Jew that we know of seriously imagined that the new covenant promises had been fulfilled - except, that is, for the small Qumran monastic sect, emerging a century and a half before Jesus, who called themselves the 'Covenanters' and who, later, after the fall of Jerusalem in AD 70, when threatened by the Roman armies, buried their precious scrolls in the caves beside the Dead Sea!

The prophetic vision awaited the arrival of God's servant who in Isaiah's words was Himself to be 'a covenant for the people' (Isa. 42:6; 49:8) as if embodying all God's covenantal investment.

DAY 171

DANIEL 9:1-19
NEHEMIAH
9:1-15,26-37

Daniel 9:1-19

BIBLE
READING

DANIEL'S PRAYER

9 In the first year of Darius, who was the son of Ahasuerus, was a Mede by birth, and was ruler over the kingdom of the Chaldeans— ²in the first year of his reign, I, Daniel, understood from the books according to the word of the LORD to Jeremiah the prophet that the number of years for the desolation of Jerusalem would be 70. ³So I turned my attention to the Lord God to seek Him by prayer and petitions, with fasting, sackcloth, and ashes.

⁴I prayed to the Lord my God and confessed:

Ah, Lord—the great and awe-inspiring God who keeps His gracious covenant with those who love Him and keep His commandments— ⁵we have sinned, done wrong, acted wickedly, rebelled, and turned away from Your commandments and ordinances. ⁶We have not listened to Your servants the prophets, who spoke in Your name to our kings, leaders, fathers, and all the people of the land.

⁷Lord, righteousness belongs to You, but this day public shame belongs to us: the men of Judah, the residents of Jerusalem, and all Israel—those who are near and those who are far, in all the countries where You have dispersed them because of the disloyalty they have shown toward You. ⁸Lord, public shame belongs to us, our kings, our leaders, and our fathers, because we have sinned against You. ⁹Compassion and forgiveness belong to the Lord our God, though we have rebelled against Him ¹⁰and have not obeyed the voice of the Lord our God by following His instructions that He set before us through His servants the prophets.

¹¹All Israel has broken Your law and turned away, refusing to obey You. The promised curse written in the law of Moses, the servant of God, has been poured out on us because we have sinned against Him. ¹²He has carried out His words that He spoke against us and against our rulers by bringing on us so great a disaster that nothing like what has been done to Jerusalem has ever been done under all of heaven. ¹³Just as it is written in the law of Moses, all this disaster has come on us, yet we have not appeased the Lord our God by turning from our injustice and paying attention to Your truth. ¹⁴So the Lord kept the disaster in mind and brought it on us, for the Lord our God is righteous in all He has done. But we have not obeyed Him.

¹⁵Now, Lord our God, who brought Your people out of the land of Egypt with a mighty hand and made Your

name [renowned] as it is this day, we have sinned, we have acted wickedly. [16]Lord, in keeping with all Your righteous acts, may Your anger and wrath turn away from Your city Jerusalem, Your holy mountain; for because of our sins and the injustices of our fathers, Jerusalem and Your people have become an object of ridicule to all those around us.

[17]Therefore, our God, hear the prayer and the petitions of Your servant. Show Your favor to Your desolate sanctuary for the Lord's sake. [18]Listen, my God, and hear. Open Your eyes and see our desolations and the city called by Your name. For we are not presenting our petitions before You based on our righteous acts, but based on Your abundant compassion. [19]Lord, hear! Lord, forgive! Lord, listen and act! My God, for Your own sake, do not delay, because Your city and Your people are called by Your name.

Nehemiah 9:1-15,26-37

BIBLE READING

NATIONAL CONFESSION OF SIN

9 On the twenty-fourth day of this month the Israelites assembled; they were fasting, [wearing] sackcloth, [and had put] dust on their heads. [2]Those of Israelite descent separated themselves from all foreigners, and they stood and confessed their sins and the guilt of their fathers. [3]While they stood in their places, they read from the book of the law of the LORD their God for a fourth of the day and [spent] another fourth of the day in confession and worship of the LORD their God. [4]Jeshua, Bani, Kadmiel, Shebaniah, Bunni, Sherebiah, Bani, and Chenani stood on the raised platform [built] for the Levites and cried out loudly to the LORD their God. [5]Then the Levites—Jeshua, Kadmiel, Bani, Hashabneiah, Sherebiah, Hodiah, Shebaniah, and Pethahiah—said:

Stand up. Bless the LORD your God
from everlasting to everlasting.
Praise Your glorious name,
and may it be exalted above all blessing and praise.

⁶ You alone are the Lord.
  You created the heavens,
   the highest heavens with all their host,
   the earth and all that is on it,
   the seas and all that is in them.
  You give life to all of them,
  and the heavenly host worships You.
⁷ You are the Lord God
  who chose Abram
  and brought him out of Ur of the Chaldeans,
  and changed his name to Abraham.
⁸ You found his heart faithful in Your sight,
  and made a covenant with him
  to give the land of the Canaanites,
  Hittites, Amorites, Perizzites,
  Jebusites, and Girgashites—
  to give it to his descendants.
  You have kept Your promise,
  for You are righteous.

⁹ You saw the oppression of our ancestors in Egypt
  and heard their cry at the Red Sea.
¹⁰ You performed signs and wonders against Pharaoh,
   all his officials, and all the people of his land,
   for You knew how arrogantly they treated our ancestors.
   You made a name for Yourself
   that endures to this day.
¹¹ You divided the sea before them,
   and they crossed through it on dry ground.
   You hurled their pursuers into the depths
   like a stone into churning waters.
¹² You led them with a pillar of cloud by day,
   and with a pillar of fire by night,
   to illuminate the way they should go.
¹³ You came down on Mount Sinai,
   and spoke to them from heaven.
   You gave them impartial ordinances,
     reliable instructions,
   and good decrees and commandments.
¹⁴ You revealed Your holy Sabbath to them,

and gave them commandments, statutes, and a law
through Your servant Moses.

¹⁵ You provided bread from heaven for their hunger;
You brought them water from the rock for their thirst.
You told them to go in and possess the land
You had sworn to give them.

＊ ＊ ＊ ＊ ＊ ＊ ＊ ＊ ＊

²⁶ But they were disobedient and rebelled against You.
They flung Your law behind their backs
and killed Your prophets
who warned them to turn them back to You.
They committed terrible blasphemies.

²⁷ So You handed them over to their enemies,
who oppressed them.
In their time of distress, they cried out to You,
and You heard from heaven.
In Your abundant compassion
You gave them deliverers, who rescued them
from the power of their enemies.

²⁸ But as soon as they had relief,
they again did what was evil in Your sight.
So You abandoned them to the power of their enemies,
who dominated them.
When they cried out to You again,
You heard from heaven and rescued them
many times in Your compassion.

²⁹ You warned them to turn back to Your law,
but they acted arrogantly
and would not obey Your commandments.
They sinned against Your ordinances,
by which a person will live if he does them.
They stubbornly resisted,
stiffened their necks, and would not obey.

³⁰ You were patient with them for many years,
and Your Spirit warned them through Your prophets,
but they would not listen.
Therefore, You handed them over to the surrounding
peoples.

³¹ However, in Your abundant compassion,

You did not destroy them or abandon them,
for You are a gracious and compassionate God.

32 So now, our God—the great, mighty,
and awe-inspiring God who keeps
    His gracious covenant—
do not view lightly all the hardships
    that have afflicted us,
our kings and leaders,
our priests and prophets,
our ancestors and all Your people,
from the days of the Assyrian kings until today.
33 You are righteous concerning all that has come on us,
because You have acted faithfully,
while we have acted wickedly.
34 Our kings, leaders, priests, and ancestors
did not obey Your law
or listen to Your commandments
and warnings You gave them.
35 When they were in their kingdom,
with Your abundant goodness You gave them,
and in the spacious and fertile land You set before them,
they would not serve You or turn
    from their wicked ways.

36 Here we are today,
slaves in the land You gave our ancestors
so that they could enjoy its fruit and its goodness.
Here we are—slaves in it!
37 Its abundant harvest goes to the kings
You have set over us,
because of our sins.
They rule over our bodies
and our livestock as they please.
We are in great distress.

TO PONDER: 'Exile' we have learned is something more than a physical separation - it is also spiritual. Even after the Israelites were back in the land given to them by God, their hearts, with few exceptions, were far from God. It is possible to draw near to God in worship (such as in church on Sundays, singing the songs or hymns, for example) while our hearts are far from Him. It's our hearts God is after!

DAY
172
MARK 1:1-15

IT IS FASCINATING to see where each Evangelist starts his story of Jesus. Matthew begins with Abraham, Luke even further back with Adam, while John links Jesus directly to the eternal God Himself. Mark starts with the Exile - with Isaiah 40 - by identifying John the Baptist as the voice in the wilderness preparing the way of the Lord. This bizarre prophetic figure lures the people to a barren landscape and urges Israel to start afresh with God. To that end, John preaches national repentance and national forgiveness, inviting Israel, through baptism, to repeat, as it were, the original Jordan crossing and so to enter the new promised land of God's long-awaited Messianic kingdom!

John prepares 'the way of the Lord' also by consistently pointing beyond himself to the One whose arrival will inaugurate the Messianic era of salvation characterised by the outpouring of the Holy Spirit of God. Himself prepared by the Spirit's anointing and the Father's approval, and His way prepared by John, Jesus finally enters Galilee, with God's good news. At last, God's time has come! God's age-old plans have come of age! The day Isaiah saw is here!

God's kingly rule is no longer a wistful dream but a close-up reality to be encountered head-on by repentance, and embraced whole-heartedly by faith.

Mark 1:1-15

THE MESSIAH'S HERALD

1 The beginning of the gospel of Jesus Christ, the Son of God. ²As it is written in Isaiah the prophet:

> "Look, I am sending My messenger ahead of You,
> who will prepare Your way.
> ³ A voice of one crying out in the wilderness:
> 'Prepare the way for the Lord;
> make His paths straight!'"

⁴John came baptizing in the wilderness and preaching a baptism of repentance for the forgiveness of sins. ⁵The whole Judean countryside and all the people of Jerusalem were flocking to him, and they were baptized by him in the Jordan River as they confessed their sins. ⁶John wore a camel-hair garment with a leather belt around his waist and ate locusts and wild honey. ⁷He was preaching: "Someone more powerful than I will come after me. I am not worthy to stoop down and untie the strap of His sandals. ⁸I have baptized you with water, but He will baptize you with the Holy Spirit."

THE BAPTISM OF JESUS

⁹In those days Jesus came from Nazareth in Galilee and was baptized in the Jordan by John. ¹⁰As soon as He came up out of the water, He saw the heavens being torn open and the Spirit descending to Him like a dove. ¹¹And a voice came from heaven:

> You are My beloved Son;
> I take delight in You!

THE TEMPTATION OF JESUS

¹²Immediately the Spirit drove Him into the wilderness. ¹³He was in the wilderness 40 days, being tempted by Satan. He was with the wild animals, and the angels began to serve Him.

MINISTRY IN GALILEE

[14]After John was arrested, Jesus went to Galilee, preaching the good news of God: [15]"The time is fulfilled, and the kingdom of God has come near. Repent and believe in the good news!"

THOUGHT: Did you realise as you read today's reading that John the Baptist through his words effectively announces the end of the Exile? What a moment this was! The dreams of the past - forgiveness and freedom from sin and the empowering of the Spirit - were about to become reality in the appearance and ministry of the soon-coming One. The Old Testament prophets said He is coming. John announces the good news: He is here!

DAY 173

LUKE 22:1-46

IN JESUS' WORDS and actions, many threads are now being drawn together.

Held at Passover time, the Last Supper points back to the foundational event of the Exodus and God's covenant with Israel. This in turn evokes hopes of a new and greater Exodus. But, since God's redemptive promise-plan always had in view the establishing of His kingdom, so, Jesus says, the Passover will find its fulfilment through a new Exodus in the kingdom of God (vv.16-18). His cross and resurrection establish the new covenant, just as sacrifice had attended the old covenant (Exod. 24:8).

Underlying everything is a deeper divine plan to establish His kingly rule in which the disciples of Jesus will share (vv.21,37).

As we have learned from Isaiah, new Exodus and new covenant occur under the rule of a new kind of servant-kingship (v.27) which is willing to suffer for sinners (v.37, quoting Isa. 53:12).

Marvellously and mysteriously, God's strategic plan is now coming to fruition in His Servant-King who, by His blood poured out as a sacrificial offering, inaugurates the new covenant agreement, initiates a new Exodus from sin and death, and guarantees the coming of God's kingdom!

And because our King rose from the dead, the Last Supper was turned into the Lord's Supper, not a funeral wake but a feast of good things still to come!

Luke 22:1-46

THE PLOT TO KILL JESUS

22 The Festival of Unleavened Bread, which is called Passover, was drawing near. [2]The chief priests and the scribes were looking for a way to put Him to death, because they were afraid of the people.

[3]Then Satan entered Judas, called Iscariot, who was numbered among the Twelve. [4]He went away and discussed with the chief priests and temple police how he could hand Him over to them. [5]They were glad and agreed to give him silver. [6]So he accepted [the offer] and started looking for a good opportunity to betray Him to them when the crowd was not present.

PREPARATION FOR PASSOVER

[7]Then the Day of Unleavened Bread came when the Passover lamb had to be sacrificed. [8]Jesus sent Peter and John, saying, "Go and prepare the Passover meal for us, so we can eat it."

[9]"Where do You want us to prepare it?" they asked Him.

[10]"Listen," He said to them, "when you've entered the city, a man carrying a water jug will meet you. Follow him into the house he enters. [11]Tell the owner of the house, 'The Teacher asks you, "Where is the guest room where I can eat the Passover with My disciples?"' [12]Then he will show you a large, furnished room upstairs. Make the preparations there."

[13]So they went and found it just as He had told them, and they prepared the Passover.

THE FIRST LORD'S SUPPER

[14]When the hour came, He reclined at the table, and the apostles with Him. [15]Then He said to them, "I have fervently desired to eat this Passover with you before I suffer. [16]For I tell you, I will not eat it again until it is fulfilled in the kingdom

of God." [17]Then He took a cup, and after giving thanks, He said, "Take this and share it among yourselves. [18]For I tell you, from now on I will not drink of the fruit of the vine until the kingdom of God comes."

[19]And He took bread, gave thanks, broke it, gave it to them, and said, "This is My body, which is given for you. Do this in remembrance of Me."

[20]In the same way He also took the cup after supper and said, "This cup is the new covenant [established by] My blood; it is shed for you. [21]But look, the hand of the one betraying Me is at the table with Me! [22]For the Son of Man will go away as it has been determined, but woe to that man by whom He is betrayed!"

[23]So they began to argue among themselves which of them it could be who was going to do this thing.

THE DISPUTE OVER GREATNESS

[24]Then a dispute also arose among them about who should be considered the greatest. [25]But He said to them, "The kings of the Gentiles dominate them, and those who have authority over them are called 'Benefactors.' [26]But it must not be like that among you. On the contrary, whoever is greatest among you must become like the youngest, and whoever leads, like the one serving. [27]For who is greater, the one at the table or the one serving? Isn't it the one at the table? But I am among you as the One who serves. [28]You are the ones who stood by Me in My trials. [29]I bestow on you a kingdom, just as My Father bestowed one on Me, [30]so that you may eat and drink at My table in My kingdom. And you will sit on thrones judging the 12 tribes of Israel.

PETER'S DENIAL PREDICTED

[31]"Simon, Simon, look out! Satan has asked to sift you like wheat. [32]But I have prayed for you that your faith may not fail. And you, when you have turned back, strengthen your brothers."

[33]"Lord," he told Him, "I'm ready to go with You both to prison and to death!"

[34]"I tell you, Peter," He said, "the rooster will not crow today until you deny three times that you know Me!"

MONEY-BAG, BACKPACK, AND SWORD

³⁵He also said to them, "When I sent you out without money-bag, traveling bag, or sandals, did you lack anything?"

"Not a thing," they said.

³⁶Then He said to them, "But now, whoever has a money-bag should take it, and also a traveling bag. And whoever doesn't have a sword should sell his robe and buy one. ³⁷For I tell you, what is written must be fulfilled in Me: And He was counted among the outlaws. Yes, what is written about Me is coming to its fulfillment."

³⁸"Lord," they said, "look, here are two swords."

"Enough of that!" He told them.

THE PRAYER IN THE GARDEN

³⁹He went out and made His way as usual to the Mount of Olives, and the disciples followed Him. ⁴⁰When He reached the place, He told them, "Pray that you may not enter into temptation." ⁴¹Then He withdrew from them about a stone's throw, knelt down, and began to pray, ⁴²"Father, if You are willing, take this cup away from Me—nevertheless, not My will, but Yours, be done."

[⁴³Then an angel from heaven appeared to Him, strengthening Him. ⁴⁴Being in anguish, He prayed more fervently, and His sweat became like drops of blood falling to the ground.] ⁴⁵When He got up from prayer and came to the disciples, He found them sleeping, exhausted from their grief. ⁴⁶"Why are you sleeping?" He asked them. "Get up and pray, so that you won't enter into temptation."

FOR FUTURE ACTION: Next time you take Communion think about this - every time you take the bread and the wine you are reiterating the start of the new covenant so long foretold and hoped for by the saints of the Old Testament. The 'Passover' you participate in eclipsed the original one by the nature of the Person whose body was broken and whose blood was shed. May your next Communion service be more wonderful than ever.

DAY 174

ACTS 2:1-21,36-47

TO THE SOUND of a windstorm, with flames flickering over every head, many voices erupt in a torrent of praise to God in languages they had never learned. At a stroke, the time-honoured rituals of the Feast of Pentecost are shattered!.

First question: what does this mean (v.12)?

Startling as the phenomena are, Peter links them to Joel's prophecy of the 'last days': 'this is what was spoken'. God's story has reached a climactic stage when God exalts His Son as King, pours out His Spirit on all flesh and saves all who call upon Him!

So, it is misleading to see Acts 2 as the 'birthday of the Church', as if the Church were an innovation. We do better to see here the emergence of that new covenant community of which the prophets spoke.

The tell-tale marks are evident: immediate access to God, forgiveness of sins, the gift of God's Spirit, an awesome, first-hand knowledge of God which results in sharing goods within a just society.

What this means is that Jesus is Israel's King and the world's Lord and now the way is open - as Joel had prophesied - for all to call on His name for salvation! Only one question remains outstanding: what shall we do (v.37)? What else can anyone do but repent, believe, be filled with God's Spirit and be baptised into this God-experiencing, love-saturated, company of God's people!

BIBLE READING

Acts 2:1-21,36-47

PENTECOST

2 When the day of Pentecost had arrived, they were all together in one place. ²Suddenly a sound like that of a violent rushing wind came from heaven, and it filled the whole house where they were staying. ³And tongues, like flames of fire that were divided, appeared to them and rested on each one of them. ⁴Then they were all filled with the Holy Spirit and began to speak in different languages, as the Spirit gave them ability for speech.

⁵There were Jews living in Jerusalem, devout men from every nation under heaven. ⁶When this sound occurred, the multitude came together and was confused because each one heard them speaking in his own language. ⁷And they were astounded and amazed, saying, "Look, aren't all these who are speaking Galileans? ⁸How is it that we hear, each of us, in our own native language? ⁹Parthians, Medes, Elamites; those who live in Mesopotamia, in Judea and Cappadocia, Pontus and Asia, ¹⁰Phrygia and Pamphylia, Egypt and the parts of Libya near Cyrene; visitors from Rome, both Jews and proselytes, ¹¹Cretans and Arabs—we hear them speaking in our own languages the magnificent acts of God." ¹²And they were all astounded and perplexed, saying to one another, "What could this be?" ¹³But some sneered and said, "They're full of new wine!"

PETER'S SERMON

¹⁴But Peter stood up with the Eleven, raised his voice, and proclaimed to them: "Jewish men and all you residents of Jerusalem, let this be known to you and pay attention to my words. ¹⁵For these people are not drunk, as you suppose, since it's only nine in the morning. ¹⁶On the contrary, this is what was spoken through the prophet Joel:

> ¹⁷ "And it will be" in the last days, says God,
>   that "I will pour out My Spirit on all humanity;
>   then your sons and your daughters will prophesy,
>   your young men will see visions,
>   and your old men will dream dreams.
> ¹⁸ I will even pour out My Spirit
>   on My male and female slaves in those days,"
>   and they will prophesy.
> ¹⁹ "I will display wonders in the heaven" above
>   "and signs on the earth" below:
>   "blood and fire and a cloud of smoke.
> ²⁰ The sun will be turned to darkness,
>   and the moon to blood,
>   before the great and remarkable day of the Lord comes;
> ²¹ then whoever calls on the name of the Lord will be saved."

• • • • • • • • •

[36]"Therefore let all the house of Israel know with certainty that God has made this Jesus, whom you crucified, both Lord and Messiah!"

FORGIVENESS THROUGH THE MESSIAH

[37]When they heard this, they were pierced to the heart and said to Peter and the rest of the apostles: "Brothers, what must we do?"

[38]"Repent," Peter said to them, "and be baptized, each of you, in the name of Jesus the Messiah for the forgiveness of your sins, and you will receive the gift of the Holy Spirit. [39]For the promise is for you and for your children, and for all who are far off, as many as the Lord our God will call." [40]And with many other words he testified and strongly urged them, saying, "Be saved from this corrupt generation!"

A GENEROUS AND GROWING CHURCH

[41]So those who accepted his message were baptized, and that day about 3,000 people were added to them. [42]And they devoted themselves to the apostles' teaching, to fellowship, to the breaking of bread, and to prayers.

[43]Then fear came over everyone, and many wonders and signs were being performed through the apostles. [44]Now all the believers were together and had everything in common. [45]So they sold their possessions and property and distributed the proceeds to all, as anyone had a need. [46]And every day they devoted themselves [to meeting] together in the temple complex, and broke bread from house to house. They ate their food with gladness and simplicity of heart, [47]praising God and having favor with all the people. And every day the Lord added to them those who were being saved.

FOR PRAISE: Lift up your heart in praise right now for the fact that Jesus is the 'true' (that is, final) Son of David who has ascended to David's throne by virtue of His resurrection from the dead. Praise Him also for pouring out the Spirit on all flesh - as He promised, for securing forgiveness of sins and giving us access to God, for establishing a new covenant community of which you are a part.

UNDER PRESSURE TO produce 'letters of recommendation' endorsing his ministry, Paul points to the Corinthians themselves as evidence for the work God has done in their lives through his ministry. In words which have significant Old Testament echoes, Paul says that the letters Christ has written through his ministry, are inscribed not on tablets of stone (like the law, Exod. 31:18) but on the heart of the Corinthian believers (combining new covenant terms from Ezek. 11:19-20; 36:26; Jer. 31:31).

The difference between old and new covenants could not be greater; it is the difference between life and death: 'the letter kills, but the Spirit produces life' (v.6). The distinction made here is not between a literal and a spiritual reading of the text, but between the fact that the law sentences sinners to death but is powerless to do anything about it, while the gospel of the new covenant brings atonement, forgiveness of sins and actually produces real covenantal life. The ministry of the Holy Spirit is indispensable in bringing this about. Joel, Ezekiel, Isaiah, each presumed this would be the case and New Testament gospel experience bears it out. We are called to enact and commend God's saving story: only the Holy Spirit can make us 'equal to such a task'.

2 Corinthians 3:1-6

BIBLE READING

3 Are we beginning to commend ourselves again? Or like some, do we need letters of recommendation to you or from you? ²You yourselves are our letter, written on our hearts, recognized and read by everyone, ³since it is plain that you are Christ's letter, produced by us, not written with ink but with the Spirit of the living God; not on stone tablets but on tablets that are hearts of flesh.

PAUL'S COMPETENCE

⁴We have this kind of confidence toward God through Christ: ⁵not that we are competent in ourselves to consider anything as coming from ourselves, but our competence is from God. ⁶He has made us competent to be ministers of a new covenant, not of the letter, but of the Spirit; for the letter kills, but the Spirit produces life.

> PRAYER: Gracious and loving heavenly Father, I am so thankful for the salvation You have brought to me through Your Son. I never tire of saying thank You, for the wonder of it grows and grows upon me day by day. May my life be a 'living letter' that will tell the story of a covenant-keeping God who alone has atoned for sin and opened up for all who will receive it lasting forgiveness and everlasting life. Amen.

DAY 176

2 CORINTHIANS 3:7-18

ALTHOUGH THAT OLD covenant associated with Sinai was glorious, it has been eclipsed by the splendour of what the Holy Spirit achieves. Paul – and all who proclaim the same gospel – are ministers of the new covenant. Where the old covenant condemned, the new covenant brings righteousness, vindicating and securing covenant membership for repentant sinners. Where the old covenant had glory, fading though it was, how much more glorious is the new covenant which is permanent!

This is one of the densest and richest passages in Paul's writings. He is clearly utilising Exodus 34:29-35 and Ezekiel 36 in order to contrast Israelites then and now with Christian believers. Then Moses had to veil his face before the glory, fading though it was. Even today when Moses is read a veil remains, except that now the veil is not over Moses' face but over the hearts of those who hear the Torah. But, as when Moses turned to the Lord in face-to-face encounter and removed his veil, so now everyone who turns to the Lord by opening up to the Lordship of the Holy

Spirit, has the veil removed and perceives God's glory in the face of Jesus Christ.

With unhardened hearts and unveiled faces, we enjoy and reflect His glory in our lives together as God's new covenant people!

2 Corinthians 3:7-18

BIBLE READING

3 Are we beginning to commend ourselves again? Or like some, do we need letters of recommendation to you or from you? ²You yourselves are our letter, written on our hearts, recognized and read by everyone, ³since it is plain that you are Christ's letter, produced by us, not written with ink but with the Spirit of the living God; not on stone tablets but on tablets that are hearts of flesh.

PAUL'S COMPETENCE

⁴We have this kind of confidence toward God through Christ: ⁵not that we are competent in ourselves to consider anything as coming from ourselves, but our competence is from God. ⁶He has made us competent to be ministers of a new covenant, not of the letter, but of the Spirit; for the letter kills, but the Spirit produces life.

NEW COVENANT MINISTRY

⁷Now if the ministry of death, chiseled in letters on stones, came with glory, so that the sons of Israel were not able to look directly at Moses' face because of the glory from his face—a fading [glory]— ⁸how will the ministry of the Spirit not be more glorious? ⁹For if the ministry of condemnation had glory, the ministry of righteousness overflows with even more glory. ¹⁰In fact, what had been glorious is not glorious in this case because of the glory that surpasses it. ¹¹For if what was fading away was glorious, what endures will be even more glorious.

¹²Therefore having such a hope, we use great boldness— ¹³not like Moses, who used to put a veil over his face so that the sons of Israel could not look at the end of what was fading away. ¹⁴But their minds were closed. For to this day, at the reading of

the old covenant, the same veil remains; it is not lifted, because it is set aside [only] in Christ. ¹⁵However, to this day, whenever Moses is read, a veil lies over their hearts, ¹⁶but whenever a person turns to the Lord, the veil is removed. ¹⁷Now the Lord is the Spirit; and where the Spirit of the Lord is, there is freedom. ¹⁸We all, with unveiled faces, are reflecting the glory of the Lord and are being transformed into the same image from glory to glory; this is from the Lord who is the Spirit.

THOUGHT: Before you slip away and attend to the duties of the day think for a few moments of how fortunate we are to live in this day and age when access to God through Jesus His Son is open to us whoever and wherever we are. No need of sacrifices, ceremonies, tabernacles, temples, etc. The veil has been removed and we have seen God's glory in the face of Jesus Christ. Think – and give thanks!

DAY 177

2 CORINTHIANS 5:1-19

IN THIS SECTION of 2 Corinthians, chapters 1-5, Paul is clearly shadowing the prophetic sequence of new covenant – new kingship – leading to new creation.

'Anointed' or 'Christed' by the Spirit, and sealed as belonging to the Messiah's people (1:21-22), we are ministers of the new covenant (3:6). As servants of our King, Jesus Christ the Lord (4:6), we already share in the 'new realm of reality' inaugurated 'in Christ' – for 'if any one is in Christ – new creation' (5:17 literal translation).

Paul's vision of 'new creation' must not be limited to mean 'born again' or 'a Christian is a new person', true though this is. Much more than this is being said! 'If any one is in Christ – new creation' means that when we come to faith in Christ we enter the realm of God's new creation. Anyone 'in Christ' becomes a sample of the world's future, a prototype of what all God's created works are set to become!

To be reconciled to God – which is our deepest need – is to have the barrier caused by sin broken down and fellowship with God restored. But this means being reconciled not to things as they are, but to things as they may become in God's new order.

Peace with God does not make us passive but exposes us to the glory that transforms. New covenant Christians do not simply keep up with the times but live 'ahead of the times'.

2 Corinthians 5:1-19

BIBLE READING

OUR FUTURE AFTER DEATH

5 For we know that if our earthly house, a tent, is destroyed, we have a building from God, a house not made with hands, eternal in the heavens. ²And, in fact, we groan in this one, longing to put on our house from heaven, ³since, when we are clothed, we will not be found naked. ⁴Indeed, we who are in this tent groan, burdened as we are, because we do not want to be unclothed but clothed, so that mortality may be swallowed up by life. ⁵And the One who prepared us for this very thing is God, who gave us the Spirit as a down payment.

⁶Therefore, though we are always confident and know that while we are at home in the body we are away from the Lord— ⁷for we walk by faith, not by sight— ⁸yet we are confident and satisfied to be out of the body and at home with the Lord. ⁹Therefore, whether we are at home or away, we make it our aim to be pleasing to Him. ¹⁰For we must all appear before the judgment seat of Christ, so that each may be repaid for what he has done in the body, whether good or bad.

¹¹Knowing, then, the fear of the Lord, we persuade people. We are completely open before God, and I hope we are completely open to your consciences as well. ¹²We are not commending ourselves to you again, but giving you an opportunity to be proud of us, so that you may have a reply for those who take pride in the outward appearance rather than in the heart. ¹³For if we are out of our mind, it is for God; if we have a sound mind, it is for you. ¹⁴For Christ's love compels us, since we have reached this conclusion: if One died for all, then all died. ¹⁵And He died for all so that those who live should no longer live for themselves, but for the One who died for them and was raised.

THE MINISTRY OF RECONCILIATION

[16]From now on, then, we do not know anyone in a purely human way. Even if we have known Christ in a purely human way, yet now we no longer know Him like that. [17]Therefore if anyone is in Christ, there is a new creation; old things have passed away, and look, new things have come. [18]Now everything is from God, who reconciled us to Himself through Christ and gave us the ministry of reconciliation: [19]that is, in Christ, God was reconciling the world to Himself, not counting their trespasses against them, and He has committed the message of reconciliation to us.

QUESTION: Are you trying to keep up with the times or living ahead of them? Do you understand that you are at this moment being exposed to 'the glory that transforms'? You are a sample of the future. Think about these questions as you go through the day and consider whether you are living in the world or above it. Let the power of the world to come, which now you have in part, influence everything you say and everything you do.

DAY
178

**2 CORINTHIANS
5:20–6:2,17-18**

GOD'S AIM IN reconciling us to Himself through Christ's cross is that we might become the righteousness of God.

In our 'great exchange' with Christ, we are saved to embody God's own world-reconciling, covenant-faithfulness and to manifest the new creation.

Paul pleads with the Corinthians to live up to this calling, 'Be reconciled to God', and so to live that the 'church is a sneak preview of the ultimate redemption of the world' (Richard Hays).

Isaiah's longed-for day of favour and salvation has dawned in Christ (6:2; Isa. 49:8). So, as the prophet did, Paul urges his hearers to break with 'Babylonian' values by coming out of cultural compromise and coming home to true covenant living (6:17; cf.Isa. 49:9; 52:11). We are not meant to hear this call as an invitation to join an exclusive, self-righteous ghetto. We hear it as a call not to be unthinkingly conformed to the culture of violence and consumerism all around us. We hear it as the call to freedom and glory.

Those who have the courage to be a counter-cultural community, God will gladly affirm as His people, wonderfully expanding the original promise in God's covenant with David to include sons and daughters (6:18; 2 Sam. 7:14). Christians are God's royal family, dared to live differently for the sake of the new world coming!

2 Corinthians 5:20-6:2,17-18

²⁰Therefore, we are ambassadors for Christ; certain that God is appealing through us, we plead on Christ's behalf, "Be reconciled to God." ²¹He made the One who did not know sin to be sin for us, so that we might become the righteousness of God in Him.

6 Working together with Him, we also appeal to you: "Don't receive God's grace in vain." ²For He says:

"In an acceptable time, I heard you,
and in the day of salvation, I helped you."

Look, now is the acceptable time; look, now is the day of salvation.

• • • • • • • • • •

¹⁷ "Therefore, come out from among them
and be separate, says the Lord;
do not touch any unclean thing,
and I will welcome you.
¹⁸ I will be a Father to you,
and you will be sons and daughters to Me,
says the Lord Almighty."

PRAYER: Gracious God and loving Father, help me understand what it means to be part of a counter-cultural community. May the men and women I rub shoulders with day by day and who do not know You see in me the glory of another world. I am in the world, belong to the world, but I serve another King, one Jesus. May that fact show and shine through me. In Christ's name I pray. Amen.

DAY
179

**HEBREWS 8:7-13;
10:11-18**

THE NEW TESTAMENT writer to the Hebrews celebrates the dawn of this new covenant era by citing Jeremiah 31:31-34 in full.

Jesus is God's unique Son, the King sharing God's throne, High Priest of heaven who, by virtue of His death and resurrection and ascension, has become the mediator of a better covenant (7:22). He eclipses Moses and the Levitical priesthood of the old order.

By His effective sacrifice, achieving what the sacrifice of animals and birds could not, Jesus is now the 'mediator of a new covenant', providing for believers an 'inheritance' which the writer has already linked to the promises made to Abraham (9:15; 6:12-13)

So, the writer argues, the old covenant is obsolete. There was nothing intrinsically wrong with it; it's simply past its 'sell-by date'. It remains as a revelation of God's will for His people: but it no longer regulates our lives, it is not the administration we are now serving under.

While the repeated sacrifices under the Old Testament system were effective for temporary forgiveness, they did not take away sins (10:11). Under the terms of the new covenant, however, Christ's one final, complete sacrifice deals finally with sin, writes the law on the heart and brings believers into a permanent state of non-condemnation (10:16-18).

Hebrews 8:7-13

A SUPERIOR COVENANT

7For if that first [covenant] had been faultless, no opportunity would have been sought for a second one. 8But finding fault with His people, He says:

> "'Look, the days are coming," says the Lord,
> "when I will make a new covenant
> with the house of Israel
> and with the house of Judah—
> 9 not like the covenant
> that I made with their fathers
> on the day I took them by their hand
> to lead them out of the land of Egypt.
> Because they did not continue in My covenant,
> I disregarded them," says the Lord.
> 10 "But this is the covenant that I will make with the house
>   of Israel
> after those days," says the Lord:
> "I will put My laws into their minds,
> and I will write them on their hearts,
> and I will be their God,
> and they will be My people.
> 11 And each person will not teach his fellow citizen,
> and each his brother, saying, 'Know the Lord,'
> because they will all know Me,
> from the least to the greatest of them.
> 12 For I will be merciful to their wrongdoing,
> and I will never again remember their sins.'"

13By saying, "a new [covenant]," He has declared that the first is old. And what is old and aging is about to disappear.

BIBLE READING

Hebrews 10:11-18

[11]Now every priest stands day after day ministering and offering time after time the same sacrifices, which can never take away sins. [12]But this man, after offering one sacrifice for sins forever, sat down at the right hand of God. [13]He is now waiting until His enemies are made His footstool. [14]For by one offering He has perfected forever those who are sanctified. [15]The Holy Spirit also testifies to us about this. For after He had said:

[16] "This is the covenant that I will make with them
after those days, says the Lord:
I will put My laws on their hearts,
and I will write them on their minds,"

[17][He adds]:

"I will never again remember
their sins and their lawless acts."

[18]Now where there is forgiveness of these, there is no longer an offering for sin.

TO PONDER: Consider as you go through the day what a joy and delight it is to be part of a new administration and to live in a permanent state of non-condemnation. Charles Wesley wrote: 'No condemnation now I dread, Jesus and all in Him is mine.' It's easy to say, but has the meaning reached deep into your soul? Say it over and over again until its truth is fixed in your soul: In Christ I am in a permanent state of non-condemnation. Hallelujah!

PAUL HERE WAXES lyrical that what the old covenant and its Torah could not do – deal with the deep problem of sin and create genuine covenant living – God has done in the sending and dying of His Son as a sin offering and by the gift of His empowering Spirit.

DAY
180
ROMANS 8

So is born the new covenant community, the company of the forgiven-forgivers, the uncondemned sons of God, who live by the Spirit.

Exodus language abounds here, but in the service of a more far-reaching redemption!

With slavery behind them, marked out as God's covenant family by receiving His Spirit, the true sons of God call on God as 'Abba, Father!'

Led, not by a pillar of fire and cloud, but by the immediate light of God's Spirit, the covenant family marches onwards towards its God-given inheritance.

Only, in this scenario, our promised land is no partial Canaan but nothing less than a redeemed earth. We are destined to occupy a transformed creation, freed from its own bondage to decay and radiant in the glorious freedom characteristic of God's own children. We, in turn, show our true identity by our willingness to suffer for the world and Messiah's sake in fellowship with Him.

Yet, purposefully and with hope, surrounded by frustration, in a world growing old, we offer ourselves as samples of that newness for which all creation longs.

Romans 8

BIBLE
READING

THE LIFE-GIVING SPIRIT

8 Therefore, no condemnation now exists for those in Christ Jesus, ²because the Spirit's law of life in Christ Jesus has set you free from the law of sin and of death. ³What the law could not do since it was limited by the flesh, God did. He condemned sin in the flesh by sending His own Son in flesh like ours under sin's domain, and as a sin offering, ⁴in order that the law's requirement would be accomplished in us who do not walk according to the flesh but according

to the Spirit. [5]For those whose lives are according to the flesh think about the things of the flesh, but those whose lives are according to the Spirit, about the things of the Spirit. [6]For the mind-set of the flesh is death, but the mind-set of the Spirit is life and peace. [7]For the mind-set of the flesh is hostile to God because it does not submit itself to God's law, for it is unable to do so. [8]Those whose lives are in the flesh are unable to please God. [9]You, however, are not in the flesh, but in the Spirit, since the Spirit of God lives in you. But if anyone does not have the Spirit of Christ, he does not belong to Him. [10]Now if Christ is in you, the body is dead because of sin, but the Spirit is life because of righteousness. [11]And if the Spirit of Him who raised Jesus from the dead lives in you, then He who raised Christ from the dead will also bring your mortal bodies to life through His Spirit who lives in you.

THE HOLY SPIRIT'S MINISTRIES

[12]So then, brothers, we are not obligated to the flesh to live according to the flesh, [13]for if you live according to the flesh, you are going to die. But if by the Spirit you put to death the deeds of the body, you will live. [14]All those led by God's Spirit are God's sons. [15]For you did not receive a spirit of slavery to fall back into fear, but you received the Spirit of adoption, by whom we cry out, "*Abba*, Father!" [16]The Spirit Himself testifies together with our spirit that we are God's children, [17]and if children, also heirs—heirs of God and co-heirs with Christ—seeing that we suffer with Him so that we may also be glorified with Him.

FROM GROANS TO GLORY

[18]For I consider that the sufferings of this present time are not worth comparing with the glory that is going to be revealed to us. [19]For the creation eagerly waits with anticipation for God's sons to be revealed. [20]For the creation was subjected to futility—not willingly, but because of Him who subjected it—in the hope [21]that the creation itself will also be set free from the bondage of corruption into the glorious freedom of God's children. [22]For we know that the whole creation has been groaning together with labor pains until now. [23]And not only that, but we ourselves who have the Spirit as the firstfruits—we also groan within ourselves, eagerly waiting for adoption, the

redemption of our bodies. ²⁴Now in this hope we were saved, yet hope that is seen is not hope, because who hopes for what he sees? ²⁵But if we hope for what we do not see, we eagerly wait for it with patience.

²⁶In the same way the Spirit also joins to help in our weakness, because we do not know what to pray for as we should, but the Spirit Himself intercedes for us with unspoken groanings. ²⁷And He who searches the hearts knows the Spirit's mind-set, because He intercedes for the saints according to the will of God.

²⁸We know that all things work together for the good of those who love God: those who are called according to His purpose. ²⁹For those He foreknew He also predestined to be conformed to the image of His Son, so that He would be the firstborn among many brothers. ³⁰And those He predestined, He also called; and those He called, He also justified; and those He justified, He also glorified.

THE BELIEVER'S TRIUMPH

³¹ What then are we to say about these things?
If God is for us, who is against us?

³² He did not even spare His own Son,
but offered Him up for us all;
how will He not also with Him grant us everything?

³³ Who can bring an accusation against God's elect?
God is the One who justifies.

³⁴ Who is the one who condemns?
Christ Jesus is the One who died, but even more,
has been raised;
He also is at the right hand of God and intercedes for us.

³⁵ Who can separate us from the love of Christ?
Can affliction or anguish or persecution
or famine or nakedness or danger or sword?

³⁶ As it is written:
"Because of You we are being put to death all day long;
we are counted as sheep to be slaughtered."

³⁷ No, in all these things we are more than victorious
through Him who loved us.

³⁸ For I am persuaded that neither death nor life,
nor angels nor rulers,

nor things present, nor things to come, nor powers,
³⁹ nor height, nor depth, nor any other created thing
will have the power to separate us
from the love of God that is in Christ Jesus our Lord!

DEDICATION: We suggest making this day a day of renewed dedication in which you offer yourself once again to the Lord for Him to do in you and through you whatever He wills. Ask Him especially to make you a sample of that 'newness for which all creation longs' and reveal through you to your friends and family what Christian living is all about. You supply the willingness; He will supply the power.

SECTION

NOAH
ALL CREATION

ABRAHAM
ALL NATIONS

ISRAEL
ONE NATION

DAVID
REPRESENTATIVE KING

NEW COVENANT
FAITHFUL COVENANT PARTNER

JESUS
FAITHFUL COVENANT PARTNER

JESUS
DAVIDIC KING
MESSIAH

JESUS
THE NEW ISRAEL

JESUS
THE WORLD'S LORD

JESUS
THE TRULY HUMAN ONE
CROWNED WITH GLORY AND HONOUR

JESUS
COSMIC RULER IN GOD'S NEW CREATION
NEW HEAVENS AND NEW EARTH

SECTION 8

THE EVANGELISTS'
REPORT

GOD IS COMMITTED TO FULFILLING ALL HIS PROMISES IN HIS SON JESUS – THE EVANGELISTS' REPORT

The genealogies which three of the Evangelists employ to show who Jesus is, make little impression on modern minds. But in ancient and Eastern cultures, a family tree can reveal much about the person being described. The Evangelists trace Jesus' predecessors for the same reason.

For them, Jesus is the fruit of all that is rooted in the Old Testament phase of God's story. One way to gauge this is to note the starting point for the Evangelists. They each connect Jesus with what God has revealed about Himself in the previous stages of the narrative.

Mark roots his story of Jesus in Isaiah's prophecy to the Babylonian exiles. Isaiah said that God would raise up a voice in the wilderness to prepare God's way back into the centre of His people's life as King. Mark is in no doubt that John the Baptist has filled that role perfectly.

Matthew says, in effect, that to tell the story of Jesus adequately, you must start further back, with Abraham. Jesus can be understood only by linking Him with God's foundational promises to Abraham that envisage saving blessings for all nations.

For his part, Luke starts even further back, with Adam. Luke shows that Jesus is the true Davidic King, who brings the Israel story to its successful conclusion and, in doing so, makes good the whole human story.

John, of course, writing later, sums up what they all agree on, that Jesus can be properly understood only by rooting Him in the very eternal nature of God. In which case the story told in Jesus is the true version of the story of the One Creator God.

Matthew in particular uses the language of 'fulfilment' in order to say that Jesus re-enacts and completes the whole pattern of Israel's history. Jesus is

THE PROMISE-PLAN OF GOD   JESUS

COVENANT WITH:

NOAH   ABRAHAM   ISRAEL/MOSES   DAVID   NEW COVENANT

God's new and true Israel, who comes out of Egypt and successfully comes through testing in the wilderness. He is the new Moses, spelling out a new covenant charter, as in Deuteronomy, to the hearers of the new Sermon on the Mount. He is the new David, anointed to proclaim the good news of God's arriving kingdom.

All the characteristic titles of Jesus have rich Old Testament meanings. All of them have larger than individual reference which incorporate the nation's destiny. Isaiah's 'servant of the Lord', the psalmist's 'son of God', and Daniel's 'son of man' are all applied to Jesus as a representative figure who acts as and for His people.

If we ask: what were Jesus' aims? – the initial answer may surprise us. Jesus' top priority is to Israel, to restore the lost sheep of the house of Israel. To this end He chooses twelve new 'tribal' heads, alters the rules of acceptance and non-acceptance, and proclaims that exile is over by forgiving sins and welcoming repentant sinners.

He challenges Israel to follow Him and take up the cross of a new way of being Israel by dying and rising with Him to the realities of a new covenant existence. He rescripts the Passover meal to focus on Himself as the one true sacrifice for sin. But alongside this grace there is a warning of judgment. Jesus looked ahead and foresaw the dreadful calamity which we now know befell Jerusalem and the Temple in AD 70-73 in the Jewish-Roman conflict. He could see it all coming. He predicted that within the lifetime of His contemporaries, foreign armies would again besiege the city so that not one stone of the Temple would be left standing. The looming shadow of AD 70 hangs over everything

Jesus says and does and gives His message a terrible urgency. This was the hour of decision. His generation was the 'terminal generation' from whom God was calling in the accounts. The judgment He envisaged was the judgment He was willing to bear for His people. But if His self-offering were refused then a dark fate awaited the nation. In the last week of His life, the questions about Him intensified into a loud clamour. Who was He anyway? What right did He have to redraw the lines of Israel's national life like this? Who was He to think of rewriting the story of God in so daring a way? By what authority does He do and say such things? If, as His friends, we ask the question that His enemies asked, then we might conclude with Matthew that no one could do and say the things Jesus did except Israel's God in Person. In Matthew's first and final word: He is Immanuel, 'God with us'. In His blood the new covenant is established and sealed. In Him are realised the promises cherished in Israel that Abraham's seed would bring blessing to the world of nations. Great David's greater Son stands tall as Israel's King and the world's Lord, His resurrection from the dead the token of a new creation.

FOR MANY MODERN people, genealogies are not an interesting way to begin a compelling story. But in older cultures – especially a Jewish culture – a person's family tree tells you a great deal about their significance. All the more so in Jesus' case. When Matthew wants to tell us the story of Jesus as he sees it, he plunges straight into the history of Israel. We ought not to be surprised by this move because already it has become clear that without the Old Testament phase of God's story we cannot begin to understand Jesus. Matthew offers us the genealogy of Jesus because he wants us to see straightaway that Jesus is the climax to the longer, earlier stages of God's story. The genealogy is not an exhaustive one but written up in the shape of three series of fourteen generations (v.17). In effect it is a condensed history of Israel, arranged into three main eras. Here are Jesus' roots. Matthew first of all connects Jesus to Abraham through whom, we recall, 'all the nations of the earth will be blessed'. He then links Him to the Davidic line of kings on whom the well-being and destiny of the people depended. The hopes of the whole world, the hopes of Israel, all rest on the shoulders of the One whose story Matthew is telling. So much depends on Jesus and we are glad to put all our trust in Him too.

DAY
181
MATTHEW 1:1-17

Matthew 1:1-17

BIBLE
READING

THE GENEALOGY OF JESUS CHRIST

1 The historical record of Jesus Christ, the Son of David, the Son of Abraham:

FROM ABRAHAM TO DAVID

² Abraham fathered Isaac,
Isaac fathered Jacob,
Jacob fathered Judah and his brothers,
³ Judah fathered Perez and Zerah by Tamar,

489

Perez fathered Hezron,
Hezron fathered Aram,
⁴ Aram fathered Aminadab,
Aminadab fathered Nahshon,
Nahshon fathered Salmon,
⁵ Salmon fathered Boaz by Rahab,
Boaz fathered Obed by Ruth,
Obed fathered Jesse,
⁶ and Jesse fathered King David.

FROM DAVID TO THE BABYLONIAN EXILE

Then David fathered Solomon by Uriah's wife,
⁷ Solomon fathered Rehoboam,
Rehoboam fathered Abijah,
Abijah fathered Asa,
⁸ Asa fathered Jehoshaphat,
Jehoshaphat fathered Joram,
Joram fathered Uzziah,
⁹ Uzziah fathered Jotham,
Jotham fathered Ahaz,
Ahaz fathered Hezekiah,
¹⁰ Hezekiah fathered Manasseh,
Manasseh fathered Amon,
Amon fathered Josiah,
¹¹ and Josiah fathered Jechoniah and his brothers
at the time of the exile to Babylon.

FROM THE EXILE TO THE MESSIAH

¹² Then after the exile to Babylon
Jechoniah fathered Salathiel,
Salathiel fathered Zerubbabel,
¹³ Zerubbabel fathered Abiud,
Abiud fathered Eliakim,
Eliakim fathered Azor,
¹⁴ Azor fathered Zadok,
Zadok fathered Achim,
Achim fathered Eliud,
¹⁵ Eliud fathered Eleazar,
Eleazar fathered Matthan,
Matthan fathered Jacob,

¹⁶ and Jacob fathered Joseph the husband of Mary,
who gave birth to Jesus who is called the Messiah.

¹⁷So all the generations from Abraham to David were 14 generations; and from David until the exile to Babylon, 14 generations; and from the exile to Babylon until the Messiah, 14 generations.

> THOUGHT: Nowadays people spend large amounts of money tracing their family tree. Sometimes they are disappointed when they discover amongst their ancestors people of ill repute. How thrilling it is that our spiritual roots, our genealogy and our family tree can be traced back to God the Father Himself. So lift up your head, throw back your shoulders. You are a child of the living God!

THE THIRD MOVE Matthew makes is to view the Jesus story as the true sequel to the Exile in Babylon five hundred years before. Nothing that had occurred in the intervening centuries had fully resolved the issue of the sin of God's people or corresponded to the prophetic hopes of salvation. Israel's continuing oppression by godless powers only seemed to reinforce the sense of still being under God's judgment. But now things are about to change. It is against this backdrop that the Evangelists highlight the significance of the Exile for Jesus. Each of them ties Jesus closely to John the Baptist whom they identify as that 'voice in the wilderness' spoken of by Isaiah as heralding the return of God as King. When he appears and speaks, it will be to declare that the long 'Exile' in sin and under judgment at last is over! The birth of a child will change everything. The child will bear the name of Israel's first conquering hero 'Joshua' who led the people into the promised land of Canaan. But this 'Yeshua' is about a bigger business. He will save His people, Israel, from her sins, and lead

DAY
182
MATTHEW 1:17-21

her - albeit through death - into the new promised land of salvation (Matt. 1:21).

Abrahamic promises, Davidic dreams, prophetic hopes at Exile - all these are coming to fruition at last in Jesus.

BIBLE READING	## Matthew 1:17-21

¹⁷So all the generations from Abraham to David were 14 generations; and from David until the exile to Babylon, 14 generations; and from the exile to Babylon until the Messiah, 14 generations.

THE NATIVITY OF THE MESSIAH

¹⁸The birth of Jesus Christ came about this way: After His mother Mary had been engaged to Joseph, it was discovered before they came together that she was pregnant by the Holy Spirit. ¹⁹So her husband Joseph, being a righteous man, and not wanting to disgrace her publicly, decided to divorce her secretly.

²⁰But after he had considered these things, an angel of the Lord suddenly appeared to him in a dream, saying, "Joseph, son of David, don't be afraid to take Mary as your wife, because what has been conceived in her is by the Holy Spirit. ²¹She will give birth to a son, and you are to name Him Jesus, because He will save His people from their sins."

TO PONDER: Those who live in the Scriptures will know that time and time again whenever God's people seemed to lose hope God would remind them of His promise that a better day lay up ahead. Do you wonder as you look around just what the world is coming to? Hold on to this - all God's great promises will be fulfilled through Jesus in the glorious dawn that awaits those whose trust is in the Saviour. Better times are coming.

IN ORDER TO show us that Jesus is the culmination of the previous phases in God's story, Matthew often uses the language of 'fulfilment' (for example, v.22). By 'fulfilment' he does not mean that a random selection of predictions from the Old Testament somehow land on target in Jesus.

Rather, on a larger scale, by 'fulfilment', Matthew seeks to show that the whole pattern of Israel's story is being gathered up and reproduced in Jesus.

That entire story is being 'filled-full' by Jesus, as Jesus is and does all that God wanted Israel to be and do. On the largest scale, the God who has always been with Israel is now with them in person to do for them – and for the world – what only God could do.

Matthew says that the birth of Jesus the 'Immanuel-child' fulfils Isaiah 7:14 as a sign – 'God with us' (1:22-23). This is not a simple proof-text that 'proves' Jesus' divine credentials.

In its original context Isaiah's message was not a Messianic prophecy but a word to King Ahaz that the imminent defeat of his enemies would be a sure sign of 'God-being-with-him'.

Reflecting on who Mary's baby really is, Matthew sees in Jesus the ultimate sign of God-being-with-His-people. After all, how much more 'with-His-people' can God get than to become one of them?

Matthew 1:22-2:12

BIBLE
READING

¹⁷So all the generations from Abraham to David were 14 generations; and from David until the exile to Babylon, 14 generations; and from the exile to Babylon until the Messiah, 14 generations.

THE NATIVITY OF THE MESSIAH

¹⁸The birth of Jesus Christ came about this way: After His mother Mary had been engaged to Joseph, it was discovered before they came together that she was

pregnant by the Holy Spirit. ¹⁹So her husband Joseph, being a righteous man, and not wanting to disgrace her publicly, decided to divorce her secretly.

²⁰But after he had considered these things, an angel of the Lord suddenly appeared to him in a dream, saying, "Joseph, son of David, don't be afraid to take Mary as your wife, because what has been conceived in her is by the Holy Spirit. ²¹She will give birth to a son, and you are to name Him Jesus, because He will save His people from their sins."

²²Now all this took place to fulfill what was spoken by the Lord through the prophet:

²³ "See, the virgin will become pregnant
  and give birth to a son,
  and they will name Him Immanuel,"

which is translated "God is with us."

²⁴When Joseph got up from sleeping, he did as the Lord's angel had commanded him. He married her ²⁵but did not know her intimately until she gave birth to a son. And he named Him Jesus.

WISE MEN SEEK THE KING

2 After Jesus was born in Bethlehem of Judea in the days of King Herod, wise men from the east arrived unexpectedly in Jerusalem, ²saying, "Where is He who has been born King of the Jews? For we saw His star in the east and have come to worship Him."

³When King Herod heard this, he was deeply disturbed, and all Jerusalem with him. ⁴So he assembled all the chief priests and scribes of the people and asked them where the Messiah would be born.

⁵"In Bethlehem of Judea," they told him, "because this is what was written by the prophet:

⁶ "'And you, Bethlehem,' in the land of Judah,
  are by no means "least among the leaders of Judah:
  because out of you will come a leader
  who will shepherd My people Israel.'"

⁷Then Herod secretly summoned the wise men and asked them the exact time the star appeared. ⁸He sent them to Bethlehem and said, "Go and search carefully for the child. When you find Him, report back to me so that I too can go and worship Him."

⁹After hearing the king, they went on their way. And there it was—the star they had seen in the east! It led them until it came and stopped above the place where the child was. ¹⁰When they saw the star, they were overjoyed beyond measure. ¹¹Entering the house, they saw the child with Mary His mother, and falling to their knees, they worshiped Him. Then they opened their treasures and presented Him with gifts: gold, frankincense, and myrrh. ¹²And being warned in a dream not to go back to Herod, they returned to their own country by another route.

> **FOR PRAISE:** There are some who view God as a distant deity, a being high up in the heavens who stands remote from His creation. In Jesus, however, God has come close to us. Through the great act of the Incarnation we can now say God is not just for us but with us. Whatever you do today, and wherever you will go – through the Holy Spirit He will be there to love, guide, comfort, deliver and save. Give God praise for that great fact.

SIMEON IS AN attractive figure in his own right. But for Luke, he also symbolises a faithful and expectant Israel, 'waiting for Israel's consolation' (vv.25,38). This expression was shorthand for the blessing and salvation of the Messianic era. Isaiah had captured the relief of the coming age in such phrases as: 'Comfort, comfort My people' (Isa. 40:1); 'For the LORD will comfort Zion' (Isa. 51:3). The divine discontent stirring within Simeon was the work of the Holy Spirit on him. He looked for interests bigger than his own. For an old man – as he seems to be – he remains sharp and forward-looking, alive and alert in the Spirit to the

DAY
184

LUKE 2:22-32

next chapter in God's big story. And the Holy Spirit prompted him to discern what God was doing in this critical and climactic stage of the story, enabling him to recognise the child in his arms as the long-awaited Christ, the goal of Israel's dreams and his own desires. His song says it all. Jesus is the culmination of what God has been preparing for a very long time. He replaces the Temple as the focal point of God's glory in Israel, and becomes the One through whom Israel is now set to achieve her purpose as God's people by being a light to the Gentile nations of the world. No wonder, that seeing Jesus, Simeon knew he had seen all he needed to see to make his life worthwhile.

BIBLE READING

Luke 2:22-32

[22] And when the days of their purification according to the law of Moses were finished, they brought Him up to Jerusalem to present Him to the Lord [23] (just as it is written in the law of the Lord: "Every firstborn male will be dedicated to the Lord") [24] and to offer a sacrifice (according to what is stated in the law of the Lord: "a pair of turtledoves or two young pigeons").

SIMEON'S PROPHETIC PRAISE

[25] There was a man in Jerusalem whose name was Simeon. This man was righteous and devout, looking forward to Israel's consolation, and the Holy Spirit was on him. [26] It had been revealed to him by the Holy Spirit that he would not see death before he saw the Lord's Messiah. [27] Guided by the Spirit, he entered the temple complex. When the parents brought in the child Jesus to perform for Him what was customary under the law, [28] Simeon took Him up in his arms, praised God, and said:

[29] Now, Master,
   You can dismiss Your slave in peace,
   according to Your word.
[30] For my eyes have seen Your salvation.
[31] You have prepared [it]

in the presence of all peoples—
³² a light for revelation to the Gentiles
and glory to Your people Israel.

PRAYER: My Father and my God, just as Simeon, when his eyes fell upon Jesus, knew that he had seen all he needed to make his life worthwhile, so this is my testimony too. The entrance of Your Son into my life has turned my life from defeat to victory, from gloom to gladness, from a life that lacked meaning to one that is now full of meaning. How I bless the day when the Saviour became *my* Saviour! Thank You, my Father. Amen.

DAY 185

LUKE 2:33-40

THE DAY OF salvation for which God has long prepared has dawned, but its coming to Israel will not be greeted with universal acclaim.

Simeon and Anna are among those who constitute a Spirit-filled 'welcome committee' for Jesus, but not all would be as receptive. The cruciality of Christ is unavoidable. Nothing and no one will escape the effects of His coming. As a quite deliberate part of God's plan, this child is destined to cause great upheaval. His effect will be to turn Israel upside down. The revolution He ushers in will inevitably flush out opposition and arouse fierce antagonism. He will act as a searching light, exposing vested interest, vainglory, hidden agendas and well-disguised hypocrisy. He will force people to show their hand and to declare themselves in their true colours. Not everyone will like Him or find satisfaction in His arrival as Simeon does. Jesus brings both judgment and grace. No one will remain neutral in His presence. And His ministry, like His birth, will cause pain. The price He pays will be felt by His mother as a sword thrust through her heart. But Simeon praised God for His coming, His parents marvelled at what was said about Him, and we, with Anna, give thanks for

Him and speak about Him to all who look for Israel's consolation and the world's salvation.

| BIBLE READING | ## Luke 2:33-40 |

²²And when the days of their purification according to the law of Moses were finished, they brought Him up to Jerusalem to present Him to the Lord ²³(just as it is written in the law of the Lord: "Every firstborn male will be dedicated to the Lord") ²⁴and to offer a sacrifice (according to what is stated in the law of the Lord: "a pair of turtledoves or two young pigeons").

SIMEON'S PROPHETIC PRAISE

²⁵There was a man in Jerusalem whose name was Simeon. This man was righteous and devout, looking forward to Israel's consolation, and the Holy Spirit was on him. ²⁶It had been revealed to him by the Holy Spirit that he would not see death before he saw the Lord's Messiah. ²⁷Guided by the Spirit, he entered the temple complex. When the parents brought in the child Jesus to perform for Him what was customary under the law, ²⁸Simeon took Him up in his arms, praised God, and said:

²⁹ Now, Master,
You can dismiss Your slave in peace,
according to Your word.
³⁰ For my eyes have seen Your salvation.
³¹ You have prepared [it]
in the presence of all peoples—
³² a light for revelation to the Gentiles
and glory to Your people Israel.

³³His father and mother were amazed at what was being said about Him. ³⁴Then Simeon blessed them and told His mother Mary: "Indeed, this child is destined to cause the fall and rise of many in Israel and to be a sign that will be opposed — ³⁵and a sword will pierce your own soul—that the thoughts of many hearts may be revealed."

ANNA'S TESTIMONY

³⁶There was also a prophetess, Anna, a daughter of Phanuel, of the tribe of Asher. She was well along in years, having lived with her husband seven years after her marriage, ³⁷and was a widow for 84 years. She did not leave the temple complex, serving God night and day with fastings and prayers. ³⁸At that very moment, she came up and began to thank God and to speak about Him to all who were looking forward to the redemption of Jerusalem.

THE FAMILY'S RETURN TO NAZARETH

³⁹When they had completed everything according to the law of the Lord, they returned to Galilee, to their own town of Nazareth. ⁴⁰The boy grew up and became strong, filled with wisdom, and God's grace was on Him.

QUESTION: Have you experienced moments when your Christian commitment has caused you to be rejected by those who reject Jesus? Most Christians have undergone such times. Whenever that happens keep in mind that though those who reject Christ may sometimes reject us, we are on the other hand gloriously accepted by God and promised a reward in heaven. The one perspective more than compensates for the other.

MATTHEW IS SHOWING us how Jesus, as it were, re-enacts the pattern of events in Israel's history in order to fulfil the purpose for which God chose Israel.

DAY
186
MATTHEW 2:13-15

In this chapter Matthew refers to both Exodus and Exile - the two traumatic events that bracket the Old Testament story of Israel: Exodus - the dramatic beginning; and Exile - the effective end of her life as an independent nation under God.

Matthew describes how parents and child escape Herod's anger by fleeing to Egypt. Matthew sees their return as fulfilling words of the prophet Hosea: 'Out of Egypt I called My Son' (2:15b; Hosea 11:1).

Hosea is here referring to the early description of Israel as God's son (Exod. 4:22). But again we have an important insight into what Matthew means by fulfilment as applied to Jesus' relation to the Old Testament prophets.

For the fulfilment here is not that of fulfilling a predictive prophecy. In fact Hosea's words have no future reference at all but are a reflection on Israel's past history, recalling the Exodus from Egypt.

Once again Matthew is making the larger point that Jesus recapitulates Israel's story by beginning where she began – in Egypt. He comes up 'out of Egypt' as God's 'Son', the true Israel of God. And immediately Matthew alerts us to the fact that a new and greater 'Exodus' is under way!

BIBLE READING

Matthew 2:13-15

THE FLIGHT INTO EGYPT

¹³After they were gone, an angel of the Lord suddenly appeared to Joseph in a dream, saying, "Get up! Take the child and His mother, flee to Egypt, and stay there until I tell you. For Herod is about to search for the child to destroy Him." ¹⁴So he got up, took the child and His mother during the night, and escaped to Egypt. ¹⁵He stayed there until Herod's death, so that what was spoken by the Lord through the prophet might be fulfilled: "Out of Egypt I called My Son."

A CHALLENGE: If there is one thing that God hates it is to see His people under the bondage of sin. The Almighty has a passion to see His people free from all that binds them. It was this passion (as we saw in earlier readings) that led Him to rescue Israel from the bondage of slavery in Egypt. Are there any bondages in your life? The Almighty is still in the 'Exodus' business. Ask Him to set you free today.

DAY 187

MATTHEW 2:16-23

MATTHEW NOW BRINGS the Exile into focus by quoting from Jeremiah in a passage where the prophet decribes the 'new covenant' and refers to Israel as God's 'precious Son' (Jer. 31:20,31ff.).

Jeremiah was responding to the pain of the Babylonian Exile, by picturing Rachel, the original mother of Israel, weeping for her descendants taken into captivity in Babylon. Matthew perceives Rachel's deep grief as being felt all over again in the agony of the mothers around Bethlehem whose children have been murdered in Herod's savage purge. The 'massacre of the innocents' is a violent intrusion into the Nativity story, showing the harshness of the world the Christ-child has come to redeem. Even His arrival to defeat evil brings pain before it brings consolation. Poignantly, the Bethlehem mothers are caught up in the larger story of Israel's Exile under judgment and God's act of redemption.

By drawing Exodus and Exile together, Matthew is already indicating the scale of what this child will achieve. It is clear that Jesus will gather up both ends of Israel's story - starting where she started, enslaved in Egypt and again in Exile - and bringing her out in a greater Exodus, by a greater redemption, returning her not merely to the land but to her God!

BIBLE READING

Matthew 2:16-23

THE FLIGHT INTO EGYPT

[13]After they were gone, an angel of the Lord suddenly appeared to Joseph in a dream, saying, "Get up! Take the child and His mother, flee to Egypt, and stay there until I tell you. For Herod is about to search for the child to destroy Him." [14]So he got up, took the child and His mother during the night, and escaped to Egypt. [15]He stayed there until Herod's death, so that what was spoken by the Lord through the prophet might be fulfilled: "Out of Egypt I called My Son."

THE MASSACRE OF THE INNOCENTS

[16]Then Herod, when he saw that he had been outwitted by the wise men, flew into a rage. He gave orders to massacre all the male children in and around Bethlehem who were two years old and under, in keeping with the time he had learned from the wise men. [17]Then what was spoken through Jeremiah the prophet was fulfilled:

[18] "A voice was heard in Ramah,
   weeping, and great mourning,
   Rachel weeping for her children;
   and she refused to be consoled,
   because they were no more."

THE HOLY FAMILY IN NAZARETH

[19]After Herod died, an angel of the Lord suddenly appeared in a dream to Joseph in Egypt, [20]saying, "Get up! Take the child and His mother and go to the land of Israel, because those who sought the child's life are dead." [21]So he got up, took the child and His mother, and entered the land of Israel. [22]But when he heard that Archelaus was ruling over Judea in place of his father Herod, he was afraid to go there. And being warned in a dream, he withdrew to the region of Galilee. [23]Then he went and settled in a town called Nazareth to fulfill what was spoken through the prophets, that He will be called a Nazarene.

PRAYER: Father, how can we thank You enough for the fact that Jesus is the beginner of our story and the concluder of Your story of salvation. He sets the slaves free and brings the exiles home to You. I am so grateful that my spiritual slavery has been abolished and that I am no longer an exile but an heir of God and a joint heir with Christ. My heart is Yours forever. Amen.

DAY
188

JESUS COMES TO the banks of the Jordan River, where the children of Israel had once stood poised to enter the promised land, in order to submit to John's baptism, joining with all those who were repenting of their sins in doing so (v.6). John is taken aback and feels the roles should be reversed because Jesus does not seem to be a sinner (vv.11,14). But Jesus has come to 'fulfill all righteousness' which in broad terms means that He has come to bring to reality God's age-old redemptive plan revealed in the Scriptures.

So, the fact that Jesus undergoes a 'baptism for sinners', when by all accounts He was not one, further shows the extent to which He would identify with Israel at this climactic moment in her history. He does so in at least two ways. In being baptised, He willingly steps into Israel's shoes to fulfil her role as God's faithful covenant partner. Secondly, He shows Himself willing to bear Israel's sin and judgment by being 'numbered with transgressors' as they confessed their sins and made ready for the arriving kingdom of God.

He was, in other words, being baptised for others – thus anticipating his 'immersion' in the atoning death of the cross. Those willing to follow Him all the way down into the river of death would emerge with sins forgiven, stepping out into the new world of salvation.

BIBLE READING

Matthew 3:1-15

THE MESSIAH'S HERALD

3 In those days John the Baptist came, preaching in the Wilderness of Judea ²and saying, "Repent, because the kingdom of heaven has come near!" ³For he is the one spoken of through the prophet Isaiah, who said:

> "A voice of one crying out in the wilderness:
> 'Prepare the way for the Lord;
> make His paths straight!'"

⁴John himself had a camel-hair garment with a leather belt around his waist, and his food was locusts and wild honey. ⁵Then [people from] Jerusalem, all Judea, and all the vicinity of the Jordan were flocking to him, ⁶and they were baptized by him in the Jordan River as they confessed their sins.

⁷When he saw many of the Pharisees and Sadducees coming to the place of his baptism, he said to them, "Brood of vipers! Who warned you to flee from the coming wrath? ⁸Therefore produce fruit consistent with repentance. ⁹And don't presume to say to yourselves, 'We have Abraham as our father.' For I tell you that God is able to raise up children for Abraham from these stones! ¹⁰Even now the ax is ready to strike the root of the trees! Therefore every tree that doesn't produce good fruit will be cut down and thrown into the fire.

¹¹"I baptize you with water for repentance, but the One who is coming after me is more powerful than I. I am not worthy to take off His sandals. He Himself will baptize you with the Holy Spirit and fire. ¹²His winnowing shovel is in His hand, and He will clear His threshing floor and gather His wheat into the barn. But the chaff He will burn up with fire that never goes out."

THE BAPTISM OF JESUS

¹³Then Jesus came from Galilee to John at the Jordan, to be baptized by him. ¹⁴But John tried to stop Him, saying, "I need to be baptized by You, and yet You come to me?"

¹⁵Jesus answered him, "Allow it for now, because this is the way for us to fulfill all righteousness." Then he allowed Him [to be baptized].

THOUGHT: Consider this before you take up the duties of the day: everything Christ did He did for us. He wore our flesh, measured its frailty, 'walked in our shoes' so to speak, was baptised as our representative, immersed Himself in death so that we might live. A good response to all this would be for us to pray the words of an ancient prayer: 'All this You have done for me; what have I done for Thee?'

WE LINGER OVER this crucial moment of Jesus' baptism on the banks of the Jordan River.

The voice from heaven endorses Jesus as the true Davidic King whose Sonship is affirmed by the anointing of the Holy Spirit as truly Messianic. The divine words are a merging of Psalm 2:7 with Isaiah 42:1 – with perhaps an echo of the offering of the only beloved son, Isaac. The words combine God's promise to the Davidic king that he would be 'God's son', with Isaiah's vision of the self-effacing servant of God who would eventually suffer in the cause of bringing salvation to others. The words from heaven, therefore, mark Jesus out as a Servant-king, set on an ambiguous and mysterious royal road which must pass through suffering and humiliation on its way to glory.

For Jesus personally, we can perhaps sense how the Father's love and approval penetrate to the depth of His heart, not only clarifying His identity and mission, but fortifying Him emotionally against the disapproval of His enemies and the misunderstanding of His friends in the three years ahead. The significance of the Holy Spirit coming in the form of a dove may derive from Genesis 8:8-12 where the dove appears as the harbinger of a new world after the Flood. The Father endorses the Son and the Spirit empowers Him to bring in the new creation!

BIBLE READING

Matthew 3:16-17

THE MESSIAH'S HERALD

3 In those days John the Baptist came, preaching in the Wilderness of Judea ²and saying, "Repent, because the kingdom of heaven has come near!" ³For he is the one spoken of through the prophet Isaiah, who said:

> "A voice of one crying out in the wilderness:
> 'Prepare the way for the Lord;
> make His paths straight!'"

[4]John himself had a camel-hair garment with a leather belt around his waist, and his food was locusts and wild honey. [5]Then [people from] Jerusalem, all Judea, and all the vicinity of the Jordan were flocking to him, [6]and they were baptized by him in the Jordan River as they confessed their sins.

[7]When he saw many of the Pharisees and Sadducees coming to the place of his baptism, he said to them, "Brood of vipers! Who warned you to flee from the coming wrath? [8]Therefore produce fruit consistent with repentance. [9]And don't presume to say to yourselves, 'We have Abraham as our father.' For I tell you that God is able to raise up children for Abraham from these stones! [10]Even now the ax is ready to strike the root of the trees! Therefore every tree that doesn't produce good fruit will be cut down and thrown into the fire.

[11]"I baptize you with water for repentance, but the One who is coming after me is more powerful than I. I am not worthy to take off His sandals. He Himself will baptize you with the Holy Spirit and fire. [12]His winnowing shovel is in His hand, and He will clear His threshing floor and gather His wheat into the barn. But the chaff He will burn up with fire that never goes out."

THE BAPTISM OF JESUS

[13]Then Jesus came from Galilee to John at the Jordan, to be baptized by him. [14]But John tried to stop Him, saying, "I need to be baptized by You, and yet You come to me?" [15]Jesus answered him, "Allow it for now, because this is the way for us to fulfill all righteousness." Then he allowed Him [to be baptized].

[16]After Jesus was baptized, He went up immediately from the water. The heavens suddenly opened for Him, and He saw the Spirit of God descending like a dove and coming down on Him. [17]And there came a voice from heaven:

This is My beloved Son.
I take delight in Him!

TO PONDER: The greatest joy in the Christian life, Dr Martyn Lloyd-Jones used to say, is not just that our sins have been forgiven, but that we have been made children of God and adopted into the royal family of heaven. Thus we are invited to hear the Father's voice saying to us, in similar words to those He said to His Son: 'I delight in you too as My child.' Read 1 John 3:1 now and ponder it throughout the day.

DAY 190

**MATTHEW 4:1-3
EXODUS 4:22-23
PSALM 2:7**

MATTHEW'S PICTURE OF Jesus as the One who re-enacts Israel's story is further underlined by the narrative describing Jesus' temptations.

Like David confronting Goliath, the newly anointed king-in-waiting strides out to meet the evil challenger to God's rule.

His test lasts a symbolic forty days in the wilderness, re-enacting, as it were, the temptations which Israel faced and failed to resist during forty years in the wilderness and thereafter in the land. This is confirmed by the fact that Jesus quotes three times from Deuteronomy, Israel's charter of national identity and behaviour. But, whereas Israel had failed the test in the wilderness, God's 'new Israel', Jesus Himself, succeeds gloriously.

Jesus is tested as 'the Son of God' – perhaps a faint echo of the privileged calling of Adam himself (as Luke implies in 3:38). Matthew's clear intention is to link Jesus with the covenantal 'sonship' of both Israel's king (2 Sam. 7:14; Psa. 2:7), and of Israel herself whom the king represented (Exod. 4:22-23; Hosea 11:1). It is interesting to notice that the wilderness period was seen as a 'test' for Israel for, Moses says, 'the LORD your God has been disciplining you just as a man disciplines his son' (Deut. 8:5). Once again everything hangs on the obedience of one man: and He doesn't fail us!

Matthew 4:1-3

THE TEMPTATION OF JESUS

4 Then Jesus was led up by the Spirit into the wilderness to be tempted by the Devil. ²After He had fasted 40 days and 40 nights, He was hungry. ³Then the tempter approached Him and said, "If You are the Son of God, tell these stones to become bread."

Exodus 4:22-23

²²Then you will say to Pharaoh: This is what the LORD says: Israel is My firstborn son. ²³I told you: Let My son go so that he may worship Me, but you refused to let him go. Now I will kill your firstborn son!"

Psalm 2:7

⁷ I will declare the LORD's decree:
He said to Me, "You are My Son;
today I have become Your Father.

FOR PRAISE: Pause before going any further and allow these thoughts to lie upon your mind until they generate a stream of praise: Jesus, our new David, our great Champion, wins the victory for us over sin and Satan's forces. Thus, we are, as Scripture says, 'more than conquerors'. A conqueror is someone who wins by fighting. Being more than a conqueror is someone who wins without fighting.

DAY
191

MATTHEW 4:3-4
HEBREWS 2:16-18

THE DEVIL'S AIM, it appears, is to distort Jesus' sense of a God-given vocation by encouraging Him to adopt ungodly methods for how it might be worked out. He first challenges Jesus' faith in God's ability to provide for Him, by tempting Him to turn stones into bread to meet His own needs. This is tantamount to magic which is the desire to harness divine power to our own ends, or to bring divine forces under our control. Jesus is being tempted to abuse His power in His own self-interest. Like Israel before Him, Jesus is tempted to the sin of unbelief, that is, to live other than by faith in God's Word. Even after a forty-day fast Jesus refuses. Even though, like John, He knows God can make stones 'talk', He refuses (cf.Matt 3:9). Jesus responds by declaring His intention of adhering to the covenant charter of how the true Israel should live, by quoting from Deuteronomy 8:3 to the effect that 'Man must not live on bread alone but on every word that comes from the mouth of God'. Jesus will wait patiently in faith for His Father to act and will not deny His call. The Holy Spirit sustains Jesus here in trust and dependency on God.

BIBLE READING

Matthew 4:3-4

THE TEMPTATION OF JESUS

4 Then Jesus was led up by the Spirit into the wilderness to be tempted by the Devil. [2]After He had fasted 40 days and 40 nights, He was hungry.

[3]Then the tempter approached Him and said, "If You are the Son of God, tell these stones to become bread."

[4]But He answered, "It is written:

'Man must not live on bread alone
but on every word that comes
from the mouth of God.'"

Hebrews 2:16-18

¹⁶For it is clear that He does not reach out to help angels, but to help Abraham's offspring. ¹⁷Therefore He had to be like His brothers in every way, so that He could become a merciful and faithful high priest in service to God, to make propitiation for the sins of the people. ¹⁸For since He Himself was tested and has suffered, He is able to help those who are tested.

PRAYER: My Father and my God, help me to honour You as did Your Son, with my trust and patient courage. May my reliance always be on You and on Your written Word. Produce in me, dear Father, the fruits of longsuffering and self-control so that I may be able to withstand all the wiles of the devil and rebut all his temptations in the power of the Holy Spirit. I ask this in and through the name of Jesus. Amen.

SECONDLY, JESUS IS urged to throw Himself from the pinnacle of the Temple, while 'naming and claiming' Psalm 91 as His protection. But such suicidal bravado is fanaticism, not true faith. Intriguingly, also, Israel's original failure in the wilderness was along these lines. It was soberly immortalised in the names Meribah ('contention') and Massah ('testing') which recalled the day when the children of Israel clamoured for water, suggesting that God was out to kill them. Moses gave the place these names because the people 'tested the Lord, saying, "Is the Lord among us or not?"' (Exod. 17:7). The memory of this tragic event was kept alive in Israel's worship with its ringing call for an obedient response 'today' (Psa. 95:7-11). As the psalmist indicates, it is tragically possible to have seen God act in mighty 'works' but not to know or walk in His 'ways'. Jesus, for His part, would always avoid doing miracles 'on demand' as proof of anything! He refuses to prove that God is with Him 'on demand'.

DAY
192

**MATTHEW 4:5-7
HEBREWS 4:14-16**

He resists what He sees as presumption, as putting God to the test, by again citing the Deuteronomy command, 'Do not test the LORD your God'. Jesus will not presume on His relationship with His Father as if God were there to serve Him rather than the reverse.

BIBLE READING

Matthew 4:5-7

THE TEMPTATION OF JESUS

4 Then Jesus was led up by the Spirit into the wilderness to be tempted by the Devil. [2]After He had fasted 40 days and 40 nights, He was hungry. [3]Then the tempter approached Him and said, "If You are the Son of God, tell these stones to become bread."
[4]But He answered, "It is written:

> 'Man must not live on bread alone
> but on every word that comes
> from the mouth of God.'"

[5]Then the Devil took Him to the holy city, had Him stand on the pinnacle of the temple, [6]and said to Him, "If You are the Son of God, throw Yourself down. For it is written:

> 'He will give His angels orders concerning you, and
> they will support you with their hands
> so that you will not strike
> your foot against a stone.'"

[7]Jesus told him, "It is also written: 'Do not test the Lord your God.'"

BIBLE READING

Hebrews 4:14-16

OUR GREAT HIGH PRIEST

[14]Therefore since we have a great high priest who has passed through the heavens—Jesus the Son of God—let us hold fast to the confession. [15]For we do not have a high priest who is unable

to sympathize with our weaknesses, but One who has been tested in every way as we are, yet without sin. ¹⁶Therefore let us approach the throne of grace with boldness, so that we may receive mercy and find grace to help us at the proper time.

TO PONDER: Is God here to serve us or are we here to serve Him? That is a question that deserves the deepest thought and consideration. Sadly, multitudes of Christians seem to think God is under an obligation to answer their every prayer and respond to their every whim. Ask yourself today: Am I walking in the obedience of faith or do I live out my days with the assumption that God exists to serve me?

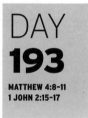

DAY
193
MATTHEW 4:8-11
1 JOHN 2:15-17

THE THIRD TEMPTATION Jesus faces is to be offered the kingdoms of the world on condition He bows down and worships Satan. We have seen from the second psalm that God's anointed King will only have to entreat His Father for the nations to become His inheritance. Worldwide rule is His for the asking! Jesus, therefore, is quick to rebut this temptation. He repudiates the idea of idolatry, insisting, again in words from Deuteronomy: 'Worship the Lord your God, and serve only Him.' We can see what the thrust of the temptation is.

'If you are the true Israel, God's "son", if you are her representative king, God's "son", then go the way of Israel and her kings before you.' But - savingly - Jesus refuses! Unbelief, presumption, idolatry - these are the sins Israel continued to be bedeviled by throughout her life in the promised land. But Jesus is saying, in effect, that where Israel failed to rise to the covenant challenge and abide by the Deuteronomic ideal, He will. His secret? Well, the Spirit led Him not only into the desert to be tested but led Him through it triumphantly.

| BIBLE READING | **Matthew 4:8-11** |

THE TEMPTATION OF JESUS

4 Then Jesus was led up by the Spirit into the wilderness to be tempted by the Devil. ²After He had fasted 40 days and 40 nights, He was hungry. ³Then the tempter approached Him and said, "If You are the Son of God, tell these stones to become bread."

⁴But He answered, "It is written:

'Man must not live on bread alone
but on every word that comes
from the mouth of God.'"

⁵Then the Devil took Him to the holy city, had Him stand on the pinnacle of the temple, ⁶and said to Him, "If You are the Son of God, throw Yourself down. For it is written:

'He will give His angels orders concerning you,
and they will support you with their hands
so that you will not strike
your foot against a stone.'"

⁷Jesus told him, "It is also written: 'Do not test the Lord your God.'"

⁸Again, the Devil took Him to a very high mountain and showed Him all the kingdoms of the world and their splendor. ⁹And he said to Him, "I will give You all these things if You will fall down and worship me."

¹⁰Then Jesus told him, "Go away, Satan! For it is written:

'Worship the Lord your God,
and serve only Him.'"

¹¹Then the Devil left Him, and immediately angels came and began to serve Him.

1 John 2:15-17

A WARNING ABOUT THE WORLD

¹⁵Do not love the world or the things that belong to the world. If anyone loves the world, love for the Father is not in him. ¹⁶For everything that belongs to the world—the lust of the flesh, the lust of the eyes, and the pride in one's lifestyle—is not from the Father, but is from the world. ¹⁷And the world with its lust is passing away, but the one who does God's will remains forever.

> QUOTATION: Chris Wright is one of the finest biblical scholars of our day and his remarks on today's theme form a helpful supplement to what has already been said. 'On the shoulders of Jesus as the Son of God lay the responsibility of being the true son, succeeding where Israel had failed, submitting to God's will where they had rebelled, obeying where they had disobeyed.' What a Saviour!

JESUS RETURNED TO Galilee, but He made His base of ministry not in Nazareth but in the more populated and influential Capernaum. He deliberately restricted His mission to the people of Israel and never embarked on a wider Gentile mission. In fact He avoided the larger, more cosmopolitan towns such as Tiberius and Sepphoris. But in returning to Galilee, Matthew sees Jesus marking out a claim, rooted in the prophecy of Isaiah, that the impact of God's Messianic King and kingdom would be felt by the nations beyond Israel. Galilee was the 'way to the sea', situated on the trade routes to the Mediterranean coast and therefore to the rest of the world. However much Jesus made Israel His first priority, what happened in Galilee and Judea would eventually light up the whole world. It was here that Jesus recruited His first disciples. He called them from fishing for

DAY
194
MATTHEW 4:12-25

fish in the local lake to fishing for people in the ocean of the world. Meanwhile He launched His Messianic ministry, preaching the good news of God's kingdom. Where God's kingdom breaks into our lives in power, demons fear and fly, the sick are healed and Jesus makes news everywhere. Jesus is still the most consistently breaking news there is!

BIBLE READING

Matthew 4:12-25

MINISTRY IN GALILEE

[12]When He heard that John had been arrested, He withdrew into Galilee. [13]He left Nazareth behind and went to live in Capernaum by the sea, in the region of Zebulun and Naphtali. [14]This was to fulfill what was spoken through the prophet Isaiah:

[15] "Land of Zebulun and land of Naphtali,
along the sea road, beyond the Jordan,
Galilee of the Gentiles!
[16] The people who live in darkness
have seen a great light,
and for those living in the shadowland of death,
light has dawned."

[17]From then on Jesus began to preach, "Repent, because the kingdom of heaven has come near!"

THE FIRST DISCIPLES

[18]As He was walking along the Sea of Galilee, He saw two brothers, Simon, who was called Peter, and his brother Andrew. They were casting a net into the sea, since they were fishermen. [19]"Follow Me," He told them, "and I will make you fish for people!" [20]Immediately they left their nets and followed Him.

[21]Going on from there, He saw two other brothers, James the son of Zebedee, and his brother John. They were in a boat with Zebedee their father, mending their nets, and He called them. [22]Immediately they left the boat and their father and followed Him.

TEACHING, PREACHING, AND HEALING

²³Jesus was going all over Galilee, teaching in their synagogues, preaching the good news of the kingdom, and healing every disease and sickness among the people. ²⁴Then the news about Him spread throughout Syria. So they brought to Him all those who were afflicted, those suffering from various diseases and intense pains, the demon-possessed, the epileptics, and the paralytics. And He healed them. ²⁵Large crowds followed Him from Galilee, Decapolis, Jerusalem, Judea, and beyond the Jordan.

THOUGHT: When Jesus said 'I am the light of the world' few people realised that His message and His gospel would illuminate the centuries and make an impact on the world greater than any other individual who has ever lived. Think of it – what He did back there 2,000 years ago has reached across the centuries to impact your life in the here and now. That's worth a shout of 'Hallelujah!' – is it not?

WHEN JESUS RETURNED to His hometown synagogue from His first preaching tour, the atmosphere was electric. Who did this carpenter's boy think he was? Jesus offers Isaiah 61 as His credentials for ministry. The 'good news' heralded by Isaiah focuses on Jesus as the anointed deliverer, who proclaims the kingdom of God.

DAY
195

LUKE 4:16-30

And this gospel is for the poor, for those who are economically impoverished and culturally marginalised.

Jesus' keynote is 'freedom'. The setting free ('release', NIV) He speaks of harks back to the unfulfilled dreams of the Jubilee year freedoms of Leviticus 25. 'Today is the day,' Jesus declares, for ancient scriptures to come good before your very eyes. Jesus proclaims release for the beggars in debt, for the bound in detention, for the blind in darkness, for the burdened under domination. This is the year of the Lord's favour announced in gracious words (v.22).

But the gospel provokes a mixed reaction. First attentive amazement (vv.20-22), then puzzlement (v.22), then furious antagonism (v.28). The idea that the freedom is for Gentiles was too much (vv.25-27). They missed God's acceptable year because it came through God's unacceptable prophet!

BIBLE READING

Luke 4:16-30

REJECTION AT NAZARETH

[16]He came to Nazareth, where He had been brought up. As usual, He entered the synagogue on the Sabbath day and stood up to read. [17]The scroll of the prophet Isaiah was given to Him, and unrolling the scroll, He found the place where it was written:

[18] "The Spirit of the Lord is on Me,
  because He has anointed Me
  to preach good news to the poor.
  He has sent Me
  to proclaim freedom to the captives
  and recovery of sight to the blind,
  to set free the oppressed,
[19] to proclaim the year of the Lord's favor."

[20]He then rolled up the scroll, gave it back to the attendant, and sat down. And the eyes of everyone in the synagogue were fixed on Him. [21]He began by saying to them, "Today as you listen, this Scripture has been fulfilled."

[22]They were all speaking well of Him and were amazed by the gracious words that came from His mouth, yet they said, "Isn't this Joseph's son?"

[23]Then He said to them, "No doubt you will quote this proverb to Me: 'Doctor, heal yourself.' 'All we've heard that took place in Capernaum, do here in Your hometown also.'"

[24]He also said, "I assure you: No prophet is accepted in his hometown. [25]But I say to you, there were certainly many widows in Israel in Elijah's days, when the sky was shut up for three years and six months while a great famine came over

all the land. ²⁶Yet Elijah was not sent to any of them—but to a widow at Zarephath in Sidon. ²⁷And in the prophet Elisha's time, there were many in Israel who had serious skin diseases, yet not one of them was healed —only Naaman the Syrian."

²⁸When they heard this, everyone in the synagogue was enraged. ²⁹They got up, drove Him out of town, and brought Him to the edge of the hill their town was built on, intending to hurl Him over the cliff. ³⁰But He passed right through the crowd and went on His way.

FOR PRAISE: James Montgomery wrote a verse of a hymn that captures some of the thoughts that have been presented to us today. Sing it or say it as your 'sacrifice' of praise to God

Hail to the Lord's anointed, Great David's greater Son!
Hail in the time appointed, His reign on earth begun
He comes to break oppression, to set the captive free
To take away transgression and rule in equity.

WE CALL IT the Sermon on the Mount and so make it sound like a polite homily from a pulpit. To those who first heard it must have sounded more like a manifesto for a revolutionary political party!

DAY 196
MATTHEW 5:1-11

Those seeking the invasion of God's kingdom to restore Israel's glory, are told that it will come but only to those who are beggars in spirit and humbly dependent on God's grace. The consolation of Israel will come but it will be paid for in repentant tears. The whole earth waits to be inherited, not by the conquering strong, but by the humble meek. Soul satisfaction is a noble quest but only those who hunger and thirst to see God's justice prevail will find it. You want mercy? Then show mercy! The sight of God is not for the elite or advantaged holders of religious office but for the pure in heart. For Israel once again to be the 'sons of God' will mean making peace not war. The kingdom belongs not to those who inflict violence but to those who endure violence for the sake of this gloriously upside-down kingdom! And the blessedness is for right now! – a deeply satisfying God-given blessing that rests upon the humble poor, the meek, the mourners, the merciful and those who long for God's righteousness, peace and justice to be seen on earth.

BIBLE READING

Matthew 5:1-11

THE SERMON ON THE MOUNT

5 When He saw the crowds, He went up on the mountain, and after He sat down, His disciples came to Him. [2]Then He began to teach them, saying:

THE BEATITUDES

[3] "Blessed are the poor in spirit,
because the kingdom of heaven is theirs.
[4] Blessed are those who mourn,
because they will be comforted.
[5] Blessed are the gentle,
because they will inherit the earth.
[6] Blessed are those who hunger
and thirst for righteousness,
because they will be filled.
[7] Blessed are the merciful,
because they will be shown mercy.
[8] Blessed are the pure in heart,
because they will see God.
[9] Blessed are the peacemakers,
because they will be called sons of God.
[10] Blessed are those who are persecuted for righteousness,
because the kingdom of heaven is theirs.

[11]"Blessed are you when they insult you and persecute you and falsely say every kind of evil against you because of Me."

PRAYER: Thank You, Father, for the great 'reversals of grace' that turn the world upside down and therefore right side up. Thank You too for the way Your Son has impacted my life and shown me how I should live. Help me function in this upside-down kingdom the way Your Son has taught me - blessing those who persecute me and giving out love when I meet hatred. In Jesus' name. Amen.

DAY 197

MATTHEW 5:13-15

LIKE A NEW Moses, Jesus issues a new Torah, not an abolition but a fulfilment of the old one, a Torah intensified and radicalised by His own presence as the fulfilment of God's promises (vv.17-20). So it was no call to return to conventional morality. Whatever its wider application, Jesus' message was originally a sharp challenge to the Israel of His day to renew their vocation as God's covenant people.

Only the 'Jesus way' of being Israel has a future in it. His teaching outlines the path of true covenant loyalty to God which fulfils the intentions of the law and the prophets.

Can His disciples rise to the challenge of becoming the new people of God? Israel had been called to be a holy nation, a royal priesthood, a light to the Gentile nations. But that salty distinctiveness has been all but obliterated. A darkened people are in no position to show the way to others. Will the disciples of Jesus be the nucleus of that new people of God who will demonstrate the light of life to the world? Will they authenticate the truth they hold by the lives they live?

Matthew 5:13-15

BIBLE READING

BELIEVERS ARE SALT AND LIGHT

¹³"You are the salt of the earth. But if the salt should lose its taste, how can it be made salty? It's no longer good for anything but to be thrown out and trampled on by men.

¹⁴"You are the light of the world. A city situated on a hill cannot be hidden. ¹⁵No one lights a lamp and puts it under a basket, but rather on a lampstand, and it gives light for all who are in the house.

TO PONDER: In Christ we are called and empowered to live lives that illuminate rather than darken the world around us, to reflect and relay the love of God to everyone we meet. Ask the Lord to help you daily to live and witness, whether through your words or through your life, in such a way that you impact the life of every unbeliever you relate to. 'It's amazing,' said Hudson Taylor, 'what God can do through one life committed to him.'

DAY
198
MATTHEW 6:5-15

THE LORD'S PRAYER has its context within the longer story we are tracing. Israel had been judged by God and sent into exile for bringing God's name into disrepute by her failure to live a covenant life. God's reputation has been tarnished by Israel's behaviour before the eyes of a watching world. When God moves to restore His people, says Ezekiel, it will be less for their sake than to restore the honour of His holy name (Ezek. 36:22). Those who know the times of restoration are at hand, will have one priority in prayer: 'Hallowed be Your name, O Lord.'

From the time of the Exile, the prophets project the hope that God would forgive His people. Isaiah says that God will blot out sins as we erase a stain, He will sweep them away like a morning mist burnt off by the sun. This longed-for forgiveness will flood an exiled people with the joy of pardon and re-acceptance by God. In such a day, Jesus says, the forgiveness sinners receive from God will overflow into forgiving one another. Grace will create a community of 'forgiven-forgivers'. The age-old Jubilee dream (Lev. 25) may yet be realised through the gospel in a society built not on debt and vindictiveness, not on extortion or resentment but on fairness, generosity and mercy.

Matthew 6:5-15

HOW TO PRAY

⁵"Whenever you pray, you must not be like the hypocrites, because they love to pray standing in the synagogues and on the street corners to be seen by people. I assure you: They've got their reward! ⁶But when you pray, go into your private room, shut your door, and pray to your Father who is in secret. And your Father who sees in secret will reward you. ⁷When you pray, don't babble like the idolaters, since they imagine they'll be heard for their many words. ⁸Don't be like them, because your Father knows the things you need before you ask Him.

THE MODEL PRAYER

⁹"Therefore, you should pray like this:

> Our Father in heaven,
> Your name be honored as holy.
> ¹⁰ Your kingdom come.
> Your will be done
> on earth as it is in heaven.
> ¹¹ Give us today our daily bread.
> ¹² And forgive us our debts,
> as we also have forgiven our debtors.
> ¹³ And do not bring us into temptation,
> but deliver us from the evil one.
> [For Yours is the kingdom and the power
> and the glory forever. Amen.]

THOUGHT: The receiving and giving of forgiveness is what the Christian life is all about. No one can call himself or herself a true believer unless he or she is willing to accept this truth and put it into practice. You have been forgiven, now if you have not yet forgiven all those who hurt or injured you then don't go any further into the day until you have done so. Only the forgiving can be forgiven.

DAY
199
MARK 2:1-12

LET'S NOT MISS the drama as Jesus pronounces forgiveness for sins (2:5). We are used to taking this personally, in the sense of having *our* sins forgiven, and we are right to do so. But it is important to remember – in the context of the ministry of Jesus – that it was God's judgment on Israel's sins which sent her into exile in Babylon and prompted the need for national forgiveness. This hope of forgiveness for Israel was part of the prophets' promise for the future (Isa. 43:25; 44:21-22). We heard both Daniel and Ezra pleading with God to forgive an Israel 'still in its sins' despite being back in the land. Isaiah offers hope to the exiles after hearing a commanding voice declaring that Israel's 'sin has been paid for' (40:1-2, NIV).

When Jesus heals and forgives one paralysed man, He is, in effect, proclaiming national healing and forgiveness. And His religious opponents were scandalised, not because they heard a human voice saying the words '... your sins are forgiven' – the priests did this in the Temple every day after the right sacrifice had been offered – but because Jesus was doing it, unauthorised, and not in the Temple but on the streets. When Jesus declared the healed man 'forgiven' He was, in effect, announcing that 'Exile was now finally over' and that the day of salvation had arrived in and through Him!

BIBLE READING

Mark 2:1-12

THE SON OF MAN FORGIVES AND HEALS

2 When He entered Capernaum again after some days, it was reported that He was at home. ²So many people gathered together that there was no more room, not even in the doorway, and He was speaking the message to them. ³Then they came to Him bringing a paralytic, carried by four men. ⁴Since they were not able to bring him to Jesus because of the crowd, they removed the roof above where He was. And

when they had broken through, they lowered the stretcher on which the paralytic was lying.

⁵Seeing their faith, Jesus told the paralytic, "Son, your sins are forgiven."

⁶But some of the scribes were sitting there, thinking to themselves: ⁷"Why does He speak like this? He's blaspheming! Who can forgive sins but God alone?"

⁸Right away Jesus understood in His spirit that they were reasoning like this within themselves and said to them, "Why are you reasoning these things in your hearts? ⁹Which is easier: to say to the paralytic, 'Your sins are forgiven,' or to say, 'Get up, pick up your stretcher, and walk'? ¹⁰But so you may know that the Son of Man has authority on earth to forgive sins," He told the paralytic, ¹¹"I tell you: get up, pick up your stretcher, and go home."

¹²Immediately he got up, picked up the stretcher, and went out in front of everyone. As a result, they were all astounded and gave glory to God, saying, "We have never seen anything like this!"

FOR PRAISE: In today's world psychiatrists are highly skilled in unearthing the things that trouble us. They can trace the sins once committed but long forgotten and bring them out into the light of day. But there is one thing they cannot do – they cannot forgive. Only God can do that. Jesus is God and therefore able to forgive all sin. No greater proof of His deity is needed. Praise Him for that glorious fact.

JESUS APPOINTED TWELVE apostles for His own good reasons. Among them, we need not doubt, was His own human need for companionship. Mark says they were appointed to 'be with Him'. He wanted friends on His journey who could share His exalted moments – as in transfiguration – or His darkest hours – as in Gethsemane.

His calling of the twelve was also born of His desire to see an extension of His ministry beyond Himself.

DAY 200
MARK 3:13-18

525

He called them so that He might 'send them out ...'. Jesus wanted agents who would share His Messianic mission. He wanted heralds who would announce the day of judgment and favour and proclaim the nearness of God's kingdom. He wanted those who could be trusted to share His authority over personal evil. But why twelve? Why not eleven or thirteen? Well, like His Old Testament namesake, He calls twelve because they represent the twelve tribes of Israel (cf.Josh. 3-4). The choice of twelve was a powerful symbolic gesture, a political statement that, in the restored Israel, the traditional religious leaders would be replaced by fisherman and other working men. He could give no clearer sign of His intention to redefine who Israel was than by re-assigning the leadership of God's people in His way to the men of His choice.

BIBLE READING

Mark 3:13-18

THE 12 APOSTLES

[13]Then He went up the mountain and summoned those He wanted, and they came to Him. [14]He also appointed 12—He also named them apostles—to be with Him, to send them out to preach, [15]and to have authority to drive out demons.

[16]He appointed the Twelve:

To Simon, He gave the name Peter;
[17] and to James the son of Zebedee,
and to his brother John,
He gave the name "Boanerges"
(that is, "Sons of Thunder");
[18] Andrew;
Philip and Bartholomew;
Matthew and Thomas;
James the son of Alphaeus,
and Thaddaeus;
Simon the Zealot,

QUESTION: How much time do you spend communing with the Saviour? Not reading about Him in books such as this, but talking to Him, as a friend talks to a friend? The Christian life rises and falls at this point. Time spent in any other way may yield rewards but it must not displace time spent with Him. So, once again: how much time do you spend really communing with the Saviour? A little or a lot?

DAY
201
MATTHEW 8:5-13

JESUS HAD LITTLE direct contact with Gentiles during His ministry, but this was a significant meeting. Roman soldiers knew all about authority and so it shows striking humility and submission for the centurion to acknowledge the authority of Jesus. Jesus was rarely taken aback by anything: only extreme lack of faith (Mark 6:6) and, as here, sheer audacity of faith, surprise him (v.10).

For now, the scope of Jesus' mission was restricted to Israel. But the centurion's bold faith heralds the day, soon to come, when the Gentiles from every corner of the globe would come streaming in to take their places at the feast of grace with Abraham and Isaac and Jacob. A military man from Rome in the West and magi from the East would sit down together at table as equal members, in Christ, of God's one covenant family. Perhaps even Abraham will be taken aback by the crowds who follow in the footsteps of his faith! But if many are included by faith, others exclude themselves by their unbelief – a sober warning to nationalist Jews in Matthew's day and complacent Christians then and now! Let's make sure we give Jesus a joyous not a sad surprise!

BIBLE READING

Matthew 8:5-13

A CENTURION'S FAITH

[5]When He entered Capernaum, a centurion came to Him, pleading with Him, [6]"Lord, my servant is lying at home paralyzed, in terrible agony!"

[7]"I will come and heal him," He told him.

[8]"Lord," the centurion replied, "I am not worthy to have You come under my roof. But only say the word, and my servant will be cured. [9]For I too am a man under authority, having soldiers under my command. I say to this one, 'Go!' and he goes; and to another, 'Come!' and he comes; and to my slave, 'Do this!' and he does it."

[10]Hearing this, Jesus was amazed and said to those following Him, "I assure you: I have not found anyone in Israel with so great a faith! [11]I tell you that many will come from east and west, and recline at the table with Abraham, Isaac, and Jacob in the kingdom of heaven. [12]But the sons of the kingdom will be thrown into the outer darkness. In that place there will be weeping and gnashing of teeth." [13]Then Jesus told the centurion, "Go. As you have believed, let it be done for you." And his servant was cured that very moment.

THOUGHT: While in a sense nothing can surprise the Lord for He sees and knows everything in advance, how pleased He must be when our love, faith and courage break out in new and delightful ways. Think of one way today you can 'surprise' the Lord with an act of love, faith or courage that will bring delight and joy to His heart. And think too of making it not just today - but every day.

JESUS HIMSELF INDICATED that His own identity was shaped by the servant songs of Isaiah (42-53). Matthew develops this here, especially in regard to the way Jesus handled people and healed them. As He recalled the ministry of Jesus, Matthew sees Isaiah's vision brought to life - particularly here the glimpse we are given in Isaiah 42.

When God's servant appears He will be unpretentious, and without the need for self-justification. He is not in 'show-business'. He is not on an ego trip needing the impetus of spin doctors or public relations experts. He is humble and self-effacing. He is not a strident propagandist, nor an overbearing personality. He brings God's revolution, but does not advance His cause by violence or by intimidatory tactics. He fosters the tiniest flicker of faith, and deals gently with those bruised and broken by life.

When God's servant Israel fails in her mission (Isa. 42:18-19), God acts to raise up one faithful person from within Israel to restore the rest of God's people (Isa. 49:5-7). This true Israelite will be willing to suffer and die in order to bear the punishment due to the whole people (Isa. 52:13-53:12).

Through such strange and paradoxical tactics, He would in due course, as the suffering servant, 'bring justice to victory'.

Matthew 12:15-21

BIBLE READING

THE SERVANT OF THE LORD

[15]When Jesus became aware of this, He withdrew from there. Huge crowds followed Him, and He healed them all. [16]He warned them not to make Him known, [17]so that what was spoken through the prophet Isaiah might be fulfilled:

[18] "Here is My Servant whom I have chosen,
My beloved in whom My soul delights;
I will put My Spirit on Him,

and He will proclaim justice to the nations.
¹⁹ He will not argue or shout,
and no one will hear His voice in the streets.
²⁰ He will not break a bruised reed,
and He will not put out a smoldering wick,
until He has led justice to victory.
²¹ The nations will put their hope in His name."

QUOTATION: 'The true way to be humble is not to stoop until you are smaller than yourself but to stand at your real height against some higher nature that will show you what the real smallness of your greatest greatness is. Stand at your very highest and then look at Christ and go away and be forever humble. Be aware that when you lose sight of Christ you yourself begin to loom large.' (Philip Brooks)

DAY 203
MATTHEW 13:1-23

THE PARABLES ARE best understood in the context of Jesus' own ministry. They are not bland, timeless, abstract truths, but the cutting-edge of God's kingdom as they challenge the people of His day. Here, the seed is the 'message of the kingdom' which Jesus speaks and embodies (v.19, NIV). God's kingdom comes not in a great blitz, but as a Word to be preached and believed. Jesus preaches the kingdom – like the prophets – as a two-edged sword, bringing both God's judgment and God's grace. His ministry provokes a very varied response. Resistant hearers show indifference, and remain hard and obdurate. Shallow hearers will soon fall away when the big trouble of AD 70 comes. Double-minded hearers find their new-found faith in Jesus choked by the preoccupations of everyday living. The quotation from Isaiah 6 shows that this mixed result is not due to bad luck or poor evangelistic methods; it is God's intention! Jesus divides Israel by forcing a decision. Some will harden in their unbelief. But there is hope. Isaiah says of the felled tree that 'the holy seed will be the stump in the land' (Isa. 6:13,

NIV). So, Jesus says, in the very entity being cut back and judged there will lodge a seed (in Jesus' disciples) that will bear a disproportionate hundred-fold harvest (vv.8,23). Have you read Acts 2 recently?

Matthew 13:1-23

THE PARABLE OF THE SOWER

13 On that day Jesus went out of the house and was sitting by the sea. ²Such large crowds gathered around Him that He got into a boat and sat down, while the whole crowd stood on the shore.

³Then He told them many things in parables, saying: "Consider the sower who went out to sow. ⁴As he was sowing, some seeds fell along the path, and the birds came and ate them up. ⁵Others fell on rocky ground, where there wasn't much soil, and they sprang up quickly since the soil wasn't deep. ⁶But when the sun came up they were scorched, and since they had no root, they withered. ⁷Others fell among thorns, and the thorns came up and choked them. ⁸Still others fell on good ground, and produced a crop: some 100, some 60, and some 30 times [what was sown]. ⁹Anyone who has ears should listen!"

WHY JESUS USED PARABLES

¹⁰Then the disciples came up and asked Him, "Why do You speak to them in parables?"

¹¹He answered them, "Because the secrets of the kingdom of heaven have been given for you to know, but it has not been given to them. ¹²For whoever has, [more] will be given to him, and he will have more than enough. But whoever does not have, even what he has will be taken away from him. ¹³For this reason I speak to them in parables, because looking they do not see, and hearing they do not listen or understand. ¹⁴Isaiah's prophecy is fulfilled in them, which says:

"You will listen and listen,
yet never understand;
and you will look and look,

yet never perceive.

15 For this people's heart has grown callous;
their ears are hard of hearing,
and they have shut their eyes;
otherwise they might see with their eyes
and hear with their ears,
understand with their hearts
and turn back—
and I would cure them."

16"But your eyes are blessed because they do see, and your ears because they do hear! 17For I assure you: Many prophets and righteous people longed to see the things you see yet didn't see them; to hear the things you hear yet didn't hear them.

THE PARABLE OF THE SOWER EXPLAINED

18"You, then, listen to the parable of the sower: 19When anyone hears the word about the kingdom and doesn't understand it, the evil one comes and snatches away what was sown in his heart. This is the one sown along the path. 20And the one sown on rocky ground—this is one who hears the word and immediately receives it with joy. 21Yet he has no root in himself, but is short-lived. When pressure or persecution comes because of the word, immediately he stumbles. 22Now the one sown among the thorns—this is one who hears the word, but the worries of this age and the seduction of wealth choke the word, and it becomes unfruitful. 23But the one sown on the good ground—this is one who hears and understands the word, who does bear fruit and yields: some 100, some 60, some 30 times [what was sown]."

FOR ACTION: Open your Bible at Acts 2 and read once again the story of the great harvest of souls that were swept into the kingdom as a result of Peter's simple but Spirit-drenched preaching. Just think of it - one sermon brought 3,000 souls to Christ. Nowadays in some parts of the Church it takes 3,000 sermons to bring one soul to Christ. Suggest reasons to yourself why this may be so.

DAY
204

MATTHEW 13:33-35

ALL THE OLD Testament scriptures – including Psalm 78 – are considered to be 'prophetic'. All of them foreshadow God's future salvation in the Messianic era. Jesus quotes the opening verse of Psalm 78 to explain what is going on in His parabolic teaching (v.35). Who better to interpret David's prophetic song than David's greater son, Jesus, to whom all these scriptures point and in whom they are all fulfilled?

Now Psalm 78 is a long recital of the turbulent history of God with Israel. That history of God's dealings with His people was with a view to the salvation of the world.

When Jesus reveals 'things kept secret from the foundation of the world' (v.35) He is not uttering vacuous spiritual soundbites for religiously minded people, nor offering greeting-card clichés in vague spirituality. No! Jesus is about His Father's bigger business. He is now claiming to unveil the strategic plan of God which has been in God's heart from the beginning. This grand design is now being revealed and enacted in His ministry. These mysteries of the kingdom revealed in the parables are what former prophets and righteous men longed to see but can now be known because that longed-for day of salvation has at last arrived (13:11,16-17). How privileged we are as His disciples to be caught up in God's big story!

BIBLE READING

Matthew 13:33-35

³³He told them another parable: "The kingdom of heaven is like yeast that a woman took and mixed into 50 pounds of flour until it spread through all of it."

USING PARABLES FULFILLS PROPHECY

³⁴Jesus told the crowds all these things in parables, and He would not speak anything to them without a parable, ³⁵so that what was spoken through the prophet might be fulfilled:

"I will open My mouth in parables;
I will declare things kept secret
from the foundation of the world."

TO PONDER: In the light of today's reading this is a good opportunity to think once again of the privilege that is ours of being caught up in God's bigger story. Has this thought gripped you yet? Of course you are able to understand it intellectually, but has it gripped you in your heart? Do you thrill to the fact that you are involved in something that is not merely terrestrial but universal? If not why not?

JESUS' PARABLES TEASE the mind, slipping through gaps in mental defences with the sharp thrust of God's kingdom.

DAY
205

MATTHEW 13:51-52
REVELATION 21:12-14

The kingdom's progress directly involves the disciples in whom the 'seed' takes root and grows. Each disciple is given a glimpse into God's big strategy ('mystery') of bringing His rule to the world in judgment and salvation. To understand this, the 'student of the kingdom' must study the previous revelation in the Old Testament and the 'new' revelation brought by Jesus. The 'new' things of Jesus don't cancel out but complete the 'old' things.

Without the Old Testament we cannot understand Jesus. But, conversely, we cannot understand the Old Testament without the newness of the gospel of Jesus. So 'old' and 'new' go together and interpret each other. There is continuity between them because the one God speaks and acts in both. Throughout the 'old' era, God commits Himself by a series of covenant arrangements in order to further His plan of salvation. There is also discontinuity. In the 'new era' all that's gone before is ransacked so as to begin to explain the revolution taking place in and through Jesus!

BIBLE READING

Matthew 13:51-52

THE STOREHOUSE OF TRUTH

⁵¹"Have you understood all these things?"

"Yes," they told Him.

⁵²"Therefore," He said to them, "every student of Scripture instructed in the kingdom of heaven is like a landowner who brings out of his storeroom what is new and what is old." ⁵³When Jesus had finished these parables, He left there.

BIBLE READING

Revelation 21:12-14

¹²[The city] had a massive high wall, with 12 gates. Twelve angels were at the gates; [on the gates], names were inscribed, the names of the 12 tribes of the sons of Israel. ¹³There were three gates on the east, three gates on the north, three gates on the south, and three gates on the west. ¹⁴The city wall had 12 foundations, and on them were the 12 names of the Lamb's 12 apostles.

PRAYER: O Father, help me understand more deeply this thought that while in Jesus there is continuity from the old, there is also discontinuity. I have tasted of His revolutionary power and I shall never be the same again. My life has been turned upside down by Him. Help me share this revolutionary message at every opportunity I am given. In His peerless name I pray. Amen.

DAY 206

MATTHEW 15:21-28

AT THIS STAGE in His ministry Jesus acknowledges the priority of Israel in the divine plan. The prophetic sequence of events in God's programme of salvation had always made it clear that first Israel then the Gentiles would come in. So Jesus confines His mission to Israel: 'I was sent only to the lost sheep of the house of Israel' (v.24). Moved with compassion, He seeks out those who have been cast out by the false shepherds of God's flock (cf.Matt. 9:36). Jesus presents Himself as the final restoration shepherd, foreseen by Ezekiel. This 'final' shepherd would be a Prince of the house of David through whom God Himself would shepherd His people (Ezek. 34). As this good shepherd, Jesus has come to regather and heal and feed the scattered, wounded, hungry sheep of God's flock.

In this light, His blunt treatment of the Canaanite woman is disturbing but just about understandable. To her credit, she remains undeterred and presses Him with admirable faith to include her in the feast of the kingdom. Already it is clear that more than enough bread is left over from feeding Israel to feed the four or five thousand and indeed the hungry multitudes across the world.

Matthew 15:21-28

BIBLE READING

A GENTILE MOTHER'S FAITH

21When Jesus left there, He withdrew to the area of Tyre and Sidon. 22Just then a Canaanite woman from that region came and kept crying out, "Have mercy on me, Lord, Son of David! My daughter is cruelly tormented by a demon."

23Yet He did not say a word to her. So His disciples approached Him and urged Him, "Send her away because she cries out after us."

24He replied, "I was sent only to the lost sheep of the house of Israel."

25But she came, knelt before Him, and said, "Lord, help me!"

26He answered, "It isn't right to take the children's bread and throw it to their dogs."

27"Yes, Lord," she said, "yet even the dogs eat the crumbs that fall from their masters' table!"

28Then Jesus replied to her, "Woman, your faith is great. Let it be done for you as you want." And from that moment her daughter was cured.

FOR THANKSGIVING: Some things are made to be broken. Bread is one of them. Left to itself it grows a green beard and goes bad. How grateful we ought to be that though our Lord's primary mission was to the nation of Israel, there was more than enough bread left over to include us in the redemptive plan. Give thanks for the fact that there is bread in our Father's house 'and to spare'.

DAY
207

MATTHEW 16:24-28
DANIEL 7

THE 'SON OF man' (as in Daniel) is Jesus' favourite and exclusive way of referring to Himself. He comes as the truly Human One to identify with the 'saints' of God fighting for their lives against evil foes. He wrestles with the wild beasts of entrenched religion and implacable political power. He emerges triumphant and is raised to a place of honour. Everything He does is for His people, as their representative. He incorporates their destiny. He defeats their enemies and is vindicated at the place of honour and judgment on their behalf. When He receives the kingdom and its authority, the saints receive it too. All that He is and does, His people are and achieve. He comes to the throne of the Ancient of Days trailing clouds of glory.

As for this future glory, it will be seen, He insists, in 'this generation', within the lifetime of 'some standing here' (v.28).

Again the earliest vision of this glory will be in transfiguration and resurrection, in ascension and the coming of the Spirit, and – as far as an unbelieving Israel was concerned – in the tragic ruin of Jerusalem and the Temple in AD 70 which would vindicate Jesus as a true prophet of God. All the more remarkable then, that this glorious and all-conquering figure will achieve God's ends by being willing to serve and in serving to suffer.

Matthew 16:24-28

TAKE UP YOUR CROSS

²⁴Then Jesus said to His disciples, "If anyone wants to come with Me, he must deny himself, take up his cross, and follow Me. ²⁵For whoever wants to save his life will lose it, but whoever loses his life because of Me will find it. ²⁶What will it benefit a man if he gains the whole world yet loses his life? Or what will a man give in exchange for his life? ²⁷For the Son of Man is going to come with His angels in the glory of His Father, and then He will reward each according to what he has done. ²⁸I assure you: There are some standing here who will not taste death until they see the Son of Man coming in His kingdom."

Daniel 7

DANIEL'S VISION OF THE FOUR BEASTS

7 In the first year of Belshazzar king of Babylon, Daniel had a dream with visions in his mind as he was lying in his bed. He wrote down the dream, and here is the summary of his account. ²Daniel said, "In my vision at night I was watching, and suddenly the four winds of heaven stirred up the great sea. ³Four huge beasts came up from the sea, each different from the other.

⁴"The first was like a lion but had eagle's wings. I continued watching until its wings were torn off. It was lifted up from the ground, set on its feet like a man, and given a human mind.

⁵"Suddenly, another beast appeared, a second one, that looked like a bear. It was raised up on one side, with three ribs in its mouth between its teeth. It was told, 'Get up! Gorge yourself on flesh.'

⁶"While I was watching, another beast appeared. It was like a leopard with four wings of a bird on its back. It had four heads and was given authority to rule.

⁷"While I was watching in the night visions, a fourth beast appeared, frightening and dreadful, and incredibly strong, with large iron teeth. It devoured and crushed, and it trampled

with its feet whatever was left. It was different from all the beasts before it, and it had 10 horns.

⁸"While I was considering the horns, suddenly another horn, a little one, came up among them, and three of the first horns were uprooted before it. There were eyes in this horn like a man's, and it had a mouth that spoke arrogantly.

THE ANCIENT OF DAYS AND THE SON OF MAN
⁹"As I kept watching,

> thrones were set in place,
> and the Ancient of Days took His seat.
> His clothing was white like snow,
> and the hair of His head like whitest wool.
> His throne was flaming fire;
> its wheels were blazing fire.
> 10 A river of fire was flowing,
> coming out from His presence.
> Thousands upon thousands served Him;
> ten thousand times ten thousand stood before Him.
> The court was convened,
> and the books were opened.

¹¹"I watched, then, because of the sound of the arrogant words the horn was speaking. As I continued watching, the beast was killed and its body destroyed and given over to the burning fire. ¹²As for the rest of the beasts, their authority to rule was removed, but an extension of life was granted to them for a certain period of time. ¹³I continued watching in the night visions,

> and I saw One like a son of man
> coming with the clouds of heaven.
> He approached the Ancient of Days
> and was escorted before Him.
> 14 He was given authority to rule,
> and glory, and a kingdom;
> so that those of every people,
> nation, and language
> should serve Him.

His dominion is an everlasting dominion
that will not pass away,
and His kingdom is one
that will not be destroyed.

INTERPRETATION OF THE VISION

[15]"As for me, Daniel, my spirit was deeply distressed within me, and the visions in my mind terrified me. [16]I approached one of those who were standing by and asked him the true meaning of all this. So he let me know the interpretation of these things: [17]"These huge beasts, four in number, are four kings who will rise from the earth. [18]But the holy ones of the Most High will receive the kingdom and possess it forever, yes, forever and ever.'

[19]"Then I wanted to know the true meaning of the fourth beast, the one different from all the others, extremely terrifying, with iron teeth and bronze claws, devouring, crushing, and trampling with its feet whatever was left. [20][I also wanted to know] about the 10 horns on its head and about the other horn that came up, before which three fell—the horn that had eyes, and a mouth that spoke arrogantly, and that was more visible than the others. [21]As I was watching, this horn made war with the holy ones and was prevailing over them [22]until the Ancient of Days arrived and a judgment was given in favor of the holy ones of the Most High, for the time had come, and the holy ones took possession of the kingdom.

[23]"This is what he said: 'The fourth beast will be a fourth kingdom on the earth, different from all the other kingdoms. It will devour the whole earth, trample it down, and crush it. [24]The 10 horns are 10 kings who will rise from this kingdom. Another, different from the previous ones, will rise after them and subdue three kings. [25]He will speak words against the Most High and oppress the holy ones of the Most High. He will intend to change religious festivals and laws, and the holy ones will be handed over to him for a time, times, and half a time. [26]But the court will convene, and his dominion will be taken away, to be completely destroyed forever. [27]The kingdom, dominion, and greatness of the kingdoms under all of heaven will be given to the people, the holy ones of the Most High. His kingdom will be an everlasting kingdom, and all rulers will serve and obey Him.'

²⁸"This is the end of the interpretation. As for me, Daniel, my thoughts terrified me greatly, and my face turned pale, but I kept the matter to myself."

> **THOUGHT:** We have referred previously to the fact that the apostle Paul uses one term over and over again to remind us of our spiritual inheritance - 'in Christ'. Let this thought lie upon your mind before you go out into the day: to be 'in Christ' is to share Christ's victory over sin and be a part of God's glorious plans for the future. You are a child of destiny. Never, never forget it.

DAY 208

JOHN 1:14-17

JOHN RELATES JESUS to the earlier stages of God's story with Israel by celebrating the 'Word made flesh'. Astonishingly, the all-powerful Word of God which gave the universe life and continues to be the reason for its existence, has come enfleshed as a real human being. God's mighty Word which reverberates down through the centuries as a promise on the lips of prophets and which currently resounds throughout the world as a gospel in the mouth of apostles, is nothing less than a glorious Person, Jesus of Nazareth.

All that the One Creator God has to say to His world is finally and fully summed up in Jesus! This Word, as John puts it in the literal translation, has 'pitched His tent' or 'tabernacled among us' - language reminiscent of God 'dwelling' in the tabernacle and filling it with his glory (Exod. 25:8-9; 40:34-35). Once, when God's glory passed before Moses, it turned out to be a glorious demonstration of His goodness which consists of steadfast love and faithfulness or truth (Exod. 33:19; 34:6). It is precisely this majestic combination of 'grace and truth' that John believes has been gloriously concentrated and displayed in Jesus. Moses is well and truly eclipsed. The Torah was a gift from God but the ultimate grace and truth is not encoded in a book but embodied in a person.

John 1:14-17

¹⁴ The Word became flesh
and took up residence among us.
We observed His glory,
the glory as the One and Only Son from the Father,
full of grace and truth.
¹⁵ (John testified concerning Him and exclaimed,
"This was the One of whom I said,
'The One coming after me has surpassed me,
because He existed before me.'")
¹⁶ Indeed, we have all received grace after grace
from His fullness,
¹⁷ for although the law was given through Moses,
grace and truth came through Jesus Christ.

QUOTATION: 'Why is Jesus called the "Word"? Well, one's words are the expression of the hidden thought. If you should stand before an audience without a word, hoping the audience would get your thought intuitively and immediately, it would end in futility. Only as the hidden thought is put into a word is the thought communicated. Jesus is God's hidden thought put into a Word.' (E. Stanley Jones)

THE STORY OF Jesus, John reminds us, is the key to the story of the world (vv.3-5,9-10). Creation cannot properly be understood except from a world-view in which Jesus is the central agent of God's creative wisdom and Word, the One by whom (and for whom) the world was made (cf.Prov. 8; Col. 1:15-20). But Jesus' story is also the climax of the story of Israel (vv.6-8,11-13,17). All that Israel was meant to be as a showcase of God's glory is now focused and concentrated in Jesus. Israel's special role in bringing the light of God's truth to the nations, is now fulfilled in the one obedient 'Son of God' (v.34). He does this

DAY
209

JOHN 1:1-18

by making His story one with our story, by taking our 'flesh and blood' humanity to Himself. The humanity He assumes is the humanity He heals. Out of His fullness we have all received, grace upon grace. The 'sons of God' are no longer determined by heredity or ethnicity or Torah but 'to all who received him, to those who believed in his name, he gave the right to become children of God - children born not of natural descent, nor of human decision or a husband's will, but born of God' (vv.12-13, NIV). All who see His glory and believe in Him are constituted as the new covenant family of the One Creator God.

BIBLE READING

John 1:1-18

1 In the beginning was the Word,
and the Word was with God,
and the Word was God.

2 He was with God in the beginning.

3 All things were created through Him,
and apart from Him not one thing was created
that has been created.

4 Life was in Him,
and that life was the light of men.

5 That light shines in the darkness,
yet the darkness did not overcome it.

6 There was a man named John
who was sent from God.

7 He came as a witness
to testify about the light,
so that all might believe through him.

8 He was not the light,
but he came to testify about the light.

9 The true light, who gives light to everyone,
was coming into the world.

10 He was in the world,
and the world was created through Him,

yet the world did not recognize Him.

¹¹ He came to His own,
and His own people did not receive Him.

¹² But to all who did receive Him,
He gave them the right to be children of God,
to those who believe in His name,

¹³ who were born,
not of blood,
or of the will of the flesh,
or of the will of man,
but of God.

¹⁴ The Word became flesh
and took up residence among us.
We observed His glory,
the glory as the One and Only Son from the Father,
full of grace and truth.

¹⁵ (John testified concerning Him and exclaimed,
"This was the One of whom I said,
'The One coming after me has surpassed me,
because He existed before me.'")

¹⁶ Indeed, we have all received grace after grace
from His fullness,

¹⁷ for although the law was given through Moses,
grace and truth came through Jesus Christ.

¹⁸ No one has ever seen God.
The One and Only Son—
the One who is at the Father's side—
He has revealed Him.

TO PONDER: Suppose the Scriptures said 'full of truth and grace' rather than 'grace and truth', what would be the difference? The emphasis would have been upon 'truth'. Truth of course is very important but the first emphasis in the Christian message is 'grace'. John got the order right: first grace then truth. We see truth through grace - grace is truth in glorious act.

DAY
210

JOHN 1:18
1 JOHN 1:1-4

ABOVE ALL, SAYS John, the story of Jesus is the story of God. God's own glory and presence, Word and wisdom, grace and truth, are incarnated fully and uniquely in Jesus. No one has ever seen God, but the One who is at the Father's side 'has revealed Him'. Jesus perfectly 'exegetes' God (v.18) – a word used elsewhere with the meaning 'to tell a story'. In Don Carson's words, 'Jesus is the narration of God'. We read God's story in the human story of Jesus because Jesus is the obedient Son who does only what He sees the Father doing and says only what He hears the Father say. Incarnation is the supreme mystery at the centre of the story. But it does not come entirely out of the blue for those who have read the clues in the story so far. There, we find a God who loves to be with His people; a God who allows Himself to be described (anthropomorphically) in human terms; a God who feels and makes Himself vulnerable. What might Israel's God look like if He emerged within the world in human flesh? If human beings bear His image, and Israel is His 'son' who represents Him in the world, then the One Creator God might well appear as a Jewish human being.

But then Jesus has been in the 'image of the invisible God' from the beginning!

BIBLE READING

John 1:18

¹⁸ No one has ever seen God.
The One and Only Son —
the One who is at the Father's side —
He has revealed Him.

BIBLE READING

1 John 1:1-4

PROLOGUE

1 What was from the beginning,
what we have heard,

what we have seen with our eyes,
what we have observed,
and have touched with our hands,
concerning the Word of life—
2 that life was revealed,
and we have seen it
and we testify and declare to you
the eternal life that was with the Father
and was revealed to us—
3 what we have seen and heard
we also declare to you,
so that you may have fellowship along with us;
and indeed our fellowship is with the Father
and with His Son Jesus Christ.
4 We are writing these things
so that our joy may be complete.

PRAYER: O Son of God, thank You for showing us the Father. We would never have known what He was like had we not looked upon Your face. Now seeing the Father in Your face we are satisfied, yet not satisfied. We are stirred to be like what we see in You. Help us become more like You in character and in attitude. For Your dear name's sake we ask it. Amen.

JOHN THE BAPTIST occupies a special place in the unfolding story because he stands on the dividing line between the old and the new order. Again John the 'plunger' is identified with the 'voice in the wilderness' who, Isaiah had said, would prepare the way of the Lord and herald the coming rule of God. John fits the bill well. He makes a way for Jesus who is the Way. John is a lamp: Jesus is the Light. John is a voice: Jesus is the Word. John testifies that Jesus is the Lamb of God, the final Passover sacrifice for sin. John baptises in water but only with a view to a greater baptism from the One who bestows the Spirit in the Messianic age. The first tentative confessions

DAY
211

JOHN 1:19-51

of faith confirm this (vv.41,45,49). More is revealed in a cryptic saying of Jesus during His encounter with Nathanael (vv.50-51).

Jacob, the founding father of Israel, who gave his name to the nation, once saw a ladder on which heavenly beings travelled in both directions. Later Jewish speculation posited the angels viewing Jacob at both ends of the ladder, so that he represents both an earthly and a heavenly Israel. But, says Jesus, it is not upon Jacob/Israel, but on Him, the Son of Man, that the ladder rests which bears the traffic between earth and heaven! On Him, the 'New Israel' God's transactions with earth are now conducted. What a claim!

BIBLE READING

John 1:19-51

JOHN THE BAPTIST'S TESTIMONY

[19]This is John's testimony when the Jews from Jerusalem sent priests and Levites to ask him, "Who are you?"

[20]He did not refuse to answer, but he declared: "I am not the Messiah."

[21]"What then?" they asked him. "Are you Elijah?"

"I am not," he said.

"Are you the Prophet?"

"No," he answered.

[22]"Who are you, then?" they asked. "We need to give an answer to those who sent us. What can you tell us about yourself?"

[23]He said, "I am a 'voice of one crying out in the wilderness: Make straight the way of the Lord'—just as Isaiah the prophet said."

[24]Now they had been sent from the Pharisees. [25]So they asked him, "Why then do you baptize if you aren't the Messiah, or Elijah, or the Prophet?"

[26]"I baptize with water," John answered them. "Someone stands among you, but you don't know [Him]. [27]He is the One coming after me, whose sandal strap I'm not worthy to untie."

[28]All this happened in Bethany across the Jordan, where John was baptizing.

THE LAMB OF GOD

[29]The next day John saw Jesus coming toward him and said, "Here is the Lamb of God, who takes away the sin of the world! [30]This is the One I told you about: 'After me comes a man who has surpassed me, because He existed before me.' [31]I didn't know Him, but I came baptizing with water so He might be revealed to Israel."

[32]And John testified, "I watched the Spirit descending from heaven like a dove, and He rested on Him. [33]I didn't know Him, but He who sent me to baptize with water told me, 'The One you see the Spirit descending and resting on—He is the One who baptizes with the Holy Spirit.' [34]I have seen and testified that He is the Son of God!"

[35]Again the next day, John was standing with two of his disciples. [36]When he saw Jesus passing by, he said, "Look! The Lamb of God!"

[37]The two disciples heard him say this and followed Jesus. [38]When Jesus turned and noticed them following Him, He asked them, "What are you looking for?"

They said to Him, "Rabbi" (which means "Teacher"), "where are You staying?"

[39]"Come and you'll see," He replied. So they went and saw where He was staying, and they stayed with Him that day. It was about 10 in the morning.

[40]Andrew, Simon Peter's brother, was one of the two who heard John and followed Him. [41]He first found his own brother Simon and told him, "We have found the Messiah!" (which means "Anointed One"), [42]and he brought [Simon] to Jesus.

When Jesus saw him, He said, "You are Simon, son of John. You will be called Cephas" (which means "Rock").

PHILIP AND NATHANAEL

[43]The next day He decided to leave for Galilee. Jesus found Philip and told him, "Follow Me!"

[44]Now Philip was from Bethsaida, the hometown of Andrew and Peter. [45]Philip found Nathanael and told him, "We have found the One Moses wrote about in the Law (and so did the prophets): Jesus the son of Joseph, from Nazareth!"

[46]"Can anything good come out of Nazareth?" Nathanael asked him.

"Come and see," Philip answered.

[47]Then Jesus saw Nathanael coming toward Him and said about him, "Here is a true Israelite; no deceit is in him."

[48]"How do you know me?" Nathanael asked.

"Before Philip called you, when you were under the fig tree, I saw you," Jesus answered.

[49]"Rabbi," Nathanael replied, "You are the Son of God! You are the King of Israel!"

[50]Jesus responded to him, "Do you believe [only] because I told you I saw you under the fig tree? You will see greater things than this." [51]Then He said, "I assure you: You will see heaven opened and the angels of God ascending and descending on the Son of Man."

FOR THANKSGIVING: O God, how can we ever thank You enough for the fact that You have given us Jesus to be our Passover Lamb, to be our Mediator between heaven and earth. He is the only Ladder between heaven and earth – all other ladders are too short. I am so grateful that I have put my feet on the first rung of that ladder. I am ready for heaven and I know that through grace heaven will be ready for me. Amen.

DAY 212

JOHN 2

IF THIS FIRST sign 'signifies' anything, it is that the time of fulfilment has arrived. The water in the pots symbolises the old order of things, told in the earlier chapters of the story, where the Torah is often likened to water. Now that old order of preparation is giving way to the new age of Messianic fulfilment, of which wine is often a potent symbol (Isa. 55:1). Symbolically, the previous stage of the relationship has now progressed to the point of the wedding, which anticipates the description of the bridegroom (3:29). Jesus is the fully matured vintage wine, kept till last, that tops all others! In Jesus, God has saved the best revelation till last (cf.Heb. 1:1). In this sign, we behold His glory (v.11).

The key to John's entire Gospel is that Jesus fulfils the meaning of the central Old Testament feasts and institutions. Nothing would more strikingly signify the 'death' of the old order than the destruction of the great Temple in Jerusalem. The zeal of those who built and maintained the Temple as the house of God would prove mere tinder for the fiery zeal for God's house that burned in Jesus. That fire eventually consumed Him in the flames of sacrificial love on the cross. But, like a phoenix, from the ashes of His dying would come the triumphant Risen Life where God is met and worshipped.

John 2

BIBLE READING

THE FIRST SIGN: TURNING WATER INTO WINE

2 On the third day a wedding took place in Cana of Galilee. Jesus' mother was there, and ²Jesus and His disciples were invited to the wedding as well. ³When the wine ran out, Jesus' mother told Him, "They don't have any wine."

⁴"What has this concern of yours to do with Me, woman?" Jesus asked. "My hour has not yet come."

⁵"Do whatever He tells you," His mother told the servants.

⁶Now six stone water jars had been set there for Jewish purification. Each contained 20 or 30 gallons.

⁷"Fill the jars with water," Jesus told them. So they filled them to the brim. ⁸Then He said to them, "Now draw some out and take it to the chief servant." And they did.

⁹When the chief servant tasted the water (after it had become wine), he did not know where it came from—though the servants who had drawn the water knew. He called the groom ¹⁰and told him, "Everybody sets out the fine wine first, then, after people have drunk freely, the inferior. But you have kept the fine wine until now."

¹¹Jesus performed this first sign in Cana of Galilee. He displayed His glory, and His disciples believed in Him.

¹²After this, He went down to Capernaum, together with His mother, His brothers, and His disciples, and they stayed there only a few days.

CLEANSING THE TEMPLE COMPLEX

¹³The Jewish Passover was near, so Jesus went up to Jerusalem. ¹⁴In the temple complex He found people selling oxen, sheep, and doves, and [He also found] the money changers sitting there. ¹⁵After making a whip out of cords, He drove everyone out of the temple complex with their sheep and oxen. He also poured out the money changers' coins and overturned the tables. ¹⁶He told those who were selling doves, "Get these things out of here! Stop turning My Father's house into a marketplace!"

¹⁷And His disciples remembered that it is written: "Zeal for Your house will consume Me."

¹⁸So the Jews replied to Him, "What sign [of authority] will You show us for doing these things?"

¹⁹Jesus answered, "Destroy this sanctuary, and I will raise it up in three days."

²⁰Therefore the Jews said, "This sanctuary took 46 years to build, and will You raise it up in three days?"

²¹But He was speaking about the sanctuary of His body. ²²So when He was raised from the dead, His disciples remembered that He had said this. And they believed the Scripture and the statement Jesus had made.

²³While He was in Jerusalem at the Passover Festival, many trusted in His name when they saw the signs He was doing. ²⁴Jesus, however, would not entrust Himself to them, since He knew them all ²⁵and because He did not need anyone to testify about man; for He Himself knew what was in man.

FOR PRAISE: No one has ever tasted true joy until they have tasted the joy that Jesus provides. Joy it must be remembered is different from happiness. Happiness depends upon what is happening. When what happens is happy then we are happy. But joy is that deep quality that remains even when unhappy times are upon us. And only a Christian has access to that. For that give Him praise.

ACCORDING TO THE other three Evangelists, Jesus was accused by false witnesses at His trial of saying that He would destroy the Temple and in three days build another. John here records the statement made by Jesus on which such a misunderstanding might be based. Jesus did not say, 'I will destroy' this building: but '[you] destroy this building and in three days I will raise it again'. Of course, to claim to rebuild such an impressive sanctuary that had been forty-six years in the making – and was still unfinished – was absurd. It amounts to a gently mocking rebuff of their demand for a miraculous sign. In fact, a sign is just what they will get, one even more extraordinary than any logic could imagine. He Himself in His own body is the ultimate manifestation and location of God on earth. In this body, the ultimate sacrifice for sin will soon be made. He would be raised from the dead in three days. And His resurrection would spell the end of the old Temple as the privileged focus of the presence and worship of God. In the Risen Jesus a new Temple, a new basis for communion with God, will be established.

DAY
213
JOHN 2:18-25

John 2:18-25

BIBLE
READING

¹⁸So the Jews replied to Him, "What sign [of authority] will You show us for doing these things?"

¹⁹Jesus answered, "Destroy this sanctuary, and I will raise it up in three days."

²⁰Therefore the Jews said, "This sanctuary took 46 years to build, and will You raise it up in three days?"

²¹But He was speaking about the sanctuary of His body. ²²So when He was raised from the dead, His disciples remembered that He had said this. And they believed the Scripture and the statement Jesus had made.

²³While He was in Jerusalem at the Passover Festival, many trusted in His name when they saw the signs He was doing. ²⁴Jesus, however, would not entrust Himself to them, since

He knew them all ²⁵and because He did not need anyone to testify about man; for He Himself knew what was in man.

PRAYER: O Father how can I ever thank You enough for the fact that my faith is not in a lifeless structure or physical building but in a resurrected and living Saviour. It was possible for Your Son to die, but not possible for Him to be held by death. Jesus is the 'new Temple' in Whom I find a new basis for worship, and a new foundation for praise. All honour and glory be to His peerless name for ever. Amen.

DAY 214
JOHN 2:23-3:8

JESUS KNOWS WHAT is going on inside people, says John, even within a man like Nicodemus, a teacher of the law. Learned in theology and Jewish thinking, Nicodemus is curious perhaps as to how Jesus fits into the scheme of things. There is continuity between Jesus and the Old Testament revelation that explains Him. But there is also a radical discontinuity as Nicodemus abruptly discovers. Jesus does emerge out of that Old Testament truth but in doing so bursts its banks. Jesus transcends the categories to which even a sympathetic Jewish teacher might try to confine Him. Nicodemus must have a heart and mind transplant to see this! He must be born again into a whole new way of looking at things in order to grasp it. He needs a spiritual regeneration and a spiritual revolution in his mind, if he is to enter into the reality of the kingdom of God as it has come in Jesus! The 'water' and 'Spirit' Jesus speaks of represent the transforming work of the Holy Spirit. What Jesus describes echoes Ezekiel's prophecy about the way in which God would wash people clean, implanting a new heart and imparting a new spirit to create God's new covenant people. Will Nicodemus – will we – allow the mysterious moving of God's Spirit to outflank all our old categories and give us a new spiritual birthday?

John 2:23-3:8

²³While He was in Jerusalem at the Passover Festival, many trusted in His name when they saw the signs He was doing. ²⁴Jesus, however, would not entrust Himself to them, since He knew them all ²⁵and because He did not need anyone to testify about man; for He Himself knew what was in man.

JESUS AND NICODEMUS

There was a man from the Pharisees named Nicodemus, a ruler of the Jews. ²This man came to Him at night and said, "Rabbi, we know that You have come from God as a teacher, for no one could perform these signs You do unless God were with him."

³Jesus replied, "I assure you: Unless someone is born again, he cannot see the kingdom of God."

⁴"But how can anyone be born when he is old?" Nicodemus asked Him. "Can he enter his mother's womb a second time and be born?"

⁵Jesus answered, "I assure you: Unless someone is born of water and the Spirit, he cannot enter the kingdom of God. ⁶Whatever is born of the flesh is flesh, and whatever is born of the Spirit is spirit. ⁷Do not be amazed that I told you that you must be born again. ⁸The wind blows where it pleases, and you hear its sound, but you don't know where it comes from or where it is going. So it is with everyone born of the Spirit."

FOR THANKSGIVING: If you were to say to a non-Christian that to become a follower of Jesus requires them to 'have a heart and mind transplant' it might cause them to question your sanity. But that is precisely what Christianity is - a revolutionary experience that equates to a heart and mind transplant. Give thanks to God for performing that miracle on you.

DAY 215

HAVING USED NEW covenant terminology - Ezekiel's 'water' and 'Spirit' - to describe the new birth necessary to enter God's kingdom, Jesus now utilises a strange old covenant story to make His point.

During the wilderness wanderings, the children of Israel grumble bitterly against God and under judgment succumb to deadly snake bites (Num. 21:4-9). Moses is told to make a bronze serpent and place it on top of a tall pole visible to the whole camp. Anyone who looks with faith upon this bronze snake is healed.

Now the same God who had made saving provision for a temporary bodily need, will make final provision of eternal life by lifting Jesus up on a cross. The key word is 'lifted up'. It implies not only physical elevation but spiritual exaltation and almost certainly reflects Isaiah's picture of the suffering servant being 'lifted up' in vindication and honour (Isa. 52:13). This is characteristic of John. In a marvellous and paradoxical sense, he sees the moment when Jesus is 'lifted up in glory' as occurring not at His resurrection or ascension but even earlier, at His crucifixion! Jesus' 'lifting up' on the cross is not just prior to, but synonymous with, His lifting up and exaltation in glory! His throne was Calvary; He reigns from the cross. Look to Him there in faith and you will live!

BIBLE READING

John 3:9-21

⁹"How can these things be?" asked Nicodemus.

¹⁰"Are you a teacher of Israel and don't know these things?" Jesus replied. ¹¹"I assure you: We speak what We know and We testify to what We have seen, but you do not accept Our testimony. ¹²If I have told you about things that happen on earth and you don't believe, how will you believe if I tell you about things of heaven? ¹³No one has ascended into heaven except the One who descended from heaven—the Son of Man. ¹⁴Just as Moses lifted up the snake in the wilderness, so the Son of Man must be lifted up, ¹⁵so that everyone who believes in

Him will have eternal life.

¹⁶"For God loved the world in this way: He gave His One and Only Son, so that everyone who believes in Him will not perish but have eternal life. ¹⁷For God did not send His Son into the world that He might condemn the world, but that the world might be saved through Him. ¹⁸Anyone who believes in Him is not condemned, but anyone who does not believe is already condemned, because he has not believed in the name of the One and Only Son of God.

¹⁹"This, then, is the judgment: the light has come into the world, and people loved darkness rather than the light because their deeds were evil. ²⁰For everyone who practices wicked things hates the light and avoids it, so that his deeds may not be exposed. ²¹But anyone who lives by the truth comes to the light, so that his works may be shown to be accomplished by God."

THOUGHT: It's interesting that a serpent is both a symbol of sin and a symbol of salvation. It is interesting also that the most effective antidote for a snakebite is the snake venom itself. The cure is that which caused the disease. When our Lord was crucified our sins were crucified in Him. He became our sin that He might be our salvation. Looking up 2 Corinthians 5:21 will enlighten you further.

WHAT A TEACHER of Israel fails to grasp, a Samaritan woman is led to see. But the setting – Jacob's well in Sychar – intentionally evokes the era of the patriarchs, and connects Jesus again with the deep covenantal roots in Israel's story.

The old water of the Torah cannot completely satisfy, but the living water can. This inspires a change in worship. Worship no longer depends on a sacred site, be it a Samaritan mountain, nor even, more shockingly, the Temple in Jerusalem!

Some scholars detect a betrothal scene here, reminiscent of how Jacob met Rachel at a well (Gen.

DAY
216
JOHN 4:1-42

29:1-10) and linking the narrative to that of the wedding in Cana (2:1-10). If Jesus is the bridegroom (3:29), who is the bride if not Israel as the Old Testament affirms?

Like the provocative parable which features an outsider, a Samaritan man who proves faithful to the Torah by caring for the wounded traveller, so here, with a Samaritan woman, Yahweh's 'marriage' is not exclusively with Israel but with all who believe in His Christ. This needy woman, unsatisfied by her sexual indulgence, is now ready to meet her seventh and perfect match in Jesus. Here is the man that she, and we, have been waiting for, the perfection and wholeness of salvation for her and her family, and indeed for men and women everywhere (vv.28-29,42).

BIBLE READING | John 4:1-42

JESUS AND THE SAMARITAN WOMAN

4 When Jesus knew that the Pharisees heard He was making and baptizing more disciples than John [2](though Jesus Himself was not baptizing, but His disciples were), [3]He left Judea and went again to Galilee. [4]He had to travel through Samaria, [5]so He came to a town of Samaria called Sychar near the property that Jacob had given his son Joseph. [6]Jacob's well was there, and Jesus, worn out from His journey, sat down at the well. It was about six in the evening.

[7]A woman of Samaria came to draw water.

"Give Me a drink," Jesus said to her, [8]for His disciples had gone into town to buy food.

[9]"How is it that You, a Jew, ask for a drink from me, a Samaritan woman?" she asked Him. For Jews do not associate with Samaritans.

[10]Jesus answered, "If you knew the gift of God, and who is saying to you, 'Give Me a drink,' you would ask Him, and He would give you living water."

[11]"Sir," said the woman, "You don't even have a bucket, and the well is deep. So where do You get this 'living water'? [12]You aren't greater than our father Jacob, are You? He gave us the

well and drank from it himself, as did his sons and livestock."

¹³ Jesus said, "Everyone who drinks from this water will get thirsty again. ¹⁴But whoever drinks from the water that I will give him will never get thirsty again—ever! In fact, the water I will give him will become a well of water springing up within him for eternal life."

¹⁵"Sir," the woman said to Him, "give me this water so I won't get thirsty and come here to draw water."

¹⁶"Go call your husband," He told her, "and come back here."

¹⁷"I don't have a husband," she answered.

"You have correctly said, 'I don't have a husband,'" Jesus said. ¹⁸"For you've had five husbands, and the man you now have is not your husband. What you have said is true."

¹⁹"Sir," the woman replied, "I see that You are a prophet. ²⁰Our fathers worshiped on this mountain, yet you [Jews] say that the place to worship is in Jerusalem."

²¹Jesus told her, "Believe Me, woman, an hour is coming when you will worship the Father neither on this mountain nor in Jerusalem. ²²You Samaritans worship what you do not know. We worship what we do know, because salvation is from the Jews. ²³But an hour is coming, and is now here, when the true worshipers will worship the Father in spirit and truth. Yes, the Father wants such people to worship Him. ²⁴God is spirit, and those who worship Him must worship in spirit and truth."

²⁵The woman said to Him, "I know that Messiah is coming" (who is called Christ). "When He comes, He will explain everything to us."

²⁶"I am [He]," Jesus told her, "the One speaking to you."

THE RIPENED HARVEST

²⁷Just then His disciples arrived, and they were amazed that He was talking with a woman. Yet no one said, "What do You want?" or "Why are You talking with her?"

²⁸Then the woman left her water jar, went into town, and told the men, ²⁹"Come, see a man who told me everything I ever did! Could this be the Messiah?" ³⁰They left the town and made their way to Him.

³¹In the meantime the disciples kept urging Him, "Rabbi, eat something."

³²But He said, "I have food to eat that you don't know about."

³³The disciples said to one another, "Could someone have brought Him something to eat?"

³⁴"My food is to do the will of Him who sent Me and to finish His work," Jesus told them. ³⁵"Don't you say, 'There are still four more months, then comes the harvest'? Listen [to what] I'm telling you: Open your eyes and look at the fields, for they are ready for harvest. ³⁶The reaper is already receiving pay and gathering fruit for eternal life, so the sower and reaper can rejoice together. ³⁷For in this case the saying is true: 'One sows and another reaps.' ³⁸I sent you to reap what you didn't labor for; others have labored, and you have benefited from their labor."

THE SAVIOR OF THE WORLD

³⁹Now many Samaritans from that town believed in Him because of what the woman said when she testified, "He told me everything I ever did." ⁴⁰Therefore, when the Samaritans came to Him, they asked Him to stay with them, and He stayed there two days. ⁴¹Many more believed because of what He said. ⁴²And they told the woman, "We no longer believe because of what you said, for we have heard for ourselves and know that this really is the Savior of the world."

PRAYER: Lord Jesus, my Saviour and my God, I am so grateful that with Wesley I can say, 'Thou O Christ art all I want, more than all in Thee I find'. For years I tried to satisfy my soul with water that failed to quench my thirst, but one draught of the water that You give has taken away the ache and given me a new zest for life - true life. My heart is Yours for ever. Amen.

ONE OF JOHN'S aims is to show how Jesus brings to full reality the major themes and events of Israel, including, here, the Sabbath. John shows us that Jesus transforms the Sabbath regulations by being, Himself, the focus of the Sabbath-rest of God. The physical (v.5) and psychological (vv.6,13) barriers to the man's healing are considerable and, in addition, the religious climate of Sabbath-keeping precluded God working in this way.

But Jesus' action shows that it is wrong to regard the Sabbath as the day when God is not at work. The Sabbath laws were not meant to curtail life but to promote it. To prevent a healing on the Sabbath is therefore to go against the whole spirit and intention of the day when, says Jesus, 'My Father is still working.' Though His original creation work was completed to His satisfaction, God remains restless and unceasing in working for redemption in a sin-spoiled world. And where His Father works, the Son works. To believe in Jesus is to enter into God's redemptive rest and into the good of His saving achievement. This is what the lame man sampled. In Jesus the day of rest becomes the day of restoration! This does not set Jesus up in competition with God – as His accusers allege – but in fact reflects His dependence and humility, as He does only what He sees the Father doing.

DAY 217

JOHN 5:1-30

John 5:1-30

BIBLE READING

THE THIRD SIGN: HEALING THE SICK

5 After this, a Jewish festival took place, and Jesus went up to Jerusalem. ²By the Sheep Gate in Jerusalem there is a pool, called Bethesda in Hebrew, which has five colonnades. ³Within these lay a multitude of the sick—blind, lame, and paralyzed [—waiting for the moving of the water, ⁴because an angel would go down into the pool from time to time and stir up the water. Then the first one who got

in after the water was stirred up recovered from whatever ailment he had].

⁵One man was there who had been sick for 38 years. ⁶When Jesus saw him lying there and knew he had already been there a long time, He said to him, "Do you want to get well?"

⁷"Sir," the sick man answered, "I don't have a man to put me into the pool when the water is stirred up, but while I'm coming, someone goes down ahead of me."

⁸"Get up," Jesus told him, "pick up your bedroll and walk!" ⁹Instantly the man got well, picked up his bedroll, and started to walk.

Now that day was the Sabbath, ¹⁰so the Jews said to the man who had been healed, "This is the Sabbath! It's illegal for you to pick up your bedroll."

¹¹He replied, "The man who made me well told me, 'Pick up your bedroll and walk.' "

¹²"Who is this man who told you, 'Pick up [your bedroll] and walk?' " they asked. ¹³But the man who was cured did not know who it was, because Jesus had slipped away into the crowd that was there.

¹⁴After this, Jesus found him in the temple complex and said to him, "See, you are well. Do not sin any more, so that something worse doesn't happen to you." ¹⁵The man went and reported to the Jews that it was Jesus who had made him well.

HONORING THE FATHER AND THE SON

¹⁶Therefore, the Jews began persecuting Jesus because He was doing these things on the Sabbath. ¹⁷But Jesus responded to them, "My Father is still working, and I am working also." ¹⁸This is why the Jews began trying all the more to kill Him: not only was He breaking the Sabbath, but He was even calling God His own Father, making Himself equal with God.

¹⁹Then Jesus replied, "I assure you: The Son is not able to do anything on His own, but only what He sees the Father doing. For whatever the Father does, the Son also does these things in the same way. ²⁰For the Father loves the Son and shows Him everything He is doing, and He will show Him greater works than these so that you will be amazed. ²¹And just as the Father raises the dead and gives them life, so the

Son also gives life to anyone He wants to. [22]The Father, in fact, judges no one but has given all judgment to the Son, [23]so that all people will honor the Son just as they honor the Father. Anyone who does not honor the Son does not honor the Father who sent Him.

LIFE AND JUDGMENT

[24]"I assure you: Anyone who hears My word and believes Him who sent Me has eternal life and will not come under judgment but has passed from death to life.

[25]"I assure you: An hour is coming, and is now here, when the dead will hear the voice of the Son of God, and those who hear will live. [26]For just as the Father has life in Himself, so also He has granted to the Son to have life in Himself. [27]And He has granted Him the right to pass judgment, because He is the Son of Man. [28]Do not be amazed at this, because a time is coming when all who are in the graves will hear His voice [29]and come out—those who have done good things, to the resurrection of life, but those who have done wicked things, to the resurrection of judgment.

[30]"I can do nothing on My own. I judge only as I hear, and My judgment is righteous, because I do not seek My own will, but the will of Him who sent Me.

QUOTATION: 'We should walk through every day with eyes wide open to see what God would have us do, with ears alert to hear what he has to say, with hands ready to do the work he would have us do. This is how Jesus lived out his days when he was here on earth and this is how we should live them out too. His secret was that he did only what the Father was doing. That must be our secret too.' (Dr Cynddylan Jones)

WITH GREAT IRONY, John presents Jesus to us as on trial to which witnesses are called.

This links with Isaiah 40-55 where Yahweh and pagan gods go on trial before the world to determine who is the true God. In this 'trial', God looks to Israel to be His witness who will give testimony on His behalf as the one true God (Isa. 41:1-4,21-29; 43:8-13; 44:6-8; 45:20-25). John puts a subtle twist on this so that Jesus becomes both the accused who is on trial, and the judge who takes on God's role of giving a verdict! The terrible irony is that Jesus' accusers are siding with the pagans in lining up against Him!

Jesus calls four witnesses in His defence: John the Baptist (vv.33-35), the work the Father has given Him to do (v.36), the Father's personal affirmation (v.37) and, above all, the Scriptures themselves (vv.39-40). Here we are on familiar ground. The entire scriptural story of God, told so far through the story of God's people, Israel, points directly to Jesus and tells His story too. Jesus is the convergence point of that earlier stage of the story. Jesus is the narrative telling of God in full and concentrated form. He gathers up all previous revelation into His own account. He is the Bible's beating heart. His is the life-story told there, and to embrace Him is to find the life that is in the story.

John 5:31-47

FOUR WITNESSES TO JESUS

[31]"If I testify about Myself, My testimony is not valid. [32]There is Another who testifies about Me, and I know that the testimony He gives about Me is valid. [33]You have sent [messengers] to John, and he has testified to the truth. [34]I don't receive man's testimony, but I say these things so that you may be saved. [35]John was a burning and shining lamp, and for a time you were willing to enjoy his light.

[36]"But I have a greater testimony than John's because of the works that the Father has given Me to accomplish. These very

works I am doing testify about Me that the Father has sent Me. ³⁷The Father who sent Me has Himself testified about Me. You have not heard His voice at any time, and you haven't seen His form. ³⁸You don't have His word living in you, because you don't believe the One He sent. ³⁹You pore over the Scriptures because you think you have eternal life in them, yet they testify about Me. ⁴⁰And you are not willing to come to Me that you may have life.

⁴¹"I do not accept glory from men, ⁴²but I know you—that you have no love for God within you. ⁴³I have come in My Father's name, yet you don't accept Me. If someone else comes in his own name, you will accept him. ⁴⁴How can you believe? While accepting glory from one another, you don't seek the glory that comes from the only God. ⁴⁵Do not think that I will accuse you to the Father. Your accuser is Moses, on whom you have set your hope. ⁴⁶For if you believed Moses, you would believe Me, because he wrote about Me. ⁴⁷But if you don't believe his writings, how will you believe My words?"

> TO PONDER: Think about this on and off throughout the day - our faith is not a vague leap in the dark but is based on the reliable evidence of Scripture and eyewitness accounts of events that happened in history. Many in these days are seeking to overturn the Bible's veracity, but stand firm on its truth. Those who lose faith in Scripture often lose faith in Jesus. And vice versa.

DAY 219

JOHN 6:1-35

ECHOES OF THE Exodus pervade this passage: the crossing of the sea (vv.1,12-21), the climbing of a mountain (v.3), the timing at Passover (v.4), the gift of bread/manna in the desert (vv.6-13,31-33). In addition, 'manna' became in later Jewish thinking a metaphor for the Torah. So the comparison being made becomes clear. Jesus is the new Moses, He Himself is the covenant provision of God's people, He is the Passover Lamb of sacrifice, He is leading God's people out in a new exodus!

The account of the walking on the water at this point strengthens the Exodus allusion and enhances the contrast being made. The stakes are high. No longer mere physical hunger needs to be assuaged. If that is all, says Jesus, you seek Me for the wrong reasons (v.26). Our energies are consumed in the search for bread but need to be exerted in the quest for what really matters, what really lasts, which is eternal life (v.27). In fact, we can do nothing to attain this except believe (v.29). Like the offer of Lady Wisdom (Prov. 9:1-6) or the invitation of the wise man (Isa. 55:1), the challenge of Jesus is to find true satisfaction in Him. Just as the woman at the well was looking for water, so now men look for bread. To drink His living water is never to thirst again; to eat His living bread is never to go hungry again (v.35).

John 6:1-35

BIBLE
READING

THE FOURTH SIGN: FEEDING 5,000

6 After this, Jesus crossed the Sea of Galilee (or Tiberias). ²And a huge crowd was following Him because they saw the signs that He was performing on the sick. ³So Jesus went up a mountain and sat down there with His disciples.

⁴Now the Passover, a Jewish festival, was near. ⁵Therefore, when Jesus looked up and noticed a huge crowd coming toward Him, He asked Philip, "Where will we buy bread so these people can eat?" ⁶He asked this to test him, for He Himself knew what He was going to do.

⁷Philip answered, "Two hundred denarii worth of bread wouldn't be enough for each of them to have a little."

⁸One of His disciples, Andrew, Simon Peter's brother, said to Him, ⁹"There's a boy here who has five barley loaves and two fish—but what are they for so many?"

¹⁰Then Jesus said, "Have the people sit down."

There was plenty of grass in that place, so they sat down. The men numbered about 5,000. ¹¹Then Jesus took the loaves, and after giving thanks He distributed them to those who were seated—so also with the fish, as much as they wanted.

¹²When they were full, He told His disciples, "Collect the leftovers so that nothing is wasted." ¹³So they collected them and filled 12 baskets with the pieces from the five barley loaves that were left over by those who had eaten.

¹⁴When the people saw the sign He had done, they said, "This really is the Prophet who was to come into the world!" ¹⁵Therefore, when Jesus knew that they were about to come and take Him by force to make Him king, He withdrew again to the mountain by Himself.

THE FIFTH SIGN: WALKING ON WATER

¹⁶When evening came, His disciples went down to the sea, ¹⁷got into a boat, and started across the sea to Capernaum. Darkness had already set in, but Jesus had not yet come to them. ¹⁸Then a high wind arose, and the sea began to churn. ¹⁹After they had rowed about three or four miles, they saw Jesus walking on the sea. He was coming near the boat, and they were afraid.

²⁰But He said to them, "It is I. Don't be afraid!" ²¹Then they were willing to take Him on board, and at once the boat was at the shore where they were heading.

THE BREAD OF LIFE

²²The next day, the crowd that had stayed on the other side of the sea knew there had been only one boat. [They also knew] that Jesus had not boarded the boat with His disciples, but that His disciples had gone off alone. ²³Some boats from Tiberias came near the place where they ate the bread after the Lord gave thanks. ²⁴When the crowd saw that neither Jesus nor His disciples were there, they got into the boats and went to Capernaum looking for Jesus.

²⁵When they found Him on the other side of the sea, they said to Him, "Rabbi, when did You get here?"

²⁶Jesus answered, "I assure you: You are looking for Me, not because you saw the signs, but because you ate the loaves and were filled. ²⁷Don't work for the food that perishes but for the food that lasts for eternal life, which the Son of Man will give you, because God the Father has set His seal of approval on Him."

²⁸"What can we do to perform the works of God?" they asked.

²⁹Jesus replied, "This is the work of God: that you believe in the One He has sent."

³⁰"What sign then are You going to do so we may see and believe You?" they asked. "What are You going to perform? ³¹Our fathers ate the manna in the wilderness, just as it is written: 'He gave them bread from heaven to eat.'"

³²Jesus said to them, "I assure you: Moses didn't give you the bread from heaven, but My Father gives you the real bread from heaven. ³³For the bread of God is the One who comes down from heaven and gives life to the world."

³⁴Then they said, "Sir, give us this bread always!"

³⁵"I am the bread of life," Jesus told them. "No one who comes to Me will ever be hungry, and no one who believes in Me will ever be thirsty again.

THOUGHT: One of the most powerful truths in the whole of Scripture and one which the Bible everywhere makes clear is this – there are desires in our souls which nothing on earth can satisfy. Not even the best things of earth. In some ways we have a kinship with the beasts, but so far as we can tell, earth satisfies them. However it does not satisfy us. We are made for God. He alone satisfies.

IN THE NEW exodus, Jesus is the living bread which comes down from heaven to feed Israel and a world which is parched and hungry in the wilderness of alienation from God. By faith He becomes the true food of the genuine 'sons of God' who are vindicated by being raised up on the last day. Can a mere carpenter from Nazareth achieve this? His accusers murmur at His origins (vv.41-42) but cannot deny that, like the manna, Jesus is a fact within history. Next, His opponents question how He will feed the entire world (v.52). Here is an even greater scandal. For this bread which is Jesus to become life for others, He must offer His flesh-and-blood body on the cross. To receive eternal life is to appropriate by faith the reality of His

DAY
220
JOHN 6:35-71

569

incarnation and sacrificial offering of His broken body and poured-out blood on the cross (v.51). If we 'take Him' into our lives, He becomes our covenant provision. If we can stomach this truth about Him, including His ascension (v.62) - which His disciples initially found difficult to do (v.60) - then a covenant bond is forged between God and us. It is a bond we renew every time we take bread and wine. Not that the materiality of flesh or bread counts for much except as vehicles for the life-giving power of the Spirit. His very words which tell us this, are charged with life and power.

BIBLE READING

John 6:35-71

³⁵"I am the bread of life," Jesus told them. "No one who comes to Me will ever be hungry, and no one who believes in Me will ever be thirsty again. ³⁶But as I told you, you've seen Me, and yet you do not believe. ³⁷Everyone the Father gives Me will come to Me, and the one who comes to Me I will never cast out. ³⁸For I have come down from heaven, not to do My will, but the will of Him who sent Me. ³⁹This is the will of Him who sent Me: that I should lose none of those He has given Me but should raise them up on the last day. ⁴⁰For this is the will of My Father: that everyone who sees the Son and believes in Him may have eternal life, and I will raise him up on the last day."

⁴¹Therefore the Jews started complaining about Him, because He said, "I am the bread that came down from heaven." ⁴²They were saying, "Isn't this Jesus the son of Joseph, whose father and mother we know? How can He now say, 'I have come down from heaven'?"

⁴³Jesus answered them, "Stop complaining among yourselves. ⁴⁴No one can come to Me unless the Father who sent Me draws him, and I will raise him up on the last day. ⁴⁵It is written in the Prophets: 'And they will all be taught by God.' Everyone who has listened to and learned from the Father comes to Me— ⁴⁶not that anyone has seen the Father except the One who is from God. He has seen the Father.

⁴⁷"I assure you: Anyone who believes has eternal life. ⁴⁸I

am the bread of life. ⁴⁹Your fathers ate the manna in the wilderness, and they died. ⁵⁰This is the bread that comes down from heaven so that anyone may eat of it and not die. ⁵¹I am the living bread that came down from heaven. If anyone eats of this bread he will live forever. The bread that I will give for the life of the world is My flesh."

⁵²At that, the Jews argued among themselves, "How can this man give us His flesh to eat?"

⁵³So Jesus said to them, "I assure you: Unless you eat the flesh of the Son of Man and drink His blood, you do not have life in yourselves. ⁵⁴Anyone who eats My flesh and drinks My blood has eternal life, and I will raise him up on the last day, ⁵⁵because My flesh is real food and My blood is real drink. ⁵⁶The one who eats My flesh and drinks My blood lives in Me, and I in him. ⁵⁷Just as the living Father sent Me and I live because of the Father, so the one who feeds on Me will live because of Me. ⁵⁸This is the bread that came down from heaven; it is not like the manna your fathers ate—and they died. The one who eats this bread will live forever."

⁵⁹He said these things while teaching in the synagogue in Capernaum.

MANY DISCIPLES DESERT JESUS

⁶⁰Therefore, when many of His disciples heard this, they said, "This teaching is hard! Who can accept it?"

⁶¹Jesus, knowing in Himself that His disciples were complaining about this, asked them, "Does this offend you? ⁶²Then what if you were to observe the Son of Man ascending to where He was before? ⁶³The Spirit is the One who gives life. The flesh doesn't help at all. The words that I have spoken to you are spirit and are life. ⁶⁴But there are some among you who don't believe." (For Jesus knew from the beginning those who would not believe and the one who would betray Him.) ⁶⁵He said, "This is why I told you that no one can come to Me unless it is granted to him by the Father."

⁶⁶From that moment many of His disciples turned back and no longer accompanied Him. ⁶⁷Therefore Jesus said to the Twelve, "You don't want to go away too, do you?"

⁶⁸Simon Peter answered, "Lord, who will we go to? You have the words of eternal life. ⁶⁹We have come to believe and know

that You are the Holy One of God!"

⁷⁰Jesus replied to them, "Didn't I choose you, the Twelve? Yet one of you is the Devil!" ⁷¹He was referring to Judas, Simon Iscariot's son, one of the Twelve, because he was going to betray Him.

FOR PRAISE: Prepare your heart to give God praise and thanksgiving for the fact that Christ is the bread that fully satisfies our souls. What better than to sing those words from the well-known hymn of William Williams, 'Guide me, O Thou great Jehovah':

Bread of heaven; Bread of heaven
Feed me now and ever more,
Feed me now and ever more.

DAY 221

ISAIAH 44:3; 55:1
JOHN 7:37-39

THE FEAST OF Tabernacles was an autumn harvest festival during which people lived in makeshift shelters or booths to commemorate the departure from Egypt and the pilgrimage in the wilderness. On each of the seven days of the Feast, a laver filled with water was poured out by the priest beside the altar. This echoes Zechariah's picture: 'living water will flow out from Jerusalem' (Zech. 14:8) which likely merges in Jesus' mind with Ezekiel's vision of living water flowing out from the Temple (Ezek. 47:1-12). These deep Old Testament allusions lie behind His cry on the last day of the Feast: 'If anyone is thirsty, he should come to Me and drink! The one who believes in Me, as the Scripture has said, will have streams of living water flow from deep within him.' When the leaders led the returned exiles in a prayer of penitence, they linked the Feast of Tabernacles with the pillar and cloud, the water from the rock, the manna in the desert, the giving of the Torah and the outpouring of God's Spirit (Neh. 8:5-18; 9:12-20). Once more the connection with vital

Old Testament traditions tells the Jesus story as one of climax and consummation. What the Feast once offered in symbol, Jesus will offer in full reality as the gift of the Holy Spirit, but only when He is glorified by death and resurrection (v.39)!

Isaiah 44:3

BIBLE READING

³ For I will pour water on the thirsty land,
    and streams on the dry ground;
    I will pour out My Spirit on your descendants
    and My blessing on your offspring.

Isaiah 55:1

BIBLE READING

COME TO THE LORD

55 "Come, everyone who is thirsty,
        come to the waters;
    and you without money,
    come, buy, and eat!
    Come, buy wine and milk
    without money and without cost!

John 7:37-39

BIBLE READING

THE PROMISE OF THE SPIRIT

³⁷On the last and most important day of the festival, Jesus stood up and cried out, "If anyone is thirsty, he should come to Me and drink! ³⁸The one who believes in Me, as the Scripture has said, will have streams of living water flow from deep within him." ³⁹He said this about the Spirit, whom those who believed in Him were going to receive, for the Spirit had not yet been received, because Jesus had not yet been glorified.

PRAYER: Loving heavenly Father, I am so grateful that You pour streams of living water into our barren lives that we may be fruitful and a source of blessing to others. I realise also that nothing can flow in unless it can get out. Grant that I will be as eager to give as much as I am to receive. I want not only my thirst to be satisfied but also to satisfy the thirst of others. Use me for that purpose I pray. Amen.

DAY 222

JOHN 8:12-59

ON THE FIRST day of the Feast of Tabernacles, the great golden candelabra were lit. Symbolism is again focused and fulfilled in Jesus. Jesus is the true and ultimate light of the whole world. He speaks and embodies that transforming revelation that saves and changes people's lives. He assumes Israel's age-long vocation of being a light to the nations (Isa. 49). He reveals God supremely. By illuminating the truth, He exposes falsehood and darkness. He is the creative energy of light. As runners carry the Olympic flame in relays to the lighting of the Olympic fire when the time for the games has come, so the lawgivers and the prophets, the sages and singers of the earlier part of the story, have relayed the flame of God's self-revelation until they plunge it into the final conflagration of truth which is Jesus. The fire that He is, gathers up what has gone before and the blaze of truth burns higher and brighter than ever before so that the whole world can see and know. But who chooses to walk in His light? So the debate rages as to who are the true sons of Abraham (a debate Paul will have with the Galatians). The natural heirs of Abraham, Jesus asserts, are in fact in slavery and need the new and greater exodus He has come to bring (v.34). Those who acknowledge Him as the truth are set free to be a true son of Abraham.

John 8:12-59

THE LIGHT OF THE WORLD

[12]Then Jesus spoke to them again: "I am the light of the world. Anyone who follows Me will never walk in the darkness but will have the light of life."

[13]So the Pharisees said to Him, "You are testifying about Yourself. Your testimony is not valid."

[14]"Even if I testify about Myself," Jesus replied, "My testimony is valid, because I know where I came from and where I'm going. But you don't know where I come from or where I'm going. [15]You judge by human standards. I judge no one. [16]And if I do judge, My judgment is true, because I am not alone, but I and the Father who sent Me [judge together]. [17]Even in your law it is written that the witness of two men is valid. [18]I am the One who testifies about Myself, and the Father who sent Me testifies about Me."

[19]Then they asked Him, "Where is Your Father?"

"You know neither Me nor My Father," Jesus answered. "If you knew Me, you would also know My Father." [20]He spoke these words by the treasury, while teaching in the temple complex. But no one seized Him, because His hour had not come.

JESUS PREDICTS HIS DEPARTURE

[21]Then He said to them again, "I'm going away; you will look for Me, and you will die in your sin. Where I'm going, you cannot come."

[22]So the Jews said again, "He won't kill Himself, will He, since He says, 'Where I'm going, you cannot come'?"

[23]"You are from below," He told them, "I am from above. You are of this world; I am not of this world. [24]Therefore I told you that you will die in your sins. For if you do not believe that I am [He], you will die in your sins."

[25]"Who are You?" they questioned.

"Precisely what I've been telling you from the very beginning," Jesus told them. [26]"I have many things to say and to judge about you, but the One who sent Me is true, and what I have heard from Him—these things I tell the world."

[27]They did not know He was speaking to them about the Father. [28]So Jesus said to them, "When you lift up the Son of Man, then you will know that I am [He], and that I do nothing on My own. But just as the Father taught Me, I say these things. [29]The One who sent Me is with Me. He has not left Me alone, because I always do what pleases Him."

TRUTH AND FREEDOM

[30]As He was saying these things, many believed in Him. [31]So Jesus said to the Jews who had believed Him, "If you continue in My word, you really are My disciples. [32]You will know the truth, and the truth will set you free."

[33]"We are descendants of Abraham," they answered Him, "and we have never been enslaved to anyone. How can You say, 'You will become free'?"

[34]Jesus responded, "I assure you: Everyone who commits sin is a slave of sin. [35]A slave does not remain in the household forever, but a son does remain forever. [36]Therefore if the Son sets you free, you really will be free. [37]I know you are descendants of Abraham, but you are trying to kill Me because My word is not welcome among you. [38]I speak what I have seen in the presence of the Father, and therefore you do what you have heard from your father."

[39]"Our father is Abraham!" they replied.

"If you were Abraham's children," Jesus told them, "you would do what Abraham did. [40]But now you are trying to kill Me, a man who has told you the truth that I heard from God. Abraham did not do this! [41]You're doing what your father does."

"We weren't born of sexual immorality," they said. "We have one Father—God."

[42]Jesus said to them, "If God were your Father, you would love Me, because I came from God and I am here. For I didn't come on My own, but He sent Me. [43]Why don't you understand what I say? Because you cannot listen to My word. [44]You are of your father the Devil, and you want to carry out your father's desires. He was a murderer from the beginning and has not stood in the truth, because there is no truth in him. When he tells a lie, he speaks from his own nature, because he is a liar and the father of liars. [45]Yet because I tell the truth, you

do not believe Me. [46]Who among you can convict Me of sin? If I tell the truth, why don't you believe Me? [47]The one who is from God listens to God's words. This is why you don't listen, because you are not from God."

JESUS AND ABRAHAM

[48]The Jews responded to Him, "Aren't we right in saying that You're a Samaritan and have a demon?"

[49]"I do not have a demon," Jesus answered. "On the contrary, I honor My Father and you dishonor Me. [50]I do not seek My glory; the One who seeks it also judges. [51]I assure you: If anyone keeps My word, he will never see death—ever!"

[52]Then the Jews said, "Now we know You have a demon. Abraham died and so did the prophets. You say, 'If anyone keeps My word, he will never taste death—ever!' [53]Are You greater than our father Abraham who died? Even the prophets died. Who do You pretend to be?"

[54]"If I glorify Myself," Jesus answered, "My glory is nothing. My Father—you say about Him, 'He is our God'—He is the One who glorifies Me. [55]You've never known Him, but I know Him. If I were to say I don't know Him, I would be a liar like you. But I do know Him, and I keep His word. [56]Your father Abraham was overjoyed that he would see My day; he saw it and rejoiced."

[57]The Jews replied, "You aren't 50 years old yet, and You've seen Abraham?"

[58]Jesus said to them, "I assure you: Before Abraham was, I am."

[59]At that, they picked up stones to throw at Him. But Jesus was hidden and went out of the temple complex.

THOUGHT: 'Light', says one dictionary, 'is the agent by which objects are made visible'. How glad we are, when we find ourselves enshrouded in darkness, to reach for an electric light switch or a torch. The world is a dark place, but Jesus brings light into that darkness. Just where would we be without Jesus? In darkness, stumbling from one day to another. Aren't you glad that He has lighted up your life?

DAY 223

LUKE 13:10-30

THE EFFECT OF Jesus' ministry is to redefine Israel so that who belongs to the true family of Abraham is determined by their response to Him.

This is why His healings are not only signs of the kingdom or acts of compassion but symbols of the healing of the nation (cf.Isa. 35).

The release of Israel from satanic oppression into the freedom of God's kingdom is embodied in the liberation of one pain-wracked woman from her crippling infirmity. The act of deliverance which heals her, at the same time rescues her from the margins of society and restores her to the full status of a true 'daughter of Abraham' (v.16).

The revolution of God's reign brought by Jesus turns upside down the entrenched social order. Those who thought they were 'insiders' may find themselves 'outsiders', while those once considered 'outside the sphere of God's grace' will, through the narrow door of repentance and faith, find a way into God's kingdom feast. What Jesus says is not, of course, an anti-Jewish statement. How could it be, seeing Jesus is a Jew. But it is a prophetic indictment of the tendency on the part of God's people to become inward-looking, self-regarding, exclusive or possessive of God's truth and salvation. Through Jesus, Abraham's worldwide family of faith is coming to birth in the radical grace of the kingdom of God.

BIBLE READING

Luke 13:10-30

HEALING A DAUGHTER OF ABRAHAM

¹⁰As He was teaching in one of the synagogues on the Sabbath, ¹¹a woman was there who had been disabled by a spirit for over 18 years. She was bent over and could not straighten up at all. ¹²When Jesus saw her, He called out to her, "Woman, you are free of your disability." ¹³Then He laid His hands on her, and instantly she was restored and began to glorify God.

¹⁴But the leader of the synagogue, indignant because Jesus

had healed on the Sabbath, responded by telling the crowd, "There are six days when work should be done; therefore come on those days and be healed and not on the Sabbath day."

¹⁵But the Lord answered him and said, "Hypocrites! Doesn't each one of you untie his ox or donkey from the feeding trough on the Sabbath and lead it to water? ¹⁶Satan has bound this woman, a daughter of Abraham, for 18 years—shouldn't she be untied from this bondage on the Sabbath day?"

¹⁷When He had said these things, all His adversaries were humiliated, but the whole crowd was rejoicing over all the glorious things He was doing.

THE PARABLES OF THE MUSTARD SEED AND OF THE YEAST

¹⁸He said therefore, "What is the kingdom of God like, and what can I compare it to? ¹⁹It's like a mustard seed that a man took and sowed in his garden. It grew and became a tree, and the birds of the sky nested in its branches."

²⁰Again He said, "What can I compare the kingdom of God to? ²¹It's like yeast that a woman took and mixed into 50 pounds of flour until it spread through the entire mixture."

THE NARROW WAY

²²He went through one town and village after another, teaching and making His way to Jerusalem. ²³"Lord," someone asked Him, "are there few being saved?"

He said to them, ²⁴"Make every effort to enter through the narrow door, because I tell you, many will try to enter and won't be able ²⁵once the homeowner gets up and shuts the door. Then you will stand outside and knock on the door, saying, 'Lord, open up for us!' He will answer you, 'I don't know you or where you're from.' ²⁶Then you will say, 'We ate and drank in Your presence, and You taught in our streets!' ²⁷But He will say, 'I tell you, I don't know you or where you're from. Get away from Me, all you workers of unrighteousness!' ²⁸There will be weeping and gnashing of teeth in that place, when you see Abraham, Isaac, Jacob, and all the prophets in the kingdom of God but yourselves thrown out. ²⁹They will come from east and west, from north and south, and recline at the table in the kingdom of God. ³⁰Note this: some are last who will be first, and some are first who will be last."

TO PONDER: What is your response to today's reading? One suggested response ought to be heartfelt gratitude to God for making you a full member of His family. Once you were an outsider, but now you are an insider. Think back to the moment (or the period) of your conversion and reflect on what God has done for you in the intervening years. Think and give thanks.

DAY
224

LUKE 19:1-10

AS WE HAVE seen, the upside-down kingdom of God inaugurated by Jesus is good news for the 'least, the last and the lost'.

The least have greatness thrust upon them by grace; the last in line come first; the lost are found. Those regarded – whether by officialdom or in popular perception – as beyond the pale through sickness or trade or poverty are now, through grace, reinstated as 'sons and daughters of Abraham'.

Tax-collectors like Zacchaeus were thought by many people to have disqualified themselves by collaborating with Rome either directly or, more likely, indirectly through working for Herod. Jesus targets such people.

His table-fellowship when He 'eats with sinners' is His way of acting out the welcome and acceptance God offers the repentant sinner.

Eating with such a notorious 'sinner' does not contaminate Jesus but 'sanctifies' Zacchaeus! 'Today salvation has come to this house' – and this without recourse to Temple or sacrificial system!

God's covenant family is being reconstituted: 'he, too, is a son of Abraham' (v.9).

The only question remains: will Jerusalem, the Temple and the once-born sons of Abraham recognise this 'today' as a visitation of God in judgment and grace (vv.41-44)?

Luke 19:1-10

JESUS VISITS ZACCHAEUS

19 He entered Jericho and was passing through. ²There was a man named Zacchaeus who was a chief tax collector, and he was rich. ³He was trying to see who Jesus was, but he was not able because of the crowd, since he was a short man. ⁴So running ahead, he climbed up a sycamore tree to see Jesus, since He was about to pass that way. ⁵When Jesus came to the place, He looked up and said to him, "Zacchaeus, hurry and come down, because today I must stay at your house."

⁶So he quickly came down and welcomed Him joyfully. ⁷All who saw it began to complain, "He's gone to lodge with a sinful man!"

⁸But Zacchaeus stood there and said to the Lord, "Look, I'll give half of my possessions to the poor, Lord! And if I have extorted anything from anyone, I'll pay back four times as much!"

⁹"Today salvation has come to this house," Jesus told him, "because he too is a son of Abraham. ¹⁰For the Son of Man has come to seek and to save the lost."

FOR PRAISE: The Gospels list three classes of people who qualify for salvation - the last, the least and the lost. In which group were you? Did you come to Christ in your later years? He promises to pay you in full. Were you deprived of education and have few talents? He gives gifts that more than compensate. Did you feel like a 'missing person'? You have been found. All good reasons for exuberant praise.

JOHN 10:1-18

DAY 225

EZEKIEL HAD ONCE savaged the false shepherds who mislead God's people, and pledged that God Himself would come to shepherd His flock. When Jesus says that He is the 'good [or genuine] shepherd', He is making, therefore, both a highly charged political claim indicting Israel's current leaders and a bold theological claim about exactly where Israel's God is currently present and active! By comparison with Him all other leaders are thieves, perhaps, seeking false ways of being Israel (cf.12:6). They are perhaps would-be revolutionaries advocating violence as the way to achieve God's kingdom – the word 'robber' is applied elsewhere to nationalistic terrorists and guerrilla fighters like Barabbas (18:40).

Ezekiel saw God coming as shepherd only on the other side of the 'death and resurrection' of the Exile. This shepherd is willing to undergo death for God's sheep that He might bring them up in resurrection to the secure pasture and abundant provision of His risen life (vv.10-11,14,18).

Like his namesake, Joshua, Jesus comes to the sheepfold of Israel (Num. 27:15-17), but now to call out His new Messianic flock. And He has other sheep scattered in all the nations whom He will bring into one fold under one shepherd, creating the one covenant family God has always desired.

BIBLE READING

John 10:1-18

THE IDEAL SHEPHERD

10 "I assure you: Anyone who doesn't enter the sheep pen by the door but climbs in some other way, is a thief and a robber. ²The one who enters by the door is the shepherd of the sheep. ³The doorkeeper opens it for him, and the sheep hear his voice. He calls his own sheep by name and leads them out. ⁴When he has brought all his own outside, he goes ahead of them. The sheep follow him because they recognize his voice. ⁵They will never follow a stranger; instead

they will run away from him, because they don't recognize the voice of strangers."

⁶Jesus gave them this illustration, but they did not understand what He was telling them.

THE GOOD SHEPHERD

⁷So Jesus said again, "I assure you: I am the door of the sheep. ⁸All who came before Me are thieves and robbers, but the sheep didn't listen to them. ⁹I am the door. If anyone enters by Me, he will be saved and will come in and go out and find pasture. ¹⁰A thief comes only to steal and to kill and to destroy. I have come that they may have life and have it in abundance.

¹¹"I am the good shepherd. The good shepherd lays down his life for the sheep. ¹²The hired man, since he is not the shepherd and doesn't own the sheep, leaves them and runs away when he sees a wolf coming. The wolf then snatches and scatters them. ¹³[This happens] because he is a hired man and doesn't care about the sheep.

¹⁴"I am the good shepherd. I know My own sheep, and they know Me, ¹⁵as the Father knows Me, and I know the Father. I lay down My life for the sheep. ¹⁶But I have other sheep that are not of this fold; I must bring them also, and they will listen to My voice. Then there will be one flock, one shepherd. ¹⁷This is why the Father loves Me, because I am laying down My life so I may take it up again. ¹⁸No one takes it from Me, but I lay it down on My own. I have the right to lay it down, and I have the right to take it up again. I have received this command from My Father."

THOUGHT: D.L. Moody once said, 'When Jesus announced that he is "the good shepherd" he sacked all the others and made it clear that the job was now his forever.' Present-day pastors and spiritual leaders are really under-shepherds, working under the direction of the good shepherd. They sometimes fail but the good shepherd never fails. His care and concern know no bounds.

DAY
226

MATTHEW 16:13-28

PETER'S CONFESSION OF Him as the Christ, draws from Jesus an amazing statement. The God-given revelation about Jesus is to form the basis of a renewed people of God. On an entirely new foundation-rock - confession of Him as the Christ - the 'ecclesia' of God will be built. In effect, Jesus is daringly reconstituting Israel around Himself!

Extraordinary as this is, even more astounding is the way in which Jesus says it will occur - as He suffers, is killed and on the third day rises again (v.21)!

Already pre-figured by Hosea (6:3) and expanded later in Ezekiel's vision of the dry bones (Ezek. 37), the restoration of the people of God will take place when 'resurrection' as a metaphor becomes resurrection as an actuality!

Jesus was throwing down the gauntlet to His contemporaries. Take up your cross and follow Me. As if to say: 'Come and be Israel My way! Come down into death with Me, the suffering servant Israel and rise up with Me your anointed Messianic King as the new covenant people of God, cleansed, forgiven and empowered to be the Israel God intended!'

Everything in God's purposes for His people Israel and through them for the world are converging on Jesus.

BIBLE READING

Matthew 16:13-28

PETER'S CONFESSION OF THE MESSIAH

¹³When Jesus came to the region of Caesarea Philippi, He asked His disciples, "Who do people say that the Son of Man is?"

¹⁴And they said, "Some say John the Baptist; others, Elijah; still others, Jeremiah or one of the prophets."

¹⁵"But you," He asked them, "who do you say that I am?"

¹⁶Simon Peter answered, "You are the Messiah, the Son of the living God!"

¹⁷And Jesus responded, "Simon son of Jonah, you are blessed because flesh and blood did not reveal this to you, but My

Father in heaven. ¹⁸And I also say to you that you are Peter, and on this rock I will build My church, and the forces of Hades will not overpower it. ¹⁹I will give you the keys of the kingdom of heaven, and whatever you bind on earth is already bound in heaven, and whatever you loose on earth is already loosed in heaven."

²⁰And He gave the disciples orders to tell no one that He was the Messiah.

HIS DEATH AND RESURRECTION PREDICTED

²¹From then on Jesus began to point out to His disciples that He must go to Jerusalem and suffer many things from the elders, chief priests, and scribes, be killed, and be raised the third day. ²²Then Peter took Him aside and began to rebuke Him, "Oh no, Lord! This will never happen to You!"

²³But He turned and told Peter, "Get behind Me, Satan! You are an offense to Me because you're not thinking about God's concerns, but man's."

TAKE UP YOUR CROSS

²⁴Then Jesus said to His disciples, "If anyone wants to come with Me, he must deny himself, take up his cross, and follow Me. ²⁵For whoever wants to save his life will lose it, but whoever loses his life because of Me will find it. ²⁶What will it benefit a man if he gains the whole world yet loses his life? Or what will a man give in exchange for his life? ²⁷For the Son of Man is going to come with His angels in the glory of His Father, and then He will reward each according to what he has done. ²⁸I assure you: There are some standing here who will not taste death until they see the Son of Man coming in His kingdom."

PRAYER: O Father, the more I contemplate Your Son's commitment to living out Your story the more my heart is drawn to praise. For Him it meant death, but through that death and resurrection a new order was established. Help me understand even more clearly that I will only truly find my life in You when, like Jesus, I am willing to give it up here on earth. In His name I pray. Amen.

DAY 227

MARK 9:2-32

JOHN STRANGELY OMITS the transfiguration, perhaps because, for him, the glory of Jesus is diffused right through his account. John's Jesus is not so much transfigured on one occasion as translucent throughout. Mark seizes on the incident with relish to capture in miniature the story of Jesus who came down from glory into a sin-infested world. Jesus' story gathers up Israel's story too. Why else would Moses and Elijah appear. Do they represent the law and the prophets paying homage to Jesus? Perhaps. But, even more, they represent the glorious beginning of Israel's story under Moses and the anticipated end of Israel's story when Elijah was expected to reappear. So Jesus gathers up in Himself both ends of Israel's story. Moses, who steps out of Israel's past, is eclipsed; Elijah stepping out of Israel's future is upstaged. Like them we are urged to listen and to look only to Jesus who is central to God's story.

The human story being acted out in the valley of the shadow of death below is one of misery, confusion, debate and even powerless disciples. But in a world at the mercy of evil forces, the deliverance of one deranged boy heralds the defeat of evil on the cross. And the raising up of one corpse-like child is a trailer for the raising up in His resurrection of a whole new creation.

BIBLE READING

Mark 9:2-32

THE TRANSFIGURATION

²After six days Jesus took Peter, James, and John and led them up on a high mountain by themselves to be alone. He was transformed in front of them, ³and His clothes became dazzling—extremely white as no launderer on earth could whiten them. ⁴Elijah appeared to them with Moses, and they were talking with Jesus.

⁵Then Peter said to Jesus, "Rabbi, it is good for us to be here! Let us make three tabernacles: one for You, one for Moses, and

one for Elijah"— [6]because he did not know what he should say, since they were terrified.

[7]A cloud appeared, overshadowing them, and a voice came from the cloud:

> This is My beloved Son;
> listen to Him!

[8]Then suddenly, looking around, they no longer saw anyone with them except Jesus alone.

[9]As they were coming down from the mountain, He ordered them to tell no one what they had seen until the Son of Man had risen from the dead. [10]They kept this word to themselves, discussing what "rising from the dead" meant.

[11]Then they began to question Him, "Why do the scribes say that Elijah must come first?"

[12]"Elijah does come first and restores everything," He replied. "How then is it written about the Son of Man that He must suffer many things and be treated with contempt? [13]But I tell you that Elijah really has come, and they did to him whatever they wanted, just as it is written about him."

THE POWER OF FAITH OVER A DEMON

[14]When they came to the disciples, they saw a large crowd around them and scribes disputing with them. [15]All of a sudden, when the whole crowd saw Him, they were amazed and ran to greet Him. [16]Then He asked them, "What are you arguing with them about?"

[17]Out of the crowd, one man answered Him, "Teacher, I brought my son to You. He has a spirit that makes him unable to speak. [18]Wherever it seizes him, it throws him down, and he foams at the mouth, grinds his teeth, and becomes rigid. So I asked Your disciples to drive it out, but they couldn't."

[19]He replied to them, "You unbelieving generation! How long will I be with you? How long must I put up with you? Bring him to Me." [20]So they brought him to Him. When the spirit saw Him, it immediately convulsed the boy. He fell to the ground and rolled around, foaming at the mouth. [21]"How long has this been happening to him?" Jesus asked his father.

"From childhood," he said. [22]"And many times it has thrown him into fire or water to destroy him. But if You can do anything, have compassion on us and help us."

²³Then Jesus said to him, "'If You can?' Everything is possible to the one who believes."

²⁴Immediately the father of the boy cried out, "I do believe! Help my unbelief."

²⁵When Jesus saw that a crowd was rapidly coming together, He rebuked the unclean spirit, saying to it, "You mute and deaf spirit, I command you: come out of him and never enter him again!"

²⁶Then it came out, shrieking and convulsing him violently. The boy became like a corpse, so that many said, "He's dead." ²⁷But Jesus, taking him by the hand, raised him, and he stood up.

²⁸After He went into a house, His disciples asked Him privately, "Why couldn't we drive it out?"

²⁹And He told them, "This kind can come out by nothing but prayer [and fasting]."

THE SECOND PREDICTION OF HIS DEATH

³⁰Then they left that place and made their way through Galilee, but He did not want anyone to know it. ³¹For He was teaching His disciples and telling them, "The Son of Man is being betrayed into the hands of men. They will kill Him, and after He is killed, He will rise three days later." ³²But they did not understand this statement, and they were afraid to ask Him.

QUOTATION: 'Reflect on this fact concerning the three who saw the transfiguration. These three amazed disciples who were eyewitnesses of his majesty, who heard the voice of God ... soon backslid. Mark this: glorious manifestations of divine power in lofty mountain ranges are not in themselves any guarantee of security against deflection and failure in the spiritual life.' (Leonard Ravenhill)

THE FIRST MAJOR section of John's Gospel (chs. 1-11) where Jesus appears to the world and to Israel is now giving way to the second half of the book where His concern is much more for the disciples and where He meets with final rejection by Israel and the world.

With chapter 11, the Book of Signs - as chapters 1-11 have been called - gives way to the so-called Book of Glory (chs. 12-21).

Some people see a pattern of six signs or miracles in chapters 1-11 which climaxes with the raising of Lazarus as the seventh and greatest sign. The Word who initiated the original creation, now, with a 'loud voice', calls forth the dead as a sign of the new creation (11:43; cf.5:25). He who had the first word on the old creation (1:1ff), now has the last word on it - resurrection. And Lazarus' resuscitation which returns him to the old world as it is - eventually to die again - turns out to be a dramatic sign of Christ's own imminent victory over death which inaugurates the new creation and releases Him into the freedom of the age to come never to die again. He is, in Himself, the resurrection and the life (v.25). But there is still to be a poignant climax to the end of the old creation. The great life-giver will give His life sacrificially in order to recreate Israel as a new covenant community and set in train the renewal of all God's creation.

John 11:1-44

LAZARUS DIES AT BETHANY

11 Now a man was sick, Lazarus, from Bethany, the village of Mary and her sister Martha. ²Mary was the one who anointed the Lord with fragrant oil and wiped His feet with her hair, and it was her brother Lazarus who was sick. ³So the sisters sent a message to Him: "Lord, the one You love is sick."

⁴When Jesus heard it, He said, "This sickness will not end in death but is for the glory of God, so that the Son of God may

be glorified through it." ⁵(Jesus loved Martha, her sister, and Lazarus.) ⁶So when He heard that he was sick, He stayed two more days in the place where He was. ⁷Then after that, He said to the disciples, "Let's go to Judea again."

⁸"Rabbi," the disciples told Him, "just now the Jews tried to stone You, and You're going there again?"

⁹"Aren't there 12 hours in a day?" Jesus answered. "If anyone walks during the day, he doesn't stumble, because he sees the light of this world. ¹⁰If anyone walks during the night, he does stumble, because the light is not in him." ¹¹He said this, and then He told them, "Our friend Lazarus has fallen asleep, but I'm on My way to wake him up."

¹²Then the disciples said to Him, "Lord, if he has fallen asleep, he will get well."

¹³Jesus, however, was speaking about his death, but they thought He was speaking about natural sleep. ¹⁴So Jesus then told them plainly, "Lazarus has died. ¹⁵I'm glad for you that I wasn't there so that you may believe. But let's go to him."

¹⁶Then Thomas (called "Twin") said to his fellow disciples, "Let's go so that we may die with Him."

THE RESURRECTION AND THE LIFE

¹⁷When Jesus arrived, He found that Lazarus had already been in the tomb four days. ¹⁸Bethany was near Jerusalem (about two miles away). ¹⁹Many of the Jews had come to Martha and Mary to comfort them about their brother. ²⁰As soon as Martha heard that Jesus was coming, she went to meet Him. But Mary remained seated in the house.

²¹Then Martha said to Jesus, "Lord, if You had been here, my brother wouldn't have died. ²²Yet even now I know that whatever You ask from God, God will give You."

²³"Your brother will rise again," Jesus told her.

²⁴Martha said, "I know that he will rise again in the resurrection at the last day."

²⁵Jesus said to her, "I am the resurrection and the life. The one who believes in Me, even if he dies, will live. ²⁶Everyone who lives and believes in Me will never die—ever. Do you believe this?"

²⁷"Yes, Lord," she told Him, "I believe You are the Messiah, the Son of God, who was to come into the world."

JESUS SHARES THE SORROW OF DEATH

[28]Having said this, she went back and called her sister Mary, saying in private, "The Teacher is here and is calling for you."

[29]As soon as she heard this, she got up quickly and went to Him. [30]Jesus had not yet come into the village but was still in the place where Martha had met Him. [31]The Jews who were with her in the house consoling her saw that Mary got up quickly and went out. So they followed her, supposing that she was going to the tomb to cry there.

[32]When Mary came to where Jesus was and saw Him, she fell at His feet and told Him, "Lord, if You had been here, my brother would not have died!"

[33]When Jesus saw her crying, and the Jews who had come with her crying, He was angry in His spirit and deeply moved. [34]"Where have you put him?" He asked.

"Lord," they told Him, "come and see."

[35]Jesus wept.

[36]So the Jews said, "See how He loved him!" [37]But some of them said, "Couldn't He who opened the blind man's eyes also have kept this man from dying?"

THE SEVENTH SIGN: RAISING LAZARUS FROM THE DEAD

[38]Then Jesus, angry in Himself again, came to the tomb. It was a cave, and a stone was lying against it. [39]"Remove the stone," Jesus said.

Martha, the dead man's sister, told Him, "Lord, he already stinks. It's been four days."

[40]Jesus said to her, "Didn't I tell you that if you believed you would see the glory of God?"

[41]So they removed the stone. Then Jesus raised His eyes and said, "Father, I thank You that You heard Me. [42]I know that You always hear Me, but because of the crowd standing here I said this, so they may believe You sent Me." [43]After He said this, He shouted with a loud voice, "Lazarus, come out!" [44]The dead man came out bound hand and foot with linen strips and with his face wrapped in a cloth. Jesus said to them, "Loose him and let him go."

THOUGHT: A pastor once asked his congregation if they knew the precise moment when Jesus used the phrase 'I am the resurrection and the life'. Most replied that it was after He was resurrected from the dead. 'No,' said the pastor. 'He said it before not after.' He went on to say, 'Jesus is not the resurrection because He rose from the dead; He rose from the dead because He is the resurrection.'

DAY
229

JOHN 11:45-12:19

HERE JOHN RECORDS a whole series of prophetic words and actions. Firstly, Caiaphas unwittingly prophesies the fruitful and effective death of Jesus. Tragically, the high priest's action would not avert the destruction of Temple and city as he hoped (11:48,51) but would seal it! Jesus would indeed die for Israel and so gather into one enlarged fold the shared Jewish-Gentile community of God (11:52)!

But where Caiaphas plots His death, Mary, in a moving prophetic action, prepares for His burial (12:7), while the foot washing done to Jesus anticipates the foot washing done by Jesus (13:1ff.). Jesus then enters Jerusalem, prophetically demonstrating what kind of king He is. He is greeted with traditional Messianic applause. But only after the resurrection did the disciples – with Holy Spirit inspired hindsight – come to put two and two scriptures together and add them up to Jesus! Then they saw – as He had already seen (12:13-15) that it took the whole Old Testament story to explain Him and He to fulfil it! And if 'the world has gone after Him' (12:19), what else should we expect, seeing that He is Israel's Messiah and the world's true Lord!

John 11:45-12:19

THE PLOT TO KILL JESUS

[45]Therefore many of the Jews who came to Mary and saw what He did believed in Him. [46]But some of them went to the Pharisees and told them what Jesus had done.

[47]So the chief priests and the Pharisees convened the Sanhedrin and said, "What are we going to do since this man does many signs? [48]If we let Him continue in this way, everybody will believe in Him! Then the Romans will come and remove both our place and our nation."

[49]One of them, Caiaphas, who was high priest that year, said to them, "You know nothing at all! [50]You're not considering that it is to your advantage that one man should die for the people rather than the whole nation perish." [51]He did not say this on his own, but being high priest that year he prophesied that Jesus was going to die for the nation, [52]and not for the nation only, but also to unite the scattered children of God. [53]So from that day on they plotted to kill Him. [54]Therefore Jesus no longer walked openly among the Jews but departed from there to the countryside near the wilderness, to a town called Ephraim. And He stayed there with the disciples.

[55]The Jewish Passover was near, and many went up to Jerusalem from the country to purify themselves before the Passover. [56]They were looking for Jesus and asking one another as they stood in the temple complex: "What do you think? He won't come to the festival, will He?" [57]The chief priests and the Pharisees had given orders that if anyone knew where He was, he should report it so they could arrest Him.

THE ANOINTING AT BETHANY

12 Six days before the Passover, Jesus came to Bethany where Lazarus was, the one Jesus had raised from the dead. [2]So they gave a dinner for Him there; Martha was serving them, and Lazarus was one of those reclining at the table with Him. [3]Then Mary took a pound of fragrant oil—pure and expensive nard—anointed Jesus' feet, and wiped His feet with her hair. So the house was filled with the fragrance of the oil.

[4]Then one of His disciples, Judas Iscariot (who was about to betray Him), said, [5]"Why wasn't this fragrant oil sold for 300 denarii and given to the poor?" [6]He didn't say this because he cared about the poor but because he was a thief. He was in charge of the money-bag and would steal part of what was put in it.

[7]Jesus answered, "Leave her alone; she has kept it for the day of My burial. [8]For you always have the poor with you, but you do not always have Me."

THE DECISION TO KILL LAZARUS

[9]Then a large crowd of the Jews learned He was there. They came not only because of Jesus, but also to see Lazarus, the one He had raised from the dead. [10]Therefore the chief priests decided to also kill Lazarus, [11]because he was the reason many of the Jews were deserting them and believing in Jesus.

THE TRIUMPHAL ENTRY

[12]The next day, when the large crowd that had come to the festival heard that Jesus was coming to Jerusalem, [13]they took palm branches and went out to meet Him. They kept shouting: "'Hosanna! Blessed is He who comes in the name of the Lord'—the King of Israel!"

[14]Jesus found a young donkey and sat on it, just as it is written: [15]"Fear no more, Daughter Zion; look! your King is coming, sitting on a donkey's colt."

[16]His disciples did not understand these things at first. However, when Jesus was glorified, then they remembered that these things had been written about Him and that they had done these things to Him. [17]Meanwhile the crowd, which had been with Him when He called Lazarus out of the tomb and raised him from the dead, continued to testify. [18]This is also why the crowd met Him, because they heard He had done this sign.

[19]Then the Pharisees said to one another, "You see? You've accomplished nothing. Look—the world has gone after Him!"

TO PONDER: Someone has called the story of the woman who took the precious perfume and poured it on Jesus' feet as 'the sweetest story in all of the Gospels'. It evoked criticism from Judas, but the woman's extravagance apparently brought great pleasure and joy to the heart of Jesus. Ask yourself now: How extravagant am I in my love for the Lord? Do you give it in thimblefuls or bucketfuls?

THE COMING OF the Greeks alerts Jesus to the hour of His going! But since the Son of Man will be granted rule over the nations only through suffering, John describes Jesus being in deep emotional turmoil like the waves of a stormy sea. Prophetically, Jesus discerns the voice of God from the alternative evaluations offered (vv.28-30). Like a prophet, Jesus announces that now is final judgment day for the world and the eviction of its demonic ruler (v.31). The long-running saga of God's redemptive plans which we have been tracing comes down to this crucial moment in Jesus' earthly life.

DAY
230
JOHN 12:20-50

The mystery is wrapped in a parable - only the dying seed brings forth fruit. Only by plunging into the obscurity of suffering will He become visible to the Greeks! Only by being lowered into the ground will He be lifted up from the earth.

As Isaiah foretold, God's original people prove unwilling to believe and so are hardened in their unbelief (12:37-49). This is within the sovereign purpose of God (vv.39-40), but fulfils the long-range view of the prophets straining to glimpse the coming glory (v.41). And the Greeks, up for the Feast, presage a multitude of others drawn like a magnet to Jesus when He is 'lifted up' in paradoxical glory on the cross (12:32).

BIBLE READING

John 12:20-50

JESUS PREDICTS HIS CRUCIFIXION

²⁰Now some Greeks were among those who went up to worship at the festival. ²¹So they came to Philip, who was from Bethsaida in Galilee, and requested of him, "Sir, we want to see Jesus."

²²Philip went and told Andrew; then Andrew and Philip went and told Jesus. ²³Jesus replied to them, "The hour has come for the Son of Man to be glorified.

²⁴"I assure you: Unless a grain of wheat falls into the ground and dies, it remains by itself. But if it dies, it produces a large crop. ²⁵The one who loves his life will lose it, and the one who hates his life in this world will keep it for eternal life. ²⁶If anyone serves Me, he must follow Me. Where I am, there My servant also will be. If anyone serves Me, the Father will honor him.

²⁷"Now My soul is troubled. What should I say—Father, save Me from this hour? But that is why I came to this hour. ²⁸Father, glorify Your name!"

Then a voice came from heaven: "I have glorified it, and I will glorify it again!"

²⁹The crowd standing there heard it and said it was thunder. Others said, "An angel has spoken to Him!"

³⁰Jesus responded, "This voice came, not for Me, but for you. ³¹Now is the judgment of this world. Now the ruler of this world will be cast out. ³²As for Me, if I am lifted up from the earth I will draw all [people] to Myself." ³³He said this to signify what kind of death He was about to die.

³⁴Then the crowd replied to Him, "We have heard from the law that the Messiah will remain forever. So how can You say, 'The Son of Man must be lifted up'? Who is this Son of Man?"

³⁵Jesus answered, "The light will be with you only a little longer. Walk while you have the light so that darkness doesn't overtake you. The one who walks in darkness doesn't know where he's going. ³⁶While you have the light, believe in the light so that you may become sons of light." Jesus said this, then went away and hid from them.

ISAIAH'S PROPHECIES FULFILLED

[37]Even though He had performed so many signs in their presence, they did not believe in Him. [38]But this was to fulfill the word of Isaiah the prophet, who said:

> "Lord, who has believed our message?
> And who has the arm of the Lord been revealed to?"

[39]This is why they were unable to believe, because Isaiah also said:

> [40] "He has blinded their eyes
> and hardened their hearts,
> so that they would not see with their eyes
> or understand with their hearts,
> and be converted,
> and I would heal them."

[41]Isaiah said these things because he saw His glory and spoke about Him.

[42]Nevertheless, many did believe in Him even among the rulers, but because of the Pharisees they did not confess Him, so they would not be banned from the synagogue. [43]For they loved praise from men more than praise from God.

A SUMMARY OF JESUS' MISSION

[44]Then Jesus cried out, "The one who believes in Me believes not in Me, but in Him who sent Me. [45]And the one who sees Me sees Him who sent Me. [46]I have come as a light into the world, so that everyone who believes in Me would not remain in darkness. [47]If anyone hears My words and doesn't keep them, I do not judge him; for I did not come to judge the world but to save the world. [48]The one who rejects Me and doesn't accept My sayings has this as his judge: the word I have spoken will judge him on the last day. [49]For I have not spoken on My own, but the Father Himself who sent Me has given Me a command as to what I should say and what I should speak. [50]I know that His command is eternal life. So the things that I speak, I speak just as the Father has told Me."

PRAYER: Gracious and loving heavenly Father, this message of dying to live is one that I find deeply challenging. Help me, I pray, to see, however, that when I am unwilling to die to self-interest and self-concern then I cannot live the life You would have me live. May I be like Jesus who aligned Himself with self-giving rather than self-saving. In His peerless and precious name I pray. Amen.

DAY 231

JOHN 13

THIS UNFORGETTABLE RECOLLECTION

of Jesus shows the humbled disciples struggling to come to terms with His self-abasement. Jesus gives an acted parable of His coming death on the cross which reveals the full extent of His love and it is more than adequate to the full extent of our need.

The 'Upper Room discourses' - as they are called - are reminiscent of Moses' farewell speeches to the children of Israel spoken on the verge of the promised land and, recorded in the book of Deuteronomy. If we keep this in mind as we reflect on the words of Jesus as He takes leave of His disciples, we can trace echoes of Deuteronomy all through this moving section of Scripture. Just as Moses rehearsed the ten commandments for God's covenant people about to possess the land, so Jesus does the same for the new covenant community being created in Him as it prepares to launch out into the world. Only this time there is only one commandment and it is new (v.34). It is not new because it has never been heard of before. It is new for two reasons. Firstly, the new age of salvation is here and love's full time has come. Secondly, and above all, Jesus' unprecedented self-giving on the cross totally redefines what love really is and becomes the new measure of it.

John 13

JESUS WASHES HIS DISCIPLES' FEET

13 Before the Passover Festival, Jesus knew that His hour had come to depart from this world to the Father. Having loved His own who were in the world, He loved them to the end.

²Now by the time of supper, the Devil had already put it into the heart of Judas, Simon Iscariot's son, to betray Him. ³Jesus knew that the Father had given everything into His hands, that He had come from God, and that He was going back to God. ⁴So He got up from supper, laid aside His robe, took a towel, and tied it around Himself. ⁵Next, He poured water into a basin and began to wash His disciples' feet and to dry them with the towel tied around Him.

⁶He came to Simon Peter, who asked Him, "Lord, are You going to wash my feet?"

⁷Jesus answered him, "What I'm doing you don't understand now, but afterwards you will know."

⁸"You will never wash my feet—ever!" Peter said.

Jesus replied, "If I don't wash you, you have no part with Me."

⁹Simon Peter said to Him, "Lord, not only my feet, but also my hands and my head."

¹⁰"One who has bathed," Jesus told him, "doesn't need to wash anything except his feet, but he is completely clean. You are clean, but not all of you." ¹¹For He knew who would betray Him. This is why He said, "You are not all clean."

THE MEANING OF FOOTWASHING

¹²When Jesus had washed their feet and put on His robe, He reclined again and said to them, "Do you know what I have done for you? ¹³You call Me Teacher and Lord. This is well said, for I am. ¹⁴So if I, your Lord and Teacher, have washed your feet, you also ought to wash one another's feet. ¹⁵For I have given you an example that you also should do just as I have done for you.

¹⁶"I assure you: A slave is not greater than his master, and a messenger is not greater than the one who sent him. ¹⁷If you know these things, you are blessed if you do them. ¹⁸I'm not

speaking about all of you; I know those I have chosen. But the Scripture must be fulfilled: The one who eats My bread has raised his heel against Me.

¹⁹"I am telling you now before it happens, so that when it does happen you will believe that I am [He]. ²⁰I assure you: 'The one who receives whomever I send receives Me, and the one who receives Me receives Him who sent Me.'"

JUDAS' BETRAYAL PREDICTED

²¹When Jesus had said this, He was troubled in His spirit and testified, "I assure you: One of you will betray Me!"

²²The disciples started looking at one another—uncertain which one He was speaking about. ²³One of His disciples, the one Jesus loved, was reclining close beside Jesus. ²⁴Simon Peter motioned to him to find out who it was He was talking about. ²⁵So he leaned back against Jesus and asked Him, "Lord, who is it?"

²⁶Jesus replied, "He's the one I give the piece of bread to after I have dipped it." When He had dipped the bread, He gave it to Judas, Simon Iscariot's son. ²⁷After [Judas ate] the piece of bread, Satan entered him. Therefore Jesus told him, "What you're doing, do quickly."

²⁸None of those reclining at the table knew why He told him this. ²⁹Since Judas kept the money-bag, some thought that Jesus was telling him, "Buy what we need for the festival," or that he should give something to the poor. ³⁰After receiving the piece of bread, he went out immediately. And it was night.

THE NEW COMMANDMENT

³¹When he had gone out, Jesus said, "Now the Son of Man is glorified, and God is glorified in Him. ³²If God is glorified in Him, God will also glorify Him in Himself and will glorify Him at once.

³³"Children, I am with you a little while longer. You will look for Me, and just as I told the Jews, 'Where I am going you cannot come,' so now I tell you.

³⁴"I give you a new commandment: love one another. Just as I have loved you, you must also love one another. ³⁵By this all people will know that you are My disciples, if you have love for one another."

PETER'S DENIALS PREDICTED

³⁶"Lord," Simon Peter said to Him, "where are You going?"

Jesus answered, "Where I am going you cannot follow Me now, but you will follow later."

³⁷"Lord," Peter asked, "why can't I follow You now? I will lay down my life for You!"

³⁸Jesus replied, "Will you lay down your life for Me? I assure you: A rooster will not crow until you have denied Me three times.

> QUOTATION: 'The account says: Jesus knew ... that he had come from God and was returning to God ... took off his outer clothing, and wrapped a towel round his waist ... and began to wash his disciples' feet ...' The consciousness of greatness was the secret of His humility. The small dare not be humble. But Jesus' greatness was rooted in God. 'Being in God made him great - and humble.' (E. Stanley Jones)

IN THESE MOVING discourses, Jesus spells out the covenant blessings and responsibilities of the new covenant people of God as their covenant-mediator gets ready to leave them. As in Deuteronomy, a new generation stands poised to revive its covenant identity and claim its promised inheritance. So Jesus lays emphasis afresh on familiar Deuteronomic keynotes but with a revolutionary twist that places Himself at the centre. Loving God and being loved by God is worked out in obedience to what God says. This was reworked by the prophets as they envisaged the new covenant and Jesus reflects this (John 14:15-21).

DAY
232
JOHN 14; 15:26-27

Jesus' greatest prayer for His disciples is that they might receive the Holy Spirit (14:16,26; 15:26; 16:6,13-15). With their master leaving, the disciples of Jesus stand on the edge of an awesome adventure. They will need to rely utterly on the Holy Spirit to be their empowering Counsellor and Teacher who leads them into all truth and never allows them to forget what Jesus said (14:16-17; 15:26). As they confront the intimidating task of proclaiming Jesus as Lord and Christ to a sceptical world, they will be encouraged to realise that they are merely a supporting cast to the Holy Spirit: our witness is always a subset of His witness (15:18-27)!

BIBLE READING

John 14

THE WAY TO THE FATHER

14 "Your heart must not be troubled. Believe in God; believe also in Me. ²In My Father's house are many dwelling places; if not, I would have told you. I am going away to prepare a place for you. ³If I go away and prepare a place for you, I will come back and receive you to Myself, so that where I am you may be also. ⁴You know the way where I am going."

⁵"Lord," Thomas said, "we don't know where You're going. How can we know the way?"

⁶Jesus told him, "I am the way, the truth, and the life. No one comes to the Father except through Me.

JESUS REVEALS THE FATHER

⁷"If you know Me, you will also know My Father. From now on you do know Him and have seen Him."

⁸"Lord," said Philip, "show us the Father, and that's enough for us."

⁹Jesus said to him, "Have I been among you all this time without your knowing Me, Philip? The one who has seen Me has seen the Father. How can you say, 'Show us the Father'? ¹⁰Don't you believe that I am in the Father and the Father is in Me? The words I speak to you I do not speak on My own. The Father who lives in Me does His works. ¹¹Believe Me that I am in the Father and the Father is in Me. Otherwise, believe because of the works themselves.

PRAYING IN JESUS' NAME

¹²"I assure you: The one who believes in Me will also do the works that I do. And he will do even greater works than these, because I am going to the Father. ¹³Whatever you ask in My

name, I will do it so that the Father may be glorified in the Son. [14]If you ask Me anything in My name, I will do it.

ANOTHER COUNSELOR PROMISED

[15]"If you love Me, you will keep My commandments. [16]And I will ask the Father, and He will give you another Counselor to be with you forever. [17]He is the Spirit of truth. The world is unable to receive Him because it doesn't see Him or know Him. But you do know Him, because He remains with you and will be in you. [18]I will not leave you as orphans; I am coming to you.

THE FATHER, THE SON, AND THE HOLY SPIRIT

[19]"In a little while the world will see Me no longer, but you will see Me. Because I live, you will live too. [20]In that day you will know that I am in My Father, you are in Me, and I am in you. [21]The one who has My commands and keeps them is the one who loves Me. And the one who loves Me will be loved by My Father. I also will love him and will reveal Myself to him."

[22]Judas (not Iscariot) said to Him, "Lord, how is it You're going to reveal Yourself to us and not to the world?"

[23]Jesus answered, "If anyone loves Me, he will keep My word. My Father will love him, and We will come to him and make Our home with him. [24]The one who doesn't love Me will not keep My words. The word that you hear is not Mine but is from the Father who sent Me.

[25]"I have spoken these things to you while I remain with you. [26]But the Counselor, the Holy Spirit—the Father will send Him in My name—will teach you all things and remind you of everything I have told you.

JESUS' GIFT OF PEACE

[27]"Peace I leave with you. My peace I give to you. I do not give to you as the world gives. Your heart must not be troubled or fearful. [28]You have heard Me tell you, 'I am going away and I am coming to you.' If you loved Me, you would have rejoiced that I am going to the Father, because the Father is greater than I. [29]I have told you now before it happens so that when it does happen you may believe. [30]I will not talk with you much longer, because the ruler of the world is coming. He has no

power over Me. ³¹On the contrary, [I am going away] so that the world may know that I love the Father. Just as the Father commanded Me, so I do.

"Get up; let's leave this place."

John 15:26-27

COMING TESTIMONY AND REJECTION

²⁶"When the Counselor comes, the One I will send to you from the Father—the Spirit of truth who proceeds from the Father—He will testify about Me. ²⁷You also will testify, because you have been with Me from the beginning.

THOUGHT: 'There are few doctrines more perplexing than the doctrine of the Holy Spirit,' said a London newspaper columnist. He should have added: 'The man without the Spirit does not accept the things that come from the Spirit of God, for they are foolishness to him, and he cannot understand them, because they are spiritually discerned' (1 Cor. 2:14, NIV). To the converted the Holy Spirit is not a puzzle but a power.

DAY
233

JOHN 15:1-17

THE IMAGERY OF the vine is derived from the picture of Israel as God's vine which was sadly often found to be unfruitful (Psa. 80:8-9; Isa. 5). By saying 'I am the true vine', Jesus is assuming the identity of what Israel was meant to be so that life and fruitfulness now flow from being attached to Him.

Sometimes, too, the vine imagery is a code for 'Israel-in-the-land' so that, as vine and vineyard Jesus may be indicating that He not only embodies Israel but is taking the place of the promised land itself! What if all along Jesus had displaced this contentious, blood-stained land as the place where God's people are to be rooted, the only source of abundance and fruitfulness that Israel - or anyone else - needs? Instead of a sanctified land, we have a sanctified

Person. Just as Jesus has supplanted the Temple and the feasts as the focal point of God's presence and worship, so Jesus is the only holy space His people need. Our inheritance is no longer territorial except as we are heirs of the whole earth.

One thing that is clear is that remaining in the Torah by keeping the commandments is now replaced by remaining in Jesus and abiding in His Word (15:4,7,9-10). Jesus is Lord of the covenant people which is determined by His choice (15:16). Graciously, though, it's not servants He wants but friends!

John 15:1-17

BIBLE
READING

THE VINE AND THE BRANCHES

15 "I am the true vine, and My Father is the vineyard keeper. ²Every branch in Me that does not produce fruit He removes, and He prunes every branch that produces fruit so that it will produce more fruit. ³You are already clean because of the word I have spoken to you. ⁴Remain in Me, and I in you. Just as a branch is unable to produce fruit by itself unless it remains on the vine, so neither can you unless you remain in Me.

⁵"I am the vine; you are the branches. The one who remains in Me and I in him produces much fruit, because you can do nothing without Me. ⁶If anyone does not remain in Me, he is thrown aside like a branch and he withers. They gather them, throw them into the fire, and they are burned. ⁷If you remain in Me and My words remain in you, ask whatever you want and it will be done for you. ⁸My Father is glorified by this: that you produce much fruit and prove to be My disciples.

CHRISTLIKE LOVE

⁹"As the Father has loved Me, I have also loved you. Remain in My love. ¹⁰If you keep My commands you will remain in My love, just as I have kept My Father's commands and remain in His love.

¹¹"I have spoken these things to you so that My joy may be in you and your joy may be complete. ¹²This is My command: love

one another as I have loved you. ¹³No one has greater love than this, that someone would lay down his life for his friends. ¹⁴You are My friends if you do what I command you. ¹⁵I do not call you slaves anymore, because a slave doesn't know what his master is doing. I have called you friends, because I have made known to you everything I have heard from My Father. ¹⁶You did not choose Me, but I chose you. I appointed you that you should go out and produce fruit and that your fruit should remain, so that whatever you ask the Father in My name, He will give you. ¹⁷This is what I command you: love one another.

> **TO PONDER:** Let that final thought lie on your mind throughout the day: 'it's not servants He wants but friends'. Do you see yourself as Christ's servant – someone who does a master's bidding, or a friend – someone who has an intimate relationship? We are of course His servants, but we are more than that – we are His friends. He is a friend to you, but are you a friend to Him?

AS IF ON holy ground, we watch in intimate close-up our Great High Priest at prayer.

Jesus models an integrity of heart and mind and will that is surrendered lovingly and obediently to God. Through knowing this perfect Priest, we know God (v.3). Jesus first prays for Himself that He may accomplish God's work to the Father's glory which He asks to share. He then prays for His disciples, especially for their protection and security. Finally, Jesus prays for all future believers whose faith depends on the faithful witness of His original disciples. For them He prays, above all, that they may be one in a way that reflects the unity which exists between Father and Son in the Godhead. The Trinity of love which is God has opened itself to us by an amazing grace so that believers are embraced with the same love with which the Father loves the Son! His is a prayer of consecration before the sacrificial self-giving

DAY
234
JOHN 17

of the cross (v.19). Our consecration takes its rise from His. Receiving us as the Father's gift to Him (v.6), and consecrating us by His own self-offering on the cross (v.19), He takes us and gives us to the world (v.18) so that - seeing the divine love and unity displayed in us - the world might come to believe (vv.21,23) and experience that Trinity-love for itself. Surely Jesus gets His prayers answered!

BIBLE READING

John 17

JESUS PRAYS FOR HIMSELF

17 Jesus spoke these things, looked up to heaven, and said:

> Father,
> the hour has come.
> Glorify Your Son
> so that the Son may glorify You,
> ² for You gave Him authority
> over all flesh;
> so He may give eternal life
> to all You have given Him.
> ³ This is eternal life:
> that they may know You, the only true God,
> and the One You have sent—Jesus Christ.
> ⁴ I have glorified You on the earth
> by completing the work You gave Me to do.
> ⁵ Now, Father, glorify Me in Your presence
> with that glory I had with You
> before the world existed.

JESUS PRAYS FOR HIS DISCIPLES

> ⁶ I have revealed Your name
> to the men You gave Me from the world.
> They were Yours, You gave them to Me,
> and they have kept Your word.
> ⁷ Now they know that all things
> You have given to Me are from You,

⁸ because the words that You gave Me,
   I have given them.
   They have received them
   and have known for certain
   that I came from You.
   They have believed that You sent Me.
⁹ I pray for them.
   I am not praying for the world
   but for those You have given Me,
   because they are Yours.
¹⁰ All My things are Yours,
   and Yours are Mine,
   and I have been glorified in them.
¹¹ I am no longer in the world,
   but they are in the world,
   and I am coming to You.
   Holy Father,
   protect them by Your name
   that You have given Me,
   so that they may be one as We are one.
¹² While I was with them,
   I was protecting them by Your name
   that You have given Me.
   I guarded them and not one of them is lost,
   except the son of destruction,
   so that the Scripture may be fulfilled.
¹³ Now I am coming to You,
   and I speak these things in the world
   so that they may have My joy completed in them.
¹⁴ I have given them Your word.
   The world hated them
   because they are not of the world,
   as I am not of the world.
¹⁵ I am not praying
   that You take them out of the world
   but that You protect them from the evil one.
¹⁶ They are not of the world,
   as I am not of the world.
¹⁷ Sanctify them by the truth;
   Your word is truth.

¹⁸ As You sent Me into the world,
  I also have sent them into the world.
¹⁹ I sanctify Myself for them,
  so they also may be sanctified by the truth.

JESUS PRAYS FOR ALL BELIEVERS

²⁰ I pray not only for these,
  but also for those who believe in Me
  through their message.
²¹ May they all be one,
  as You, Father, are in Me and I am in You.
  May they also be one in Us,
  so the world may believe You sent Me.
²² I have given them the glory You have given Me.
  May they be one as We are one.
²³ I am in them and You are in Me.
  May they be made completely one,
  so the world may know You have sent Me
  and have loved them as You have loved Me.
²⁴ Father,
  I desire those You have given Me
  to be with Me where I am.
  Then they will see My glory,
  which You have given Me
  because You loved Me before the world's foundation.
²⁵ Righteous Father!
  The world has not known You.
  However, I have known You,
  and these have known that You sent Me.
²⁶ I made Your name known to them
  and will make it known,
  so the love You have loved Me with
  may be in them and I may be in them.

PRAYER: Gracious Father, as I see Jesus at prayer and hearken to His words I realise that He models a way of praying that leaves me feeling somewhat ashamed. How I long to echo His consecration and commitment. Dear Lord, work in me so that I might be a more consecrated person – consecrated to all that Jesus prayed for, especially the unity of His people. In Jesus' name. Amen.

RETURNING TO MATTHEW'S narrative,

we note again that Jesus' entry into Jerusalem and the Temple are both symbolic actions, reflecting Zechariah's image of the royal temple builder (Zech. 6:12; 9:9). The so-called 'cleansing of the Temple' spells far more than a mere spring-clean; it is an explicitly prophetic action which heralds the doom and end of the Temple (cf.Matt. 12:6,25-29). The further acted parable of the cursing of the fig tree confirms this. In the Old Testament the fig tree symbolises Israel when blessed. Withering the fig tree speaks of Israel under the covenantal curse of God's judgment! Jesus' strong words and actions are matched by what He says about the mountain cast into the sea. Though often taken as a generalised lesson in faith, His words need to be seen in context. Jesus does not say *a* mountain but *this* mountain, which must refer either to Mount Zion or the Temple Mount. Can you have the faith to see this removed and survive? The crisis for the Temple is not a crisis for God, in fact He's bringing it about. Don't put all your faith in the God-in-the-Temple-God – that current presumption on Israel's part is doomed. Faith can envisage a whole new order of things, not dependent on a material Temple in Jerusalem. Faith like this can move anything.

DAY
235
MATTHEW 21:1-21

BIBLE READING

Matthew 21:1-21

THE TRIUMPHAL ENTRY

21 When they approached Jerusalem and came to Bethphage at the Mount of Olives, Jesus then sent two disciples, ²telling them, "Go into the village ahead of you. At once you will find a donkey tied there, and a colt with her. Untie them and bring them to Me. ³If anyone says anything to you, you should say that the Lord needs them, and immediately he will send them."

⁴This took place so that what was spoken through the prophet might be fulfilled:

⁵ "Tell Daughter Zion,
   'See, your King is coming to you,
   gentle, and mounted on a donkey,
   even on a colt,
   the foal of a beast of burden.'"

⁶The disciples went and did just as Jesus directed them. ⁷They brought the donkey and the colt; then they laid their robes on them, and He sat on them. ⁸A very large crowd spread their robes on the road; others were cutting branches from the trees and spreading them on the road. ⁹Then the crowds who went ahead of Him and those who followed kept shouting:

   "*Hosanna*" to the Son of David!
   "Blessed is He who comes
   in the name of the Lord!
   Hosanna" in the highest heaven!

¹⁰When He entered Jerusalem, the whole city was shaken, saying, "Who is this?" ¹¹And the crowds kept saying, "This is the prophet Jesus from Nazareth in Galilee!"

CLEANSING THE TEMPLE COMPLEX

¹²Jesus went into the temple complex and drove out all those buying and selling in the temple. He overturned the money changers' tables and the chairs of those selling doves. ¹³And He

said to them, "It is written, 'My house will be called a house of prayer.' But you are making it a 'den of thieves!'"

CHILDREN CHEER JESUS

[14]The blind and the lame came to Him in the temple complex, and He healed them. [15]When the chief priests and the scribes saw the wonders that He did and the children in the temple complex cheering, "*Hosanna* to the Son of David!" they were indignant [16]and said to Him, "Do You hear what these [children] are saying?"

"Yes," Jesus told them. "Have you never read:

'You have prepared praise
from the mouths of children and nursing infants'?"

[17]Then He left them, went out of the city to Bethany, and spent the night there.

THE BARREN FIG TREE

[18]Early in the morning, as He was returning to the city, He was hungry. [19]Seeing a lone fig tree by the road, He went up to it and found nothing on it except leaves. And He said to it, "May no fruit ever come from you again!" At once the fig tree withered.

[20]When the disciples saw it, they were amazed and said, "How did the fig tree wither so quickly?"

[21]Jesus answered them, "I assure you: If you have faith and do not doubt, you will not only do what was done to the fig tree, but even if you tell this mountain, 'Be lifted up and thrown into the sea,' it will be done.

THOUGHT: Christians can often be heard praying that God would help them cultivate a great faith that will be able to move mountains. However, mountains are not removed by a great faith, but by a small faith. Actually it is more biblical to pray for a small faith - a mustard seed faith - than a great faith. We do not need a great faith in God but a small mustard seed faith in a great God.

DAY 236

MATTHEW 21:23-32

THE PARABLES OF Jesus, we note again, are not generalised stories about timeless truths, but powerful weapons in the conflict at hand. These stories are 'Israel-specific', told in a time when Israel is being brought a final national decision. Stories which feature a 'son' are especially appropriate to the occasion because, we recall, Israel was termed God's 'firstborn son' (Exod. 4:22). Parables that speak of two sons are raising the issue of a divided Israel. They force the nation to face the split in its allegiance to God and the direction it is taking (cf.Luke 15:11-32). In telling them, Jesus cleverly poses the question: 'Which kind of Israel is in line with God's will and which kind of Israel will the nation choose to be?'

You - the chief priest and scribes - say 'yes' to doing God's will but don't actually do it! They - the sinners and outcasts - initially say 'no' to God's will but repent and do it! What a challenge this story is to the leaders of God's people who are failing to recognise God's salvation as it comes in Jesus - a ministry to which outsiders and misfits are eagerly responding! The leaders couldn't see it in John the Baptist's ministry, and they can't see it now even when such dramatic change in sinners is happening right in front of their noses.

BIBLE READING

Matthew 21:23-32

MESSIAH'S AUTHORITY CHALLENGED

²³When He entered the temple complex, the chief priests and the elders of the people came up to Him as He was teaching and said, "By what authority are You doing these things? Who gave You this authority?"

²⁴Jesus answered them, "I will also ask you one question, and if you answer it for Me, then I will tell you by what authority I do these things. ²⁵Where did John's baptism come from? From heaven or from men?"

They began to argue among themselves, "If we say, 'From

heaven,' He will say to us, 'Then why didn't you believe him?' ²⁶But if we say, 'From men,' we're afraid of the crowd, because everyone thought John was a prophet." ²⁷So they answered Jesus, "We don't know."

And He said to them, "Neither will I tell you by what authority I do these things.

THE PARABLE OF THE TWO SONS

²⁸"But what do you think? A man had two sons. He went to the first and said, 'My son, go, work in the vineyard today.'

²⁹"He answered, 'I don't want to!' Yet later he changed his mind and went. ³⁰Then the man went to the other and said the same thing.

"'I will, sir,' he answered. But he didn't go.

³¹"Which of the two did his father's will?"

"The first," they said.

Jesus said to them, "I assure you: Tax collectors and prostitutes are entering the kingdom of God before you! ³²For John came to you in the way of righteousness, and you didn't believe him. Tax collectors and prostitutes did believe him, but you, when you saw it, didn't even change your minds then and believe him.

> TO PONDER: One of the things that seemed often to frustrate Jesus was the fact that so many people said 'Yes' to God with their lips but 'No' to Him in their hearts. God does not look for lips expressing words of obedience but hearts performing acts of obedience. How about you? Are you a lip responder or a heart responder? It's an issue worth pondering.

THIS PARABLE ONCE more directly addresses Israel, previously pictured as God's vine (Psa. 80:8; Isa. 5:2; Jer. 2:21). God has sent many prophets to appeal to His people but to no avail (vv.34-36). Last of all He sends His own son to call in the final accounts. In killing the son, the tenants 'take his inheritance' for themselves (v.38). This strongly implies that Israel's

DAY
237
MATTHEW 21:33-46

sonship was only held on trust, and was meant to be yielded up when the true Son and Heir appeared!

Jesus' words about the 'stone that the builders rejected' picks up the song of pilgrims coming up to the Temple for the Feast (Psa. 118:22-23). It echoes Isaiah where the 'stone' is used of God's ultimate Temple in the Messianic age (Isa. 8:14; 28:16). There may even be a play on words here since the Hebrew word for stone (*eben*) sounds like the word for son (*ben*). The rejected Son is the chief headstone of the new Temple complex that God is building through Him. The Temple is being drastically redefined through His rejection in death and vindication in resurrection.

And no question who this powerful parable with its sting in the tail was aimed at. The religious leaders 'knew He was speaking about them' (v.45)! The kingdom will pass to others in judgment and grace. But this is the Lord's doing and 'is wonderful in our eyes' (v.42)!

BIBLE READING

Matthew 21:33-46

THE PARABLE OF THE VINEYARD OWNER

[33]"Listen to another parable: There was a man, a landowner, who planted a vineyard, put a fence around it, dug a winepress in it, and built a watchtower. He leased it to tenant farmers and went away. [34]When the grape harvest drew near, he sent his slaves to the farmers to collect his fruit. [35]But the farmers took his slaves, beat one, killed another, and stoned a third. [36]Again, he sent other slaves, more than the first group, and they did the same to them. [37]Finally, he sent his son to them. 'They will respect my son,' he said.

[38]"But when the tenant farmers saw the son, they said among themselves, 'This is the heir. Come, let's kill him and take his inheritance!' [39]So they seized him and threw him out of the vineyard, and killed him. [40]Therefore, when the owner of the vineyard comes, what will he do to those farmers?"

[41]"He will completely destroy those terrible men," they told Him, "and lease his vineyard to other farmers who will give

him his produce at the harvest."

⁴²Jesus said to them, "Have you never read in the Scriptures:

'The stone that the builders rejected
has become the cornerstone.
This came from the Lord
and is wonderful in our eyes?'

⁴³Therefore I tell you, the kingdom of God will be taken away from you and given to a nation producing its fruit. [⁴⁴Whoever falls on this stone will be broken to pieces; but on whomever it falls, it will grind him to powder!"]

⁴⁵When the chief priests and the Pharisees heard His parables, they knew He was speaking about them. ⁴⁶Although they were looking for a way to arrest Him, they feared the crowds, because they regarded Him as a prophet.

FOR PRAISE: A tinge of sadness lies on the spirit of all Christians when they see how our Lord was rejected by those who should have eagerly accepted Him. But it is also a cause for rejoicing that the rejected One is now the Chief Cornerstone of a new Temple complex in which we have a part. The One whom others rejected is the Rock upon which God's promises to us rest.

MATTHEW HERE NEATLY mirrors Deuteronomy 27-28 so that the 'blessings' (Matt. 5:3-12) are now matched by 'woes' (23:13-32). The point is clear. Just as Moses brought God's people to a moment of covenantal choice, so, even more, Jesus brings Israel to its final covenantal crisis. Israel must choose: blessing or curse!

It makes sense, then, to see all the parables Jesus told in the last week of His life (21:28-46; 25:1-46), and the vision of the end (ch. 24), as primarily referring not to His second coming but to His first coming and its immediate repercussions in the

DAY
238

MATTHEW 23

imminent judgment of God during the Jewish-Roman War of AD 70-73.

That war did leave 'not one stone of the Temple standing' - except, that is, for a supporting wall of the outer court which still remains sacred to Jews today as the Western or Wailing Wall.

All of Israel's previous covenantal unfaithfulness is now being laid at the door of this, the terminal generation (v.36).

But, like a hen sheltering her chicks under her wings, so God (Jesus speaks here as a prophet for God) longs to gather His people to Himself in salvation. But the 'house [primarily the Temple] is left to you desolate'. The only hope is to welcome Jesus by blessing Him who comes in the name of the Lord as the ultimate pilgrim to Jerusalem!

BIBLE READING

Matthew 23

RELIGIOUS HYPOCRITES DENOUNCED

23 Then Jesus spoke to the crowds and to His disciples: [2]"The scribes and the Pharisees are seated in the chair of Moses. [3]Therefore do whatever they tell you and observe [it]. But don't do what they do, because they don't practice what they teach. [4]They tie up heavy loads that are hard to carry and put them on people's shoulders, but they themselves aren't willing to lift a finger to move them. [5]They do everything to be observed by others: They enlarge their phylacteries and lengthen their tassels. [6]They love the place of honor at banquets, the front seats in the synagogues, [7]greetings in the marketplaces, and to be called 'Rabbi' by people.

[8]"But as for you, do not be called 'Rabbi,' because you have one Teacher, and you are all brothers. [9]Do not call anyone on earth your father, because you have one Father, who is in heaven. [10]And do not be called masters either, because you have one Master, the Messiah. [11]The greatest among you will be your servant. [12]Whoever exalts himself will be humbled, and whoever humbles himself will be exalted.

[13]"But woe to you, scribes and Pharisees, hypocrites! You

lock up the kingdom of heaven from people. For you don't go in, and you don't allow those entering to go in.

[¹⁴"Woe to you, scribes and Pharisees, hypocrites! You devour widows' houses and make long prayers just for show. This is why you will receive a harsher punishment.]

¹⁵"Woe to you, scribes and Pharisees, hypocrites! You travel over land and sea to make one proselyte, and when he becomes one, you make him twice as fit for hell as you are!

¹⁶"Woe to you, blind guides, who say, 'Whoever takes an oath by the sanctuary, it means nothing. But whoever takes an oath by the gold of the sanctuary is bound by his oath.' ¹⁷Blind fools! For which is greater, the gold or the sanctuary that sanctified the gold? ¹⁸Also, 'Whoever takes an oath by the altar, it means nothing. But whoever takes an oath by the gift that is on it is bound by his oath.' ¹⁹Blind people! For which is greater, the gift or the altar that sanctifies the gift? ²⁰Therefore the one who takes an oath by the altar takes an oath by it and by everything on it. ²¹The one who takes an oath by the sanctuary takes an oath by it and by Him who dwells in it. ²²And the one who takes an oath by heaven takes an oath by God's throne and by Him who sits on it.

²³"Woe to you, scribes and Pharisees, hypocrites! You pay a tenth of mint, dill, and cumin, yet you have neglected the more important matters of the law—justice, mercy, and faith. These things should have been done without neglecting the others. ²⁴Blind guides! You strain out a gnat, yet gulp down a camel!

²⁵"Woe to you, scribes and Pharisees, hypocrites! You clean the outside of the cup and dish, but inside they are full of greed and self-indulgence! ²⁶Blind Pharisee! First clean the inside of the cup, so the outside of it may also become clean.

²⁷"Woe to you, scribes and Pharisees, hypocrites! You are like whitewashed tombs, which appear beautiful on the outside, but inside are full of dead men's bones and every impurity. ²⁸In the same way, on the outside you seem righteous to people, but inside you are full of hypocrisy and lawlessness.

²⁹"Woe to you, scribes and Pharisees, hypocrites! You build the tombs of the prophets and decorate the monuments of the righteous, ³⁰and you say, 'If we had lived in the days of our fathers, we wouldn't have taken part with them in shedding

the prophets' blood.' ³¹You therefore testify against yourselves that you are sons of those who murdered the prophets. ³²Fill up, then, the measure of your fathers' sins!

³³"Snakes! Brood of vipers! How can you escape being condemned to hell? ³⁴This is why I am sending you prophets, sages, and scribes. Some of them you will kill and crucify, and some of them you will flog in your synagogues and hound from town to town. ³⁵So all the righteous blood shed on the earth will be charged to you, from the blood of righteous Abel to the blood of Zechariah, son of Berechiah, whom you murdered between the sanctuary and the altar. ³⁶I assure you: All these things will come on this generation!

JESUS' LAMENTATION OVER JERUSALEM

³⁷"Jerusalem, Jerusalem! The city who kills the prophets and stones those who are sent to her. How often I wanted to gather your children together, as a hen gathers her chicks under her wings, yet you were not willing! ³⁸See, your house is left to you desolate. ³⁹For I tell you, you will never see Me again until you say, 'Blessed is He who comes in the name of the Lord!'"

THOUGHT: In our relationship with God we are called to make a choice. Israel had to choose – blessing or curse. Though we have the freedom to choose, things will go better for us when we make a choice for freedom. Freedom is often misunderstood. One Bible teacher defines it thus: 'Freedom is not the right do what we want but the power to do what we ought.' It is.

DAY
239

JOHN 19:1-22

THIS ABUSED MAN, in the regalia of a king, seems a parody of the royal human vocation of being God's partners in ruling over the world (Gen. 1:26-28). Despite human sin and failure, this calling refuses to die (cf.Psa. 8). Created for dominion, we have rebelled against our high calling. We wear no longer a crown of honour but of shame. A 'crown of thorns' is a fitting symbol of our human disgrace. The thorns are signs of God's curse on the ground on which His disobedient sons and daughters walk in rebellion (Gen. 3:17-19). Through sin, we have twisted our humanness out of shape and misused our God-given gifts and abilities. The face in which God aimed to see His reflection, is spat upon and disfigured by blows. In all this the 'Word-made-flesh' endures the universal humiliation of the victim of oppression, and the special mockery devised for Jews. Israel represents God's image-bearing humanity, and in abusing Israel, our humanness and God's image are being attacked. But Jesus atones for us all by taking our shame, bearing our sins and wearing our crown of disgrace so that He might wear again for us the crown of human honour and so bring many sons to the glory from which we fell. 'Behold the Man! ... Behold your King!' (vv.5,14, NKJV)!

John 19:1-22

BIBLE READING

JESUS FLOGGED AND MOCKED

19 Then Pilate took Jesus and had Him flogged. ²The soldiers also twisted together a crown of thorns, put it on His head, and threw a purple robe around Him. ³And they repeatedly came up to Him and said, "Hail, King of the Jews!" and were slapping His face.

⁴Pilate went outside again and said to them, "Look, I'm bringing Him outside to you to let you know I find no grounds for charging Him."

PILATE SENTENCES JESUS TO DEATH

⁵Then Jesus came out wearing the crown of thorns and the purple robe. Pilate said to them, "Here is the man!"

⁶When the chief priests and the temple police saw Him, they shouted, "Crucify! Crucify!"

Pilate responded, "Take Him and crucify Him yourselves, for I find no grounds for charging Him."

⁷"We have a law," the Jews replied to him, "and according to that law He must die, because He made Himself the Son of God."

⁸When Pilate heard this statement, he was more afraid than

ever. [9]He went back into the headquarters and asked Jesus, "Where are You from?" But Jesus did not give him an answer. [10]So Pilate said to Him, "You're not talking to me? Don't You know that I have the authority to release You and the authority to crucify You?"

[11]"You would have no authority over Me at all," Jesus answered him, "if it hadn't been given you from above. This is why the one who handed Me over to you has the greater sin."

[12]From that moment Pilate made every effort to release Him. But the Jews shouted, "If you release this man, you are not Caesar's friend. Anyone who makes himself a king opposes Caesar!"

[13]When Pilate heard these words, he brought Jesus outside. He sat down on the judge's bench in a place called the Stone Pavement (but in Hebrew *Gabbatha*). [14]It was the preparation day for the Passover, and it was about six in the morning. Then he told the Jews, "Here is your king!"

[15]But they shouted, "Take Him away! Take Him away! Crucify Him!"

Pilate said to them, "Should I crucify your king?"

"We have no king but Caesar!" the chief priests answered.

[16]So then, because of them, he handed Him over to be crucified.

THE CRUCIFIXION

Therefore they took Jesus away. [17]Carrying His own cross, He went out to what is called Skull Place, which in Hebrew is called *Golgotha*. [18]There they crucified Him and two others with Him, one on either side, with Jesus in the middle. [19]Pilate also had a sign lettered and put on the cross. The inscription was:

JESUS THE NAZARENE THE KING OF THE JEWS

[20]Many of the Jews read this sign, because the place where Jesus was crucified was near the city, and it was written in Hebrew, Latin, and Greek. [21]So the chief priests of the Jews said to Pilate, "Don't write, 'The King of the Jews,' but that He said, 'I am the King of the Jews.'"

[22]Pilate replied, "What I have written, I have written."

PRAYER: Lord Jesus Christ, how can I ever put into words the gratitude my heart feels for wearing on Your brow the crown of our human shame so that we may share the crown of Your honour and glory. My heart cries out: 'All this You did for me; what have I done for Thee?' I know I cannot pay You back for what You have done for me, but help me show my gratitude by living a life that honours You. Amen.

IN A FINAL prophetic action, Jesus 'breathed on them and said, "Receive the Holy Spirit" ' (v.22). This graphic action immediately evokes the narrative of Genesis where God breathes the life of the first creation into Adam and constitutes him a living being (Gen. 2:7). It echoes the symbolic action of the prophet Elijah when he stretched out on the corpse of the widow of Zarephath's son and breathed the breath of new life into the lifeless boy (1 Kings 17:21). It connects too with Ezekiel's stunning vision of the breath or wind of God seeping down into the reassembled bodies of the slain of Israel to reanimate them and turn them into a living army again (Ezek. 37). So Jesus breathes upon the 'dead' of Israel and the world and breathes new, invigorating resurrection-life into them! The covenant purposes of God have reached their climax. In the small group gathered round Jesus is a nucleus of new covenant community and a new creation humanity to whom the last Adam imparts His life. Ending as he began, John unites creation and redemption. The Word by whom the world was made took flesh and dwelt among us. The Word-made-flesh was crucified, dead and buried, but on the third day rose again with a new world in His nail-pierced hands. To as many as received Him He imparted the life of the new creation (cf.1:12–13).

DAY
240

JOHN 20:19-23

BIBLE READING

John 20:19-23

THE DISCIPLES COMMISSIONED

¹⁹In the evening of that first day of the week, the disciples were [gathered together] with the doors locked because of their fear of the Jews. Then Jesus came, stood among them, and said to them, "Peace to you!"

²⁰Having said this, He showed them His hands and His side. So the disciples rejoiced when they saw the Lord.

²¹Jesus said to them again, "Peace to you! As the Father has sent Me, I also send you." ²²After saying this, He breathed on them and said, "Receive the Holy Spirit. ²³If you forgive the sins of any, they are forgiven them; if you retain [the sins of] any, they are retained."

TO PONDER: When Jesus breathed upon His disciples and said 'Receive the Holy Spirit', was that the moment when they were baptised in the Spirit? Or was that 'breathing' the moment of their regeneration? If so what exactly happened at Pentecost? Bible teachers are divided on this issue. It is hard to think Jesus' action did not have some effect. What do you think?

DAY 241

MATTHEW 28:16-20

MATTHEW, LIKE JOHN at times, has presented his work as a new Deuteronomy with Israel facing a life-or-death challenge in her confrontation with Jesus. So Matthew ends his story with Jesus – Moses-like – gathering the remnant of Israel around Himself on a mountain top. But the contrast is remarkable.

What had Moses urged Israel to do? In effect, Moses had said: 'Go into the promised land, observe the Torah and Yahweh will be with you always.' Now Jesus stands on a mountain to commission His small disciple band: 'Go, not just into a promised land but into the promised world; teach people not what Torah says but what I have commanded you' and – even more remarkably – the pledge is not, 'Yahweh will go with you', but 'I will be with you to the end of the age'! Matthew thus ends his Gospel where he began it, with 'Immanuel, God-with-us'. So if we ask again as His friends the question asked by His enemies: Who is this person?; with Matthew and with hindsight we have to say: 'No one has the authority to do and say these things except Israel's God in person.' Jesus both embodies Israel's mission and incarnates her God.

At His royal command a new covenant people is launched on the world with a restored Abrahamic mission to bring the blessings of God's salvation and grace to all the nations.

Matthew 28:16-20

THE GREAT COMMISSION

[16]The 11 disciples traveled to Galilee, to the mountain where Jesus had directed them. [17]When they saw Him, they worshiped, but some doubted. [18]Then Jesus came near and said to them, "All authority has been given to Me in heaven and on earth. [19]Go, therefore, and make disciples of all nations, baptizing them in the name of the Father and of the Son and of the Holy Spirit, [20]teaching them to observe everything I have commanded you. And remember, I am with you always, to the end of the age."

THOUGHT: A Christian magazine once researched the favourite story that preachers like to tell. It was this: When Jesus returned to heaven after His time on earth the angels asked Him how He planned to make the gospel message known. 'I have commissioned my followers for the task,' He replied. 'What if they fail?' asked the angels. Solemnly Jesus replied, 'Then I have no other plan.'

SECTION

NOAH
ALL CREATION

ABRAHAM
ALL NATIONS

ISRAEL
ONE NATION

DAVID
REPRESENTATIVE KING

NEW COVENANT
FAITHFUL COVENANT PARTNER

JESUS
FAITHFUL COVENANT PARTNER

JESUS
DAVIDIC KING MESSIAH

JESUS
THE NEW ISRAEL

JESUS
THE WORLD'S LORD

JESUS
THE TRULY HUMAN ONE
CROWNED WITH GLORY AND HONOUR

JESUS
COSMIC RULER IN GOD'S NEW CREATION
NEW HEAVENS AND NEW EARTH

SECTION 9

PAUL'S WORLD-VIEW
PART 1

GOD IS COMMITTED TO BRINGING EVERYTHING UNDER THE LORDSHIP OF JESUS – PAUL'S APOSTOLIC VISION

Paul is a master storyteller. This assessment may surprise those who think of him as writing only in logical concepts and propositions. But behind the penetrating logic and passionate argument lurks an overarching storyline which shapes all that he says. Paul has a 'narrative mindset'. He sees the world through the lens of God's big story, told progressively in the story of Israel and climactically in the story of Jesus. This story of the One Creator God's involvement with His world, starts redemptively with the call of Abraham in faith to be the channel of God's blessings to all nations. It extends through the covenantal history of Israel and her kings, expands in the critique and hopeful vision of Israel's prophets, and is finally established in the death and resurrection of God's Son, Jesus, Israel's Messiah and the world's Lord. By the Holy Spirit, through Christian apostles, prophets and 'saints in ordinary', God is writing the conclusive chapters in the story which is heading for a total renovation of His universe! Everything Paul says and writes, however practical or pastoral its immediate intention, stems from this larger vision and all-embracing narrative of what God is doing in the earth.

He views the history of Israel as a catalogue of covenantal privilege and failure. Tragically, God's 'son', Israel, has been shown to share the sin of the whole world. But as Paul tells the Romans, God's covenant faithfulness – His 'righteousness' – has gone forth to save His people and restore His creation. God has acted to save in the death and resurrection of His Son through whom He has begun to create the one covenant family of faithful disciples from all nations that He promised Abraham. This family is made up of those

who put their trust in the faithfulness of God at work in the faithfulness of Jesus! Those who believe in this way, God justifies. He vindicates them or declares them to be His own covenant people, judged before the final day to be 'righteous' – that is, in covenant relationship with Him. So emerges that new covenant community, first envisaged by the prophets of the Exile. These forgiven and Spirit-led 'sons of God', the sample new humanity, are making their new exodus through a groaning world, heading for the new world that is coming.

Along the way, the history of Jew and Gentile mysteriously interweaves as God works out His purpose to heal the nations and restore His creation. This overarching narrative of salvation is entirely God's doing. It flows from His grace, is worked out through His power and tends to His ultimate glory. By grace, we are called to participate in this great drama by our faith, our prayers and our suffering.

It is against this storyline that Paul measures the health of the churches to which he writes. Problems arise in those he deals with when Christians lose the plot and mislocate themselves in the narrative flow of God's history. So the Galatians were under pressure to re-locate themselves in an earlier pre-Christian stage of the story and so come back under the dominion of the law. To do that, says Paul, is to fail to understand where you are in the story. Since Christ has come, the law has changed its role. It no longer lords it over us; Christ does. Know your place, then, in the story. The Corinthians' case is similar. In their charismatic enthusiasm, they were 'getting above themselves', believing they were in some way superior, even to Paul! This was because they were getting ahead of themselves in the storyline. They assumed they were further down the road than it is possible to be before Jesus returns. They thought they could pre-empt the end of the story, bypass the normal human weakness and Christian suffering which is inevitable in this as yet unredeemed world, and so arrive at a state of perfection and completion. Paul has to remind them of their place in the story and to pull them back from their over-triumphalist 'there and then' into the realistic 'here and now'. We do enjoy the fullness of the Spirit now, he agrees, but we have not yet arrived at final salvation. We still live by hope in what remains as the future gift of God. For their part, the Thessalonians were unsure about the way the story ends for believers in Christ and so Paul has to rehearse with them as much as he knows about Christ's coming for His people whether living or dead.

Above all, the storyline calls for a radical new unity of Jew and Gentile to overcome the age-old divisions of tribe and race that stain the human story. From one angle, the whole reason for writing his letter to the Romans is to urge Jewish and Gentile Christians to be at peace with one another. He reminds them that all have sinned, that Israel's exclusive story was meant to bear fruit for the whole world, that the ground is level at the foot of the cross and that, in order to be saved, everyone, everywhere, can and must call on the name of the same Lord, the One Lord who is over all, for salvation.

Paul admits to knowing all this only because God has revealed to him the 'mystery of His will' centred in Jesus Christ. This 'mystery' is the open secret of God's strategic plan to save the world through Him. It is this 'mystery' Paul longs to tell and lives to implement.

MOST OF US love a good mystery. Some readers relish a good crime mystery. Scientists probe the 'mystery of life'.

Paul obviously relishes a good mystery too: he uses the word three times in this short section. (Eph. 3:3,4,9).

The word 'mystery' – '*musterion*' in Greek – was a technical term used for the secret initiation rites of the so-called 'mystery-religions' of the Greco-Roman world.

The English translation 'mystery' conjures up something spooky, dark, even incomprehensible.

The ancient philosophers graded '*musterion*' at the upper end of the knowledge scale attainable only by the persistent and ultra-clever disciple. But in Paul's use of the word we are not to think of the solution to a mysterious crime or entry to a mystery religion or elevation to an exclusive academy of higher knowledge. When Paul uses this term, he is drawing on Jewish and Old Testament categories. For him *musterion* is a secret that lies beyond the reach of human reason; a secret which could never be uncovered or known unless God Himself took the initiative and made it known to us.

And that, Paul declares, is precisely what God has done! In the gospel God has made known or revealed to us His deepest and most secret intentions. In short, 'mystery' is Paul's shorthand for 'God's Strategic Plan'.

DAY 242

EPHESIANS 3:1-9

Ephesians 3:1-9

BIBLE READING

PAUL'S MINISTRY TO THE GENTILES

3 For this reason, I, Paul, the prisoner of Christ Jesus on behalf of you Gentiles— ²you have heard, haven't you, about the administration of God's grace that He gave to me for you? ³The mystery was made known to me by revelation, as I have briefly written above. ⁴By reading this you are able to understand my insight about the mystery of the Messiah. ⁵This was not made known to people in other generations as it

is now revealed to His holy apostles and prophets by the Spirit: [6]the Gentiles are co-heirs, members of the same body, and partners of the promise in Christ Jesus through the gospel. [7]I was made a servant of this [gospel] by the gift of God's grace that was given to me by the working of His power.

[8]This grace was given to me—the least of all the saints!—to proclaim to the Gentiles the incalculable riches of the Messiah, [9]and to shed light for all about the administration of the mystery hidden for ages in God who created all things.

PRAYER: Loving heavenly Father, how I praise You that You are not a keeper of secrets but a revealer of mysteries. How I praise You, too, that by Your Holy Spirit You have unveiled the wonder of Your Son to me and now I am Yours - saved, surrendered and satisfied. The greatest wonder to my heart is that the initiative was all Yours. You came looking for me. My heart is Yours for all eternity. Amen.

DAY 243

EPHESIANS 1:3-10

THIS 'MYSTERY' IS God's single plan of salvation, born in eternity, disclosed in history.

We learn about this redemptive plan only because God has chosen to reveal it to us. God's grace has been 'lavished on us' to give us a share in His own 'wisdom and understanding' (v.8).

For Paul this mystery is no mystery at all: it's an open secret!

Paul has been given the inside story, been taken behind the scenes and shown a glimpse of God's secret strategy for human history!

Paul celebrates God's revelation of the 'mystery of His will' at the start of this letter (1:9-10). The scope of God's strategy is breathtaking. In Eugene Peterson's stirring paraphrase: God 'set it all out before us in Christ, a long-range plan in which everything would be brought together and summed up in him, everything in deepest heaven, everything on planet earth' (*The Message*).

All believers - not just an elite - have been initiated

into this 'mystery'. We have had a tip-off from unimpeachable sources; a leak from the highest authority has come to our notice: a file marked 'Top Secret' has fallen into our possession: classified 'inside information' is now in our hands – and hearts!

Ephesians 1:3-10

BIBLE
READING

GOD'S RICH BLESSINGS

³Blessed be the God and Father of our Lord Jesus Christ, who has blessed us with every spiritual blessing in the heavens, in Christ; ⁴for He chose us in Him, before the foundation of the world, to be holy and blameless in His sight. In love ⁵He predestined us to be adopted through Jesus Christ for Himself, according to His favor and will, ⁶to the praise of His glorious grace that He favored us with in the Beloved.

⁷In Him we have redemption through His blood, the forgiveness of our trespasses, according to the riches of His grace ⁸that He lavished on us with all wisdom and understanding. ⁹He made known to us the mystery of His will, according to His good pleasure that He planned in Him ¹⁰for the administration of the days of fulfillment —to bring everything together in the Messiah, both things in heaven and things on earth in Him.

AN ADDED PERSPECTIVE: 'So richly God has lavished upon us his grace, granting us complete insight and understanding of the open secret of his will showing us how it was the purpose of his design so to order it in the fullness of the ages that all things in heaven and alike should be gathered up in Christ – in the Christ in whom we have our inheritance allotted to us' (Eph. 1:9-11, Moffatt).

DAY
244

EPHESIANS 1:11-14

PAUL IS CELEBRATING that there is an overall plan God is working out. We are not at the cold mercy of the stars or in the grip of a heartless fate. There is a loving purpose behind the human story and a saving thread woven through it. Life is not meaningless. There is meaning and so there is hope. In Jesus Christ we discover God's saving plan and find out who we are and what we are here for. Our past history of sin has been cleansed at the cross. The forgiven have a future. We have been re-rooted and replanted in the grace that chose us before time began. Amid lies and distortions and fantasy, we have heard God speak His 'word of truth' (v.13) to us in the gospel of Jesus. When we responded to God's grace by believing, we were 'included in Christ' (v.13, NIV). 'In Christ' is Paul's favourite way of describing our salvation. When we believe, our personal stories are included in the saving story of Jesus Christ.

Our current experience of the Holy Spirit confirms us in this. The Spirit is the downpayment on our future salvation, the pledge of our coming inheritance when the narrative is satisfactorily concluded.

The Holy Spirit in us guarantees that we shall participate in the successful outcome of the story which is the praise of God's glory (1:13-14).

BIBLE READING

Ephesians 1:11-14

GOD'S RICH BLESSINGS

³Blessed be the God and Father of our Lord Jesus Christ, who has blessed us with every spiritual blessing in the heavens, in Christ; ⁴for He chose us in Him, before the foundation of the world, to be holy and blameless in His sight. In love ⁵He predestined us to be adopted through Jesus Christ for Himself, according to His favor and will, ⁶to the praise of His glorious grace that He favored us with in the Beloved.

⁷In Him we have redemption through His blood, the

forgiveness of our trespasses, according to the riches of His grace [8]that He lavished on us with all wisdom and understanding. [9]He made known to us the mystery of His will, according to His good pleasure that He planned in Him [10]for the administration of the days of fulfillment—to bring everything together in the Messiah, both things in heaven and things on earth in Him.

[11]In Him we were also made His inheritance, predestined according to the purpose of the One who works out everything in agreement with the decision of His will, [12]so that we who had already put our hope in the Messiah might bring praise to His glory.

[13]In Him you also, when you heard the word of truth, the gospel of your salvation—in Him when you believed—were sealed with the promised Holy Spirit. [14]He is the down payment of our inheritance, for the redemption of the possession, to the praise of His glory.

FOR THANKSGIVING: Reflect further on the thought that we are not meteorites speeding across the universe to burn out on the edge of some gravitational field; we are beings made in the image of God, an important part of God's bigger story, with a destiny that will ultimately see us joined to Jesus Christ in a marriage which will last for all eternity. How wonderful! How truly wonderful!

PAUL'S PRAYER IS our prayer for you as you travel through God's story with us. We pray that you may grow in understanding of the glorious redemptive plan of God for the world and your place in it. With Paul, we pray that you may be given 'a spirit of wisdom and revelation' to know God better, to know God's plans better, to know God's future better.

Paul prays that we might have our inner eyes – the 'eyes of your heart' (v.18) – opened to the heart-warming vision of God's future. Then we can live with our eyes on the end of the story. It might seem that

DAY
245

EPHESIANS 1:15-23

to know how a story ends would make life tediously predictable, like knowing the punch line of a joke. But not in this case. We are in an adventure story, marching on with hope in our hearts and the Voice that calls us ringing in our ears. Hope is sure because God has invested richly in our lives (v.18). We stay confident that the God who raised Jesus from the dead has the power to bring the story of salvation to a successful conclusion. Final victory has already been won. The name of Jesus is above every name that can be named. Jesus is the Truly Human One who already occupies the human place of dominion with all creation laid in tribute beneath His feet. Jesus is Head of the Church which shares His fullness but does not contain Him because He fills everything with His lordly presence.

BIBLE READING

Ephesians 1:15-23

GOD'S RICH BLESSINGS

³Blessed be the God and Father of our Lord Jesus Christ, who has blessed us with every spiritual blessing in the heavens, in Christ; ⁴for He chose us in Him, before the foundation of the world, to be holy and blameless in His sight. In love ⁵He predestined us to be adopted through Jesus Christ for Himself, according to His favor and will, ⁶to the praise of His glorious grace that He favored us with in the Beloved.

⁷In Him we have redemption through His blood, the forgiveness of our trespasses, according to the riches of His grace ⁸that He lavished on us with all wisdom and understanding. ⁹He made known to us the mystery of His will, according to His good pleasure that He planned in Him ¹⁰for the administration of the days of fulfillment—to bring everything together in the Messiah, both things in heaven and things on earth in Him.

¹¹In Him we were also made His inheritance, predestined according to the purpose of the One who works out everything in agreement with the decision of His will,

[12]so that we who had already put our hope in the Messiah might bring praise to His glory.

[13]In Him you also, when you heard the word of truth, the gospel of your salvation—in Him when you believed—were sealed with the promised Holy Spirit. [14]He is the down payment of our inheritance, for the redemption of the possession, to the praise of His glory.

PRAYER FOR SPIRITUAL INSIGHT

[15]This is why, since I heard about your faith in the Lord Jesus and your love for all the saints, [16]I never stop giving thanks for you as I remember you in my prayers. [17][I pray] that the God of our Lord Jesus Christ, the glorious Father, would give you a spirit of wisdom and revelation in the knowledge of Him. [18][I pray] that the eyes of your heart may be enlightened so you may know what is the hope of His calling, what are the glorious riches of His inheritance among the saints, [19]and what is the immeasurable greatness of His power to us who believe, according to the working of His vast strength.

GOD'S POWER IN CHRIST

[20]He demonstrated [this power] in the Messiah by raising Him from the dead and seating Him at His right hand in the heavens— [21]far above every ruler and authority, power and dominion, and every title given, not only in this age but also in the one to come. [22]And "He put everything under His feet" and appointed Him as head over everything for the church, [23]which is His body, the fullness of the One who fills all things in every way.

THOUGHT: 'A small boy in Sunday School who had recently given his heart to the Lord was asked by his teacher what was his goal for the future ... what he wanted more than anything in life. His teacher was surprised when he said, "To know God better". The "Spirit of wisdom and revelation" was already at work in that little boy's life. Is it at work in you, giving you that same desire - to know God better?'

DAY 246

EPHESIANS 1:19; 2:10; 3:20; 4:16

THE MORE WE are drawn into God's story, the more we come to realise that God is at work. In the modern world it is difficult to conceive of a God who is the chief actor in the drama. We are so used to running our own lives, and so absorbed with what we are doing and deciding, that we find it hard to imagine a world in which God does the most important things, not just on the big occasions like Exodus and resurrection, but every day, in every place.

In the opening burst of praise in this letter, Paul celebrates the initiatives God has taken to bless and save us. We are on the receiving end of what God has planned, decided, destined, done and made known. Because God is a relational Being - Father, Son and Holy Spirit - His actions are directed to personal ends. We are in the grip, not of inexorable laws, but of a loving purpose. Philosophical speculation about how God 'predestines' is best left to one side in favour of the helpful insight that such activity 'frees us to do human things, leaving God to do divine things' (Eugene Peterson). God is working powerfully for us (1:19), ahead of us (2:10), in us (3:20) and through us (4:16) in order to accomplish what He has planned to do (1:19-20; 3:11). And if there is one word that describes God's *modus operandi* - His telltale way of working - it is 'grace'.

BIBLE READING

Ephesians 1:19

¹⁹... and what is the immeasurable greatness of His power to us who believe, according to the working of His vast strength.

BIBLE READING

Ephesians 2:10

¹⁰For we are His creation—created in Christ Jesus for good works, which God prepared ahead of time so that we should walk in them.

Ephesians 3:20

²⁰Now to Him who is able to do above and beyond all that we ask or think—according to the power that works in you—

Ephesians 4:16

¹⁶From Him the whole body, fitted and knit together by every supporting ligament, promotes the growth of the body for building up itself in love by the proper working of each individual part.

TO PONDER: Throughout time the subject of God's sovereignty and mankind's freedom is one on which there has never been any full agreement. Our reading today suggests we leave such thoughts aside in favour of seeing that the Almighty 'frees us to do human things, leaving God to do divine things'. You can always depend on God to do His part, can He depend on you to do yours?

GOD WORKS EVERYTHING by His grace; His unsolicited gifts and unprompted initiatives. The story of God's grace in action is told by considering when it was He saved us. It was when we were dead in sins, dominated by the godless world system, drifting on the tides of fashion, driven by the sin-corrupted natural appetites and doomed under the wrath of God! But God who is rich in mercy, acted to save us by making us who were dead alive with Christ. He has raised us up and out of the dominion of darkness into the Lordship of His Son Jesus. He has seated us with Christ in the place of spiritual ascendancy over the powers that governed our lives. He is reclaiming our God-given drives and turning us into the paths of righteousness, recreating us for good works. This is God's gift to us which we receive by faith.

DAY
247
EPHESIANS 2:1-10

639

All of this happens to us as a result of our relationship to Jesus Christ. Our appreciation of His grace grows, when we realise that God has saved us in this way, so that we might be His showpiece in the future (2:7-9). Amazingly, God plans to put saved sinners on exhibit to show the splendour of His grace for ever. Meanwhile we are His 'workmanship'. He is working on us as a craftsman works on his chosen material. God even sets 'traps' of good works for us to walk right into every day! What a story this is.

BIBLE READING

Ephesians 2:1-10

FROM DEATH TO LIFE

2 And you were dead in your trespasses and sins [2]in which you previously walked according to this worldly age, according to the ruler of the atmospheric domain, the spirit now working in the disobedient. [3]We too all previously lived among them in our fleshly desires, carrying out the inclinations of our flesh and thoughts, and by nature we were children under wrath, as the others were also. [4]But God, who is abundant in mercy, because of His great love that He had for us, [5]made us alive with the Messiah even though we were dead in trespasses. By grace you are saved! [6]He also raised us up with Him and seated us with Him in the heavens, in Christ Jesus, [7]so that in the coming ages He might display the immeasurable riches of His grace in [His] kindness to us in Christ Jesus. [8]For by grace you are saved through faith, and this is not from yourselves; it is God's gift— [9]not from works, so that no one can boast. [10]For we are His creation—created in Christ Jesus for good works, which God prepared ahead of time so that we should walk in them.

PRAYER: How can I ever thank You enough, dear Father, for the fact that what I have received from You is not a reward for my effort but the result of Your undeserved love and infinite grace. You have saved me to 'show me off' to the universe as an exhibit of how grace can turn a hell-deserving sinner into a saint. All glory and honour be to Your wonderful name. Amen.

PAUL EMPHASISES THAT it was God's grace to share this secret with him (3:2-3). Paul makes no claim that he deserved to receive this privileged information. On the Damascus Road, God broke open Paul's world-view and blinded him with an amazing revelation of Jesus.

DAY
248

EPHESIANS 3:1-4

Why is he raising this here? Paul writes to the Ephesian believers in order to raise their awareness of the dimensions of their salvation and the high privileges of their Christian identity. Paul himself is evidence of a career, a ministry and a destiny passionately absorbed by this secret strategy of God.

This 'mystery' - this strategic plan of God's - is Paul's magnificent obsession! If we are going to track down God's secret strategy (vv.1-6), the first move we must make is to discover that it centres on Jesus Christ, on who He is, what has been achieved through Him and what is projected for Him (v.4). This is the reason why 'in Christ' is Paul's instinctive way of describing the central reality of our lives as Christians.

Everything of our saving involvement in this plan occurs 'in Christ'.

Everything that God destines for the redemption and perfecting of His creation is 'in Christ'.

Ephesians 3:1-4

BIBLE
READING

PAUL'S MINISTRY TO THE GENTILES

3 For this reason, I, Paul, the prisoner of Christ Jesus on behalf of you Gentiles— ²you have heard, haven't you, about the administration of God's grace that He gave to me for you? ³The mystery was made known to me by revelation, as I have briefly written above. ⁴By reading this you are able to understand my insight about the mystery of the Messiah.

THOUGHT: The Bible makes so much of Jesus because without Him there would be no eternal story. He is the hero of that story because He is the one who saves. A newspaper report told how a man saved a little boy from drowning. It said little about the boy but a lot about the one who saved him. The glory always goes to the one who saves. Isn't that how it should be?

DAY
249
ACTS 9:1-20

WHAT TURNED SAUL, the law-enforcing Pharisee into Paul, the gospel-storytelling apostle, centred on Jesus Christ?

Well, what did Paul think of Jesus when he set out for Damascus? For Saul, Jesus was a dead and discredited Messianic pretender. His followers – following the so-called Way – were on the wrong track altogether and deserved to be persecuted as heretics. What happened on the road? Saul's companions saw light and heard sound, but to Saul the light was vision and the sound a voice!

He saw, as the dying Stephen had seen, a man about his own age, shining with transcendent glory. The voice asked him: 'Saul, Saul, why are you persecuting Me?' (v.4). Dazzled and disorientated, Saul asks: 'Who are You, Lord?' The answer is devastating: 'I am Jesus, whom you are persecuting.' And right there, Saul made two startling discoveries about Jesus. Firstly, Jesus was alive when Saul had thought Him dead and buried and forgotten. And if Jesus was alive, then He was vindicated by God as the person He and His followers claimed Him to be! Far from being disgraced, Jesus was now honoured by sharing the very glory of the One Creator God. Stephen had been right; Saul had been wrong. Saul's slanted version of the story of God, Israel and the world, began to unravel and reform around Jesus the Christ.

Acts 9:1-20

THE DAMASCUS ROAD

9 Meanwhile Saul, still breathing threats and murder against the disciples of the Lord, went to the high priest ²and requested letters from him to the synagogues in Damascus, so that if he found any who belonged to the Way, either men or women, he might bring them as prisoners to Jerusalem. ³As he traveled and was nearing Damascus, a light from heaven suddenly flashed around him. ⁴Falling to the ground, he heard a voice saying to him, "Saul, Saul, why are you persecuting Me?"

⁵"Who are You, Lord?" he said.

"I am Jesus, whom you are persecuting," He replied. ⁶"But get up and go into the city, and you will be told what you must do."

⁷The men who were traveling with him stood speechless, hearing the sound but seeing no one. ⁸Then Saul got up from the ground, and though his eyes were open, he could see nothing. So they took him by the hand and led him into Damascus. ⁹He was unable to see for three days, and did not eat or drink.

SAUL'S BAPTISM

¹⁰Now in Damascus there was a disciple named Ananias. And the Lord said to him in a vision, "Ananias!"

"Here I am, Lord!" he said.

¹¹"Get up and go to the street called Straight," the Lord said to him, "to the house of Judas, and ask for a man from Tarsus named Saul, since he is praying there. ¹²In a vision he has seen a man named Ananias coming in and placing his hands on him so he may regain his sight."

¹³"Lord," Ananias answered, "I have heard from many people about this man, how much harm he has done to Your saints in Jerusalem. ¹⁴And he has authority here from the chief priests to arrest all who call on Your name."

¹⁵But the Lord said to him, "Go! For this man is My chosen instrument to carry My name before Gentiles, kings, and the sons of Israel. ¹⁶I will certainly show him how much he must suffer for My name!"

¹⁷So Ananias left and entered the house. Then he placed his hands on him and said, "Brother Saul, the Lord Jesus, who appeared to you on the road you were traveling, has sent me so you may regain your sight and be filled with the Holy Spirit."

¹⁸At once something like scales fell from his eyes, and he regained his sight. Then he got up and was baptized. ¹⁹And after taking some food, he regained his strength.

SAUL PROCLAIMING THE MESSIAH

Saul was with the disciples in Damascus for some days. ²⁰Immediately he began proclaiming Jesus in the synagogues: "He is the Son of God."

FOR ACTION: 'Conversion,' said someone, 'is the discovery that what we thought was a theory or an illusion is actually true.' Saul of Tarsus discovered that, and so no doubt have you. Just in case you haven't had your own personal moment of conversion we invite you now to accept Jesus with this simple prayer: 'Lord Jesus, come into my heart, forgive my sin and make me Your child. In Jesus' name. Amen.'

If you said this prayer and meant it, write to us and we will send you a free copy of *Every Day with Jesus for New Christians*.

DAY
250

ACTS 22

SAUL'S SECOND DISCOVERY came when Jesus said: 'Why are you persecuting Me?' It seeped into Saul's baffled mind that in hurting Christians he had in fact been hurting Jesus. Paul learned in a raw moment of experience what he later refined as a profound theology – that Jesus was as closely identified with His followers as a head is with its body! Paul was shattered to realise that he had been fighting God and opposing His Messiah! But if Jesus was the God-vindicated Christ then Paul's grasp of the biblical story was turned inside-out. Was this a conversion or a commission? Not a conversion in the sense of changing religions. Far from it. Paul now began to come to terms with the fact that the story of Jesus was the climax and centrepiece of the longer, larger story of God's dealings with the world focused in the story of Israel which he had always believed. This was a conversion to a Christ-centred view of things. It was certainly a commission, a drastic role reversal. A Rabbinic Jew, once dedicated to guarding jealously the exclusiveness of Israel, now finds himself selected to take the gospel to the Gentile world of 'lesser breeds without the law'.

As he did so Paul would realise that he was an agent of the one story that from Abraham onwards God had always been writing, with Jesus now at its heart.

Acts 22

BIBLE READING

22 ¹"Brothers and fathers, listen now to my defense before you." ²When they heard that he was addressing them in the Hebrew language, they became even quieter. ³He continued, "I am a Jewish man, born in Tarsus of Cilicia, but brought up in this city at the feet of Gamaliel, and educated according to the strict view of our patriarchal law. Being zealous for God, just as all of you are today, ⁴I persecuted this Way to the death, binding and putting both men and women in jail, ⁵as both the high priest and the whole council of elders can testify about me. Having received letters from them to the brothers, I was traveling to Damascus to bring those who were prisoners there to be punished in Jerusalem.

PAUL'S TESTIMONY

⁶"As I was traveling and near Damascus, about noon an intense light from heaven suddenly flashed around me. ⁷I fell to the ground and heard a voice saying to me, 'Saul, Saul, why are you persecuting Me?'

⁸"I answered, 'Who are You, Lord?'

"He said to me, 'I am Jesus the Nazarene, whom you are persecuting!' ⁹Now those who were with me saw the light, but they did not hear the voice of the One who was speaking to me.

¹⁰"Then I said, 'What should I do, Lord?'

"And the Lord told me, 'Get up and go into Damascus, and there you will be told about everything that is assigned for you to do.'

¹¹"Since I couldn't see because of the brightness of that light, I was led by the hand by those who were with me, and came into Damascus. ¹²Someone named Ananias, a devout man according to the law, having a good reputation with all the Jews residing there, ¹³came to me, stood by me, and said, 'Brother Saul, regain your sight.' And in that very hour I looked up and saw him. ¹⁴Then he said, 'The God of our fathers has appointed you to know His will, to see the Righteous One, and to hear the sound of His voice. ¹⁵For you will be a witness for Him to all people of what you have seen and heard. ¹⁶And now, why delay? Get up and be baptized, and wash away your sins by calling on His name.'

¹⁷"After I came back to Jerusalem and was praying in the temple complex, I went into a visionary state ¹⁸and saw Him telling me, 'Hurry and get out of Jerusalem quickly, because they will not accept your testimony about Me!'

¹⁹"But I said, 'Lord, they know that in synagogue after synagogue I had those who believed in You imprisoned and beaten. ²⁰And when the blood of Your witness Stephen was being shed, I myself was standing by and approving, and I guarded the clothes of those who killed him.'

²¹"Then He said to me, 'Go, because I will send you far away to the Gentiles.'"

PAUL'S ROMAN PROTECTION

²²They listened to him up to this word. Then they raised their voices, shouting, "Wipe this person off the earth—it's a disgrace for him to live!"

²³As they were yelling and flinging aside their robes and throwing dust into the air, ²⁴the commander ordered him to be brought into the barracks, directing that he be examined with the scourge, so he could discover the reason they were shouting against him like this. ²⁵As they stretched him out for the lash, Paul said to the centurion standing by, "Is it legal for you to scourge a man who is a Roman citizen and is uncondemned?"

26When the centurion heard this, he went and reported to the commander, saying, "What are you going to do? For this man is a Roman citizen."

27The commander came and said to him, "Tell me—are you a Roman citizen?"

"Yes," he said.

28The commander replied, "I bought this citizenship for a large amount of money."

"But I myself was born a citizen," Paul said.

29Therefore, those who were about to examine him withdrew from him at once. The commander too was alarmed when he realized Paul was a Roman citizen and he had bound him.

PAUL BEFORE THE SANHEDRIN

30The next day, since he wanted to find out exactly why Paul was being accused by the Jews, he released him and instructed the chief priests and all the Sanhedrin to convene. Then he brought Paul down and placed him before them.

PRAYER: Heavenly Father, I may never have done this before but today I want to thank You for the way You brought Paul to Yourself. What an impact his conversion has made on history - and also on me. Almost half the books of the New Testament are from his pen - and what I have learned from them is beyond all telling. So thank You, dear Lord, for that most wonderful conversion. And also for mine. Amen.

WHEN PAUL ARRIVED in Damascus it was with letters of authority from the high priest in Jerusalem to discredit Jesus and His followers. When he left the city it was as an ambassador accredited to the court of King Jesus. If this Messianic claimant, Jesus, had been resurrected, then, as a shrewd Pharisee, Paul knew that Jesus had received God's ultimate stamp of approval. Paul now proclaims Jesus as God's royal 'Son' who is exalted to a place of honour and Lordship which fulfils the promises made before to the Davidic dynasty (9:20).

DAY
251
ACTS 9:19b-31

Jesus must be Israel's long-awaited Messiah (9:22). Much still remained to be revealed to Paul, but the Damascus Road experience was his 'Copernical revolution'. His sun no longer circled the earth; the earth circled the sun. No longer did eternal reality centre on the Torah and the Temple as defining Israel's unique identity, but everything to do with God, salvation and the future revolves around Jesus Christ. Paul did not change his Judaism for another religion but he changed his Judaism! Everything that Abraham had been promised and with which Israel had been entrusted, was now made good, Paul saw, in Abraham's seed and Israel's Messiah, Jesus. He came from Jerusalem to take prisoners; he returned with only one: himself – a newly captured prisoner of Jesus.

BIBLE READING

Acts 9:19b-31

SAUL PROCLAIMING THE MESSIAH

Saul was with the disciples in Damascus for some days. [20]Immediately he began proclaiming Jesus in the synagogues: "He is the Son of God."

[21]But all who heard him were astounded and said, "Isn't this the man who, in Jerusalem, was destroying those who called on this name, and then came here for the purpose of taking them as prisoners to the chief priests?"

[22]But Saul grew more capable, and kept confounding the Jews who lived in Damascus by proving that this One is the Messiah.

[23]After many days had passed, the Jews conspired to kill him, [24]but their plot became known to Saul. So they were watching the gates day and night intending to kill him, [25]but his disciples took him by night and lowered him in a large basket through [an opening in] the wall.

SAUL IN JERUSALEM

[26]When he arrived in Jerusalem, he tried to associate with the disciples, but they were all afraid of him, since they did

not believe he was a disciple. ²⁷Barnabas, however, took him and brought him to the apostles and explained to them how, on the road, Saul had seen the Lord, and that He had talked to him, and how in Damascus he had spoken boldly in the name of Jesus. ²⁸Saul was coming and going with them in Jerusalem, speaking boldly in the name of the Lord. ²⁹He conversed and debated with the Hellenistic Jews, but they attempted to kill him. ³⁰When the brothers found out, they took him down to Caesarea and sent him off to Tarsus.

³¹So the church throughout all Judea, Galilee, and Samaria had peace, being built up and walking in the fear of the Lord and in the encouragement of the Holy Spirit, and it increased in numbers.

THOUGHT: Contemplate the fact that after Paul met Jesus Christ everything changed. The way he thought about God was changed. How he viewed Jesus was changed. His understanding of salvation was changed. And he had a new understanding too of the concept of freedom. An old hymn puts it: 'Make me a captive Lord, and then I shall be free'. Has salvation changed you? How much?

IF PAUL'S VIEW of Jesus changed as a result of his encounter on the Damascus Road, so did his view of the cross. Once, he had considered the Christians preaching of a crucified Messiah as a scandal, almost a blasphemy. For him, anyone who had hung on a cross was a law-breaker, an outcast, someone dying under the curse of God. But if Jesus had been raised from the dead, then He had been exonerated. The curse He bore must have been our curse so that blessing might come to us. Above all what had been a stumbling-block to him became the centre-piece of his message. Crucifixion had seemed the final denial that Jesus fitted into God's scheme of things. Now the cross placed Jesus at the very centre of God's saving strategy.

DAY
252

1 CORINTHIANS
1:18-25

The all-wise power of God working out His purposes in history is explosively concentrated in the conquering weakness of the cross. The almighty wisdom of God that is fashioning the complete recovery of His creation is most convincingly demonstrated in the foolishness of the cross (1:25). No one else would have dreamt up a plan that involved saving the world through a crucified carpenter. But God did. And God did it this way quite deliberately in order to shatter the idolatrous demands of the human mind that God should act, on our terms, in ways we deem to be clever or powerful (1:19-22). What an amazing plan this is!

BIBLE READING

1 Corinthians 1:18-25

CHRIST THE POWER AND WISDOM OF GOD

[18]For to those who are perishing the message of the cross is foolishness, but to us who are being saved it is God's power. [19]For it is written:

> "I will destroy the wisdom of the wise,
> and I will set aside the understanding of the experts."

[20]Where is the philosopher? Where is the scholar? Where is the debater of this age? Hasn't God made the world's wisdom foolish? [21]For since, in God's wisdom, the world did not know God through wisdom, God was pleased to save those who believe through the foolishness of the message preached. [22]For the Jews ask for signs and the Greeks seek wisdom, [23]but we preach Christ crucified, a stumbling block to the Jews and foolishness to the Gentiles. [24]Yet to those who are called, both Jews and Greeks, Christ is God's power and God's wisdom, [25]because God's foolishness is wiser than human wisdom, and God's weakness is stronger than human strength.

FOR PRAISE: Many years ago Sir John Bowring when sailing through the South China Sea saw a cross on a headland and was inspired to write this hymn:

In the Cross of Christ I glory, towering o'er the wrecks of time
All the light of sacred story, gathers round its head sublime.

In your own way and in your own words give God thanks for what one writer calls 'the radiant cross'.

DAY 253

1 CORINTHIANS 2:6-16

PAUL ONCE MORE employs his key term 'musterion'. The words 'we speak of God's secret wisdom' (2:7, NIV), more literally translated, come out as 'we speak God's wisdom in a mystery'. Recall that this strategic plan of God would have remained unknown unless He revealed it to us. God's plan to save the world, now focused in the cross of Jesus, baffles all godless minds. The rulers of the world certainly had no inkling when they contrived to have Jesus killed that they were crucifying the very Lord of glory. They no doubt went to bed on Good Friday satisfied with a day's work well done, having rid themselves of a troublesome prophet and Messianic pretender. But the unaided natural mind cannot understand that the world's salvation is achieved through the cross. The depths of God's wisdom are demonstrated at the cross. But only the Holy Spirit can show us this. The cross is the culmination of what God has been preparing for those who love Him. And what no eye has seen, no ear heard, no heart imagined or mind conceived, God has revealed to us by the Holy Spirit. The Holy Spirit searches the deep things in God and He comes up with nothing deeper than the cross. No higher wisdom can be found than God's redemptive plan in the cross. Those who see this are not the intellectually superior but those who love God!

651

BIBLE READING

1 Corinthians 2:6-16

SPIRITUAL WISDOM

[6]However, among the mature we do speak a wisdom, but not a wisdom of this age, or of the rulers of this age, who are coming to nothing. [7]On the contrary, we speak God's hidden wisdom in a mystery, which God predestined before the ages for our glory. [8]None of the rulers of this age knew it, for if they had known it, they would not have crucified the Lord of glory. [9]But as it is written:

> "What no eye has seen and no ear has heard,
> and what has never come into a man's heart,
> is what God has prepared for those who love Him."

[10]Now God has revealed them to us by the Spirit, for the Spirit searches everything, even the deep things of God. [11]For who among men knows the concerns of a man except the spirit of the man that is in him? In the same way, no one knows the concerns of God except the Spirit of God. [12]Now we have not received the spirit of the world, but the Spirit who is from God, in order to know what has been freely given to us by God. [13]We also speak these things, not in words taught by human wisdom, but in those taught by the Spirit, explaining spiritual things to spiritual people. [14]But the natural man does not welcome what comes from God's Spirit, because it is foolishness to him; he is not able to know it since it is evaluated spiritually. [15]The spiritual person, however, can evaluate everything, yet he himself cannot be evaluated by anyone. [16]For:

> "who has known the Lord's mind,
> that he may instruct Him?"

But we have the mind of Christ.

QUOTATION: 'If a spotlight from outer space was to be pointed at the most important place on our planet it would fall upon a hill called Calvary. But the cross that was lifted up there at a point in time was done so that we might see that really it is timeless. There was a cross in the heart of God before there was a cross uplifted at Calvary. He is the Lamb slain from "before the foundation of the world".' (E. Stanley Jones)

DAY 254

2 CORINTHIANS 4:4-6

HOWEVER INTENSE THE visible light that dazzled him, it was the piercing inner illumination that Paul never got over. For him, that experience was like the dawn of creation when God said, 'Let there be light'. Paul looked into the radiant face of Jesus Christ and knew that what shone there was the very glory of God. He saw what James and John and Peter had seen on the Mount of Transfiguration which showed that Jesus was the summary and fulfilment of all God's previous revelation. The very 'shekinah' glory of God was no longer concentrated in the Jerusalem Temple, available only to the priests, but was streaming from the face of Jesus Christ into all believing hearts. The outshining of God's inner holiness was no longer, as the Pharisees had claimed, shining on those gathered round to study the Torah. It was to be found reflected in the eyes of those who read the open book of Jesus' life and death and resurrection. The glory Abraham glimpsed, the glory Moses longed to see, the glory that filled the tabernacle and prevented priests from ministering in the Temple – that glory which irradiated earlier phases of the story, has now 'shone in our hearts to give the light of the knowledge of the glory of God in the face of Jesus Christ'.

BIBLE READING

2 Corinthians 4:4-6

⁴For I am not conscious of anything against myself, but I am not justified by this. The One who evaluates me is the Lord. ⁵Therefore don't judge anything prematurely, before the Lord comes, who will both bring to light what is hidden in darkness and reveal the intentions of the hearts. And then praise will come to each one from God.

THE APOSTLES' EXAMPLE OF HUMILITY

⁶Now, brothers, I have applied these things to myself and Apollos for your benefit, so that you may learn from us the saying: "Nothing beyond what is written." The purpose is that none of you will be inflated with pride in favor of one person over another.

> **PRAYER:** Lord Jesus Christ, the Lamb slain before the foundation of the world, how glad I am that I too have looked into Your face, seen the glory of God shining through You to me, and that now I am a recipient of Your grace. Grace sought me, grace bought me, grace taught me, grace caught me – and now grace has me for ever. I am more grateful than words can convey. Amen.

DAY
255

EPHESIANS 3:1-6

IF GOD'S PLAN centres on Christ (3:4), our next move to stay on the track of this mystery is to discover here that it was not revealed to previous generations as it has now been revealed to God's holy apostles and prophets (3:5).

And the 'not' means not disclosed until now. With hindsight, the 'mystery' is seen to be the actual fulfilment in a particular time and person of the Old Testament's prophetic promises. Paul is not indulging in some mystical spirituality, but is dealing with what has happened in history. There was a time when this secret was hidden: now it is out in the open!

That God's secret has been entrusted 'to His holy apostles and prophets by the Spirit' makes an important point about the divine authority of the New Testament as Scripture here.

In the Old Testament, God's 'secret' was disclosed only to His prophets who stood in God's privy council or secret assembly (Amos 3:7; Jer. 23:22).

Just as, by the Spirit, their revelation became foundational Scripture so, by analogy, those who receive and transmit the '*musterion*' of God - namely the New Testament apostles and the prophetic figures associated with them - by the same Spirit, lay the foundation for the New Testament as authoritative Scripture (Eph. 2:20).

Ephesians 3:1-6

BIBLE READING

PAUL'S MINISTRY TO THE GENTILES

3 For this reason, I, Paul, the prisoner of Christ Jesus on behalf of you Gentiles— ²you have heard, haven't you, about the administration of God's grace that He gave to me for you? ³The mystery was made known to me by revelation, as I have briefly written above. ⁴By reading this you are able to understand my insight about the mystery of the Messiah. ⁵This was not made known to people in other generations as it is now revealed to His holy apostles and prophets by the Spirit: ⁶the Gentiles are co-heirs, members of the same body, and partners of the promise in Christ Jesus through the gospel.

THOUGHT: In giving God glory for Christ and His cross we must not forget (as we have been reminded today) the work of the Holy Spirit. He is referred to in Scripture by various terms - among others by the term, '*paraclete*'. It is a Greek term made up of two words - '*para*' meaning 'alongside' and '*kaleo*' meaning 'to summon or call'. We call and He comes alongside. Simple, but so sublime!

DAY
256

ROMANS 16:25-27

PAUL IS INSISTENT that the revelation of the mystery is not an insight into perennial truths but a breaking open of a long-guarded secret. It does not deal in vague abstractions but is disclosed in a particular person who lived and died and rose again in a particular stage of the story. This is what gives his gospel its special shape, as a story to tell to the nations.

The prophets sowed the seeds of this mystery, but only with the coming of Jesus have these seeds sprung up into visible fruit. With the Word made flesh, the Old Testament Scriptures find their true voice. With His coming, the prophetic writings come alive and, in the gospel of Christ preached by the apostles, speak clearly as never before. In other words, once more, we see that the story of Jesus makes sense of the Old Testament story of God's dealings with Israel. It was at 'God's command' that all was revealed in Christ at this time. And what God aims for is what He has had in mind since He made promises to Abraham, that all nations should hear, believe and obey and so be written into the story of the One Creator God and Jesus the world's true Lord and Saviour.

BIBLE READING

Romans 16:25-27

GLORY TO GOD

²⁵Now to Him who has power to strengthen you according to my gospel and the proclamation of Jesus Christ, according to the revelation of the sacred secret kept silent for long ages, ²⁶but now revealed and made known through the prophetic Scriptures, according to the command of the eternal God, to advance the obedience of faith among all nations— ²⁷to the only wise God, through Jesus Christ—to Him be the glory forever! Amen.

TO PONDER: Once again, the issue of making this message of Christ's death and resurrection known to the whole world is before us. 'Evangelism,' said someone, 'is not complete until the evangelised become evangelists.' Has your reception of Christ's salvation stirred you to share it with others? The only way people can be saved is when they hear the message. Has anyone ever heard it from your lips?

PAUL REMINDS THE Colossians that just as he has been appointed to 'fill up' his quota in the sufferings associated with Christ in the Messianic age (cf.Rom. 8:22), so he is commissioned to preach the fullness of God's Word. In one sense, the Word of God, enshrined in the message of the gospel, remains incomplete and unfulfilled until it is embraced by the Gentiles. The time for this has now come.

DAY
257

COLOSSIANS 1:24-2:5

At the heart of this 'secret plan' is the revelation that in Christ the scope of God's plans is not restricted to Jews but expands to include all nations. The rich fabric of God's glory is demonstrated when God clothes the whole world in His grace and affirms the universal Lordship of Jesus Christ. The presence of Christ in and among Gentile believers is the basis of their own hope of sharing in the glory of God. To see God's glory shining in the Temple or diffused among His chosen people, Israel, was one thing; to see God's glory shimmering through previously pagan nations as the name of Jesus is confessed, is cause for even greater wonder. God's plan, centring on Jesus, is far-reaching and aims to fill the whole earth with His glory 'as the waters cover the sea' (Isa. 11:9, NIV).

We are invited to explore the central mystery which is Jesus who embodies the wisdom by which God made the world (2:2-3; cf.1:15-20).

BIBLE READING

Colossians 1:24-2:5

PAUL'S MINISTRY

[24]Now I rejoice in my sufferings for you, and I am completing in my flesh what is lacking in Christ's afflictions for His body, that is, the church. [25]I have become its minister, according to God's administration that was given to me for you, to make God's message fully known, [26]the mystery hidden for ages and generations but now revealed to His saints. [27]God wanted to make known to those among the Gentiles the glorious wealth of this mystery, which is Christ in you, the hope of glory. [28]We proclaim Him, warning and teaching everyone with all wisdom, so that we may present everyone mature in Christ. [29]I labor for this, striving with His strength that works powerfully in me.

2 For I want you to know how great a struggle I have for you, for those in Laodicea, and for all who have not seen me in person. [2][I want] their hearts to be encouraged and joined together in love, so that they may have all the riches of assured understanding, and have the knowledge of God's mystery—Christ. [3]In Him all the treasures of wisdom and knowledge are hidden.

CHRIST VERSUS THE COLOSSIAN HERESY

[4]I am saying this so that no one will deceive you with persuasive arguments. [5]For I may be absent in body, but I am with you in spirit, rejoicing to see your good order and the strength of your faith in Christ.

FOR PRAISE: God's glory no longer shines through a temple in Jerusalem but through the lives of Christ's followers throughout the world, of which you are one. Give God thanks in your own way now for putting the glow and glory of His presence in your heart and ask Him that nothing in your life may ever prevent the light and glory of His presence shining through.

IN OUR NEXT move in pursuing the 'mystery', we stumble right on the particular aspect of the secret Paul is relishing (3:6).

What Paul is marvelling over here is the formation of an unprecedented new community embracing the two groups who represent the bitterest divisions which tear the human race apart – Jews and Gentiles.

Throughout his apostolic career, Paul consistently fought for this aspect of the big mystery of God bringing all things under the Lordship of Christ. He warned the Galatians about the danger of Jewish Christian exclusivism and legalism: he upbraided the Roman Church for Gentile Christian arrogance.

Grace not race, faith not law, Spirit-motivated obedience from the heart not external signs like circumcision – these are the true identity-markers of the new covenant people of God.

For Paul, Israel, in line with Noah and Abraham before her, had always a larger vocation, not to be displaced but to be the nucleus of a world-wide covenant family of faith!

So startling is this new unity in the Church that Paul coins three new words especially for it, each with a prefix – which in the Greek language means 'with' or 'joint': '*sun-kleronoma*' ('joint heirs'), '*sussoma*' ('joint-body'), '*summetoxa*' ('joint sharers')!

Ephesians 3:5-6

BIBLE
READING

⁵This was not made known to people in other generations as it is now revealed to His holy apostles and prophets by the Spirit:

⁶the Gentiles are co-heirs, members of the same body, and partners of the promise in Christ Jesus through the gospel.

BIBLE READING

Acts 10:44-48

GENTILE CONVERSION AND BAPTISM

⁴⁴While Peter was still speaking these words, the Holy Spirit came down on all those who heard the message. ⁴⁵The circumcised believers who had come with Peter were astounded, because the gift of the Holy Spirit had been poured out on the Gentiles also. ⁴⁶For they heard them speaking in [other] languages and declaring the greatness of God.

Then Peter responded, ⁴⁷"Can anyone withhold water and prevent these from being baptized, who have received the Holy Spirit just as we have?" ⁴⁸And he commanded them to be baptized in the name of Jesus Christ. Then they asked him to stay for a few days.

THOUGHT: Some Christians are thrilled that God unites them to Christ but not so thrilled that He unites them with others who may not be as likeable. But that's what grace is for. It is given to us to love those we may not naturally even like. If you are having troubles in your relationships it is not because grace is not flowing; it can only be because it is not being received.

DAY 259

EPHESIANS 2:11-22

IN CHRIST AND through His peace-making cross, there has come about an unprecedented unity of Jew and Gentile which Paul celebrates here.

The inclusion of 'uncircumcised' Gentiles on an equal footing with Jewish believers, in the one family of God through faith in Christ, is especially notable because they were previously 'excluded from citizenship in Israel and strangers to the covenants of the promise' (2:12, NRSV).

The plural 'covenants' and the singular 'promise' indicate again that the several covenants serve to implement the one overarching promise-plan of God. In the single strategy of God, the Gentiles have been welcomed into 'the social novelty of the covenant of grace' (John Yoder).

Created by the grace of God, the cross of Jesus and the genius of the Holy Spirit, this new body is the place where pride and exclusiveness are overcome, where the ethnic hatred and religious bigotry that still bedevil our world are swallowed up in Christ. Here is revealed the down-to-earth, incarnational, relational reality and victory of God's strategic plan – here where former bitter enemies can join hands and lives in Jesus Christ. No wonder He calls it a new human race (2:15)! Through Jesus alone, we all have access to the one Father by the one Spirit. Together we make up the living temple of God.

Ephesians 2:11-22

BIBLE READING

UNITY IN CHRIST

[11]So then, remember that at one time you were Gentiles in the flesh—called "the uncircumcised" by those called "the circumcised," done by hand in the flesh. [12]At that time you were without the Messiah, excluded from the citizenship of Israel, and foreigners to the covenants of the promise, with no hope and without God in the world. [13]But now in Christ Jesus, you who were far away have been brought near by the blood of the Messiah. [14]For He is our peace, who made both groups one and tore down the dividing wall of hostility. In His flesh, [15]He did away with the law of the commandments in regulations, so that He might create in Himself one new man from the two, resulting in peace. [16][He did this so] that He might reconcile both to God in one body through the cross and put the hostility to death by it. [17]When [Christ] came, He proclaimed the good news of peace to you who were far away and peace to those who were near. [18]For through Him we both have access by one Spirit to the Father. [19]So then you are no longer foreigners and strangers, but fellow citizens with the saints, and members of God's household, [20]built on the foundation of the apostles and prophets, with Christ Jesus Himself as the cornerstone. [21]The whole building is being

fitted together in Him and is growing into a holy sanctuary in the Lord, ²²in whom you also are being built together for God's dwelling in the Spirit.

TO PONDER: The issue of racial distinctions flares up from time to time in different parts of the world, and sometimes even in the Church. Take a moment to read John 17 focusing on our Lord's prayer for unity amongst His people. In your own words form a prayer for Christian unity and present it to the Lord. Prayer really does change things. Never let go of that important truth.

TODAY, WE FIND that God's plan is a working-out of His heart-felt intention in creating the world in the first place (3:9c).

DAY
260

EPHESIANS 3:6-9
TITUS 1:1-3

God, the Holy Father, gave us being with a view to our becoming His faithful children, in loving and obedient partnership with Him, and a perfect creaturely counterpart to His eternal Son – in short a Bride for Christ (1:4-5; 5:25ff.).

The One Creator God always intended to fulfil His creation's potential and to bring it to perfection in alliance with His mature sons. Since our Great Rebellion, under the terms our sin has set, this destiny must pass through suffering and go the way of the cross before it can again enter into its appointed glory.

It has always been His aim, undeflected by sin, to redeem His creation, not to replace it with something else.

Once again we are reminded that there is no plan-B; it's always been plan-A!

All this flows out of the Fatherly heart of a God who took the responsibility for creating this world knowing He had the power and love to redeem it.

In Christ, the Father is set to achieve that world-wide family in a perfected creation which before the Fall, before even creation itself, He had set His heart on. Through the gospel, in the revelation of this 'mystery' we are in touch with the ultimate purpose of all reality.

BIBLE READING

Ephesians 3:6-9

[6]the Gentiles are co-heirs, members of the same body, and partners of the promise in Christ Jesus through the gospel. [7]I was made a servant of this [gospel] by the gift of God's grace that was given to me by the working of His power.

[8]This grace was given to me—the least of all the saints!—to proclaim to the Gentiles the incalculable riches of the Messiah, [9]and to shed light for all about the administration of the mystery hidden for ages in God who created all things.

BIBLE READING

Titus 1:1-3

GREETING

1 Paul, a slave of God, and an apostle of Jesus Christ for the faith of God's elect and the knowledge of the truth that leads to godliness, [2]in the hope of eternal life that God, who cannot lie, promised before time began, [3]and has in His own time revealed His message in the proclamation that I was entrusted with by the command of God our Savior:

PRAYER: O Father, the thought of me, a hell-deserving sinner, being close to You in heaven is almost more than my mind can take in, but to be actually joined to Jesus Christ in that mysterious union that a bride and bridegroom enjoy is even more mind-blowing. And it's not because of my merit but because of Your mercy. Eternity will be too short to express my gratitude and praise. Thank You, my Father. Amen.

BEFORE WE KNOW where we are, as we stay on the trail of this mystery, we find ourselves tracking down the impact of this secret plan on the cosmic forces in the heavenly realms (3:10).

And it is through the Church that the revolution rumbles round the heavenly realms.

Did Paul really say: 'through the church'! Yes, despite everything, it is by a Church in which the ability of the powers to divide and rule and destroy has been broken by the cross of Christ, that God's 'multi-coloured wisdom' is flaunted before their disbelieving eyes.

As a sample of the 'new human race' the Church is called to exhibit a startling new unity which overcomes the deep racial and cultural divisions in society. We defeat the 'powers' of evil by this show of unity and herald to them that their division of the universe into rival wills is doomed to fail. Our unity in the relationships of family, of work and in the Church, radiates outwards from our reconciliation with God until its 'peace' touches and confounds the spiritual forces of wickedness.

Our oneness demonstrates to the cosmic powers, and to the human institutions which welcome them, that God is wise enough to find ways of bringing about His ultimate purpose to unite all things in Christ (1:10-11).

DAY 261

EPHESIANS 3:10-13

Ephesians 3:10-13

BIBLE READING

[8]This grace was given to me—the least of all the saints!—to proclaim to the Gentiles the incalculable riches of the Messiah, [9]and to shed light for all about the administration of the mystery hidden for ages in God who created all things.

[10]This is so that God's multi-faceted wisdom may now be made known through the church to the rulers and authorities in the heavens. [11]This is according to the purpose of the ages, which He made in the Messiah, Jesus our Lord, [12]in whom we

have boldness, access, and confidence through faith in Him. [13]So then I ask you not to be discouraged over my afflictions on your behalf, for they are your glory.

> QUOTATION: 'I stood one evening in front of the Niagara Falls and watched with bated breath as a floodlight was turned on, slowly changing colours from blue to red, from red to yellow, from yellow to green and so on. I came away reflecting on the multi-coloured wisdom that God delights to display through His Church and thought how sad that so much of it is not seen because of our lack of unity.' (Tom Rees)

DAY 262

EPHESIANS 3:11-21

WHAT A BREATHTAKING mystery story this is – God's strategic plan!

But the mystery is not mere mystification! It is a secret that can be received, grasped and communicated. Yet it remains a mystery for all that in so far as it partakes of the transcendence and infinity of God Himself.

It cannot therefore be contained. Though it can be known, it surpasses knowledge (3:19). The riches of Christ are unsearchable (3:8), as are the riches of the Father's glory (3:16). The ways and wisdom of this gracious God are multi-faceted and past finding out, confounding the evil intelligence of the cosmic powers (3:10). The mysterious will of love in Christ has heights and depths and lengths and breadth which are unfathomable (3:18) and which only all the saints across all the ages can begin together to quantify. Only through prayer do we have access to this realm of mystery. The secret of the Lord is for those who love, for those who together with all the saints experience the dimensions of God's love.

The fullness to be experienced is the immeasurable fullness of God Himself (3:19b). The fullness of what this God is able to do lies beyond anything we can ask or imagine (3:20). The glory that radiates in the Church will need eternal ages for justice to be done to it (3:21).

Ephesians 3:11-21

⁸This grace was given to me—the least of all the saints!—to proclaim to the Gentiles the incalculable riches of the Messiah, ⁹and to shed light for all about the administration of the mystery hidden for ages in God who created all things. ¹⁰This is so that God's multi-faceted wisdom may now be made known through the church to the rulers and authorities in the heavens.

¹¹This is according to the purpose of the ages, which He made in the Messiah, Jesus our Lord, ¹²in whom we have boldness, access, and confidence through faith in Him. ¹³So then I ask you not to be discouraged over my afflictions on your behalf, for they are your glory.

PRAYER FOR SPIRITUAL POWER

¹⁴For this reason I bow my knees before the Father ¹⁵from whom every family in heaven and on earth is named. ¹⁶[I pray] that He may grant you, according to the riches of His glory, to be strengthened with power through His Spirit in the inner man, ¹⁷and that the Messiah may dwell in your hearts through faith. [I pray that] you, being rooted and firmly established in love, ¹⁸may be able to comprehend with all the saints what is the length and width, height and depth [of God's love], ¹⁹and to know the Messiah's love that surpasses knowledge, so you may be filled with all the fullness of God.

²⁰Now to Him who is able to do above and beyond all that we ask or think—according to the power that works in you—²¹to Him be glory in the church and in Christ Jesus to all generations, forever and ever. Amen.

THOUGHT: 'Come you surveyors and mathematicians,' cried C.H. Spurgeon one evening from his pulpit in the Metropolitan Tabernacle, 'bring your measuring instruments and see if you can measure the love of God.' How can you measure the immeasurable, define the indefinable, limit the illimitable? It's best not to try - just simply bask in its wonder and be thankful to God that He is who He is.

DAY 263

EPHESIANS 4:17-5:2

EVERYTHING WE DO as believers 'in Christ' makes sense. It does so because we are connected to the big story of who God is, who we are in Christ and what we are here for. And what we are here for is to 'image-forth' God's character and story. The 'new self' we put on when we were made alive in Christ is 'created to be like God in true righteousness and holiness' (4:23-24, NIV).

Our audaciously high calling, restored by redemption, is to copy God (5:1)! Why work in order to give to others, rather than steal and rob (4:28)? Because God is a working God who made the world in six days, who looked forward to the weekend and could enjoy it all the more for having achieved something worthwhile. Which is just the reason we need not only to work but to rest and take a Sabbath.

Why tell the truth? Not because it will always make people like you; they may get enraged. Not because it will guarantee your children will like you or because it will advance your career prospects with the company. We are to tell the truth because that is the kind of people we have learned to be in the school of Jesus (4:21,25).

Why forgive? Because, Paul reminds the Ephesians, it re-enacts the gracious story of how 'God in Christ forgave you' (4:32, NIV).

The point is clear: if you know who you are in the big story, you know what you're here for.

BIBLE READING

Ephesians 4:17-5:2

LIVING THE NEW LIFE

[17]Therefore, I say this and testify in the Lord: You should no longer walk as the Gentiles walk, in the futility of their thoughts. [18]They are darkened in their understanding, excluded from the life of God, because of the ignorance that is in them and because of the hardness of their hearts. [19]They became callous and gave themselves over to promiscuity for the practice of every kind of impurity with a desire for more and more.

²⁰But that is not how you learned about the Messiah, ²¹assuming you heard Him and were taught by Him, because the truth is in Jesus: ²²you took off your former way of life, the old man that is corrupted by deceitful desires; ²³you are being renewed in the spirit of your minds; ²⁴you put on the new man, the one created according to God's [likeness] in righteousness and purity of the truth.

²⁵Since you put away lying, "Speak the truth, each one to his neighbor," because we are members of one another. ²⁶"Be angry and do not sin." Don't let the sun go down on your anger, ²⁷and don't give the Devil an opportunity. ²⁸The thief must no longer steal. Instead, he must do honest work with his own hands, so that he has something to share with anyone in need. ²⁹No rotten talk should come from your mouth, but only what is good for the building up of someone in need, in order to give grace to those who hear. ³⁰And don't grieve God's Holy Spirit, who sealed you for the day of redemption. ³¹All bitterness, anger and wrath, insult and slander must be removed from you, along with all wickedness. ³²And be kind and compassionate to one another, forgiving one another, just as God also forgave you in Christ.

5 Therefore, be imitators of God, as dearly loved children. ²And walk in love, as the Messiah also loved us and gave Himself for us, a sacrificial and fragrant offering to God.

TO PONDER: Is it becoming clearer why we have embarked upon this theme of God's story? We have the opportunity of being microcosms of the Godhead demonstrating to all around us on earth how God functions in heaven. He forgives, so should we. He offers unconditional love, so should we. He works, so should we. He speaks truth, so should we. That's why we are here - and that is why God keeps us here.

DAY 264

EPHESIANS 5:25-33

LIVING OUT THE story is the Christian reason for every action and relationship. It is with this in mind that Paul views Christian marriage as a vivid sign of the greater 'mystery' of Christ and Church (5:31-33)! Today, the question is not so much whether we should allow divorce and remarriage but the bigger question: why get married at all?

The final New Testament answer would appear to be: because the covenant commitment of marriage enshrines the great mystery and tells out something essential about God's big story.

To commit and to vow, to be faithful in keeping covenant, until death or desertion breaks that covenant, is to tell the story of the One Creator God who kept covenant with His creation even after the Flood. This God bonded with Israel and remained - as Hosea did - obstinately determined to redeem His love - even if it cost Him the life of His only Son on the cross.

Pretty soon it will be a definite Christian act of faith and testimony to get married. Why? Because it only makes sense to get married at all if marriage is connected to the big story of God's covenant love for His people, Christ's sacrificial passion for His bride the Church!

Husbands, then, sacrifice for their wives because Christ did: wives submit to husbands who do that - and both live to tell the tale!

BIBLE READING

Ephesians 5:25-33

²⁵Husbands, love your wives, just as also Christ loved the church and gave Himself for her, ²⁶to make her holy, cleansing her in the washing of water by the word. ²⁷He did this to present the church to Himself in splendor, without spot or wrinkle or any such thing, but holy and blameless. ²⁸In the same way, husbands should love their wives as their own bodies. He who loves his wife loves himself. ²⁹For no one ever hates his own flesh, but provides and cares for it,

just as Christ does for the church, ³⁰since we are members of His body.

³¹ "For this reason a man will leave his father and mother
and be joined to his wife,
and the two will become one flesh."

³²This mystery is profound, but I am talking about Christ and the church. ³³To sum up, each one of you is to love his wife as himself, and the wife is to respect her husband.

PRAYER: O God, in an age when it seems marriage is no longer seen in the light it once was, help us as Your people to show the world by our own marriages what fidelity, commitment and covenant are all about. Dear Father, You have kept Your covenant with us, help us keep our covenants with one another. Pour Your Spirit upon us that we might show the world the way to live. In Jesus' name. Amen.

ENTRUSTED WITH GOD'S plans, Paul's role

in this is as God's secret agent. God's agents live by grace alone - a grace which calls and commissions and flows in and out of Paul as a mighty power (3:7-8).

Grace could carry the day with Paul because he regarded himself in humility as the 'least of all the saints'.

Grace has been given to me - Paul insists - to preach the unsearchable riches of Christ. No limit therefore can be put on such resources. Now that is a mystery!

And Paul receives grace in order to make plain to everyone the 'administration of the mystery' (3:9).

What Paul does with God's secret is exactly the opposite of what the cults do with their murky mysteries. They hide them away in dark rites and obscure sanctuaries which only the special few can enter. But the Christian gospel which discloses the mystery of God's strategic plan is an open secret for everyone to share!

DAY
265

EPHESIANS 3:6-9
2 TIMOTHY 1:8-11

The gospel blows the lid off the stale and murky mysteries of the cults and sects and blows the bracing fresh air of freedom through every nook and cranny of our tired and musty world – even the prison cells where God's special agents are held!

The God whose eternal purpose is being worked out in Christ is a God whom we may approach 'with freedom and confidence' (3:12, NIV) so that we may boldly come to, and boldly go from, God's presence.

BIBLE READING

Ephesians 3:6-9

⁶the Gentiles are co-heirs, members of the same body, and partners of the promise in Christ Jesus through the gospel. ⁷I was made a servant of this [gospel] by the gift of God's grace that was given to me by the working of His power.

⁸This grace was given to me—the least of all the saints!—to proclaim to the Gentiles the incalculable riches of the Messiah, ⁹and to shed light for all about the administration of the mystery hidden for ages in God who created all things.

BIBLE READING

2 Timothy 1:8-11

NOT ASHAMED OF THE GOSPEL

⁸So don't be ashamed of the testimony about our Lord, or of me His prisoner. Instead, share in suffering for the gospel, relying on the power of God,

⁹ who has saved us and called us with a holy calling,
not according to our works, but according to His own
   purpose and grace,
which was given to us in Christ Jesus before time began.
¹⁰ This has now been made evident
through the appearing of our Savior Christ Jesus,
   who has abolished death
and has brought life and immortality to light
   through the gospel.

[11] For this [gospel] I was appointed a herald, apostle, and teacher,

FOR PRAISE: What if Paul had kept to himself the secrets God revealed to him? Doubtless God would have raised up someone else, but be that as it may, let's give praise to God for the fact that the secret is out – God has a plan for the universe, a plan in which we play a part. We are now God's secret agents – not to keep His secrets but to reveal them to whoever will listen.

PAUL'S 'SUFFERING' IN the course of duty alerts us to the dangers faced by a special agent inside enemy territory. We must never let down our guard or lose contact with base. We remain subversives with the 'gospel of peace'. The story we are caught up in is not a fantasy in virtual reality but a real battle with hostile forces. We need the whole armour of God to sustain the fight.

DAY
266
EPHESIANS 6:19-20

But we need not be discouraged by those of our agents who, operating behind enemy lines, suffer pain and imprisonment for their daring deeds, as Paul did (3:1; 6:20). To recount the noble company of apostles and martyrs is to perpetuate the memory of those of our agents who are 'missing – presumed dead'.

Praying in the Spirit, praying at all times, praying alertly, praying for God's special emissaries – this is the strange and paradoxical way in which God works out through us His sovereign plan. 'Boldness' ('fearlessly' NIV) is a favourite attitude of Paul. Secret agent he may be, but there is nothing secret about his message. Paul asks for prayer that he might freely and publicly proclaim the 'open secret' of God's redemptive plan for which he is 'an ambassador in chains' (6:19-20). Strange state for an ambassador to be in! But that's part of the mystery, too; prison bars cannot stop this gospel or impede God's plan.

Ephesians 6:19-20

¹⁹Pray also for me, that the message may be given to me when I open my mouth to make known with boldness the mystery of the gospel. ²⁰For this I am an ambassador in chains. Pray that I might be bold enough in Him to speak as I should.

FOR ACTION: In the light of today's reading, in which the power of persevering prayer has been highlighted, spend at least 15 minutes in prayer for those 'operating behind enemy lines' - those special agents whose lives are often in danger as they work to share the gospel in countries where the Christian faith is opposed. It may be a cliché but it is true - prayer changes things. It really does.

DAY 267

EPHESIANS 1:6,12,14; 3:21

AND THE END of all things? 'To Him be glory in the church ... forever and ever' (3:21). Every aspect of this sovereign strategy moves majestically to magnify His grace and glory (1:6,12,14).

The Father's eternal plan (1:5-6) to gather a family in love moves into our time and space worlds to pick us up in His saving hand and it's all 'to the praise of His glorious grace' (1:6).

His historic action in Bethlehem and Calvary (1:6-7), redeeming us in Christ at the cost of His blood, forgiving us by grace, sharing with us His stupendous strategy for the world, fills us with unspeakable wonder so that we exist 'for the praise of his glory' (1:12, NIV).

His invasion of our lives by His Holy Spirit's empowering presence, leaving the indelible stamp of His claim upon us, continues to redound 'to the praise of His glory' (1:14).

The end of all things is to share in the Trinity-life of the One Creator God, to know with all the saints the four-dimensional love of this God in Christ; in the Spirit, to be embraced for ever by the same love with which the Father eternally loves the Son – this is the end of all things.

This is the eco-system of the divine life. This is the glory of God's love and will flow out to us and back to God again in loving praise and covenant faithfulness. God's is the true love which makes the world go round!

Ephesians 1:6,12,14

BIBLE READING

⁶to the praise of His glorious grace that He favored us with in the Beloved.

. . . .

¹²so that we who had already put our hope in the Messiah might bring praise to His glory.

. . . .

¹⁴He is the down payment of our inheritance, for the redemption of the possession, to the praise of His glory.

Ephesians 3:21

BIBLE READING

²¹to Him be glory in the church and in Christ Jesus to all generations, forever and ever. Amen.

THOUGHT: The fact that God is working in us and through us to the praise of His glory may sometimes produce mixed emotions in us – especially when He works to rid us of those things that hinder His image being seen in us. C.S. Lewis described this as 'God's intolerable compliment'. As the old saying goes: God loves us as we are but too much to let us stay as we are.

DAY
268

GALATIANS 2:15-21

IN PAUL'S VIEW, when God justifies us, He declares on the basis of our faith in Christ's atoning death that we are acceptable to Him and that we belong to His covenant family.

'Works of the law' ('observing the law', NIV) here probably means doing those works of the law, laws such as circumcision and the food laws that played so prominent a part in distinguishing Jews in the ancient world from their Gentile neighbours. Some in the churches in Galatia were trying to impose these works of the law on newly converted Gentile Christians (cf.6:12). And Paul is furious! No one is justified this way, it is only by faith (2:15-16). Paul personalises the issue.

If I move outside the law to go into Christ, I become technically 'a sinner' (2:17). Not that Jesus encourages sin! On the contrary, says Paul, if I attempt to rebuild the bridge that I tore down back into reliance on the law, then I show that I am a transgressor (2:18), unable to keep all the law (cf.3:10) and disloyal to Jesus! Through the law's own condemnation of me as a sinner, Paul goes on, I died to the law as lord of my life, and came alive to God. Co-crucified with Christ, I now live defined and motivated by the faithfulness of Jesus Christ who loved me and gave Himself for me. To do anything else would to give up on grace.

But Paul has burnt his bridges and is not going back!

BIBLE READING

Galatians 2:15-21

[15]We are Jews by birth and not "Gentile sinners"; [16]yet we know that no one is justified by the works of the law but by faith in Jesus Christ. And we have believed in Christ Jesus, so that we might be justified by faith in Christ and not by the works of the law, because by the works of the law no human being will be justified. [17]But if, while seeking to be justified by Christ, we ourselves are also found to be sinners, is Christ then a promoter of sin? Absolutely not! [18]If I rebuild those things that I tore down, I show myself to be

a lawbreaker. ¹⁹For through the law I have died to the law, that I might live to God. I have been crucified with Christ; ²⁰and I no longer live, but Christ lives in me. The life I now live in the flesh, I live by faith in the Son of God, who loved me and gave Himself for me. ²¹I do not set aside the grace of God; for if righteousness comes through the law, then Christ died for nothing.

PRAYER: O Father, I am so thankful that through Your Holy Spirit I have come to see that the bridge of 'good works' could never cross the gulf that separated You from me. You did for me what I could not do for myself and flung across the great divide the Person of Your own dear Son. Now I am reconciled, justified, and I stand in Your presence just as if I had never sinned. Blessed be Your name forever. Amen.

FOR PAUL, THE gospel was preached 'beforehand' in the promises given to Abraham through whom God's saving blessings would reach all nations. The new covenant life enjoyed in Christ is the fulfilment of God's covenant with Abraham. Both have the same basis – faith, whether for circumcised or uncircumcised. Both involve children given by God, and a promise about the world, not just the land.

DAY 269

GALATIANS
3:10-14,26-29

This fulfilment has been achieved through the death of Jesus and the outpouring of the Spirit. Jesus hangs on the cross under a curse (3:13 cf.Deut. 21:23). An Israel, unfaithful to her covenant vocation to be an agent of blessing for nations, would incur the curses of God culminating in exile from the land (Deut. 28:63; 29:25-28)

Jesus, 'the faithful Israel', the true covenant partner of God, dies this cursed death instead of Israel. Dying as an exile and outcast, He absorbs the curse of judgment, and so the blessing promised to Abraham can now flow to the world by the gift of the Spirit (3:13-14).

By faith in Jesus Christ, the one, singular 'seed' of

Abraham, the one covenant people of the One God is formed (3:16,20,28).

Neither race, nor gender, nor social status bars anyone who believes from entering into Christ's body and therefore becoming a member of the one covenant family God promised to Abraham!

BIBLE READING

Galatians 3:10-14,26-29

LAW AND PROMISE

[10]For all who [rely on] the works of the law are under a curse, because it is written: "Cursed is everyone who does not continue doing everything written in the book of the law." [11]Now it is clear that no one is justified before God by the law, because "the righteous will live by faith." [12]But the law is not based on faith; instead, "the one who does these things will live by them." [13]Christ has redeemed us from the curse of the law by becoming a curse for us, because it is written: "Cursed is everyone who is hung on a tree." [14]The purpose was that the blessing of Abraham would come to the Gentiles in Christ Jesus, so that we could receive the promise of the Spirit through faith.

• • • • • • • • • •

[26]for you are all sons of God through faith in Christ Jesus.

SONS AND HEIRS

[27]For as many of you as have been baptized into Christ have put on Christ. [28]There is no Jew or Greek, slave or free, male or female; for you are all one in Christ Jesus. [29]And if you are Christ's, then you are Abraham's seed, heirs according to the promise.

TO PONDER: How mysterious yet how amazing is this principle seen in both Testaments – the principle of faith. Let the wonder of it lie upon your mind as you move through the day. One definition of faith as we observed earlier, based on the acrostic F.A.I.T.H. is this: Forsaking All I Trust Him. Abraham believed like that, Paul believed like that and so eventually did the blundering Simon Peter. How about you?

DAY 270

GALATIANS 3:15-26

AS A NARRATIVE thinker, Paul notes that in the big biblical storyline, Abraham received God's promises 400 years before the giving of the law. When the law came it did not nullify the previous promise of covenant. It is seen to have functioned as a temporary and parenthetical provision until Christ should come in the fullness of time (3:19,23-24; 4:1-4).

The law was God-given ('through angels' reflects a current Jewish belief), and mediated by Moses. But Moses' role was a divisive one ('is not of one') since Gentiles were excluded from the Sinai covenant. But God is One and ultimately seeks one people from all nations.

The law is further limited in that it cannot produce the life it demands. Paradoxically, by condemning sinners and – as it were – shutting them up as prisoners of their sin, the law drives people to trust in God's promise as the only way to be saved. The principle of faith with which Abraham sustained a covenant relationship with God has now finally come into its own with the advent of Christ. The role of the law has changed. While the law remains as a revelation of God's will for His covenant people, it no longer governs our lives as it did before Christ came to bring us under His Lordship and that of the Holy Spirit.

BIBLE READING

Galatians 3:15-26

[15]Brothers, I'm using a human illustration. No one sets aside even a human covenant that has been ratified, or makes additions to it. [16]Now the promises were spoken to Abraham and to his seed. He does not say "and to seeds," as though referring to many, but and to your seed, referring to one, who is Christ. [17]And I say this: the law, which came 430 years later, does not revoke a covenant that was previously ratified by God, so as to cancel the promise. [18]For if the inheritance is from the law, it is no longer from the promise; but God granted it to Abraham through the promise.

THE PURPOSE OF THE LAW

[19]Why the law then? It was added because of transgressions until the Seed to whom the promise was made would come. [The law] was ordered through angels by means of a mediator. [20]Now a mediator is not for just one person, but God is one. [21]Is the law therefore contrary to God's promises? Absolutely not! For if a law had been given that was able to give life, then righteousness would certainly be by the law. [22]But the Scripture has imprisoned everything under sin's power, so that the promise by faith in Jesus Christ might be given to those who believe. [23]Before this faith came, we were confined under the law, imprisoned until the coming faith was revealed. [24]The law, then, was our guardian until Christ, so that we could be justified by faith. [25]But since that faith has come, we are no longer under a guardian, [26]for you are all sons of God through faith in Christ Jesus.

THOUGHT: While we rejoice in the fact that the impossible demands of the law no longer rule and govern our lives as God's people, that does not mean that we can now ignore God's commands. The Ten Commandments have never been repealed. The difference between law and grace is this; the law said do this and you will live. Grace says I will do it for you.

PAUL ARGUES FIERCELY throughout Galatians against those who would impose Torah-observance on Christian believers in order to guarantee their covenant membership. No, Paul asserts, only faith is necessary to be included in God's covenant family. But surely, Paul's opponents might then have argued: if law-keeping is not the way to become God's covenant people, then it is the law which governs how covenant people live? No, says Paul! Freedom is what marks God's people in Christ, not because they live 'law-less' lives but because the law is fulfilled in those who live in Christ and are controlled by the Holy Spirit.

What the law can never do, Christ and the Spirit can now produce, achieving in 'crucified' believers that quality of life expected of God's covenant people (cf.5:16-26). This is gospel ethics!

Paul utilises the old story of Sarah and Hagar, Isaac and Ishmael to illustrate his point. Sarah represents the Abrahamic covenant and the Jerusalem above; Hagar is made to stand for Mount Sinai and the present Jerusalem including those who want to impose the law on Christian believers in Galatia. If Abraham is our 'father in faith' so Sarah is a our 'mother in faith and freedom'. We are like Isaac, children born of God's promised miracle of grace and God Himself is our 'Abba, Father'!

DAY
271
GALATIANS 4

Galatians 4

BIBLE READING

4 Now I say that as long as the heir is a child, he differs in no way from a slave, though he is the owner of every-thing. ²Instead, he is under guardians and stewards until the time set by his father. ³In the same way we also, when we were children, were in slavery under the elemental forces of the world. ⁴But when the completion of the time came, God sent His Son, born of a woman, born under the law, ⁵to redeem those under the law, so that we might receive adoption as sons.

[6]And because you are sons, God has sent the Spirit of His Son into our hearts, crying, "*Abba*, Father!" [7]So you are no longer a slave, but a son; and if a son, then an heir through God.

PAUL'S CONCERN FOR THE GALATIANS

[8]But in the past, when you didn't know God, you were enslaved to things that by nature are not gods. [9]But now, since you know God, or rather have become known by God, how can you turn back again to the weak and bankrupt elemental forces? Do you want to be enslaved to them all over again? [10]You observe [special] days, months, seasons, and years. [11]I am fearful for you, that perhaps my labor for you has been wasted.

[12]I beg you, brothers: become like me, for I also became like you. You have not wronged me; [13]you know that previously I preached the gospel to you in physical weakness, [14]and though my physical condition was a trial for you, you did not despise or reject me. On the contrary, you received me as an angel of God, as Christ Jesus [Himself].

[15]What happened to this blessedness of yours? For I testify to you that, if possible, you would have torn out your eyes and given them to me. [16]Have I now become your enemy by telling you the truth? [17]They are enthusiastic about you, but not for any good. Instead, they want to isolate you so you will be enthusiastic about them. [18]Now it is always good to be enthusiastic about good—and not just when I am with you. [19]My children, again I am in the pains of childbirth for you until Christ is formed in you. [20]I'd like to be with you right now and change my tone of voice, because I don't know what to do about you.

SARAH AND HAGAR: TWO COVENANTS

[21]Tell me, you who want to be under the law, don't you hear the law? [22]For it is written that Abraham had two sons, one by a slave and the other by a free woman. [23]But the one by the slave was born according to the flesh, while the one by the free woman was born as the result of a promise. [24]These things are illustrations, for the women represent the two covenants. One is from Mount Sinai and bears children into slavery—this is Hagar. [25]Now Hagar is Mount Sinai in Arabia and corresponds to the present Jerusalem, for she is in slavery with her children.

²⁶But the Jerusalem above is free, and she is our mother. ²⁷For it is written:

> "Rejoice, O barren woman
> who does not give birth.
> Break forth and shout,
> you who are not in labor,
> for the children of the desolate are many,
> more numerous than those
> of the woman who has a husband."

²⁸Now you, brothers, like Isaac, are children of promise. ²⁹But just as then the child born according to the flesh persecuted the one born according to the Spirit, so also now. ³⁰But what does the Scripture say?

> "Throw out the slave and her son, for the son of the slave will never inherit with the son of the free woman."

³¹Therefore, brothers, we are not children of the slave but of the free woman.

FOR PRAISE: When we contrast our lives today with those of the Old Testament saints, we see how wonderful it is to live a life of 'freedom'. We defined 'freedom' the other day as 'not the right to do what we want but the power to do what we ought'. Because the Spirit lives in our hearts He motivates us to do what we ought to do. Living the life God wants us to live is not a pressure but a possibility.

GENTILE BELIEVERS IN Galatia were, it seems, being pressurised by some zealous Jewish Christians to submit to the detailed requirements of the law, especially circumcision.

To do such a thing, Paul argues, would be to fall away from grace (5:4) and to barter your new-found freedom in Christ for a spurious sense of assurance.

DAY
272

GALATIANS 5:1-6;
6:12-16

683

To go back under the law would be to lose the plot and to regress to an earlier outmoded stage of the story. It would be like turning back the spiritual clock. It would be as good as denying that Christ had come to fulfil the law by dying for us. In the glorious reality of new covenant living, it no longer matters whether or not you are circumcised (5:6; 6:15). In Christ, such signs of belonging to God are obsolete. All that matters now is faith and the Spirit expressed in us through love and humility. We are all humbled by this. Exclusive Jews have to humble themselves to accept Gentiles on an equal footing in God's covenant family. Proud Gentiles have to humble themselves to accept a Jewish Messiah as the Saviour and Lord of the world. In short, we all have to die, crucified with Christ.

But this as a price well worth paying for it ushers us into God's sparkling 'new creation' life (6:15).

BIBLE READING — Galatians 5:1-6

FREEDOM OF THE CHRISTIAN

5 Christ has liberated us into freedom. Therefore stand firm and don't submit again to a yoke of slavery. [2]Take note! I, Paul, tell you that if you get circumcised, Christ will not benefit you at all. [3]Again I testify to every man who gets circumcised that he is obligated to keep the entire law. [4]You who are trying to be justified by the law are alienated from Christ; you have fallen from grace! [5]For by the Spirit we eagerly wait for the hope of righteousness from faith. [6]For in Christ Jesus neither circumcision nor uncircumcision accomplishes anything; what matters is faith working through love.

BIBLE READING — Galatians 6:12-16

[12]Those who want to make a good showing in the flesh are the ones who would compel you to be circumcised—but only to avoid being persecuted for the cross of Christ. [13]For even

the circumcised don't keep the law themselves; however, they want you to be circumcised in order to boast about your flesh. ¹⁴But as for me, I will never boast about anything except the cross of our Lord Jesus Christ, through whom the world has been crucified to me, and I to the world. ¹⁵For both circumcision and uncircumcision mean nothing; [what matters] instead is a new creation. ¹⁶May peace be on all those who follow this standard, and mercy also be on the Israel of God!

TO PONDER: There is a great tendency in the human heart to cling to rituals and ceremonies as these things are visible. The challenge of those who live by faith is not to rest on visual aids but to put one's trust in the unseen, in the innocent sufferings of Christ and Christ alone. How dependent are you on rituals and ceremonies? It's an issue worth pondering.

DAY
273
ROMANS 1:1-16

PAUL CARRIES IN his mind all the time the one storyline of the Creator God's relationship with Israel and looks at every issue through that lens. So Romans is not a series of random theological topics but a coherent argument which shadows the biblical story of God and Israel. In chapters 1-4 Paul shows that in Jesus the Messiah – and especially through His cross – God has demonstrated His covenant faithfulness to Israel by dealing with Israel and the world's sin, in order to create a world-wide community of faith in line with His promises to Abraham. Chapters 5-8 show that this faith-community, undergoing a new exodus to fulfil Israel's vocation and to rewrite Adam's story by bearing the hallmarks of a new humanity, is heading now for the promised land of renewed creation.

Where Israel's traditional story fits with this is faced in chapters 9-11. There Paul is shown that Jews and Gentiles mysteriously interact as factors in God's overall saving plan for the world. Israel's vocation is enacted by Jesus and her failure borne by Him so that the way is open for Gentiles along with Jews to enjoy the blessings of salvation by trusting Christ.

This new covenant community is called – as chapters 12-16 make clear – to be a sample of what a new humanity looks like in living a life of unity and love.

BIBLE READING

Romans 1:1-16

GOD'S GOOD NEWS FOR ROME

1 Paul, a slave of Christ Jesus, called as an apostle and singled out for God's good news— ²which He promised long ago through His prophets in the Holy Scriptures— ³concerning His Son, Jesus Christ our Lord, who was a descendant of David according to the flesh ⁴and was established as the powerful Son of God by the resurrection from the dead according to the Spirit of holiness. ⁵We have received grace and apostleship through Him to bring about the obedience of faith among all the nations, on behalf of His name, ⁶including yourselves who are also Jesus Christ's by calling:

⁷To all who are in Rome, loved by God, called as saints.

Grace to you and peace from God our Father and the Lord Jesus Christ.

THE APOSTLE'S DESIRE TO VISIT ROME

⁸First, I thank my God through Jesus Christ for all of you because the news of your faith is being reported in all the world. ⁹For God, whom I serve with my spirit in [telling] the good news about His Son, is my witness that I constantly mention you, ¹⁰always asking in my prayers that if it is somehow in God's will, I may now at last succeed in coming to you. ¹¹For I want very much to see you, that I may impart to you some spiritual gift to strengthen you, ¹²that is, to be mutually encouraged by each other's faith, both yours and mine.

¹³Now I want you to know, brothers, that I often planned to come to you (but was prevented until now) in order that I might have a fruitful ministry among you, just as among the rest of the Gentiles. ¹⁴I am obligated both to Greeks and barbarians, both to the wise and the foolish. ¹⁵So I am eager to preach the good news to you also who are in Rome.

THE RIGHTEOUS WILL LIVE BY FAITH

¹⁶For I am not ashamed of the gospel, because it is God's power for salvation to everyone who believes, first to the Jew, and also to the Greek.

PRAYER: Loving heavenly Father, the truth that You have been working through Israel towards a wider community – the goal that was in Your heart in the beginning – fills me with wonder and joy. As the story unfolds I find myself thrilling more and more to the fact that I am part of it. A small part perhaps, but an important part. For there is nothing unimportant in Your story. Thank You, dear Father. Amen.

DAY 274
ROMANS 1:17-32

THE GOSPEL WHICH tells the story of God's covenant faithfulness acting to save, also exposes the sad history of sin and God's wrathful judgment on it.

Paul's devastating analysis of how sin ruins a society is not a knee-jerk moralistic reaction to how bad things have become. Rather, Paul shows how sin turns the narrative of creation upside down, so that we humans refuse to reflect God's image but sinfully look for other options for self-fulfilment and other objects of worship. But in bowing down to self-made images, we fall victim to believing a lie. Our human story is bent cruelly out of shape.

Homosexuality is no more subject to God's wrath than the other sins mentioned. But it is a more graphic sign than most that a society has lost the plot. Perverted sexual activity is itself a sign ('God gave them over ...' v.24, NIV) that a society is under God's judgment. We are called to reflect God's image in a polar male–female relationship. To pervert this is to distort God's image and to destroy our humanness. It is as if the original creation story has been scrambled by human rebellion into a confusing code of language. The gospel re-translates our human story back into its original language of partnership with God and then re-inserts this human story into the larger narrative of a good and gracious God.

BIBLE READING

Romans 1:17-32

GOD'S GOOD NEWS FOR ROME

1 Paul, a slave of Christ Jesus, called as an apostle and singled out for God's good news— [2]which He promised long ago through His prophets in the Holy Scriptures— [3]concerning His Son, Jesus Christ our Lord, who was a descendant of David according to the flesh [4]and was established as the powerful Son of God by the resurrection from the dead according to the Spirit of holiness. [5]We have received grace and apostleship through Him to bring about the obedience of faith among all the nations, on behalf of His name, [6]including yourselves who are also Jesus Christ's by calling:

[7]To all who are in Rome, loved by God, called as saints. Grace to you and peace from God our Father and the Lord Jesus Christ.

THE APOSTLE'S DESIRE TO VISIT ROME

[8]First, I thank my God through Jesus Christ for all of you because the news of your faith is being reported in all the world. [9]For God, whom I serve with my spirit in [telling] the good news about His Son, is my witness that I constantly mention you, [10]always asking in my prayers that if it is somehow in God's will, I may now at last succeed in coming to you. [11]For I want very much to see you, that I may impart to you some spiritual gift to strengthen you, [12]that is, to be mutually encouraged by each other's faith, both yours and mine.

[13]Now I want you to know, brothers, that I often planned to come to you (but was prevented until now) in order that I might have a fruitful ministry among you, just as among the rest of the Gentiles. [14]I am obligated both to Greeks and barbarians, both to the wise and the foolish. [15]So I am eager to preach the good news to you also who are in Rome.

THE RIGHTEOUS WILL LIVE BY FAITH

[16]For I am not ashamed of the gospel, because it is God's power for salvation to everyone who believes, first to the Jew, and also to the Greek.

[17]For in it God's righteousness is revealed from faith to faith, just as it is written: "The righteous will live by faith."

THE GUILT OF THE GENTILE WORLD

[18]For God's wrath is revealed from heaven against all godlessness and unrighteousness of people who by their unrighteousness suppress the truth, [19]since what can be known about God is evident among them, because God has shown it to them. [20]From the creation of the world His invisible attributes, that is, His eternal power and divine nature, have been clearly seen, being understood through what He has made. As a result, people are without excuse. [21]For though they knew God, they did not glorify Him as God or show gratitude. Instead, their thinking became nonsense, and their senseless minds were darkened. [22]Claiming to be wise, they became fools [23]and exchanged the glory of the immortal God for images resembling mortal man, birds, four-footed animals, and reptiles.

[24]Therefore God delivered them over in the cravings of their hearts to sexual impurity, so that their bodies were degraded among themselves. [25]They exchanged the truth of God for a lie, and worshiped and served something created instead of the Creator, who is blessed forever. Amen.

FROM IDOLATRY TO DEPRAVITY

[26]This is why God delivered them over to degrading passions. For even their females exchanged natural sexual intercourse for what is unnatural. [27]The males in the same way also left natural sexual intercourse with females and were inflamed in their lust for one another. Males committed shameless acts with males and received in their own persons the appropriate penalty for their perversion.

[28]And because they did not think it worthwhile to have God in their knowledge, God delivered them over to a worthless mind to do what is morally wrong. [29]They are filled with all unrighteousness, evil, greed, and wickedness. They are full of

envy, murder, disputes, deceit, and malice. They are gossips, [30]slanderers, God-haters, arrogant, proud, boastful, inventors of evil, disobedient to parents, [31]undiscerning, untrustworthy, unloving, and unmerciful. [32]Although they know full well God's just sentence—that those who practice such things deserve to die—they not only do them, but even applaud others who practice them.

THOUGHT: C.S. Lewis once used the word 'bentness' to describe the core problem sin has produced in the universe. 'Bentness' is when the creature is 'bent' in the direction of created things rather than the Creator. We are designed to stand upright and worship the Creator. Sin has 'bent' us in the direction of earth. We must decide whether we stand up straight or remain 'bent'.

DAY 275
ROMANS 2

A SAD FEATURE of the human tragedy of sin, exposed by the prophets of old and highlighted now by the gospel, is that Israel is shown to be as much part of the problem as she is part of the answer.

Not, of course, that every Jew is a robber or a murderer. The problem with Israel, as Jesus and Paul found, is a national pride in its exclusive relationship with God. But how can a nation brag of being a light to the nations when it is darkened by its own sinfulness (2:19)? Israel is still in 'exile' for her sins, still bearing the reproach levelled at her by the prophet Ezekiel of 'dishonouring the name of God' (NIV) by her unbelief and misconduct (2:24). In such a condition, having the outward sign of being God's people – circumcision – counts for nothing. But there is a gleam of hope that a people can emerge who, while not circumcised, will truly be God's covenant people and will keep God's law (2:27). The description of people changed from the inside-out with hearts remade to love and obey God, sounds very much like Jeremiah's and Ezekiel's picture of the new covenant community. And it is. Thankfully, the story of creation gone wrong and the story of Israel falling from grace, is not the end of the story. Already we catch a glimpse of a new people of God in whose hearts the Holy Spirit has worked miracles (2:29).

Romans 2

GOD'S RIGHTEOUS JUDGMENT

2 Therefore, anyone of you who judges is without excuse. For when you judge another, you condemn yourself, since you, the judge, do the same things. ²We know that God's judgment on those who do such things is based on the truth. ³Do you really think—anyone of you who judges those who do such things yet do the same—that you will escape God's judgment? ⁴Or do you despise the riches of His kindness, restraint, and patience, not recognizing that God's kindness is intended to lead you to repentance? ⁵But because of your hardness and unrepentant heart you are storing up wrath for yourself in the day of wrath, when God's righteous judgment is revealed. ⁶He "will repay each one according to his works:" ⁷eternal life to those who by patiently doing good seek for glory, honor, and immortality; ⁸but wrath and indignation to those who are self-seeking and disobey the truth, but are obeying unrighteousness; ⁹affliction and distress for every human being who does evil, first to the Jew, and also to the Greek; ¹⁰but glory, honor, and peace for everyone who does good, first to the Jew, and also to the Greek. ¹¹There is no favoritism with God.

¹²All those who sinned without the law will also perish without the law, and all those who sinned under the law will be judged by the law. ¹³For the hearers of the law are not righteous before God, but the doers of the law will be declared righteous. ¹⁴So, when Gentiles, who do not have the law, instinctively do what the law demands, they are a law to themselves even though they do not have the law. ¹⁵They show that the work of the law is written on their hearts. Their consciences testify in support of this, and their competing thoughts either accuse or excuse them ¹⁶on the day when God judges what people have kept secret, according to my gospel through Christ Jesus.

JEWISH VIOLATION OF THE LAW

[17]Now if you call yourself a Jew, and rest in the law, and boast in God, [18]and know His will, and approve the things that are superior, being instructed from the law, [19]and are convinced that you are a guide for the blind, a light to those in darkness, [20]an instructor of the ignorant, a teacher of the immature, having in the law the full expression of knowledge and truth— [21]you then, who teach another, do you not teach yourself? You who preach, "You must not steal"—do you steal? [22]You who say, "You must not commit adultery"—do you commit adultery? You who detest idols, do you rob their temples? [23]You who boast in the law, do you dishonor God by breaking the law? [24]For, as it is written: "The name of God is blasphemed among the Gentiles because of you."

CIRCUMCISION OF THE HEART

[25]For circumcision benefits you if you observe the law, but if you are a lawbreaker, your circumcision has become uncircumcision. [26]Therefore if an uncircumcised man keeps the law's requirements, will his uncircumcision not be counted as circumcision? [27]A man who is physically uncircumcised, but who fulfills the law, will judge you who are a lawbreaker in spite of having the letter [of the law] and circumcision. [28]For a person is not a Jew who is one outwardly, and [true] circumcision is not something visible in the flesh. [29]On the contrary, a person is a Jew who is one inwardly, and circumcision is of the heart—by the Spirit, not the letter. His praise is not from men but from God.

FOR PRAISE: The thrust of God's workings in the Old Testament was from the outside in (generally speaking) but in the New it is from the inside out. The Holy Spirit has come to reside and preside within us and has given us 'circumcised' hearts that are free to love in the way God wants us to love. How thankful we ought to be to God that He has gone to such lengths to set us free.

DAY 276

ROMANS 3:1-20

ISRAEL'S PRIVILEGE WAS to be the one nation entrusted with the very words of God. But if Israel fails, does God's Word fail? Does the faithlessness of the covenant people discredit the faithfulness of the covenant God? Does God scrap plan-A in favour of plan-B? 'No,' says Paul (3:4). Two things follow. Firstly, Israel is no less part of the problem of sin than the Gentile world to which Israel was meant to bring God's saving revelation. There is no one righteous. As the psalmist had foreseen, all the world is exposed as sinful and under God's judgment. In the imaginary law court where the case is presented, no one has any defence to offer. Every mouth is silenced (3:19). All excuses, all rationalisations, all pride, all evasions, are cut off. We sinners stand mute before a holy God with nothing left to say for ourselves.

Not even Jewish national pride in possessing the law is of any avail. In fact possessing it only serves to highlight what sin is and how guilty we all are (cf.Rom. 5:20; 7:7-8).

But if God is to remain faithful to His promise to bless the world through His covenant people, then He must find a true Israel through whom to do the job. A faithful Israel(ite) is required at this point. Step forward Jesus ('God presented him' 3:25) who is exactly what the situation demands.

BIBLE READING

Romans 3:1-20

PAUL ANSWERS AN OBJECTION

3 So what advantage does the Jew have? Or what is the benefit of circumcision? ²Considerable in every way. First, they were entrusted with the spoken words of God. ³What then? If some did not believe, will their unbelief cancel God's faithfulness? ⁴Absolutely not! God must be true, but everyone is a liar, as it is written:

"That You may be justified in Your words
and triumph when You judge."

⁵But if our unrighteousness highlights God's righteousness, what are we to say? I use a human argument: Is God unrighteous to inflict wrath? ⁶Absolutely not! Otherwise, how will God judge the world? ⁷But if by my lie God's truth is amplified to His glory, why am I also still judged as a sinner? ⁸And why not say, just as some people slanderously claim we say, "Let us do evil so that good may come"? Their condemnation is deserved!

THE WHOLE WORLD GUILTY BEFORE GOD

⁹What then? Are we any better? Not at all! For we have previously charged that both Jews and Gentiles are all under sin, ¹⁰as it is written:

"There is no one righteous, not even one;
¹¹ there is no one who understands,
there is no one who seeks God.
¹² All have turned away,
together they have become useless;
there is no one who does good,
there is not even one.
¹³ Their throat is an open grave;
they deceive with their tongues.
Vipers' venom is under their lips.
¹⁴ Their mouth is full of cursing and bitterness.
¹⁵ Their feet are swift to shed blood;
¹⁶ ruin and wretchedness are in their paths,
¹⁷ and the path of peace they have not known.
¹⁸ There is no fear of God before their eyes."

¹⁹Now we know that whatever the law says speaks to those who are subject to the law, so that every mouth may be shut and the whole world may become subject to God's judgment. ²⁰For no flesh will be justified in His sight by the works of the law, for through the law [comes] the knowledge of sin.

WORSHIP: Nothing gathers up the truth of our inability to meet God's standards like this verse from Toplady's well-known hymn, 'Rock of Ages'. If you know it sing it; if not, say it:

Nothing in my hands I bring,
Simply to Thy Cross I cling ...
Foul I to the fountain fly
Wash me, Saviour, or I die.

In Jesus He has cleansed us. For that give Him the worship that is due to His name.

DAY 277

ACTS 13:34-39
ROMANS 3:21-22

IN THE COMING cross and resurrection of Jesus, God's covenant faithfulness has come to the rescue.

This salvation works 'apart from the law' in the sense that it is not achieved by law-keeping or in a way exclusive to Jews. At the same time it is something to which the Torah and the prophets bear witness so that it has impeccable Old Testament roots.

God's covenant faithfulness ('righteousness') has acted to save. God has achieved His own ends through the 'faithfulness of Jesus Christ', the one true covenant partner. Whoever puts their faith in this faithful Jesus is 'justified' in the sense of being owned by God, as belonging to God's covenant people.

What was supposed to happen at the end of history has happened in the middle of history. The verdict of the last day has been brought forward and announced in the present. God 'justifies' or 'vindicates' His people by finding in their favour. God declares that all those who trust in Christ for forgiveness of sins are His covenant people. The proof that God has made a 'pre-emptive strike' in favour of His people is that He has raised Jesus from the dead. The ultimate sign of His own people's vindication and justification will be their own 'resurrection' of which Jesus' resurrection is the guarantee (see 4:25).

Acts 13:34-39

³⁴Since He raised Him from the dead, never to return to decay, He has spoken in this way, "I will grant you the faithful covenant blessings made to David." ³⁵Therefore He also says in another passage, "You will not allow Your Holy One to see decay." ³⁶For David, after serving his own generation in God's plan, fell asleep, was buried with his fathers, and decayed. ³⁷But the One whom God raised up did not decay. ³⁸Therefore, let it be known to you, brothers, that through this man forgiveness of sins is being proclaimed to you, ³⁹and everyone who believes in Him is justified from everything, which you could not be justified from through the law of Moses.

Romans 3:21-22

GOD'S RIGHTEOUSNESS THROUGH FAITH

²¹But now, apart from the law, God's righteousness has been revealed—attested by the Law and the Prophets ²²—that is, God's righteousness through faith in Jesus Christ, to all who believe, since there is no distinction.

PRAYER: I am so thankful, dear heavenly Father, for this 'pre-emptive strike' I have read about today. And as You raised Jesus from the dead so, too, have I been raised from the dead to live this life that is just too wonderful to put into words. I am so glad that You have saved me and all I long for is that my life might show forth the 'fruits' of Your favour. Help me, my Father. In Jesus' name. Amen.

DAY
278
ROMANS 3:23-31

WHEN GOD FORGIVES sins He does it on the basis of the blood of Jesus. His gracious covenant integrity moves out in saving love to put people who believe right with Him. The cross is the crux of His action to save the world, the final demonstration of God's faithfulness to the covenant. God has dealt with the sin that spoils His creation and undermines Israel's vocation by means of the sacrificial, substitutionary death of Jesus, the Messiah. By Jesus' death for sinners, God is vindicated, because He is both seen to have dealt with sin and, at the same time, is shown to have faithfully kept His covenant commitments. There is no room then for the kind of boasting a Jew might indulge in who was proud of His exclusive relationship with God. Ethnicity is no longer an advantage card. Those works of law that marked out Israel as different are effectively sidelined when it comes to salvation and faith. God is not the God of Jews only but the One Creator God who aims to create one people for Himself out of both the 'circumcised' and 'uncircumcised' – Jew and Gentile. Yet though the law is marginalised as a means of marking out who God's people are, it is upheld because in it is taught the principle of faith through the foundational story of Abraham. It is to this story that Paul next turns to bolster his case.

BIBLE READING

Romans 3:23-31

GOD'S RIGHTEOUSNESS THROUGH FAITH

²¹But now, apart from the law, God's righteousness has been revealed—attested by the Law and the Prophets ²²—that is, God's righteousness through faith in Jesus Christ, to all who believe, since there is no distinction.

²³For all have sinned and fall short of the glory of God. ²⁴They are justified freely by His grace through the redemption that is in Christ Jesus. ²⁵God presented Him as

a propitiation through faith in His blood, to demonstrate His righteousness, because in His restraint God passed over the sins previously committed. [26]He presented Him to demonstrate His righteousness at the present time, so that He would be righteous and declare righteous the one who has faith in Jesus.

BOASTING EXCLUDED

[27]Where then is boasting? It is excluded. By what kind of law? By one of works? No, on the contrary, by a law of faith. [28]For we conclude that a man is justified by faith apart from works of law. [29]Or is God for Jews only? Is He not also for Gentiles? Yes, for Gentiles too, [30]since there is one God who will justify the circumcised by faith and the uncircumcised through faith. [31]Do we then cancel the law through faith? Absolutely not! On the contrary, we uphold the law.

> QUOTATION: 'The church ... has become increasingly accustomed to Christianity without a cross ... or at best with one hanging harmlessly in the background. We have forgotten that in the middle of this Gospel stands a cross ... the splinters of which are largely ignored by a contemporary Christian world eager to tell mostly the good part of the story.' (John Fischer)

PAUL IS MIRRORING the Old Testament storyline of God's promises and covenant faithfulness. Abraham, then, is not merely a random example of faith, but the key figure through whom God established that faith is the one factor which governs a right relationship with God. This occurred long before the giving of the law and even before circumcision was enjoined. This strengthens Paul's argument that it is not by law-keeping but by trust in God that a covenant people, both then and now, is born and sustained (4:3,9,22-23; Gen. 15:6). This principle applies to us ('but also for us' 4:24).

DAY
279

ROMANS 4

The blessedness of sins forgiven which David enjoyed comes to all who believe (4:6-9).

Abraham is the father of a universal family of faith whether Jew or Gentile (4:11-12). The scope of his inheritance is not restricted to the promised land but extends to the whole earth (4:13, anticipating 8:18-21). God gives life to the dead – including a 'dead' Israel – and calls things that are not – even the 'non-existent' Gentiles – as though they were. Faith in such a God honours grace (4:16), gives God glory (4:20) and engenders hope (4:18-20). We believe in God who raised Jesus from the dead who died for our sins and rose again to guarantee our vindication as God's people (4:25).

BIBLE READING

Romans 4

ABRAHAM JUSTIFIED BY FAITH

4 What then can we say that Abraham, our forefather according to the flesh, has found? ²If Abraham was justified by works, then he has something to brag about—but not before God. ³For what does the Scripture say?

> "Abraham believed God,
> and it was credited to him for righteousness."

⁴Now to the one who works, pay is not considered as a gift, but as something owed. ⁵But to the one who does not work, but believes on Him who declares righteous the ungodly, his faith is credited for righteousness.

DAVID CELEBRATING THE SAME TRUTH

⁶Likewise, David also speaks of the blessing of the man to whom God credits righteousness apart from works:

⁷ "How happy those whose lawless acts are forgiven
and whose sins are covered!
⁸ How happy the man whom
the Lord will never charge with sin!"

ABRAHAM JUSTIFIED BEFORE CIRCUMCISION

⁹Is this blessing only for the circumcised, then? Or is it also for the uncircumcised? For we say, "Faith was credited to Abraham for righteousness." ¹⁰How then was it credited—while he was circumcised, or uncircumcised? Not while he was circumcised, but uncircumcised. ¹¹And he received the sign of circumcision as a seal of the righteousness that he had by faith while still uncircumcised. This was to make him the father of all who believe but are not circumcised, so that righteousness may be credited to them also. ¹²And he became the father of the circumcised, not only to those who are circumcised, but also to those who follow in the footsteps of the faith our father Abraham had while still uncircumcised.

THE PROMISE GRANTED THROUGH FAITH

¹³For the promise to Abraham or to his descendants that he would inherit the world was not through the law, but through the righteousness that comes by faith. ¹⁴If those who are of the law are heirs, faith is made empty and the promise is canceled. ¹⁵For the law produces wrath; but where there is no law, there is no transgression.

¹⁶This is why the promise is by faith, so that it may be according to grace, to guarantee it to all the descendants—not only to those who are of the law, but also to those who are of Abraham's faith. He is the father of us all ¹⁷in God's sight. As it is written: "I have made you the father of many nations." He believed in God, who gives life to the dead and calls things into existence that do not exist. ¹⁸Against hope, with hope he believed, so that he became "the father of many nations," according to what had been spoken: "So will your descendants be." ¹⁹He considered his own body to be already dead (since he was about a hundred years old), and the deadness of Sarah's womb, without weakening in the faith. ²⁰He did not waver in unbelief at God's promise, but was strengthened in his faith and gave glory to God, ²¹because he was fully convinced that what He had promised He was also able to perform. ²²Therefore, "it was credited to him for righteousness." ²³Now "it was credited to him" was not written for Abraham alone, ²⁴but also for us. It will be credited to us who believe in Him who raised Jesus our Lord from the dead. ²⁵He was delivered up for our trespasses and raised for our justification.

THOUGHT: We just cannot get away from 'faith'. Wherever we turn either in the Old Testament or the New we keep bumping into this word. And why? Because without faith, as the writer to the Hebrews tells us, 'it is impossible to please God'. A similar word to 'faith' is 'trust'. It's one thing to 'trust' God for salvation, but what about other aspects of your life? Worth thinking about!

DAY 280

ROMANS 5

PAUL HAS SHOWN that God has one covenant family, rooted in Abraham's faith, and now being created in Christ Jesus from both Jew and Gentile. Family members enjoy peace with God and rejoice in hope of once again sharing the glory of God (5:1-2; cf.3:23).

We have been reconciled to God by the undeserved covenant love of God through the death of Jesus by which God's wrath against sin has been turned aside. Paul now stands back to see the global picture (5:12-21). Within the overall narrative of what God is doing, the stories of Adam, Israel and Jesus interact.

God's work in Jesus Christ, Israel's Messiah, finally overcomes Adam's sin and disobedience. In fact Christ has done more than merely reverse Adam's fall. Jesus has not only offered the obedience that Adam didn't offer, but He exhibits the true covenant love and faithfulness that Israel was called to show. Either way, we owe everything to the obedience of Jesus. The law served a special role in concentrating sin in Israel - and then in her representative figure of the Messiah - where it could be dealt with once and for all (5:20).

This is not just the rebranding but the remaking of the human race. Once sin reigned over us resulting in sure and certain death. Now God's grace rules our lives resulting in sure and certain life, now and in the future.

Romans 5

FAITH TRIUMPHS

5 Therefore, since we have been declared righteous by faith, we have peace with God through our Lord Jesus Christ. ²Also through Him, we have obtained access by faith into this grace in which we stand, and we rejoice in the hope of the glory of God. ³And not only that, but we also rejoice in our afflictions, because we know that affliction produces endurance, ⁴endurance produces proven character, and proven character produces hope. ⁵This hope does not disappoint, because God's love has been poured out in our hearts through the Holy Spirit who was given to us.

THOSE DECLARED RIGHTEOUS ARE RECONCILED

⁶For while we were still helpless, at the appointed moment, Christ died for the ungodly. ⁷For rarely will someone die for a just person—though for a good person perhaps someone might even dare to die. ⁸But God proves His own love for us in that while we were still sinners Christ died for us! ⁹Much more then, since we have now been declared righteous by His blood, we will be saved through Him from wrath. ¹⁰For if, while we were enemies, we were reconciled to God through the death of His Son, [then how] much more, having been reconciled, will we be saved by His life! ¹¹And not only that, but we also rejoice in God through our Lord Jesus Christ, through whom we have now received reconciliation.

DEATH THROUGH ADAM AND LIFE THROUGH CHRIST

¹²Therefore, just as sin entered the world through one man, and death through sin, in this way death spread to all men, because all sinned. ¹³In fact, sin was in the world before the law, but sin is not charged to one's account when there is no law. ¹⁴Nevertheless, death reigned from Adam to Moses, even over those who did not sin in the likeness of Adam's transgression. He is a prototype of the Coming One.

¹⁵But the gift is not like the trespass. For if by the one man's trespass the many died, how much more have the grace of God and the gift overflowed to the many by the grace of

the one man, Jesus Christ. ¹⁶And the gift is not like the one man's sin, because from one sin came the judgment, resulting in condemnation, but from many trespasses came the gift, resulting in justification. ¹⁷Since by the one man's trespass, death reigned through that one man, how much more will those who receive the overflow of grace and the gift of righteousness reign in life through the one man, Jesus Christ.

¹⁸So then, as through one trespass there is condemnation for everyone, so also through one righteous act there is life-giving justification for everyone. ¹⁹For just as through one man's disobedience the many were made sinners, so also through the one man's obedience the many will be made righteous. ²⁰The law came along to multiply the trespass. But where sin multiplied, grace multiplied even more, ²¹so that, just as sin reigned in death, so also grace will reign through righteousness, resulting in eternal life through Jesus Christ our Lord.

FOR PRAISE: We have been reminded once again that 'we owe everything to the obedience of Jesus'. What if He had failed? The consequences of such a failure are too frightening to contemplate. But He did not fail and because of His triumph we are saved, redeemed and reconciled to God. Right now give the Lord your thanks for such perfect obedience.

DAY
281
ROMANS 6

IF ANYONE IS tempted to presume on God's grace and persist in wilful sinning, then they have not grasped the first thing about what it means to be in Christ. We have been immersed in the drama of Jesus' dying and rising and can be expected to live a cruciform life.

You are living out of a different story now, Paul says, so don't think or behave as if you were playing a part in the unredeemed Adam story.

There are surely echoes here of the crossing of the Red Sea and the escape from slavery in Egypt (6:6-7,16-22). In the larger story, Pharaoh's role is now played by sin. Freed from slavery to sin, we have become slaves of righteousness as servants of God. Paul celebrates the reality of living in the new covenant by speaking of an obedience from the heart to that 'form of teaching to which you were entrusted' (v.17, NIV). The apostolic teaching is not just a series of beliefs we assent to but the pattern our lives are now to be conformed to and shaped by. In other words, we are placed in a new story, the story of the dying-rising Jesus.

If Paul, in telling the new exodus story of human redemption, is mirroring Israel's story, then we might expect to be brought next in the story to Mount Sinai and to the law of God. This is just what happens in chapter 7.

Romans 6

THE NEW LIFE IN CHRIST

6 What should we say then? Should we continue in sin in order that grace may multiply? [2]Absolutely not! How can we who died to sin still live in it? [3]Or are you unaware that all of us who were baptized into Christ Jesus were baptized into His death? [4]Therefore we were buried with Him by baptism into death, in order that, just as Christ was raised from the dead by the glory of the Father, so we too may walk in a new way of life. [5]For if we have been joined with Him in the likeness of His death, we will certainly also be in the likeness of His resurrection. [6]For we know that our old self was crucified with Him in order that sin's dominion over the body may be abolished, so that we may no longer be enslaved to sin, [7]since a person who has died is freed from sin's claims. [8]Now if we died with Christ, we believe that we will also live with Him, [9]because we know that Christ, having been raised from the dead, no longer dies. Death no longer rules over Him. [10]For in that He died, He died to sin once for all; but in that He lives, He lives to God. [11]So, you too consider yourselves dead to sin, but alive to God in Christ Jesus.

[12]Therefore do not let sin reign in your mortal body, so

that you obey its desires. [13]And do not offer any parts of it to sin as weapons for unrighteousness. But as those who are alive from the dead, offer yourselves to God, and all the parts of yourselves to God as weapons for righteousness. [14]For sin will not rule over you, because you are not under law but under grace.

FROM SLAVES OF SIN TO SLAVES OF GOD

[15]What then? Should we sin because we are not under law but under grace? Absolutely not! [16]Do you not know that if you offer yourselves to someone as obedient slaves, you are slaves of that one you obey—either of sin leading to death or of obedience leading to righteousness? [17]But thank God that, although you used to be slaves of sin, you obeyed from the heart that pattern of teaching you were entrusted to, [18]and having been liberated from sin, you became enslaved to righteousness. [19]I am using a human analogy because of the weakness of your flesh. For just as you offered the parts of yourselves as slaves to moral impurity, and to greater and greater lawlessness, so now offer them as slaves to righteousness, which results in sanctification. [20]For when you were slaves of sin, you were free from allegiance to righteousness. [21]And what fruit was produced then from the things you are now ashamed of? For the end of those things is death. [22]But now, since you have been liberated from sin and become enslaved to God, you have your fruit, which results in sanctification—and the end is eternal life! [23]For the wages of sin is death, but the gift of God is eternal life in Christ Jesus our Lord.

PRAYER: Father, once again I come to You with praise and thanksgiving in my heart for the fact that You have taken me out of the old story - 'the unredeemed Adam story' - and made me a part of the redeemed story - Your story. Grant that my behaviour and all my thinking shall be such that fits in with the thrilling story You are telling. In Jesus' name. Amen.

THIS CONTENTIOUS PASSAGE is also best seen in the light of the stories Paul is telling.

Paul is then not concerned here with any supposed second stage of Christian blessing or with the inner dynamics of the Christian experience. The subject throughout is the law, the Torah, given at Sinai, and how Paul now views it. Ironically, the law is part of the bondage sinners need to be freed from. And through dying with Christ, we are released from any 'marriage' to the law (7:1-3). In classic new covenant language, Paul describes how we can serve God fruitfully in the Spirit (7:4-6). Where does this leave the law? Although God-given, good, holy and righteous, the law has the effect of inciting inveterate sinners to more sin which incurs more guilt and condemnation and hardens us in our sinful condition (7:12-13).

Paul speaks in the first person, not to show that his present Christian experience is an internal 'civil war' between two supposed natures within him, no, rather, as a representative Jew, and from the standpoint of being 'in Christ', he looks back with new eyes, on what it was like to be under God's law. Paul sees the deficiencies in his pre-Christian story but now rejoices in being part of a new story, the story of the dying-rising Jesus (7:25).

DAY
282
ROMANS 7

Romans 7

BIBLE
READING

AN ILLUSTRATION FROM MARRIAGE

7 Since I am speaking to those who understand law, brothers, are you unaware that the law has authority over someone as long as he lives? ²For example, a married woman is legally bound to her husband while he lives. But if her husband dies, she is released from the law regarding the husband. ³So then, if she gives herself to another man while her husband is living, she will be called an adulteress. But if her husband dies, she is free from that law. Then, if she gives herself to another man, she is not an adulteress.

[4]Therefore, my brothers, you also were put to death in relation to the law through the [crucified] body of the Messiah, so that you may belong to another—to Him who was raised from the dead—that we may bear fruit for God. [5]For when we were in the flesh, the sinful passions operated through the law in every part of us and bore fruit for death. [6]But now we have been released from the law, since we have died to what held us, so that we may serve in the new way of the Spirit and not in the old letter of the law.

SIN'S USE OF THE LAW

[7]What should we say then? Is the law sin? Absolutely not! On the contrary, I would not have known sin if it were not for the law. For example, I would not have known what it is to covet if the law had not said, Do not covet. [8]And sin, seizing an opportunity through the commandment, produced in me coveting of every kind. For apart from the law sin is dead. [9]Once I was alive apart from the law, but when the commandment came, sin sprang to life [10]and I died. The commandment that was meant for life resulted in death for me. [11]For sin, seizing an opportunity through the commandment, deceived me, and through it killed me. [12]So then, the law is holy, and the commandment is holy and just and good.

THE PROBLEM OF SIN IN US

[13]Therefore, did what is good cause my death? Absolutely not! On the contrary, sin, in order to be recognized as sin, was producing death in me through what is good, so that through the commandment sin might become sinful beyond measure. [14]For we know that the law is spiritual; but I am made out of flesh, sold into sin's power. [15]For I do not understand what I am doing, because I do not practice what I want to do, but I do what I hate. [16]And if I do what I do not want to do, I agree with the law that it is good. [17]So now I am no longer the one doing it, but it is sin living in me. [18]For I know that nothing good lives in me, that is, in my flesh. For the desire to do what is good is with me, but there is no ability to do it. [19]For I do not do the good that I want to do, but I practice the evil that I do not want to do. [20]Now if I do what I do not want, I am no longer the one doing it, but it is

the sin that lives in me. ²¹So I discover this principle: when I want to do good, evil is with me. ²²For in my inner self I joyfully agree with God's law. ²³But I see a different law in the parts of my body, waging war against the law of my mind and taking me prisoner to the law of sin in the parts of my body. ²⁴What a wretched man I am! Who will rescue me from this body of death? ²⁵I thank God through Jesus Christ our Lord! So then, with my mind I myself am a slave to the law of God, but with my flesh, to the law of sin.

FOR THANKSGIVING: The controversial nature of this passage has already been noted, but do not miss the indisputable truth that the passage brings us, namely that God gives us the victory over the condemnation of the law on sinners. Keep this simple and sublime thought before you - you are not under law but under grace. Form now your own prayer of thanksgiving for this fact and offer it to God.

AS WE HAVE seen, the problem is not with God's law but with the sinful people who are meant to live by it. What the 'law could not do' (v.3, NKJV) was to produce the kind of covenant life it described. Sin prevented God's people living out the 'righteous requirements of the law' or enjoying the life of the covenant which was the aim of the Torah. Our 'flesh' (v.3) - here used in the negative sense of our disposition to disobey God - weakened the law fatally. But what the law could not do, God has done by sending His Son in the likeness of our sinful 'flesh' to offer Himself as a sacrifice for sin on the cross. God condemned sin in Jesus, doing what the law also could not do, which was to deal a fatal blow to sin. God did this so that the true intention of Torah might finally be fulfilled in the creating of a new covenant people. This people no longer lives 'under the law', dominated by sin, but lives under the Lordship of Jesus and is controlled by the Holy Spirit. In Christ

DAY
283

ROMANS 8:1-11

Jesus we relish the freedom from the law which spelt only sin and death. Uncondemned, we live by the law of the Spirit who gives life. If the immediate sign of our being God's covenant people is that God's Spirit is in us, then the ultimate sign will be our resurrection from the dead (8:11). That Spirit of future resurrection hope reverberates within us right now!

BIBLE READING

Romans 8:1-11

THE LIFE-GIVING SPIRIT

8 Therefore, no condemnation now exists for those in Christ Jesus, ²because the Spirit's law of life in Christ Jesus has set you free from the law of sin and of death. ³What the law could not do since it was limited by the flesh, God did. He condemned sin in the flesh by sending His own Son in flesh like ours under sin's domain, and as a sin offering, ⁴in order that the law's requirement would be accomplished in us who do not walk according to the flesh but according to the Spirit. ⁵For those whose lives are according to the flesh think about the things of the flesh, but those whose lives are according to the Spirit, about the things of the Spirit. ⁶For the mind-set of the flesh is death, but the mind-set of the Spirit is life and peace. ⁷For the mind-set of the flesh is hostile to God because it does not submit itself to God's law, for it is unable to do so. ⁸Those whose lives are in the flesh are unable to please God. ⁹You, however, are not in the flesh, but in the Spirit, since the Spirit of God lives in you. But if anyone does not have the Spirit of Christ, he does not belong to Him. ¹⁰Now if Christ is in you, the body is dead because of sin, but the Spirit is life because of righteousness. ¹¹And if the Spirit of Him who raised Jesus from the dead lives in you, then He who raised Christ from the dead will also bring your mortal bodies to life through His Spirit who lives in you.

THOUGHT: Today's reading makes crystal clear just why the law, though good, brought us into bondage. We just could not live up to it. The intervention of Jesus on our behalf means that what the law could not do – deal a fatal blow to sin – has now been accomplished through Christ's death. The law rendered us helpless but the Spirit now helps us live the life God always wanted for us.

ONCE AGAIN WE catch the allusions to the first Exodus story as Paul shows how Israel's story and the human story have been taken up into the drama of God's salvation in Jesus.

DAY
284

ROMANS 8:12-30

Israel's bondage in Egypt was, after all, only a sign of all humanity's deeper bondage to sin and death. Both stories are redeemed by the story of Jesus.

God's sons are led by the Spirit through the present unredeemed world as the cloud and fire led God's 'son', Israel, through the wilderness. On our pilgrimage, as we share His sufferings, we can cry out to 'Abba, Father' at times of stress, as Jesus did.

God groans in and with His pilgrim people in a groaning world that waits for redemption as they march towards the new world coming.

Canaan was viewed in the Old Testament as a larger-scale version of Eden and, in turn, points forward as a metaphor for the whole earth renewed as the scene of God's glory for which we are heading. Our freedom from slavery mysteriously interacts with the freeing of a creation bound to decay and death.

On the way to that promised future, the Holy Spirit works in every circumstance towards the 'good' that God intends for us – which is to make us like Jesus. Seeing the end of the story from the beginning, our final glorification is as sure an outcome to our story as the Author's pre-set plans for us.

BIBLE READING

Romans 8:12-30

THE LIFE-GIVING SPIRIT

8 Therefore, no condemnation now exists for those in Christ Jesus, [2]because the Spirit's law of life in Christ Jesus has set you free from the law of sin and of death. [3]What the law could not do since it was limited by the flesh, God did. He condemned sin in the flesh by sending His own Son in flesh like ours under sin's domain, and as a sin offering, [4]in order that the law's requirement would be accomplished in us who do not walk according to the flesh but according to the Spirit. [5]For those whose lives are according to the flesh think about the things of the flesh, but those whose lives are according to the Spirit, about the things of the Spirit. [6]For the mind-set of the flesh is death, but the mind-set of the Spirit is life and peace. [7]For the mind-set of the flesh is hostile to God because it does not submit itself to God's law, for it is unable to do so. [8]Those whose lives are in the flesh are unable to please God. [9]You, however, are not in the flesh, but in the Spirit, since the Spirit of God lives in you. But if anyone does not have the Spirit of Christ, he does not belong to Him. [10]Now if Christ is in you, the body is dead because of sin, but the Spirit is life because of righteousness. [11]And if the Spirit of Him who raised Jesus from the dead lives in you, then He who raised Christ from the dead will also bring your mortal bodies to life through His Spirit who lives in you.

THE HOLY SPIRIT'S MINISTRIES

[12]So then, brothers, we are not obligated to the flesh to live according to the flesh, [13]for if you live according to the flesh, you are going to die. But if by the Spirit you put to death the deeds of the body, you will live. [14]All those led by God's Spirit are God's sons. [15]For you did not receive a spirit of slavery to fall back into fear, but you received the Spirit of adoption, by whom we cry out, "*Abba*, Father!" [16]The Spirit Himself testifies together with our spirit that we are God's children, [17]and if children, also heirs—heirs of God and co-heirs with Christ—

seeing that we suffer with Him so that we may also be glorified with Him.

FROM GROANS TO GLORY

[18]For I consider that the sufferings of this present time are not worth comparing with the glory that is going to be revealed to us. [19]For the creation eagerly waits with anticipation for God's sons to be revealed. [20]For the creation was subjected to futility—not willingly, but because of Him who subjected it—in the hope [21]that the creation itself will also be set free from the bondage of corruption into the glorious freedom of God's children. [22]For we know that the whole creation has been groaning together with labor pains until now. [23]And not only that, but we ourselves who have the Spirit as the firstfruits—we also groan within ourselves, eagerly waiting for adoption, the redemption of our bodies. [24]Now in this hope we were saved, yet hope that is seen is not hope, because who hopes for what he sees? [25]But if we hope for what we do not see, we eagerly wait for it with patience.

[26]In the same way the Spirit also joins to help in our weakness, because we do not know what to pray for as we should, but the Spirit Himself intercedes for us with unspoken groanings. [27]And He who searches the hearts knows the Spirit's mind-set, because He intercedes for the saints according to the will of God.

[28]We know that all things work together for the good of those who love God: those who are called according to His purpose. [29]For those He foreknew He also predestined to be conformed to the image of His Son, so that He would be the firstborn among many brothers. [30]And those He predestined, He also called; and those He called, He also justified; and those He justified, He also glorified.

PRAYER: Gracious and loving Father, it is a privilege to be a part of Your creation and an even greater privilege to be counted as one of Your servants. To be called Your child, to be considered as one of Your family, to be able to call You Abba Father is a truth that I just can't get over. Once again all I can say is 'Thank You'. I shall go on saying it again and again and again. Amen.

DAY
285

CAN WE SUM up Paul's vision? It heralds the arrival of God's new covenant people, founded on the death of Jesus, and in which the Spirit of God is triumphantly at work. The Spirit enables believers to fulfil the just requirements of the law, to defeat the flesh and to live as God intends His covenant people to live. The Spirit joins us to the character and destiny of Jesus and so guarantees our final resurrection. The Spirit assures us of our sonship, evoking within us a heartfelt appeal to God as Father especially during times of crisis. The Spirit inspires hope and helps us to pray in line with God's will. The Spirit groans within us as we share a divine discontent for a better world. In every way, the Spirit sustains us in the weakness of life in the present age, and assures us of future glory.

As the Spirit floods our hearts with God's love, we know that no opposition can defeat us since Christ is our covenant protector. No deprivation can threaten us for God is our provider. No accusation can be made against us because God vindicates us. No condemnation can doom us because Christ is our advocate with the Father. And, above all, on the way to the promised future, nothing in the world as it is or in the world as it may become, can come between us and the unquenchable covenant-love of God in Jesus Christ.

BIBLE READING

Romans 8:31-39

THE BELIEVER'S TRIUMPH

³¹ What then are we to say about these things?
If God is for us, who is against us?

³² He did not even spare His own Son,
but offered Him up for us all;
how will He not also with Him grant us everything?

³³ Who can bring an accusation against God's elect?
God is the One who justifies.

³⁴ Who is the one who condemns?
  Christ Jesus is the One who died, but even more,
    has been raised;
  He also is at the right hand of God and intercedes for us.
³⁵ Who can separate us from the love of Christ?
  Can affliction or anguish or persecution
  or famine or nakedness or danger or sword?
³⁶ As it is written:
  "Because of You we are being put to death all day long;
  we are counted as sheep to be slaughtered."
³⁷ No, in all these things we are more than victorious
  through Him who loved us.
³⁸ For I am persuaded that neither death nor life,
  nor angels nor rulers,
  nor things present, nor things to come, nor powers,
³⁹ nor height, nor depth, nor any other created thing
  will have the power to separate us
  from the love of God that is in Christ Jesus our Lord!

QUESTION: How do you feel about the fact that nothing can separate you from the love of Christ? If you have never given deep thought to this issue then do so now. Think of it – no shortcoming, no circumstance, no opposition, no person, place or thing can come between us and the love which Christ has for us. Once again – how do you feel about that? Express those feelings in prayer, praise or perhaps even song.

PAUL'S CELEBRATION OF God's enduring covenant-love leaves a question hanging in the air: Is there any place for ethnic Israel in the plot?

Paul's answer is to the effect that the story of Israel has not been written out of God's larger story but transformed and enlarged in and through her Messiah, Jesus.

Paul's own mind seems stretched to breaking point here both by the agony of the issue and by the breathtaking answers the Holy Spirit was giving him.

DAY
286

ROMANS 9:1-13

715

Israel's failure to embrace Jesus as Messiah is all the more tragic when you recall her unique God-given privileges and status (9:4) – all derived from the promises made to the patriarchs. Above all, nothing can ever take from them the privilege of being the forebears of the Messiah who is 'God over all' (9:5).

But an even bigger question remains: does Israel's failure mean that God's covenant promises have fallen to the ground? Paul answers with a decisive 'no'. Whoever else has failed, God has not failed and nor has His Word of promise (9:6).

In fact, there has always been an ambiguity about Israel; there has always been an 'Israel' within Israel (9:7-13). Genealogical descent from Abraham never did count for much, only being children of the promise. Always what matters is the promise of God which shapes the story, and what our response is to it.

BIBLE READING

Romans 9:1-13

9 I speak the truth in Christ—I am not lying; my conscience is testifying to me with the Holy Spirit — ²that I have intense sorrow and continual anguish in my heart. ³For I could wish that I myself were cursed and cut off from the Messiah for the benefit of my brothers, my countrymen by physical descent. ⁴They are Israelites, and to them belong the adoption, the glory, the covenants, the giving of the law, the temple service, and the promises. ⁵The forefathers are theirs, and from them, by physical descent, came the Messiah, who is God over all, blessed forever. Amen.

GOD'S GRACIOUS ELECTION OF ISRAEL

⁶But it is not as though the word of God has failed. For not all who are descended from Israel are Israel. ⁷Neither are they all children because they are Abraham's descendants. On the contrary, "in Isaac your seed will be called." ⁸That is, it is not the children by physical descent who are God's children, but the children of the promise are considered seed. ⁹For this is the statement of the promise: "At this time I will come, and Sarah

will have a son." [10]And not only that, but also when Rebekah became pregnant by Isaac our forefather [11](for though they had not been born yet or done anything good or bad, so that God's purpose according to election might stand, [12]not from works but from the One who calls) she was told: "The older will serve the younger. [13]As it is written: Jacob I have loved, but Esau I have hated."

FOR PRAISE: Are you familiar with the following verse? It summarises the enduring nature of God's promises. If you know it sing it (or say it) as your response to today's reading:

Standing, standing,
Standing on the promises
of God my Saviour
Standing, standing
I'm standing on the promises of God.

(R. Kelso Carter, 1849-1928)

DAY
287
ROMANS 9:14-33

PAUL'S CONCERN IS with the fate of Israel but even more with the character and integrity of God. In the narrowing of Abraham's seed to the line of Isaac is God unjust? In the golden calf incident, (9:14-15 citing Exod. 33:19), as with God's treatment of Pharaoh, the over-riding consideration is God's glory and the honour of His name (vv.16-18). As Israel's own prophets testify, God would be unable to affirm Israel as she stood and would need to subject her to His judgment and mercy in order to change and restore her (9:19-29). Tragically, Israel has become 'objects of wrath ready for destruction', but God has borne with His people patiently with a view to demonstrating His mercy in the creation of an amazingly enlarged people of God - made up of both Jews and Gentiles - who respond to His call.

The greater tragedy is that more Gentiles than Jews are presently entering God's new covenant family, while Israel is preoccupied with pursuing the law in her own nationalistic and exclusive way (9:30-32). This misuse of the law has, in turn, led Israel to stumble over the Messiah (9:33). But the very fact that this 'stumbling' of Israel was foreseen by the prophets holds out the tough but mysterious hope that Israel's failure, and with it her future destiny, is, somehow, incorporated into God's plan from the start!

| BIBLE READING | **Romans 9:14-33** |

9 I speak the truth in Christ—I am not lying; my conscience is testifying to me with the Holy Spirit— ²that I have intense sorrow and continual anguish in my heart. ³For I could wish that I myself were cursed and cut off from the Messiah for the benefit of my brothers, my countrymen by physical descent. ⁴They are Israelites, and to them belong the adoption, the glory, the covenants, the giving of the law, the temple service, and the promises. ⁵The forefathers are theirs, and from them, by physical descent, came the Messiah, who is God over all, blessed forever. Amen.

GOD'S GRACIOUS ELECTION OF ISRAEL

⁶But it is not as though the word of God has failed. For not all who are descended from Israel are Israel. ⁷Neither are they all children because they are Abraham's descendants. On the contrary, "in Isaac your seed will be called." ⁸That is, it is not the children by physical descent who are God's children, but the children of the promise are considered seed. ⁹For this is the statement of the promise: "At this time I will come, and Sarah will have a son." ¹⁰And not only that, but also when Rebekah became pregnant by Isaac our forefather ¹¹(for though they had not been born yet or done anything good or bad, so that God's purpose according to election might stand, ¹²not from works but from the One who calls) she was told: "The older will serve the younger. ¹³As it is written: Jacob I have loved, but Esau I have hated."

GOD'S SELECTION IS JUST

[14]What should we say then? Is there injustice with God? Absolutely not! [15]For He tells Moses:

> "I will show mercy to whom I show mercy,
> and I will have compassion on whom have compassion."

[16]So then it does not depend on human will or effort, but on God who shows mercy. [17]For the Scripture tells Pharaoh:

> "For this reason I raised you up:
> so that I may display My power in you,
> and that My name may be proclaimed in all the earth."

[18]So then, He shows mercy to whom He wills, and He hardens whom He wills.

[19]You will say to me, therefore, "Why then does He still find fault? For who can resist His will?" [20]But who are you—anyone who talks back to God? Will what is formed say to the one who formed it, "Why did you make me like this?" [21]Or has the potter no right over His clay, to make from the same lump one piece of pottery for honor and another for dishonor? [22]And what if God, desiring to display His wrath and to make His power known, endured with much patience objects of wrath ready for destruction? [23]And [what if] He did this to make known the riches of His glory on objects of mercy that He prepared beforehand for glory— [24]on us whom He also called, not only from the Jews but also from the Gentiles? [25]As He also says in Hosea:

> "I will call 'Not-My-People,' 'My-People,'
> and she who is 'Unloved,' 'Beloved.'
> [26] And it will be in the place where they were told,
> you are not My people,
> there they will be called sons of the living God."

[27]But Isaiah cries out concerning Israel:

> "Though the number of Israel's sons is like
> the sand of the sea,

only the remnant will be saved;
28 for the Lord will execute His sentence
completely and decisively on the earth."

29 And just as Isaiah predicted:

"If the Lord of Hosts had not left us a seed,
we would have become like Sodom,
and we would have been made like Gomorrah."

ISRAEL'S PRESENT STATE

30 What should we say then? Gentiles, who did not pursue righteousness, have obtained righteousness—namely the righteousness that comes from faith. 31 But Israel, pursuing the law for righteousness, has not achieved the law. 32 Why is that? Because they did not pursue it by faith, but as if it were by works. They stumbled over the stumbling stone. 33 As it is written:

"Look! I am putting a stone in Zion to stumble over,
and a rock to trip over,
yet the one who believes on Him will not
be put to shame."

THOUGHT: One of the most intriguing truths to be found in Scripture is that God is able to take the stumbles and blunders of His people and incorporate them into His purposes. Nothing can outwit the mind of the Almighty or out-manoeuvre His strategies. As Ian Sewter puts it: 'God's plans for us can never be thwarted by our failures as He includes them from the start.'

PAUL NOW FURTHER explains the strange twist in the story of redemption caused by Israel's ignorance of what God has been faithfully doing throughout her covenant history. Israel has grasped for her 'own' exclusive righteousness, as if Israel said: 'The covenant righteousness is ours alone.' In doing this, first-century Israel lost the plot of God's big story and failed to recognise the climactic stage of the story when it dawned in Jesus.

DAY
288
ROMANS 10

Jesus is the 'end' of the law. Negatively, He 'ends' the law by bearing the judgment on sin it prescribes. He is the 'end' of the law, positively, because He keeps all its covenant demands. He is the 'end' of the law in that everything that the law patterns and promises Jesus fulfils. Jesus is the climax of God's covenant intention for which the law was given. The law was a good thing, fitted for a particular stage in the story. Now, its time is up. The goal of the law has arrived and it is a person, Jesus. There can now be no question of anyone hijacking the covenant for themselves. In Christ it is open to 'everyone who believes', whatever their nationality. Wasn't this exactly what God told Abraham He wanted at the start of our story?

Romans 10

BIBLE
READING

RIGHTEOUSNESS BY FAITH ALONE

10 Brothers, my heart's desire and prayer to God concerning them is for their salvation! [2]I can testify about them that they have zeal for God, but not according to knowledge. [3]Because they disregarded the righteousness from God and attempted to establish their own righteousness, they have not submitted to God's righteousness. [4]For Christ is the end of the law for righteousness to everyone who believes. [5]For Moses writes about the righteousness that is from the law: "The one who does these things will live by them." [6]But the righteousness that comes from faith speaks like this: "Do not say in your heart, 'Who will go up to heaven?'" that is, to bring

Christ down [7]or, "'Who will go down into the abyss?'" that is, to bring Christ up from the dead. [8]On the contrary, what does it say? "The message is near you, in your mouth and in your heart." This is the message of faith that we proclaim: [9]if you confess with your mouth, "Jesus is Lord," and believe in your heart that God raised Him from the dead, you will be saved. [10]With the heart one believes, resulting in righteousness, and with the mouth one confesses, resulting in salvation. [11]Now the Scripture says, "No one who believes on Him will be put to shame," [12]for there is no distinction between Jew and Greek, since the same Lord of all is rich to all who call on Him. [13]For "everyone who calls on the name of the Lord will be saved."

ISRAEL'S REJECTION OF THE MESSAGE

[14]But how can they call on Him in whom they have not believed? And how can they believe without hearing about Him? And how can they hear without a preacher? [15]And how can they preach unless they are sent? As it is written: "How welcome are the feet of those who announce the gospel of good things!" [16]But all did not obey the gospel. For Isaiah says, "Lord, who has believed our message?" [17]So faith comes from what is heard, and what is heard comes through the message about Christ. [18]But I ask, "Did they not hear?" Yes, they did:

> "Their voice has gone out to all the earth,
>   and their words to the ends of the inhabited world."

[19]But I ask, "Did Israel not understand?" First, Moses said:

> "I will make you jealous of those who are not a nation;
> I will make you angry by a nation that lacks
>   understanding."

[20]And Isaiah says boldly:

> "I was found by those who were not looking for Me;
> I revealed Myself to those who were not asking for Me."

[21]But to Israel he says: "All day long I have spread out My hands to a disobedient and defiant people."

TO PONDER: If there is one thing Scripture emphasises again and again it is this - God delights to bless us. He gets great delight out of making His people happy. But He requires always that His blessings be shared with others, whether given to Abraham, Israel or the Church. Count your own blessings at this moment. Now consider, how much of what God has given you have you given to others?

DAY
289
ROMANS 10:5-21

PAUL HAS TRACED the covenant purpose of God from Abraham down as far as the Exile in Babylon (9:6-33).

Then he recalls the hope offered by Moses that Israel would be restored after Exile (Deut. 30). This enables Paul to show that the Deuteronomy way of 'doing the law' (10:5) is, in fact, the way of faith!

In this paradoxical way, the law can be said to be fulfilled whenever Christ is preached and people respond in faith. In what is perhaps the earliest Christian confession of faith that exists, the way to be saved is to confess that 'Jesus is Lord' and to believe that God raised Him from the dead (10:9). Believing 'with your heart' (NIV) once again picks up the new covenant theme (Deut. 30:6; Jer. 33).

Joel's prophecy (10:13; Joel 2:32) is applied to the Jews and Gentiles who are putting their faith in Christ and acknowledging him as Lord (10:11-14). The era of restoration and salvation which Isaiah saw announced by the herald with the 'beautiful feet' running over the mountain with the good news of the kingdom of God (Isa. 52:7), has well and truly come. Sadly, most Jews remain resistant to the message of the gospel, though in doing so they ironically fulfil their own Scriptures (10:16-21). But a hope remains that Israel may even be stirred to jealousy by a people of God who know Israel's Messiah as the key to God's story (10:19).

BIBLE READING

Romans 10:5-21

⁵For Moses writes about the righteousness that is from the law: "The one who does these things will live by them." ⁶But the righteousness that comes from faith speaks like this: "Do not say in your heart, 'Who will go up to heaven?'" that is, to bring Christ down ⁷or, "'Who will go down into the abyss?'" that is, to bring Christ up from the dead. ⁸On the contrary, what does it say? "The message is near you, in your mouth and in your heart." This is the message of faith that we proclaim: ⁹if you confess with your mouth, "Jesus is Lord," and believe in your heart that God raised Him from the dead, you will be saved. ¹⁰With the heart one believes, resulting in righteousness, and with the mouth one confesses, resulting in salvation. ¹¹Now the Scripture says, "No one who believes on Him will be put to shame," ¹²for there is no distinction between Jew and Greek, since the same Lord of all is rich to all who call on Him. ¹³For "everyone who calls on the name of the Lord will be saved."

ISRAEL'S REJECTION OF THE MESSAGE

¹⁴But how can they call on Him in whom they have not believed? And how can they believe without hearing about Him? And how can they hear without a preacher? ¹⁵And how can they preach unless they are sent? As it is written: "How welcome are the feet of those who announce the gospel of good things!" ¹⁶But all did not obey the gospel. For Isaiah says, "Lord, who has believed our message?" ¹⁷So faith comes from what is heard, and what is heard comes through the message about Christ. ¹⁸But I ask, "Did they not hear?" Yes, they did:

> "Their voice has gone out to all the earth,
> and their words to the ends of the inhabited world."

¹⁹But I ask, "Did Israel not understand?" First, Moses said:

> "I will make you jealous of those who are not a nation;
> I will make you angry by a nation that lacks
> understanding."

²⁰And Isaiah says boldly:

> "I was found by those who were not looking for Me;
> I revealed Myself to those who were not asking for Me."

²¹But to Israel he says: "All day long I have spread out My hands to a disobedient and defiant people."

FOR ACTION: We have been told something today that while bringing to every Christian heart a tinge of sadness should also stir us to deeper intercessory prayer, namely that most Jews remain resistant to the gospel. Notwithstanding that, many Jews come to Christ each year. Some reports say as many as half a million. Spend a few minutes today interceding for Jews who do not yet know Jesus.

IN EXPLORING FURTHER the covenant faithfulness of God in Christ, Paul here seems to be answering two implied questions.

To the question 'Are any Jews being saved at all?' Paul answers with the notion, derived from the prophets, of the 'remnant' who believe, Paul among them. For their part, Gentile Christians are warned against arrogantly forgetting their Jewish roots in the patriarchal promises and covenants. There is only one olive tree, one people of God to whom Gentiles have been added by grace and some Jews removed by judgment. But the one should not presume nor the other despair. Will any more Jews be saved? Though some may continue to respond, a hardening has settled over Jewish hearts until the fullness of the Gentiles has come in. In this way 'all Israel' – the whole people of God – will be saved through embracing the new covenant promise of God (11:26; Isa. 27:9; 59:20-21; Jer. 31:33-34). The deliverer comes out of Zion and appeals to Zion to be forgiven and restored as a new covenant people.

This strange interaction of Jews and Gentiles is

DAY
290
ROMANS 11:1-32

central to the 'mystery' of God's strategic plan that Paul unveils (11:26).

Whether this involves the conversion of Israel on a national scale prior to the second coming of Jesus is an open question. Paul seems more concerned for what is happening 'now' (11:31).

But one way or another, it's all a miracle of grace.

| BIBLE READING | **Romans 11:1-32** |

11 I ask, then, has God rejected His people? Absolutely not! For I too am an Israelite, a descendant of Abraham, from the tribe of Benjamin. ²God has not rejected His people whom He foreknew. Or do you not know what the Scripture says in the Elijah section—how he pleads with God against Israel?

> ³ "Lord, they have killed Your prophets, torn down
> Your altars;
> and I am the only one left, and they are trying to take
> my life!"

⁴But what was God's reply to him? "I have left 7,000 men for Myself who have not bowed down to Baal." ⁵In the same way, then, there is also at the present time a remnant chosen by grace. ⁶Now if by grace, then it is not by works; otherwise grace ceases to be grace.

⁷What then? Israel did not find what it was looking for, but the elect did find it. The rest were hardened, ⁸as it is written:

> "God gave them a spirit of stupor,
> eyes that cannot see and ears that cannot hear,
> to this day."

⁹And David says:

> "Let their feasting become a snare and a trap,
> a pitfall and a retribution to them.
> ¹⁰ Let their eyes be darkened so they cannot see,
> and their backs be bent continually."

ISRAEL'S REJECTION NOT FINAL

[11]I ask, then, have they stumbled so as to fall? Absolutely not! On the contrary, by their stumbling, salvation has come to the Gentiles to make Israel jealous. [12]Now if their stumbling brings riches for the world, and their failure riches for the Gentiles, how much more will their full number bring!

[13]Now I am speaking to you Gentiles. In view of the fact that I am an apostle to the Gentiles, I magnify my ministry, [14]if I can somehow make my own people jealous and save some of them. [15]For if their being rejected is world reconciliation, what will their acceptance mean but life from the dead? [16]Now if the firstfruits offered up are holy, so is the whole batch. And if the root is holy, so are the branches.

[17]Now if some of the branches were broken off, and you, though a wild olive branch, were grafted in among them, and have come to share in the rich root of the cultivated olive tree, [18]do not brag that you are better than those branches. But if you do brag—you do not sustain the root, but the root sustains you. [19]Then you will say, "Branches were broken off so that I might be grafted in." [20]True enough; they were broken off by unbelief, but you stand by faith. Do not be arrogant, but be afraid. [21]For if God did not spare the natural branches, He will not spare you either. [22]Therefore, consider God's kindness and severity: severity toward those who have fallen, but God's kindness toward you—if you remain in His kindness. Otherwise you too will be cut off. [23]And even they, if they do not remain in unbelief, will be grafted in, because God has the power to graft them in again. [24]For if you were cut off from your native wild olive, and against nature were grafted into a cultivated olive tree, how much more will these—the natural branches—be grafted into their own olive tree?

[25]So that you will not be conceited, brothers, I do not want you to be unaware of this mystery: a partial hardening has come to Israel until the full number of the Gentiles has come in. [26]And in this way all Israel will be saved, as it is written:

> "The Liberator will come from Zion;
> He will turn away godlessness from Jacob.
> [27] And this will be My covenant with them,
> when I take away their sins."

²⁸Regarding the gospel, they are enemies for your advantage, but regarding election, they are loved because of their forefathers, ²⁹since God's gracious gifts and calling are irrevocable. ³⁰As you once disobeyed God, but now have received mercy through their disobedience, ³¹so they too have now disobeyed, [resulting] in mercy to you, so that they also now may receive mercy. ³²For God has imprisoned all in disobedience, so that He may have mercy on all.

PRAYER: Heavenly Father, the more I read Your Word the more I realise that everything we receive from You is all because of Your grace. The Jews with their rebellious hearts were undeserving of Your grace but then so are those of us who are Gentiles. If we had our just deserts then we would be cast into outer darkness. But grace has intervened. Glory be to Your wondrous name for ever. Amen.

DAY 291

ROMANS 11:28-36

'GOD MOVES IN a mysterious way his wonders to perform.' This is not a puzzle to be figured out but a providence to be marvelled at.

Because they opposed the preaching of Jesus, Paul can regard his fellow Jews only as enemies of the gospel. But does God still have a special love for His ancient people? Yes, He does. God does not go back on His gifts and calling. But God has special love for Israel not because she has a specially reserved, fast-track into God's kingdom in the future that by-passes Jesus but because of His own historical commitments to the patriarchs!

Once more little is said here about the future of Israel as a nation. Paul's concern is with the wider picture of what God is doing in His world. As a result of Jewish disobedience, the Gentiles have received mercy. So now disobedient Jews may receive mercy because of God's mercy to the Gentiles! God's forgiving heart is open to all (11:32). Through a mysterious interplay between Jews and Gentiles God will achieve His breathtaking purpose.

When even Israel's failure, rejection and disobedience are woven into God's plan of salvation then we can only stand back and wonder at this strangely sovereign and covenant-keeping God. From His grace, through His power, to His glory explains it all. All that's left is our worship.

Romans 11:28-36

²⁸Regarding the gospel, they are enemies for your advantage, but regarding election, they are loved because of their forefathers, ²⁹since God's gracious gifts and calling are irrevocable. ³⁰As you once disobeyed God, but now have received mercy through their disobedience, ³¹so they too have now disobeyed, [resulting] in mercy to you, so that they also now may receive mercy. ³²For God has imprisoned all in disobedience, so that He may have mercy on all.

A HYMN OF PRAISE

³³ Oh, the depth of the riches
both of the wisdom and the knowledge of God!
How unsearchable His judgments
and untraceable His ways!

³⁴ "For who has known the mind of the Lord?
Or who has been His counselor?

³⁵ Or who has ever first given to Him,
and has to be repaid?"

³⁶ For from Him and through Him and to Him
are all things.
To Him be the glory forever. Amen.

THOUGHT: 'From His grace, through His power, to His glory.' That pregnant phrase sums up the whole of Scripture. The consideration of that stupendous fact leaves us with just one thing to do - fall to our knees in worship. Nothing in us gave rise to God's love and grace, and nothing in us can extinguish it. Never forget - His love for us is based not on our faultless character, but on His forgiving nature.

729

DAY
292

ROMANS 12:1-8

WHEN OUR WHOLE beings are gripped by God's grace (as in 11:33-36), we can only respond by the offering of our whole selves to God in worship. Our sacrifice, of course, is living, not dead like animals; holy, as we dedicate our entire life to God; and spiritual or reasonable, in that we make an intelligent and fitting response to grace.

This covers all of life. How is this done? First, Paul says, refuse to let the 'world squeeze you into its own mould' (J.B. Phillips). We become non-conformist in our thinking and behaving, by rejecting the story told by this present evil age. Being 'transformed' by the 'renewing' of our minds once again describes authentic new covenant living with a new heart, and God's law implanted in our minds. It is an affront to proud intellectuals to learn that sin has affected our minds, distorting our thinking and darkening our understanding, so that when the things of God are first presented to us as sinners, we 'just don't get it'. And this re-programming of our minds is a life-long process which starts when we humble them before God. It continues as we bend every mental and intellectual power we possess to the joyous task of loving God with our minds and growing in understanding of His plan of salvation! This journey through God's big story is designed to help you do just that!

BIBLE READING

Romans 12:1-8

A LIVING SACRIFICE

12 Therefore, brothers, by the mercies of God, I urge you to present your bodies as a living sacrifice, holy and pleasing to God; this is your spiritual worship. ²Do not be conformed to this age, but be transformed by the renewing of your mind, so that you may discern what is the good, pleasing, and perfect will of God.

MANY GIFTS BUT ONE BODY

³For by the grace given to me, I tell everyone among you

not to think of himself more highly than he should think. Instead, think sensibly, as God has distributed a measure of faith to each one. ⁴Now as we have many parts in one body, and all the parts do not have the same function, ⁵in the same way we who are many are one body in Christ and individually members of one another. ⁶According to the grace given to us, we have different gifts:

If prophecy, use it according to the standard of faith;
⁷ if service, in service; if teaching, in teaching;
⁸ if exhorting, in exhortation; giving, with generosity;
leading, with diligence; showing mercy,
with cheerfulness.

TO PONDER: There is a great deal of anti-intellectualism in some parts of today's Church. One Christian put it like this: 'Sometimes when I go to church I might as well unscrew my head and put it under the seat. The emphasis is on feeling good and there is no attempt to engage with my brain.' Remember we are commanded to love God not just with all our hearts but also with all our minds.

PAUL HERE DISCUSSES the vexed question of what Christians can legitimately disagree about and how they can live together in unity when they do! The 'strong' have a robust sense of their freedom in Christ and so have few scruples about what they eat or do. The 'weak' are those who do have scruples about many things and feel some areas of life are 'off limits'. Such matters as feast days and food laws are matters on which Christians may rightly differ. What must not happen is for the 'weak' to judge and condemn the 'strong' or for the 'strong' to look down patronisingly on the 'weak'.

Both parties are called to realise that they are in God's story which rolls inexorably on towards final resolution.

DAY
293
ROMANS 14:7-12

No one is in a position to judge another because we shall all stand before God's judgment seat (14:10-11).

Above all, the story of Jesus stands at the heart of God's big story and ours. Crucial to our grasp of that story is the recognition that Jesus died and rose again to become Lord of the dead and the living, Lord of our present and our future. The onus is on the 'strong' Christians to make the story of the cross their central dynamic by acting sensitively towards a brother 'for whom Christ died' (14:15). Living out the story together in this way honours its Author and commends it to outsiders (14:18).

BIBLE READING

Romans 14:7-12

⁷For none of us lives to himself, and no one dies to himself. ⁸If we live, we live to the Lord; and if we die, we die to the Lord. Therefore, whether we live or die, we belong to the Lord. ⁹Christ died and came to life for this: that He might rule over both the dead and the living. ¹⁰But you, why do you criticize your brother? Or you, why do you look down on your brother? For we will all stand before the judgment seat of God. ¹¹For it is written:

> "As I live, says the Lord,
> every knee will bow to Me,
> and every tongue will give praise to God."

¹²So then, each of us will give an account of himself to God.

FOR ACTION: In the light of the fact that Scripture calls us to 'maintain the unity of the Spirit in the bonds of peace' and live in harmony with one another, this issue must be treated seriously. Is there anyone in your circle of friends or relationships with whom you have a difference of opinion that has caused a rift to come between you? If so, before the sun goes down determine to seek a reconciliation.

CHRISTIAN HOPE DERIVES from the Scriptures (15:4) and from the Holy Spirit (15:13).

DAY
294
ROMANS 15:4-13

We are enriched by seeing that the Old Testament is not a static book but rather has a powerful momentum that presses towards God's future. Dark as some passages may seem, the narrative points forward to find its final meaning in Jesus. In other words, the ancient Scriptures generate enormous hope.

Reading the Old Testament in this way should give us hope that, despite appearances to the contrary, history is going God's way. This especially encourages those non-Jewish participants in the story who were originally not addressed by the hopeful visions offered by the Old Testament prophets. Only when Jesus Christ comes to make good those promises do Gentile believers find a new history for themselves. While Jews rejoice, therefore, that God is a truthful God who keeps His word, Gentile believers glorify God for the mercy that includes them in His saving plans on an equal footing. Through Jesus, God has kept his age-old promise to Abraham to bring blessing to all nations. And Gentile believers can't thank Him enough!

Jew and Gentile hope knows no bounds, fed as it is by prophetic scriptures, fixed as it is on Jesus the Messiah (15:12) and overflowing as it does by the Spirit's power in one united chorus of praise.

Romans 15:4-13

BIBLE
READING

⁴For whatever was written before was written for our instruction, so that through our endurance and through the encouragement of the Scriptures we may have hope. ⁵Now may the God of endurance and encouragement grant you agreement with one another, according to Christ Jesus, ⁶so that you may glorify the God and Father of our Lord Jesus Christ with a united mind and voice.

GLORIFYING GOD TOGETHER

[7]Therefore accept one another, just as the Messiah also accepted you, to the glory of God. [8]Now I say that Christ has become a servant of the circumcised on behalf of the truth of God, to confirm the promises to the fathers, [9]and so that Gentiles may glorify God for His mercy. As it is written:

"Therefore I will praise You among the Gentiles,
and I will sing psalms to Your name."

[10]Again it says: Rejoice, you Gentiles, with His people! [11]And again:

"Praise the Lord, all you Gentiles;
all the peoples should praise Him!"

[12]And again, Isaiah says:

"The root of Jesse will appear,
the One who rises to rule the Gentiles;
in Him the Gentiles will hope."

[13]Now may the God of hope fill you with all joy and peace in believing, so that you may overflow with hope by the power of the Holy Spirit.

FOR PRAISE: Join in praise to God right now along with the many thousands who will read these lines, people from all nationalities, who have been saved by grace and washed in the blood of Christ. Praise Him for the fact that from all nations, with all their differences and cultures, He has formed, through Jesus, one family who is to the praise of His glory.

IN ROMANS, THE gospel is the good news that God's covenant faithfulness ('His righteousness') is revealed in the preaching of Jesus. As Messiah, Jesus has dealt a death blow to the sin which ruins God's good creation and holds both Jew and Gentile in its thrall. God's covenant faithfulness has acted to save by overcoming in His Son's death and resurrection all the negative factors that oppose the truly human life – namely, sin, death, the flesh and, surprisingly, the law of God itself. But through Christ, God reverses Adam's plight and offers the prospect of a new humanity in Christ. This newly human, new covenant community, is leading the way through a groaning world to the new creation God. God's plan mysteriously interweaves the stories of Israel and the world and wraps them up in the story of Jesus.

God's covenant-love writes a new chapter in the human story, with new characters, forgiven and empowered by the Spirit, who are learning their parts in the new drama of being human. Whether Jew or Gentile, these new covenant people sing from the same songsheet of love and worship with one voice. The ordinary saints Paul greets at the end of this letter are the real heroes in the story. In the end, the mystery of God's strategic plan evokes astonished praise of the One and 'only wise God'.

DAY
295
ROMANS 15:14-16:27

Romans 15:14-16:27

FROM JERUSALEM TO ILLYRICUM

[14]Now, my brothers, I myself am convinced about you that you also are full of goodness, filled with all knowledge, and able to instruct one another. [15]Nevertheless, to remind you, I have written to you more boldly on some points because of the grace given me by God [16]to be a minister of Christ Jesus to the Gentiles, serving as a priest of God's good news. My purpose is that the offering of the Gentiles may be acceptable, sanctified by the Holy Spirit. [17]Therefore I have reason to boast in Christ

Jesus regarding what pertains to God. ¹⁸For I would not dare say anything except what Christ has accomplished through me to make the Gentiles obedient by word and deed, ¹⁹by the power of miraculous signs and wonders, and by the power of God's Spirit. As a result, I have fully proclaimed the good news about the Messiah from Jerusalem all the way around to Illyricum. ²⁰So my aim is to evangelize where Christ has not been named, in order that I will not be building on someone else's foundation, ²¹but, as it is written:

> "Those who had no report of Him will see,
> and those who have not heard will understand."

PAUL'S TRAVEL PLANS

²²That is why I have been prevented many times from coming to you. ²³But now I no longer have any work to do in these provinces, and I have strongly desired for many years to come to you ²⁴whenever I travel to Spain. For I do hope to see you when I pass through, and to be sent on my way there by you, once I have first enjoyed your company for a while. ²⁵Now, however, I am traveling to Jerusalem to serve the saints; ²⁶for Macedonia and Achaia were pleased to make a contribution to the poor among the saints in Jerusalem. ²⁷Yes, they were pleased, and they are indebted to them. For if the Gentiles have shared in their spiritual benefits, then they are obligated to minister to Jews in material needs. ²⁸So when I have finished this and safely delivered the funds to them, I will go by way of you to Spain. ²⁹But I know that when I come to you, I will come in the fullness of the blessing of Christ.

³⁰Now I implore you, brothers, through the Lord Jesus Christ and through the love of the Spirit, to agonize together with me in your prayers to God on my behalf: ³¹that I may be rescued from the unbelievers in Judea, that my service for Jerusalem may be acceptable to the saints, ³²and that, by God's will, I may come to you with joy and be refreshed together with you.

³³The God of peace be with all of you. Amen.

PAUL'S COMMENDATION OF PHOEBE

16 I commend to you our sister Phoebe, who is a servant of the church in Cenchreae. ²So you should welcome her in the Lord in a manner worthy of the saints, and assist her in whatever matter she may require your help. For indeed she has been a benefactor of many—and of me also.

GREETING TO ROMAN CHRISTIANS

³ Give my greetings to Prisca and Aquila, my co-workers in Christ Jesus, ⁴ who risked their own necks for my life. Not only do I thank them, but so do all the Gentile churches.

⁵ Greet also the church that meets in their home. Greet my dear friend Epaenetus, who is the first convert to Christ from Asia.

⁶ Greet Mary, who has worked very hard for you.

⁷ Greet Andronicus and Junia, my fellow countrymen and fellow prisoners. They are outstanding among the apostles, and they were also in Christ before me.

⁸ Greet Ampliatus, my dear friend in the Lord.

⁹ Greet Urbanus, our co-worker in Christ, and my dear friend Stachys.

¹⁰ Greet Apelles, who is approved in Christ. Greet those who belong to the household of Aristobulus.

¹¹ Greet Herodion, my fellow countryman. Greet those who belong to the household of Narcissus who are in the Lord.

¹² Greet Tryphaena and Tryphosa, who have worked hard in the Lord. Greet my dear friend Persis, who has worked very hard in the Lord.

¹³ Greet Rufus, chosen in the Lord; also his mother—and mine.

¹⁴ Greet Asyncritus, Phlegon, Hermes, Patrobas, Hermas, and the brothers who are with them.

¹⁵ Greet Philologus and Julia, Nereus and his sister, and Olympas, and all the saints who are with them.

¹⁶ Greet one another with a holy kiss. All the churches of Christ send you greetings.

WARNING AGAINST DIVISIVE PEOPLE

¹⁷Now I implore you, brothers, watch out for those who cause dissensions and pitfalls contrary to the doctrine you

have learned. Avoid them; [18]for such people do not serve our Lord Christ but their own appetites, and by smooth talk and flattering words they deceive the hearts of the unsuspecting.

PAUL'S GRACIOUS CONCLUSION

[19]The report of your obedience has reached everyone. Therefore I rejoice over you. But I want you to be wise about what is good, yet innocent about what is evil. [20]The God of peace will soon crush Satan under your feet. The grace of our Lord Jesus be with you.

[21]Timothy, my co-worker, and Lucius, Jason, and Sosipater, my fellow countrymen, greet you.

[22]I Tertius, who penned this epistle in the Lord, greet you.

[23]Gaius, who is host to me and to the whole church, greets you. Erastus, the city treasurer, and our brother Quartus greet you.

[[24]The grace of our Lord Jesus Christ be with you all.]

GLORY TO GOD

[25]Now to Him who has power to strengthen you according to my gospel and the proclamation of Jesus Christ, according to the revelation of the sacred secret kept silent for long ages, [26]but now revealed and made known through the prophetic Scriptures, according to the command of the eternal God, to advance the obedience of faith among all nations— [27]to the only wise God, through Jesus Christ—to Him be the glory forever! Amen.

PRAYER: O Father, the more I understand Your ways and purposes in the past, and the more I learn of Your plans for the future, the more confident I am of living in the present. Help me realise even more fully that when I feel as if there is not much happening in my life You are at work nevertheless. Often You do Your greatest work in secret. Blessed be Your name for ever. Amen.

NOAH
ALL CREATION

ABRAHAM
ALL NATIONS

ISRAEL
ONE NATION

DAVID
REPRESENTATIVE KING

NEW COVENANT
FAITHFUL COVENANT PARTNER

JESUS
FAITHFUL COVENANT PARTNER

JESUS
DAVIDIC KING MESSIAH

JESUS
THE NEW ISRAEL

JESUS
THE WORLD'S LORD

JESUS
THE TRULY HUMAN ONE
CROWNED WITH GLORY
AND HONOUR

JESUS
COSMIC RULER IN GOD'S NEW CREATION
NEW HEAVENS AND NEW EARTH

SECTION 10 PAUL'S WORLD-VIEW
PART 2

DAY
296

**PHILIPPIANS 1:1-5
1 THESSALONIANS
1:2-10**

PHILIPPIANS MUST BE the most famous thank-you note in history!

While Paul does warn against false teachers and disunity, his main reason for writing is to thank the Philippians for their long-term sponsorship of his ministry through prayer and financial support.

In short, Paul rejoices that the Philippians have come alive to the part they are called to play in the ongoing story of the gospel. He rejoices in praying for the Philippians because of their 'partnership in the gospel from the first day until now'.

The word '*koinonia*' is often translated 'fellowship' or, as here, 'partnership' and implies 'to share in' something, to 'hold something in common' – whether an experience or an activity.

In the Christian case, this is not just a sharing together but a sharing together in something else – in Christ and in the Holy Spirit and in our common story.

Koinonia originally described those in business partnership and implies bonds of commitment and co-operation. This is Paul's emphasis here. He applauds the Philippians for their faithful participation with him in the cause of the gospel. They have taken out shares in the mission of the gospel. Nothing gives greater joy.

BIBLE READING

Philippians 1:1-5

GREETING

Paul and Timothy, slaves of Christ Jesus:

To all the saints in Christ Jesus who are in Philippi, including the overseers and deacons.

²Grace to you and peace from God our Father and the Lord Jesus Christ.

THANKSGIVING AND PRAYER

³I give thanks to my God for every remembrance of you, ⁴always praying with joy for all of you in my every prayer, ⁵because of your partnership in the gospel from the first day until now.

1 Thessalonians 1:2-10

THANKSGIVING

²We always thank God for all of you, remembering you constantly in our prayers. ³We recall, in the presence of our God and Father, your work of faith, labor of love, and endurance of hope in our Lord Jesus Christ, ⁴knowing your election, brothers loved by God. ⁵For our gospel did not come to you in word only, but also in power, in the Holy Spirit, and with much assurance. You know what kind of men we were among you for your benefit, ⁶and you became imitators of us and of the Lord when, in spite of severe persecution, you welcomed the message with the joy from the Holy Spirit. ⁷As a result, you became an example to all the believers in Macedonia and Achaia. ⁸For the Lord's message rang out from you, not only in Macedonia and Achaia, but in every place that your faith in God has gone out, so we don't need to say anything. ⁹For they themselves report about us what kind of reception we had from you: how you turned to God from idols to serve the living and true God, ¹⁰and to wait for His Son from heaven, whom He raised from the dead—Jesus, who rescues us from the coming wrath.

FOR ACTION: A devotional moment consists of more than just focusing on God and His goodness; it also means being thankful to those whom God has used to bring blessing into our lives. Philippians, we are told, is the most famous thank-you note in history. When did you last write a thank-you note to someone who was a 'minister of the Lord' to you? If you have not done so, sit down and write one today.

DAY 297

**PHILIPPIANS 1:6
JUDE 20-25**

THE AUTHOR OF the story has the stamina to see it through to a satisfactory ending. The 'good work' which God began might refer to the Philippians' support for Paul's ministry. But the mention of the 'day of Christ Jesus' makes it more likely that it refers to the saving work of grace begun in their lives at conversion - of which their backing for Paul is, of course, evidence.

What God begins He completes. You may feel you are in the middle of a slow movement right now but God composes no 'unfinished symphonies'. What He starts, He continues. God never grows weary in well-doing, or downs tools. He does not repent of His sacrifices. His purposes for our lives cannot be thwarted. What a comfort this is. Jesus laid a sure foundation on the cross and God is committed to completing what is built on it. Tracing God's big story has shown that God's covenant commitments are permanent. We are saved in three tenses - we have been saved, we are being saved, we will be saved. God's good work covers all three - from commencement through continuation to completion! What grace!

'All's well that starts well!'

BIBLE READING

Philippians 1:6

GREETING

1 Paul and Timothy, slaves of Christ Jesus:
To all the saints in Christ Jesus who are in Philippi, including the overseers and deacons.
²Grace to you and peace from God our Father and the Lord Jesus Christ.

THANKSGIVING AND PRAYER

³I give thanks to my God for every remembrance of you, ⁴always praying with joy for all of you in my every prayer, ⁵because of your partnership in the gospel from the first day until now.

⁶I am sure of this, that He who started a good work in you will carry it on to completion until the day of Christ Jesus.

Jude 20-25

EXHORTATION AND BENEDICTION

²⁰But you, dear friends, building yourselves up in your most holy faith and praying in the Holy Spirit, ²¹keep yourselves in the love of God, expecting the mercy of our Lord Jesus Christ for eternal life. ²²Have mercy on some who doubt; ²³save others by snatching [them] from the fire; on others have mercy in fear, hating even the garment defiled by the flesh.

²⁴Now to Him who is able to protect you from stumbling and to make you stand in the presence of His glory, blameless and with great joy, ²⁵to the only God our Savior, through Jesus Christ our Lord, be glory, majesty, power, and authority before all time, now, and forever. Amen.

THOUGHT: You cannot be sure of many things in this world. Projects are started and then laid aside. People make promises and then forget them. However, when it comes to God, you can bank on this - whatever He starts He finishes. The Almighty 'never downs tools'. Let this thought be your anchor - what God has started in your life He is committed to finishing. Yes 'all's well that starts well'.

TODAY WE STAND back, to see the end of the story from the beginning.

God has set alight in the heart of every true believer an 'inextinguishable blaze' which is God's own burning passion to see His story succeed.

Knowing that God always takes the initiative in salvation makes us confident that the 'good work' begun in our lives cannot be thwarted. Where our human decisions might prove unreliable, God's unshakeable resolutions give hope.

DAY
298

PHILIPPIANS 1:6
1 THESSALONIANS 5:23-28

When Christian saw water being poured on the fire in *Pilgrim's Progress*, he feared that the devil was quenching God's work of grace. Wondering why the flames burned 'higher and hotter', he was shown the 'backside of the wall where a man was pouring oil secretly into the fire. This, it was explained to him, was Christ who continually with the oil of grace maintains the work already begun in the heart'.

I had a tight deadline to meet for this book. And there is a day of completion for the big story itself, a 'deadline' if we can call it that when it is so full of life! The 'day of Christ' will be not just a judgment day of quality control on our lives, but a glorious day of completion and consummation, a splendid coming-out parade of these to whom God has applied the finishing touches, a proud curtain call at the end of this act of the drama.

BIBLE READING

Philippians 1:6

GREETING

1 Paul and Timothy, slaves of Christ Jesus:
To all the saints in Christ Jesus who are in Philippi, including the overseers and deacons.
²Grace to you and peace from God our Father and the Lord Jesus Christ.

THANKSGIVING AND PRAYER

³I give thanks to my God for every remembrance of you, ⁴always praying with joy for all of you in my every prayer, ⁵because of your partnership in the gospel from the first day until now.

⁶I am sure of this, that He who started a good work in you will carry it on to completion until the day of Christ Jesus.

1 Thessalonians 5:23-28

²³Now may the God of peace Himself sanctify you completely. And may your spirit, soul, and body be kept sound and blameless for the coming of our Lord Jesus Christ. ²⁴He who calls you is faithful, who also will do it. ²⁵Brothers, pray for us also. ²⁶Greet all the brothers with a holy kiss. ²⁷I charge you by the Lord that this letter be read to all the brothers. ²⁸May the grace of our Lord Jesus Christ be with you!

FOR PRAISE: How grateful we ought to be for the fact that the fire God lights in our hearts can never be put out by the devil's cold water. Do you remember this verse from Wesley's great hymn?

> There let it burn with holy fire
> And inextinguishable blaze
> And trembling to its source aspire
> In humble prayer and fervent praise.

Sing it with joy and praise in your heart remembering thousands of others will be singing it too.

THIS REMARKABLE PASSAGE again speaks volumes for the way in which being in God's story transforms our view of reality.

Paul would argue that even prison looks different if you can see it as providing strange opportunities for the furtherance of the gospel. He's not in prison for crime but for Christ!

Providence is a dull word for such a sparkling truth. God's overarching strategy is very flexible in its tactics. God is infinitely adaptable and can work out His sovereign will in the most unfavourable conditions. Knowing this makes Paul remarkably resilient. Trying to tame him is like trying to take a tiger by the tail!

DAY
299

PHILIPPIANS 1:12-18

What an irrepressible prisoner Paul is!

Paul mentions three effects of his imprisonment: it evangelises his enemies; it encourages his friends; it is being exploited by his rivals.

But as long as Christ is preached, Paul is content that the true story is being told of what the One Creator God has done for His world.

Paul is spiritually buoyant. Suppressing this man is like trying to sink a cork in a bath! But Paul would only say, it's all Christ's doing and He can do the same for any believer in Him. The Holy Spirit can make you irrepressible whatever your circumstances. Whatever has happened to you, can you believe with Paul that it might somehow tend to the furtherance of the gospel?

BIBLE READING

Philippians 1:12-18

ADVANCE OF THE GOSPEL

[12]Now I want you to know, brothers, that what has happened to me has actually resulted in the advancement of the gospel, [13]so that it has become known throughout the whole imperial guard, and to everyone else, that my imprisonment is for Christ. [14]Most of the brothers in the Lord have gained confidence from my imprisonment and dare even more to speak the message fearlessly. [15]Some, to be sure, preach Christ out of envy and strife, but others out of good will. [16]These do so out of love, knowing that I am appointed for the defense of the gospel; [17]the others proclaim Christ out of rivalry, not sincerely, seeking to cause [me] trouble in my imprisonment. [18]What does it matter? Just that in every way, whether out of false motives or true, Christ is proclaimed. And in this I rejoice. Yes, and I will rejoice

QUESTION: Do you believe God can make you 'irrepressible' whatever your circumstances? It's easy to say but not so easy to put into practice. Paul's secret lay in the fact he believed, as he put it in Romans 8, that all things were working together for good to him because he loved God. When you believe (really believe) that nothing can work successfully against you then you too will be irrepressible. Try it and see.

THESE WORDS ARE a veritable tapestry of grace woven from strange threads.

DAY
300
PHILIPPIANS 1:19-20

Although imprisoned, Paul believes that whatever happens to him is in God's hands, and can only work for his ultimate good.

We may recall the similar attitude of Joseph (Gen. 45:5-8; 50:19-20) or Job whose very words – 'this will lead to my deliverance' – Paul quotes (Job 13:16).

This is the poise of the Christ-centred life. After all, when Paul was first imprisoned in Philippi the walls fell down; but not this time.

Paul believes this will turn out for his vindication so that he will 'not be ashamed' in the sense of being let down by God. Whether in the short term or in the longer eternal sense, deliverance will come. Like Job he knows that his redeemer lives and that he will stand in that day! Paul is sustained by the prayers of others and by his own experience of the Holy Spirit. God 'choreographs' the drama to supply the needed resources of the Spirit to Paul.

God sovereignly and mysteriously interweaves our intercession and His interventions into the final tapestry of His strategic purpose.

Our prayers count for something in God's big scheme of things, usually in ways beyond our knowing. We are not puppets on a divine string, but free and willing partners in the story God is enacting.

BIBLE READING

Philippians 1:19-20

ADVANCE OF THE GOSPEL

[12]Now I want you to know, brothers, that what has happened to me has actually resulted in the advancement of the gospel, [13]so that it has become known throughout the whole imperial guard, and to everyone else, that my imprisonment is for Christ. [14]Most of the brothers in the Lord have gained confidence from my imprisonment and dare even more to speak the message fearlessly. [15]Some, to be sure, preach Christ out of envy and strife, but others out of good will. [16]These do so out of love, knowing that I am appointed for the defense of the gospel; [17]the others proclaim Christ out of rivalry, not sincerely, seeking to cause [me] trouble in my imprisonment. [18]What does it matter? Just that in every way, whether out of false motives or true, Christ is proclaimed. And in this I rejoice. Yes, and I will rejoice

[19]because I know this will lead to my deliverance through your prayers and help from the Spirit of Jesus Christ. [20]My eager expectation and hope is that I will not be ashamed about anything, but that now as always, with all boldness, Christ will be highly honored in my body, whether by life or by death.

TO PONDER: Some time ago research amongst a group of Christians showed that 99% believed the most important discipline was prayer, and the same number claimed it formed the greatest challenge in their lives in terms of time, inclination etc. Consider this as you go through your day - if God weaves His interventions with our intercessions how many deliverances will not take place today?

NOTHING IS MORE remarkable than the way God's story brings perspective to the Christian's confrontation with death.

Here the question is raised: Is death a plus or a minus?

Paul looks death in the face and confronts the ultimate question: 'Will death add to you or only take away?' Paul's answer is clear: 'For to me, to live is Christ, and to die is gain' (NIV). For those for whom living means Christ, death will only gain us more of Him.

Paul expresses a new valuation of death, asserts a victory over death and expects vindication after death.

With similar confidence, our Christian forebears looked death in the face. Imminence of death concentrates the mind wonderfully on what is vital. As the old adage goes: we must deal with death or it will kill us! Paul's deliberations about whether to stay or go sound as if he's negotiating with God. But he is not bargaining with God here. Rather he is exercising the unique freedom of someone who, long ago, handed over complete control of his life and reputation to the Lord Jesus and is not now about to take it back!

To use business jargon, Paul is in a 'win-win' situation. He can't lose because he is totally committed to Christ being magnified in his body whether by life or death. Death is not the last chapter in the story we are in, for its author is the Author of life!

Philippians 1:21

BIBLE
READING

ADVANCE OF THE GOSPEL

[12]Now I want you to know, brothers, that what has happened to me has actually resulted in the advancement of the gospel, [13]so that it has become known throughout the whole imperial guard, and to everyone else, that my imprisonment is for Christ. [14]Most of the brothers in the Lord have gained confidence from my imprisonment and dare even more to speak the message fearlessly. [15]Some, to be sure, preach Christ out of envy and strife, but others

out of good will. ¹⁶These do so out of love, knowing that I am appointed for the defense of the gospel; ¹⁷the others proclaim Christ out of rivalry, not sincerely, seeking to cause [me] trouble in my imprisonment. ¹⁸What does it matter? Just that in every way, whether out of false motives or true, Christ is proclaimed. And in this I rejoice. Yes, and I will rejoice ¹⁹because I know this will lead to my deliverance through your prayers and help from the Spirit of Jesus Christ. ²⁰My eager expectation and hope is that I will not be ashamed about anything, but that now as always, with all boldness, Christ will be highly honored in my body, whether by life or by death.

LIVING IS CHRIST

²¹For me, living is Christ and dying is gain.

> QUOTATION: 'The best man who ever lived went down through death and came back, and the first thing He said was, "Fear not" there is nothing here to fear. He who was so right in everything else, the ages being witness, is He wrong here? He who never lets us down in one single area of life, will He let us down in this central area? It is impossible.' (E.S. Jones)

DAY 302

PHILIPPIANS 1:27-30

JUST AS PAUL read his circumstances in the perspective of the story of the gospel, so now he urges the Philippians to make the same gospel the narrative pattern on which to base their lives. The imperative 'Live your life ...' or 'Let your conduct be ...' uses a unique political verb which means 'live as citizens of a kingdom'.

Anticipating 3:20, Paul gives here the Christian Citizens Charter. The gospel of Jesus is not only good news to be received and believed but has the power to shape our behaviour and lifestyle.

Conduct 'worthy of the gospel' is characterised especially by a serious commitment to Christian unity: 'standing firm in one spirit' as if in warfare; 'striving together for the faith of the gospel' (NASB) as if in an athletic contest. Disunity in the Church still mars our witness to the gospel. If only we could remember that we are committed to a common cause as citizens of the same city, athletes playing in the same team, soldiers fighting on the same side. Unity would make us fearless in the face of any opposition. The increasing conflict that is coming to the Church will surely test how united we are but will expose the difference between those who are perishing and those who are being saved. We shall count it as a privilege to be found worthy to suffer for the sake of the gospel as Paul did.

Philippians 1:27-30

²⁷Just one thing: live your life in a manner worthy of the gospel of Christ. Then, whether I come and see you or am absent, I will hear about you that you are standing firm in one spirit, with one mind, working side by side for the faith of the gospel, ²⁸not being frightened in any way by your opponents. This is evidence of their destruction, but of your deliverance— and this is from God. ²⁹For it has been given to you on Christ's behalf not only to believe in Him, but also to suffer for Him, ³⁰having the same struggle that you saw I had and now hear about me.

THOUGHT: The New Testament fairly bulges with the importance of Christian unity. Our Lord in John 17 prayed that His people might be one in order that the world might believe. 'We appear to suffer from a pathological inability to get on with one another,' says John Stott, 'or to co-operate in the cause of the Kingdom of God. We ought not to make light of this grievous situation.'

DAY 303

PHILIPPIANS 2:5-11

WE INVITE YOU to spend a number of days reflecting on this one rich passage of Scripture.

In what may be an early Christian 'hymn to Christ', Paul dwells on the mindset of Jesus 'who, though he was in the form of God, did not regard equality with God as something to be exploited, but emptied himself, taking the form of a slave, being born in human likeness. And being found in human form, he humbled himself and became obedient to the point of death – even death on a cross.

'Therefore God also highly exalted him and gave him the name that is above every name, so that at the name of Jesus every knee should bend in heaven and on earth and under the earth, and every tongue should confess that Jesus Christ is Lord to the glory of God the Father' (NRSV).

This memorable passage tells a number of stories as one story. It will help you if you refer back to Day 12 to refresh your memory on how the whole Bible works this way. Now let's consider how the five circles apply here.

At one level it is of course the story of Jesus.

But then again this story is told, by way of contrast, as the true story of Adam.

The story told here is also telling of the strange but climactic fulfilment of the story of Israel.

And then again what is truly remarkable is that Paul is telling this story as the story of God!

What is being told finally is the story of the world.

BIBLE READING

Philippians 2:5-11

CHRIST'S HUMILITY AND EXALTATION

[5]Make your own attitude that of Christ Jesus,

[6] who, existing in the form of God, did not consider equality with God
as something to be used for His own advantage.
[7] Instead He emptied Himself by assuming the form

of a slave,
taking on the likeness of men.
And when He had come as a man in His external form,
8 He humbled Himself by becoming obedient
to the point of death—even to death on a cross.
9 For this reason God also highly exalted Him
and gave Him the name that is above every name,
10 so that at the name of Jesus every knee should bow—
of those who are in heaven and on earth
and under the earth—
11 and every tongue should confess
that Jesus Christ is Lord,
to the glory of God the Father.

PRAYER: Gracious Father, once again I give You thanks for allowing me to be one of the characters in Your story. I see today that one of the purposes of my involvement in Your story is to be part of the great hymn of worship to Your Son. Today, as all over the world men and women give You praise I gladly add my own. Blessed Trinity I give You my heartfelt worship. In Jesus' name. Amen.

THE FIRST STORY this passage tells is, of course, the story of Jesus.

Jesus is described as 'being equal with God' and 'being in the form of God' which both express full-scale divinity.

But does Paul imply of Jesus that this is something He does not yet have but is seeking to grasp or snatch (as in the NIV)?

Or should it be taken as referring to what someone already has but chooses not to exploit or use 'for His own advantage' (as here)?

The latter is undoubtedly the best way of reading the text and has considerable implications. Christ 'did not regard equality with God as something to be exploited ...'

In other words, Christ refused to exploit to His own

DAY
304

PHILIPPIANS 2:5-11
JOHN 13:3-5

advantage the position of equality with God which He already had.

Christ never stops 'being equal with God' or 'in the form of God'. What happens is that such states are dramatically re-interpreted in unexpected ways.

Without ceasing to be what He was, the Lord Jesus did not take advantage of His exalted position, He did not exploit it for His own selfish purposes. When He came among us He did not dazzle us with displays of overwhelming divine power nor did He intimidate us with bullying tactics. He never acted in possessive or exploitative ways. He was secure enough and humble enough to look us in the eye and meet us at our own level.

BIBLE READING

Philippians 2:5-11

CHRIST'S HUMILITY AND EXALTATION

⁵Make your own attitude that of Christ Jesus,

⁶ who, existing in the form of God, did not consider
equality with God
as something to be used for His own advantage.
⁷ Instead He emptied Himself by assuming the form
of a slave,
taking on the likeness of men.
And when He had come as a man in His external form,
⁸ He humbled Himself by becoming obedient
to the point of death—even to death on a cross.
⁹ For this reason God also highly exalted Him
and gave Him the name that is above every name,
¹⁰ so that at the name of Jesus every knee should bow—
of those who are in heaven and on earth
and under the earth—
¹¹ and every tongue should confess
that Jesus Christ is Lord,
to the glory of God the Father.

John 13:3-5

³Jesus knew that the Father had given everything into His hands, that He had come from God, and that He was going back to God. ⁴So He got up from supper, laid aside His robe, took a towel, and tied it around Himself. ⁵Next, He poured water into a basin and began to wash His disciples' feet and to dry them with the towel tied around Him.

TO PONDER: Did God have to become human in order to save us? The answer of course must be 'Yes'. We see something of God in nature, but we do not see Him fully, except in the life of Jesus. 'Jesus,' said a little boy in Sunday School, 'is the best photograph God ever had taken.' 'Jesus,' said one theologian, 'puts a face on God.' We would never know what God is truly like had we not seen Him in the Son.

IN SOME TRANSLATIONS, Jesus is said to have 'emptied Himself'. This may mislead us into asking, 'emptied of what?'

The answer usually supplied is that Jesus laid aside divine attributes such as omnipotence and omniscience. But Paul is almost certainly using the word 'emptied' in the sense of 'rendering something powerless', or 'emptying it of apparent significance' (cf.Rom. 4:14; 1 Cor. 1:17).

The translations 'but made Himself of no reputation' (NKJV) or 'made himself nothing' (NIV) are not far short of the mark. Even better, perhaps, to say 'He poured Himself out'.

Paul is celebrating the stunning story of God's utter self-giving of Himself in Jesus Christ. When he looks at Jesus from manger to cross, Paul sees a life poured out in lavish self-expenditure for the sake of others. The one glorious pre-incarnate life of God poured itself into a human life at Bethlehem and poured out

DAY
305

PHILIPPIANS 2:5-11
2 CORINTHIANS 8:9

in sacrificial death at Easter. We can perhaps hear an echo of Isaiah 53:12 where the servant of the Lord 'poured out his soul unto death' (KJV). His life and death taxed His deepest inner resources. For the sake of us prodigals our Eldest Brother entered the far country of rebellion and death and squandered His life in righteous living and redemptive dying. Thank God He did.

BIBLE READING

Philippians 2:5-11

CHRIST'S HUMILITY AND EXALTATION

⁵Make your own attitude that of Christ Jesus,

⁶ who, existing in the form of God, did not consider
    equality with God
  as something to be used for His own advantage.
⁷ Instead He emptied Himself by assuming the form
    of a slave,
  taking on the likeness of men.
  And when He had come as a man in His external form,
⁸ He humbled Himself by becoming obedient
  to the point of death—even to death on a cross.
⁹ For this reason God also highly exalted Him
  and gave Him the name that is above every name,
¹⁰ so that at the name of Jesus every knee should bow—
  of those who are in heaven and on earth
    and under the earth—
¹¹ and every tongue should confess
  that Jesus Christ is Lord,
  to the glory of God the Father.

BIBLE READING

2 Corinthians 8:9

⁹For you know the grace of our Lord Jesus Christ: although He was rich, for your sake He became poor, so that by His poverty you might become rich.

FOR PRAISE: Does it not evoke within you the deepest praise when you consider that Jesus was born not in a mansion but in a manger, that He lived the life not of a celebrity, but a carpenter? Think of it also in this way - He forsook the glory of heaven that you and I might have a part in God's story. Dwell on that thought before you move away and do other things. And give Him praise.

DAY
306

PHILIPPIANS 2:5-11
HEBREWS 2:5-10

THE STORY OF Jesus being told here is also, by way of contrast, the true story of Adam, our human story.

Adam - made in the image of God - grasped at being equal with God, a status which was not his to have. But Jesus, the Last Adam, refused to cling on to His divine status, voluntarily renouncing what He had every right to.

Where Adam in pride sought to become like God, Christ in humility becomes human.

This is the truly human life. In Jesus, the Truly Human One achieved that destiny which was always envisaged for Adam's sons - sharing with God's dominion as 'Lord' over the world (v.10).

It is usually assumed that being God and being human are inherently incompatible states. God is, of course, the Creator and we are mere creatures, but they are essentially compatible (Gen. 1:26-28). It is, then, strangely appropriate for God to come into His world in human form in Jesus.

It is wonderful to realise that our human nature is a vehicle designed by God as a means through which He can express Himself! God called humans to be the sovereign-wise rulers of this world so that He might be the sovereign-wise ruler of the world by becoming human Himself!

This is the only authentic and truly human story, which fulfils every human potential to the glory of the Father.

Philippians 2:5-11

CHRIST'S HUMILITY AND EXALTATION

⁵Make your own attitude that of Christ Jesus,

⁶ who, existing in the form of God, did not consider
  equality with God
  as something to be used for His own advantage.
⁷ Instead He emptied Himself by assuming the form
  of a slave,
  taking on the likeness of men.
  And when He had come as a man in His external form,
⁸ He humbled Himself by becoming obedient
  to the point of death—even to death on a cross.
⁹ For this reason God also highly exalted Him
  and gave Him the name that is above every name,
¹⁰ so that at the name of Jesus every knee should bow—
  of those who are in heaven and on earth
  and under the earth—
¹¹ and every tongue should confess
  that Jesus Christ is Lord,
  to the glory of God the Father.

Hebrews 2:5-10

JESUS AND HUMANITY

⁵For He has not subjected to angels the world to come that we are talking about. ⁶But one has somewhere testified:

  "What is man, that You remember him,
    or the son of man, that You care for him?
⁷ You made him lower than the angels for a short time;
  You crowned him with glory and honor
⁸ and subjected everything under his feet."

For in "subjecting everything" to him, He left nothing not subject to him. As it is, we do not yet see "everything subjected" to him. ⁹But we do see Jesus—"made lower than the angels for a short time" so that by God's grace He might taste death for everyone—crowned with glory and honor because of the suffering of death.

^{10}For it was fitting, in bringing many sons to glory, that He, for whom and through whom all things exist, should make the source of their salvation perfect through sufferings.

> PRAYER: O God, the more I think of the stoop made by Your Son from heaven to earth, the more my soul is filled with unutterable joy. I do not have to knock at the gates of heaven, Jesus has come knocking at the door of my heart. What grace, what humility, what love. What I dare not dream of - that Jesus the Son of God should come to me - has happened. And I am more grateful than words can convey. Amen.

DAY 307

PHILIPPIANS 2:5-11
ACTS 3:18-20,24-26

THE THIRD STORY embedded in this profound 'hymn' is the strange but climactic fulfilment of the story of Israel.

Called out of slavery to be God's servant partner for the salvation of the world, Israel refused the way of humility and obedience.

As a result Israel plunged down into the 'ignominious death' of exile, ending up ironically enslaved again in the very place from which Abraham had first come at the beginning of her story!

As Israel's Messiah, Jesus re-runs the Israel story successfully.

Jesus particularly moulds Himself to that concentrated version of the story which is told in Isaiah 40-55. There, God's agent brings God's salvation through humble servanthood and willing obedience to death. How differently might Israel's story have unfolded if Israel had gone the way of God's servant Jesus; how Israel's story might look if it passed through the prism of Christ's humble death and triumphant vindication told in the parallel story of Paul in 3:1-21.

It involves not being obsessed with acquiring status

and glory. It means not acting in self-regarding or exploitative ways. It means exhibiting the self-less, other-regarding humility, born in those who have been immersed in baptism into the story of this dying and rising Jesus.

Philippians 2:5-11

BIBLE READING

CHRIST'S HUMILITY AND EXALTATION

⁵Make your own attitude that of Christ Jesus,

⁶ who, existing in the form of God, did not consider
equality with God
as something to be used for His own advantage.
⁷ Instead He emptied Himself by assuming the form
of a slave,
taking on the likeness of men.
And when He had come as a man in His external form,
⁸ He humbled Himself by becoming obedient
to the point of death—even to death on a cross.
⁹ For this reason God also highly exalted Him
and gave Him the name that is above every name,
¹⁰ so that at the name of Jesus every knee should bow—
of those who are in heaven and on earth
and under the earth—
¹¹ and every tongue should confess
that Jesus Christ is Lord,
to the glory of God the Father.

Acts 3:18-20,24-26

BIBLE READING

¹⁸But what God predicted through the mouth of all the prophets—that His Messiah would suffer—He has fulfilled in this way. ¹⁹Therefore repent and turn back, that your sins may be wiped out so that seasons of refreshing may come from the presence of the Lord, ²⁰and He may send Jesus, who has been appointed Messiah for you.

● ● ● ● ● ● ● ● ●

²⁴"In addition, all the prophets who have spoken, from Samuel and those after him, have also announced these days. ²⁵You are the sons of the prophets and of the covenant that God made with your forefathers, saying to Abraham, "And in your seed all the families of the earth will be blessed." ²⁶God raised up His Servant and sent Him first to you to bless you by turning each of you from your evil ways."

THOUGHT: 'Everyone's life is a story,' said Eugene Peterson, 'whether God is in it or not.' However, what a different story we have to tell when God is in it. Imagine recounting the story of your life if Jesus had not saved you. Doubtless there have been good times and bad times, light and shade - but without Jesus there is no sense of destiny. Destiny is what makes the difference.

DAY
308

PHILIPPIANS 2:5-11
ISAIAH 45:21-23

WHAT IS TRULY remarkable is that Paul is telling this story as the story of God!

What does it feel like to be a god and to behave like one?

Telling the story of Jesus like this is a way of telling the story of the One True God! The astonishing thing about the humility with which Jesus stooped to conquer us is that the Person who never stopped being equal with God, chose to walk such a path of lowliness.

The narrative of Jesus from manger to cross is therefore the definitive revelation of God! This story throws totally fresh light on God.

The climax which quotes Isaiah (v.11; Isa. 45:23) applies to Jesus the name Lord which was reserved in the Old Testament exclusively for the One Creator God, Yahweh. This is not only God's stamp of approval on Jesus as sharing the very 'Godness' of God. It is God's way of telling us what 'being equal with God' really looks like - it looks like this!

God is shown to be selfless, pouring out His life

for the sake of others. In Christ God has told His real autobiographical story. God is not a being gripped with the lust to exploit His advantages; He is motivated not by the love of power but the power of love.

Here is the truth about Christ, about God, and about universal humanity, all wrapped up in a very particular Jewish story.

Philippians 2:5-11

CHRIST'S HUMILITY AND EXALTATION

⁵Make your own attitude that of Christ Jesus,

⁶ who, existing in the form of God, did not consider
equality with God
as something to be used for His own advantage.
⁷ Instead He emptied Himself by assuming the form
of a slave,
taking on the likeness of men.
And when He had come as a man in His external form,
⁸ He humbled Himself by becoming obedient
to the point of death—even to death on a cross.
⁹ For this reason God also highly exalted Him
and gave Him the name that is above every name,
¹⁰ so that at the name of Jesus every knee should bow—
of those who are in heaven and on earth
and under the earth—
¹¹ and every tongue should confess
that Jesus Christ is Lord,
to the glory of God the Father.

Isaiah 45:21-23

²¹ Speak up and present [your case] —
yes, let them take counsel together.
Who predicted this long ago?
Who announced it from ancient times?
Was it not I, the LORD?

There is no other God but Me,
a righteous God and Savior;
there is no one except Me.
22 Turn to Me and be saved,
all the ends of the earth.
For I am God,
and there is no other.
23 By Myself I have sworn;
Truth has gone from My mouth,
a word that will not be revoked:
Every knee will bow to Me,
every tongue will swear allegiance.

TO PONDER: Some children in a Christian school were asked to write on the subject: What is God like? Their answers included words like - power, majesty, authority, greatness and so on. Astonishingly no one used words like humility, gentleness, graciousness, love. It is these latter words however that endear Him to us. Perhaps this might be a good time to ask yourself: what is my picture of God?

DAY 309

PHILIPPIANS 2:5-11
ROMANS 10:9-13

ONE LAST REFLECTION on the stories being told here in Paul's celebration of Jesus Christ.

Finally what is being told, by contrast, is the world's story - in particular the story of the world Paul knew, of Roman imperial power and might. And that world is being subverted because Jesus Christ is the Last Emperor!

For the early Christians, Jesus was the Jewish 'Messiah', 'the Christ'. Psalm 2 had declared God's intention to make His King in Jerusalem the Lord of the whole world. As a result of His obedience unto the death of the cross, Jesus has been exalted and given the name above every name. This name, in context, can only be 'Lord' - the very name applied in the Greek Old Testament to God Himself (Isa. 45:21)! When Jesus is announced then all must bow the knee and confess that 'He is Lord'.

Caesar's empire, like every subsequent imitation, is a parody of the real thing!

While Paul wrote, the Caesars were annexing for themselves the title '*kurios*' or 'Lord'. Nowhere outside of Rome would this have been felt more keenly than in the Roman Colony of Philippi. But the Christians there had heard and believed a different script in which Jesus, not Caesar, is Lord of the world. No wonder so many of the first apostles ended up in prison or that so many Christians now as then give their lives for Jesus.

Philippians 2:5-11

BIBLE READING

CHRIST'S HUMILITY AND EXALTATION

⁵Make your own attitude that of Christ Jesus,

⁶ who, existing in the form of God, did not consider
    equality with God
  as something to be used for His own advantage.
⁷ Instead He emptied Himself by assuming the form
    of a slave,
  taking on the likeness of men.
  And when He had come as a man in His external form,
⁸ He humbled Himself by becoming obedient
  to the point of death—even to death on a cross.
⁹ For this reason God also highly exalted Him
  and gave Him the name that is above every name,
¹⁰ so that at the name of Jesus every knee should bow—
  of those who are in heaven and on earth
    and under the earth—
¹¹ and every tongue should confess
    that Jesus Christ is Lord,
    to the glory of God the Father.

BIBLE READING

Romans 10:9-13

⁹if you confess with your mouth, "Jesus is Lord," and believe in your heart that God raised Him from the dead, you will be saved. ¹⁰With the heart one believes, resulting in righteousness, and with the mouth one confesses, resulting in salvation. ¹¹Now the Scripture says, "No one who believes on Him will be put to shame," ¹²for there is no distinction between Jew and Greek, since the same Lord of all is rich to all who call on Him. ¹³For "everyone who calls on the name of the Lord will be saved."

QUESTION: What does the Lordship of Christ mean to you? Is it merely a biblical doctrine or does it relate to the way you live, the way you think, everything you do? 'You call me Lord, Lord,' said Jesus to the people of His day, 'but you do not do what I say.' Someone has put it like this: 'If we do not crown Him Lord of all, we do not crown Him Lord at all.' Is Jesus Lord of all that goes on in your life?

DAY 310

PHILIPPIANS 2:12-13
HEBREWS 13:20-21

PAUL'S UNFORGETTABLE TELLING of the Jesus story comes with a 'so then' or 'therefore' (NIV) attached, calling us to respond. We do so not simply by drawing a logical conclusion or even by following an example, but by being connected to a power which changes our life.

Of course, there is no hint that we can achieve our own salvation. Salvation is God's gift. But we are urged to 'work out our salvation' in the sense of living out the life we possess in Christ.

No passive 'let go and let God' attitude will do. We are participants in the drama not spectators of it.

We must co-operate with the power of God working in us.

Deep within the springs of each Christian's personality, God is at work re-directing our wills and rejuvenating our motivation to do His will!

This is the glorious reality of the new covenant life once promised by Jeremiah and made good by the Holy Spirit.

Do you hear your inner self saying: 'I can't do God's will, I'm too weak, I keep failing'? God says, 'I am working actively inside you to will and to work what pleases Me. I am continuing the good work I began in you and will bring it to completion.'

How awesome! 'Danger – God at work!' No wonder Paul reacts with 'fear and trembling', not because he has a nervous disposition, but at the thought that the mighty Creator God is working in and through him!

Philippians 2:12-13

BIBLE READING

CHRIST'S HUMILITY AND EXALTATION

[5]Make your own attitude that of Christ Jesus,

[6] who, existing in the form of God, did not consider equality with God
as something to be used for His own advantage.
[7] Instead He emptied Himself by assuming the form of a slave,
taking on the likeness of men.
And when He had come as a man in His external form,
[8] He humbled Himself by becoming obedient
to the point of death—even to death on a cross.
[9] For this reason God also highly exalted Him
and gave Him the name that is above every name,
[10] so that at the name of Jesus every knee should bow—
of those who are in heaven and on earth
and under the earth—
[11] and every tongue should confess
that Jesus Christ is Lord,
to the glory of God the Father.

LIGHTS IN THE WORLD

[12]So then, my dear friends, just as you have always obeyed, not only in my presence, but now even more in my absence,

work out your own salvation with fear and trembling. [13]For it is God who is working in you, [enabling you] both to will and to act for His good purpose.

BIBLE READING

Hebrews 13:20-21

BENEDICTION AND FAREWELL

[20]Now may the God of peace, who brought up from the dead our Lord Jesus—the great Shepherd of the sheep—with the blood of the everlasting covenant, [21]equip you with all that is good to do His will, working in us what is pleasing in His sight, through Jesus Christ, to whom be glory forever and ever. Amen.

> **THOUGHT**: Someone has said, 'Whenever you see the word "therefore" [translated as 'so then' in the HCSB] in the Bible always ask yourself what it is there for'. The 'therefore' in this passage, as the writer has pointed out, calls us to respond by connecting to the power which operated in the life of Jesus. The Christian life it has often been said is not our responsibility but our response to His ability. How well connected are you?

DAY 311

PHILIPPIANS 2:14-16

IN TODAY'S WORLD celebrities are famous merely for being famous. But to be a star in God's eyes demands no heroic exploits except the major feats of not grumbling or complaining, both of which cast a slur on the reputation of God! God's new covenant people are called to avoid the mistakes of the earlier phase of the story.

Paul recalls the tiresome attitude of the children of Israel in the wilderness which so severely put God to the test. But, as Daniel hoped, one day the righteous will 'shine like stars'.

Darkness is defined as the 'crooked and perverted generation' - a term once applied to a rebellious Israel (Deut. 32:5).

Christians are one with God's Old Testament people and are now challenged to live with uncomplaining patience and to hold firm the Word of Life by believing and testifying to its truth.

Paul often describes in sacrificial terms Christian ministry which exhausts our energies and entails suffering. But this 'sacrifice' is not dragged from him reluctantly but is part of his joyful self-offering in the cause of the gospel. Yet his outpouring of life is a drink offering that climaxes their sacrifice, not his! Amazingly, the self-offering of apostles and martyrs is only the crowning seal of value placed on your faith as Christ's people.

Philippians 2:14-16

BIBLE
READING

CHRIST'S HUMILITY AND EXALTATION

⁵Make your own attitude that of Christ Jesus,

⁶ who, existing in the form of God, did not consider
    equality with God
as something to be used for His own advantage.

⁷ Instead He emptied Himself by assuming the form
    of a slave,
taking on the likeness of men.
And when He had come as a man in His external form,

⁸ He humbled Himself by becoming obedient
to the point of death—even to death on a cross.

⁹ For this reason God also highly exalted Him
and gave Him the name that is above every name,

¹⁰ so that at the name of Jesus every knee should bow—
of those who are in heaven and on earth
    and under the earth—

¹¹ and every tongue should confess
    that Jesus Christ is Lord,
to the glory of God the Father.

LIGHTS IN THE WORLD

¹²So then, my dear friends, just as you have always

obeyed, not only in my presence, but now even more in my absence, work out your own salvation with fear and trembling. ¹³For it is God who is working in you, [enabling you] both to will and to act for His good purpose.

¹⁴Do everything without grumbling and arguing, ¹⁵so that you may be blameless and pure, children of God who are faultless in a crooked and perverted generation, among whom you shine like stars in the world. ¹⁶Hold firmly the message of life. Then I can boast in the day of Christ that I didn't run in vain or labor for nothing.

> PRAYER: O Father, living as I am in a darkened society, help me I pray to shine out as a bright light reflecting the glory of Your presence and the power of Your love. Help me also to have complete confidence in Your Word and to live uncomplainingly, sacrificially, counting it all joy to suffer for You if and when necessary and pouring out my life as did the apostle Paul as a 'drink offering' to You. Amen.

DAY 312

PHILIPPIANS 2:19-30

HOW DO ANCIENT travel plans end up in Holy Writ? Because even our small-scale domestic stories are vital to God's big story. The genius of the gospel is that it sanctifies the mundane and makes the ordinary sublime. Timothy will arrive at Philippi soon, while Epaphroditus is coming later; of such is the kingdom of heaven. God's story is not all about headline names and incredible feats. It's curiously heartening that some of the apostles rate only half a line of Scripture while these two 'saints in ordinary' rate half a chapter!

Timothy and Epaphroditus are Paul's friends as well as his co-workers, and two of the gospel's countless 'unsung heroes'.

Timothy was a role-model in seeking the interests of others rather than his own and was as near to a son as Paul ever had.

Epaphroditus was evidently missing home and worrying how the Philippians might be reacting to news of his illness. How very human!

Welcome him back, says Paul, without thinking he has let you down by returning when in fact he risked his neck for me. All in all this is a wonderful sample of how redemption transfigures everyday events and the Holy Spirit inspires a practical down-to-earth spirituality. Who you are, what you are doing and even where you are going today, matters to the Lord and contributes crucially to His story.

Philippians 2:19-30

TIMOTHY AND EPAPHRODITUS

[19]Now I hope in the Lord Jesus to send Timothy to you soon so that I also may be encouraged when I hear news about you. [20]For I have no one else like-minded who will genuinely care about your interests; [21]all seek their own interests, not those of Jesus Christ. [22]But you know his proven character, because he has served with me in the gospel ministry like a son with a father. [23]Therefore, I hope to send him as soon as I see how things go with me. [24]And I am convinced in the Lord that I myself will also come quickly.

[25]But I considered it necessary to send you Epaphroditus—my brother, co-worker, and fellow soldier, as well as your messenger and minister to my need— [26]since he has been longing for all of you and was distressed because you heard that he was sick. [27]Indeed, he was so sick that he nearly died. However, God had mercy on him, and not only on him but also on me, so that I would not have one grief on top of another. [28]For this reason, I am very eager to send him so that you may rejoice when you see him again and I may be less anxious. [29]Therefore, welcome him in the Lord with all joy and hold men like him in honor, [30]because he came close to death for the work of Christ, risking his life to make up what was lacking in your ministry to me.

FOR THANKSGIVING: A man said to a preacher after he had heard him preach on the theme 'Giving Thanks': 'I have nothing to be thankful for.' Nothing to be thankful for? What about our five senses, reason unimpaired, the gift of God's own Son and so on. Then of course there's this drawn from our reading today – everyone matters to God be they pensioner or preacher, accountant or apostle, child or king! Give thanks.

DAY
313

PHILIPPIANS 3:1-2
DEUTERONOMY 30:6
ROMANS 2:28-29

PAUL DERISIVELY DENOUNCES those he calls 'dogs' who if you let them cut your body, will mutilate your faith! Who is this fierce talk aimed at and why?

Like the Galatians, the Philippians are being troubled by some Jewish Christians who want to impose on Gentile Christians the specific marks of Jewishness – particularly circumcision.

We recall that circumcision was the outward sign, in males at least, of being in God's covenant family, especially important for Jews living outside the promised land, and a contentious issue in the apostolic mission.

'Circumcision' stands here for 'covenant people' or status.

But circumcision was always meant to signify a deeper 'circumcision of the heart' (Deut. 10:16; 30:6; Jer. 4:4; 9:25 cf.Rom. 2:28-29). And, since Christ has come, it no longer counts for anything in a believer's relationship with God. To say otherwise is to threaten the freedom of the gospel of grace. So, when so much is at stake, Paul does not mince his words.

For Paul, faith in Christ is now the only indelible sign of being in God's covenant family. He reacts strongly to anything that says knowing Jesus is not enough and seeks to drag believers back to an earlier outmoded stage of the story. God's story is now an open book and freedom is the chapter we are in.

Philippians 3:1-2

KNOWING CHRIST

3 Finally, my brothers, rejoice in the Lord. To write to you again about this is no trouble for me and is a protection for you.

²Watch out for "dogs," watch out for evil workers, watch out for those who mutilate the flesh.

Deuteronomy 30:6

⁶The LORD your God will circumcise your heart and the hearts of your descendants, and you will love Him with all your heart and all your soul, so that you will live.

Romans 2:28-29

²⁸For a person is not a Jew who is one outwardly, and [true] circumcision is not something visible in the flesh. ²⁹On the contrary, a person is a Jew who is one inwardly, and circumcision is of the heart—by the Spirit, not the letter. His praise is not from men but from God.

TO PONDER: One of the greatest temptations we Christians face, said C.S. Lewis is, 'Christianity and ...' What did he mean? Christianity and something else. Christianity and psychology; Christianity and good works; Christianity and human effort. Some Jewish Christians in Paul's day said Christianity and circumcision. Faith in Christ is all that is needed for salvation. Make sure there are no 'ands' in your life.

DAY
314

PHILIPPIANS 3:3
ROMANS 8:1-4

PAUL CELEBRATES THE fact that the Philippian Christians – whether Jewish or Gentile – are bone fide members of God's new covenant community. The trademark of physical circumcision operative from Abraham's day has become obsolete and the real 'circumcised ones' can now be defined as those who enjoy the privileges of the new covenant relationship promised by the prophets long ago.

Christians now serve or worship God 'in the Spirit'. To live 'in the flesh' is to live centred on oneself and without God. In this case 'in the flesh' is particularly apt since the problem people are those who are trusting to a literal cut in the flesh! On the other hand, to live 'in the Spirit' is to live a human life in all its aspects controlled and empowered by the Spirit of God.

Our worship, too, is characterised by the way 'we boast in Christ Jesus'.

Trusting Christ and experiencing the Spirit are the only genuine signs of being in God's covenant family. Our trademark is that we exuberantly exult in the glory of the Person of Jesus Christ, totally repudiating any confidence in the flesh. Our status before God does not depend on any inherited patterns of privilege or achievements of our own piety but solely on Christ and the Spirit. We are in God's covenant family through grace. This is our story, this is our song!

BIBLE READING

Philippians 3:3

KNOWING CHRIST

3 Finally, my brothers, rejoice in the Lord. To write to you again about this is no trouble for me and is a protection for you.

²Watch out for "dogs," watch out for evil workers, watch out for those who mutilate the flesh.

³For we are the circumcision, the ones who serve by the Spirit of God, boast in Christ Jesus, and do not put confidence in the flesh—

Romans 8:1-4

THE LIFE-GIVING SPIRIT

8 Therefore, no condemnation now exists for those in Christ Jesus, ²because the Spirit's law of life in Christ Jesus has set you free from the law of sin and of death. ³What the law could not do since it was limited by the flesh, God did. He condemned sin in the flesh by sending His own Son in flesh like ours under sin's domain, and as a sin offering, ⁴in order that the law's requirement would be accomplished in us who do not walk according to the flesh but according to the Spirit.

FOR PRAISE: You will no doubt know the following song by Fanny Crosby, that Billy Graham made famous. To sing it seems an appropriate response to today's reading:

This is my story, this is my song
Praising my Saviour all the day long
This is my story, this is my song,
Praising my Saviour all the day long.

PERSONAL STORIES ARE transformed when they are caught up in God's larger drama of salvation. Paul's autobiography is especially instructive because it mirrors that of Jesus (Phil. 2:5-11) and, as the story of a representative Jew, shows what Israel might be if it followed his example.

Paul never denigrates his Jewish heritage, only the false confidence he had once placed in it. By his own account, he loved the patriarchs, honoured the Torah, worshipped at Temple and synagogue, and soaked himself in the Hebrew Scriptures as the living oracles of the One Creator God. He never denigrates these things in themselves, only the false confidence he had once placed in them.

DAY
315

PHILIPPIANS 3:4-6
GALATIANS 2:19-21

His zeal for the law, he sadly recalls, had led him to persecute the Church, but in other respects he could claim to be 'blameless', not in the sense of being faultless but in scrupulously using the law's prescribed remedies when he sinned. But his law-keeping has become distorted into his 'own righteousness'.

Paul's past was fine but had no future in it!

Of course, there should have been because that previous narrative was meant to lead somewhere, in fact to the feet of Christ. Paul for one has found the rainbow of salvation at the end of the trail and sees absolutely no need to retrace his steps.

BIBLE READING

Philippians 3:4-6

KNOWING CHRIST

3 Finally, my brothers, rejoice in the Lord. To write to you again about this is no trouble for me and is a protection for you.

²Watch out for "dogs," watch out for evil workers, watch out for those who mutilate the flesh. ³For we are the circumcision, the ones who serve by the Spirit of God, boast in Christ Jesus, and do not put confidence in the flesh—

⁴although I once had confidence in the flesh too. If anyone else thinks he has grounds for confidence in the flesh, I have more: ⁵circumcised the eighth day; of the nation of Israel, of the tribe of Benjamin, a Hebrew born of Hebrews; as to the law, a Pharisee; ⁶as to zeal, persecuting the church; as to the righteousness that is in the law, blameless.

BIBLE READING

Galatians 2:19-21

¹⁹For through the law I have died to the law, that I might live to God. I have been crucified with Christ; ²⁰and I no longer live, but Christ lives in me. The life I now live in the flesh, I live by faith in the Son of God, who loved me and gave Himself for

me. ²¹I do not set aside the grace of God; for if righteousness comes through the law, then Christ died for nothing.

FOR PRAYER: Father, help me to appreciate and value all that Christians owe to the Jews in giving us our Bible and their Messiah. But help me, too, to value Jesus above everything else as the gold at the end of every rainbow.

PAUL'S IMMERSION IN the saving story of Jesus has led him to draw up his profit and loss account. In his 'revised balance-sheet', the apostle reveals that his old status and privileges did not, in any way, add up to the joys of salvation in Christ. In fact all that was previously profitable to him he has decisively written off, consigning them to the 'rubbish dump'!

DAY 316

PHILIPPIANS 3:7-8
MATTHEW 16:24-27

This is tough talk again from Paul especially about things that were once so precious to him. But knowing Jesus surpasses everything else.

Note again how closely Paul's testimony mirrors the story told of Jesus in 2:5-11. Like his Lord, Paul too has renounced a privileged status, suffered loss, undergone humiliation. In other words this is the cruciform, Christ-pattern worked out in the history of one Jewish man.

As such Paul exemplifies the way all his fellow-Jews might go to fulfil their destiny and achieve their true identity. And if we were to ask Paul, 'Was it worth it?', he would surely reply with a resounding 'Yes!' Right now he has gained a relationship with Christ; in that decisive future he is sure he will be 'found in Christ' with covenant membership not guaranteed by law but given by God to those who believe in Jesus. How much richer can anyone be?

BIBLE READING

Philippians 3:7-8

KNOWING CHRIST

3 Finally, my brothers, rejoice in the Lord. To write to you again about this is no trouble for me and is a protection for you.

²Watch out for "dogs," watch out for evil workers, watch out for those who mutilate the flesh. ³For we are the circumcision, the ones who serve by the Spirit of God, boast in Christ Jesus, and do not put confidence in the flesh—⁴although I once had confidence in the flesh too. If anyone else thinks he has grounds for confidence in the flesh, I have more: ⁵circumcised the eighth day; of the nation of Israel, of the tribe of Benjamin, a Hebrew born of Hebrews; as to the law, a Pharisee; ⁶as to zeal, persecuting the church; as to the righteousness that is in the law, blameless.

⁷But everything that was a gain to me, I have considered to be a loss because of Christ. ⁸More than that, I also consider everything to be a loss in view of the surpassing value of knowing Christ Jesus my Lord. Because of Him I have suffered the loss of all things and consider them filth, so that I may gain Christ ...

BIBLE READING

Matthew 16:24-27

TAKE UP YOUR CROSS

²⁴Then Jesus said to His disciples, "If anyone wants to come with Me, he must deny himself, take up his cross, and follow Me. ²⁵For whoever wants to save his life will lose it, but whoever loses his life because of Me will find it. ²⁶What will it benefit a man if he gains the whole world yet loses his life? Or what will a man give in exchange for his life? ²⁷For the Son of Man is going to come with His angels in the glory of His Father, and then He will reward each according to what he has done."

FOR ACTION: Have you ever drawn up a spiritual profit and loss account? Do so now. Think of all your achievements, credits, degrees, wealth, your status in society - everything that the world regards as important. Then think of the fact that you are an heir of God and a joint heir with Jesus Christ. Would you be willing to count all you possess as loss in order to win Christ? If the answer is 'Yes' then you are growing.

IN THE NEW script being written of his life-story, Paul rejoices that he has discovered a new way of 'righteousness' which here means something like 'vindication'.

God vindicates those who take their stand with the crucified Messiah, Jesus.

For Jews, like Paul, it means that they are no longer taking their stand with Torah or any of its works, like circumcision, but wholly and finally casting in their lot with God's crucified and exalted servant, Jesus, who has Himself been vindicated in resurrection and exaltation to the place of supreme Lordship.

As a result, they too are vindicated and declared to be His covenant people.

But the move cost Paul everything. Like his Lord, Paul has stepped down into disgrace in order to step up into God's life and glory. Like his Lord, Paul found that his privileges advantaged him nothing, nor could he exploit his privileged status for any gain that accrued to him.

This humbled him and recalled him to Israel's original servant vocation.

In embracing this, Paul obediently submitted to immersion in his Messiah's humiliating death. But because Christ was raised and exalted to final vindication, Paul too looks forward to ultimate vindication in final resurrection through Christ. His story becomes our future!

DAY
317

PHILIPPIANS 3:9
ACTS 13:38-39

Philippians 3:9

KNOWING CHRIST

3 Finally, my brothers, rejoice in the Lord. To write to you again about this is no trouble for me and is a protection for you.

²Watch out for "dogs," watch out for evil workers, watch out for those who mutilate the flesh. ³For we are the circumcision, the ones who serve by the Spirit of God, boast in Christ Jesus, and do not put confidence in the flesh—⁴although I once had confidence in the flesh too. If anyone else thinks he has grounds for confidence in the flesh, I have more: ⁵circumcised the eighth day; of the nation of Israel, of the tribe of Benjamin, a Hebrew born of Hebrews; as to the law, a Pharisee; ⁶as to zeal, persecuting the church; as to the righteousness that is in the law, blameless.

⁷But everything that was a gain to me, I have considered to be a loss because of Christ. ⁸More than that, I also consider everything to be a loss in view of the surpassing value of knowing Christ Jesus my Lord. Because of Him I have suffered the loss of all things and consider them filth, so that I may gain Christ

⁹and be found in Him, not having a righteousness of my own from the law, but one that is through faith in Christ—the righteousness from God based on faith.

Acts 13:38-39

³⁸Therefore, let it be known to you, brothers, that through this man forgiveness of sins is being proclaimed to you, ³⁹and everyone who believes in Him is justified from everything, which you could not be justified from through the law of Moses.

THOUGHT: Clearly there is a reproach in the gospel. The writer to the Hebrews bears down on this point: 'Let us then go to Him outside the camp, bearing His disgrace' (Heb. 13:13). There is a shame at the heart of the cross and it must be borne. Paul experienced it and so must we. Our commitment to Christ may immerse us in His 'shame' but we shall be immersed also in His 'glory'.

DAY 318

PHILIPPIANS 3:10-11
HEBREWS 12:1-3

PAUL HAS A completely new ambition: he wants above all to 'know' Jesus more and more. But notice that knowing Jesus involves entering more and more deeply into an experience both of His risen power and His suffering death!

Paul looked back on the price of knowing Jesus as a cost infinitely worth counting. He wrote in his journal: 'All my intellectual and moral achievements gasped their final breath when I had that breathtaking encounter with Jesus, crucified and risen; the old me died and a new Paul arose as if from the dead.'

So when Paul speaks of knowing Christ more he is speaking out of an already profound and firsthand experience.

He already knows Christ as a moral power penetrating to the depths of his personality. He knows Christ as the living Lord who gives him the surge of courage to face an angry mob. He knows Christ as the captivating Saviour turning the moral effort of a legal past into a life-stretching adventure with the Holy Spirit. He knows how Christ fills the wings of his abilities and ambitions. No wonder he still wants 'to know Him'!

Having been enrolled in the curriculum of Christ's sufferings, Paul is willing, for the further joy set before him, to be a graduate of the 'school of Calvary' whatever it costs.

BIBLE READING

Philippians 3:10-11

KNOWING CHRIST

3 Finally, my brothers, rejoice in the Lord. To write to you again about this is no trouble for me and is a protection for you.

²Watch out for "dogs," watch out for evil workers, watch out for those who mutilate the flesh. ³For we are the circumcision, the ones who serve by the Spirit of God, boast in Christ Jesus, and do not put confidence in the flesh—⁴although I once had confidence in the flesh too. If anyone else thinks he has grounds for confidence in the flesh, I have more: ⁵circumcised the eighth day; of the nation of Israel, of the tribe of Benjamin, a Hebrew born of Hebrews; as to the law, a Pharisee; ⁶as to zeal, persecuting the church; as to the righteousness that is in the law, blameless.

⁷But everything that was a gain to me, I have considered to be a loss because of Christ. ⁸More than that, I also consider everything to be a loss in view of the surpassing value of knowing Christ Jesus my Lord. Because of Him I have suffered the loss of all things and consider them filth, so that I may gain Christ ⁹and be found in Him, not having a righteousness of my own from the law, but one that is through faith in Christ—the righteousness from God based on faith.

¹⁰[My goal] is to know Him and the power of His resurrection and the fellowship of His sufferings, being conformed to His death, ¹¹assuming that I will somehow reach the resurrection from among the dead.

BIBLE READING

Hebrews 12:1-3

THE CALL TO ENDURANCE

12 Therefore since we also have such a large cloud of witnesses surrounding us, let us lay aside every weight and the sin that so easily ensnares us, and run with endurance the race that lies before us, ²keeping our eyes on Jesus, the source and perfecter of our faith, who for the joy that lay before Him endured a cross and despised the shame, and has sat down at the right hand of God's throne.

FATHERLY DISCIPLINE

³For consider Him who endured such hostility from sinners against Himself, so that you won't grow weary and lose heart.

> TO PONDER: One of the exciting aspects of the Christian life is that there is always 'more'. However well we know Christ, there is always more to know of Him. It may be an arguable point but perhaps Paul knew Jesus better – if not better than anyone who has ever lived. Yet he wanted to know more. Are you satisfied with what you know of the Saviour or do you, like Paul, long to know more?

THE DEEPEST INSIDE knowledge of the story of Jesus comes through 'holding shares in His sufferings'.

DAY
319

**PHILIPPIANS 3:10-11
ROMANS 4:24-25**

Paul has made a re-investment of his life. Having written off all his previous assets as a Pharisee, he has declared himself bankrupt, gone into voluntary liquidation and is now resolved to invest his life's capital in the ongoing sufferings of Christ!

The resurrection does not cancel out the cross, so that Jesus did all the dying while we do all the triumphing. No! By raising Jesus from the dead God endorsed the whole self-giving, servant lifestyle that had taken Him to the cross. Consequently, if we enjoy the power of His resurrection operating in us – and by the Spirit we certainly do – then we must realise it is meant to empower us precisely to enter into the fellowship of His sufferings in the real world. This is what knowing Jesus means.

Note again how the language of 2:5-11 is echoed here as Paul talks of being 'conformed' to the cruciform pattern of the way Jesus died. Finally, as with Jesus,

Paul hopes to 'attain to the resurrection from the dead' which, as the prophets knew, is the way God ultimately vindicates His people and shows they are really His. In this strange but true love story, the way of the cross leads home; the way of death leads to life; the way down is the way up.

BIBLE READING

Philippians 3:10-11

KNOWING CHRIST

3 Finally, my brothers, rejoice in the Lord. To write to you again about this is no trouble for me and is a protection for you.

[2]Watch out for "dogs," watch out for evil workers, watch out for those who mutilate the flesh. [3]For we are the circumcision, the ones who serve by the Spirit of God, boast in Christ Jesus, and do not put confidence in the flesh—[4]although I once had confidence in the flesh too. If anyone else thinks he has grounds for confidence in the flesh, I have more: [5]circumcised the eighth day; of the nation of Israel, of the tribe of Benjamin, a Hebrew born of Hebrews; as to the law, a Pharisee; [6]as to zeal, persecuting the church; as to the righteousness that is in the law, blameless.

[7]But everything that was a gain to me, I have considered to be a loss because of Christ. [8]More than that, I also consider everything to be a loss in view of the surpassing value of knowing Christ Jesus my Lord. Because of Him I have suffered the loss of all things and consider them filth, so that I may gain Christ [9]and be found in Him, not having a righteousness of my own from the law, but one that is through faith in Christ—the righteousness from God based on faith.

[10][My goal] is to know Him and the power of His resurrection and the fellowship of His sufferings, being conformed to His death, [11]assuming that I will somehow reach the resurrection from among the dead.

Romans 4:24-25

²⁴but also for us. It will be credited to us who believe in Him who raised Jesus our Lord from the dead. ²⁵He was delivered up for our trespasses and raised for our justification.

> QUOTATION: 'When we shrink from suffering we deprive ourselves of the joy of knowing God more deeply. Suffering produces pain (I am not referring necessarily to physical pain) but we emerge through the pain to be a new person. The apostle Paul knew the brokenness that came from suffering for Christ and it was this that made him the great man he was. Only broken people truly know God.' (Evan Roberts; Welsh Revivalist)

ONE FEATURE OF being caught up in an ongoing story is that we never stand still.

To encourage us to keep pace with God, Paul gives us a vivid insight into his own spiritual progress. He makes two virtually parallel statements built around the metaphor of a race in which the central message is: 'I make every effort', or 'I press on', which is emphasised twice in the NIV. Paul brackets this intense sense of purpose with three disclaimers which give a realistic context for his aspirations: he has not yet obtained; he has not yet been made complete; he does not consider himself to have taken hold of his final destiny.

Paul is under no illusions about the present life. He is 'betwixt and between'. He has gained Christ but there is so much more to know and his eye is on the well-stocked future of God's story as a goal to be reached.

Paul was apprehended at the crime scene by Jesus on the Damascus Road and now he presses on to take hold of that for which Christ took hold of him. Paul's career was turned around. Jesus now sets the agenda for what is important to Paul; God's purposes

DAY
320

**PHILIPPIANS 3:12
2 TIMOTHY 2:3-7**

not Paul's plans matter most. The goal and the prize that await at the finishing tape – whatever way you look at them – can only be that ultimate experience of 'knowing Jesus' which he has already told us is his over-riding ambition. May God help us to live at 'full stretch' for Him.

BIBLE READING

Philippians 3:12

[7]But everything that was a gain to me, I have considered to be a loss because of Christ. [8]More than that, I also consider everything to be a loss in view of the surpassing value of knowing Christ Jesus my Lord. Because of Him I have suffered the loss of all things and consider them filth, so that I may gain Christ [9]and be found in Him, not having a righteousness of my own from the law, but one that is through faith in Christ—the righteousness from God based on faith.

[10][My goal] is to know Him and the power of His resurrection and the fellowship of His sufferings, being conformed to His death, [11]assuming that I will somehow reach the resurrection from among the dead.

REACHING FORWARD TO GOD'S GOAL

[12]Not that I have already reached [the goal] or am already fully mature, but I make every effort to take hold of it because I also have been taken hold of by Christ Jesus.

BIBLE READING

2 Timothy 2:3-7

[3]Share in suffering as a good soldier of Christ Jesus. [4]To please the recruiter, no one serving as a soldier gets entangled in the concerns of everyday life. [5]Also, if anyone competes as an athlete, he is not crowned unless he competes according to the rules. [6]It is the hardworking farmer who ought to be the first to get a share of the crops. [7]Consider what I say, for the Lord will give you understanding in everything.

THOUGHT: We do not all travel along the road of Christian discipleship at the same rate. We grow old at the same rate. A year is as long for a lad in his teens as a man in his seventies, but progress in the things of God is not made at a fixed rate. Paul has been described by one writer as 'a pace-maker'. He sped along the path of discipleship at speed. And why? Read Romans 5:17 for the answer.

WE LIVE LIFE forwards and understand life backwards. In God's fast-moving narrative, we are swept up in a momentum not of our own.

Inevitably we must leave some things behind, even cherished landmarks.

Contrary to common practice, it is perhaps wise not to put too much of a psychological slant on Paul's forgetting what lies behind.

It's certainly true that we must never allow needless regrets or memories or failures or limited education or handicaps of birth to stop us pressing forwards with Jesus. But when Paul uses the athletic imagery to refer to his apostolic ministry, the likely point at issue here is that he refuses to rest on past successes but concentrates on pressing on towards the goal. He wants to do this without distractions. So we need to keep the race metaphor simple. Whatever else you do, don't look back over your shoulder.

'Keep on keeping on' as the saying goes. As the great nineteenth-century scholar, J.B. Lightfoot, paraphrases: 'Do not mistake me, I hold the language of hope not of assurance ... forgetting the landmarks already passed and straining every nerve and muscle in the onward race, I press forward toward the goal.'

In this way we are invited to turn the landmarks into signposts to the future.

DAY 321
PHILIPPIANS 3:13-14

BIBLE READING

Philippians 3:13-14

[7]But everything that was a gain to me, I have considered to be a loss because of Christ. [8]More than that, I also consider everything to be a loss in view of the surpassing value of knowing Christ Jesus my Lord. Because of Him I have suffered the loss of all things and consider them filth, so that I may gain Christ [9]and be found in Him, not having a righteousness of my own from the law, but one that is through faith in Christ—the righteousness from God based on faith.

[10][My goal] is to know Him and the power of His resurrection and the fellowship of His sufferings, being conformed to His death, [11]assuming that I will somehow reach the resurrection from among the dead.

REACHING FORWARD TO GOD'S GOAL

[12]Not that I have already reached [the goal] or am already fully mature, but I make every effort to take hold of it because I also have been taken hold of by Christ Jesus.

[13]Brothers, I do not consider myself to have taken hold of it. But one thing I do: forgetting what is behind and reaching forward to what is ahead, [14]I pursue as my goal the prize promised by God's heavenly call in Christ Jesus.

PRAYER: Lord Jesus Christ, help me to keep keeping on, I pray. Don't let me look back over my shoulder to focus on the things of the past or to see who is coming up behind me. Help me to keep my eyes on You and to run the race with no distractions - past or present. You are my goal, Lord Jesus, and I want to grow more and more like You until that day when I shall see You and be transformed into Your Image. Amen.

ALTHOUGH PAUL USES strong language to warn of the twisted truth these 'enemies of the cross' exemplify, he weeps for them at the same time. These are the only tears in the letter of joy, showing that Paul is torn apart by the thought of Christians living like pagans and 'idolising their bellies' in the process! What they delight in, is what Paul considers they should be ashamed of.

As before in this letter, Paul targets the mindset behind such behaviour. Their failure is that 'their minds are set on earthly things' (NRSV). 'Earthly things' in this context are not the practical affairs of everyday life but things that characterise a worldly outlook which is in opposition to God. An 'earthbound mindset' will involve both personal sins and those social sins which destroy unity and community in the Church. This is the tragic outcome of lowering our sights and forgetting the over-arching and transcendent narrative that defines who we are as Christians.

Paul has commended the mindset of Jesus as the only authentic criterion of a godly and truly human life. To live by any other story than the cross-shaped one is to court destruction. To abandon the cross is to forfeit the future inheritance. The narrow way of following Jesus leads to life. Anything else is a dead end.

DAY 322

PHILIPPIANS 3:17-19
COLOSSIANS 3:1-4

Philippians 3:17-19

BIBLE READING

[17]Join in imitating me, brothers, and observe those who live according to the example you have in us. [18]For I have often told you, and now say again with tears, that many live as enemies of the cross of Christ. [19]Their end is destruction; their god is their stomach; their glory is in their shame. They are focused on earthly things,

Colossians 3:1-4

THE LIFE OF THE NEW MAN

3 So if you have been raised with the Messiah, seek what is above, where the Messiah is, seated at the right hand of God. ²Set your minds on what is above, not on what is on the earth. ³For you have died, and your life is hidden with the Messiah in God. ⁴When the Messiah, who is your life, is revealed, then you also will be revealed with Him in glory.

TO PONDER: Not all are willing to admit that their minds need to be transformed. 'What's wrong with my mind?' they say. 'I am a perfectly normal person.' But there is an enormous difference between what the world thinks of as normal and what the Bible teaches as normal. The Christian mind (or mindset) is a mind set on God and His purposes. Do you have a 'mind' like this?

DAY
323

**PHILIPPIANS 3:20
JOHN 18:36**

IN STARK CONTRAST to those whose horizon is limited by this world, Paul now affirms that a true Christian's 'citizenship is in heaven'. James Moffatt's famous version of this, 'you are a colony of heaven', though strictly not an accurate translation, brilliantly catches the flavour of what Paul is saying.

This was apt language to employ in this letter because Philippi was a military colony of Rome. Nowhere outside Italy was there any city more thoroughly Roman. Its motto might well have been: 'When in Philippi do as the Romans do'! But the Christians in Philippi know they owe allegiance to a different Emperor and another kingdom. Their rule of conduct is: 'When in Philippi do as Christ did'!

New followers of Jesus become citizens of another kingdom, called to a wholly new politics of thinking and behaving. Sadly this has often been misconstrued, by us as much as by our critics, as if we exist in a time-warp, intent only on preserving old values, and permanently behind the times. But a colony of heaven is not backward-looking, representing only 'the forces of conservatism'.

On the contrary we represent the future as citizens of the coming kingdom. Christians ought more often to be taken for revolutionaries than traditionalists!

Philippians 3:20

BIBLE READING

¹⁷Join in imitating me, brothers, and observe those who live according to the example you have in us. ¹⁸For I have often told you, and now say again with tears, that many live as enemies of the cross of Christ. ¹⁹Their end is destruction; their god is their stomach; their glory is in their shame. They are focused on earthly things,

²⁰but our citizenship is in heaven, from which we also eagerly wait for a Savior, the Lord Jesus Christ.

John 18:36

BIBLE READING

³⁶"My kingdom is not of this world," said Jesus. "If My kingdom were of this world, My servants would fight, so that I wouldn't be handed over to the Jews. As it is, My kingdom does not have its origin here."

QUOTATION: 'A quaint old Yorkshire Christian, whenever anyone would ask him where his home was, would reply, "My home is in heaven, but my residence is in the city of Leeds." What do you see as "home"? Heaven or the place of your residence here on earth? If some discerning soul called at your residence would they say to themselves: "This is a colony of Jesus Christ"? If not why not?' (Taken from a church newsletter.)

DAY
324

WE REMIND OURSELVES that the genuinely Christian mindset is not one which is focused on 'earthly things'.

Enemies of the cross cannot be friends of the resurrection!

But because our 'citizenship is in heaven' our hopes and horizons, destiny and dreams are bound up with heaven and 'we eagerly await a Saviour from there, the Lord Jesus Christ'. The Caesars and other significant benefactors in the ancient world were, at this very time, expropriating the title 'saviour' for their own self-glory. When they visited a provincial town, on their arrival (know as a '*parousia*'), they were accorded VIP treatment. But believers are awaiting the arrival of the MIP (Most Important Person)!

Our place in the bigger story reminds us that our salvation is predominantly a future event and experience. Our life in Christ however vibrant now is but a tiny foretaste of what is yet to come!

And this future hope is a decidedly earthly hope. Salvation is ultimately not about our going to heaven when we die; rather, heaven is coming here in the Person of the Saviour bent on reclaiming and renewing His entire creation.

That's why we'll need – and will assuredly receive – brand-new, resurrection bodies. But to say that is to take a sneak look at the last page of the exciting final chapter in the different story we are enacting.

BIBLE READING

Philippians 3:20-4:7

[20]but our citizenship is in heaven, from which we also eagerly wait for a Savior, the Lord Jesus Christ. [21]He will transform the body of our humble condition into the likeness of His glorious body, by the power that enables Him to subject everything to Himself.

PRACTICAL COUNSEL

4 So then, in this way, my dearly loved brothers, my joy and crown, stand firm in the Lord, dear friends. ²I urge Euodia and I urge Syntyche to agree in the Lord. ³Yes, I also ask you, true partner, to help these women who have contended for the gospel at my side, along with Clement and the rest of my co-workers whose names are in the book of life. ⁴Rejoice in the Lord always. I will say it again: Rejoice! ⁵Let your graciousness be known to everyone. The Lord is near. ⁶Don't worry about anything, but in everything, through prayer and petition with thanksgiving, let your requests be made known to God. ⁷And the peace of God, which surpasses every thought, will guard your hearts and your minds in Christ Jesus.

THOUGHT: Many Christians think that the final hope of the Christian is to be with Jesus in heaven. That of course is quite true, but there is to be a new earth we are told in Scripture, for God is going to renew the whole of His creation. However, as the writer says, 'that's taking a sneak look at the last page of the story'. See it just as a taster. The banquet will come later.

AT TIMES IN its history the Church has sadly downplayed the value of the material creation and, in particular, of our physical bodies. But we do not become more spiritual by denigrating the physical which God saw as good and our Saviour saw fit to assume at Bethlehem.

Paul is not contrasting our 'lowly' body with something 'higher' or more spiritual. He is contrasting our present 'body of humiliation' with our future 'body of glory'.

For sin, disease and ageing do humiliate us. Anyone who has stood by the hospital bed of a loved one whose body was shrivelled up by cancer, or watched a beloved parent's dignity reduced by Alzheimer's, knows this only too well.

DAY
325
PHILIPPIANS 3:18-21

Yet it was such physicality that the Son of God honoured in His Incarnation, and offered on the cross for our salvation.

By His bodily resurrection from the dead, He majestically affirmed the goodness of God's original creation even as He magnificently inaugurated the new creation.

This is our sure and certain hope for all who die 'in Christ'. Again the match with 2:5-11 assures us that the Father's glory which Jesus went through death to share, He will share with us in resurrection.

Our first creation body may be ravaged by age and disease and succumb to death, but our new creation body is guaranteed to be resplendent with glory. Praise the Lord!

BIBLE READING

Philippians 3:18-21

[18]For I have often told you, and now say again with tears, that many live as enemies of the cross of Christ. [19]Their end is destruction; their god is their stomach; their glory is in their shame. They are focused on earthly things, [20]but our citizenship is in heaven, from which we also eagerly wait for a Savior, the Lord Jesus Christ. [21]He will transform the body of our humble condition into the likeness of His glorious body, by the power that enables Him to subject everything to Himself.

PRAYER: Thank You, dear Lord, for reminding me of the fact that this body of humiliation which now enwraps me is to be changed into a glorious body - one that will never age, never run out of energy, and never die. No more headaches, or aches and pains. The prospect of this makes me feel like shouting: O day of joy and delight, delay not your dawning. Let the angels be sent forth to gather the elect. Even so, come Lord Jesus.

THE THOUGHT OF God's lavish giving moves Paul to a characteristic burst of praise as if he were punching the air as winners do today.

Like all Paul's letters, Philippians ends, as it began, on the note of grace. It is God's grace which begins a good work in our lives and is pledged to complete it at the day of Christ.

God's providential grace can turn prisons into preaching centres, and enable His people to face death with extraordinary equanimity.

Above all, recall the amazing grace of our Lord Jesus Christ in not exploiting His advantages, in humbling Himself to be a servant and becoming obedient unto death.

And only grace could break a proud Pharisee and make a Christ-obsessed apostle.

Celebrate the grace that makes us citizens of heaven's kingdom and raises our sights to a coming Saviour. Hope for transforming grace by which He changes our despised, death-ridden earthly bodies into radiant, resurrection bodies modelled on His.

Grace begins and sustains the story; resilient grace that makes us ready for anything: gracious supply that means we lack for nothing!

Grace flows from start to finish. Grace in the end is 'The grace of our Lord Jesus Christ be with you all. Yes!'

Philippians 4:19-23

BIBLE READING

¹⁹And my God will supply all your needs according to His riches in glory in Christ Jesus. ²⁰Now to our God and Father be glory forever and ever. Amen.

FINAL GREETINGS

²¹Greet every saint in Christ Jesus. Those brothers who are with me greet you. ²²All the saints greet you, but especially those from Caesar's household. ²³The grace of the Lord Jesus Christ be with your spirit.

TO PONDER: How interesting that Paul in prison should end not with 'grace to me', but 'grace be with you'. That shows how other-centred the great apostle was. He could say this because grace was not just a theory to him but a living fact. He was saved by grace, he lived by grace and he dispensed grace to everyone he met. As you go through the day may grace be with you from start to finish.

SECTION

NOAH
ALL CREATION

ABRAHAM
ALL NATIONS

ISRAEL
ONE NATION

DAVID
REPRESENTATIVE KING

NEW COVENANT
FAITHFUL COVENANT PARTNER

JESUS
FAITHFUL COVENANT PARTNER

JESUS
DAVIDIC KING MESSIAH

JESUS
THE NEW ISRAEL

JESUS
THE WORLD'S LORD

JESUS
THE TRULY HUMAN ONE
CROWNED WITH GLORY AND HONOUR

JESUS
COSMIC RULER IN GOD'S
NEW CREATION
NEW HEAVENS AND NEW EARTH

SECTION 11   JOHN'S FINAL VISION

GOD IS COMMITTED TO RENEWIN THE WHOLE OF HIS CREATION – JOHN'S FINAL VISION ON PATMO

Our curiosity about the future is insatiable.

Eagerly, if somewhat sheepishly, we read our horoscopes, gaze into our crystal balls and try to sneak a look into what lies ahead. More pretentiously, big businesses hire expensive trend-analysts or futurologists in an attempt to predict the market. It's all a bit of a lottery; and we don't always get the weather forecast right!

This is where John shouts his good news to us of what he has glimpsed of the final state of affairs. Swept up by the prophetic inspiration of God's Spirit, he is taken to a high-mountain vantage-point and shown a stunning vision of the future (Rev. 21:10). They say 'on a clear day, you can see for ever' and this is an exceptionally clear day!

As if from far below, we shout up to John on his lonely pinnacle of vision: 'What can you see from there, John?'

John replies: 'I can see a sparkling new world, a whole new creation.'

'What does it look like?' we enquire.

'It looks like a city! But a city which is stretched out in all directions! It's like a new kind of Jerusalem teeming with people from every nation as if up for an international festival, enjoying the presence of God.'

'What else can you see?'

'I can see that no one is crying, there are no cemeteries, no prisons; I can see no one in pain or suffering any disease; and I think I can see God's face! And yet everything is radiating such a glorious light that I am not sure what I see; when I stare at the face of God, more often than not, I see the human face of Jesus.'

This is John's seventh and final vision; this is the ultimate vision. We might shout to him to be more specific but we'll shout ourselves hoarse.

Once again we are reminded that 'people are not changed by moral exhortation but by transformed imagination'. Nowhere is this insight more necessary than when approaching John's Revelation. Otherwise, crassly literal minds will be blinded to the truth.

Intriguing images, dazzling visions, majestic metaphors, stunning symbols – these are the currency of trade here. These images sharpen and fade, merge and separate before our very eyes as if on a giant computer screen. These visions dazzle us at the same time as they enlighten us. Yet what they portray is not less real but even more real for being given to us in this way; because it is these intensely poetic words that, we are assured, are trustworthy (faithful, NIV) and true (21:5) and can be submitted to as conveying divine authority and disclosure.

John celebrates the ultimate victory of the Lamb and His martyrs, together with all His faithful followers who have not loved 'their lives so much as to shrink from death' (12:11, NIV). He visualises the ultimate environment for redeemed people, a new heaven and new earth, and holds out the prospect of attaining the ultimate prize of looking on God's face.

DAY
327

REVELATION 21:1
ISAIAH 65:17; 66:22-23

WHEN JOHN PEERS into the future he sees in one dazzling vision an entirely new creation: 'I saw a new heaven and a new earth' (21:1).

All of God's strategic covenant commitments and dramatic redemptive intrusions; the continuous energising of His creative Spirit and the never-ceasing flow of His Word – it has all been leading to this – both Hebrew prophets and Jewish Christian apostles agree.

Isaiah hears God say: 'Behold, I will create new heavens and a new earth. The former things will not be remembered' (Isa. 65:17, NIV; cf.66:22). Creation and redemption are held together (Isa. 40-55); it is the Creator who redeems and in redeeming creates again.

The apostle Peter has seen in the cross and resurrection of Jesus the death and rebirth of the world.

Answering critics of God's slowness in keeping His promises, Peter re-affirms Isaiah's vision. Even though the cosmos is melted down to its constituent elements, in judgment and resolution, 'based on His promise, we wait for new heavens and a new earth, where righteousness will dwell' (2 Pet. 3:11-13). Paul, too, sees this present world released into the freedom God's sons already enjoy (Rom. 8:18-22). God has not written off His good creation. The Christian's future environment is not heaven in an ethereal sense but a redeemed earth.

BIBLE
READING

Revelation 21:1

THE NEW CREATION

21 Then I saw a new heaven and a new earth, for the first heaven and the first earth had passed away, and the sea existed no longer.

Isaiah 65:17

A NEW CREATION

¹⁷ "For I will create a new heaven and a new earth;
the past events will not be remembered or come
to mind.

Isaiah 66:22-23

²² "For just as the new heavens and the new earth,
which I will make,
will endure before Me"—

the LORD's declaration—

"so will your offspring and your name endure.
²³ All mankind will come to worship Me,
from one New Moon to another,
and from one Sabbath to another,"
says the LORD.

PRAYER: Gracious and loving Lord, I see that this glorious new life You have given me here on earth is only a precursor to a glorious new world, a new heaven and a new earth. Help me never forget that in that new world You are going to create I have a part to play - a part that was predestined for me before the foundation of the world. My gratitude knows no bounds. Thank You, my Father. Amen.

JOHN SUMS UP the whole biblical vision of what lies ahead as not some merely spiritual salvation but the ultimate reconciliation of spirit and matter, the reclaiming and restoring of God's own good creation.

John's 'no longers' ('no mores' NIV) say it well. He reports that in the final new creation there will be no more sea (21:1). This could sound disappointing to sailors and lovers of oceans. But the 'sea' in Scripture

DAY
328

REVELATION 21:1,4
2 PETER 3:11-13

represents the forces of chaos brought under control at the first creation. John is shown a resplendent landscape from which the untamed restlessness of evil and disorder has been banished for ever.

It follows, as the greatest miracle of all, that there is no more death (21:4). And no more death means no mourning, no crying, no pain, no disease, no cot-deaths, no cancer, no Alzheimer's, no widows and orphans. The God who stooped once to wash the dust from tired feet, will wipe away every tear from every grief-stricken eye – the 'old order passing away'.

But this will not just be 'paradise regained' as if all will be returned to how it was before – everything will be transformed and enhanced: better than before, with every potential fulfilled and every seed bearing fruit.

This is the Christian hope – a redeemed earth for which you and I will need, and receive, brand-new resurrection bodies.

BIBLE READING

Revelation 21:1,4

THE NEW CREATION

21 Then I saw a new heaven and a new earth, for the first heaven and the first earth had passed away, and the sea existed no longer.

. . . .

[4]He will wipe away every tear from their eyes.
Death will exist no longer;
grief, crying, and pain will exist no longer,
because the previous things have passed away.

BIBLE READING

2 Peter 3:11-13

[11]Since all these things are to be destroyed in this way, [it is clear] what sort of people you should be in holy conduct and godliness [12]as you wait for and earnestly desire the coming of the day of God, because of which the heavens

will be on fire and be dissolved, and the elements will melt with the heat. [13]But based on His promise, we wait for new heavens and a new earth, where righteousness will dwell.

QUOTATION: 'A little girl who had been born blind, received her sight through the miracle of modern-day surgery. She clapped her hands with delight and said "Mummy why didn't you tell me it was so beautiful?" "I tried my darling," said her mother, "but I just didn't have the words." That's John's predicament in Revelation 21: he tries to tell us of heaven's beauty but ... [it] will be more wonderful than words can convey.' (David Evans)

IT IS A fundamental feature of our Christian hope that, ultimately, we are not going to heaven: heaven is coming here!

This is reinforced by the second great image John sees in which the new creation is viewed as a city. Note again that this is flexible imagery. There are not two entities: a city within a creation; but the new creation is viewed as a city.

'I also saw the Holy City, new Jerusalem, coming down out of heaven from God ...' (21:2).

It comes to a mountain top (21:10). Here are echoes of the ancient myth of the mountain of the gods merged with Mount Zion in the vision of the Hebrew psalmist when he sang: 'Great is the LORD, and most worthy of praise, in the city of our God, his holy mountain' (Psa. 48:1, NIV). According to Ezekiel, the Garden of Eden was set also on a mountain (Ezek. 28:12-16) so that what we have is a fusion of images, Jerusalem with Paradise restored!

The Jerusalem John sees is a city which comes 'down out of heaven from God' (21:2,10).

Again it is emphasised, heaven is coming here – 'from God' for this is a God-designed and God-made city.

DAY 329

REVELATION 21:2,9-10

It was to see this that Abraham left Ur, the epitome of Babylonian civilisation, turning his back on the city man was building, setting out on the great faith adventure, 'looking forward to the city that has foundations, whose architect and builder is God' (Heb. 11:10).

BIBLE READING

Revelation 21:2,9-10

²I also saw the Holy City, new Jerusalem, coming down out of heaven from God, prepared like a bride adorned for her husband.

• • • • • • • • • •

THE NEW JERUSALEM

⁹Then one of the seven angels, who had held the seven bowls filled with the seven last plagues, came and spoke with me: "Come, I will show you the bride, the wife of the Lamb." ¹⁰He then carried me away in the Spirit to a great and high mountain and showed me the holy city, Jerusalem, coming down out of heaven from God ...

THOUGHT: The heavenly city described in Revelation 21 is clearly a place without fault or flaw. Imagine living in a world where all is perfect. Here there is something wrong with everything; there nothing is wrong with anything. The grand reason for that of course is because God is its Architect. Whatever the Almighty builds is faultless. It is sin that spoils things and there no sin will ever be found.

THE NEW JERUSALEM is a holy city – the dwelling place of the holy God (21:2,10). This is the significance of its remarkable shape – as wide and high as it is long (21:16). The symbolism of the shape derives from the Holy of Holies in the Temple which was a perfect cube (1 Kings 6:20). There, on one sacred spot on earth, God was manifest in concentrated form. But what was once compressed into one place, now pervades the whole. In other words, in this new world everything is holy space, everywhere is filled to the same intensity with the holy presence of God. No wonder a temple is redundant there (21:22).

The city John sees is a glorious city – brilliant with the radiant glory of God Himself (21:11). This is in stark contrast to the city of Babylon, which represents all that humankind has built without God. Babylon was built for self-glorification. Its idolatry made it vulnerable to demonic infiltration so that it became the home or 'a dwelling for demons' (18:2). But God's new Jerusalem is the dwelling-place of God and shines to His glory.

The Bible is a 'tale of two cities' – Babylon and Jerusalem: salvation rests on coming out of the one culture and becoming a citizen in the other, so that your name is enrolled in the 'Lamb's book of life' (21:27). A place in the new city is not to be missed.

DAY
330

REVELATION 21:11
1 KINGS 6:11-22

Revelation 21:11

BIBLE
READING

THE NEW JERUSALEM

⁹Then one of the seven angels, who had held the seven bowls filled with the seven last plagues, came and spoke with me: "Come, I will show you the bride, the wife of the Lamb." ¹⁰He then carried me away in the Spirit to a great and high mountain and showed me the holy city, Jerusalem, coming down out of heaven from God, ¹¹arrayed with God's glory. Her radiance was like a very precious stone, like a jasper stone, bright as crystal.

BIBLE READING

1 Kings 6:11-22

[11]The word of the LORD came to Solomon: [12]"As for this temple you are building—if you walk in My statutes, execute My ordinances, and keep all My commandments by walking in them, I will fulfill My promise to you, which I made to your father David. [13]I will live among the Israelites and not abandon My people Israel."

[14]When Solomon finished building the temple, [15]he paneled the interior temple walls with cedar boards; from the temple floor to the surface of the ceiling he overlaid the interior with wood. He also overlaid the floor with cypress boards. [16]Then he lined 30 feet of the rear of the temple with cedar boards from the floor to the surface of the ceiling, and he built the interior as an inner sanctuary, the most holy place. [17]The temple, that is, the sanctuary in front of the most holy place, was 60 feet long. [18]The cedar paneling inside the temple was carved with [ornamental] gourds and flower blossoms. Everything was cedar; not a stone could be seen.

[19]He prepared the inner sanctuary inside the temple to put the ark of the LORD's covenant there. [20]The interior of the sanctuary was 30 feet long, 30 feet wide, and 30 feet high; he overlaid it with pure gold. He also overlaid the cedar altar. [21]Next, Solomon overlaid the interior of the temple with pure gold, and he hung gold chains across the front of the inner sanctuary and overlaid it with gold. [22]So he added the gold overlay to the entire temple until everything was completely finished, including the entire altar that belongs in the inner sanctuary.

PRAYER: O God my Father, how can I tell out the feeling that surges within me when I realise that my name has been enrolled in the Lamb's book of life? There is a place in that new city just for me. And I have it not because of my merit but because of Your mercy. Blessed be Your name forever. How I long that my unsaved friends and loved ones will be there also. Save them, dear Lord. In Jesus' name. Amen.

THE NEW JERUSALEM is an inclusive city, which welcomes true believers from before and after Christ's coming, Old and New Testament believers who trust God for the coming of the Christ. The city's gates are inscribed with the twelve tribes of Israel and its foundation stones with the names of the twelve apostles (21:12,14). John has heard the songs of Moses and the Lamb (15:3).

This is an international city, fulfilling and far exceeding what Abraham was promised – descendants as innumerable as the stars in the night sky, as the grains of sand on the seashore – in whom all the nations of the earth would be blessed.

John hears that there are 144,000 in this company (7:4) – in other words, that God's covenant family is complete, no one in who shouldn't be there, no one out who should be in. But when he looks, he sees a multitude which no one could number from every nation, tribe, people and language group!

And to this city the nations and their kings bring tribute. Again, this symbolically contrasts with Babylon. A man-made culture is ultimately self-defeating. It consumes all in its quest for self-glory and self-gratification. But in the new Jerusalem, every human potential will be realised, all seeds will bear fruit, all history and culture will be redeemed and made good to the glory of the Creator.

DAY
331

REVELATION 22:12-27

Revelation 22:12-27

BIBLE
READING

¹²"Look! I am coming quickly, and My reward is with Me to repay each person according to what he has done. ¹³I am the Alpha and the Omega, the First and the Last, the Beginning and the End.

¹⁴"Blessed are those who wash their robes, so that they may have the right to the tree of life and may enter the city by the gates. ¹⁵ Outside are the dogs, the sorcerers, the sexually immoral, the murderers, the idolaters, and everyone who

loves and practices lying.

¹⁶ "I, Jesus, have sent My angel to attest these things to you for the churches. I am the Root and the Offspring of David, the Bright Morning Star."

¹⁷Both the Spirit and the bride say, "Come!" Anyone who hears should say, "Come!" And the one who is thirsty should come. Whoever desires should take the living water as a gift.

¹⁸I testify to everyone who hears the prophetic words of this book: If anyone adds to them, God will add to him the plagues that are written in this book. ¹⁹And if anyone takes away from the words of this prophetic book, God will take away his share of the tree of life and the holy city, written in this book.

²⁰He who testifies about these things says, "Yes, I am coming quickly."

Amen! Come, Lord Jesus!

²¹The grace of the Lord Jesus be with all the saints. Amen.

TO PONDER: Today you will step out into a world that is consumed with self-glory and self-gratification. Doubtless at some point you will meet with frustration or difficulty that will cause you to realise that though the world is beautiful there are evidences that it has been spoilt by sin. The world you are heading for in the future however is different. No frustration, no difficulties, no sin. Keep hope alive!

DAY
332
REVELATION 22:1-3

JOHN IS FINALLY shown the new Jerusalem as a garden-city. Its flowering completes the movement from first creation to new creation. There is, in effect, a restoring of the Garden of Eden without going back to it (22:1-2).

Here is development and expansion from a mere garden to a garden-city – one with all the benefits of urban living and all the joys of country life. There may be no more sea, but the river of true life runs sparkling through the city-centre. To this city, by the Spirit, we have already come as worshippers (Heb. 12:22f.); towards this city, by faith, we continue to march as pilgrims.

'... there will no longer be any curse' says it all (22:3). God's judgmental curse, once pronounced over the whole earth because of Adam's disobedience, is now rescinded. A thornless world appears. Creation is finally released into the liberty and blessing already tasted by the redeemed children of the One Creator God (Rom. 8:19ff.).

This is the new environment prepared for this new covenant people. And it is this company, purified and redeemed, which is the bride of the Lamb; the people who are in every way the perfect complement to Jesus. For this reason the city is portrayed as a beautiful bridal city (21:2,9).

But how can a city be a bride? The answer to that, John sees, is in those who live there.

Revelation 22:1-3

THE SOURCE OF LIFE

22 Then he showed me the river of living water, sparkling like crystal, flowing from the throne of God and of the Lamb [2]down the middle of the broad street [of the city]. On both sides of the river was the tree of life bearing 12 kinds of fruit, producing its fruit every month. The leaves of the tree are for healing the nations, [3]and there will no longer be any curse. The throne of God and of the Lamb will be in the city, and His servants will serve Him.

THOUGHT: Though metaphors seem to clash with each other in John's description of the Holy City this again shows how language is inadequate to describe the glory that awaits us. A beautiful environment awaits a beautiful people. And the beauty of the people of God arises not from their own efforts but rather because they have been made beautiful through the grace and power of Jesus Christ.

DAY
333

JOHN IS SHOWN the inhabitants of the city, God's new covenant community: 'Look! God's dwelling is with men, and He will live with them. They will be His people, and God Himself will ... be their God.' God finally has the people He always set His heart on.

This is the God we should have known about throughout the biblical story – who loves people and longs to be with them, and who had quiet walks and conversation with Adam and Eve in the garden in the cool of the afternoon. This is a God who camped and decamped all those years with Israel in the wilderness, marking His presence with a pillar of cloud by day and fire by night, who showed up in the sanctuary built for Him with the golden mist of His Shekinah glory and who gave Himself an earthly address in the Temple in Jerusalem.

And here is the great summary covenant statement: 'I will be their God and they will be My people' which runs like a recurring thread through all His dealings in history (cf.Lev. 26:11-12). Here are those who have slaked their eternal thirst at His fountain (21:6).

Verse 7, 'I will be his God, and he will be My son' takes the amazing covenantal promise made to David that he and his descendants could enjoy a unique Father-son relationship with God, and extends it to all! So at last, God's people reign with Him on the earth (22:5).

BIBLE READING

Revelation 21:3-7

³Then I heard a loud voice from the throne:

> Look! God's dwelling is with men,
> and He will live with them.
> They will be His people,
> and God Himself will be with them and be their God.
> ⁴ He will wipe away every tear from their eyes.
> Death will exist no longer;
> grief, crying, and pain will exist no longer,
> because the previous things have passed away.

⁵Then the One seated on the throne said, "Look! I am making everything new." He also said, "Write, because these words are faithful and true." ⁶And He said to me, "It is done! I am the Alpha and the Omega, the Beginning and the End. I will give to the thirsty from the spring of living water as a gift. ⁷The victor will inherit these things, and I will be his God, and he will be My son.

PRAYER: Father, the more I contemplate the glory that lies ahead the more wondrous it seems. I have read today that You are a God who loves people and longs to be with them. I am so glad that I am one of the people You long to be with. I long to be with You too, my Father. My thirst has been slaked at Your fountain and my heart rejoices to know that I will never thirst again. Thank You dear Lord. In Jesus' name. Amen.

DAY
334
REVELATION 21:5-6

THE LAST WORD on human history is spoken by the voice of Him who sits on the throne: 'I am making all things new' (21:5, NRSV). It seems as if the One Creator God is so brimful of vitality that He cannot do anything else but create. His final word declares that 'It is done!' (21:6). This declaration introduces the splendid sight given next of the new Jerusalem (21:9-22:11), just as it had closed the account of the downfall of the unholy city, Babylon (16:17-21). When it comes to judgment or salvation, only God can say 'It is done'. The old creation is wrapped up, the old order of things is passing away; the new creation, the new city, are ready and waiting to be unveiled (21:6). The joy of tracing the biblical story is to realise that God is the beginning and end of it. Our God had the first and last word on the old creation and the first word on the new creation. We may live ambiguously and sometimes anxiously 'between the times'. How near the end we are we do not know for sure. Is there meaning to be found? Meaning is to be found in God who is not only the A and the Z but the whole alphabet in between; in the One who, standing in the middle of history, proclaimed its end - 'It is finished' - and then breathed the Spirit of a new beginning into those who staked their future and eternal destiny on His cross and resurrection.

BIBLE READING

Revelation 21:5-6

⁵Then the One seated on the throne said, "Look! I am making everything new." He also said, "Write, because these words are faithful and true." ⁶And He said to me, "It is done! I am the Alpha and the Omega, the Beginning and the End. I will give to the thirsty from the spring of living water as a gift.

FOR PRAISE: Some psychologists claim that what is wrong with the human soul is that it lacks a sense of identity and meaning. We don't know who we are (as we said earlier) because we don't know whose we are. Our meaning and identity as children of God lies in knowing whose we are - we belong to Jesus. We may not know everything the future holds but we know Jesus. And that is enough.

DAY 335

REVELATION 21:7-8; 12:10-12

IT IS THE 'victors' ('overcomers', NIV) who inherit all these things (21:7); who are they?

If the rest of the book of Revelation is anything to go by, they are very definitely not some spiritual equivalent of the Marine Corps, not the few super-powered macho Christians.

The overcomers are all who fight the fight of faith and win on a daily basis some minute victory; those who have put all their faith in the blood of the Lamb to save them, who faithfully confess the Lordship of this Jesus, and who do not love their lives so much they shrink from death (12:11)!

The followers of the Lamb, through their own suffering and self-giving love, share in the implementation of His victory over evil and death. They have glimpsed the coming glory and been captivated by John's vision. They live as heralds of the new day, harbingers of a new world, samples of the world's future.

For this you keep fighting the fight of faith, achieve minor victories of integrity and patience and prayer. And this is your inheritance. Soberly, John allows himself a terrible glance over his shoulder into the abyss (21:8) at the fate of those who have debarred themselves from being part of this!

But the angels who have supervised the judgmental destruction of Babylon and the old order of things want to show him something better. Who in their right minds would want to miss that?

Revelation 21:7-8

BIBLE READING

⁷The victor will inherit these things, and I will be his God, and he will be My son. ⁸But the cowards, unbelievers, vile, murderers, sexually immoral, sorcerers, idolaters, and all liars—their share will be in the lake that burns with fire and sulfur, which is the second death."

Revelation 12:10-12

BIBLE READING

¹⁰Then I heard a loud voice in heaven say:

The salvation and the power and the kingdom
of our God
and the authority of His Messiah have now come,
because the accuser of our brothers has been thrown out:
the one who accuses them before our God day and night.
¹¹ They conquered him by the blood of the Lamb
and by the word of their testimony,
for they did not love their lives in the face of death.
¹² Therefore rejoice, O heavens, and you who dwell
in them!
Woe to the earth and the sea,

for the Devil has come down to you with great fury, because he knows he has a short time.

> **THOUGHT**: Amongst the most penetrating and exciting words Jesus ever gave us were these: 'In the world you will have tribulation; but be of good cheer, I have overcome the world' (John 16:33, NKJV). One preacher suggests that we are so one with Christ that when we see the Lord we might say: 'Why, Lord, did I overcome the world or did You?', We will hear Him answer gently: 'Why we both did, for My victory is your victory.'

DAY 336

REVELATION 22:1-16

WHAT STIRS JOHN most of all is the prospect held out to us all of a new vision of God Himself: 'They will see His face ...' (22:4). This surely is the ultimate prize, the final vision. Yet if one thing is clear throughout John's Patmos experience it is that whenever he looks to see the One Creator God, it is the Lamb who comes into focus!

The Lamb receives the bride, the Lamb lays the foundations of the city, the Lamb is the temple and the light in it, the Lamb shares the throne of God. The slain Lamb who now stands to rule keeps coming into view.

To see the very face of God surely would be heaven on earth: the 'beatific vision' as the medieval mystics called it. But John gives the distinct impression throughout his 'revelation' that whenever he peered closer to look into the face of God, what came into focus was the human face of Jesus – so much do they have in common. So Jesus shares with the One God the fullness of deity as Alpha and Omega, the Beginning and the End (22:13 cf.1:8). As the final fruit from David's root, the King of kings, Jesus is the Morning Star of the eternal day of God's kingdom, one empire, at least, on which the sun never sets.

With his own visionary experience dazzling his eyes and the sublime heavenly voice ringing in his ears, John falls down to worship (22:8).

Revelation 22:1-16

THE SOURCE OF LIFE

22 Then he showed me the river of living water, sparkling like crystal, flowing from the throne of God and of the Lamb ²down the middle of the broad street [of the city]. On both sides of the river was the tree of life bearing 12 kinds of fruit, producing its fruit every month. The leaves of the tree are for healing the nations, ³and there will no longer be any curse. The throne of God and of the Lamb will be in the city, and His servants will serve Him. ⁴They will see His face, and His name will be on their foreheads. ⁵Night will no longer exist, and people will not need lamplight or sunlight, because the Lord God will give them light. And they will reign forever and ever.

THE TIME IS NEAR

⁶Then he said to me, "These words are faithful and true. And the Lord, the God of the spirits of the prophets, has sent His angel to show His servants what must quickly take place."

⁷"Look, I am coming quickly! Blessed is the one who keeps the prophetic words of this book."

⁸I, John, am the one who heard and saw these things. When I heard and saw them, I fell down to worship at the feet of the angel who had shown them to me. ⁹But he said to me, "Don't do that! I am a fellow slave with you, your brothers the prophets, and those who keep the words of this book. Worship God." ¹⁰He also said to me, "Don't seal the prophetic words of this book, because the time is near. ¹¹Let the unrighteous go on in unrighteousness; let the filthy go on being made filthy; let the righteous go on in righteousness; and let the holy go on being made holy."

¹²"Look! I am coming quickly, and My reward is with Me to repay each person according to what he has done. ¹³I am the Alpha and the Omega, the First and the Last, the Beginning and the End.

¹⁴"Blessed are those who wash their robes, so that they may have the right to the tree of life and may enter the city by the gates. ¹⁵ Outside are the dogs, the sorcerers, the sexually immoral, the murderers, the idolaters, and everyone who loves and practices lying.

¹⁶ "I, Jesus, have sent My angel to attest these things to you for the churches. I am the Root and the Offspring of David, the Bright Morning Star."

FOR WORSHIP: I wonder do you know the words of this old but famous hymn. You might sing it (or say it) as your response to today's reading:

Face to face with Christ my Saviour. Face to face - what will it be,
When with rapture I behold Him, Jesus Christ who died for me?
Face to face we shall behold Him, Far beyond the starry sky;
Face to face in all His glory, I shall see Him by and by!

DAY
337
REVELATION 22:17-21

JOHN'S CLOSING EXHORTATIONS are a fitting lesson in how to respond to God's big story.

John's instinctive response of worship is surely right, even if he over-estimated the value of his angelic vision-bearer (22:8)!

He urges the Church not to lose its distinctive edge (22:14-15) or to lose hope that the story ends well, fixing our hopes and eyes not on dates or world events but on Jesus and His coming (22:7,12,17,20).

He warns against adding to or subtracting from the revelation he has passed on to us - the vision he has shared with us is too true to tamper with and too good to miss.

For this Noah overcame fear and stepped into the ark and with even more faith stepped out of it again.

For this Abraham launched into the great unknown trusting the Word of God.

For this Israel was chosen, loved, delivered and covenanted with.

For this David left his father's flock, and was anointed king.

For this the prophets were persecuted as they pictured God's future in stunning pictures and powerful words.

For this the Lamb came and lived among us. For this He chose twelve apostles, entered Jerusalem and laid down His life to displace the Temple. For this He died and rose again with a new world in His nail-pierced hands. For this He shares God's throne and intercedes, and for this He is coming again.

Revelation 22:17-21

THE SOURCE OF LIFE

22 Then he showed me the river of living water, sparkling like crystal, flowing from the throne of God and of the Lamb ²down the middle of the broad street [of the city]. On both sides of the river was the tree of life bearing 12 kinds of fruit, producing its fruit every month. The leaves of the tree are for healing the nations, ³and there will no longer be any curse. The throne of God and of the Lamb will be in the city, and His servants will serve Him. ⁴They will see His face, and His name will be on their foreheads. ⁵Night will no longer exist, and people will not need lamplight or sunlight, because the Lord God will give them light. And they will reign forever and ever.

THE TIME IS NEAR

⁶Then he said to me, "These words are faithful and true. And the Lord, the God of the spirits of the prophets, has sent His angel to show His servants what must quickly take place."
⁷"Look, I am coming quickly! Blessed is the one who keeps the prophetic words of this book."
⁸I, John, am the one who heard and saw these things. When I heard and saw them, I fell down to worship at the feet of the angel who had shown them to me. ⁹But he said to me, "Don't do that! I am a fellow slave with you, your brothers the prophets, and those who keep the words of this book. Worship God." ¹⁰He also said to me, "Don't seal the prophetic words of this book, because the time is near. ¹¹Let the unrighteous go on in

unrighteousness; let the filthy go on being made filthy; let the righteous go on in righteousness; and let the holy go on being made holy."

[12]"Look! I am coming quickly, and My reward is with Me to repay each person according to what he has done. [13]I am the Alpha and the Omega, the First and the Last, the Beginning and the End.

[14]"Blessed are those who wash their robes, so that they may have the right to the tree of life and may enter the city by the gates. [15] Outside are the dogs, the sorcerers, the sexually immoral, the murderers, the idolaters, and everyone who loves and practices lying.

[16] "I, Jesus, have sent My angel to attest these things to you for the churches. I am the Root and the Offspring of David, the Bright Morning Star."

[17]Both the Spirit and the bride say, "Come!" Anyone who hears should say, "Come!" And the one who is thirsty should come. Whoever desires should take the living water as a gift.

[18]I testify to everyone who hears the prophetic words of this book: If anyone adds to them, God will add to him the plagues that are written in this book. [19]And if anyone takes away from the words of this prophetic book, God will take away his share of the tree of life and the holy city, written in this book.

[20]He who testifies about these things says, "Yes, I am coming quickly."

Amen! Come, Lord Jesus!

[21]The grace of the Lord Jesus be with all the saints. Amen.

TO PONDER: 'Everyone,' it has been said, 'needs a guiding vision, something to aim at, something to live for.' What guides you? Is it climbing to the top of your career, ensuring you have enough in your old age? There's nothing wrong with those things of course but a Christian has something to aim for beyond those aspirations – seeing Jesus. Is that your 'guiding vision'?

SECTION 12 RESPONDING TO GOD'S BIG STORY

This is the challenge and invitation then: to discover your place in God's strategic plan and redemptive story.

What is your place in Noah's story?

As part of the new creation 'in Christ', you are called to keep your feet firmly on this old ground, respecting the earth but travelling through it as a pilgrim, walking keenly towards the future new heavens and new earth 'all landscaped with righteousness' (*The Message*).

Where are you in Abraham's adventure?

Following in the footsteps of faith, you are challenged to live counter-culturally, not wedded to the society man is building, but to the city God is building, living daringly by faith not sight, confident in trusting Jesus 'the seed of Abraham' and serving His mission to bring blessing to an accursed world.

Where are you in Israel's vocation?

By grace, grafted onto the stock of the Old Testament people of God, revering your Jewish roots but living free from the burden of Torah, you are enabled to keep covenant with God through the death of Christ and the indwelling power of the Holy Spirit as members of a 'chosen race, and royal priesthood', called to praise before the world the God who has brought you out of darkness into His marvellous light.

Where are you in David's destiny?

By redemptive transfer from the kingdom of darkness, you now find yourself in Messiah's kingdom and community, confessing Jesus as Lord of the world, learning with others how to be 'kings and priests' unto

God for the sake of the world.

Where are you in the prophetic hope?
Enjoying the blessing of the new covenant in Christ's
blood, you relish being forgiven, your heart responsive
to God, His will your growing delight, His Spirit within
you as God's empowering presence, among the new
people who serve one another as the true temple of
the Living God.

Where are you, above all, in the Jesus story?
This for all of us is the crucial question.
    Have I repented and embraced Him as the Master-
story of my life?
    Will I be His disciple? Am I a follower of Jesus Christ?
    In order to become one, we must first 'repossess'
our own stories repentantly, by acknowledging our
past as our responsibility. We have to learn to say, 'I
did that'. Then we must bow the knee to Jesus, and
'immerse ourselves in His story', dying with Him and
rising with Him to a new life. This is what faith and
baptism involve. As for the future, we stay honest
by continuing to 'own' our own stories. We own the
successes and failures, the trophies and the scars, the
glorious pages and the sad or bad chapters. All the
while, it is helpful to realise that 'my' story is now 'our'
story. I didn't begin the story and, in all likelihood, will
not be asked to finish it, but only to take my part in it
faithfully, joyfully, wholeheartedly and with others.

    When the day comes, then - as it surely will - when
the red book is handed to you which says, 'This is your
life', what will it add up to?

821

What story, or better whose story, will it tell?

In the words of St Columba: 'Since all the world is but a story, it were well for thee to buy the more enduring story, rather than the story that is less enduring.'

Fame is a fleeting phenomenon in our celebrity-conscious media-driven, modern world. The writer to the Hebrews celebrates the heroes of faith. But none of them achieved fame merely by being celebrities. They are famous for being faithful.

Noah and Abraham and Moses, David, the prophets and all the unsung heroes of the faith, were often insignificant players on the world stage. They were made famous by God's story. And so are we all. Yet, 'Not one of these people, even though their lives of faith were exemplary, got their hands on what was promised. God had a better plan for us: that their faith and our faith would come together to make one completed whole, their lives of faith not complete apart from ours' (Heb. 11:39–40, *The Message*).

FOR OVER 200 years in the modern Western world we have been sold a story other than God's story, with a script written by philosophers, scientists and evolutionary thinkers, and in which the leading role is played by human reason. Nothing can be treated as true that cannot be proved by reason.

Now, in our so-called postmodern world, these confident overarching narratives have broken down so that many people now assume that there is no story, no overall plot-line, that makes sense of anything. 'Life is a string of pearls whose thread is broken.' We are cast back on our own self-made stories.

Is there a bigger, better story that will show us who we are? Paul says 'yes, there is' and he proceeds to tell it at Antioch: This story is told in the Bible: it is God's story and it is God who is the chief actor in it.

Notice how Paul emphasises God's actions and initiatives. God chose our fathers; He made the people prosper in Egypt. He led them out; He endured for forty years; He overthrew seven nations; He conquered Canaan; He gave Israel judges; He installed and removed Saul; He raised up King David – 'a man after My heart'; He brought to Israel, from this man's descendants, a Saviour ... (vv.16-23).

DAY
338
ACTS 13:13-25

Acts 13:13-25

BIBLE
READING

PAUL'S SERMON IN ANTIOCH OF PISIDIA

¹³Paul and his companions set sail from Paphos and came to Perga in Pamphylia. John, however, left them and went back to Jerusalem. ¹⁴They continued their journey from Perga and reached Antioch in Pisidia. On the Sabbath day they went into the synagogue and sat down. ¹⁵After the reading of the Law and the Prophets, the leaders of the synagogue sent [word] to them, saying, "Brothers, if you have any message of encouragement for the people, you can speak."

¹⁶Then standing up, Paul motioned with his hand and spoke: "Men of Israel, and you who fear God, listen! ¹⁷The God of this

people Israel chose our forefathers, exalted the people during their stay in the land of Egypt, and led them out of it with a mighty arm. [18]And for about 40 years He put up with them in the desert; [19]then after destroying seven nations in the land of Canaan, He gave their land to them as an inheritance. [20]This all took about 450 years. After this, He gave them judges until Samuel the prophet. [21]Then they asked for a king, so God gave them Saul the son of Kish, a man of the tribe of Benjamin, for 40 years. [22]After removing him, He raised up David as their king, of whom He testified: "'I have found David" the son of Jesse, "a man after My heart," who will carry out all My will.'

[23]"From this man's descendants, according to the promise, God brought the Savior, Jesus, to Israel. [24]Before He came to public attention, John had previously proclaimed a baptism of repentance to all the people of Israel. [25]Then as John was completing his life work, he said, 'Who do you think I am? I am not the One. But look! Someone is coming after me, and I am not worthy to untie the sandals on His feet.'"

THOUGHT: At no other time in history has the need for 'story' been more necessary. As you observed in today's reading 'people now assume there is no story, no overall plot-line that makes sense of anything'. How refreshing it is to realise that against the background of pessimism and gloom a cosmic story is being worked out - one in which God plays the lead part. What a thought to begin a day!

DAY
339
ACTS 13:26-31

PAUL REMINDS US that the story of Jesus (13:26-37), though not the end of the ongoing story, is the climax of the earlier stage of the story of God's covenant relationship with His people Israel (v.23).

Like Matthew, Paul employs the idea of fulfilment to say this (vv.27,29,33). 'To fulfil', we recall, is 'to bring something to its intended goal' - in other words, to complete, or to fill full with meaning. The gospel Paul proclaims is the fulfilment of God's plan in a Person who fulfils the promise of God.

It is the fulfilment of a plan (vv.26-27) which the first-born 'sons of Abraham' should have known about since it began with Abraham. God's ground plan is, as we have seen, to bring blessing to the whole world through one family, one nation and its King.

The deep irony is that the religious leaders in Jerusalem unwittingly fulfilled this previously stated plan of God by rejecting Jesus. Mysteriously, we see hinted at again that even the failure of Israel seems to have been accommodated in God's plan from the beginning. This plan was fulfilled in a Person for all that was written was 'written about Him' (v.29).

This whole saving narrative pivots on the dramatic events of Jesus' death and resurrection from the dead - viewed by Paul as a mighty creative act of God (v.30).

Acts 13:26-31

BIBLE READING

PAUL'S SERMON IN ANTIOCH OF PISIDIA

[13]Paul and his companions set sail from Paphos and came to Perga in Pamphylia. John, however, left them and went back to Jerusalem. [14]They continued their journey from Perga and reached Antioch in Pisidia. On the Sabbath day they went into the synagogue and sat down. [15]After the reading of the Law and the Prophets, the leaders of the synagogue sent [word] to them, saying, "Brothers, if you have any message of encouragement for the people, you can speak."

[16]Then standing up, Paul motioned with his hand and spoke: "Men of Israel, and you who fear God, listen! [17]The God of this people Israel chose our forefathers, exalted the people during their stay in the land of Egypt, and led them out of it with a mighty arm. [18]And for about 40 years He put up with them in the desert; [19]then after destroying seven nations in the land of Canaan, He gave their land to them as an inheritance. [20]This all took about 450 years. After this, He gave them judges until Samuel the prophet. [21]Then they asked for a king, so God gave them Saul the son of Kish, a man of the tribe of

Benjamin, for 40 years. [22]After removing him, He raised up David as their king, of whom He testified: "'I have found David" the son of Jesse, "a man after My heart," who will carry out all My will.'

[23]"From this man's descendants, according to the promise, God brought the Savior, Jesus, to Israel. [24]Before He came to public attention, John had previously proclaimed a baptism of repentance to all the people of Israel. [25]Then as John was completing his life work, he said, 'Who do you think I am? I am not the One. But look! Someone is coming after me, and I am not worthy to untie the sandals on His feet.'

[26]"Brothers, sons of Abraham's race, and those among you who fear God, the message of this salvation has been sent to us. [27]For the residents of Jerusalem and their rulers, since they did not recognize Him or the voices of the prophets that are read every Sabbath, have fulfilled their words by condemning Him. [28]Though they found no grounds for the death penalty, they asked Pilate to have Him killed. [29]When they had fulfilled all that had been written about Him, they took Him down from the tree and put Him in a tomb. [30]But God raised Him from the dead, [31]and He appeared for many days to those who came up with Him from Galilee to Jerusalem, who are now His witnesses to the people."

PRAYER: Gracious and loving Father, I see again even more clearly that the pivotal point of Your story is the death and resurrection of Your Son. Help me not to take this for granted, but with gratitude. Had Jesus not come to this world, died for my sins and risen again I would still be in my sins - condemned to a lost eternity. I am grateful to the very core of my being. Thank You, my Father. In Jesus' name. Amen.

DAY 340

ACTS 13:32-37

THE EASTER EVENTS, Paul proclaims, were the fulfilment of a promise (v.32). Paul sums up the gospel as the 'good news of the promise' which God originally made to the fathers, Abraham, Isaac and Jacob, and especially confirmed to David.

He recalls God's promise to David – recorded in 2 Samuel 7:14 – of a throne, a dynasty, a kingdom which will last for ever and, above all, of a special Father-son relationship with God. This was further spelt out in the coronation psalm (Psa. 2), confessional song (Psa. 16) and prophetic testimony (Isa. 55).

But it was not King David himself who fulfilled God's dreams; he's dead and buried. It was Jesus, the Anointed One, who is no longer dead and buried: He did die but is very much alive and ruling.

Paul now presses home his case, issuing a challenge and an invitation. It is, he urges, through this Person that you can be written into the story of salvation. The challenge of God's story is that it offers every one of us a bigger, better, story to be part of, to be drawn into what He has been doing, is doing and will do in human history and on this earth!

Why stay in amateur dramatics in the school hall when we are summoned to appear on Broadway or in the West End?

BIBLE READING

Acts 13:32-37

²⁶"Brothers, sons of Abraham's race, and those among you who fear God, the message of this salvation has been sent to us. ²⁷For the residents of Jerusalem and their rulers, since they did not recognize Him or the voices of the prophets that are read every Sabbath, have fulfilled their words by condemning Him. ²⁸Though they found no grounds for the death penalty, they asked Pilate to have Him killed. ²⁹When they had fulfilled all that had been written about Him, they took Him down from the tree and put Him in a tomb. ³⁰But God

raised Him from the dead, ³¹and He appeared for many days to those who came up with Him from Galilee to Jerusalem, who are now His witnesses to the people.

³²And we ourselves proclaim to you the good news of the promise that was made to our forefathers. ³³God has fulfilled this to us their children by raising up Jesus, as it is written in the second Psalm:

'You are My Son;
today I have become Your Father.'

³⁴Since He raised Him from the dead, never to return to decay, He has spoken in this way, 'I will grant you the faithful covenant blessings made to David.' ³⁵Therefore He also says in another passage, 'You will not allow Your Holy One to see decay.' ³⁶For David, after serving his own generation in God's plan, fell asleep, was buried with his fathers, and decayed. ³⁷But the One whom God raised up did not decay."

FOR PRAISE: It might sound repetitive to keep reminding ourselves that we have been invited to be a part of God's big story and to be drawn into what He is doing, but is there in earth or heaven anything bigger and better than this? This is a promise - the more you dwell on this thought the more it will grip you. And the more it grips you the more you will want to praise the Lord. So once again - think and give thanks.

THE GOSPEL DECLARES that we can be freed from our own self-made stories whatever their failure. On the basis of Christ's death on the cross, God offers us forgiveness for our sins. He invites us to trade in the old, dog-eared, much corrected script of our own life for a brand-new one He'll help us write. God is seemingly more interested in setting people free than in controlling them!

Yet, the invitation, however personal, is not to embark on a solo career but to join the rest of the cast as they

DAY
341

ACTS 13:38-39

seek to live out this story together (vv.39-48). Come and join the cast of thousands who are repentantly, enthusiastically, sometimes blunderingly, but always hopefully, learning their parts in this greatest story ever told.

Paul is here test-driving his characteristic term which derives from the Old Testament concept of righteousness. There God is 'righteous' because He is faithful to the covenant, and people are 'righteous' who live faithfully within the covenant. When God 'justifies' then, He 're-righteous them' by restoring them to covenant membership.

In this gospel 'everyone who believes', is justified by faith and joins the community of faith (v.39) and so makes the story their own.

BIBLE READING

Acts 13:38-39

[26]"Brothers, sons of Abraham's race, and those among you who fear God, the message of this salvation has been sent to us. [27]For the residents of Jerusalem and their rulers, since they did not recognize Him or the voices of the prophets that are read every Sabbath, have fulfilled their words by condemning Him. [28]Though they found no grounds for the death penalty, they asked Pilate to have Him killed. [29]When they had fulfilled all that had been written about Him, they took Him down from the tree and put Him in a tomb. [30]But God raised Him from the dead, [31]and He appeared for many days to those who came up with Him from Galilee to Jerusalem, who are now His witnesses to the people.
[32]And we ourselves proclaim to you the good news of the promise that was made to our forefathers. [33]God has fulfilled this to us their children by raising up Jesus, as it is written in the second Psalm:

'You are My Son;

today I have become Your Father.'

[34]Since He raised Him from the dead, never to return to decay, He has spoken in this way, 'I will grant you the

faithful covenant blessings made to David.' ³⁵Therefore He also says in another passage, 'You will not allow Your Holy One to see decay.' ³⁶For David, after serving his own generation in God's plan, fell asleep, was buried with his fathers, and decayed. ³⁷But the One whom God raised up did not decay.

³⁸Therefore, let it be known to you, brothers, that through this man forgiveness of sins is being proclaimed to you, ³⁹and everyone who believes in Him is justified from everything, which you could not be justified from through the law of Moses."

> **TO PONDER**: Have things gone wrong in your life? Does it seem like the story of your past is a battered script, unworthy to be read? Then consider this – now you are a Christian you have a new role and a new part to play in a story that will go on playing throughout all eternity. So, shoulders back, lift up your head, you are a player in the greatest production the world has and can ever know. 'Rejoice. And again I say rejoice!'

GOD IS FAITHFUL and utterly to be depended on but He is not predictable. He can do startlingly new things which even His people, used to His normal ways of working, may find disconcerting or even unacceptable. The dramatic story of Jesus explodes in the middle of history to shatter preconceived ideas about God. As the prophet warned, God's people who should know better, can find themselves on the same cynical side as sneering unbelievers (13:41; cf.17:32).

DAY 342

ACTS 13:40-52

Some opponents will make life difficult for those who respond to the story, and verbal abuse may intensify into open hostility (vv.45,50). But others are enthralled by the story, and can't wait to hear more (13:42).

As for the newly recruited 'actors', they can't disguise their joy in the undeserved 'grace' of God (13:43c).

The servant's mission to bring light to the Gentiles (13:47; cf.Isa. 49:6; Luke 2:32) strengthens the apostles' resolve to take the gospel to the pagan world, where they find a ready response. New believers buzz with the vitality of life with an eternal quality (v.48), and share exuberantly in the divine energy that has been let loose in the world as they are 'filled with joy and the Holy Spirit' (v.52).

These disciples relish the fact that the story is an on-going story and that the cast list grows by the day (v.48)!

BIBLE READING

Acts 13:40-52

[26]"Brothers, sons of Abraham's race, and those among you who fear God, the message of this salvation has been sent to us. [27]For the residents of Jerusalem and their rulers, since they did not recognize Him or the voices of the prophets that are read every Sabbath, have fulfilled their words by condemning Him. [28]Though they found no grounds for the death penalty, they asked Pilate to have Him killed. [29]When they had fulfilled all that had been written about Him, they took Him down from the tree and put Him in a tomb. [30]But God raised Him from the dead, [31]and He appeared for many days to those who came up with Him from Galilee to Jerusalem, who are now His witnesses to the people.

[32]And we ourselves proclaim to you the good news of the promise that was made to our forefathers. [33]God has fulfilled this to us their children by raising up Jesus, as it is written in the second Psalm:

'You are My Son;

today I have become Your Father.'

[34]Since He raised Him from the dead, never to return to decay, He has spoken in this way, 'I will grant you the faithful covenant blessings made to David.' [35]Therefore He also says in another passage, 'You will not allow Your Holy One to see decay.' [36]For David, after serving his own generation in God's plan, fell asleep, was buried with his fathers, and decayed. [37]But the One whom God raised up did not decay.

[38]Therefore, let it be known to you, brothers, that

through this man forgiveness of sins is being proclaimed to you, ³⁹and everyone who believes in Him is justified from everything, which you could not be justified from through the law of Moses.

⁴⁰So beware that what is said in the prophets does not happen to you:

⁴¹ 'Look, you scoffers,
marvel and vanish away,
because I am doing a work in your days,
a work that you will never believe,
even if someone were to explain it to you.'"

PAUL AND BARNABAS IN ANTIOCH

⁴²As they were leaving, they begged that these matters be presented to them the following Sabbath. ⁴³After the synagogue had been dismissed, many of the Jews and devout proselytes followed Paul and Barnabas, who were speaking with them and persuading them to continue in the grace of God.

⁴⁴The following Sabbath almost the whole town assembled to hear the message of the Lord. ⁴⁵But when the Jews saw the crowds, they were filled with jealousy and began to oppose what Paul was saying by insulting him.

⁴⁶Then Paul and Barnabas boldly said: "It was necessary that God's message be spoken to you first. But since you reject it, and consider yourselves unworthy of eternal life, we now turn to the Gentiles! ⁴⁷For this is what the Lord has commanded us:

'I have appointed you as a light for the Gentiles,
to bring salvation to the ends of the earth.'"

⁴⁸When the Gentiles heard this, they rejoiced and glorified the message of the Lord, and all who had been appointed to eternal life believed. ⁴⁹So the message of the Lord spread through the whole region. ⁵⁰But the Jews incited the religious women of high standing and the leading men of the city. They stirred up persecution against Paul and Barnabas and expelled them from their district. ⁵¹But shaking the dust off their feet against them, they proceeded to Iconium. ⁵²And the disciples were filled with joy and the Holy Spirit.

THOUGHT: One of the issues which trouble some Christians is the unpredictability of God. They want a God who is 'safe', one who acts and behaves in ways that can be anticipated. Lindsey Glegg, a famous Christian who rose to prominence in the early twentieth century used to say: 'God is a God of surprises. Just when you think you have figured Him out you will find you haven't.' Perhaps He has a surprise waiting for you today.

DAY
343

HEBREWS 1:1
JOHN 1:1-16

NOWHERE IN THE New Testament is there a better summary of the relationship between Old and New Testaments than here.

In the earlier stage of the story, God spoke in fragmentary and varied ways. Now in these 'last days' He has spoken His final Word in Jesus. Once more we see that Jesus is the summation of all that God has previously said about Himself and His people in the Old Testament Scriptures.

Note, too, that while no one can be sure whether we are approaching history's final day or hour, the New Testament is clear that we have been in the 'last days' ever since Jesus came.

We see elements of both continuity and discontinuity here. There is continuity because it is the same God who speaks then and now. And those who respond to His Word form one continuous story of faith, as Hebrews chapter 11 especially highlights. Throughout his letter, the writer assumes that what was said then to God's people in the earlier part of the story continues to apply to us now.

But there is a sharp discontinuity too, in the unfolding story of God's self-revelation. What was partial ('fragmentary'), is now full. What was provisional ('in the past'), is now final ('in these last days'). Above all, what was spoken through God's servants ('by the prophets'), has now been uttered in His Son.

Hebrews 1:1

THE NATURE OF THE SON

1 Long ago God spoke to the fathers by the prophets at different times and in different ways.

John 1:1-16

1 In the beginning was the Word,
and the Word was with God,
and the Word was God.
2 He was with God in the beginning.
3 All things were created through Him,
and apart from Him not one thing was created
that has been created.
4 Life was in Him,
and that life was the light of men.
5 That light shines in the darkness,
yet the darkness did not overcome it.

6 There was a man named John
who was sent from God.
7 He came as a witness
to testify about the light,
so that all might believe through him.
8 He was not the light,
but he came to testify about the light.
9 The true light, who gives light to everyone,
was coming into the world.

10 He was in the world,
and the world was created through Him,
yet the world did not recognize Him.
11 He came to His own,
and His own people did not receive Him.
12 But to all who did receive Him,
He gave them the right to be children of God,
to those who believe in His name,

¹³ who were born,
not of blood,
or of the will of the flesh,
or of the will of man,
but of God.

¹⁴ The Word became flesh
and took up residence among us.
We observed His glory,
the glory as the One and Only Son from the Father,
full of grace and truth.
¹⁵ (John testified concerning Him and exclaimed,
"This was the One of whom I said,
'The One coming after me has surpassed me,
because He existed before me.'")
¹⁶ Indeed, we have all received grace after grace
from His fullness ...

QUOTATION: People unread in comparative religions like to say, 'One religion is as good as another'. It sounds broad-minded. Actually it is a judgment of ignorance. 'Christianity is in a category by itself. We claim for the religion of Jesus Christ that it is unique, unsurpassed and unparalleled, the word not of a prophet but the Son Himself. Jesus is God's last word to His people.' (W.E. Sangster)

DAY
344

HEBREWS 1:2-3; 8:1-6

THE INHERITANCE RIGHTS of 'sonship', once partially and provisionally attached to Israel and her kings (cf.Exod. 4:22-23; 2 Sam. 7:14), now pass to their intended recipient, the eternal Son, Jesus. The eternal Son who radiates God's glory became the embodied Son who exactly represents God's Being and thereafter exists as the exalted Son who sits enthroned as God's right-hand man.

This rich language is mined from various parts of the Old Testament and Jewish writings, where it is applied to the eternal wisdom of God by which He made and sustains His creation.

The third Old Testament category which the writer uses here, and fully develops throughout the letter, is that of priesthood. The writer skilfully blends Old Testament prophecies and psalms to make the link between 'Son' and 'King' and 'priest' (2 Sam. 7; Psa. 2; Psa. 110 cf.1:5,13).

We may well marvel that there is a God who has broken the seemingly eternal silence and spoken to us His life-giving Word. And Jesus, the Son of God, is God's central message. In reviewing creation's origins and ultimate destiny – Jesus is the wise agent and trusted heir.

And in the cleansing that is indispensable if a sin-spoiled world is to be restored to its full potential – Jesus is the one effective sacrifice and ever-efficient priest of God's salvation.

Hebrews 1:2-3

BIBLE READING

THE NATURE OF THE SON

1 Long ago God spoke to the fathers by the prophets at different times and in different ways.

²In these last days, He has spoken to us by [His] Son, whom He has appointed heir of all things and through whom He made the universe. ³He is the radiance of His glory, the exact expression of His nature, and He sustains all things by His powerful word. After making purification for sins, He sat down at the right hand of the Majesty on high.

Hebrews 8:1-6

BIBLE READING

A HEAVENLY PRIESTHOOD

8 Now the main point of what is being said is this: we have this kind of high priest, who sat down at the right hand of the throne of the Majesty in the heavens, ²a minister of the sanctuary and the true tabernacle, which the Lord set up, and not man. ³For every high priest is appointed to

offer gifts and sacrifices; therefore it was necessary for this [priest] also to have something to offer. [4]Now if He were on earth, He wouldn't be a priest, since there are those offering the gifts prescribed by the law. [5]These serve as a copy and shadow of the heavenly things, as Moses was warned when he was about to complete the tabernacle. For He said, "Be careful that you make everything according to the pattern that was shown to you on the mountain." [6]But Jesus has now obtained a superior ministry, and to that degree He is the mediator of a better covenant, which has been legally enacted on better promises.

> **PRAYER:** Lord Jesus Christ, how perfectly You fulfil all the Old Testament prophecies and roles of Son, King, Priest and Sacrificial Lamb. What a destiny I have and what a story to tell – all the roles You fitted into were in order to save me, sanctify me and make me fit for heaven. And if I were the only one to receive salvation You would have done it just for me. Thank You, dear Saviour. Amen.

DAY 345

HEBREWS 1:5-14

HERE SEVERAL OLD Testament threads are woven into a chorus of praise in honour of Jesus. Varied voices from the earlier stage of the story are heard singing from the same songsheet the glory of God's plan now unveiled as the glorious Person, Jesus.

Notice once again how crucial in the outworking of God's saving plan was His covenant commitment to David (2 Sam. 7; Psa. 2). Again we see that scriptures are drawn together because the writers discern the underlying connections between them that form a coherent pattern and promise. This particular interweaving of quotations has been described as a 'coronation liturgy' in which God declares that the King is His Son (1:5). It heralds His acclamation, as the King is presented to His people (1:6-12) and His anointing and enthronement (1:9,13).

Notice too how the quotations match the statements of verses 1-3: verses 5-9 mirror verse 2; verse 10 mirrors verse 2; verses 11-12 mirror verse 3a; and verse 13 mirrors verse 3c.

Amid first-century fascination with angels, the writer places Jesus far above the angels, with a greater name (v.5, Son), a loftier dignity (v.6, worthy of worship), a higher status (vv.7-12 as the unchanging One), and a superior function (vv.13-14, He reigns at God's right hand, while they serve).

Hebrews 1:5-14

THE SON SUPERIOR TO ANGELS

[5]For to which of the angels did He ever say, "You are My Son; today I have become Your Father," or again, "I will be His Father, and He will be My Son"? [6]When He again brings His firstborn into the world, He says, "And all God's angels must worship Him." [7]And about the angels He says:

> "He makes His angels winds,
> and His servants a fiery flame;"

[8]but about the Son:

> "Your throne, O God, is forever and ever,
> and the scepter of Your kingdom is a scepter of justice.
> [9] You have loved righteousness and hated lawlessness;
> this is why God, Your God, has anointed You,
> rather than Your companions, with the oil of joy."

[10]And:

> "In the beginning, Lord, You established the earth,
> and the heavens are the works of Your hands;
> [11] they will perish, but You remain.
> They will all wear out like clothing;
> [12] You will roll them up like a cloak,
> and they will be changed like a robe.

But You are the same,
and Your years will never end."

¹³Now to which of the angels has He ever said:

"Sit at My right hand
until I make Your enemies Your footstool?"

¹⁴Are they not all ministering spirits sent out to serve those who are going to inherit salvation?

FOR ACTION: Of all the descriptions given to Jesus none is greater than the fact He is King. How are we to proclaim His Kingship? The words of an old hymn provide an answer:

Rise up O men of God,
Have done with lesser things.
Give heart and soul and mind and strength
To serve the King of kings.

(William P. Merrill)

DAY 346

HEBREWS 2:5-9

THAT GOD BRINGS His 'firstborn into the world' (1:6) is not a reference to the incarnation but to the ascension. Just as God brought His first-born people, Israel, into the promised land, so He has brought His eternal Son made flesh through death up into the realm of eternal salvation. He has entered ahead of us the 'world to come' (2:5).

The one Son's humiliation is set to achieve glory for God's many 'sons'. Psalm 8 is itself a lyrical expansion of Genesis 1:26-28. The writer now expounds it to show that the eternal Son of God assumed the human condition, with its vulnerability to death, in order to bring humanity through to its intended glory. Once more, the original and overarching plan of God is revealed as made good in and through Jesus. The eternal Son was willing in His incarnation to be made temporarily 'lower than the angels' and so was crowned with the honour due to a victorious humanity to whom all things in creation are subject. In a rebellious and sin-torn world, we do not yet, of course, see the final outcome of God's plan to subject the world to a redeemed human race. But we do see Jesus, the truly Human One, who has gone ahead of us and who guarantees our ultimate inclusion in the triumph of God's design. Jesus shares our humanity, dies our death, bears our sins, and now wears our crown!

Hebrews 2:5-9

BIBLE READING

JESUS AND HUMANITY

[5]For He has not subjected to angels the world to come that we are talking about. [6]But one has somewhere testified:

> "What is man, that You remember him,
>   or the son of man, that You care for him?
> [7] You made him lower than the angels for a short time;
>   You crowned him with glory and honor
> [8] and subjected everything under his feet."

For in "subjecting everything" to him, He left nothing not subject to him. As it is, we do not yet see "everything subjected" to him. [9]But we do see Jesus—"made lower than the angels for a short time" so that by God's grace He might taste death for everyone—crowned with glory and honor because of the suffering of death.

THOUGHT: Have you ever thought about the vulnerability of Jesus and what that meant for Him? Then think about it for a few moments now. Vulnerability means 'open to emotional or physical attack'. The Saviour voluntarily put Himself in a position where He could be attacked by both human and devilish forces and be subject to pain and death. And He did it all for you.

DAY 347

HEBREWS 2:10
JOHN 16:31-33

GOD'S PURPOSE IS to redeem His original creation. He aims to bring 'many sons' in a new exodus not just to the promised land but to the glory of shared dominion with Him. That God is achieving this through the incarnation and suffering of Jesus, in identification with sinful humanity, is thus described as strangely 'fitting' to God (2:10).

Doing it this way fits God's nature as the source and agent of all things in creation and salvation. Only such a God could have initiated such a staggering plan and carried it through. So the whole execution of the plan is consistent with His character as a God of 'grace' (2:9).

Its outcome, too, is entirely appropriate to Him, in being not some panic-driven emergency which He might be embarrassed to acknowledge as His own but, in fact, the very pre-determined way in which He intended to maximise His glory.

And if it was 'fitting' to God, then it was 'necessary' for Jesus to suffer in our humanness for us, if He were to be the source of our salvation. This He achieved through His suffering as God's obedient Son (cf.Heb. 5:8). This vivid word 'source' may variously be translated 'author' - the One who writes the script of our savation - or 'leader' or 'pioneer' which suits the pilgrimage theme so favoured by the writer (3:7-4:11). Even better, perhaps, it means 'champion' so that it highlights the heroic struggle Jesus fought in order to bring our human story through to God's intended conclusion.

BIBLE READING

Hebrews 2:10

JESUS AND HUMANITY

⁵For He has not subjected to angels the world to come that we are talking about. ⁶But one has somewhere testified:

"What is man, that You remember him,
or the son of man, that You care for him?
⁷You made him lower than the angels for a
short time;

You crowned him with glory and honor
⁸and subjected everything under his feet."

For in "subjecting everything" to him, He left nothing not subject to him. As it is, we do not yet see "everything subjected" to him. ⁹But we do see Jesus—"made lower than the angels for a short time" so that by God's grace He might taste death for everyone—crowned with glory and honor because of the suffering of death.

¹⁰For it was fitting, in bringing many sons to glory, that He, for whom and through whom all things exist, should make the source of their salvation perfect through sufferings.

John 16:31-33

³¹Jesus responded to them, "Do you now believe? ³²Look: An hour is coming, and has come, when each of you will be scattered to his own home, and you will leave Me alone. Yet I am not alone, because the Father is with Me. ³³I have told you these things so that in Me you may have peace. You will have suffering in this world. Be courageous! I have conquered the world."

QUOTATION: 'A pioneer is someone who goes ahead of others, opens up new territory, makes a path along which others can follow. This is precisely what Jesus has done for us; He went through the darkest regions of death which was a most trackless area, and fought with adversaries which we will never have to fight. He is the Champion of champions; the Pioneer of all pioneers. Blessed be His wonderful name.' (David Thomas)

DAY 348

HEBREWS 2:11-13

WHEN THE STORY of Jesus was grafted onto our sinful, rebellious story, suffering was a inevitable outcome for Him. His sufferings were the means by which He was 'made perfect', not in a moral but a functional sense. In other words, His willingness to endure sufferings fully equipped Him for the task of being our champion and priestly Saviour. To be so closely identified with us qualified Him to be our Priest.

The One who consecrates is, in the Old Testament, God (Exod. 31:13; Lev. 20:8), but here it is a role assigned to Jesus (cf.Heb. 13:12). He makes His perfection ours. Consecration has a necessary corollary in cleansing from sin and defilement, for those set apart for God must first be purified from sin.

So even though Jesus shares deep solidarity with us, He remains distinct from us as the One who consecrates (cf.Heb. 4:15; 7:26-28).

Yet we are said to share a common origin with Him. This may be read as from 'one stock' or one 'family' or one 'ancestor' like Adam or Abraham. It may mean simply that we both derive from the One God!

Christ and His covenant people share the same family, the same Father, which is why He is not ashamed to call them brothers!

BIBLE READING

Hebrews 2:11-13

JESUS AND HUMANITY

⁵For He has not subjected to angels the world to come that we are talking about. ⁶But one has somewhere testified:

"What is man, that You remember him,
or the son of man, that You care for him?
⁷You made him lower than the angels for a
short time;
You crowned him with glory and honor
⁸and subjected everything under his feet."

For in "subjecting everything" to him, He left nothing not subject to him. As it is, we do not yet see "everything subjected" to him. ⁹But we do see Jesus—"made lower than the angels for a short time" so that by God's grace He might taste death for everyone—crowned with glory and honor because of the suffering of death.

¹⁰For it was fitting, in bringing many sons to glory, that He, for whom and through whom all things exist, should make the source of their salvation perfect through sufferings.

¹¹For the One who sanctifies and those who are sanctified all have one Father. That is why He is not ashamed to call them brothers, ¹²saying:

> "I will proclaim Your name to My brothers;
> I will sing hymns to You in the congregation."

¹³Again, "I will trust in Him." And again, "Here I am with the children God gave Me."

TO PONDER: Wouldn't you think that Jesus, being who He is, perfect, unsullied by sin and the delight of His Father's heart, would be more tentative in relating to us as 'brothers'? Not so, however. We are told that He is not ashamed to call us brothers. Not ashamed? What amazing grace! What astonishing acceptance! Nothing in heaven or earth can equal this.

WITH JESUS, GOD'S final Word, the prophetic hopes are an 'idea whose time has come'. This convergence of the Jesus story and the human story can be told through three Old Testament references.

The prophetic assertion; 'I will proclaim Your name to my brothers' (Psa. 22:22) is put in the mouth of the singing Jesus who leads us in praising God. In this way, we find our voice in His voice. We praise in and through His praise. We join in worship that Jesus is already leading.

The prophetic vow: 'I will put my trust in him' (Isa. 8:17, NIV) becomes His pledge of total reliance on God, so

DAY
349

HEBREWS 2:12-13

that He leads us in confident trust in God. We put our faith in His faithfulness, we trust in His trust. We believe in God through Him.

The prophetic willingness in dark days to stand up and be counted as God's servant: 'Here I am with the children the LORD has given me' (Isa. 8:18) becomes His rallying call to us, His spiritual 'offspring', to bravely make ourselves available with Him for whatever God wants us to be and do.

He lived these words. He sang this psalm on the cross from its opening minor key of God-forsakenness to its major key of praise. On the cross, He entrusted His spirit to His Father's tender hands and said to Mary, 'Here is your son' and to John, 'Here is your mother'.

In this way He qualified to be the head of the whole family of faith.

BIBLE READING

Hebrews 2:12-13

JESUS AND HUMANITY

[5]For He has not subjected to angels the world to come that we are talking about. [6]But one has somewhere testified:

"What is man, that You remember him,
or the son of man, that You care for him?
[7]You made him lower than the angels for a
    short time;
You crowned him with glory and honor
[8]and subjected everything under his feet."

For in "subjecting everything" to him, He left nothing not subject to him. As it is, we do not yet see "everything subjected" to him. [9]But we do see Jesus—"made lower than the angels for a short time" so that by God's grace He might taste death for everyone—crowned with glory and honor because of the suffering of death.

[10]For it was fitting, in bringing many sons to glory, that He, for whom and through whom all things exist, should make the source of their salvation perfect through sufferings.

[11]For the One who sanctifies and those who are sanctified

all have one Father. That is why He is not ashamed to call them brothers, ¹²saying:

"I will proclaim Your name to My brothers;
I will sing hymns to You in the congregation."

¹³Again, "I will trust in Him." And again, "Here I am with the children God gave Me."

> **FOR PRAISE:** As you open your heart in praise and worship to God right now keep in mind that Jesus is the leader of all the praise and worship that ascends to the Father. 'We praise in and through His praise.' Whatever words you use as you praise Him are merged into the stream of praise that Christ co-ordinates. Multitudes all over the world are praising God through Jesus at this moment. Let's join them.

DAY 350
HEBREWS 2:14-18

ALTHOUGH JESUS IS the chief actor in God's story and ours, His humanity is no actor's mask! He is not a god dressed up as a man. He bleeds real blood and tears real flesh. He feels and suffers as truly one of us even to the point of death.

By doing this, He aims to destroy, or nullify, the power of the devil. This is not the power to kill us indiscriminately but the devil's cunning in making death his ally against sinful men and women, both to consign them to final judgment and damnation and to hold them in perpetual fear.

But we have a champion whose death was not a sentence of death on His own rebellion but the consecration of an obedient life to God's will to save sinners (cf.10:5-7).

The 'second Adam to the fight and rescue came' as our 'David', defeating our ultimate 'Goliath'.

The nature which He assumed in order to achieve this was not angelic but human, and especially Jewish.

847

He stood in line as Abraham's 'seed' to fulfil the faith story Abraham began. Being made like His human brothers in every respect save sin was essential to Him – that He might qualify to be a High Priest – and was vital to us – in order to bear God's wrath upon our sin and so propitiate it.

He is merciful enough to come to the aid of the tempted because He resisted temptation, remaining faithful to God despite suffering.

BIBLE READING

Hebrews 2:14-18

JESUS AND HUMANITY

[5]For He has not subjected to angels the world to come that we are talking about. [6]But one has somewhere testified:

> "What is man, that You remember him,
> or the son of man, that You care for him?
> [7]You made him lower than the angels for a
>   short time;
> You crowned him with glory and honor
> [8]and subjected everything under his feet."

For in "subjecting everything" to him, He left nothing not subject to him. As it is, we do not yet see "everything subjected" to him. [9]But we do see Jesus—"made lower than the angels for a short time" so that by God's grace He might taste death for everyone—crowned with glory and honor because of the suffering of death.

[10]For it was fitting, in bringing many sons to glory, that He, for whom and through whom all things exist, should make the source of their salvation perfect through sufferings.

[11]For the One who sanctifies and those who are sanctified all have one Father. That is why He is not ashamed to call them brothers, [12]saying:

> "I will proclaim Your name to My brothers;
> I will sing hymns to You in the congregation."

[13]Again, "I will trust in Him." And again, "Here I am with the children God gave Me."

[14]Now since the children have flesh and blood in common,

He also shared in these, so that through His death He might destroy the one holding the power of death—that is, the Devil— ¹⁵and free those who were held in slavery all their lives by the fear of death. ¹⁶For it is clear that He does not reach out to help angels, but to help Abraham's offspring. ¹⁷Therefore He had to be like His brothers in every way, so that He could become a merciful and faithful high priest in service to God, to make propitiation for the sins of the people. ¹⁸For since He Himself was tested and has suffered, He is able to help those who are tested.

PRAYER: How thankful I am, dear Father, that when I come to You through Jesus I am coming to One who knows my every feeling, One who has worn my flesh, measured its frailty and can sympathise with my every emotion. And He did all this without sin. He knows my condition because He has been in my condition. My gratitude will just not go into words. Blessed Trinity. Thank You. Amen.

THE WRITER TELLS his readers: You have a champion, Jesus. He is the faithful Son over God's house. Jesus is contrasted with Moses.

DAY
351
HEBREWS 3:1-6

As God's 'apostle', sent with God's final message (cf.1:1; 2:1-4), and as 'high priest' (cf.1:4; 2:17), He eclipses Moses who was called the 'sent one' (Exod. 3:10) and was associated with priestly functions (Psa. 99:6). Yet again we see how Jesus gathers up, expands and enriches all that went before in the Old Testament.

Hebrews is a sustained exposition of the superiority of Jesus over all previous revelation and institutions. In the writer's eyes, Jesus is 'better' than the prophets, 'better' than angels, 'better' than Moses, Joshua and Aaron. He establishes a 'better' priesthood, based on a 'better' sacrifice which inaugurates a 'better' covenant and introduces a 'better' hope of a 'better' resurrection!

He is superior to Moses - the faithful founder of the nation - and has greater glory because He is not merely a servant 'in' the house but the Son 'over' God's house - in the same way that the builder of the house has greater honour than the house itself.

In the flow of God's story, everything is owed to the faithfulness of Christ. Our challenge is to play our part in the story as members of God's house by staying faithful.

BIBLE READING

Hebrews 3:1-6

OUR APOSTLE AND HIGH PRIEST

3 Therefore, holy brothers and companions in a heavenly calling, consider Jesus, the apostle and high priest of our confession; [2]He was faithful to the One who appointed Him, just as Moses was in all God's household. [3]For Jesus is considered worthy of more glory than Moses, just as the builder has more honor than the house. [4]Now every house is built by someone, but the One who built everything is God. [5]Moses was faithful as a servant in all God's household, as a testimony to what would be said [in the future]. [6]But Christ was faithful as a Son over His household, whose household we are if we hold on to the courage and the confidence of our hope.

THOUGHT: A man looked at some pictures in a famous gallery and said to the attendant; 'I don't think much of these pictures.' The attendant replied, 'Excuse me, sir, but the pictures are not on trial.' It was the people who viewed them who were. It is the same with Jesus, when we look at Him He is not on trial - we are. We judge ourselves by our judgment of Him. He is the best character in God's story, the One who brings it to life.

THE WRITER TO the Hebrews has a dynamic view of Scripture. Unlike Paul, he never introduces an Old Testament quotation with 'It is written' but prefers 'He says' or 'He is speaking'.

Like Paul, he believes there is one continuous story unfolded in Scripture, so that what the Holy Spirit said then is said now. This enables him to recall the crisis of faith which Israel had in the wilderness, in order to challenge his readers to reaffirm their own commitment to Jesus.

The original story told in the book of Numbers (chs. 12-14) shows both the unfaithfulness of Israel and the faithfulness of God. The story is recorded as a prophetic warning in Psalm 95 which was in regular use as an introit to the synagogue liturgy. Those who rebelled were privileged to have been led out of Egypt and had seen God's works but had not embraced His ways. God was angry with that whole generation and they never made it to the 'rest' of the promised land.

Don't share their unbelief, says the writer, or doubt, as they did, that God is with you. Encourage one another as long as 'today' lasts. And don't throw away your confidence.

Between past redemption and future rest there is much ground to cover. The story is not over yet. Heed 'today's' voice and keep moving on in faith.

Hebrews 3:7-19

OUR APOSTLE AND HIGH PRIEST

3 Therefore, holy brothers and companions in a heavenly calling, consider Jesus, the apostle and high priest of our confession; ²He was faithful to the One who appointed Him, just as Moses was in all God's household. ³For Jesus is considered worthy of more glory than Moses, just as the builder has more honor than the house. ⁴Now every house is built by someone, but the One who built everything is God. ⁵Moses was faithful as a servant in all God's household, as a testimony to what would be said [in the future]. [6]But Christ was faithful as a Son over His household, whose household we are if we hold on to the courage and the confidence of our hope.

WARNING AGAINST UNBELIEF

[7]Therefore, as the Holy Spirit says:

> "Today, if you hear His voice,
> [8] do not harden your hearts as in the rebellion,
>   on the day of testing in the desert,
> [9] where your fathers tested Me, tried [Me],
>   and saw My works [10]for 40 years.
>   Therefore I was provoked with this generation
>   and said, 'They always go astray in their hearts,
>   and they have not known My ways.'
> [11] So I swore in My anger,
>   'They will not enter My rest.'"

[12]Watch out, brothers, so that there won't be in any of you an evil, unbelieving heart that departs from the living God. [13]But encourage each other daily, while it is still called "today," so that none of you is hardened by sin's deception. [14]For we have become companions of the Messiah if we hold firmly until the end the reality that we had at the start. [15]As it is said:

> "Today, if you hear His voice,
>   do not harden your hearts as in the rebellion."

[16]For who heard and rebelled? Wasn't it really all who came out of Egypt under Moses? [17]And with whom was He "provoked for 40 years"? Was it not with those who sinned, whose bodies fell in the desert? [18]And to whom did He "swear that they would not enter His rest," if not those who disobeyed? [19]So we see that they were unable to enter because of unbelief.

FOR ACTION: Consider this: Scripture bids us encourage one another not every year, every month or every week, but every day. Many of your fellow Christians are dying on the vine simply because of a lack of encouragement. People don't despair because so many bad things happen to them; they despair because so few good things happen to them. Go out of your way to encourage someone this very hour.

DAY
353
HEBREWS 4:1-14

THE STORY OF the people of God is bracketed by an original promised 'rest' and an ultimate future 'rest'.

Entering the 'rest' of God has both a literal and metaphorical reference. There is rest that is already assured which is the creation-rest God enjoys since completing His first creation work (Heb. 4:3-5; Gen. 2:2) and which is the goal of all His creation.

There was a 'rest' which Israel achieved through conquering and entering into the 'rest' of the land of Canaan (Heb. 3:18-19 but cf.Heb. 4:8; Josh. 1:13; 21:44). But, in a figurative way, this Canaan-rest anticipates the 'rest' of consummation (4:9-11) when as believers we will have completed our work and will enjoy the festivity of final salvation in the heavenly realm.

There remains a 'rest' available now to those who put their total confidence and trust in the completed work of God in Christ. The Holy Spirit contemporises this, offering us a satisfying foretaste of that future 'rest' if 'today' we will hear His voice and obey.

If heaven overflows with joy at one sinner who repents, how much more over a whole world restored? That will be a party to beat all parties and God will be the life and soul of it! To be outside of this would be hell; to be inside it will be the very heaven of heavens.

BIBLE READING

Hebrews 4:1-14

THE PROMISED REST

4 Therefore, while the promise remains of entering His rest, let us fear so that none of you should miss it. [2]For we also have received the good news just as they did; but the message they heard did not benefit them, since they were not united with those who heard it in faith [3](for we who have believed enter the rest), in keeping with what He has said:

> "So I swore in My anger,
> they will not enter My rest."

And yet His works have been finished since the foundation of the world, [4]for somewhere He has spoken about the seventh day in this way:

> "And on the seventh day
> God rested from all His works."

[5]Again, in that passage [He says], "They will never enter My rest." [6]Since it remains for some to enter it, and those who formerly received the good news did not enter because of disobedience, [7]again, He specifies a certain day—"today"—speaking through David after such a long time, as previously stated:

> "Today if you hear His voice,
> do not harden your hearts."

[8]For if Joshua had given them rest, He would not have spoken later about another day. [9]A Sabbath rest remains, therefore, for God's people. [10]For the person who has entered His rest has rested from his own works, just as God did from His. [11]Let us then make every effort to enter that rest, so that no one will fall into the same pattern of disobedience.

[12]For the word of God is living and effective and sharper than any two-edged sword, penetrating as far as to divide soul, spirit, joints, and marrow; it is a judge of the ideas and thoughts of the heart. [13]No creature is hidden from Him, but

all things are naked and exposed to the eyes of Him to whom we must give an account.

OUR GREAT HIGH PRIEST

¹⁴Therefore since we have a great high priest who has passed through the heavens—Jesus the Son of God—let us hold fast to the confession.

> TO PONDER: Many Christians are puzzled by the concept of 'God's rest' which is referred to several times in Scripture. To be 'in Christ' is to be in rest. No more struggling to come up to standard, no more striving to be good. The Spirit within us empowers us for that purpose. Our souls find a place of rest through faith 'today' that is merely a foretaste of things to come. A taster now, the full banquet later.

HEBREWS CAN INTIMIDATE us with all its talk of priests, sanctuaries and sacrificial ritual, so much of which seems remote to us. We may ask – what does all this religious language have to do with reality? Hebrews answers: in one sense, nothing at all.

DAY
354
HEBREWS 9:23-10:10

That's just the point – Christ is the only Priest, altar and sacrifice we need for a lasting relationship with God. But apart from Israel's story and God-given worship we would lack this rich vision of who Jesus is and what He has achieved.

The writer sums up his vision by noting the impact of the three 'appearings' of Jesus (9:23-28).

Jesus has 'appeared once ... to do away with sin' (NIV) - this is an unrepeatable historically based fact (9:25-26). Jesus now 'appears' after His ascension in the heavenly sanctuary to represent us in God's very presence (9:24).

He will 'appear a second time, not to bear sin, but to bring salvation to those who are waiting for Him' (9:28).

What gives His ministry saving power - past, present and future - is that it is not the unwilling sacrifice of a dumb animal but a man's willing and conscious self-sacrifice in service to God's will (10:5-10). This carries God's story forward into a wholly new phase of fulfilment and establishes us on a wholly new covenant basis with God (10:8-10).

| BIBLE READING | **Hebrews 9:23–10:10** |

²³Therefore it was necessary for the copies of the things in the heavens to be purified with these [sacrifices], but the heavenly things themselves [to be purified] with better sacrifices than these. ²⁴For the Messiah did not enter a sanctuary made with hands (only a model of the true one) but into heaven itself, that He might now appear in the presence of God for us. ²⁵He did not do this to offer Himself many times, as the high priest enters the sanctuary yearly with the blood of another. ²⁶Otherwise, He would have had to suffer many times since the foundation of the world. But now He has appeared one time, at the end of the ages, for the removal of sin by the sacrifice of Himself. ²⁷And just as it is appointed for people to die once— and after this, judgment— ²⁸so also the Messiah, having been offered once to bear the sins of many, will appear a second time, not to bear sin, but to bring salvation to those who are waiting for Him.

THE PERFECT SACRIFICE

10 Since the law has [only] a shadow of the good things to come, and not the actual form of those realities, it can never perfect the worshipers by the same sacrifices they continually offer year after year. ²Otherwise, wouldn't they have stopped being offered, since the worshipers, once purified, would no longer have any consciousness of sins? ³But in the sacrifices there is a reminder of sins every year. ⁴For it is impossible for the blood of bulls and goats to take away sins.

⁵Therefore, as He was coming into the world, He said:

"You did not want sacrifice and offering,
but You prepared a body for Me.
⁶ You did not delight

in whole burnt offerings and sin offerings.
⁷ Then I said, 'See, I have come—
it is written about Me
in the volume of the scroll—
to do Your will, O God!'"

⁸After He says above, "You did not desire or delight in sacrifices and offerings, whole burnt offerings and sin offerings," (which are offered according to the law), ⁹He then says, "See, I have come to do Your will." He takes away the first to establish the second. ¹⁰By this will, we have been sanctified through the offering of the body of Jesus Christ once and for all.

PRAYER: O Father, how wonderful it is to be living in a day and age when an animal sacrifice is no longer needed. The best those sacrifices could do was to cover sin, but the sacrifice of Jesus my Saviour not only covers it, but cleanses it and makes my conscience clean. I am so grateful for this, my Father. Accept my praise and worship – worship that comes from a heart made clean. Amen.

WHERE DO WE fit in 'God's honours list', 'God's roll-call of fame'?

DAY 355

HEBREWS 10:32–11:1

Note that the writer starts not with the Old Testament heroes but with his readers' own vigorous faith (10:32). In other words, you are in the same story, the same arena as them (12:1). Their witness is not meant to intimidate you but to inspire you.

In uncertain times we need encouragement to keep our nerve. The writer addresses such a time and need.

For Jewish Christians far away from the impending disaster about to strike Jerusalem, these were deeply disturbing days. Their old securities were literally being swept away, as much of their Jewish heritage was threatened with extinction by the pagan Romans. Nearer to home was even more uncertainty. Living in the capital of the Roman Empire, they were also threatened with persecution for their new-found faith.

With every foundation outside of Christ being shaken, this great pastoral writer offers them his word of exhortation and encouragement (13:20-22). He does it by reminding them and us of what gives significance to our lives. And what gives deep and lasting significance to our lives is to be an active participant in the on-going story of faith.

BIBLE READING

Hebrews 10:32-11:1

[32]Remember the earlier days when, after you had been enlightened, you endured a hard struggle with sufferings. [33]Sometimes you were publicly exposed to taunts and afflictions, and at other times you were companions of those who were treated that way. [34]For you sympathized with the prisoners and accepted with joy the confiscation of your possessions, knowing that you yourselves have a better and enduring possession. [35]So don't throw away your confidence, which has a great reward. [36]For you need endurance, so that after you have done God's will, you may receive what was promised.

[37] For in yet "a very little while,
the Coming One will come and not delay.
[38] But My righteous one will live by faith;
and if he draws back,
My soul has no pleasure in him."

[39]But we are not those who draw back and are destroyed, but those who have faith and obtain life.

HEROES OF FAITH

11 Now faith is the reality of what is hoped for, the proof of what is not seen.

QUOTATION: 'Hebrews 11 has been described by someone as "The Westminster Abbey of the Bible" as it honours the names of some of the illustrious men and women of Scripture. And remember, they were there not simply because of their exploits, but because they acted in faith. Nothing delights God more than trust and confidence in Him. Nothing. Remember that the next time you worry that you are an "unknown".' (Wendell Smith)

HEBREWS CHAPTER 11 is, in fact, a special re-reading of the story of Israel and her ancestors. The writer could have listed the long catalogue of unbelief – as in chapter 4 – but here he lights on the gripping examples of radical obedience and passionate trust that are also true of the same story.

DAY
356
HEBREWS 10:35-11:1

The closest parallel to Hebrews 11 is the list of heroes in the Jewish Book of Sirach (Ecclesiasticus).

Sirach, written about 180 BC, celebrates Israel's famous – from Enoch, and Noah, right down to the kings.

Interestingly the story climaxes with a glowing portrait of a contemporary of the writer – Simeon II, son of Jonathan – who held office as high priest from 219-196 BC, emerging from the splendid and ordered worship of the Temple (Ecclus. 50:5-7, 12-21).

Hebrews, however, re-writes the story to show that its true climax is Jesus, the splendid and glorious and ultimate High Priest who, having made the final effective sacrifice, officiates in the heavenly sanctuary where He lives to bless His people, and from where He will re-appear at history's end. Hebrews 11 then is not an isolated message about faith but serves to reinforce its whole message that Jesus is the final Word and fulfilment of every Old Testament office and institution.

BIBLE READING

Hebrews 10:35-11:1

³²Remember the earlier days when, after you had been enlightened, you endured a hard struggle with sufferings. ³³Sometimes you were publicly exposed to taunts and afflictions, and at other times you were companions of those who were treated that way. ³⁴For you sympathized with the prisoners and accepted with joy the confiscation of your possessions, knowing that you yourselves have a better and enduring possession.

³⁵So don't throw away your confidence, which has a great reward. ³⁶For you need endurance, so that after you have done God's will, you may receive what was promised.

> ³⁷ For in yet "a very little while,
>   the Coming One will come and not delay.
> ³⁸ But My righteous one will live by faith;
>   and if he draws back,
>   My soul has no pleasure in him."

³⁹But we are not those who draw back and are destroyed, but those who have faith and obtain life.

HEROES OF FAITH

11 Now faith is the reality of what is hoped for, the proof of what is not seen. ²For by it our ancestors were approved.

FOR PRAISE: Hebrews, as you have gathered by now, was written to show the supremacy of Jesus over every other person in the universe. He is the hero of God's story. As you survey the great list of heroes and personages, remember that He is out there ahead of them all – leading the procession because of His outstanding faith and confidence in His heavenly Father. Give Him glory and praise.

SO WHAT, BRIEFLY, are the implications for our faith? That faith is essentially a future-orientated assurance of things hoped for (11:1)!

Faith is not fuelled by gratitude for past mercies. Gratitude is good and natural but even the godless can be grateful. The faith talked about here reaches forward for the power of God because we trust Him to keep His Word and promises.

It is - in the title of John Piper's memorable book - 'faith in future grace'. You can believe in future grace because it is its own evidence. Faith opens our closed eyes to understand creation. It does so intuitively, as we recognise God's power behind the world (cf.Rom. 1:19-20). And faith responds to God's revelation that He is the One Creator whose Word brought the world into being (Gen. 1:1f.). The creational scale of God's big story is vital if our faith is to stretch beyond our domestic concerns to embrace the God who creates worlds.

Faith is the only difference - so far as we can tell - between Cain and Abel. Cain's lack of it, led him to silence his brother. Abel's faith enables his blood still to speak. By faith Enoch walked with God right out of this world and into the next. But then Enoch's faith was not self-serving but expressed his desire to please God. Such faith will always write new chapters in faith's story.

Hebrews 11:1-5

BIBLE
READING

HEROES OF FAITH

11 Now faith is the reality of what is hoped for, the proof of what is not seen. ²For by it our ancestors were approved.

³By faith we understand that the universe was created by the word of God, so that what is seen has been made from things that are not visible.

⁴By faith Abel offered to God a better sacrifice than Cain [did]. By this he was approved as a righteous man, because God approved his gifts, and even though he is dead, he still speaks through this.

⁵By faith, Enoch was taken away so that he did not experience death, and "he was not to be found because God took him away." For prior to his transformation he was approved, having pleased God.

> **THOUGHT:** New chapters similar to Hebrews 11 are being written every day by people like you who go out into the day trusting in the Holy Spirit to hold them, and living out their lives in response to divine grace. Don't just look back to great people of the past, look forward to the day that is ahead and determine by God's grace to draw by faith from the great resources of God. Today you can write a new chapter in faith's story.

DAY 358

HEBREWS 11:6-7

IF YOU HAVE travelled with us through the year thus far, I trust your faith has enjoyed firsthand experience of the trustworthiness of God's character.

Faith believes in God not as a vague backdrop to life but as an active responder to the appetite for Him which He Himself whets in our hearts. God is a rewarder not a refuser. God is not a God who has off days or gets moody. This is no lottery. God is a covenant-making, covenant-keeping God. For this reason, true faith-people are God-orientated, God-obsessed, passionate pleasers of God. The current self-absorption of much popular Christianity compares poorly with such radically counter-cultural faith. We want to be able to control our own destiny, and to reduce everything to manageable proportions. Our pride is hurt by the realisation that we don't know all the answers.

We want to plan our schedules, and we feel insecure when we are told that the life of Jesus was 'plan-less'.

No wonder Noah condemned the world by faith. His foolish obedience was a standing contradiction to a culture that was taken up with eating, drinking and family-making and which was not in the least bit concerned with saving anything up for what turned out to be an exceptionally rainy day!

Hebrews 11:6-7

HEROES OF FAITH

11 Now faith is the reality of what is hoped for, the proof of what is not seen. ²For by it our ancestors were approved.

³By faith we understand that the universe was created by the word of God, so that what is seen has been made from things that are not visible.

⁴By faith Abel offered to God a better sacrifice than Cain [did]. By this he was approved as a righteous man, because God approved his gifts, and even though he is dead, he still speaks through this.

⁵By faith, Enoch was taken away so that he did not experience death, and "he was not to be found because God took him away." For prior to his transformation he was approved, having pleased God.

⁶Now without faith it is impossible to please God, for the one who draws near to Him must believe that He exists and rewards those who seek Him.

⁷By faith Noah, after being warned about what was not yet seen, in reverence built an ark to deliver his family. By this he condemned the world and became an heir of the righteousness that comes by faith.

TO PONDER: Where is your life's focus? On yourself or on Christ? We bring great pleasure to our Lord when we focus on Him in a response of faith and obedience rather than focusing upon ourselves in self-absorption. It should be noted that self-absorption is different from self-consideration. There is nothing wrong with considering yourself; just don't be absorbed by yourself. Be absorbed by Him.

DAY **359**

HEBREWS 11:8-12

IF YOU HAVE some confidence that God's bigger story gives perspective to your own personal drama then you can put your faith in God even without knowing where you're going (v.8). We walk as children of the light but sometimes in the dark for we walk by faith not sight. It was in the deep and dreadful darkness of a God-induced trance-like sleep that Abraham received a prophetic vision of the troubled centuries ahead.

He lived in the promised land as if he were a stranger in it, feeling rootless and unsettled and incomplete. He erected his tents every night, no doubt wondering as he did so if there was anything permanent! His faith was stretched – as ours is – by living in 'transition'.

And knowing you are part of God's big story stirs you to believe God even without knowing how (vv.11-12)! Abraham and Sarah confronted the reality of their own bodies and faced the impossible. But from what was considered 'as good as dead' new life sprung.

The seed grows, said Jesus, secretly, and even the experienced farmer 'doesn't know how' it happens (Mark 4:27). Of such is the kingdom of God.

BIBLE READING

Hebrews 11:8-12

HEROES OF FAITH

11 Now faith is the reality of what is hoped for, the proof of what is not seen. ²For by it our ancestors were approved.

³By faith we understand that the universe was created by the word of God, so that what is seen has been made from things that are not visible.

⁴By faith Abel offered to God a better sacrifice than Cain [did]. By this he was approved as a righteous man, because God approved his gifts, and even though he is dead, he still speaks through this.

⁵By faith, Enoch was taken away so that he did not

experience death, and "he was not to be found because God took him away." For prior to his transformation he was approved, having pleased God. [6]Now without faith it is impossible to please God, for the one who draws near to Him must believe that He exists and rewards those who seek Him.

[7]By faith Noah, after being warned about what was not yet seen, in reverence built an ark to deliver his family. By this he condemned the world and became an heir of the righteousness that comes by faith.

[8]By faith Abraham, when he was called, obeyed and went out to a place he was going to receive as an inheritance; he went out, not knowing where he was going. [9]By faith he stayed as a foreigner in the land of promise, living in tents with Isaac and Jacob, co-heirs of the same promise. [10]For he was looking forward to the city that has foundations, whose architect and builder is God.

[11]By faith even Sarah herself, when she was barren, received power to conceive offspring, even though she was past the age, since she considered that the One who had promised was faithful. [12]And therefore from one man—in fact, from one as good as dead—came offspring as numerous as the stars of heaven and as innumerable as the grains of sand by the seashore.

PRAYER: Heavenly Father I do not know quite where You will lead me in the future, but my faith is not in a planned destination but in a faithful companion and guide - the Lord Jesus Christ Himself. Loving Father, Your reign in my life is my realisation, Your rule my release. Knowing You will be there in my future gives me a confidence and joy that nothing can take away. I am so deeply grateful. Amen.

DAY
360

HEBREWS 11:13-15

YOU CAN ENJOY faith in future grace without knowing 'when' (11:13).

Abraham's faith was stretched to breaking point before Isaac arrived. But the city never did arrive.

Abraham was the first of a line of heroes of faith of which it is said: 'These all died in faith' (11:13, NKJV). What a wonderful epitaph: not 'died disillusioned, embittered, nostalgic for the glories of the past', but died still believing. Isaac, of whom we know so little, and even Jacob, a mixed character if ever there was one, are famed for this. And noble Joseph spoke believingly about the future grace coming to his people (11:20-22).

When faith is harnessed to God's larger, long-term redemptive story, it is no longer motivated by short-term goals or fixed on short-term gains. Faith looks beyond the visible and the immediate, creating waves beyond its own life-span which influence the future. Without seeking to control the future, or manipulate God, faith makes a difference to those following on in the continuing story.

Such faith reaches up and beyond the kitsch glitter of contemporary culture to the mountain peaks of a more abiding city (v.10), an alternative homeland (v.14), a better country (v.16), a more lasting reward, solid joys and lasting treasure (v.26), a better resurrection in a superior kingdom.

BIBLE READING

Hebrews 11:13-15

HEROES OF FAITH

11 Now faith is the reality of what is hoped for, the proof of what is not seen. ²For by it our ancestors were approved.

³By faith we understand that the universe was created by the word of God, so that what is seen has been made from things that are not visible.

⁴By faith Abel offered to God a better sacrifice than

Cain [did]. By this he was approved as a righteous man, because God approved his gifts, and even though he is dead, he still speaks through this.

[5]By faith, Enoch was taken away so that he did not experience death, and "he was not to be found because God took him away." For prior to his transformation he was approved, having pleased God. [6]Now without faith it is impossible to please God, for the one who draws near to Him must believe that He exists and rewards those who seek Him.

[7]By faith Noah, after being warned about what was not yet seen, in reverence built an ark to deliver his family. By this he condemned the world and became an heir of the righteousness that comes by faith.

[8]By faith Abraham, when he was called, obeyed and went out to a place he was going to receive as an inheritance; he went out, not knowing where he was going. [9]By faith he stayed as a foreigner in the land of promise, living in tents with Isaac and Jacob, co-heirs of the same promise. [10]For he was looking forward to the city that has foundations, whose architect and builder is God.

[11]By faith even Sarah herself, when she was barren, received power to conceive offspring, even though she was past the age, since she considered that the One who had promised was faithful. [12]And therefore from one man—in fact, from one as good as dead—came offspring as numerous as the stars of heaven and as innumerable as the grains of sand by the seashore.

[13]These all died in faith without having received the promises, but they saw them from a distance, greeted them, and confessed that they were foreigners and temporary residents on the earth. [14]Now those who say such things make it clear that they are seeking a homeland. [15]If they had been remembering that land they came from, they would have had opportunity to return.

QUOTATION: 'There is a grave in the Swiss Alps in which the body of a climber who fell to his death whilst attempting to climb the Matterhorn lies. His grave is marked with these three simple words: "He died climbing". When you die will the same be said of you – in a spiritual sense I mean? Reach continually for the skies, in the true sense of that word. Always look up, never down.' (R.B. Jones)

DAY 361

HEBREWS 11:17-22

THE MYSTERY IN the story of faith, which believes 'not knowing how', deepens into 'not knowing why' (11:12-19).

Does it make sense to sacrifice Isaac the child of promise on whom the whole promise-plan hinged? Did Abraham wonder how he would return with Isaac?

The writer here construes it – perceptively – as Abraham's faith in a God who can raise the dead! This God defies the odds, surmounts the arguments, does wonders to faith. Faith is tested most when God seems mysterious or even contradictory in His purpose. Then we are tempted to elevate principles or dogma above a relationship with the living God and to say: this can't happen or this can't be true when it is.

If Abraham had been a slave to his own logical consistency he would have rejected the angel's veto as wishful thinking and Isaac would have died right there and then. But fanaticism isn't faith. And Abraham trusted enough to listen.

It was George Muller who said: 'Save me from pride in my own consistency' (ie always wanting to be proved right).

Hebrews speaks compellingly to Christians tempted by a hostile society to blunt the cutting edge of commitment to the uniqueness of Jesus Christ. Faith is the gift to trust God as the Author of the story, whatever the turbulence and contradictions on the way.

Hebrews 11:17-22

¹⁷By faith Abraham, when he was tested, offered up Isaac; he who had received the promises was offering up his unique son, ¹⁸about whom it had been said, "In Isaac your seed will be called." ¹⁹He considered God to be able even to raise someone from the dead, from which he also got him back as an illustration.

²⁰By faith Isaac blessed Jacob and Esau concerning things to come. ²¹By faith Jacob, when he was dying, blessed each of the sons of Joseph, and, "he worshiped, leaning on the top of his staff." ²²By faith Joseph, as he was nearing the end of his life, mentioned the exodus of the sons of Israel and gave instructions concerning his bones.

THOUGHT: Nothing tests faith more than confusion. Confusion erodes our sense of competence and of being in control. But it is also the context in which we can develop the muscles of our faith. Faith in God when everything is clear is one thing, but faith in Him when all around is utter confusion is another. Remember when you are struggling to hold on to God He is holding on to you. Trust.

MOSES WAS BORN into a faithful family who saved his infant life because they believed the story of God's people which gave them a different view of the world to the one offered by Egypt's power.

Moses early on refused in faith to let that Egypt define who he was. His later choices were just as socially provocative. He preferred partnership in suffering with God's people to the usual pleasure-seeking lifestyle promoted by Pharaoh's media. Moses opted for disgrace in the will of God which he regarded as a better bet that all the accumulated wealth and wisdom, kudos and perks of a high-flying career in the Egyptian diplomatic service!

DAY
362
HEBREWS 11:23-27

His faith made him more sure of the invisible than the visible, and incited him to forego short-term satisfaction for God's long-term reward. Faith emboldened him to defy a tyrant. Faith made him obediently implement the details of God's saving plan for Israel.

No doubt Moses' example of faith inspired a normally reluctant people's willingness to cross the Red Sea. And Moses, no doubt, shared the people's surprise at their own faith which saw Jericho's walls fall and, even more, the faith of the foreign whore, Rahab! These remarkable testimonies bear witness to the way in which our lives are transformed by being taken up into God's saving story.

| BIBLE READING | **Hebrews 11:23-27** |

[17]By faith Abraham, when he was tested, offered up Isaac; he who had received the promises was offering up his unique son, [18]about whom it had been said, In "Isaac your seed will be called." [19]He considered God to be able even to raise someone from the dead, from which he also got him back as an illustration.

[20]By faith Isaac blessed Jacob and Esau concerning things to come. [21]By faith Jacob, when he was dying, blessed each of the sons of Joseph, and, "he worshiped, leaning on the top of his staff." [22]By faith Joseph, as he was nearing the end of his life, mentioned the exodus of the sons of Israel and gave instructions concerning his bones.

[23]By faith Moses, after he was born, was hidden by his parents for three months, because they saw that the child was beautiful, and they didn't fear the king's edict. [24]By faith Moses, when he had grown up, refused to be called the son of Pharaoh's daughter [25]and chose to suffer with the people of God rather than to enjoy the short-lived pleasure of sin. [26]For he considered reproach for the sake of the Messiah to be greater wealth than the treasures of Egypt, since his attention was on the reward.

[27]By faith he left Egypt behind, not being afraid of the king's anger, for he persevered, as one who sees Him who is invisible.

TO PONDER: Here's something to chew on, so to speak, throughout the day: are you as sure of the invisible as you are of the visible? Ian Sewter, who contributed to these devotional thoughts says: 'Faith is the catalyst that transforms our lives to reject visible worldly pleasures in order to embrace the invisible rewards of being taken up into God's story.' How sure are you of that?

GIDEON, BARAK, SAMSON, Jephthah, David and Samuel – unlikely heroes, flawed heroes, but all famous because they played their part in the story at crucial moments in the drama. The writer claims to have run out of time to tell all the stories he has to hand! But his summary gives us vivid glimpses of extraordinary, death-defying, risk-taking audacity.

DAY
363
HEBREWS 11:32-40

No wonder the writer says the 'world was not worthy of' such believers (v.38). The world doesn't deserve them! How could it? The world has no standard of measurement that can assess such people's true worth; they go right off the top of the scale! But what matters is 'God is not ashamed to be called their God' (11:16b).

For our part, we may not know where or how or even why or when but, like them, we know who. He dazzles us, we seek; He calls, we answer; He leads, we follow; He challenges, we obey; He dares, we risk; He invests all in us, we stake all on Him.

Our story of faith is the same as theirs: without us they are not part of a complete story (11:40).

Ecclesiasticus gave its roll-call of honour by inviting us: 'Let us now praise famous men.' Hebrews says the heroes of the Old Testament stage of the story were famous not for being celebrities but for being faithful. Hebrews wants us, like them, to be 'made famous' by the story.

BIBLE READING

Hebrews 11:32-40

³²And what more can I say? Time is too short for me to tell about Gideon, Barak, Samson, Jephthah, of David and Samuel and the prophets, ³³who by faith conquered kingdoms, administered justice, obtained promises, shut the mouths of lions, ³⁴quenched the raging of fire, escaped the edge of the sword, gained strength after being weak, became mighty in battle, and put foreign armies to flight. ³⁵Women received their dead raised to life again. Some men were tortured, not accepting release, so that they might gain a better resurrection, ³⁶and others experienced mockings and scourgings, as well as bonds and imprisonment. ³⁷They were stoned, they were sawed in two, they died by the sword, they wandered about in sheepskins, in goatskins, destitute, afflicted, and mistreated. ³⁸The world was not worthy of them. They wandered in deserts, mountains, caves, and holes in the ground.

³⁹All these were approved through their faith, but they did not receive what was promised, ⁴⁰since God had provided something better for us, so that they would not be made perfect without us.

FOR ACTION: What are your thoughts and feelings now as you come to the closing days of our meditations? We said earlier that expression deepens impression. Take a sheet of paper and in approximately fifty words write down what these daily meditations have done for you. You will be surprised how a summarised statement will clarify what has been happening in your soul over these last twelve months.

ONE ENORMOUS CONSOLATION as we come to the close of this survey of God's strategic plan is that we did not start this story and we aren't expected to finish it.

Only one person has ever been able to say with total sincerity: 'I have accomplished all that you gave me to do'; only one person could, in death, say, 'It is totally finished'. But then of course He is the author and finisher of your faith and mine. He also began the race and finishes it as we run it with Him.

Faith is therefore supremely demonstrated in the story of Jesus Himself, our champion who fought the good fight of faith and brought faith to its full and complete expression. He brought the whole dimension of faith to a new level of completion in His death and resurrection.

Jesus brings the story of Israel's faith to its destined climax by His own faith and endurance, leading those who believe from all nations into the abiding presence and worship of the One True God. He did this 'for the sake' of the joy before Him or – if we read the preposition another way – 'instead of' the joy set before Him. That is, Jesus forwent the joy of being spared death but went through the terrible and shameful death by crucifixion.

So faith rises in our hearts when we consider His story. Because He fought the good fight, and finished His race, so we can we.

DAY
364

HEBREWS 12:1-3

Hebrews 12:1-3

BIBLE
READING

THE CALL TO ENDURANCE

12 Therefore since we also have such a large cloud of witnesses surrounding us, let us lay aside every weight and the sin that so easily ensnares us, and run with endurance the race that lies before us, ²keeping our eyes on Jesus, the source and perfecter of our faith, who for the joy that lay before Him endured a cross and despised the shame, and has sat down at the right hand of God's throne.

FATHERLY DISCIPLINE

³For consider Him who endured such hostility from sinners against Himself, so that you won't grow weary and lose heart.

> **FOR PRAISE**: Let your thoughts dwell for a moment on the fact that our faith is not a product of our own intellect or disposition - Jesus is both its Author and Perfector. This means, does it not, that we are what we are because Jesus is who He is. It's all because of Jesus that we have a part in His story. Once more open your heart in praise and gratitude to Him for that most glorious fact.

DAY 365

ROMANS 11:28-36

HAVING TRACED GOD'S story during the past twelve months, what should be our settled response to God's story?

Firstly, Paul marvels at God's 'depth' of resources and that He is especially 'rich in mercy' (11:12,30-33; Eph. 2:4).

Paul marvels at God's wisdom, though, like Job, it is often only when unjust suffering disrupts our normal story that we connect with the deeper story an all-wise God is working out. Paul recognises God's infinite knowledge and asks: 'Who has ever given to God, that God should repay him?' (v.35, NIV).

Secondly, Paul ponders how unsearchable are God's judgments, and asks, 'who has been His counselor?' (v.34).

Thirdly, Paul exclaims, that God's paths are past finding out! God's plan was often a hidden stream flowing beneath the surface of events, not always obvious to the participants themselves (eg Joseph: Gen. 45:4-5; 50:19-20). Who knows His mind except Jesus and the Spirit given to us (1 Cor. 2:16)? We cannot find God's ways, but they find us!

It is this paradoxical wisdom which Paul celebrates as he tries to grasp the breathtaking strategy of God in history.

This is the story of this strange, angular God; an

untameable God; a tough-loving and tender-talking, compassionate and unquenchable God. This God's redemptive love is alone adequate to the great tragedies of the world. Let's worship Him and never lose the 'Oh!'

Romans 11:28-36

²⁸Regarding the gospel, they are enemies for your advantage, but regarding election, they are loved because of their forefathers, ²⁹since God's gracious gifts and calling are irrevocable. ³⁰As you once disobeyed God, but now have received mercy through their disobedience, ³¹so they too have now disobeyed, [resulting] in mercy to you, so that they also now may receive mercy. ³²For God has imprisoned all in disobedience, so that He may have mercy on all.

A HYMN OF PRAISE
33   Oh, the depth of the riches
     both of the wisdom and the knowledge of God!
     How unsearchable His judgments
     and untraceable His ways!
34   "For who has known the mind of the Lord?
     Or who has been His counselor?
35   Or who has ever first given to Him,
     and has to be repaid?"
36   For from Him and through Him and to Him
         are all things.
     To Him be the glory forever. Amen.

PRAYER: My Father and my God, how can I thank You enough for what You have revealed to me through Your Word as I have meditated upon it day by day? May the wisdom of Your Word that has been pouring into my soul now translate itself into my witness, my work and my worship. And from now on may I indeed never lose the 'Oh!'. In Jesus' name I ask it. Amen and Amen!

NATIONAL DISTRIBUTORS

UK: (and countries not listed below)
CWR, Waverley Abbey House, Waverley Lane, Farnham, Surrey GU9 8EP.
Tel: (01252) 784700 Outside UK (44) 1252 784700 Email: mail@cwr.org.uk

AUSTRALIA: KI Entertainment, Unit 21 317-321 Woodpark Road, Smithfield,
New South Wales 2164. Tel: 1 800 850 777 Fax: 02 9604 3699
Email: sales@kientertainment.com.au

CANADA: David C Cook Distribution Canada, PO Box 98, 55 Woodslee Avenue,
Paris, Ontario N3L 3E5.Tel: 1800 263 2664 Email: swansons@cook.ca

GHANA: Challenge Enterprises of Ghana, PO Box 5723, Accra.
Tel: (021) 222437/223249 Fax: (021) 226227 Email: ceg@africaonline.com.gh

HONG KONG: Cross Communications Ltd, 1/F, 562A Nathan Road, Kowloon.
Tel: 2780 1188 Fax: 2770 6229 Email: cross@crosshk.com

INDIA: Crystal Communications, 10-3-18/4/1, East Marredpalli,
Secunderabad – 500026, Andhra Pradesh. Tel/Fax: (040) 27737145
Email: crystal_edwj@rediffmail.com

KENYA: Keswick Books and Gifts Ltd, PO Box 10242-00400, Nairobi.
Tel: (254) 20 312639/3870125 Email: keswick@swiftkenya.com

MALAYSIA: Canaanland, No. 25 Jalan PJU 1A/41B, NZX Commercial Centre,
Ara Jaya, 47301 Petaling Jaya, Selangor.
Tel: (03) 7885 0540/1/2 Fax: (03) 7885 0545 Email: info@canaanland.com.my

Salvation Book Centre (M) Sdn Bhd, 23 Jalan SS 2/64, 47300 Petaling Jaya, Selangor. Tel:
(03) 78766411/78766797 Fax: (03) 78757066/78756360
Email: info@salvationbookcentre.com

NEW ZEALAND: KI Entertainment, Unit 21 317-321 Woodpark Road, Smithfield,
New South Wales 2164, Australia. Tel: 0 800 850 777 Fax: +612 9604 3699
Email: sales@kientertainment.com.au

NIGERIA: FBFM, Helen Baugh House, 96 St Finbarr's College Road, Akoka, Lagos.
Tel: (01) 7747429/4700218/825775/827264 Email: fbfm@hyperia.com

PHILIPPINES: OMF Literature Inc, 776 Boni Avenue, Mandaluyong City.
Tel: (02) 531 2183 Fax: (02) 531 1960 Email: gloadlaon@omflit.com

SINGAPORE: Alby Commercial Enterprises Pte Ltd, 95 Kallang Avenue #04-00,
AIS Industrial Building, 339420. Tel: (65) 629 27238 Fax: (65) 629 27235
Email: marketing@alby.com.sg

SOUTH AFRICA: Struik Christian Books, 80 MacKenzie Street, PO Box 1144,
Cape Town 8000. Tel: (021) 462 4360 Fax: (021) 461 3612
Email: info@struikchristianmedia.co.za

SRI LANKA: Christombu Publications (Pvt) Ltd, Bartleet House, 65 Braybrooke Place,
Colombo 2. Tel: (9411) 2421073/2447665 Email: dhanad@bartleet.com

USA: David C Cook Distribution Canada, PO Box 98, 55 Woodslee Avenue,
Paris, Ontario N3L 3E5, Canada. Tel: 1800 263 2664 Email: swansons@cook.ca

CWR is a Registered Charity – Number 294387
CWR is a Limited Company registered in England – Registration Number 1990308

Day and Residential Courses
Counselling Training
Leadership Development
Biblical Study Courses
Regional Seminars
Ministry to Women
Daily Devotionals
Books and DVDs
Conference Centre

Trusted all Over the World

CWR HAS GAINED A WORLDWIDE reputation as a centre of excellence for Bible-based training and resources. From our headquarters at Waverley Abbey House, Farnham, England, we have been serving God's people for over 40 years with a vision to help apply God's Word to everyday life and relationships. The daily devotional *Every Day with Jesus* is read by nearly a million readers an issue in more than 150 countries, and our unique courses in biblical studies and pastoral care are respected all over the world. Waverley Abbey House provides a conference centre in a tranquil setting.

For free brochures on our seminars and courses, conference facilities, or a catalogue of CWR resources, please contact us at the following address.
CWR, Waverley Abbey House, Waverley Lane, Farnham, Surrey GU9 8EP, UK

Telephone: +44 (0)1252 784700
Email: mail@cwr.org.uk
Website: www.cwr.org.uk

CWR Applying God's Word *to everyday life and relationships*

Take an exciting journey through the whole Bible

With *Cover to Cover Complete* you will see God's strategic promise-plan unfold across the centuries as you read through God's Word chronologically.

The full text of the flowing Holman Christian Standard translation arranged in 15-minute daily reading segments provides a highly motivating reading experience. Beautiful illustrations, maps, charts, diagrams, a timeline and key verses help make the Bible's complexity manageable, and devotional thoughts make each day's reading relevant and meaningful.

Additional information is available in a special section on our website.

Makes an ideal Bible-reading programme for individuals or churches.

Take your whole church on a *Journey of Discovery* – visit **www.cwr.org.uk/c2cc**

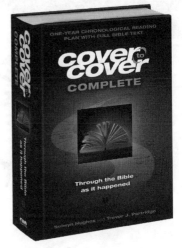

Cover to Cover Complete

1,600-page hardback, with ribbon markers, 140x215mm

ISBN: 978-1-85345-433-2

£19.99

An enriching way to read the Bible

The *Every Day with Jesus One Year Bible* will motivate you to read the entire Bible in a year by breaking it up into dated, daily portions easily read.

Each day's reading comprises short readings from the Old Testament, New Testament, Psalms and Proverbs, so there is plenty of variety every day.

The inspiring devotional writing will help you to see Scripture's relevance to your daily life and to contemporary issues. Thoughtful prayers will help you to apply what you learn, and suggestions for further study will enrich your understanding and inspire you to dig deeper into God's Word.

Great for individuals and for small groups or entire churches to use together!

Take the Bible in a Year Church Challenge – visit **www.cwr.org.uk/bibleinayear**

Prices correct at time of printing

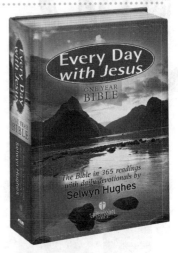

Every Day with Jesus One Year Bible

1,594-page, hardback with ribbon marker 140x215mm

ISBN: 978-1-85345-342-7

£15.99

Written with you in mind.

CWR's range of seven daily Bible-reading notes is written with the aim of offering something suitable for everyone, whatever their age or interest.

So make your choice today to be encouraged and inspired from this wide and ever popular range of Bible-reading notes – *all written with you in mind.*

CWR **Applying God's Word**
to everyday life and relationships

THEMED DEVOTIONAL	FOR WOMEN	LIFE APPLICATION	DEEPER BIBLE STUDY	FOR 14–18s	FOR 11–15s	FOR 7–11s

**Available from CWR on 01252 784710 or
by visiting our online store at www.cwr.org.uk/store**
Also available from your local Christian bookshop.